DEMOCRACY IN AMERICA

J. P. Mayer is a noted Tocqueville scholar. He is author of many books on political science and sociology and is currently teaching at the University of Reading in England.

Other Anchor Press books edited by J. P. Mayer include:

JOURNEY TO AMERICA

RECOLLECTIONS OF ALEXIS DE TOCQUEVILLE (edited with A. P. Kerr)

Alexis de Tocqueville

DEMOCRACY IN AMERICA

Edited by
J. P. MAYER

A NEW TRANSLATION BY GEORGE LAWRENCE

Anchor Books

DOUBLEDAY & COMPANY, INC.

Garden City, New York

The George Lawrence translation of *Democracy in America* was originally published by Harper & Row in 1966. The Anchor Books edition is published by agreement with Harper & Row. The author has written a new Note on the Anchor Edition.

Anchor Books edition: 1969

SYNOPTIC TABLE OF CONTENTS

FOREWORD

Since 1968, seven large editions of this book have appeared. In agreement, therefore, with the publishers and editor of Anchor Books, I thought that I should make a few additional comments to the new impression.

The Johnson administration has been succeeded by that of President Nixon. The war in Vietnam has ended—will the "peace with honour" last?—how will the war veterans adapt themselves to civil life? New foreign policies, in particular with regard to Russia and China, have been initiated. American industrial power has strengthened its immense influence on the greater part of Europe. Is the new student generation less inclined to opt out of its social and cultural commitment, as was the case in 1968, or has cynicism born of despair merely reduced the stridency of their protest? New civic orientations are attempting to put a brake on the vastly increased and overcentralised State power, not only in the United States but also in Europe.

Perhaps the recent Watergate affair may prove to be a turning point in the constitutional development of America. It will perhaps be possible to reestablish the balance between judicial, legislative, and executive power envisaged by the framers of the American Constitution.

Nor should we forget that unlimited economic "progress" is now increasingly questioned and that "the limits of growth" are vital for the younger generation and for the generations to come. In addition, the socio-psychological impact of television on our lives is more readily recognised. New value-attitudes must be formulated—and, above all, lived. All this is still in flux and no one can say what the future will hold for us all.

Yet it is evident that Tocqueville's masterpiece is still widely accepted as an example of a global interpretation of the meaning of American civilisation, for America herself, and also for Europe. This twofold point of view was ever-present in Tocqueville's mind. He was, like Montesquieu, a comparative sociologist.

It is perhaps worth noting that our edition of Tocqueville's notebooks which he kept while travelling through the United States (see Tocqueville, *Journey to America,* Anchor Books, 1971) makes the author's purpose and insight even more evident. They show how the immediate observations were elaborated in the completed work.

During further journeys to the United States, I have had discussions with American friends of whom I mention only Edward F. D'Arms, Anne Freedgood, Stanley Hoffmann, Daniel Lerner, and David Riesman. As a result, I have been strengthened in my conviction that Tocqueville's view of socio-historical phenomena has still many unexplored lessons for us.

For a bibliography, up to 1966, which is specifically centred around Tocqueville studies and works complementary to Tocquevillian ideas, the reader may wish to refer to the hardcover edition of this work, published by Harper & Row in 1966. Moreover, my French edition in the Complete Works, reprinted in 1967, also gives additional bibliographical material.

J. P. MAYER

Tocqueville Research Centre
University of Reading
January 1974

P.S.   Since these lines were written, as a consequence of the American Supreme Court decision of 24th July 1974, President Nixon had to resign and Gerald Ford became the new President of the United States. Does this chain of events not prove Tocqueville's dictum: "There is hardly a political question in the United States which does not sooner or later turn into a judicial one"? (See the present edition, p. 270).

March 1975

It was in 1957 when I decided to do a new edition of the DEMOC-RACY IN AMERICA. Two years later, the centenary year of Tocque-ville's death, I was invited by several American universities to give lectures on Tocqueville. I felt, however, I needed a deeper knowledge of America. From the end of 1959 to 1960 I was appointed as NATO Professor of History at the University of Washington; the Ford Foundation generously gave me two travel awards to travel through the United States; another appointment in 1962 at the University of Colorado as professor of sociology and political science gave me the welcome opportunity of deepening my comprehension of the American scene.

By 1960 the publishers had advanced the necessary funds for the translation, and my friend George Lawrence set to work. Lawrence had already proved his rare gift as a Tocqueville translator by having done my edition of Tocqueville's *Journey to America*. Once Lawrence had completed his gigantic task, I read his text, compared it with the original, and put many queries down on paper. Lawrence and I went over these queries together, and we hope we confront the reader with a faithful text.

Indeed the most authoritative statement for the need of a new translation comes from the author himself. On November 15, 1839, Tocqueville wrote to his translator, Henry Reeve, in London: "I am writing in a country and for a country where the cause for equality is from now on won—without the possibility of a return toward aristocracy. In this state of affairs I felt it my duty to stress particularly the bad tendencies which equality may bring about in order to prevent my contemporaries surrendering to them. This is the only honorable task for those who write in a country where the struggle has come to an end. I therefore say often very severe truths on the French society of our days and on democratic societies in general, but I say these things as friend and not as censor. Just because I am a friend do I dare to say these things. Your translation must maintain my attitude; this I demand not only from the translator, but from the man. It has seemed to me that in the translation of the last book [Tocqueville refers here to Volume I of *Democracy in America*] you have, without wanting it, following the instinct of your opinions, very lively colored what was contrary to democracy and rather appeased what could do wrong to aristocracy. I beg you earnestly to struggle against yourself on this point and to preserve my book its character, which is a veritable impartiality in the theoretical judgment of the two societies, the old and the new, and even the sincere wish to see the new one to establish itself." (Cf. *Œuvres Complètes,* J. P. Mayer, ed., Vol. VI, 1, pp. 47 f.)

I believe I have taken great pains, together with George Lawrence, to comply with the author's wish.

In other respects too, the present edition has novel features: I have verified quotations by Tocqueville and given precise references. Thus, for instance, Tocqueville's references to Story's and Kent's commentaries of the American Constitution; and we have inserted the original texts by Jefferson instead of as Reeve has done, printing them in a retranslated version from the French; etc.

Nearly all the books and documents to which Tocqueville refers have been consulted. Thus it will now be possible to study Tocqueville as an outstanding legal historian, a brilliant anthropologist, and a classic sociologist, fully equipped with the knowledge of his time. Our task would have been impossible without the unfailing and everready help by the staff of the British Museum and the Bibliothèque Nationale in Paris; to the librarians of the University of California at Santa Barbara, Donald C. Davidson and Donald E. Fitch, I am particularly obligated. They have helped to trace some Americana that could not be found in European libraries and they have even sent us volumes by air mail to facilitate our work. I am deeply grateful for their expertise and generosity. Lola Mayer with her great experience in bibliographical work and by her perseverance has greatly contributed to our purpose.

Occasionally some minor obvious errors in Tocqueville's page references have been corrected. More serious mistakes, for instance wrong names or faulty references to texts, have been indicated—not to criticize Tocqueville's scholarship, but to facilitate the use of his sources. Tocqueville's masterly use of his sources is by no means impaired by such minor inexactitudes. He wrote in the tradition of a still partly aristocratic age, before Teutonic thoroughness became victorious in the humanities. Editor's notes have been indicated by brackets.

Our text is based on the second revised and corrected text of my 1961 French edition. This text includes Tocqueville's report on Cherbuliez' book *On Democracy in Switzerland,* which he read before the Academy of Moral and Political Sciences at Paris on January 15, 1848 (Appendix II), and his famous speech in the Chamber of Deputies of January 27, 1848 (Appendix III). The last edition, published by Tocqueville himself, had included these two texts, and I felt compelled to follow the author's final intention . . .

January, 1965   J. P. MAYER

AUTHOR'S PREFACE TO THE TWELFTH EDITION[1]

HOWEVER sudden and momentous be the events which have just taken place so swiftly, the author of this book can claim that they have not taken him by surprise. This work was written fifteen years ago with a mind constantly preoccupied by a single thought: the thought of the approaching irresistible and universal spread of democracy throughout the world. On reading it again, one finds on every page a solemn warning that society is changing shape, that mankind lives under changing conditions, and new destinies are impending.

In the introduction it was stated that: "The gradual progress of equality is something fated. The main features of this progress are the following: it is universal and permanent; it is daily passing beyond human control, and every event and every man helps it along. Is it wise to suppose that a movement of society which has been so long in train can be halted by one generation? Does anyone imagine that democracy, which has destroyed the feudal system and vanquished kings, will fall back before the middle classes and the rich? Will it stop now, when it has grown so strong and its adversaries so weak?"

He who wrote these lines, proved prophetic under a monarchy strengthened rather than shaken by the Revolution of July, 1830, need feel no diffidence now in again calling public attention to his work. It is not out of place to add that the circumstances of the moment give this book a topical interest and practical utility which it did not have when it first appeared.

We then had a royal house, which is now abolished. American institutions, which for France under the monarchy were simply a subject of curiosity, ought now to be studied by republican France. It is not force alone, but rather good laws, which make a new government secure.

[1] [This preface was written in 1848 for the next-to-last edition during Tocqueville's lifetime. It was reprinted in the 13th edition of 1850; this edition forms the basis of ours. Apart from Appendix II, which had also been added to the twelfth edition, the author further added his speech on January 27, 1848: our Appendix III. Cf. Tocqueville's letter to Henry Reeve, his first English translator, of November 27, 1851, in Œuvres Complètes, ed. J. P. Mayer, VI, p. 118.]

After the battle comes the lawgiver. The one destroys; the other builds up. Each has his function. It is not a question now of finding out whether we are to have monarchy or republic in France; but we still want to know whether it is to be an agitated or a tranquil republic, an orderly or a disorderly republic, pacific or warlike, liberal or oppressive, a republic which threatens the sacred rights of property and of the family, or one which recognizes and honors them. It is a fearful problem concerning, not France alone, but the whole civilized world. If we can save ourselves, we shall at the same time save all the nations around us. If we fail, we shall bring them all down with us. According as we establish either democratic liberty or democratic tyranny, the fate of the world will be different. Indeed, one may say that it depends on us whether in the end republics will be established everywhere, or everywhere abolished.

Now this problem, newly posed for us, was solved in America sixty years ago. For sixty years the principle of the sovereignty of the people, which we have introduced but yesterday, has prevailed unchallenged there. It is put in practice in the most direct, unlimited, and absolute way. For sixty years that people who has made it the common fount of all their laws has increased in population, territory, and wealth; and, let it be noted, throughout that period it has been not only the most prosperous but also the most stable of all the peoples in the world. While all the nations of Europe have been ravaged by war or torn by civil strife, the American people alone in the civilized world have remained pacific. Almost the whole of Europe has been convulsed by revolutions; America has not even suffered from riots. There the republic, so far from disturbing them, has preserved all rights. Private property is better guaranteed there than in any other land on earth. Anarchy is as unknown as despotism.

Where else can we find greater cause of hope or more valuable lessons? Let us not turn to America in order slavishly to copy the institutions she has fashioned for herself, but in order that we may better understand what suits us; let us look there for instruction rather than models; let us adopt the principles rather than the details of her laws. The laws of the French republic can be and, in many cases, should be different from those prevailing in the United States. But the principles on which the constitutions of the American states rest, the principles of order, balance of powers, true liberty, and sincere and deep respect for law, are indispensable for all republics; they should be common to them all; and it is safe to forecast that where they are not found the republic will soon have ceased to exist.

1848

Volume One

CONTENTS OF VOLUME ONE

PART II

AUTHOR'S INTRODUCTION

No NOVELTY in the United States struck me more vividly during my stay there than the equality of conditions. It was easy to see the immense influence of this basic fact on the whole course of society. It gives a particular turn to public opinion and a particular twist to the laws, new maxims to those who govern and particular habits to the governed.

I soon realized that the influence of this fact extends far beyond political mores and laws, exercising dominion over civil society as much as over the government; it creates opinions, gives birth to feelings, suggests customs, and modifies whatever it does not create.

So the more I studied American society, the more clearly I saw equality of conditions as the creative element from which each particular fact derived, and all my observations constantly returned to this nodal point.

Later, when I came to consider our own side of the Atlantic, I thought I could detect something analogous to what I had noticed in the New World. I saw an equality of conditions which, though it had not reached the extreme limits found in the United States, was daily drawing closer thereto; and that same democracy which prevailed over the societies of America seemed to me to be advancing rapidly toward power in Europe.

It was at that moment that I conceived the idea of this book.

A great democratic revolution is taking place in our midst; everybody sees it, but by no means everybody judges it in the same way. Some think it a new thing and, supposing it an accident, hope that they can still check it; others think it irresistible, because it seems to them the most continuous, ancient, and permanent tendency known to history.

I should like for a moment to consider the state of France seven hundred years ago; at that time it was divided up between a few families who owned the land and ruled the inhabitants. At that time the right to give orders descended, like real property, from generation to generation; the only means by which men controlled each other was force; there was only one source of power, namely, landed property.

But then the political power of the clergy began to take shape and soon to extend. The ranks of the clergy were open to all, poor or rich, commoner or noble; through the church, equality began to insinuate itself into the heart of government, and a man who would have vegetated as a serf in eternal servitude could, as a priest, take his place among the nobles and often take precedence over kings.

As society became more stable and civilized, men's relations with one another became more numerous and complicated. Hence the need for civil laws was vividly felt, and the lawyers soon left their obscure tribunals and dusty chambers to appear at the king's court side by side with feudal barons dressed in chain mail and ermine.

While kings were ruining themselves in great enterprises and nobles wearing each other out in private wars, the commoners were growing rich by trade. The power of money began to be felt in affairs of state. Trade became a new way of gaining power and financiers became a political force, despised but flattered.

Gradually enlightenment spread, and a taste for literature and the arts awoke. The mind became an element in success; knowledge became a tool of government and intellect a social force; educated men played a part in affairs of state.

In proportion as new roads to power were found, the value of birth decreased. In the eleventh century, nobility was something of inestimable worth; in the thirteenth it could be bought; the first ennoblement took place in 1270, and equality was finally introduced into the government through the aristocracy itself.

During the last seven hundred years it has sometimes happened that, to combat the royal authority or dislodge rivals from power, nobles have given the people some political weight.

Even more often we find kings giving the lower classes in the state a share in government in order to humble the aristocracy.

In France the kings proved the most active and consistent of levelers. When they were strong and ambitious they tried to raise the people to the level of the nobles, and when they were weak and diffident they allowed the people to push past them. The former monarchs helped democracy by their talents, the latter by their vices. Louis XI and Louis XIV were at pains to level everyone below the throne, and finally Louis XV with all his court descended into the dust.

As soon as citizens began to hold land otherwise than by feudal tenure, and the newly discovered possibilities of personal property could also lead to influence and power, every invention in the arts and every improvement in trade and industry created fresh elements tending toward equality among men. Henceforward every new invention, every new need occasioned thereby, and every new desire craving satisfaction were steps towards a general leveling. The taste for luxury, the love of war, the dominion of fashion, all the most superficial and profound passions of the human heart, seemed to work together to impoverish the rich and enrich the poor.

Once the work of the mind had become a source of power and wealth, every addition to knowledge, every fresh discovery, and every new idea became a germ of power within reach of the people. Poetry, eloquence, memory, the graces of the mind, the fires of the imagination and profundity of thought, all things scattered broad-cast by heaven, were a profit to democracy, and even when it was the adversaries of democracy who possessed these things, they still served its cause by throwing into relief the natural greatness of man. Thus its conquests spread along with those of civilization and enlighten-ment, and literature was an arsenal from which all, including the weak and poor, daily chose their weapons.

Running through the pages of our history, there is hardly an im-portant event in the last seven hundred years which has not turned out to be advantageous for equality.

The Crusades and the English wars decimated the nobles and divided up their lands. Municipal institutions introduced democratic liberty into the heart of the feudal monarchy; the invention of fire-arms made villein and noble equal on the field of battle; printing offered equal resources to their minds; the post brought enlighten-ment to hovel and palace alike; Protestantism maintained that all men are equally able to find the path to heaven. America, once dis-covered, opened a thousand new roads to fortune and gave any obscure adventurer the chance of wealth and power.

If, beginning at the eleventh century, one takes stock of what was happening in France at fifty-year intervals, one finds each time that a double revolution has taken place in the state of society. The noble has gone down in the social scale, and the commoner gone up; as the one falls, the other rises. Each half century brings them closer, and soon they will touch.

And that is not something peculiar to France. Wherever one looks one finds the same revolution taking place throughout the Chris-tian world.

Everywhere the diverse happenings in the lives of peoples have turned to democracy's profit; all men's efforts have aided it, both those who intended this and those who had no such intention, those who fought for democracy and those who were the declared enemies thereof; all have been driven pell-mell along the same road, and all have worked together, some against their will and some unconsciously, blind instruments in the hands of God.

Therefore the gradual progress of equality is something fated. The main features of this progress are the following: it is universal and permanent, it is daily passing beyond human control, and every event and every man helps it along. Is it wise to suppose that a movement which has been so long in train could be halted by one generation? Does anyone imagine that democracy, which has destroyed the feudal system and vanquished kings, will fall back before the middle classes and the rich? Will it stop now, when it has grown so strong and its adversaries so weak?

Whither, then, are we going? No one can tell, for already terms of comparison are lacking; in Christian lands now conditions are nearer equality than they have ever been before at any time or in any place; hence the magnitude of present achievement makes it impossible to forecast what may still be done.

This whole book has been written under the impulse of a kind of religious dread inspired by contemplation of this irresistible revolution advancing century by century over every obstacle and even now going forward amid the ruins it has itself created.

God does not Himself need to speak for us to find sure signs of His will; it is enough to observe the customary progress of nature and the continuous tendency of events; I know, without special revelation, that the stars follow orbits in space traced by His finger.

If patient observation and sincere meditation have led men of the present day to recognize that both the past and the future of their history consist in the gradual and measured advance of equality, that discovery in itself gives this progress the sacred character of the will of the Sovereign Master. In that case effort to halt democracy appears as a fight against God Himself, and nations have no alternative but to acquiesce in the social state imposed by Providence.

To me the Christian nations of our day present an alarming spectacle; the movement which carries them along is already too strong to be halted, but it is not yet so swift that we must despair of directing it; our fate is in our hands, but soon it may pass beyond control.

The first duty imposed on those who now direct society is to educate democracy; to put, if possible, new life into its beliefs; to purify its mores; to control its actions; gradually to substitute understanding of statecraft for present inexperience and knowledge of its true interests for blind instincts; to adapt government to the needs of time and place; and to modify it as men and circumstances require.

A new political science is needed for a world itself quite new.

But it is just that to which we give least attention. Carried away by a rapid current, we obstinately keep our eyes fixed on the ruins still in sight on the bank, while the stream whirls us backward— facing toward the abyss.

This great social revolution has made more rapid progress with us than with any other nation of Europe, but the progress has always been haphazard.

The leaders of the state have never thought of making any preparation by anticipation for it. The progress has been against their will or without their knowledge. The most powerful, intelligent, and moral classes of the nation have never sought to gain control of it in order to direct it. Hence democracy has been left to its wild instincts; it has grown up like those children deprived of parental care who school themselves in our town streets and know nothing of society but its vices and wretchedness. Men would seem still unaware of its existence, when suddenly it has seized power. Then all submit like slaves to its least desires; it is worshiped as the idol of strength; thereafter, when it has been weakened by its own excesses, the lawgivers conceive the imprudent project of abolishing it instead of trying to educate and correct it, and without any wish to teach it how to rule, they only strive to drive it out of the government.

As a result the democratic revolution has taken place in the body of society without those changes in laws, ideas, customs, and mores which were needed to make that revolution profitable. Hence we have our democracy without those elements which might have mitigated its vices and brought out its natural good points. While we can already see the ills it entails, we are as yet unaware of the benefits it might bring.

When royal power supported by aristocracies governed the nations of Europe in peace, society, despite all its wretchedness, enjoyed several types of happiness which are difficult to appreciate or conceive today.

The power of some subjects raised insuperable obstacles to the tyranny of the prince. The kings, feeling that in the eyes of the crowd they were clothed in almost divine majesty, derived, from the very extent of the respect they inspired, a motive for not abusing their power.

The nobles, placed so high above the people, could take the calm and benevolent interest in their welfare which a shepherd takes in his flock. Without regarding the poor as equals, they took thought for their fate as a trust confided to them by Providence.

Having never conceived the possibility of a social state other than the one they knew, and never expecting to become equal to their leaders, the people accepted benefits from their hands and did not question their rights. They loved them when they were just and merciful and felt neither repugnance nor degradation in submitting to their severities, which seemed inevitable ills sent by God. Furthermore, custom and mores had set some limits to tyranny and established a sort of law in the very midst of force.

Because it never entered the noble's head that anyone wanted to snatch away privileges which he regarded as legitimate, and since the serf considered his inferiority as an effect of the immutable order of nature, one can see that a sort of goodwill could be established between these two classes so differently favored by fortune. At that time one found inequality and wretchedness in society, but men's souls were not degraded thereby.

It is not exercise of power or habits of obedience which deprave men, but the exercise of a power which they consider illegitimate and obedience to a power which they think usurped and oppressive.

On the one side were wealth, strength, and leisure combined with farfetched luxuries, refinements of taste, the pleasures of the mind, and the cultivation of the arts; on the other, work, coarseness, and ignorance.

But among this coarse and ignorant crowd lively passions, generous feelings, deep beliefs, and untamed virtues were found.

The body social thus ordered could lay claim to stability, strength, and above all, glory.

But distinctions of rank began to get confused, and the barriers separating men to get lower. Great estates were broken up, power shared, education spread, and intellectual capacities became more equal. The social state became democratic, and the sway of democracy was finally peacefully established in institutions and in mores.

At that stage one can imagine a society in which all men, regarding the law as their common work, would love it and and submit to it without difficulty; the authority of the government would be respected as necessary, not as sacred; the love felt toward the head of the state would be not a passion but a calm and rational feeling. Each man having some rights and being sure of the enjoyment of those rights, there would be established between all classes a manly confidence and a sort of reciprocal courtesy, as far removed from pride as from servility.

Understanding its own interests, the people would appreciate that in order to enjoy the benefits of society one must shoulder its obligations. Free association of the citizens could then take the place of the individual authority of the nobles, and the state would be protected both from tyranny and from license.

I appreciate that in a democracy so constituted society would not be at all immobile; but the movements inside the body social could be orderly and progressive; one might find less glory there than in an aristocracy, but there would be less wretchedness; pleasures would be less extreme, but well-being more general; the heights of knowledge might not be scaled, but ignorance would be less common; feelings would be less passionate, and manners gentler; there would be more vices and fewer crimes.

Without enthusiasm or the zeal of belief, education and experience would sometimes induce the citizens to make great sacrifices; each man being equally weak would feel a like need for the help of his companions, and knowing that he would not get their support without supplying his, he would easily appreciate that for him private interest was mixed up with public interest.

The nation as a body would be less brilliant, less glorious, and perhaps less strong, but the majority of the citizens would enjoy a more prosperous lot, and the people would be pacific not from despair of anything better but from knowing itself to be well-off.

Though all would not be good and useful in such a system of things, society would at least have appropriated all that it could of the good and useful; and men, by giving up forever the social advantages offered by aristocracy, would have taken from democracy all the good things that it can provide.

But in abandoning our ancestors' social state and throwing their institutions, ideas, and mores pell-mell behind us, what have we put in their place?

The prestige of the royal power has vanished but has not been replaced by the majesty of the law; nowadays the people despise authority but fear it, and more is dragged from them by fear than was formerly granted through respect and love.

I notice that we have destroyed those individual powers which were able singlehanded to cope with tryanny, but I see that it is the government alone which has inherited all the prerogatives snatched from families, corporations, and individuals; so the sometimes oppressive but often conservative strength of a small number of citizens has been succeeded by the weakness of all.

The breakup of fortunes has diminished the distance between rich and poor, but while bringing them closer, it seems to have provided them with new reasons for hating each other, so that with mutual fear and envy they rebuff each other's claims to power. Neither has any conception of rights, and for both force is the only argument in the present or guarantee for the future.

The poor have kept most of the prejudices of their fathers without their beliefs, their ignorance without their virtues; they accept the doctrine of self-interest as motive for action without understanding that doctrine; and their egotism is now as unenlightened as their devotion was formerly.

Society is tranquil, but the reason for that is not that it knows its strength and its good fortune, but rather that it thinks itself weak and feeble; it fears that a single effort may cost its life; each man feels what is wrong, but none has the courage or energy needed to seek something better; men have desires, regrets, sorrows, and joys which produce no visible or durable result, like old men's passions ending in impotence.

Thus we have abandoned whatever good things the old order of society could provide but have not profited from what our present state can offer; we have destroyed an aristocratic society, and settling down complacently among the ruins of the old building, we seem to want to stay there like that forever.

What is now taking place in the world of the mind is just as deplorable.

French democracy, sometimes hindered in its progress and at others left uncontrolled to its disorderly passions, has overthrown everything it found in its path, shaking all that it did not destroy. It has not slowly gained control of society in order peacefully to establish its sway; on the contrary, its progress has ever been amid the disorders and agitations of conflict. In the heat of the struggle each partisan is driven beyond the natural limits of his own views by the views and the excesses of his adversaries, loses sight of the very aim he was pursuing, and uses language which ill corresponds to his real feelings and to his secret instincts.

Hence arises that strange confusion which we are forced to witness.

I search my memory in vain, and find nothing sadder or more pitiable than that which happens before our eyes; it would seem that we have nowadays broken the natural link between opinions and tastes, acts and beliefs; that harmony which has been observed throughout history between the feelings and the ideas of men seems to have been destroyed, and one might suppose that all the laws of moral analogy had been abolished.

There are still zealous Christians among us who draw spiritual nourishment from the truths of the other life and who no doubt will readily espouse the cause of human liberty as the source of all moral greatness. Christianity, which has declared all men equal in the sight of God, cannot hesitate to acknowledge all citizens equal before the law. But by a strange concatenation of events, religion for the moment has become entangled with those institutions which democracy overthrows, and so it is often brought to rebuff the equality which it loves and to abuse freedom as its adversary, whereas by taking it by the hand it could sanctify its striving.

Alongside these religious men I find others whose eyes are turned more to the earth than to heaven; partisans of freedom, not only because they see in it the origin of the most noble virtues, but even more because they think it the source of the greatest benefits, they sincerely wish to assure its sway and allow men to taste its blessings. I think these latter should hasten to call religion to their aid, for they must know that one cannot establish the reign of liberty without that of mores, and mores cannot be firmly founded without beliefs. But they have seen religion in the ranks of their adversaries, and that is enough for them; some of them openly attack it, and the others do not dare to defend it.

In past ages we have seen low, venal minds advocating slavery, while independent, generous hearts struggled hopelessly to defend human freedom. But now one often meets naturally proud and noble men whose opinions are in direct opposition to their tastes and who vaunt that servility and baseness which they themselves have never known. Others, on the contrary, speak of freedom as if they could feel its great and sacred quality and noisily claim for humanity rights which they themselves have always scorned.

I also see gentle and virtuous men whose pure mores, quiet habits, opulence, and talents fit them to be leaders of those who dwell around them. Full of sincere patriotism, they would make great sacrifices for their country; nonetheless they are often adversaries of civilization; they confound its abuses with its benefits; and in their minds the idea of evil is indissolubly linked with that of novelty.

Besides these, there are others whose object is to make men materialists, to find out what is useful without concern for justice, to have science quite without belief and prosperity without virtue. Such men are called champions of modern civilization, and they insolently put themselves at its head, usurping a place which has been abandoned to them, though they are utterly unworthy of it.

Where are we, then?

Men of religion fight against freedom, and lovers of liberty attack religions; noble and generous spirits praise slavery, while low, servile minds preach independence; honest and enlightened citizens are the enemies of all progress, while men without patriotism or morals make themselves the apostles of civilization and enlightenment!

Have all ages been like ours? And have men always dwelt in a world in which nothing is connected? Where virtue is without genius, and genius without honor? Where love of order is confused with a tyrant's tastes, and the sacred cult of freedom is taken as scorn of law? Where conscience sheds but doubtful light on human actions? Where nothing any longer seems either forbidden or permitted, honest or dishonorable, true or false?

Am I to believe that the Creator made man in order to let him struggle endlessly through the intellectual squalor now surrounding us? I cannot believe that; God intends a calmer and more stable future for the peoples of Europe; I do not know His designs but shall not give up believing therein because I cannot fathom them, and should prefer to doubt my own understanding rather than His justice.

There is one country in the world in which this great social revolution seems almost to have reached its natural limits; it took place in a simple, easy fashion, or rather one might say that that country sees the results of the democratic revolution taking place among us, without experiencing the revolution itself.

The emigrants who colonized America at the beginning of the seventeenth century in some way separated the principle of democracy from all those other principles against which they contended when living in the heart of the old European societies, and transplanted that principle only on the shores of the New World. It could there grow in freedom and, progressing in conformity with mores, develop peacefully within the law.

It seems to me beyond doubt that sooner or later we, like the Americans, will attain almost complete equality of conditions. But I certainly do not draw from that the conclusion that we are necessarily destined one day to derive the same political consequences as the Americans from the similar social state. I am very far from believing that they have found the only form possible for democratic government; it is enough that the creative source of laws and mores is the same in the two countries, for each of us to have a profound interest in knowing what the other is doing.

So I did not study America just to satisfy curiosity, however legitimate; I sought there lessons from which we might profit. Anyone who supposes that I intend to write a panegyric is strangely mistaken; any who read this book will see that that was not my intention at all; nor have I aimed to advocate such a form of government in general, for I am one of those who think that there is hardly ever absolute right in any laws; I have not even claimed to judge whether the progress of the social revolution, which I consider irresistible, is profitable or prejudicial for mankind. I accept that revolution as an accomplished fact, or a fact that soon will be accomplished, and I selected of all the peoples experiencing it that nation in which it has come to the fullest and most peaceful completion, in order to see its natural consequences clearly, and if possible, to turn it to the profit of mankind. I admit that I saw in America more than America; it was the shape of democracy itself which I sought, its inclinations, character, prejudices, and passions; I wanted to understand it so as at least to know what we have to fear or hope therefrom.

Therefore, in the first part of this book I have endeavored to show the natural turn given to the laws by democracy when left in America to its own inclinations with hardly any restraint on its instincts, and to show its stamp on the government and its influence on affairs in general. I wanted to know what blessings and what ills it brings forth. I have inquired into the precautions taken by the Americans to direct it, and noticed those others which they have neglected, and I have aimed to point out the factors which enable it to govern society.

I had intended in a second part to describe the influence in America of equality of conditions and government by democracy upon civil society, customs, ideas, and mores, but my urge to carry out this plan has cooled off. Before I could finish this self-imposed task, it would have become almost useless. Another author is soon to portray the main characteristics of the American people and, casting a thin veil over the seriousness of his purpose, give to truth charms I could not rival.[1]

I do not know if I have succeeded in making what I saw in America intelligible, but I am sure that I sincerely wished to do so and that I never, unless unconsciously, fitted the facts to opinions instead of subjecting opinions to the facts.

Wherever there were documents to establish facts, I have been at pains to refer to the original texts or the most authentic and reputable works.[2] I have cited my authorities in the notes, so those

[1] At the time when the first edition of this work was being published, M. Gustave de Beaumont, my traveling companion in America, was still working on his book *Marie, or Slavery in the United States,* which has since been published. M. de Beaumont's main object was to draw emphatic attention to the condition of the Negroes in Anglo-American society. His book threw new and vivid light on the question of slavery, a vital question for the united republics. I may be mistaken, but I think M. de Beaumont's book, after arousing the vivid interest of those who sought emotions and descriptions therein, should have a more solid and permanent success with those readers who seek, above all, true appreciations and profound truths. [Cf. now Gustave de Beaumont, *Marie, or Slavery in the United States,* with an Introduction by A. L. Tinnin, Stanford, 1958.]

[2] I shall always remember with gratitude the kindness with which I was furnished with legislative and administrative documents. Among the American officials who aided my researches I would especially mention Mr. Edward Livingston, at that time Secretary of State and subsequently Minister Pleni-

who wish can check them. Where opinions, political customs, and mores were concerned, I have tried to consult the best-informed people. In important or doubtful cases I was not content with the testimony of one witness, but based my opinions on that of several.

The reader must necessarily take my word for that. I could often have supported my views with the authority of names he knows, or which at least are worth knowing, but I have abstained from doing so. A stranger often hears important truths at his host's fireside, truths which he might not divulge to his friends; it is a relief to break a constrained silence with a stranger whose short stay guarantees his discretion. I noted down all such confidences as soon as I heard them, but they will never leave my notebooks; I would rather let my comments suffer than add my name to the list of those travelers who repay generous hospitality with worries and embarrassments.

I realize that despite the trouble taken, nothing will be easier than to criticize this book, if anyone thinks of doing so.

Those who look closely into the whole work will, I think, find one pregnant thought which binds all its parts together. But the diversity of subjects treated is very great, and whoever chooses can easily cite an isolated fact to contradict the facts I have assembled, or an isolated opinion against my opinions. I would therefore ask for my book to be read in the spirit in which it was written and would wish it to be judged by the general impression it leaves, just as I have formed my own judgments not for any one particular reason but in conformity with a mass of evidence.

It must not be forgotten that an author who wishes to be understood is bound to derive all the theoretical consequences from each of his ideas and must go to the verge of the false and impracticable, for while it is sometimes necessary to brush rules of logic aside in action, one cannot do so in the same way in conversation, and a man finds it almost as difficult to be inconsequent in speech as he generally finds it to be consistent in action.

To conclude, I will myself point out what many readers will consider the worst defect of this work. This book is not precisely suited to anybody's taste; in writing it I did not intend to serve or to combat any party; I have tried to see not differently but further than any party; while they are busy with tomorrow, I have wished to consider the whole future.

---

potentiary in Paris. During my stay in Washington he kindly provided me with most of the documents I possess concerning the federal government. Mr. Livingston is one of those rare men whose writings inspire affection, so that we admire and respect them even before we know them, and we are glad to owe them a debt of gratitude.

PART I

Chapter 1

PHYSICAL CONFIGURATION OF NORTH AMERICA

North America divided into two vast regions, one sloping toward the pole, the other toward the equator. Mississippi valley and its geology. The Atlantic coast and the foundation of the English colonies. Contrast between North and South America at the time of discovery. North American forests and prairies. Nomadic native tribes and their appearance, mores, and languages. Traces of an unknown people.

NORTH AMERICA has striking geographical features which can be appreciated at first glance.

Land and water, mountains and valleys, seem to have been separated with systematic method, and the simple majesty of this design stands out amid the confusion and immense variety of the scene.

The continent is divided into two vast and almost equal regions.

One region is bounded by the North Pole and the great oceans to east and west, while to the south it stretches down in an irregular triangle to the Great Lakes of Canada.

The second starts where the other ends and covers the rest of the continent.

One region slopes gently toward the pole, the other toward the equator.

The lands to the north of the first region slope so imperceptibly that they may almost be described as plains, and there are no high mountains or deep valleys in the whole of this vast level expanse.

Chance seems to trace the serpentine courses of the streams; great rivers mingle, separate, and meet again; they get lost in a thousand marshes, meandering continually through the watery labyrinth they have formed, and only after innumerable detours do they finally reach the Arctic sea. The Great Lakes, which bring this region to an end, are not framed, as are most lakes in the Old World, by hills or rocks; their banks are level, hardly rising more than a few feet above the water. So each is like a huge cup filled to the brim. The slightest change of global structure would tilt their waters to the pole or to the tropics.

The second region is broken up more and is better suited as a permanent home for man. Two mountain chains run right across it; the Alleghenies parallel to the Atlantic, and the Rockies to the Pacific.

The area between these two mountain chains is 1,341,649 square miles,[1] or about six times that of France.[2]

But the whole of this vast territory is a single valley sloping down from the smooth summits of the Alleghenies and stretching up to the peaks of the Rocky Mountains, with no obstacles in the way.

An immense river flows along the bottom of this valley, and all the waters falling on the mountains on every side drain into it.

Formerly the French called it the St. Louis River, in memory of their distant fatherland, and the Indians in their grandiloquent tongue named it the Father of Waters, the Mississippi.

The Mississippi rises in the borderland between our two regions, not far from the highest point in the plain which links them.

Another river[3] which rises nearby flows down into the polar seas. The Mississippi itself sometimes seems in doubt which way to go; it twists backward several times, and only after slowing down in lakes and marshes seems finally to make up its mind and meander on toward the south.

Sometimes gently flowing along the clay bed which nature has carved out for it, and sometimes swollen by storms, the Mississippi waters some twenty-five hundred square miles.[4]

Thirteen hundred and sixty-four miles[5] above its mouth, the river already has a mean depth of fifteen feet, and ships of three hundred tons can go over four hundred and fifty miles up it.

Fifty-seven large navigable rivers flow into it. Among the tributaries of the Mississippi are one river thirteen hundred leagues long,[6] another of nine hundred leagues,[7] another of six hundred,[8] another

---

[1] 1,341,649 miles. See Darby's *View of the United States,* p. 499 [Philadelphia, 1828; Tocqueville has used the French edition: *Description statistique, historique et politique des États-Unis de l'Amérique septentrionale . . .* par D. B. Warden, 5 vols., Paris, 1820; a copy of this work is to be found among Tocqueville's books at the Chateau de Tocqueville. In the French text the square miles here and hereafter were turned into leagues of two thousand *toises*].

[2] France has 35,181 square leagues.

[3] Red River.

[4] 2,500 miles, 1,032 leagues. See *Description of the United States,* by Warden, Vol. I, p. 166.

[5] 1,364 miles, 563 leagues. See *ibid.,* Vol. I, p. 169.

[6] The Missouri. See *ibid.,* Vol. I, p. 132 (1,278 leagues).

[7] The Arkansas. See *ibid.,* Vol. I, p. 188 (877 leagues).

[8] The Red River. See *ibid.,* Vol. I, p. 190 (598 leagues).

of five hundred;[9] there are four other rivers of two hundred leagues,[10] not to mention the innumerable small streams on every side which augment its flood.

The valley watered by the Mississippi seems created for it alone; it dispenses good and evil at will like a local god. Near the river nature displays an inexhaustible fertility; the further you go from its banks, the sparser the vegetation and the poorer becomes the soil, and everything wilts or dies. Nowhere have the great convulsions of the world left more evident traces than in the valley of the Mississippi. The aspect of the whole countryside bears witness to the waters' work. Its sterility as well as its abundance is their work. Deep layers of fertile soil accumulated under the primeval ocean and had time to level out. On the right bank of the river there are huge plains as level as a rolled lawn. But nearer the mountains the land becomes more and more uneven and sterile; the soil is punctured in a thousand places by primitive rocks sticking out here and there like the bones of a skeleton when sinews and flesh have perished. The surface of the earth is covered with granitic sand and irregularly shaped stones, through which a few plants just manage to force their way; it looks like a fertile field covered by the ruins of some vast structure. Analysis of this sand and these rocks easily demonstrates that they are exactly like those on the bare and jagged peaks of the Rocky Mountains. No doubt the rains which washed all the soil down to the bottom of the valley, in the end brought portions of the rocks too; they were rolled down the neighboring slopes, and after they had been dashed one against another, were scattered at the base of the mountains from which they had fallen. (See Appendix I, A.)

All things considered, the valley of the Mississippi is the most magnificent habitation ever prepared by God for man, and yet one may say that it is still only a vast wilderness.

On the eastern slopes of the Alleghenies, between the mountains and the Atlantic, there is a long strip of rock and sand which seems to have been left behind by the retreating ocean. This strip is only forty-eight leagues[11] broad on the average, but three hundred and ninety leagues long.[12] The soil in this part of the American continent can be cultivated only with difficulty. The vegetation is scanty and uniform.

It was on that inhospital shore that the first efforts of human

[9] The Ohio. See *ibid.*, Vol. I, p. 192 (490 leagues).

[10] The Illinois, St. Pierre, St. Francis, and Des Moines. In the foregoing measurements I have taken as basis the statute mile and the French post league of two thousand *toises*.

[11] One hundred miles.

[12] About 900 miles.

industry were concentrated. That tongue of arid land was the cradle of those English colonies which were one day to become the United States of America. The center of power still remains there, while in the land behind them are assembling, almost in secret, the real elements of the great people to whom the future of the continent doubtless belongs.

When the Europeans landed on the shores of the West Indies, and later of South America, they thought themselves transported to the fabled lands of the poets. The sea sparkled with the fires of the tropics; for the first time the extraordinary transparency of the water disclosed the ocean's depths to the navigators.[13] Here and there little scented islands float like baskets of flowers on the calm sea. Everything seen in these enchanted islands seems devised to meet man's needs or serve his pleasures. Most of the trees were loaded with edible fruits, while those which were least useful to man delighted him by the brilliance of their varied colors. In groves of fragrant lemon trees, wild figs, round-leafed myrtles, acacias, and oleanders, all interlaced with flowering lianas, a multitude of birds unknown to Europe displayed their bright azure and purple feathers and mingled the concert of their song with the harmony of a world teeming with vivid life. (See Appendix I, B.)

Death lay concealed beneath this brilliant cloak, but it was not noticed then, and moreover, there prevailed in the air of these climates some enervating influence which made men think only of the present, careless of the future.

North America seemed very different; everything there was grave and serious and solemn; one might say that it had been created to be the domain of the intelligence, as the other was that of the senses.

A stormy, foggy ocean washed its shores; it was girt round by granite rocks and wide tracts of sand; woods of somber and melancholy trees covered its shores; there was hardly anything but pine, larch, ilex, wild olive, and laurel.

Having broken through that first barrier, one came to the shades of the central forest; there the largest trees of either hemisphere grow

13 Malte-Brun (Vol. III, p. 726) [in fact its reference is to be found in Vol. V, p. 726] says that the water is so clear in the Caribbean that corals and fish can be seen at a depth of sixty fathoms. The ship seems to float in air, and the traveler turns a little giddy as he looks through the crystal water down into submarine gardens where shells and golden fish shine among tufts of seawrack and bushes of seaweed. [*Précis de la Géographie universelle au Description de toutes les parties du Monde* . . . par M. Malte-Brun, Vol. V, Paris, 1817. It is this edition which Tocqueville has used. Vol. VI, to which he refers below, was published in 1826. The whole work is in eight volumes: Paris, 1810–1829.]

side by side; the plane, catalpa, sugar maple, and Virginia poplar twined their branches with those of oak, beech, and lime.

Here, as in forests tamed by man, death was striking constantly, but it was no man's duty to remove the resulting debris, which piled up faster than time could reduce it to powder and make room for new growth. New growth, however, was constantly forcing its way through this debris, with creepers and plants of every sort struggling toward the light, climbing along fallen trunks and into the rotting wood, lifting the cracking bark, and opening the way for their young shoots. Thus death in some way helped life forward, as face to face they seemed to wish to mingle and confuse their functions.

In the dark and gloomy depths of the forests the air was always damp from the thousands of streams flowing through them, as yet uncontrolled by man. There was nothing but some flowers, berries, or birds.

The only sounds breaking the silence of nature were the falling of a dead tree, a waterfall, the lowing of buffalo, and the soughing of the wind.

To the east of the great river the forest begins to disappear, and endless prairies to take its place. Whether nature in her infinite variety refused to allow the seeds of trees to grow there or whether a forest which formerly covered them has been destroyed by the hand of man is a question which neither tradition nor scientific research has answered.

However, these vast wildernesses were not completely unvisited by man; for centuries some nomads had lived under the dark forests or on the meadows of the prairies. From the mouth of the St. Lawrence to the Mississippi delta, from the Atlantic to the Pacific, the savages had some points of resemblance testifying to a common origin. But, apart from that they were different from all known races of men;[14]

---

[14] Since this was written, some resemblances have been observed between the North American Indians and the Tungus, Manchus, Mongols, Tartars, and other nomadic peoples of Asia. These tribes lived near the Bering Straits, which suggests the hypothesis that they may long ago have crossed that way to populate the empty continent of America. But research has not yet made the matter clear. See Malte-Brun, Vol. V; the words of [Alexander von] Humboldt; Fischer, *Conjectures sur l'origine des Américains* [Perhaps J. E. Fischer, *De L'Origine des Américains*, Petersbourgh, 1771; cf. Sabin, *Dictionary of Books Relating to America*, New York, 1873, Vol. VI, p. 432.] Adair *History of the American Indians.* [*The History of the American Indians; Particularly Those Nations Adjoining to the Mississippi, East and West Florida, Georgia, South and North Carolina, and Virginia: Containing an Account of Their Origin, Language, Manners, Religious and Civil Customs, Laws, Form of Government, Punishments, Conduct in War and Domestic Life; Their Habits, Diet, Agriculture, Manufactures, Disease and Methods of Cure and Other Particulars . . .* by James Adair, London, 1775.]

they were neither white like Europeans nor yellow like most Asiatics
nor black like the Negroes; their skin was reddish, their hair long and
glossy, their lips thin, and their cheekbones very high. The words
of the various languages of the savage peoples of America were different, but they all had the same rules of grammar. The rules differed
in several respects from those previously supposed to shape the formation of language among men.

These American languages seem to be the product of new combinations; those who invented them must have possessed an intellectual
drive of which present day Indians hardly seem capable. (See Appendix I, C.)

The social state of these tribes was also different in many respects
from anything known in the Old World. They would seem to have
multiplied freely in their wildernesses without contact with races
more civilized than themselves. Hence they were untroubled by those
muddled and incoherent concepts of good and evil and by that deep
corruption which generally mingles with roughness and ignorance
among once civilized peoples relapsed into barbarism. The Indian
owed nothing to anybody but himself; his virtues, vices, and prejudices were all his own; his nature had matured in wild freedom.

In well-organized countries the coarseness of the common people is
not due solely to ignorance and poverty, but is also affected by the
fact that, being poor and ignorant, they are in daily contact with the
wealthy and educated.

Their ill fortune and weakness, constantly contrasted with the prosperity and power of some of their fellows, inspire both anger and fear
in their hearts; they are vexed and humiliated by the sense of their
inferiority and dependence. Their mores and language reflect this
state of soul; they are both servile and insolent.

The truth of this can easily be proved by observation. The people
are coarser in aristocratic countries than elsewhere, and coarser in
wealthy cities than in the countryside.

Where there are such rich and powerful men, the poor and weak
feel themselves weighed down by their inferiority; seeing no prospect
of regaining equality, they quite give up hope for themselves and
allow themselves to fall below the proper dignity of mankind.

But there is no such vexatious contrast in savage life; the Indians,
all poor and all ignorant, are also all equal and free.

When the Europeans first landed, the natives of North America
were still unaware of the value of wealth and showed themselves
indifferent to the prosperity acquired by civilized man therewith. But
nothing coarse was seen in them; on the contrary, there was in their
manners a habitual reserve and a sort of aristocratic courtesy.

Gentle and hospitable in peace, in war merciless even beyond the known limits of human ferocity, the Indian would face starvation to succor the stranger who knocked in the evening on the door of his hut, but he would tear his prisoner's quivering limbs to pieces with his own hands. No famed republic of antiquity could record firmer courage, prouder spirit, or more obstinate love of freedom than lies concealed in the forests of the New World.[15] The Europeans made but little impression when they landed on the shore of North America; they were neither feared nor envied. What hold could they have on such men? The Indian knew how to live without wants, to suffer without complaint, and to die singing.[16] In common, too, with all other members of the great human family, these savages believed in the existence of a better world, and under different names worshiped God, Creator of the universe. Their conceptions of the great intellectual truths were in general simple and philosophical. (See Appendix I, D.)

Primitive as was the character of the people just described, there can be no doubt that another people, more civilized and in all respects more advanced, preceded them in these same regions.

A dim tradition, but one found among most of the Indian tribes on the Atlantic coast, says that these tribes once lived to the west of the Mississippi. Along the banks of the Ohio and throughout the central

[15] We learn from President Jefferson (*Notes on the State of Virginia*, p. 148) that among the Iroquois, when attacked by stronger forces, old men would scorn to fly or to survive the destruction of their country and braved death like the Romans when the Gauls sacked Rome.

Further on (p. 150) he tells us that there is no example of an Indian who, having fallen into the hands of his enemies, begged for his life; on the contrary, the prisoner would invite death at his captors' hands by all manner of insults and provocations. [The passages to which Tocqueville refers are to be found in Jefferson's *Notes on the State of Virginia* (Boston, 1832), p. 213: "that they are timorous and cowardly is a character with which there is little reason to charge them, when we recollect the manner in which the Iroquois met Mons. . . . , who marched into their country, in which the old men, who scorned to fly or to survive the capture of their own, braved death, like the old Romans in the time of the Gauls. . . . But above all, the unshaken fortitude with which they bear the most excruciating tortures and death when taken prisoners ought to exempt them from that character."]

[16] See *Histoire de la Louisiane,* par Lepage-Dupratz; [cf. *The History of Louisiana or of the Western Parts of Virginia and Carolina* . . . by M. Le Page du Pratz, 2 vols.; London, 1763. French edition: *Histoire de la Louisiane* par M. Le Page du Pratz, 3 vols., Paris, 1758]; Charlevoix, *Histoire de la Nouvelle France; Letters* of the Rev. G. Heckewelder, *Transactions of the American Philosophical Society,* Vol. I [cf. Appendix I.C.]; Jefferson, *Notes on Virginia,* pp. 135–190. Great weight attaches to what Jefferson records because of the personal distinction of the writer, his particular situation, and the matter-of-fact age in which he lived.

plain, man-made tumuli are continually coming to light. It is said
that if one excavates to the center of these tumuli, one almost always
finds human bones, strange instruments, weapons, and utensils of all
kinds either made of some metal or destined for some use unknown
to the present inhabitants.

Present-day Indians can supply no information about this unknown
people. Those who lived three hundred years ago, when America
was first discovered, have said nothing from which even a hypothesis
could be inferred. Traditions, those frail but constantly renewed
monuments of the primitive world, provide no light. There, however,
thousands of our fellow men did live; we cannot doubt that. When
did they come there and what was their origin, history, and fate?
No man can answer.

It is a strange thing that peoples should have so completely vanished
from the earth, that even the memory of their name is lost; their
languages are forgotten and their glory has vanished like a sound
without an echo; but I doubt that there is any which has not left
some tomb as a memorial of its passage. So, of all man's work, the
most durable is that which best records his nothingness and his misery.

Beckett

Although the huge territories just described were inhabited by
many native tribes, one can fairly say that at the time of discovery
they were no more than a wilderness. The Indians occupied but did
not possess the land. It is by agriculture that man wins the soil, and
the first inhabitants of North America lived by hunting. Their
unconquerable prejudices, their indomitable passions, their vices, and
perhaps still more their savage virtues delivered them to inevitable
destruction. The ruin of these peoples began as soon as the Europeans
landed on their shores; it has continued ever since and is coming to
completion in our own day. Providence, when it placed them amid
the riches of the New World, seems to have granted them a short lease
only; they were there, in some sense, *only waiting*. Those coasts so
well suited for trade and industry, those deep rivers, that inexhaustible valley of the Mississippi—in short, the whole continent—
seemed the yet empty cradle of a great nation.

It was there that civilized man was destined to build society on new
foundations, and for the first time applying theories till then unknown or deemed unworkable, to present the world with a spectacle
for which past history had not prepared it.

U.S. as not just terra incognita,
    but tabula (terra) rasa —
quite a justification
    for the slaughter
        to come...

Chapter 2

CONCERNING THEIR POINT OF DEPARTURE AND ITS IMPORTANCE FOR THE FUTURE OF THE ANGLO-AMERICANS

The need to understand the point of departure of a nation in order to appreciate its social condition and laws—America is the only country where we can clearly see the point of departure of a great nation. Respects in which the immigrants to the English parts of America were alike. Respects in which they differed. Remarks applicable to all Europeans who established themselves on the shores of the New World. Colonization of Virginia and of New England. Original character of the first inhabitants of New England. Their arrival. Their first laws. Social contract. Penal code borrowed from Mosaic law. Religious ardor. Republican spirit. Intimate connection between the spirit of religion and the spirit of freedom.

WHEN A CHILD IS BORN, his first years pass unnoticed in the joys and activities of infancy. As he grows older and begins to become a man, then the doors of the world open and he comes into touch with his fellows. For the first time notice is taken of him, and people think they can see the germs of the virtues and vices of his maturity taking shape.

That, if I am not mistaken, is a great error.

Go back; look at the baby in his mother's arms; see how the outside world is first reflected in the still hazy mirror of his mind; consider the first examples that strike his attention; listen to the first words which awaken his dormant powers of thought; and finally take notice of the first struggles he has to endure. Only then will you understand the origin of the prejudices, habits, and passions which are to dominate his life. The whole man is there, if one may put it so, in the cradle.

Something analogous happens with nations. Peoples always bear some marks of their origin. Circumstances of birth and growth affect all the rest of their careers.

If we could go right back to the elements of societies and examine the very first records of their histories, I have no doubt that we should there find the first cause of their prejudices, habits, dominating passions, and all that comes to be called the national character. We should there be able to discover the explanation of customs which now seem contrary to the prevailing mores, of laws which seem opposed to recognized principles, and of incoherent opinions still found here and there in society that hang like the broken chains still occasionally dangling from the ceiling of an old building but carrying nothing. This would explain the fate of certain peoples who seem borne by an unknown force toward a goal of which they themselves are unaware. But up till now evidence is lacking for such a study. The taste for analysis comes to nations only when they are growing old, and when at last they do turn their thoughts to their cradle, the mists of time have closed round it, ignorance and pride have woven fables round it, and behind all that the truth is hidden.

America is the only country in which we can watch the natural quiet growth of society and where it is possible to be exact about the influence of the point of departure on the future of a state.

At the time when Europeans first landed on the shores of the New World, features of national character were already clearly shaped; each nation had a distinct physiognomy; and since they had by then reached the stage of civilization inducing men to study themselves, they have left us a faithful record of their opinions, mores, and laws. We know the men of the fifteenth century almost as well as our own contemporaries. So America shows in broad daylight things elsewhere hidden from our gaze by the ignorance or barbarism of the earliest times.

We seem now destined to see further into human history than could the generations before us; we are close enough to the time when the American societies were founded to know in detail the elements of which they were compounded, and far enough off to judge what these seeds have produced. Providence has given us a light denied to our fathers and allowed us to see the first causes in the fate of nations, causes formerly concealed in the darkness of the past.

When, after careful study of the history of America, we turn with equal care to the political and social state there, we find ourselves deeply convinced of this truth, that there is not an opinion, custom, or law, nor, one might add, an event, which the point of departure will not easily explain. So this chapter provides the germ of all that is to follow and the key to almost the whole work.

The immigrants who came at different times to occupy what is now the United States were not alike in many respects; their aims were not the same, and they ruled themselves according to different principles.

But these men did have features in common, and they all found themselves in analogous circumstances.

Language is perhaps the strongest and most enduring link which unites men. All the immigrants spoke the same language and were children of the same people. Born in a country shaken for centuries by the struggles of parties, a country in which each faction in turn had been forced to put itself under the protection of the laws, they had learned their political lessons in that rough school, and they had more acquaintance with notions of rights and principles of true liberty than most of the European nations at that time. At the time of the first immigrations, local government, that fertile germ of free institutions, had already taken deep root in English ways, and therewith the dogma of the sovereignty of the people had slipped into the very heart of the Tudor monarchy.

That was the time of religious quarrels shaking Christendom. England plunged vehemently forward in this new career. The English, who had always been staid and deliberate, became austere and argumentative. These intellectual battles greatly advanced education and a more profound culture. Absorption in talk about religion led to chaster mores. All these general characteristics of the nation were more or less the same among those of its sons who sought a new future on the far side of the ocean.

Moreover, one observation, to which we shall come back later, applies not to the English only, but also to the French, Spaniards, and all Europeans who came in waves to plant themselves on the shores of the New World; all these new European colonies contained the germ, if not the full growth, of a complete democracy. There were two reasons for this; one may say, speaking generally, that when the immigrants left their motherlands they had no idea of any superiority of some over others. It is not the happy and the powerful who go into exile, and poverty with misfortune is the best-known guarantee of equality among men. Nonetheless, it did happen several times that as a result of political or religious quarrels great lords went to America. Laws were made there to establish the hierarchy of ranks, but it was soon seen that the soil of America absolutely rejected a territorial aristocracy. It was obvious that to clear this untamed land nothing but the constant and committed labor of the landlord himself would serve. The ground, once cleared, was by no means fertile enough to make both a landlord and a tenant rich. So the land was naturally broken up into little lots which the owner himself cultivated. But it is land that is the basis of an aristocracy, giving it both roots and support; privileges by themselves are not enough, nor is birth, but only land handed down from generation to generation. There may be huge fortunes and grinding poverty in a nation; but if that wealth is not landed, one may find rich and poor, but not, using words strictly, an aristocracy.

Hence there was a strong family likeness between all the English colonies as they came to birth. All, from the beginning, seemed destined to let freedom grow, not the aristocratic freedom of their motherland, but a middle-class and democratic freedom of which the world's history had not previously provided a complete example.

But within this general picture there were some very pronounced nuances which need to be mentioned.

There were two main branches of the great Anglo-American family which have, so far, grown up together without completely mingling —one in the South, and the other in the North.

Virginia was the first of English colonies, the immigrants arriving in 1607. At that time Europe was still peculiarly preoccupied with the notion that mines of gold and silver were the basis of the wealth of nations. That was a fatal notion that did more to impoverish the European nations deluded by it and cost more lives in America than were caused by war and all bad laws combined. It was therefore gold-seekers who were sent to Virginia,[1] men without wealth or standards whose restless, turbulent temper endangered the infant colony[2] and made its progress vacillating. Craftsmen and farm laborers came later; they were quieter folk with better morals, but there was hardly any respect in which they rose above the level

[1] The charter granted by the English Crown in 1609 contained, among other clauses, a provision that the colonists should pay a fifth of the output of gold and silver mines to the Crown. See Marshall's *Life of Washington*, Vol. I, pp. 18–66. [Tocqueville refers here to the French edition of Marshall's *Life of Washington*, 5 vols., Paris, 1807.]

[2] According to Stith's *History of Virginia*, a large proportion of the new colonists were unruly children of good family whose parents sent them off to escape from ignominy at home; for the rest there were dismissed servants, fraudulent bankrupts, debauchees, and others of that sort, people more apt to pillage and destroy than to consolidate the settlement. Seditious leaders easily enticed this band into every kind of extravagance and excess. For the history of Virginia see the following works:

History of Virginia from the First Settlements in the Year 1624, by Smith. [John Smith? See Appendix I, F.]

History of the First Discovery and Settlement of Virginia, by William Stith. [See Appendix I, F.]

History of Virginia from the Earliest Period, by Beverley, translated into French in 1807. [See Appendix I, F.]

of the English lower classes.³ No noble thought or conception above gain presided over the foundation of the new settlements. The colony had hardly been established when slavery was introduced.⁴ That was the basic fact destined to exert immense influence on the character, laws, and future of the whole South.

Slavery, as we shall show later, dishonors labor; it introduces idleness into society and therewith ignorance and pride, poverty and luxury. It enervates the powers of the mind and numbs human activity. Slavery, combined with the English character, explains the mores and social condition of the South.

In the North the English background was the same, but every nuance led the opposite way. Of this some detailed explanation is required.

It was in the English colonies of the North, better known as the states of New England,⁵ that the two or three main principles now forming the basic social theory of the United States were combined.

New England principles spread first to the neighboring states and then in due course to those more distant, finally penetrating everywhere throughout the confederation. Their influence now extends beyond its limits over the whole American world. New England civilization has been like beacons on mountain peaks whose warmth is first felt close by but whose light shines to the farthest limits of the horizon.

The foundation of New England was something new in the world, all the attendant circumstances being both peculiar and original.

In almost all other colonies the first inhabitants have been men without wealth or education, driven from their native land by poverty or misconduct, or else greedy speculators and industrial entrepreneurs. Some colonies cannot claim even such an origin as this; San Domingo was founded by pirates, and in our day the English courts of justice are busy populating Australia.

But all the immigrants who came to settle on the shores of New England belonged to the well-to-do classes at home. From the start, when they came together on American soil, they presented the un-

³ It was only later that some rich landowners came to settle in the colony.
⁴ Slavery was first introduced about the year 1620 by a Dutch ship, which landed twenty Negroes on the banks of the James River. See Chalmer. [Perhaps Tocqueville refers here to George Chalmers, *Opinions on Interesting Subjects; Arising from American Independence,* London, 1785, or by the same author, *An Introduction to the History of the Revolt of the Colonies,* London, 1782.]
⁵ The states of New England are those states which lie east of the Hudson, and there are now six of them: Connecticut, Rhode Island, Massachusetts, Vermont, New Hampshire, and Maine.

usual phenomenon of a society in which there were no great lords, no common people, and, one may almost say, no rich or poor. In proportion to their numbers, these men had a greater share of accomplishments than could be found in any European nation now. All, perhaps without a single exception, had received a fairly advanced education, and several had made a European reputation by their talents and their knowledge. The other colonies had been founded by unattached adventurers, whereas the immigrants to New England brought with them wonderful elements of order and morality; they came with their wives and children to the wilds. But what most distinguished them from all others was the very aim of their enterprise. No necessity forced them to leave their country; they gave up a desirable social position and assured means of livelihood; nor was their object in going to the New World to better their position or accumulate wealth; they tore themselves away from home comforts in obedience to a purely intellectual craving; in facing the inevitable sufferings of exile they hoped for the triumph of *an idea.*

The immigrants, or as they so well named themselves, the Pilgrims, belonged to that English sect whose austere principles had led them to be called Puritans. Puritanism was not just a religious doctrine; in many respects it shared the most absolute democratic and republican theories. That was the element which had aroused its most dangerous adversaries. Persecuted by the home government, and with their strict principles offended by the everyday ways of the society in which they lived, the Puritans sought a land so barbarous and neglected by the world that there at last they might be able to live in their own way and pray to God in freedom.

A few quotations will make the spirit of these pious adventurers clearer than anything I could say.

Nathaniel Morton, historian of the early years of New England, thus opens the subject:[6]

"I have for some length of time looked upon it as a duty incumbent, especially on the immediate successors of those that have had so large experience of those many memorable and signal demonstrations of God's goodness, viz. the first beginners of this plantation in New England, to commit to writing his gracious dispensations on that behalf; having so many inducements thereunto, not only otherwise, but so plentifully in the sacred Scriptures, that so, what we have seen, and what our fathers have told us, we may not hide from our children, shewing to the generations to come the praises of the Lord. (Psalm 78. 3,4.) That especially the seed of Abraham his

[6] *New England's Memorial* (Boston, 1826), p. 13 [f.]. See also Hutchinson's *History,* Vol. II, p. 440 [page ref. dubious].

servant, and the children of Jacob his chosen, may remember his marvelous works (Psalm 105. 5,6) in the beginning and progress of the planting of New England, his wonders, and the judgments of his mouth; how that God brought a vine into the wilderness; that he cast out the heathen and planted it; and he made also room for it, and he caused it to take deep root, and it filled the land. . . . (Psalm 80. 8,9.) And not only so, but also that he has guided his people by his strength to his holy habitation, and planted them in the mountain of his inheritance (Exodus 15. 13) . . . that as especially God may have the glory of all, unto whom it is most due; so also some rays of glory may reach the names of those blessed saints that were the main instruments of the beginning of this happy enterprise."

Any reader of this opening paragraph must in spite of himself sense the solemn religious feeling thereof; one seems to breathe the atmosphere of antiquity and to inhale a sort of Biblical fragrance.

The author's conviction heightens his language. In our eyes, as in his, it is not just a little party of adventurers going to seek their fortunes overseas; it is the scattering of the seed of a great people which God with His own hands is planting on a predestined shore.

The author goes on to describe the departure of the first immigrants thus:[7]

". . . so they left that goodly and pleasant city (Delft Haven), which had been their resting-place above eleven years; but they knew that they were pilgrims and strangers here below, and looked not much on these things, but lifted up their eyes to heaven, their dearest country, where God has prepared for them a city . . . and therein quieted their spirits. When they came to the place, they found the ship and all things ready; and such of their friends as could not come with them, followed after them. . . . One night was spent with little sleep with the most, but with friendly entertainment, and Christian discourse, and other real expressions of true Christian love. The next day, the wind being fair, they went on board, and their friends with them, where truly doleful was the sight of that sad and mournful parting, to hear what sighs and sobs and prayers did sound amongst them; what tears did gush from every eye, and pithy speeches pierced each other's heart, that sundry of . . . strangers . . . could not refrain from tears. . . . But the tide . . . calling them away . . . their reverend pastor falling down on his knees, and they all with him, with watery cheeks commended them with most fervent prayers unto the Lord and His blessing; and then with mutual embraces, and many tears, they took their leave one of another, which proved to be the last leave to many of them."

[7] *Ibid.*, p. 23 [f.].

The immigrants, including women and children, numbered about one hundred and fifty. Their object was to found a colony on the banks of the Hudson; but after long wandering over the ocean, they were finally forced to land on the arid coast of New England, on the spot where the town of Plymouth now stands. The rock on which the Pilgrims disembarked is still shown.[8]

"But before we pass on," our chronicler continues, "let the reader, with me, make a pause, and seriously consider this poor people's present condition, the more to be raised up to admiration of God's goodness toward them in their preservation:[9] for being now past the vast ocean . . . they had now no friends to welcome them, no inns to entertain or refresh them, no houses, much less towns, to repair unto to seek for succor. . . . It was winter, and they knew the winters of the country, knew them to be sharp and violent, subject to cruel and fierce storms, dangerous to travel to known places, much more to search unknown coasts. Besides, what could they see but a hideous and desolate wilderness, full of wild beasts and wild men? And what multitude of them there were, they then knew not. . . . Summer being ended, all things stand in appearance with a weather-beaten face, and the whole country, full of woods and thickets, represented a wild and savage hue; if they looked behind them, there was the mighty ocean which . . . was now as a main bar and gulf to separate them from all the civil parts of the world. . . . Which way soever they turned their eyes (save upward to heaven), they could have little solace or content."[10]

It must not be imagined that the piety of the Puritans was merely speculative, taking no notice of the course of worldly affairs. Puritanism, as already remarked, was almost as much a political theory as a religious doctrine. No sooner had the immigrants landed on that inhospitable coast described by Nathaniel Morton than they made it their first care to organize themselves as a society. They immediately passed an act which stated:[11]

[8] This rock has become an object of veneration in the United States. I have seen fragments carefully preserved in several American cities. Does not that clearly prove that man's power and greatness resides entirely in his soul? A few poor souls trod for an instant on this rock, and it has become famous; it is prized by a great nation; fragments are venerated, and tiny pieces distributed far and wide. What has become of the doorsteps of a thousand palaces? Who cares about them?

[9] *New England's Memorial*, p. 35 [f.].

[10] [The last sentence seems to paraphrase Morton's text.]

[11] The immigrants who founded the state of Rhode Island in 1638, those who settled at New Haven in 1637, the first inhabitants of Connecticut in 1639, and the founders of Providence in 1640 all began by publishing a social con-

"We whose names are underwritten . . . having undertaken for the glory of God, and advancement of the Christian faith, and the honor of our king and country a voyage to plant the first colony in the northern parts of Virginia, do by these presents solemnly and mutually, in the presence of God and one another, convenant and combine ourselves together into a civil body politic, for our better ordering and preservation, and furtherance of the ends aforesaid; and by virtue hereof, do enact, constitute, and frame such just and equal laws, ordinances, acts, constitutions, and officers, from time to time, as shall be thought most meet and convenient for the general good of the colony, unto which we promise all due submission and obedience." [Cf. Morton, *New England's Memorial,* Boston, 1826, p. 37 f.]

That happened in 1620. From that time onward immigration never ceased. The religious and political passions which ravaged the British Empire throughout the reign of Charles I drove fresh swarms of dissenters across to America every year. In England the nucleus of the Puritan movement continued to be in the middle classes, and it was from those classes that most of the emigrants sprang. The population of New England grew fast, and while in their homeland men were still despotically divided by class hierarchies, the colony came more and more to present the novel phenomenon of a society homogeneous in all its parts. Democracy more perfect than any of which antiquity had dared to dream sprang full-grown and fully armed from the midst of the old feudal society.

The English government watched untroubled the departure of so many emigrants, glad to see the seeds of discord and of fresh revolutions dispersed afar. Indeed it did everything to encourage it and seemed to have no anxiety about the fate of those who sought refuge from its harsh laws on American soil. It seemed to consider New England as a land given over to the fantasy of dreamers, where innovators should be allowed to try out experiments in freedom.

The English colonies—and that was one of the main reasons for their prosperity—have always enjoyed more internal freedom and political independence than those of other nations; nowhere was this principle of liberty applied more completely than in the states of New England.

---

tract which was submitted for approval to every person concerned. Pitkin's *History,* pp. 42 and 47. [Timothy Smith, *A Political and Civil History of the United States of America from the Year 1763 to the Close of the Administration of President Washington, in March 1797: Including a Summary View of the Political and Civil State of the North American Colonies Prior to That Period,* 2 vols., New Haven, 1828.]

It was at that time generally recognized that the lands of the New World belonged to that nation who first discovered them.

In that way almost the whole of the North American coast became an English possession toward the end of the sixteenth century. The means used by the British government to people these new domains were of various sorts; in some cases the king chose a governor to rule some part of the New World, administering the land in his name and under his direct orders;[12] that was the colonial system adopted in the rest of Europe. In others he granted ownership of some portion of the land to an individual or to a company.[13] In those cases all civil and political powers were concentrated in the hands of one man or a few individuals, who, subject to the supervision and regulation of the Crown, sold the land and ruled the inhabitants. Under the third system a number of immigrants were given the right to form a political society under the patronage of the motherland and allowed to govern themselves in any way not contrary to her laws. This mode of colonization, so favorable to liberty, was put into practice only in New England.[14]

In 1628[15] a charter of that sort was granted by Charles I to the emigrants who were going to found the colony of Massachusetts.

But generally charters were only granted to the New England colonies long after their existence had become an established fact. Plymouth, Providence, New Haven, and the states of Connecticut and Rhode Island[16] were founded without the help and, in a sense, without the knowledge of the motherland. The new settlers, without denying the supremacy of the homeland, did not derive from thence

[12] This was the case in the state of New York.

[13] Maryland, the Carolinas, Pennsylvania, and New Jersey were in this category. See Pitkin's *History*, Vol. I, pp. 11–31 [13–30. Tocqueville is not always exact in his page references].

[14] See the work entitled *Historical Collections, Consisting of State Papers and Other Authentic Documents Intended as Materials for an History of the United States of America, by Ebenezar Hazard, Printed at Philadelphia MDCCXCII*, which contains a great many valuable authentic documents concerning the early history of the colonies, including the various charters granted to them by the English Crown and the first acts of their governments.

See also the analysis of all these charters by Mr. Story, judge of the Supreme Court of the United States, in the introduction to his *Commentary on the Constitution of the United States*. [Cf. the abridged edition, Boston, 1833, which Tocqueville has used: pp. 8–83.]

It emerges from all these documents that the principles of representative government and the external forms of political liberty were introduced into all the colonies almost as soon as they came into being. These principles were developed further in the North than in the South, but they existed everywhere.

[15] See Pitkin's *History*, Vol. I, p. 35. And see *The History of the Colony of Massachusetts*, by Hutchinson, Vol. I, p. 9.

[16] See *ibid.*, pp. 42, 47.

the source of their powers, and it was only thirty or forty years afterward, under Charles II, that a royal charter legalized their existence.[17]

For this reason it is often difficult, when studying the earliest historical and legislative records of New England, to detect the link connecting the immigrants with the land of their forefathers. One continually finds them exercising rights of sovereignty; they appointed magistrates, made peace and war, promulgated police regulations, and enacted laws as if they were dependent on God alone.

Nothing is more peculiar or more instructive than the legislation of this time; there, if anywhere, is the key to the social enigma presented to the world by the United States now.

Among these records one may choose as particularly characteristic the code of laws enacted by the little state of Connecticut in 1650.[18]

The Connecticut[19] lawgivers turned their attention first to the criminal code and, in composing it, conceived the strange idea of borrowing their provisions from the text of Holy Writ: "If any man after legal conviction shall have or worship any other God but the Lord God, he shall be put to death."

There follow ten or twelve provisions of the same sort taken word for word from Deuteronomy, Exodus, or Leviticus.

Blasphemy, sorcery, adultery,[20] and rape are punished by death;

[17] In shaping their criminal and civil laws and their procedures and courts of justice, the inhabitants of Massachusetts diverged from English usages; in 1650 the king's name no longer headed judicial orders. See Hutchinson, Vol. I, p. 452.

[18] *Code of 1650,* p. 28 [f.] (Hartford, 1830). [The Library of Congress catalogue gives the following entry which describes the work to which Tocqueville refers.

Connecticut (Colony). Laws, statutes, etc.

The code of 1650, being a compilation of the earliest laws and orders of the General Court of Connecticut: also, the constitution, or civil compact, entered into and adopted by the towns of Windsor, Hartford, and Wethersfield in 1638–9. To which is added some extracts from the laws and judicial proceedings of New-Haven colony, commonly called Blue laws. Hartford, S. Andrus, 1830.

119 p. incl. front. 15 cm.

We have used a copy of this work that appears to be nearly identical with the work just described, except that it bears the imprint: Cincinnati, Published by U. P. James (no date). Title and pagination are the same.]

[19] See also in Hutchinson's *History,* Vol. I, pp. 435–455, the analysis of the penal code adopted by the colony of Massachusetts in 1648; its principles are analogous to those of Connecticut.

[20] The laws of Massachusetts also imposed the death penalty for adultery, and Hutchinson (Vol. I, p. 441) says that several people were actually executed for that crime; in this context he quotes a strange story of something which happened in 1663. A married woman had a love affair with a young man; her

a son who outrages his parents is subject to the same penalty. Thus the legislation of a rough, half-civilized people was transported into the midst of an educated society with gentle mores; as a result the death penalty has never been more frequently prescribed by the laws or more seldom carried out.

The framers of these penal codes were especially concerned with the maintenance of good behavior and sound mores in society, so they constantly invaded the sphere of conscience, and there was hardly a sin not subject to the magistrate's censure. The reader will have noticed the severity of the penalties for adultery and rape. Simple intercourse between unmarried persons was likewise harshly repressed. The judge had discretion to impose a fine or a whipping or to order the offenders to marry.[21] If the records of the old courts of New Haven are to be trusted, prosecutions of this sort were not uncommon; under the date May 1, 1660, we find a sentence imposing a fine and reprimand on a girl accused of uttering some indiscreet words and letting herself be kissed.[22] The code of 1650 is full of preventive regulations. Idleness and drunkenness are severely punished.[23] Innkeepers may give each customer only a certain quantity of wine; simple lying, if it could do harm,[24] is subject to a fine or a whipping. In other places the lawgivers, completely forgetting the great principle of religious liberty which they themselves claimed in Europe, enforced attendance at divine service by threat of fines[25] and went so far as to impose severe penalties,[26] and often the death

husband died and she married him; several years passed; at length the public came to suspect the intimacy which had earlier existed between the spouses, and criminal proceedings were brought against them; they were thrown into prison, and both were very near being condemned to death.

[21] Code of 1650, p. 48. It would seem that sometimes the judges would impose more than one of these penalties, as is seen in a judicial sentence of 1643 (*New Haven Antiquities, p. 114*) [We have been unable to trace this work. Several American libraries assisted us with this problem, but although we found one or more works of similar title, none corresponded with what Tocqueville quotes.] which directs that Margaret Bedford, convicted of loose conduct, be whipped and afterward compelled to marry her accomplice, Nicholas Jemmings.

[22] *New Haven Antiquities*, p. 104. See also Hutchinson's *History*, Vol. I, p. 436, for several other equally extraordinary sentences.

[23] Code of 1650, pp. 50, 57.

[24] *Ibid.*, p. 64.

[25] *Ibid.*, p. 44.

[26] This was not peculiar to Connecticut. See, *inter alia*, the Massachusetts law of September 13, 1644, which condemned the Anabaptists to banishment (*Historical Collection of State Papers*, Vol. I, p. 538). See also the law passed on October 14, 1656, against the Quakers: "Whereas there is a pernicious sect, commonly called Quakers, lately arisen . . ." [Cf. *The Charters and General*

penalty, on Christians who chose to worship God with a ritual other than their own.[27] Finally, sometimes the passion for regulation which possessed them led them to interfere in matters completely unworthy of such attention. Hence there is a clause in the same code forbidding the use of tobacco.[28] We must not forget that these ridiculous and tyrannical laws were not imposed from outside—they were voted by the free agreement of all the interested parties themselves—and that their mores were even more austere and puritanical than their laws. In 1649 an association was solemnly formed in Boston to check the worldly luxury of long hair.[29] (See Appendix I, E.)

Such deviations undoubtedly bring shame on the spirit of man; they attest the inferiority of our nature, which, unable to hold firmly to what is true and just, is generally reduced to choosing between two excesses.

Alongside this criminal code so strongly marked by narrow sectarian spirit and all the religious passions, stimulated by persecution and still seething in the depths of men's souls, was a body of political laws, closely bound up with the penal law, which, though drafted two hundred years ago, still seems very far in advance of the spirit of freedom of our own age.

All the general principles on which modern constitutions rest, principles which most Europeans in the seventeenth century scarcely understood and whose dominance in Great Britain was then far from complete, are recognized and given authority by the laws of New England; the participation of the people in public affairs, the free voting of taxes, the responsibility of government officials, individual freedom, and trial by jury—all these things were established without question and with practical effect.

These pregnant principles were there applied and developed in a way that no European nation has yet dared to attempt.

In Connecticut the electoral body consisted, from the beginning, of all the citizens, and that is readily understood.[30] In that nascent

---

Laws of the Colony and Province of Massachusetts Bay, Boston, 1814, p. 123.] There follow provisions imposing very heavy fines on the captains of ships bringing Quakers to the country. Quakers who succeed in coming in are to be whipped and shut up in prison to work there. Those who defend their opinions will first be fined, then imprisoned, and finally driven out of the province. (*Historical Collection of State Papers,* Vol. I, p. 630).

[27] Under the penal law of Massachusetts a Catholic priest who sets foot in the state after he has been driven out therefrom is subject to the death penalty.

[28] Code of 1650, p. 96.

[29] *New England's Memorial,* p. 316.

[30] Constitution of 1638 [*Code of 1650*], p. 17.

community there prevailed an almost perfect equality of wealth and even greater intellectual equality.[31]

At that time in Connecticut all executive officials were elected, including the governor[32] of the state.

Citizens over sixteen years of age were obliged to bear arms; they formed a national militia which appointed its officers and was bound to be ready to march at any time to the country's defense.[33]

In the laws of Connecticut and of all the other states of New England we see the birth and growth of that local independence which is still the mainspring and lifeblood of American freedom.

In most European nations political existence started in the higher ranks of society and has been gradually, but always incompletely, communicated to the various members of the body social.

Contrariwise, in America one may say that the local community was organized before the county, the county before the state, and the state before the Union.

In New England, local communities had taken complete and definite shape as early as 1650. Interests, passions, duties, and rights took shape around each individual locality and were firmly attached thereto. Inside the locality there was a real, active political life which was completely democratic and republican. The colonies still recognized the mother country's supremacy; legally the state was a monarchy, but each locality was already a lively republic.

The towns appointed their own magistrates of all sorts, assessed themselves, and imposed their own taxes.[34] The New England towns adopted no representative institutions. As at Athens, matters of common concern were dealt with in the marketplace and in the general assembly of the citizens.

When one studies in detail the laws promulgated in this early period of the American republics, one is struck by their understanding of problems of government and by the advanced theories of the lawgivers.

Clearly they had a higher and more comprehensive conception of the duties of society toward its members than had the lawgivers of Europe at that time, and they imposed obligations upon it which were still shirked elsewhere. There was provision for the poor from

[31] In 1641 the general assembly of Rhode Island declared unanimously that the government of the state was a democracy and that power resided in the body of free men, who alone had the right to make the laws and provide for their enforcement. Code of 1650, p. 70. [Should refer to p. 12.]

[32] Pitkin's *History*, p. 47.

[33] Constitution of 1638 [*Code of 1650*], p. 12. [The reference should read p. 70.]

[34] Code of 1650, p. 80.

the beginning in the states of New England;[35] there were strict regulations for the maintenance of roads, with officials appointed to supervise them;[36] the townships had public registers recording the conclusions of public deliberations and the births, deaths, and marriages of the citizens;[37] there were clerks whose duty it was to keep these records;[38] officials were appointed, some to look after intestate property, others to determine the boundaries of inherited lands, and many more whose chief function was to maintain public order.[39]

The law anticipates and provides in great detail for a multitude of social needs of which in France we are still now but vaguely conscious.

But it is the provisions for public education which, from the very first, throw into clearest relief the originality of American civilization.

The Code states: "It being one chief project of that old deluder, Satan, to keep men from the knowledge of the scriptures, as in former times, keeping them in an unknown tongue, so in these latter times, by persuading them from the use of tongues, so that at least, the true sense and meaning of the original might be clouded with false glosses of saint seeming deceivers; and that learning may not be buried in the grave of our forefathers, in church and commonwealth, the Lord assisting our endeavors . . ."[40] Provisions follow establishing schools in all townships, and obliging the inhabitants, under penalty of heavy fines, to maintain them. In the same way, high schools are founded in the more densely populated districts. The municipal officials are bound to see that parents send their children to the schools, and can impose fines on those who refuse to do so; if the parents remain recalcitrant, society can take over the charge of the children from the family, depriving the parents of those natural rights which they abused.[41] No doubt the reader has noticed the preamble to these regulations; in America it is religion which leads to enlightenment and the observance of divine laws which leads men to liberty.

If one turns from this rapid survey of the America of 1650 and considers European, especially Continental European, society at that same time, one finds the contrast profoundly astonishing. Everywhere on the Continent at the beginning of the seventeenth century absolute monarchies stood triumphantly on the ruins of the feudal or

---

[35] *Ibid.*, p. 78.
[36] *Ibid.*, p. 49.
[37] See Hutchinson's *History*, Vol. I, p. 455.
[38] Code of 1650, p. 86.
[39] *Ibid.*, p. 40[f.].
[40] *Ibid.*, p. 90[f.].
[41] *Ibid.*, p. 83 [pp. 39(?) and 91].

oligarchic freedom of the Middle Ages. Amid the brilliance and the
literary achievements of Europe, then, the conception of rights
was perhaps more completely misunderstood than at any other time;
the peoples had never taken less part in political life; notions of true
liberty had never been less in men's minds. And just at that time
these very principles, unknown to or scorned by the nations of Europe,
were proclaimed in the wildernesses of the New World, where they
were to become the watchwords of a great people. In this apparently
lowly society the boldest speculations of humanity were put into
practice, while no statesman, we may be sure, deigned to take notice
of them. With free rein given to its natural originality, human imagination there improvised unprecedented legislation. In that uncon-
sidered democracy which had as yet produced neither generals, nor
philosophers, nor great writers, a man could stand up in front of a
free people and gain universal applause for this fine definition of
freedom:

"Nor would I have you to mistake in the point of your own *liberty*.
There is a *liberty* of corrupt nature, which is affected by *men* and
beasts to do what they list; and this *liberty* is inconsistent with
authority, impatient of all restraint; by this *liberty, Sumus Omnes
Deteriores,* 'tis the grand enemy of *truth* and *peace,* and all the
ordinances of God are bent against it. But there is a civil, a moral,
a federal *liberty,* which is the proper end and object of *authority;*
it is a *liberty* for that only which is *just* and *good;* for this *liberty*
you are to stand with the hazard of your very *lives. . . .* This
liberty is maintained in a way of *subjection* to *authority;* and the
authority set over you will in all administrations for your good be
quietly submitted unto, by all but such as have a disposition to *shake
off the yoke,* and lose their true *liberty,* by their murmuring at the
honour and power of *authority."*[42]

I have already said enough to put Anglo-American civilization in
its true light. It is the product (and one should continually bear in
mind this point of departure) of two perfectly distinct elements
which elsewhere have often been at war with one another but which
in America it was somehow possible to incorporate into each other,

---

[42] Mather's *Magnalia Christi Americana,* Vol. II, p. 13. [Tocqueville's reference is faulty. The passage is to be found in the 1820 Hartford edition, which
Tocqueville used, Vol. I, p. 116 f.] Winthrop is speaking; he had been accused
of arbitrary behavior as a magistrate; when the speech of which the above
forms part was finished, he was acquitted amid applause, and thereafter he
was always reelected as governor of the state. See Marshall, Vol. I, p. 166. [*The
Life of George Washington,* Vol. I, London 1804; Governor Winthrop is mentioned on p. 173.]

forming a marvelous combination. I mean the *spirit of religion* and the *spirit of freedom.*

The founders of New England were both ardent sectarians and fanatical innovators. While held within the narrowest bounds by fixed religious beliefs, they were free from all political prejudices.

Ahhh...

Hence two distinct but not contradictory tendencies plainly show their traces everywhere, in mores and in laws.

For the sake of a religious conviction men sacrifice their friends, their families, and their fatherland; one might suppose them entirely absorbed in pursuit of that intellectual prize for which they had just paid so high a price. Yet it is with almost equal eagerness that they seek either material wealth or moral delights, either heaven in the next world or prosperity and freedom in this.

Under their manipulation political principles, laws, and human institutions seem malleable things which can at will be adapted and combined. The barriers which hemmed in the society in which they were brought up fall before them; old views which have ruled the world for centuries vanish; almost limitless opportunities lie open in a world without horizon; the spirit of man rushes forward to explore it in every direction; but when that spirit reaches the limits of the world of politics, it stops of its own accord; in trepidation it renounces the use of its most formidable faculties; it forswears doubt and renounces innovation; it will not even lift the veil of the sanctuary; and it bows respectfully before truths which it accepts without discussion.

Thus, in the moral world everything is classified, coordinated, foreseen, and decided in advance. In the world of politics everything is in turmoil, contested, and uncertain. In the one case obedience is passive, though voluntary; in the other there is independence, contempt of experience, and jealousy of all authority.

Far from harming each other, these two apparently opposed tendencies work in harmony and seem to lend mutual support.

Religion regards civil liberty as a noble exercise of men's faculties, the world of politics being a sphere intended by the Creator for the free play of intelligence. Religion, being free and powerful within its own sphere and content with the position reserved for it, realizes that its sway is all the better established because it relies only on its own powers and rules men's hearts without external support.

Freedom sees religion as the companion of its struggles and triumphs, the cradle of its infancy, and the divine source of its rights. Religion is considered as the guardian of mores, and mores are regarded as the guarantee of the laws and pledge for the maintenance of freedom itself. (See Appendix I, F.)

But religion can also guarantee the maintenance of oppression...

Reasons for Some Peculiarities in the Laws and Customs of the Anglo-Americans

Some relics of aristocratic institutions amid the most complete democracy. Why? Need to make a careful distinction between that which is Puritan in origin and that which is English.

The reader should not draw exaggeratedly general and exclusive conclusions from what has been said before. The social condition, religion, and mores of the first settlers certainly exercised an immense influence on the fate of their new country. Nevertheless, it was not open to them to found a society with no other point of departure besides themselves; no man can entirely detach himself from the past; perhaps unintentionally, perhaps unconsciously, they did mingle with their own ideas and habits others which derived from their education and the national tradition of the homeland.

So, if we are to understand the Anglo-Americans of our own day, we must make a careful distinction between elements of Puritan and elements of English origin.

One often finds laws and customs in the United States which contrast with the rest of their surroundings. Such laws seem to have been drafted in a spirit opposed to the prevailing genius of American legislation, and such mores seem to run counter to the whole tone of society. If the English colonies had been founded in an age of darkness and their origins had been lost in the night of time, the problem would have been insoluble.

I will quote just one example to make my meaning clear.

The civil and criminal procedure of the Americans relies on two modes of action only, *committal* or *bail*. The first step in any lawsuit is to get bail from the defendant or, if he refuses that, to put him in prison; only after that is the validity of the title or the gravity of the charge discussed.

Clearly such a procedure is hard on the poor and favors the rich only.

A poor man cannot always raise bail even in a civil case, and if he has to wait in prison for the hearing of the matter, his enforced idleness soon reduces him to destitution.

But if it is a civil suit, the rich man never has to go to prison, and, more important, if he has committed a crime, he can easily escape the proper punishment, for having given bail, he disappears. So, as far as he is concerned, the law actually imposes no penalty worse than a fine.[43] What could be more aristocratic than such legislation?

Yet, in America, it is the poor who make the laws, and usually they reserve the greatest benefits of society for themselves.

One must look to England for the explanation of this phenomenon, for these laws are English.[44] The Americans have not changed them at all, although they are repugnant to their laws in general, and to the bulk of their ideas.

After its customs, the thing which a people changes the least is its civil law. Only lawyers—that is to say, those who have a direct interest in keeping them as they are, good or bad, simply because they know them—are familiar with civil laws. The nation at large hardly knows about them; people see them in action only in particular cases, have difficulty in appreciating their implications, and submit to them unthinkingly.

I have quoted one example, but I could have mentioned many more.

One might put it this way. The surface of American society is covered with a layer of democratic paint, but from time to time one can see the old aristocratic colors breaking through.

[43] Of course there are crimes for which bail is not allowed, but they are very few.

[44] See Blackstone and Delolme, Book I, chapter 10. [The last reference seems to refer to De Lolme's work.]

Chapter 3

SOCIAL STATE OF THE ANGLO-AMERICANS

THE SOCIAL STATE is commonly the result of circumstances, sometimes of laws, but most often of a combination of the two. But once it has come into being, it may itself be considered as the prime cause of most of the laws, customs, and ideas which control the nation's behavior; it modifies even those things which it does not cause.

Therefore one must first study their social state if one wants to understand a people's laws and mores.

The Striking Feature in the Social Condition of the Anglo-Americans Is That It Is Essentially Democratic

First immigrants to New England. Equal among themselves. Aristocratic laws introduced in the South. Period of the Revolution. Change in the laws of inheritance. Results of that change. Equality carried to extreme limits in the new states of the West. Equality of mental endowments.

There are many important things to be said about the social condition of the Anglo-Americans, but one feature dominates all the others.

The social state of the Americans is eminently democratic. It has been like that ever since the birth of the colonies but is even more so now.

I said in the last chapter that a high degree of equality prevailed among the immigrants who first settled on the coast of New England. In that part of the states even the seeds of aristocracy were never planted. There only intellectual power could command influence, and the people came to respect certain names as symbols of enlightenment and virtue. The views of some citizens carried such weight that if it had invariably passed from father to son, their influence might reasonably have been called aristocratic.

That was the case to the east of the Hudson. To the southwest of that river and right down to the Floridas things were different.

Great English landowners had come to settle in most of the states southwest of the Hudson. They brought with them aristocratic principles, including the English law of inheritance. I have explained the reasons that made it impossible ever to establish a powerful aristocracy in America. Those reasons applied southwest of the Hudson too, but with less force than to the east thereof. In the South one man and his slaves could cultivate a wide extent of land. So there were rich landowners in that part of the country. But their influence was not exactly aristocratic, in the sense in which that word is used in Europe, for they had no privileges, and the use of slaves meant that they had no tenants and consequently no patronage. However, the great landowners south of the Hudson did form an upper class, with its own ideas and tastes, and in general it did concentrate political activity in its hands. It was a sort of aristocracy not very different from the bulk of the people whose passions and interests it easily embraced, arousing neither love nor hate. It was, to conclude, weak and unlikely to last. That was the class which, in the South, put itself at the head of the rebellion; it provided the best leaders of the American Revolution.

At that time society was shaken to the core. The people, in whose name the war had been fought, became a power and wanted to act on their own; democratic instincts awoke; the English yoke had been broken, and a taste for every form of independence grew; little by little the influence of individuals ceased to carry weight; customs and laws began to march in step toward the same goal.

But it was the law of inheritance which caused the final advance of equality.

I am surprised that ancient and modern writers have not attributed greater importance to the laws of inheritance[1] and their effect on the progress of human affairs. They are, it is true, civil laws, but they should head the list of all political institutions, for they have an un-believable influence on the social state of peoples, and political laws are no more than the expression of that state. Moreover, their way of influencing society is both sure and uniform; in some sense they lay hands on each generation before it is born. By their means man is armed with almost supernatural power over the future of his fellows. When the lawgiver has once fixed the law of inheritance,

[1] By laws of inheritance I mean all those laws whose principal object is to control the fate of property after its owner's death.

The law of entail is among these; it does, of course, also have the effect of preventing a landowner disposing of his property before his death, but its only object in making him keep it is to see that it passes on intact to his heir. Therefore the main aim of the law of entail is to control the fate of property after its owner's death; its other provisions are merely means to that end.

he can rest for centuries; once the impulse has been given to his handiwork, he can take his hand away; the mechanism works by its own power and apparently spontaneously aims at the goal indicated beforehand. If it has been drafted in a certain way, it assembles, concentrates, and piles up property, and soon power too, in the hands of one man; in a sense it makes an aristocracy leap forth from the ground. Guided by other principles and directed toward other goals, its effect is even quicker; it divides, shares, and spreads property and power; then sometimes people get frightened at the speed of its progress; despairing of stopping its motion, men seek at least to put obstacles and difficulties in its way; there is an attempt to balance its action by measures of opposite tendency. But all in vain! It grinds up or smashes everything that stands in its way; with the continual rise and fall of its hammer strokes, everything is reduced to a fine, impalpable dust, and that dust is the foundation for democracy.

When the law of inheritance allows or, *a fortiori,* ordains the equal sharing of a father's property among his children, the results are of two sorts, which need to be distinguished, though they both tend toward the same end.

Owing to the law of inheritance, the death of each owner causes a revolution in property; not only do possessions change hands, but their very nature is altered, as they are continually broken up into smaller fractions.

That is the direct physical effect of the law. So in countries where equal shares are the rule, property, particularly landed property, has a permanent tendency to grow less. However, the effects of such legislation would only be felt in the fullness of time if the effects of the law were simply left to work themselves out, for in families with not more than two children (and the average of families with a population pattern such as France is said to be only three), those children sharing their father's and their mother's fortune would not be poorer than either of the latter individually.

But the rule of equal shares does not affect only the fate of property; it also affects the very soul of the landowner and brings his passions into play. It is these indirect effects which rapidly break up great fortunes, especially landed property.

In nations where the law of inheritance is based on primogeniture, landed estates generally pass undivided from one generation to another. Hence family feeling finds a sort of physical expression in the land. The family represents the land, and the land the family, perpetuating its name, origin, glory, power, and virtue. It is an imperishable witness to the past and a precious earnest of the future.

When the law ordains equal shares, it breaks that intimate connection between family feeling and preservation of the land; the land no longer represents the family, for, as it is bound to be divided up at the end of one or two generations, it is clear that it must continually diminish and completely disappear in the end. The sons of a great landowner, if they are few, or if fortune favors them, may still hope to be no less rich than their parent, but they cannot expect to possess the same lands; their wealth is bound to be composed of different elements from his.

Now, as soon as landowners are deprived of their strong sentimental attachment to the land, based on memories and pride, it is certain that sooner or later they will sell it, for they have a powerful pecuniary interest in so doing, since other forms of investment earn a higher rate of interest and liquid assets are more easily used to satisfy the passions of the moment.

Once divided, great landed estates do not come together again; for, proportionately, a smallholder gets a better income from his fields[2] than a great landlord from his, and so he sells it too at a much higher price. Thus the same economic calculation which induced the rich man to sell vast properties will even more powerfully dissuade him from buying up small holdings to make a great one again.

What passes for family feeling is often based on an illusion of personal selfishness; a man seeks to perpetuate himself and, in some sense, to make himself immortal through his great-grandchildren. Where family feeling is at an end, personal selfishness turns again to its real inclinations. As the family is felt to be a vague, indeterminate, uncertain conception, each man concentrates on his immediate convenience; he thinks about getting the next generation established in life, but nothing further.

Hence a man does not seek to perpetuate his family, or at least he seeks other means than landed estates to do so.

Thus the law of inheritance not only makes it difficult for families to retain the same domains intact, but takes away their wish to try to do so and, in a sense, leads them to cooperate with the law in their own ruin.

The law of equal shares progresses along two paths: by acting upon things, it affects persons; by acting on persons, it has its effect on things.

---

[2] I do not mean to say that the smallholder cultivates the land better, but he does so with greater eagerness and energy, making up by hard work for anything he lacks in skill.

By both these means it strikes at the root of landed estates and quickly breaks up both families and fortunes.[3]

It is certainly not for us, Frenchmen of the nineteenth century, who are daily witness of the political and social changes caused by the law of inheritance, to doubt its power. Every day we see its influence coming and going over our land, knocking down the walls of our houses in its path, and throwing down the fences of our fields. But though the law of inheritance has done much among us, it still has much to do. Our memories, thoughts, and habits still put substantial obstacles in its way.

In the United States its work of destruction has almost been brought to an end. It is there that one can study its chief effects.

The English law concerning succession to property was abolished in almost all the states at the time of the Revolution.

The law of entail was so modified that it hardly put any restraint on the free sale of land. (See Appendix I, G.)

The first generation passed away; land began to be divided. As time passed, the change grew faster and faster. Now, hardly sixty years later, the aspect of society is already hard to recognize; the families of the great landowners have almost mingled with the common mass. In the state of New York, where formerly there were many, only two still keep their heads above the waters which are ready to swallow them too. The sons of these wealthy citizens are now merchants, lawyers, or doctors. Most of them have fallen into the most complete obscurity. The last trace of hereditary ranks and distinctions has been destroyed; the law of inheritance has everywhere imposed its dead level.

It is not that in the United States, as everywhere, there are no rich; indeed I know no other country where love of money has such a grip on men's hearts or where stronger scorn is expressed for the theory of permanent equality of property. But wealth circulates there with incredible rapidity, and experience shows that two successive generations seldom enjoy its favors.

[3] Land being the most solid type of property, one does sometimes find rich men ready to make great sacrifices to acquire it, voluntarily giving up a large part of their income to make the rest safe. But those are exceptional cases. It is in general only among the poor that love of land is something normal. The smallholder with less education, less imagination, and fewer passions than the large landowner is usually bent on nothing but increasing his holding, and it often happens that inheritance, marriage, or the chances of trade gradually provide him with the means for this.

So besides the tendency which leads men to divide up land, there is another tendency leading them to accumulate it. That tendency, which is enough to prevent the division of land ad infinitum, is not strong enough to form great territorial fortunes, still less to maintain them in the same families.

This picture, which some may think overdrawn, would give only a very imperfect impression of what goes on in the new states of the West and Southwest.

At the end of the last century a few bold adventurers began to penetrate into the Mississippi valley. It was like a new discovery of America; soon most of those who were immigrating went there; previously unheard of communities suddenly sprang up in the wilderness. States that had not even been names a few years before took their places in the American Union. It is in the West that one can see democracy in its most extreme form. In these states, in some sense improvisations of fortune, the inhabitants have arrived only yesterday in the land where they dwell. They hardly know one another, and each man is ignorant of his nearest neighbor's history. So in that part of the American continent the population escapes the influence not only of great names and great wealth but also of the natural aristocracy of education and probity. No man there enjoys the influence and respect due to a whole life spent publicly in doing good. There are inhabitants already in the new states of the West, but not as yet a society.

But it is not only fortunes that are equal in America; equality to some extent affects their mental endowments too.

I think there is no other country in the world where, proportionately to population, there are so few ignorant and so few learned individuals as in America.

Primary education is within reach of all; higher education is hardly available to anybody.

That is easily understood and is indeed the necessary consequence of what has been said before.

Almost all Americans enjoy easy circumstances and can so easily acquire the basic elements of human knowledge.

There are few rich men in America; hence almost all Americans have to take up some profession. Now, every profession requires an apprenticeship. Therefore the Americans can devote only the first years of life to general education; at fifteen they start on a career, so their education generally ends at the age when ours begins. If it is continued beyond that point, it aims only at some specialized and profitable objective; science is studied in the same spirit as one takes up a trade; and only matters of immediate and recognized practical application receive attention.

In America most rich men began by being poor; almost all men of leisure were busy in their youth; as a result, at the age when one might have a taste for study, one has not the time; and when time is available, the taste has gone.

So there is no class in America in which a taste for intellectual pleasures is transmitted with hereditary wealth and leisure and which holds the labors of the mind in esteem.

Both the will and the power to engage in such work are lacking.

A middling standard has been established in America for all human knowledge. All minds come near to it, some by raising and some by lowering their standards.

As a result one finds a vast multitude of people with roughly the same ideas about religion, history, science, political economy, legislation, and government.

Intellectual inequalities come directly from God, and man cannot prevent them existing always.

But it results from what we have just been explaining, that, though mental endowments remain unequal as the Creator intended, the means of exercising them are equal.

Therefore, in America now the aristocratic element, which was from the beginning weak, has been, if not destroyed, at least made feebler still, so that one can hardly attribute to it any influence over the course of things.

On the other hand, time, circumstances, and laws have made the democratic element not merely preponderant but, one might say, exclusive.

One cannot trace any family or corporate influence; it is often hard even to discover any durable individual influence.

So the social state of America is a very strange phenomenon. Men there are nearer equality in wealth and mental endowments, or, in other words, more nearly equally powerful, than in any other country of the world or in any other age of recorded history.

Political Consequences of the Social State of the Anglo-Americans

It is easy to deduce the political consequences of such a social state.

By no possibility could equality ultimately fail to penetrate into the sphere of politics as everywhere else. One cannot imagine that men should remain perpetually unequal in just one respect though equal in all others; within a certain time they are bound to become equal in all respects.

Now, I know of only two ways of making equality prevail in the political sphere; rights must be given either to every citizen or to nobody.

So, for a people who have reached the Anglo-Americans' social state, it is hard to see any middle course between the sovereignty of all and the absolute power of one man.

One must not disguise it from oneself that the social state I have just described may lead as easily to the one as to the other of those results.

There is indeed a manly and legitimate passion for equality which rouses in all men a desire to be strong and respected. This passion tends to elevate the little man to the rank of the great. But the human heart also nourishes a debased taste for equality, which leads the weak to want to drag the strong down to their level and which induces men to prefer equality in servitude to inequality in freedom. It is not that peoples with a democratic social state naturally scorn freedom; on the contrary, they have an instinctive taste for it. But freedom is not the chief and continual object of their desires; it is equality for which they feel an eternal love; they rush on freedom with quick and sudden impulses, but if they miss their mark they resign themselves to their disappointment; but nothing will satisfy them without equality, and they would rather die than lose it.

On the other hand, when the citizens are all more or less equal, it becomes difficult to defend their freedom from the encroachments of power. No one among them being any longer strong enough to struggle alone with success, only the combination of the forces of all is able to guarantee liberty. But such a combination is not always forthcoming.

So, nations can derive either of two great political consequences from the same social state; these consequences differ vastly from each other, but both originate from the same fact.

The Anglo-Americans who were the first to be faced with the above-mentioned alternatives were lucky enough to escape absolute power. Circumstances, origin, education, and above all mores allowed them to establish and maintain the sovereignty of the people.

Chapter 4

THE PRINCIPLE OF THE SOVEREIGNTY OF THE PEOPLE IN AMERICA

It dominates the whole of American society. How the Americans applied this principle even before their Revolution. Its growth as a result of the Revolution. Gradual and irresistible lowering of voting qualifications.

ANY DISCUSSION of the political laws of the United States must always begin with the dogma of the sovereignty of the people.

The principle of the sovereignty of the people, which is always to be found, more or less, at the bottom of almost all human institutions, usually remains buried there. It is obeyed without being recognized, or if for one moment it is brought out into the daylight, it is hastily thrust back into the gloom of the sanctuary.

"The will of the nation" is one of the phrases most generally abused by intriguers and despots of every age. Some have seen the expression of it in the bought votes of a few agents of authority, others in the votes of an interested or frightened minority, and some have even discovered it in a people's silence, thinking that the *fact* of obedience justified the *right* to command.

But in America the sovereignty of the people is neither hidden nor sterile as with some other nations; mores recognize it, and the laws proclaim it; it spreads with freedom and attains unimpeded its ultimate consequences.

If there is one country in the world where one can hope to appreciate the true value of the dogma of the sovereignty of the people, study its application to the business of society, and judge both its dangers and its advantages, that country is America.

I have already said that from the beginning the principle of the sovereignty of the people was the creative principle of most of the English colonies in America.

But it was far from dominating the government of society then as it does now.

Two obstacles, one external and the other internal, checked its encroachments.

It could not be ostensibly proclaimed in the laws, as the colonies were then still bound to obey the motherland; it had therefore to lie hidden in the provincial assemblies, especially that of the township. There it spread secretly.

American society at that time was by no means ready to accept it with all its consequences. In New England, education, and south of the Hudson, wealth, as mentioned in the last chapter, long exercised a sort of aristocratic influence which tended to keep the exercise of social power in a few hands. It was far from being the case that all public officials were elected and all citizens electors. Everywhere voting rights were restricted within certain limits and subject to some property qualification. That qualification was very low in the North but quite considerable in the South.

The American Revolution broke out. The dogma of the sovereignty of the people came out from the township and took possession of the government; every class enlisted in its cause; the war was fought and victory obtained in its name; it became the law of laws.

A change almost as rapid took place within society. The law of inheritance succeeded in breaking down local influences.

Just when all could see this effect of the laws and the Revolution, democracy's victory had already been irrevocably pronounced. Circumstances put power into its hands. It was not even permissible to struggle against it any longer. So the upper classes submitted without complaint or resistance to an evil which had by then become inevitable. They suffered the usual fate of fallen powers; each followed his own selfish interests; as there was no longer a chance of snatching power from the people's hands, and as they did not detest them enough to take pleasure in flaunting them, their only thought was to gain their goodwill at any price. Consequently the most democratic laws were voted by the very men whose interests they impaired. In this way the upper classes aroused no popular passions against themselves, but they themselves hastened the triumph of the new order. This had the singular result that the impulse toward democracy was most irresistible in those states in which aristocracy had deepest roots.

The state of Maryland, which had been founded by great lords, was the first to proclaim universal suffrage[1] and introduced the most democratic procedures throughout its government.

Once a people begins to interfere with the voting qualification, one can be sure that sooner or later it will abolish it altogether. That is one of the most invariable rules of social behavior. The further the

[1] Amendments introduced into the constitution of Maryland in 1801 and 1809. [Cf. Article XIV of the 1776 Constitution, ratified in 1810.]

limit of voting rights is extended, the stronger is the need felt to spread
them still wider; for after each new concession the forces of democracy are strengthened, and its demands increase with its augmented
power. The ambition of those left below the qualifying limit increases
in proportion to the number of those above it. Finally the exception
becomes the rule; concessions follow one another without interruption, and there is no halting place until universal suffrage has been
attained.

In the United States in our day the principle of the sovereignty of
the people has been adopted in practice in every way that imagination could suggest. It has been detached from all fictions in which it
has elsewhere been carefully wrapped; it takes on every possible
form that the exigencies of the case require. Sometimes the body of
the people makes the laws, as at Athens; sometimes deputies, elected
by universal suffrage, represent it and act in its name under its almost
immediate supervision.

There are countries in which some authority, in a sense outside the
body social, influences it and forces it to progress in a certain direction.

There are others in which power is divided, being at the same time
within the society and outside it. Nothing like that is to be seen in
the United States; there society acts by and for itself. There are no
authorities except within itself; one can hardly meet anybody who
would dare to conceive, much less to suggest, seeking power elsewhere. The people take part in the making of the laws by choosing
the lawgivers, and they share in their application by electing the
agents of the executive power; one might say that they govern themselves, so feeble and restricted is the part left to the administration,
so vividly is that administration aware of its popular origin, and so
obedient is it to the fount of power. The people reign over the
American political world as God rules over the universe. It is the
cause and the end of all things; everything rises out of it and is
absorbed back into it. (See Appendix I, H.)

Chapter 5

THE NEED TO STUDY WHAT HAPPENS IN THE STATES BEFORE DISCUSSING THE GOVERNMENT OF THE UNION

THIS CHAPTER WILL examine the form of government established in America on the principle of the sovereignty of the people, its means of action, impediments, advantages, and dangers.

A preliminary difficulty must be faced; the United States has a complex Constitution; there are two distinct social structures connected and, as it were, encased one within the other; one finds two completely separate and almost independent governments; the one is the ordinary and undefined government which provides for the daily needs of society, while the other is exceptional and circumscribed and only concerned with certain general interests. In a word, there are twenty-four little sovereign nations who together form the United States.

To study the Union before studying the state is to follow a path strewn with obstacles. The federal government was the last to take shape in the United States; the political principles on which it was based were spread throughout society before its time, existed independently of it, and only had to be modified to form the republic. Moreover, as I have just said, the federal government is something of an exception, whereas the government of each state is the normal authority. A writer who tried to paint the whole before he has described the parts would necessarily be obscure and repeat himself.

The great political principles which now rule American society were born and grew up in the *state;* there is no room for doubt about that. So one must understand the state to gain the key to the rest.

The states which now compose the American Union all have institutions with the same external aspect. Political and administrative life is concentrated in three active centers, which could be compared to the various nervous centers that control the motions of the human body.

The township is the first in order, then the county, and last the state.

The American System of Townships

Why the writer begins his examination of political institutions with the township. There are townships in every nation. Difficulty of establishing and maintaining their communal freedom. Its importance. Why the writer has chosen the organization of the New England township as the main subject to examine.

It is not by chance that I consider the township first.

The township is the only association so well rooted in nature that wherever men assemble it forms itself.

Communal society therefore exists among all peoples, whatever be their customs and their laws; man creates kingdoms and republics, but townships seem to spring directly from the hand of God. But though townships are coeval with humanity, local freedom is a rare and fragile thing. A nation can always establish great political assemblies, because it always contains a certain number of individuals whose understanding will, to some extent, take the place of experience in handling affairs. But the local community is composed of coarser elements, often recalcitrant to the lawgiver's activity. The difficulty of establishing a township's independence rather augments than diminishes with the increase of enlightenment of nations. A very civilized society finds it hard to tolerate attempts at freedom in a local community; it is disgusted by its numerous blunders and is apt to despair of success before the experiment is finished.

Of all forms of liberty, that of a local community, which is so hard to establish, is the most prone to the encroachments of authority. Left to themselves, the institutions of a local community can hardly struggle against a strong and enterprising government; they cannot defend themselves with success unless they have reached full development and have come to form part of national ideas and habits. Hence, until communal freedom has come to form part of mores, it can easily be destroyed, and it cannot enter into mores without a long-recognized legal existence.

So communal freedom is not, one may almost say, the fruit of human effort. It is seldom created, but rather springs up of its own accord. It grows, almost in secret, amid a semibarbarous society. The continual action of laws, mores, circumstances, and above all time may succeed in consolidating it. Among all the nations of continental Europe, one may say that there is not one that understand communal liberty.

However, the strength of free peoples resides in the local community. Local institutions are to liberty what primary schools are to science; they put it within the people's reach; they teach people to appreciate its peaceful enjoyment and accustom them to make use of it. Without local institutions a nation may give itself a free government, but it has not got the spirit of liberty. Passing passions, momentary interest, or chance circumstances may give it the external shape of independence, but the despotic tendencies which have been driven into the interior of the body social will sooner or later break out on the surface.

To help the reader understand the general principles on which the political organization of townships and counties in the United States depends, I thought it would be useful to take one particular state as an example and examine in detail what happens there, subsequently taking a quick look at the rest of the country.

I have chosen one of the states of New England.

Townships and counties are not organized in the same way in all parts of the Union; nevertheless, one can easily see that throughout the Union more or less the same principles have guided the formation of both township and county.

Now, I thought that in New England these principles had been carried further with more far-reaching results than elsewhere. Consequently they stand out there in higher relief and are easier for a foreigner to observe.

The local institutions of New England form a complete and regular whole; they are ancient; law and, even more, mores make them strong; and they exercise immense influence over the whole of society.

For all these reasons they deserve our attention.

Limits of the Township

The New England township is halfway between a *canton* and a *commune* in France. It generally has from two to three thousand inhabitants;[1] it is therefore not too large for all the inhabitants to have roughly the same interests, but is big enough to be sure of finding the elements of a good administration within itself.

Powers of the New England Township

The people as the origin of power in the township as elsewhere. They handle their principal affairs themselves. No municipal coun-

[1] In 1830 there were 305 townships in Massachusetts; the population was 610,014; that gives an average of about 2,000 for each township.

*cil. The greater part of municipal authority concentrated in the
hands of the "selectmen." How the selectmen function. Town
meeting. List of all municipal officials. Obligatory and paid functions.*

In the township, as everywhere else, the people are the source of
power, but nowhere else do they exercise their power so directly. In
America the people are a master who must be indulged to the utmost
possible limits.

In New England the majority works through representatives when
it is dealing with the general affairs of the state. It was necessary that
that should be so; but in the township, where both law and administration are closer to the governed, the representative system has not
been adopted. There is no municipal council; the body of the
electors, when it has chosen the officials, gives them directions in everything beyond the simple, ordinary execution of the laws of the state.[2]

Such a state of affairs is so contrary to our ideas and opposed to
our habits that some examples are needed to make it understandable.

Public duties in the township are extremely numerous and minutely
divided, as we shall see later on, but most of the administrative power
is concentrated in the hands of a few yearly elected individuals called
"selectmen."[3]

The general laws of the state impose certain duties on the selectmen. In administering these they do not require the authorization
of the governed, and it is their personal responsibility if they neglect
them. For example, the state law charges them to draw up the
municipal voting lists, and if they fail to do so, they are guilty of
an offense. But in all matters within the township's control the
selectmen carry out the popular will, just as our mayors execute the

[2] The same rules do not apply to the large townships. Those generally have
a mayor and a municipal body divided into two branches, but a law is needed
to authorize such an exception. See the law of February 23, 1822, regulating
the powers of the city of Boston. *Laws of Massachusetts,* Vol. II, p. 588. [*The
General Laws of Massachusetts,* Vol. II, Boston, 1823, p. 588 ff.] That applies
to the large towns. Small towns also often have a particular administration. In 1832 104 such municipal administrations were counted in the state of
New York. (*Williams's New York Annual Register.*) [*The New York Annual
Register for the Year of Our Lord 1832,* by Edwin Williams, New York, 1832.]

[3] There are three selectmen in the smallest townships and nine in the largest.
See *The Town Officer,* p. 186. [Tocqueville refers here to a book by Isaac
Goodwin, *Town Officer or Law of Massachusetts* (Worcester, 1829), which in-
cidentally is to be found among the volumes of his library at the Château de
Tocqueville.] See also the main laws of Massachusetts concerning selectmen:
Law of February 20, 1786, Vol. I, p. 219; February 24, 1796, Vol. I, p. 488;
March 7, 1801, Vol. II, p. 45; June 16, 1795, Vol. I, p. 475; March 12, 1808,
Vol. II, p. 186; February 28, 1787, Vol. I, p. 302; June 22, 1797, Vol. I, p.
539.

decisions of the municipal council. Usually they act on their own responsibility, merely putting into practice principles already approved by the majority. But if they want to make any change in the established order to start some new undertaking, they must go back to the source of their power. Suppose they want to start a school; the selectmen summon all the voters to a meeting on a fixed day and place; they there explain the need felt; they state the means available for the purpose, how much it will cost, and the site suggested. The meeting, consulted on all these points, accepts the principle, decides the site, votes the tax, and leaves the selectmen to carry out its orders.

Only the selectmen have the right to call a town meeting, but they may be required to do so. If ten owners of property conceive some new project and wish to submit it to the approval of the township, they demand a general meeting of the inhabitants; the selectmen are bound to agree to this and preserve only the right to preside over the meeting.[4]

Such political mores and social customs are certainly far removed from ours. I do not, at this moment, want to pass judgment on them or to reveal the hidden reasons causing them and giving them life; it is enough to describe them.

The selectmen are elected every year in April or May. At the same time, the town meeting also elects many other municipal officials[5] to take charge of important administrative details. There are assessors to rate the township and collectors to bring the taxes in. The constable must organize the police, take care of public places, and take a hand in the physical execution of the laws. The town clerk must record all resolutions; he keeps a record of the proceedings of the civil administration. The treasurer looks after the funds of the township. There are also overseers of the poor whose difficult task it is to execute the provisions of the Poor Laws; school commissioners in charge of public education; and surveyors of highways, who look after roads both large and small, to complete the list of the main administrative officials of the township. But the division of functions does not stop there; among municipal officials one also finds parish commissioners responsible for the expenses of public worship, fire wardens to direct the citizens' efforts in case of fire, tithing men, hog reeves, fence viewers, timber measurers, and sealers of weights and measures.[6]

4 See *Laws of Massachusetts,* Vol. I, p. 150; law of March 25, 1786.
5 *Ibid.*
6 All these officials really do exist. To find out the details of all their duties see *The Town Officer,* by Isaac Goodwin (Worcester, 1829), and the *General Laws of Massachusetts* in 3 vols. (Boston, 1823).

Altogether there are nineteen main officials in a township. Every inhabitant is bound, on pain of fine, to accept these various duties; but most of them also carry some remuneration so that poorer citizens can devote their time to them without loss. Furthermore, it is not the American system to give any fixed salary to officials. In general, each official act has a price, and men are paid in accordance with what they have done.

Life in the Township

Each man the best judge of his own interest. Corollary of the principle of the sovereignty of the people. How American townships apply these doctrines. The New England township sovereign in all that concerns itself alone, subordinate in all else. Duties of the township toward the state. In France the government lends officials to the commune. In America the township lends its officials to the government.

I have said before that the principle of the sovereignty of the people hovers over the whole political system of the Anglo-Americans. Every page of this book will point out new applications of this doctrine.

In nations where the dogma of the sovereignty of the people prevails, each individual forms an equal part of that sovereignty and shares equally the government of the state.

Each individual is assumed to be as educated, virtuous, and powerful as any of his fellows.

Why, then, should he obey society, and what are the natural limits of such obedience?

He obeys society not because he is inferior to those who direct it, nor because he is incapable of ruling himself, but because union with his fellows seems useful to him and he knows that that union is impossible without a regulating authority.

Therefore, in all matters concerning the duties of citizens toward each other he is subordinate. In all matters that concern himself alone he remains the master; he is free and owes an account of his actions to God alone. From this derives the maxim that the individual is the best and only judge of his own interest and that society has no right to direct his behavior unless it feels harmed by him or unless it needs his concurrence.

This doctrine is universally accepted in the United States. Elsewhere I will examine its general influence on the ordinary actions of life; here and now I am concerned only with townships.

The township, taken as a whole in relation to the central government, resembles any other individual to whom the theory just mentioned applies.

So in the United States municipal liberty derives straight from the dogma of the sovereignty of the people; all the American republics have recognized this independence more or less, but there were circumstances particularly favorable to its growth among the people of New England.

In that part of the Union political life was born in the very heart of the townships; one might almost say that in origin each of them was a little independent nation. Later, when the kings of England claimed their share of sovereignty, they limited themselves to taking over the central power. They left the townships as they had found them. Now the New England townships are subordinate, but in the beginning this was not so, or hardly so. Therefore they have not received their powers; on the contrary, it would seem that they have surrendered a portion of their powers for the benefit of the state; that is an important distinction which the reader should always bear in mind.

In general the townships are subordinate to the state only where some interest that I shall call *social* is concerned, that is to say, some interest shared with others.

In all that concerns themselves alone the townships remain independent bodies, and I do not think one could find a single inhabitant of New England who would recognize the right of the government of the state to control matters of purely municipal interest.

Hence one finds the New England townships buying and selling, suing and being sued, increasing or reducing their budgets, and no administrative authority whatsoever thinks of standing in their way.[7]

But there are social duties which they are bound to perform. Thus, if the state needs money, the township is not free to grant or refuse its help.[8] If the state wants to open a road, the township cannot bar its territory. If there is a police regulation, the township must carry it out. If the government wants to organize education on a uniform plan throughout the country, the township must establish the schools required by the law.[9] We shall see, when we come to speak of the administration of the United States, how and by whom, in these various cases, the townships are constrained to obedience.

[7] See *Laws of Massachusetts,* law of March 23, 1786, Vol. I, p. 250.

[8] *Ibid.,* law of February 20, 1786, Vol. I, p. 217.

[9] See the same collection, law of June 25, 1789, Vol. I, p. 367, and March 10, 1827, Vol. III, p. 179.

Here I only wish to establish the fact of the obligation. Strict as this obligation is, the government of the state imposes it in principle only, and in its performance the township resumes all its independent rights. Thus taxes are, it is true, voted by the legislature, but they are assessed and collected by the township; the establishment of a school is obligatory, but the township builds it, pays for it, and controls it.

In France the state tax collector receives the communal taxes; in America the township tax collector collects state taxes.

So, whereas with us the central government lends its agents to the commune, in America the township lends its agents to the government. That fact alone shows how far the two societies differ.

Spirit of the Township in New England

Why the new England township wins the affection of the inhabitants. Difficulty of creating municipal spirit in Europe. In America municipal rights and duties concur in forming that spirit. The homeland has more characteristic features in America than elsewhere. How municipal spirit manifests itself in New England. What happy results it produces there.

In America not only do municipal institutions exist, but there is also a municipal spirit which sustains and gives them life.

The New England township combines two advantages which, wherever they are found, keenly excite men's interest; they are independence and power. It acts, it is true, within a sphere beyond which it cannot pass, but within that domain its movements are free. This independence alone would give a real importance not warranted by size or population.

It is important to appreciate that, in general, men's affections are drawn only in directions where power exists. Patriotism does not long prevail in a conquered country. The New Englander is attached to his township not so much because he was born there as because he sees the township as a free, strong corporation of which he is part and which is worth the trouble of trying to direct.

It often happens in Europe that governments themselves regret the absence of municipal spirit, for everyone agrees that municipal spirit is an important element in order and public tranquillity, but they do not know how to produce it. In making municipalities strong and independent, they fear sharing their social power and exposing the state to risks of anarchy. However, if you take power and independence from a municipality, you may have docile subjects but you will not have citizens.

Another important fact must be noted. The New England township is shaped to form the nucleus of strong attachments, and there is meanwhile no rival center close by to attract the hot hearts of ambitious men.

County officials are not elected and their authority is limited. Even a state is only of secondary importance, being an obscure and placid entity. Few men are willing to leave the center of their interests and take trouble to win the right to help administer it.

The federal government does confer power and renown on those who direct it, but only a few can exercise influence there. The high office of President is hardly to be reached until a man is well on in years; as for other high federal offices, there is a large element of chance about attaining to them, and they go only to those who have reached eminence in some other walk of life. No ambitious man would make them the fixed aim of his endeavors. It is in the township, the center of the ordinary business of life, that the desire for esteem, the pursuit of substantial interests, and the taste for power and self-advertisement are concentrated; these passions, so often troublesome elements in society, take on a different character when exercised so close to home and, in a sense, within the family circle.

With much care and skill power has been broken into fragments in the American township, so that the maximum possible number of people have some concern with public affairs. Apart from the voters, who from time to time are called on to act as the government, there are many and various officials who all, within their sphere, represent the powerful body in whose name they act. Thus a vast number of people make a good thing for themselves out of the power of the community and are interested in administration for selfish reasons.

The American system, which distributes local power among so many citizens, is also not afraid to multiply municipal duties. Americans rightly think that patriotism is a sort of religion strengthened by practical service.

Thus daily duties performed or rights exercised keep municipal life constantly alive. There is a continual gentle political activity which keeps society on the move without turmoil.

Americans love their towns for much the same reasons that highlanders love their mountains. In both cases the native land has emphatic and peculiar features; it has a more pronounced physiognomy than is found elsewhere.

In general, New England townships lead a happy life. Their government is to their taste as well as of their choice. With profound peace and material prosperity prevailing in America, there are few storms in municipal life. The township's interests are easy to manage. Moreover, the people's political education has been completed long ago, or rather they were already educated when they settled there. In New England there is not even a memory of distinctions in rank, so there is no part of the community tempted to oppress the rest, and injustices which affect only isolated individuals are forgotten in the general contentment. The government may have defects, and indeed they are easy to point out, but they do not catch the eye because the government really does emanate from the governed, and so long as it gets along somehow or other, a sort of parental pride protects it. Besides, there is no basis of comparison. Formerly England ruled the colonies as a group, but the people always looked after municipal affairs. So the sovereignty of the people in the township is not ancient only, but primordial.

The New Englander is attached to his township because it is strong and independent; he has an interest in it because he shares in its management; he loves it because he has no reason to complain of his lot; he invests his ambition and his future in it; in the restricted sphere within his scope, he learns to rule society; he gets to know those formalities without which freedom can advance only through revolutions, and becoming imbued with their spirit, develops a taste for order, understands the harmony of powers, and in the end accumulates clear, practical ideas about the nature of his duties and the extent of his rights.

The New England County

The New England county corresponds to the French arrondissement.
It was created for purely administrative reasons. It has no representation. It is administered by non-elected officials.

The American county is very like the French *arrondissement*. As in the case of the latter, its limits have been arbitrarily fixed; there are no necessary links between its different parts; and neither affection, nor memories, nor communal life holds it together.

The township was too small for the adminstration of justice to be included in its functions. So the county is the primary judical center. Each county has a law court,[10] a sheriff to execute its decisions, and a prison for criminals.

[10] See the law of February 14, 1821, *Laws of Massachusetts*, Vol. II, p. 551.

Some needs were felt almost equally by all the townships in a county, and so it was natural that a central authority should provide for them. In Massachusetts authority to do this rests in the hands of certain magistrates appointed by the governor of the state on the advice[11] of his council.[12]

The powers of the county officials are limited and apply only to predetermined matters, which, by exception, are put under their charge. The state and the township suffice for the ordinary run of business. The county officials prepare only their budget, which is voted on by the legislature.[13] There is no assembly directly or indirectly representing the county.

So, strictly speaking, the county has no real political existence.

In most American constitutions one notices a tendency to divide up executive power but to concentrate legislative power. The New England township has a natural vitality which has not been curtailed; but such vitality would have had to be artificially contrived in the county, and no one felt the need to do so; it is only in the state, the center of all national powers, that all the townships are represented; apart from the activity of township and nation, one may say that only the efforts of individuals count.

Administration in New England

One is not conscious of the administration in America. Why? Europeans believe that liberty is promoted by depriving the social power of some of its rights, whereas the Americans believe in dividing up the exercise of them. Almost all administration, using the word strictly, is confined to the township and divided up among its officials. There is no trace of an administrative hierarchy, either in the township or at higher levels. Why that is so. How the state is nonetheless administered in uniform fashion. Whose duty it is to make the administrations of township and county obey the law. Judicial power introduced into administration. Result of the principle of election applied to all officials. The justices of the peace in New England. Who appoints them. They administer the county and supervise the administration of the township. Court of sessions. How it acts. Who brings matters before it. The rights of supervision and of complaint broken up like all other administrative functions. Informers encouraged by a share in fines.

[11] See the law of February 20, 1819, *ibid.*, Vol. II, p. 494.
[12] The governor's council is an elected body.
[13] See the law of November 2, 1781, *Laws of Massachusetts*, Vol. I, p. 61.

Nothing strikes a European traveler in the United States more than the absence of what we would call government or administration. One knows that there are written laws there and sees them put into execution every day; everything is in motion around you, but the motive force is nowhere apparent. The hand directing the social machine constantly slips from notice.

However, just as every people, to express its thoughts, must have some grammar shaping its language, so all societies, in order to exist, must submit to some authority without which they would relapse into anarchy. There are various ways in which that authority may be distributed, but it must exist somewhere or other.

There are two ways in which the power of authority in a nation may be diminished.

The first way is to weaken the very basis of power by depriving society of the right or the capacity to defend itself in certain circumstances. In Europe to weaken authority in this way is generally thought equivalent to establishing liberty.

But there is another way of diminishing the influence of authority without depriving society of some of its rights or paralyzing its efforts by dividing the use of its powers among several hands. Functions can be multiplied and each man given enough authority to carry out his particular duty. Among some nations such a division of social powers might lead to anarchy, but in itself it is by no means anarchic. By sharing authority in this way its power becomes, it is true, both less irresistible and less dangerous, but it is far from being destroyed.

The Revolution in the United States was caused by a mature and thoughtful taste for freedom, not by some vague, undefined instinct for independence. No disorderly passions drove it on; on the contrary, it proceeded hand in hand with a love of order and legality.

No one in the United States has pretended that, in a free country, a man has the right to do everything; on the contrary, more varied social obligations have been imposed on him than elsewhere; no one thought to attack the very basis of social power or contest its rights; the object was only to divide up the right to exercise it. By this means it was hoped that authority would be made great, but officials small, so that the state could still be well regulated and remain free.

In no country in the world are the pronouncements of the law more categorical than in America, and in no other country is the right to enforce it divided among so many hands.

There is nothing centralized or hierarchic in the constitution of American administrative power, and that is the reason why one is not at all conscious of it. The authority exists, but one does not know where to find its representative.

We have already seen that the New England townships were not under guardianship, but looked after their own interests.

So the municipal magistrates were generally given the responsibility to execute the laws of the state or to see that they were executed.[14]

Apart from general laws, the state sometimes imposes general police regulations; but generally it is the townships and their officers who, aided by the justices of the peace, and having regard to local needs, look after the details of social existence and promulgate the regulations necessary for public health, good order, and morality of the citizens.[15]

Last the municipal magistrates, on their own initiative and without outside prompting, see to those unforseen emergencies with which society is so often faced.[16]

As a result of what we have just said, in Massachusetts almost all administrative power is in the hands of the township,[17] but divided among many individuals.

In a French commune there is really only one administrative officer, the mayor.

We have seen that there were at least nineteen in a New England township.

These nineteen officials are generally not dependent one on another. The law has carefully defined the limited sphere of authority entrusted to each of these officials. Within that sphere they have all the power needed to carry out the duties of their office, and they do not depend on any municipal authority.

If one looks higher than the township, one scarcely finds the trace of an administrative hierarchy. It sometimes happens that the county officers amend a decision taken by the townships or their

[14] See *The Town Officer*, particularly under the words "Selectmen," "Assessors," "Collectors," "Schools," "Surveyors of highways." One example in a thousand: the state forbids traveling on Sunday without a reason. The "tithing men," municipal officials, are specially charged to pay attention to obedience to this law. See the law of March 8, 1792, *Laws of Massachusetts*, Vol. I, p. 410. The selectmen had to prepare the voting lists for the election of the governor and transmit the result of the poll to the secretary of the republic. Law of February 24, 1796, *ibid.*, p. 488.

[15] Example: the selectmen authorize the construction of sewers and fix the location of slaughterhouses and other trades which may be a nuisance to their neighbors. See the law of June 7, 1785, *ibid.*, p. 193.

[16] Example: the selectmen look after public health in cases of contagious diseases, taking the necessary measures in conjunction with the justices of the peace. Law of June 22, 1797, *ibid.*, p. 539.

[17] I say "almost" because there are several aspects of communal life regulated by the justices of the peace, either in their individual capacity or as a body meeting at the county town. Example: it is the justices of the peace who grant licenses. See the law of February 27, 1787, *ibid.*, p. 297.

officials,[18] but in general one can say that the county officials have no right to control the behavior of those of the township.[19] They only give them orders in matters concerning the county.

In a very small number of previously defined cases, the township and county officials are bound to communicate the results of their actions to the officers of the central government.[20] But there is no central-government official with the duty to make general police regulations or ordinances for the execution of the laws, to keep in routine communication with the township and county officials, or to supervise their conduct, direct their behavior, and punish their faults.

So there is no central point on which the radii of administrative power converge.

How, then, is the business of society conducted on a more or less uniform plan? How can obedience be imposed on the counties and their officials and on the townships and theirs?

In the states of New England the legislative power embraces more subjects than it does with us. In a sense the legislature penetrates to the very heart of the administration; the law descends into minute details; it prescribes both principles and the way in which they are to be applied; in this way the secondary authorities are tied down by a multitude of detailed obligations strictly defined.

As a result, provided that all the secondary authorities and their officials conform to the law, society proceeds in a uniform manner throughout; but we still need to know how the secondary authorities and their officials can be forced to obey the law.

Generally speaking, society has only two ways of making officials obey its laws.

It can entrust them with discretionary power to control all the others and dismiss them, if they disobey.

Or it can give the courts power to inflict judicial penalties on offenders.

[18] Example: licenses are granted only to people who can produce a certificate of good conduct from the selectmen. If the selectmen refuse to give this, the petitioner can appeal to the justices of the peace meeting in the court of sessions, who may grant it. See the law of March 12, 1808, *ibid.*, Vol. II, p. 186.

The townships have the right to make bylaws and enforce their observation by fines of fixed amounts. But these bylaws must be approved by the court of sessions. See the law of March 23, 1786, *ibid.*, Vol. I, p. 254.

[19] In Massachusetts the county officers are frequently called on to review the actions of the officials of the township, but we shall see later that they do this as a judicial authority, not as an administrative one.

[20] Example: the township educational committees are bound to send an annual report on the schools to the secretary of the republic. See the law of March 10, 1827, *ibid.*, Vol. III, p. 183.

One is not always free to choose either the one or the other of these methods.

The right to control an official assumes the right to dismiss him, if he does not follow the orders given and to promote him if he carries out all his duties zealously. Now, one can neither dismiss nor promote an elected official. It is the nature of elected offices to be irrevocable before the end of the mandate. In practice, the elected official has nothing to hope or fear except from the electors when all public offices are elective. It is therefore impossible for any true hierarchy to exist between these officials, for one and the same man cannot combine the right to order and the right effectively to punish disobedience; he cannot both command and reward and punish.

Therefore peoples who make use of elections to fill the secondary grades in their government are bound greatly to rely on judical punishments as a weapon of administration.

That is something which does not strike one at first glance. Rulers regard it as a first concession to make offices elective, and they think it a second concession to make the elected official subject to the judges. They are equally afraid of both these innovations, and as they are urged more to grant the first than the second, they allow the official to be elected and leave him independent of the judge. However, one of these two measures is the only possible counterweight to the other. It is important to realize than an elective office not subject to the judicial power will sooner or later either escape from all control or be destroyed. The courts are the only possible intermediary between the central power and an elective administrative body. They alone can force the elected official to obey the law without infringing the voter's rights.

Therefore the extension of judicial power over the political field should be correlative to the extension of elected power. If these two elements do not progress together, the state will end in anarchy or servitude.

In all ages it has been noticed that judicial habits will prepare men to exercise administrative power.

The Americans have borrowed from their English forefathers the conception of an institution which has no analogy with anything we know on the Continent, that of justices of the peace.

A justice of the peace is halfway between a man of the world and a magistrate, an administrator and a judge. A justice of the peace is an educated citizen but does not necessarily have any knowledge of the laws. For that reason his responsibility is only to be society's policeman, a matter requiring good sense and integrity more than knowledge. When a justice of the peace has a share in the administration, he brings with him a taste for formalities and for publicity, which renders him a most inconvenient instrument for a despotism; but he is not the slave of these legal superstitions which make magistrates so little capable of administration.

The Americans have taken over the institution of justices of the peace but have deprived it of that aristocratic character which marked it in their motherland.

The governor of Massachusetts[21] appoints a certain number of justices of the peace for all the counties with a seven-year term of office.[22]

Furthermore, he chooses three justices of the peace from each county who form what is called the *court of sessions*.

Individually the justices of the peace take part in public administration. Sometimes they are entrusted with administrative functions[23] jointly with elected officials; sometimes they form a tribunal before which officials can summarily prosecute refractory citizens, or a citizen can complain of the misdeeds of officials. But it is in the court of sessions that the justices of the peace perform their most important administrative functions. The court of sessions meets twice a year in the main town of the county. In Massachusetts that court is responsible for ensuring the obedience of most[24] of the public officials.[25]

It is important to note that in Massachusetts the court of sessions is both an administrative body properly so called and a political tribunal.

[21] We shall see later what the governor is; here it is enough to note that he represents the whole executive power of the state.

[22] See the Constitution of Massachusetts, Chapter II, section 1, paragraph 9, and Chapter II, paragraph 3.

[23] One example among many: a stranger arrives in a township coming from a country where a contagious disease is raging. He falls ill. On the advice of the selectmen, two justices of the peace can order the county sheriff to have him sent away and to look after him. *Laws of Massachusetts*, law of June 22, 1797, Vol. I, p. 540. In general, justices of the peace take part in all important administrative acts and so give them a semijudicial character.

[24] I say "most" because some administrative offenses are put under the jurisdiction of the ordinary courts. Example: when a township refuses to provide the funds necessary for its schools or to appoint the education committee, it is liable to a very considerable fine. That fine is imposed by a court called the supreme judicial court, or the court of common pleas. See the law of March 10, 1827, *ibid.*, Vol. III, p. 192. The same applies when a township fails to supply munitions of war. Law of February 21, 1822, *ibid.*, Vol. II, p. 573.

[25] In their individual capacity justices of the peace take part in the government of townships and counties. The most important acts of communal life cannot be performed without the concurrence of one of them.

It has been mentioned that the county[26] is a purely administrative division. The court of sessions has jurisdiction over that small number of cases which, as they concern several or all the townships in a county, cannot be dealt with by one of them alone.

As far as the county is concerned, the duties of the court of sessions are purely administrative, and if their procedure does often make use of judicial formalities, that is only done to aid it to get the matter clear[27] and to guarantee its fairness before the public. But when it is concerned with the administration of a township, it almost always functions as a judicial body and only rarely as an administrative one.

The first difficulty to be faced is that of making the township itself, an almost independent authority, obey the general laws of state.

We have seen that the townships are bound annually to appoint a certain number of officials, called assessors, to levy the taxes. Suppose a township tries to evade paying the tax by failing to appoint assessors. The court of sessions imposes a heavy fine.[28] The fine is levied individually on all the inhabitants. The county sheriff, an officer of justice, sees that the decision is executed. Thus, in the United States, government authority seems anxiously bent on keeping out of sight. An administrative order is almost always concealed under a judicial mandate; thereby it is all the more powerful, having that almost irresistible force which men accord to due process of law.

This procedure is easy to follow and to understand. What is demanded from the township is, in general, clear and definite; it turns on a simple, not a complex, fact, and a principle, not its detailed application.[29] But difficulties begin when it is a question of exacting obedience not from the township but from its officers.

[26] The subjects concerning the county which come before the court of sessions may be grouped under the following headings: (1) Erection of prisons and courts of justice; (2) the preparation of the county budget (it is the state legislature which votes it); (3) the division of the taxes thus voted; (4) grants of certain patents; (5) the making and repair of county roads.

[27] Thus, when a road is in question, the court of sessions, aided by a jury, deals with almost all the practical difficulties.

[28] See *Laws of Massachusetts,* the law of February 20, 1786, Vol. I, p. 217.

[29] There is an indirect method of forcing obedience from a township. The townships are obliged by law to keep their roads in good repair. If they fail to vote the funds necessary for their upkeep, the town surveyor is then authorized, *ex officio,* to levy the required sum. As he is himself responsible vis-à-vis individual citizens for the bad state of the roads and can be sued by them in the court of sessions, one can be sure that he will make use of the extraordinary power which the law has given him against the township. In this way, by threatening the official, the court of sessions enforces obedience by the township. See the law of March 5, 1787, *ibid.,* p. 305.

All the possible offenses that a public official can commit must fall under one of the following headings:

He may perform what the law commands without zeal or eagerness.

He may not do what the law commands.

Finally, he may do what law forbids.

Only the last two cases come within a tribunal's scope. There must be some positive recognizable fact to serve as the basis of judical action.

Thus, if the selectmen omit the legal formalities prescribed for municipal elections, they can be fined.[30]

But when a public official does his duty stupidly, when he obeys the laws' prescriptions without energy or zeal, he is quite outside the reach of judicial proceedings.

The court of sessions, though invested with administrative attributes, is powerless in this case to make him do his whole duty. Only the fear of dismissal can prevent such quasi offenses, and municipal powers are not derived from the court of sessions; it cannot dismiss officials which does not appoint.

Moreover, to be certain that there has been negligence or lack of zeal, it would be necessary to keep the subordinate official under continual supervision. But the court of sessions sits only twice a year; it supervises nothing; it judges such misdeeds as are brought to its notice.

An arbitrary power to dismiss public officials is the only guarantee of that sort of active and enlightened obedience which no judicial sanction can impose.

In France we seek that ultimate guarantee in the *administrative hierarchy;* in America *election* fills that role.

To sum up shortly what I have just stated:

If a public official in New England commits a *crime* in the exercise of his duty, the ordinary courts are *always* called on to try him.

If he is guilty of an *administrative fault,* a purely administrative tribunal is responsible for punishing him; and if the matter is serious or urgent, a judge may perform what the official should have done.[31]

Finally, if such an officer is guilty of one of those intangible offenses which human justice can neither define nor judge, he appears annually before a tribunal from which there is no appeal and which can suddenly reduce him to impotence; for with this mandate, his power goes.

[30] *Ibid.,* Vol. II, p. 45 [March 7, 1801].

[31] Example: if a township is recalcitrant about appointing assessors, the court of sessions appoints them, and the officials so chosen are clothed in all the authority of elected officers. See *ibid.,* the law already quoted, February 20, 1786.

There are certainly great advantages in this system, but there is a practical difficulty in its execution which needs to be pointed out.

I have already noted that the administrative tribunal, called the court of sessions, has no right to supervise the officials of the township; it can act only when, to use the legal expression, it is *seized* of the matter. That is the weak point in the system.

The New Englanders have never appointed a public prosecutor attached to the court of sessions,[32] and one must appreciate how difficult it would have been for them to do so. If they had merely appointed a public prosecutor in each county town without providing him with subordinates in the townships, how would he have known more about what was going on in the county than the members of the court of sessions themselves? If he had been given subordinates in each township, the most formidable of powers, that of judicial administration, would have been centralized in his hands. Moreover, laws are the children of custom, and there was nothing similar in the English legal system.

So, as with all other administrative functions, the Americans have broken up the right of supervision and of complaint. The grand jury is bound by law to apprise the court to which it is attached of all offenses of every sort committed in its county.[33] There are certain major administrative offenses which the normal public prosecutor must officially prosecute;[34] most often the duty of punishing delinquents is imposed on the treasury official, who must collect the amount of the fine; in this way the treasurer of the township is responsible for prosecuting most of the administrative offenses that take place to his knowledge.

But American legislation appeals mainly to private interest;[35] that is the great principle which one finds again and again when one studies the laws of the United States.

American legislators show little confidence in human honesty, but they always assume that men are intelligent. So they generally rely on personal interest to see to the execution of the laws.

When an individual is actually positively harmed by an adminis-

[32] I said "attached to the court of sessions." There is an officer attached to the ordinary courts who performs some of the functions of a public prosecutor.

[33] For instance, grand juries are obliged to call attention to the bad state of roads. *Laws of Massachusetts,* Vol. I, p. 308.

[34] If, for example, the county treasurer does not furnish his accounts. *Ibid.,* p. 406.

[35] One example among a thousand: a private individual damages his carriage or is injured on an ill-kept road; he can sue the township or county responsible for damages before the court of sessions. *Ibid.,* p. 309.

trative offense, it is assumed that personal interest will be sure to make him lodge a complaint.

But it is easy to foresee that in the case of some legal regulation that, although useful to society, has not the sort of usefulness that an individual can actually feel, each man will hesitate to stand up as the accuser. In this way, by a sort of tacit agreement, laws might easily fall into disuse.

Reduced by their system to this extremity, the Americans are obliged in certain cases to encourage informers by offering them a share in the fines.[36]

That is a dangerous expedient which insures the execution of the laws at the cost of degrading *mores*.

Above the level of the county officials there is really no administrative power, but only the power of the government.

General Ideas Concerning Administration in the United States

Differences in the systems of administration in the various states of the Union. Municipal life less full and active the farther one goes south. There the power of officials is greater and that of the voters less. Administration passes from the township to the county. States of New York, Ohio, and Pennsylvania. Administrative principles which apply to the whole Union. Election of public officials or irremovability of their offices. Absence of hierarchy. Introduction of judicial procedures into the administration.

I have previously stated that after a detailed examination of township and county in New England I would take a broad look at the rest of the Union.

[36] In the event of an invasion or insurrection, if officers of a township fail to furnish the militia with the necessary supplies and munitions, the township may be fined from two hundred to five hundred dollars. One can easily suppose that in such a case no one would have any interest or desire to take the role of prosecutor. So the law adds that: "All citizens shall have the right to prosecute for the punishment of such offenses, and half of the fine shall belong to the prosecutor." [Tocqueville summarizes] See the law of March 6, 1810, *ibid.*, Vol. II, p. 236. That same provision is very often repeated in the laws of Massachusetts. Sometimes it is not private persons whom the law thus incites to prosecute public officials, but the public official is encouraged in this way to punish private persons. Example: an inhabitant refuses to carry out the share of work on a main road assigned to him. The surveyor of highways ought to prosecute him; and if he gets him condemned, half the fine goes to him. See the law quoted above, Vol. I, p. 308.

There are townships and municipal life in each state, but nowhere else in the Union do we find townships exactly similar to those of New England.

As one goes farther south, one finds a less active municipal life; the township has fewer officials, rights, and duties; the population does not exercise such a direct influence on affairs; the town meetings are less frequent and deal with fewer matters. For this reason the power of the elected official is comparatively greater and that of the voter less; municipal spirit is less wide-awake and less strong.[37]

One begins to notice these differences in the state of New York; in Pennsylvania they are already much in evidence; but they become less striking as one goes farther to the northwest. Most of the immigrants who founded the northwestern states came from New England, and they brought the administrative habits of their old home to the new. A township in Ohio is very like one in Massachusetts.

We have seen that in Massachusetts the township is the mainspring of public administration. It is the center of men's interests and of their affections. But this ceases to be so as one travels down to those states in which good education is not universally spread and where, as a result, there are fewer potential administrators and less assurance that the township will be wisely governed. Hence, the farther one goes from New England, the more the county tends to take the place of the township in communal life. The county becomes the great administrative center and the intermediary between the government and the plain citizen.

I have mentioned that in Massachusetts the county's affairs are handled by the court of sessions. The court of sessions is composed of a certain number of officials nominated by the governor and his council; the county has no representative assembly, and its budget is voted by the national legislature.

But in the great state of New York, and in Ohio and Pennsylvania, the inhabitants of each county do choose a certain number of rep-

[37] For details see *The Revised Statutes of the State of New York,* part I, chapter XI, entitled "Of the Powers, Duties and Privileges of Towns, Vol. I, pp. 336–364 [Albany, 1829]. In the *Digest of the Laws of Pennsylvania,* look under the words "Assessors," "Collectors," "Constables," "Overseers of the poor," and "Supervisors of highways." [The latter are to be found under Roads; cf. *Digest of the Laws of Pennsylvania,* by John W. Purdon, Philadelphia, 1831.] And in the *Acts of a General Nature of the State of Ohio,* the law of February 25, 1834, concerning townships, on page 412. And then the particular provisions concerning various municipal officials, such as: "Township clerks," "Trustees," "Overseers of the poor," "Fence viewers," "Appraisers of property," "Township's treasurer," "Constables," "Supervisors of highways."

resentatives; the meeting of these representatives forms the assembly of the county.[38]

The county assembly has the right, within certain limits, to tax the inhabitants; in that respect it is a true legislature; it also exercises executive power in the county, and in several fields directs the administration of the townships, restricting their powers within much narrower limits than in Massachusetts.

Those are the main differences between the constitutions of town and county in the various states. If one was to go into the details of the means of execution, there would be many more differences to point out. But it is not my aim to write a treatise on American administrative law.

I think I have said enough to indicate the general principles on which American administration rests. These principles are variously applied; they work out differently in different places; but basically they are everywhere the same. The laws vary; their form changes; but the same spirit gives them all life.

County and township are not constituted everywhere in the same way, but one can say that the organization of township and county in the United States everywhere depends on the same idea, viz., that each man is the best judge of his own interest and the best able to satisfy his private needs. So township and county are responsible for their special interests. The state rules but does not administer. One finds exceptions to that principle, but no contradictory principle.

The first consequence of this doctrine was for the inhabitants themselves to choose all the administrators of town and county, or at least for them to be chosen exclusively from among them.

These officials being elected, or at least irremovable, it has never been possible to introduce rules of hierarchy anywhere. Hence there are almost as many independent officials as there are functions. Administrative power is spread among a multitude of people.

Officials being elected and irremovable before the termination of their mandate, and there being no hierarchy, the courts had to be brought into the administration to greater or lesser extent. The system of fines by which secondary authorities or their representatives are forced to obey the law derives from that. One finds that system from one end of the Union to the other.

Moreover, power to punish administrative offenses or to execute

[38] See *Revised Statutes of the State of New York,* Part I, chapter XI, Vol. I, p. 340, and chapter XII, p. 366; also in *The Acts of the State of Ohio,* the law of February 25, 1824, concerning county commissioners, p. 263. See the *Digest of the Laws of Pennsylvania,* under the words "County rates" and "Levies," p. 170. In the state of New York each township elects a commissioner to take part in the administration of both county and township.

administrative acts, where necessary, has not been granted in all states to the same judges.

All Anglo-Americans derive the institution of justices of the peace from the same source, and they are found in all the states. But they have not the same duties everywhere.

Everywhere the justices of the peace share in the administration of township and county,[39] either directly as administrators or by repressing some administrative misdeeds; but in the majority of states the most serious offenses come under the ordinary courts.

Hence, election of administrative officers, irremovability from office, absence of administrative hierarchy, and the use of judicial weapons to control secondary authorities are the chief characteristics of American administration from Maine to the Floridas.

There are some states in which we can begin to find traces of administrative centralization. The state of New York has gone furthest along this road.

In the state of New York, in some cases, the state government officials do exercise a sort of supervision and control over the behavior of secondary authorities.[40] In other cases they form a sort of court of appeal to decide matters.[41] In that state judicial penalties

[39] There are even states in the South where county court judges are responsible for all details of administration. See *The Statutes of the State of Tennessee,* under the headings "Judiciary," "Taxes," etc. [Cf. *The Statute Laws of the State of Tennessee of a Public and General Nature,* by John Haywood and Robert L. Cobbs, 2 vols., Knoxville, Tenn., 1831.]

[40] Example: control of public education is centralized in the hands of the government. The legislature appoints the *regents* of the university with the state governor and lieutenant governor as *ex officio* members. (*Revised Statutes,* Vol. I, p. 456 [Albany 1829.]) The regents of the university visit all the colleges and academies every year and make an annual report to the legislature; their supervision is no mere formality for the following reasons: the colleges, in order to become *corporations* able to buy, sell, and own property, need charters; now a charter is granted only by the legislature on the advice of the regents. The state annually distributes the interest on a special fund created to encourage education to the colleges and academies. It is the regents who apportion that money. See chapter XV, "Public Education," in *Revised Statutes,* Vol. I, p. 455. Each year the commissioners of public schools must send in a report about them to the superintendent of the republic. *Ibid.,* p. 488. A similar report must be sent to him annually concerning the number and condition of the poor. *Ibid.,* p. 631.

[41] If anyone feels himself injured by any act of the school commissioners (who are municipal officials), he can appeal to the superintendent of primary schools, whose decision is final. *Ibid.,* p. 487.

Here and there in the laws of the state of New York one finds provisions similar to those above quoted. But, generally speaking, such attempts at centralization are feeble and not very profitable. While giving the chief officials in the state the right to supervise and control the subordinate officials, they give

are used less than elsewhere as a means of administration. Also the right to prosecute administrative offenses is placed there in fewer hands.[42]

There are faint indications of the same tendency in some other states.[43] But one can say that, in general, the striking feature of American public administration is its extraordinary decentralization.

Of the State

I have spoken about the township and about administration; it remains to discuss the state and government.

This is ground I may pass over rapidly without fear of being misunderstood. What I want to say is all set out clearly in written constitutions which anyone interested can easily obtain.[44] The constitutions are, moreover, based on a simple and rational theory.

Most of their provisions have been adopted by all nations with constitutional governments and so have become familiar to us.

Here I need only give a brief summary. Later I shall try to judge what I am now going to describe.

Legislative Power of the State

Division of the legislature into two chambers. Senate. House of Representatives. Different attributes of these two bodies.

The legislative power of the state is entrusted to two bodies; the first is generally called the Senate.

---

them no right to reward or punish them. It is hardly ever the same man's duty to give the order and to punish disobedience; he therefore has the right to command but not the ability to make himself obeyed.

In 1830 the superintendent of schools complained in his annual report to the legislature that several school commissioners had not, in spite of reminders, sent him the due statements of account. "If this omission continues," he added, "I shall be reduced to prosecuting them, as the law provides, before the competent courts."

[42] Example: the district attorney is responsible for recovering all fines above fifty dollars unless the law has expressly made some other official responsible for them. *Revised Statutes,* part I, chapter X [XII], Vol. I, p. 383.

[43] There are several traces of administrative centralization in Massachusetts. Example: the committees of municipal schools are bound to send an annual report to the secretary of the state. *Laws of Massachusetts,* Vol. I, p. 367.

[44] See the text of the Constitution of New York. [1835 edition]

The Senate is generally a legislative body, but it sometimes becomes an administration or judicial one.

It takes a part in administration in various ways under the different constitutions.[45] But usually it is its concurrence in the appointment of officials that brings it into the executive sphere.

It has judicial functions in that it judges political offenses, and it sometimes also decides certain civil cases.[46]

Its membership is always small.

The other branch of the legislature, generally called the House of Representatives, has no share in administrative power, and its only judicial function is to prosecute public officers before the Senate.

Almost everywhere the same conditions of eligibility apply to members of both chambers. Both are elected in the same way and by the same citizens.

The only difference between them is that generally the senators have a longer term of office than the representatives. The latter seldom remain in office for more than one year, but the former usually for two or three.

By extending the senators' term of office to several years, and by reelecting them *seriatim*, the law has been at pains to keep within the legislature a body of men accustomed to public affairs, who can exercise a useful influence on the newcomers.

In dividing the legislative body into two branches, the Americans had no intention to create one hereditary assembly and another elected one; they did not mean to make the one an aristocratic body and the other a representative of democracy; nor yet did they mean to make the first a bulwark of authority, while the other should give scope to the interests and passions of the people.

To divide the legislative power and thus to slow down the movement of the political assemblies and create an appeal tribunal for the revision of laws were the only advantages resulting from the actual Constitution of the United States with its two chambers.

Time and experience have convinced the Americans that although these are its only two advantages, the division of legislative powers is yet a necessity of the first order. Alone among all the united republics, Pennsylvania had at first tried to establish a single assembly. Franklin himself, carried away by the logical consequences of the dogma of the sovereignty of the people, had concurred in this measure. But it was soon necessary to change the law and establish two chambers. That was the final consecration of the principle of the division of legislative power; henceforth the need to share

45 In Massachusetts the Senate has no administration function.
46 As in the state of New York.

legislative activity between several bodies has been regarded as a demonstrated truth. This theory, hardly known to the republics of antiquity, introduced into the world almost by chance, like most great truths, and misunderstood by several modern nations, has at last become an axiom of political science in our day.

The Executive Power of the State

The position of the governor in an American state. His relation to the legislature. His rights and duties. His dependence on the people.

The governor is the representative of the executive power of the state.

I have not chosen the word "representative" casually. The governor of the state does indeed represent the executive power, but he exercises only some of its rights.

That supreme officer, called the governor, is placed beside the legislature as a moderator and adviser. He is armed with a suspensive veto, which allows him to check its movements or at least to slow them down at will. He explains the country's needs to the legislative body and suggests the means he thinks advisable to provide for them; he is the natural executor of its will in all matters that concern the whole nation.[47] In the absence of the legislature, the governor is bound to take all necessary measures to protect the state against violent shocks and unforeseen dangers.

All the military power of the state is in the governor's hands. He is the commander of the militia and head of the armed forces.

When the authority, due by general consent to the laws, is disregarded, the governor marches out at the head of the physical power of the state; he breaks down resistance and reestablishes accustomed order.

For the rest, the governor plays no part in the administration of township or county, or at least he does so only very indirectly by appointing justices of the peace, whom he cannot then dismiss.[48]

The governor is an elected officer. In general his term of office is carefully limited to one or two years; in this way he is always closely dependent on the majority who elected him.

---

[47] In practice it is not always the governor who executes the plans conceived by the legislature, for the latter often appoints special agents to supervise their execution, at the same time as it votes the measure in principle.

[48] In several states the justices of the peace are not nominated by the governor.

Political Effects of Administrative Decentralization in the United States

Distinction to be made clear between governmental and administrative centralization. In the United States there is no administrative centralization, but very great centralization of government. Some troublesome effects resulting in the United States from extreme administrative decentralization. Administrative advantages from this order of things. The force which administers society is less well regulated, less enlightened, and less wise than in Europe, but it is much stronger. Political advantages from this same order of things. In the United States one is everywhere conscious of the nation. Support of the governed for the government. Provincial institutions increasingly necessary as social conditions become more democratic. Why?

"Centralization" is now a word constantly repeated but is one that, generally speaking, no one tries to define accurately.

There are, however, two very distinct types of centralization, which need to be well understood.

Certain interests, such as the enactment of general laws and the nation's relations with foreigners, are common to all parts of the nation.

There are other interests of special concern to certain parts of the nation, such, for instance, as local enterprises.

To concentrate all the former in the same place or under the same directing power is to establish what I call governmental centralization.

To concentrate control of the latter in the same way is to establish what I call administrative centralization.

There are some points where these two sorts of centralization become confused. But by broadly classifying the matters that fall more particularly within the province of each, the distinction can easily be made.

One appreciates that centralization of government acquires immense strength when it is combined with administrative centralization. In that way it accustoms men to set aside their own wills constantly and completely, to obey not just once and in one respect but always in everything. Then they are not only tamed by force, but their habits too are trained; they are isolated and then dropped one by one into the common mass.

These two types of centralization give each other mutual support and have a mutual attraction, but I cannot believe that they are inseparable.

Under Louis XIV France reached the greatest possible degree of centralization of government that can be conceived, for one man made the general laws and had the power to interpret them, and he represented France abroad and acted in her name. "I am the state," he said, and he was right.

However, under Louis XIV there was much less administrative centralization than there is now.

In our own day we see one power, England, which has reached a very high degree of centralization of government; there the state seems to move as a single man; at will it can raise vast masses of men and assemble and carry its might wherever it wishes.

England, which has done such great things in the last fifty years, has no administrative centralization.

For my part, I cannot conceive that a nation can live, much less prosper, without a high degree of centralization of government.

But I think that administrative centralization only serves to enervate the peoples that submit to it, because it constantly tends to diminish their civic spirit. Administrative centralization succeeds, it is true, in assembling, at a given time and place, all the available resources of the nation, but it militates against the increase of those resources. It brings triumph on the day of battle, but in the long run diminishes a nation's power. So it can contribute wonderfully to the ephemeral greatness of one man but not to the permanent prosperity of a people.

One must note carefully that when it is said that a nation cannot act because it has no centralization, people are almost always talking of governmental centralization without realizing it. The German Empire, people keep saying, has never been able to take full advantage of its powers. Agreed. But why? Because the national power has never been centralized, because the state has never been able to enforce obedience to its general laws, because the separate parts of this great body have always had the right and the ability to refuse their cooperation to the representatives of the common authority even in matters of common interest; in other words, because it has never had any centralization of government. The same remark applies to the Middle Ages; the cause of all the miseries of feudal society was that power, not just administration, but of government, was divided among a thousand people and broken up in a thousand ways; the absence of all governmental centralization then prevented the nations of Europe from advancing energetically toward any goal.

We have seen that in the United States there was no administrative centralization. There is scarcely a trace of a hierarchy. There decentralization has been carried to a degree that no European nation would tolerate, I think, without profound discomfort, and even in America it has produced some troublesome results. But there is a high degree of governmental centralization in the United States. It would be easy to demonstrate that national power is more concentrated there than it ever was in any of the ancient European monarchies. Not only is there but one legislative body in each state, not only is there but one single authority that can create political life around it, but generally crowded assemblies of districts or of counties have been avoided for fear that such assemblies might be tempted to step beyond their administrative functions and interfere with the working of the government. In America the legislature of each state is faced by no power capable of resisting it. Nothing can check its progress, neither privileges, nor local immunities, nor personal influence, nor even the authority of reason, for it represents the majority, which claims to be the unique organ of reason. So its own will sets the sole limits to its action. Beside it and under its power is the representative of executive authority, who, with the aid of physical force, has the duty to compel the discontented to obedience.

Weakness is found only in certain details of government action. The American republics have no permanent armed force with which to overawe minorities, but so far no minority has been reduced to an appeal to arms, and the necessity for an army has not yet been felt. The state usually employs officials of the townships or counties in dealings with the citizens. Thus in New England, for example, it is a township's assessor who fixes the taxes and its collector who receives them; the treasurer of the township hands over the money raised to the public treasury, and claims arising therefrom are submitted to the ordinary courts. Such a method of collecting taxes is slow and clumsy; it would be a constant embarrassment to any government requiring large sums of money. In general, it is desirable that a government should have in all matters, essential to its existence, its own officers, appointed by it and dismissable by it, and should have speedy methods of procedure. But a central power organized like that of America will always find it easy to introduce more energetic and effective methods of action when needed.

The republics of the New World are not going to perish, as is often asserted, for lack of centralization; so far from being inadequately centralized, one can assert that the American governments carry it much too far; that I will demonstrate later. The legislative assemblies are constantly absorbing various remnants of governmental powers; they tend to appropriate them all to themselves, as the French Convention did. The social power thus centralized is constantly changing hands, for it is subject to the people's power. It often lacks wisdom and foresight, because it can do anything. That is its danger. It is because of its very strength, not its weakness, that it is threatened with destruction one day.

Administrative decentralization produces several diverse effects in America.

We have seen that the Americans have almost entirely isolated the administration from the government; in doing this they seem to have overstepped the limits of sane reason, for order, even in secondary matters, is still a national interest.[49]

As the state has no administrative officers of its own, stationed at fixed points in its territory, to whom it can give a common impulse, it seldom tries to establish general police regulations. Yet the need for such regulations is acutely felt. Europeans often notice the lack. This apparent disorder prevailing on the surface convinces them, at first glance, that there is complete anarchy in society; it is only when they examine the background of things that they are undeceived.

There are some enterprises concerning the whole state which cannot be carried out because there is no national administration to control them. Left to the care of townships or elected and temporary officers, they lead to no result, or nothing durable.

The partisans of centralization in Europe maintain that the government administers localities better than they can themselves; that may be true when the central government is enlightened and the local authorities are not, when it is active and they lethargic, when it is accustomed to command and they to obey. One can, moreover, appreciate that as centralization increases, that tendency is intensified, the capacity of the one and the incapacity of the other becoming striking.

But I deny that that is so when, as in America, the people are en-

[49] The authority which represents the state, even when it does not administer, should not, I think, surrender its right to supervise the local administration. Suppose, for instance, that a government officer were posted at some fixed spot in every county and could bring before the courts offenses committed in the townships or the county; would not that ensure more uniform good order without compromising local independence? However, nothing of that sort exists in America. There is nothing above the county courts, and it is, in a sense, only by chance that those courts take cognizance of the administrative offenses which they should suppress.

lightened, awake to their own interests, and accustomed to take thought for them.

On the contrary, I am persuaded that in that case the collective force of the citizens will always be better able to achieve social prosperity than the authority of the government.

I admit that it is difficult to suggest a sure method of awakening a slumbering people so as to supply the passions and enlightenment they lack; to persuade people to take an interest in their own affairs is, I know well, an arduous enterprise. It would often be easier to get them interested in the details of court etiquette than in the repair of their common dwelling.

But I also think that when the central administration claims completely to replace the free concurrence of those primarily concerned, it is deceiving itself, or trying to deceive you.

A central power, however enlightened and wise one imagines it to be, can never alone see to all the details of the life of a great nation. It cannot do so because such a task exceeds human strength. When it attempts unaided to create and operate so much complicated machinery, it must be satisfied with very imperfect results or exhaust itself in futile efforts.

It is true that centralization can easily succeed in imposing an external uniformity on men's behavior and that that uniformity comes to be loved for itself without reference to its objectives, just as the pious may adore a statue, forgetting the divinity it represents. Centralization easily imposes an aspect of regularity on day-to-day business; it can regulate the details of social control skillfully; check slight disorders and petty offenses; maintain the status quo of society, which cannot properly be called either decadence or progress; and keep society in that state of administrative somnolence which administrators are in the habit of calling good order and public tranquillity.[50] In a word, it excels at preventing, not at doing. When it is a question of deeply stirring society or of setting it a rapid pace, its strength deserts it. Once its measures require any aid from individuals, this vast machine turns out to be astonishingly feeble; suddenly it is reduced to impotence.

Sometimes a centralized government does try, in despair, to sum-

[50] China seems to offer the classic example of the sort of social prosperity with which a very centralized administration can provide a submissive people. Travelers tell us that the Chinese have tranquillity without happiness, industry without progress, stability without strength, and material order without public morality. With them society always gets along fairly well, never very well. I imagine that when China is opened to Europeans, they will find it the finest model of administrative centralization in the world.

mon the citizens to its aid; but it addresses them thus: "You must do what I want, as much as I want, and in precisely the way I require. You must look after the details without aspiring to direct the whole; you will work in the dark and later you will be able to judge my work by its results." It is not on such terms that one wins the concurrence of human wills. Men must walk in freedom, responsible for their acts. Humanity is so constituted that it prefers to stay still rather than march forward without independence toward an unknown goal.

I will not deny that in the United States one often regrets the absence of those uniform rules which constantly regulate our lives in France.

Occasionally one encounters gross instances of social indifference and neglect there. Very occasionally major blemishes appear completely at variance with the surrounding civilization.

Useful undertakings requiring continuous care and rigorous exactitude for success are often abandoned in the end, for in America as elsewhere, the people proceed by sudden impulses and momentary exertions.

Europeans, accustomed to the close and constant presence of officials interfering in almost everything, find it difficult to get used to the different machinery of municipal administration. Generally speaking, one may say that those little details of social regulations which make life smooth and comfortable are neglected in America, but the guarantees essential to man as a member of society exist there as everywhere. In America the force behind the state is much less well regulated, less enlightened, and less wise, but it is a hundred times more powerful than in Europe. Without doubt there is no other country on earth where people make such great efforts to achieve social prosperity. I know of no other people who have founded so many schools or such efficient ones, or churches more in touch with the religious needs of the inhabitants, or municipal roads better maintained. So it is no good looking in the United States for uniformity and permanence of outlook, minute care of details, or perfection of administrative procedures;[51] what one does find is a picture of

[51] A talented writer who, in comparing the financial systems of France and of the United States, has proved that intelligence cannot always supply the place of knowledge of facts rightly reproaches the Americans for the type of confusion prevailing in their municipal budgets, and after citing the example of a departmental budget in France, adds: "Thanks to centralization, the wonderful creation of a great man, municipal budgets from one end of the kingdom to the other, in the smallest communes as well as in the great cities, are all equally orderly and methodical." That is certainly an achievement I admire; but I see most of those French communes, whose accounting system

power, somewhat wild perhaps, but robust, and a life liable to mishaps but full of striving and animation.

Granting, for the sake of argument, that the villages and counties of the United States would be more efficiently administered by a central authority from outside, remaining a stranger to them, than by officials chosen from their midst, I will, if you insist, admit that there would be more security in America and that social resources would be more wisely and judiciously employed, if the administration of the whole country were concentrated in one pair of hands. But the *political* advantages derived by the Americans from a system of decentralization would make me prefer that to the opposite system.

What good is it to me, after all, if there is an authority always busy to see to the tranquil enjoyment of my pleasures and going ahead to brush all dangers away from my path without giving me even the trouble to think about it, if that authority, which protects me from the smallest thorns on my journey, is also the absolute master of my liberty and of my life? If it monopolizes all activity and life to such an extent that all around it must languish when it languishes, sleep when it sleeps, and perish if it dies?

There are countries in Europe where the inhabitant feels like some sort of farm laborer indifferent to the fate of the place where he dwells. The greatest changes may take place in his country without his concurrence; he does not even know precisely what has happened; he is in doubt; he has heard tell by chance of what goes on. Worse still, the condition of his village, the policing of his road, and the repair of his church and parsonage do not concern him; he thinks that all those things have nothing to do with him at all, but belong to a powerful stranger called the government. For his part, he enjoys what he has as tenant, without feeling of ownership or any thought of improvement. His detachment from his own fate goes so far that if his own safety or that of his children is in danger, instead of trying to ward the peril off, he crosses his arms and waits for the

---

is so excellent, plunged in profound ignorance of their true interests and overtaken by such invincible apathy that society there seems to vegetate rather than live; on the other hand, I see in those American townships, with their untidy budgets lacking all uniformity, an enlightened, active, and enterprising population; there I perceive a society always at work. This contrast astonishes me, for to my mind the object of good government is to ensure the welfare of a people and not to establish a certain order in the midst of their misery. I wonder if the same cause may not be responsible for the prosperity of the American township and for the apparent disorder of its finances, and conversely, for the wretchedness of the French commune and for its immaculate budget. In any case, I distrust a good mingled with so many ills and gladly put up with evil compensated by so many benefits.

whole nation to come to his aid. Furthermore, this man who has so completely sacrificed his freedom of will does not like obedience more than the next man. He submits, it is true, to the caprice of a clerk, but as soon as force is withdrawn, he will vaunt his triumph over the law as over a conquered foe. Thus he oscillates the whole time between servility and license.

When nations reach that point, either they must modify both laws and mores or they will perish, for the fount of public virtues has run dry; there are subjects still, but no citizens.

I say that such nations are made ready for conquest. If they do not vanish from the world's scene it is because they are surrounded by peoples like or inferior to themselves or because they still have some sort of indefinable instinct of patriotism, some unconscious pride in the name they bear, some vague memory of past glory which, though not attached to anything in particular, does give them, when pressed, an urge for self-preservation.

It would be a mistake to find reassurance by remembering that certain peoples have made prodigious efforts to defend a country in which they lived almost as strangers. If one looks carefully, one will find that religion was almost always the main motive force in such cases.

For them the permanence, glory, and prosperity of the nation had become sacred dogmas, and in defending their country they defended also that holy city in which they were all citizens.

The Turkish peoples have never taken any part in the control of society's affairs; nevertheless, they accomplish immense undertakings so long as they saw the triumph of the religion of Muhammad in the conquests of the sultans. Now their religion is departing; despotism alone remains; and they are falling.

Montesquieu, in attributing a peculiar force to despotism, did it an honor which, I think, it did not deserve. Despotism by itself can maintain nothing durable. When one looks close, one sees that what made absolute governments long prosperous was religion, not fear.

Look where you will, you will never find true power among men except in the free concurrence of their wills. Now, patriotism and religion are the only things in the world which will make the whole body of citizens go persistently forward toward the same goal.

No laws can bring back life to fading beliefs, but laws can make men care for the fate of their countries. It depends on the laws to awaken and direct that vague instinct of patriotism which never leaves the human heart, and by linking it to everyday thoughts, passions, and habits, to make it a conscious and durable sentiment. And one should never say that it is too late to attempt that; nations do not grow old as men do. Each fresh generation is new material for the lawgiver to mold.

What I most admire in America is not the *administrative* but the *political* effects of decentralization. In the United States the motherland's presence is felt everywhere. It is a subject of concern to the village and to the whole Union. The inhabitants care about each of their country's interests as if it were their own. Each man takes pride in the nation; the successes it gains seem his own work, and he becomes elated; he rejoices in the general prosperity from which he profits. He has much the same feeling for his country as one has for one's family, and a sort of selfishness makes him care for the state.

Often to a European a public official stands for force; to an American he stands for right. It is therefore fair to say that a man never obeys another man, but justice, or the law.

Moreover, he has conceived an opinion of himself which is often exaggerated but almost always salutary. He trusts fearlessly in his own powers, which seem to him sufficient for everything. Suppose that an individual thinks of some enterprise, and that enterprise has a direct bearing on the welfare of society; it does not come into his head to appeal to public authority for its help. He publishes his plan, offers to carry it out, summons other individuals to aid his efforts, and personally struggles against all obstacles. No doubt he is often less successful than the state would have been in his place, but in the long run the sum of all private undertakings far surpasses anything the government might have done.

Administrative authority arouses neither jealousy nor hatred, for it is close to the governed and in a sense represents them. As its means of action are limited, each man feels that he cannot rely solely upon it.

So when an official intervenes in his proper sphere, he is not left to his own resources as in Europe. Private people do not think that their duties have ceased because the representative of the public has come to take action. On the contrary, everyone guides, supports, and sustains him.

These efforts of private individuals combined with those of the authorities often accomplish things which the most concentrated and vigorous administration would be unable to achieve. (See Appendix I, I.)

I could cite many facts in support of what I am saying, but I prefer to select one only, and that the one I know best.

In America the means available to the authorities for the discovery of crimes and arrest of criminals are few.

There is no administrative police force, and passports are unknown. The criminal police in the United States cannot be compared to that of France; the officers of the public prosecutor's office are few, and the initiative in prosecutions is not always theirs; and the examination of prisoners is rapid and oral. Nevertheless, I doubt whether in any other country crime so seldom escapes punishment.

The reason is that everyone thinks he has an interest in furnishing proofs of an offense and in arresting the guilty man.

During my stay in the United States I have seen the inhabitants of a county where a serious crime had been committed spontaneously forming committees with the object of catching the criminal and handing him over to the courts.

In Europe the criminal is a luckless man fighting to save his head from the authorities; in a sense the population are mere spectators of the struggle. In America he is an enemy of the human race and every human being is against him.

I think that provincial institutions are useful for all peoples, but none have a more real need of them than those whose society is democratic.

In an aristocracy one can always be sure that a certain degree of order will be maintained in freedom.

The ruling class has much to lose, and order is an important interest for the rulers.

It is also fair to say that in an aristocracy the people are always defended from the excesses of despotism, for there are always organized forces ready to resist a despot.

A democracy without provincial institutions has no guarantee against such ills.

How can liberty be preserved in great matters among a multitude that has never learned to use it in small ones?

How can tyranny be resisted in a country where each individual is weak and where no common interest unites individuals?

Those who fear license and those who are afraid of absolute power should both, therefore, desire the gradual growth of provincial liberties.

Moreover, I am convinced that no nations are more liable to fall under the yoke of administrative centralization than those with a democratic social condition.

Several causes contribute to this result, among which are the following:

It is a permanent tendency in such nations to concentrate all governmental power in the hands of the only power which directly repre-sents the people, because apart from the people there is nothing to be seen but equal individuals mingled in a common mass.

Now, when one sole authority is already armed with all the attri-butes of government, it is very difficult for it not to try and penetrate into all the details of administration, and in the long run it hardly ever fails to find occasion to do so. We have seen this happen in France.

In the French Revolution there were two opposite tendencies which must not be confused; one favored freedom, the other despotism.

Under the ancient monarchy the king alone made the law. Beneath his sovereign power there were some half-ruined remains of provin-cial institutions. These provincial institutions were incoherent, ill-regulated, and often absurd. In the hands of the aristocracy they had sometimes been instruments of oppression.

The Revolution pronounced at the same time against royalty and against provincial institutions. Revolutionary hatred was directed indiscriminately against all that had gone before, both the absolute power and those elements which could temper its rigors. The Revolu-tion was both republican and centralizing.

This ambivalent character of the French Revolution was a fact of which the lovers of absolute power took great pains to make use. When you see them defending administrative centralization, do you think they are working in the interests of despotism? Not at all; they are defending one of the great conquests of the Revolution. (See Appendix I, K.) In that way a man may retain popularity while being an enemy of the rights of the people; he may be the hidden servant of tryanny and the avowed lover of liberty.

I have traveled in those two countries where provincial liberties have reached their fullest growth, and I have listened to the views of the parties dividing those nations.

In America I have found men who secretly aspire to destroy the democratic institutions of their country. In England I have met others who loudly attack the aristocracy. But I have not met a single man who did not regard provincial freedom as a great blessing.

In both countries I have heard the ills of the state attributed to an infinite variety of causes, but never to local freedom.

I have heard citizens attribute the greatness and prosperity of their country to a multitude of reasons, but I found they all put the advantages of provincial freedom first and foremost of all.

Am I to believe that men who are naturally so divided that they agree neither on religious doctrines nor on political theories, but who do agree on one point, and that the matter they can best judge since they see its daily operation, are yet mistaken on that point?

Only peoples having few provincial institutions or none deny the usefulness of them; that is to say, it is only those who know nothing of them who slander them.

Chapter 6

JUDICIAL POWER IN THE UNITED STATES AND ITS EFFECT ON POLITICAL SOCIETY

The Anglo-Americans have preserved all the characteristics of judicial power common to other nations. They have, however, made it a powerful political force. How? In what way the Anglo-American judiciary differs from all others. Why American judges have the right to declare laws unconstitutional. How they make use of that right. Precautions taken by the legislature against the abuse of that right.

I HAVE THOUGHT IT RIGHT to devote a separate chapter to the power of the judges. For had I only mentioned it in passing, its great political importance might be lessened in the reader's eyes.

Confederations have existed in other countries besides America, and there are republics elsewhere than on the shores of the New World; the representative system of government has been adopted in several European states; but, so far, I do not think that any other nation in the world has organized judicial power in the same way as the Americans.

The judicial organization of the United States is the hardest thing there for a foreigner to understand. He finds judicial authority invoked in almost every political context, and from that he naturally concludes that the judge is one of the most important political powers in the United States. But when he then begins to examine the constitution of the courts, at first glance he sees nothing but judicial attributes and procedures. The judges seem to intervene in public affairs only by chance, but that chance recurs daily.

When the Parliament of Paris remonstrated and refused to register an edict, or when it summoned a dishonest official to its bar, one could see the political function of the judiciary in action. But nothing similar occurs in the United States.

The Americans have preserved all the usually accepted characteristics of judicial authority and have precisely limited its sphere of action in the normal way.

In all nations the judge's primary function is to act as arbitrator.

Rights must be contested to warrant the intervention of the court. An action must be brought before a judge can decide it. As long as a law leads to no dispute, the judges have no occasion to consider it. It may exist without being noticed. When a judge, in a given case, attacks a law relative to that case, he stretches the sphere of his influence but does not go beyond it, for he was, in a sense, bound to judge the law in order to decide the case. But if he pronounces upon a law without reference to a particular case, he steps right beyond his sphere and invades that of the legislature.

The second characteristic of judicial power is that it pronounces on particular cases and not on general principles. If a judge, in deciding a particular question, destroys a general principle, because one is quite sure that all consequences deriving from that principle will be alike undermined, and so the principle becomes barren, he stays within the natural sphere of his authority. But when a judge directly attacks the general principle and destroys it without having any particular case in view, he goes beyond the sphere to which all peoples have agreed to limit his authority; he becomes something more important and perhaps more useful than a magistrate, but he no longer represents judicial power.

The third characteristic of judicial power is that it can act only when called upon, or in legal language, when it is seised of the matter. That characteristic is not so generally found as the other two. But despite the exceptions, I think one may consider it as essential. There is nothing naturally active about judicial power; to act, it must be set in motion. When a crime is denounced to it, it punishes the guilty party; when it is called on to redress an injustice, it redresses it; when an act requires interpretation, it interprets it; but it does not on its own prosecute criminals, seek out injustices, or investigate facts. In a sense judicial power would do violence to its passive nature if it should take the initiative and establish itself as censor of the laws.

The Americans have preserved these three distinctive characteristics of judicial power. An American judge can pronounce a decision only when there is litigation. He never concerns himself with anything except a particular case, and to act he must have cognizance of the matter.

So an American judge is exactly like the magistrates of other nations. Nevertheless, he is invested with immense political power.

How does this come about? He moves within the same sphere employing the same means as other judges. Why does he have a power which the others have not?

The reason lies in this one fact: the Americans have given their judges the right to base their decisions on the *Constitution* rather than on the *laws*. In other words, they allow them not to apply laws which they consider unconstitutional.

I know that a similar right has sometimes been claimed by courts in other lands, but it has never been conceded. In America it is recognized by all the authorities; one finds neither party nor individual who contests it.

The explanation of this is found in the very basis of the American constitutions.

In France the Constitution is, or is supposed to be, immutable. No authority can change anything in it; that is the accepted theory. (See Appendix, I, L.)

In England Parliament has the right to modify the Constitution. In England, therefore, the Constitution can change constantly, or rather it does not exist at all. Parliament, besides being the legislative body, is also the constituent one. (See Appendix I, M.)

American political theories are simpler and more rational.

The American Constitution is not considered immutable, as in France; it cannot be changed by the ordinary authorities of society as in England. It is a thing apart; it represents the will of the whole people and binds the legislators as well as plain citizens, but it can be changed by the will of the people, in accordance with established forms in anticipated eventualities.

So in America the Constitution can change, but so long as it exists, it is the fount of all authority. The dominant power belongs to it alone.

It is easy to see that these differences must influence the standing and rights of the judges in the three countries mentioned.

If in France the courts could disobey the laws on the ground that they found them unconstitutional, the constitution-making power would really be in their hands, as they alone would have the right to interpret a constitution whose provisions no one could change. In that way they would take the nation's place and be the dominant power in society, so far as the inherent weakness of judicial power would allow them to play that part.

I appreciate that by refusing to give the judges the power to declare laws unconstitutional we indirectly give the legislative body the power to change the constitution, since there is no legal barrier to restrain it. But it is still better to give the power to change the people's constitution to men who, however imperfectly, represent the people's will, than to others who represent nobody but themselves.

It would be even more unreasonable to give English judges the right to resist the will of the legislature, since Parliament, which makes the laws, also shapes the constitution, and consequently in no case could one call a law emanating from king, Lords, and Commons unconstitutional.

Neither of these two arguments applies to America.

In America the Constitution rules both legislators and simple citizens. It is therefore the primary law and cannot be modified by a law. Hence it is right that the courts should obey the Constitution rather than all the laws. This touches the very essence of judicial power; it is in a way the natural right of a judge to choose among legal provisions that which binds him most strictly.

In France also the Constitution is the first of laws, and the judges there, too, have the right to take it as the basis of their decisions; but in exercising this right they would be bound to encroach on another right more sacred than their own, namely, the right of society in whose name they act. In this case ordinary reason must give way to reasons of state.

In America, where the nation always can, by changing the Constitution, reduce the judges to obedience, such a danger is not to be feared. So on this point politics and logic agree, and both the people and the judges can keep their proper privileges.

Therefore, if anyone invokes in an American court a law which the judge considers contrary to the Constitution, he can refuse to apply it. That is the only power peculiar to an American judge, but great political influence derives from it.

In practice few laws can long escape the searching analysis of the judges, for there are very few that do not injure some private interest and which advocates cannot or should not question before the courts.

Now, as soon as a judge refuses to apply a law in a case, it loses at once part of its moral force. Those who are harmed by it are notified of a means of escaping from its obligations; lawsuits multiply, and that law becomes ineffective. Then one of two things happens: either the people change the Constitution or the legislature repeals the law.

So, then, the Americans have given their courts immense political power; but by obliging them to attack the laws by judicial means, they have greatly lessened the dangers of that power.

If the judges had been able to attack laws in a general and theoretical way, if they could have taken the initiative and censored legislation, they would have played a prominent part on the political scene; a judge who had become the champion or the adversary of a party would have stirred all the passions dividing the country to take part in the struggle. But when a judge attacks a law in the course of an obscure argument in a particular case, he partly hides the importance of his attack from public observation. His decision is just intended to affect some private interest; only by chance does the law find itself harmed.

Moreover, the law thus censured is not abolished; its moral force is diminished, but its physical effect is not suspended. It is only gradually, under repeated judicial blows, that it finally succumbs.

Furthermore, it is easy to see that by entrusting it to private interest to bring about the censure of the laws, and closely linking proceedings against the law with proceedings against a man, there is a guarantee that legislation will not lightly be attacked. Under this system legislation is not daily exposed to the attacks of parties. In pointing out the lawmakers' mistakes, a real need is met; to serve as the basis for a case, one must start from a positive and definite fact.

I wonder if this way in which American courts behave is not both the best way of preserving public order and the best way of favoring liberty.

If a judge could only attack the lawmakers directly, there are occasions when he would be afraid to do so; on other occasions party spirit might drive him to do so continually. Thus it would come about that laws would be attacked when the authority from which they derive was feeble, and people would submit without complaint when it was strong; that is to say, people would often attack laws just when it would be most desirable to respect them, and they would be respected just when it became easy to be oppressive in their name.

But the American judge is dragged in spite of himself onto the political field. He only pronounces on the law because he has to judge a case, and he cannot refuse to decide the case. The political question he has to decide is linked to the litigants' interests, and to refuse to deal with it would be a denial of justice. It is by fulfilling the narrow duties imposed by his status as a judge that he also acts as a citizen. It is true that under this system judicial censorship of the laws in court cannot cover all laws without exception, for there are some laws which can never give rise to that sort of clearly formulated argument called a lawsuit. And sometimes where such argument is possible there may be no one who wishes to bring it to the cognizance of the court.

The Americans have often noted this inconvenience, but they have left the remedy incomplete rather than risk making it in all cases dangerously effective.

Restricted within its limits, the power granted to American courts to pronounce on the constitutionality of laws is yet one of the most powerful barriers ever erected against the tyranny of political assemblies.

Other Powers Given to American Judges

In the United States all citizens have the right to prosecute public officials before the ordinary courts. How they make use of that right. Article 75 of the French Constitution of the year VIII. Americans and English alike fail to understand the meaning of that article.

It is so natural that I do not know if it is necessary to state that among a free people such as the Americans all citizens have the right to prosecute public officials before the ordinary judges and that all judges have the right to condemn public officials.

It is no extra privilege granted to the courts to allow them to punish the agents of the executive when they break the law. To forbid it would be taking away a natural right.

It does not seem to me that the energy of the American government has been weakened by making all officials responsible before the courts.

On the contrary, I think that by so doing the Americans have increased the respect due to executive officers, since the latter are much more careful to avoid criticism.

Nor did I observe that many political trials take place in the United States, and I can easily explain the reason. Whatever its nature, a lawsuit is always a difficult and expensive matter. It is easy to accuse a public man in the newspapers, but only serious reasons induce anybody to prosecute him in court. Therefore, one must have just cause of complaint before starting judicial proceedings against an official; but, with the fear of prosecution, officials hardly ever give ground for such complaint.

This does not depend on the republican form of government adopted by the Americans, for the same thing can be noted any day in England.

These two nations have not thought to assure their liberty by allowing the main agents of the executive to be brought to trial. They have rather thought that little everyday lawsuits within the scope of the least of the citizens were a better guarantee of liberty than those pompous procedures to which one never has recourse or which are used too late.

In the Middle Ages, it being very difficult to catch criminals, when the judges did seize a few they often inflicted terrible punishments on these unfortunates. But that did not lessen the number of the guilty. It has subsequently been found that by making justice both more sure and milder, it has also been made more effective.

The Americans and English think that oppression and tyranny should be treated like theft, by making prosecution easier and the penalty lighter.

Article 75 of the French Republican Constitution of the year VIII reads as follows: "The agents of the government, other than ministers, cannot be prosecuted for matters relating to their functions except by virtue of a decision of the Council of State; in that case the prosecution will take place before the ordinary courts."[1]

The Constitution of the year VIII passed away, but not that article, which survived after it; and every day it still stands in the way of the citizens' just complaints.

I have often tried to explain the meaning of that Article 75 to Americans and to English people, and I have always found that very hard to do.

The thing they first noticed was that the French Council of State is a great court sitting in the center of the kingdom; there was something of tyranny in sending all complaints before it as a preliminary step.

But when I tried to make them understand that the Council of State was not a judicial body in the ordinary sense of the term, but an administrative one whose members depended on the king, so that the king, having used his sovereign power to order one of his servants, called the prefect, to commit an injustice, could then authoritatively order another of his servants, called the Council of State, to prevent the former from being punished; when I explained how the citizen, harmed by the prince's order, was reduced to asking the prince himself to allow him to obtain justice, they refused to believe such enormities and accused me of lying or of ignorance.

It often happened under the old monarchy that the Parliament decreed the arrest of a public official guilty of an offense. Sometimes the royal authority intervened to annul the proceedings. In that case despotism showed itself openly, and in obeying, men only submitted to force.

We have gone back far behind the point reached by our ancestors, for we allow under color of justice and consecrate in the name of the law that which was imposed on them by naked force.

[1] [Cf. *Les Constitutions et les principales Lois politiques de la France depuis 1789*, par L. Duguit, H. Monnier, and R. Bonnard, seventh edition, Paris, 1952, p. 116. For an admirable analysis of the constitution of the year VIII, see M. Prélot, *Institutions politiques et Droit Constitutionnel*, pp. 340 ff., Paris, 1961.]

Chapter 7

POLITICAL JURISDICTION IN
THE UNITED STATES

What the author means by political jurisdiction. How political jurisdiction is understood in France, England, and the United States. In America the political judge is concerned only with public officials. He pronounces dismissal from office rather than penalties. Political jurisdiction an ordinary means of government. Political jurisdiction such as is found in the United States is, in spite of or perhaps because of its mildness, a very powerful weapon in the hands of the majority.

By "POLITICAL JURISDICTION" I mean the decisions pronounced by a political body temporarily endowed with the right to judge.

Under absolute governments it is pointless to introduce extraordinary procedures for jurisdiction; the prince, in whose name the accused is prosecuted, being master of the courts as of everything else, has no need of any guarantee beyond the felt weight of his power. His only conceivable fear is that even the external appearances of justice will not be maintained and that his authority will be brought into dishonor by those seeking to assert it.

But in most free countries where the majority can never influence the courts as an absolute prince can, it is sometimes necessary temporarily to put judicial power into the hands of the representatives of society themselves. It has been thought better to merge these powers for a moment rather than to violate the necessary principle of unity of government. England, France, and the United States have introduced political jurisdiction into their laws, and it is curious to see the different use these three great nations have made of it.

In England and France the House of Peers forms the highest criminal court in the land.[1] It does not in fact judge all political offenses, but it can do so.

Another political body has the right of bringing accusations before

[1] In England the House of Lords is also the highest court of appeal in certain civil cases. See Blackstone, Book III, chapter 4. [*Commentaries on the Laws of England*, Vol. III, London, 1809, p. 57.]

the peers; the only difference between the two countries in this respect is that in England the Commons can impeach anybody they like before the Lords, whereas in France they can prosecute only ministers of the Crown in this way.

In both countries the House of Peers can use all the provisions of the penal laws to punish offenders.

In the United States, as in Europe, one of the two branches of the legislature has the right to prosecute and the other branch to judge. The House of Representatives denounces the offender, and the Senate punishes him.

But the Senate cannot be seised of the matter except at the prompting of the *House of Representatives,* and only *public officials* can be brought before the Senate. Therefore the Senate has a more restricted jurisdiction than the Court of Peers in France, and the representatives have a wider power of impeachment than the French deputies.

But the greatest difference between Europe and America lies in this: in Europe the political courts can apply the provisions of the criminal law; in America, when the offender has had his public status taken away and been declared unworthy to hold any political position in future, their jurisdiction is at an end and that of the ordinary courts begins.

Suppose the President of the United States has committed high treason.

The House of Representatives impeaches him, and the Senate pronounces his dismissal. After that he appears before a jury, who alone can deprive him of life or liberty.

This throws vivid light on the subject we are considering.

In introducing political jurisdiction into their laws, the Europeans wished to reach great criminals, no matter what their birth, rank, or power in the state. To this end they momentarily granted all the prerogatives of the courts to a great political body.

The legislator is then transformed into a judge; he has power to establish the crime, classify it, and punish it. In giving him the powers of a judge, the law has also imposed all the obligations of that office and made him observe all legal formalities.

When a French or English political tribunal tries a public official and condemns him, it *ipso facto* deprives him of his office and may declare him unworthy to hold any other in future; but in this case the political interdict is a consequence of the sentence and not the sentence itself.

So in Europe the political judgment is more a judicial act than an administrative measure.

The opposite is the case in America, where it is easy to see that the political judgment is much more an administrative measure than a judicial act.

It is true that the Senate's decision is judicial in form; in pronouncing it the senators are bound to conform to the solemn formalities of procedure. It is also judicial in the motives on which it is based; the Senate is generally obliged to take an offense at common law as the basis of its decision. But it is administrative in its objective.

If American lawgivers had really intended to arm a political body with great judicial power, they would not have restricted its authority to the sphere of public officials, for the most dangerous enemies of the state may not hold any office; that is particularly the case in republics, where the favor of parties is the strongest of powers and where one is often all the more formidable when one does not exercise any legal power.

If the American legislators had wished to give society itself the power to restrain great crimes, according to the practice of ordinary justice, by the fear of punishment they would have put all the resources of the penal code at the disposal of the political tribunals; but they were provided only with an incomplete weapon, and one which could not reach the most dangerous of criminals. For a decree of deprivation of political rights matters little to one who intends to overthrow the laws themselves.

So the main object of political jurisdiction in the United States is to take power away from a man who makes ill use of it and to prevent such a man from attaining it in future. It is, as one sees, an administrative act which has been clothed in the solemnity of a judgment.

In this matter the Americans have created a mixed system; the formalities of a political trial are required for administrative dismissal, and political jurisdiction has been deprived of its severest sanctions.

This point established, everything else follows; one now discovers why American constitutions subject all civil officials to the jurisdiction of the Senate, while exempting the soldiers whose crimes are nevertheless more to be feared. In the American civil administration one may almost say that no officials can be dismissed; some are irremovable, and others hold office by a mandate which cannot be revoked. So, in order to deprive them of power, they must be brought to trial. The soldiers depend on the head of state, who is himself a civil official. When the head of state is condemned, the same blow strikes them all.[2]

[2] An officer cannot be deprived of his rank, but his command can be taken from him.

If one then goes on to compare the effects which do or may result from the European and American systems, one finds the differences no less marked.

In France and England political jurisdiction is regarded as an extraordinary weapon which society should use only to save itself in moments of great peril.

One cannot deny that political jurisdiction, as understood in Europe, violates the protecting principle of the division of powers and continually threatens men's lives and liberty.

Political jurisdiction in the United States holds only an indirect threat to the principle of division of powers; it is no threat to the citizen's existence; it does not, as in Europe, hover over all heads, for it touches only those who, by accepting public office, have submitted in advance to its rigors.

It is both less formidable and less effective.

So American legislators have not regarded it as an extreme remedy for the great ills of society, but as a habitual means of government.

In this respect it may have more real influence on society in America than in Europe. One must not be taken in by the apparent mildness of American legislation where political jurisdiction is concerned. In the first place, one should note that in the United States the tribunal which pronounces judgment in such cases is composed of the same elements, subject to the same influences, as the body responsible for impeachment, and that gives an almost irresistible impulse to the vindictive passions of parties. While American political judges cannot impose as severe penalities as those of Europe can, there is also much less chance of being acquitted by them. Condemnation is less to be feared, but more certain.

In establishing political tribunals, Europeans chiefly intended to *punish* the guilty, the Americans to *take away their power*. In the United States a political judgment is in a sense a preventive measure. The judge must therefore not be tied down by overexact definitions of crime.

There is nothing more terrifying than the vagueness of American laws when they are defining political crimes properly so called. "The President, Vice-President, and all civil officers of the United States shall be removed from office on impeachment for and conviction of treason, bribery, or other high crimes and misdemeanors," states the Constitution of the United States, Article II, section 4. Most of the state constitutions are even more obscure.

"The senate shall be a court," says the Constitution of Massachusetts, "with full authority to hear and determine all impeachments made by the House of Representatives against any officer or officers of the commonwealth for misconduct and maladministration in their offices."[3] "All officers offending against the state," declares the Constitution of Virginia, "either by maladministration, corruption, neglect of duty, or any other high crime or misdemeanor, shall be impeachable by the House of Delegates." There are constitutions which do not specify any crime, so that an unlimited responsibility may weigh upon public officers.[4]

But what makes American laws so formidable in this matter is, I dare assert, their very mildness.

We have seen that in Europe dismissal from office and deprivation of political rights were among the consequences of the penalty; in America they are the penalty. The result is as follows: in Europe political tribunals are endowed with terrible attributes which they often do not know how to use, so it may happen that they do not punish, for fear of punishing too much. But in America no one shrinks back from a penalty which does not make humanity groan; to condemn a political enemy to death in order to take away his power is, in the eyes of all men, a horrible assassination; to declare one's adversary unworthy to possess that power and to take it away from him, while leaving him life and liberty, may seem the honest result of the struggle.

But that judgment, so easy to pronounce, is nonetheless the summit of misfortune for the general run of those to whom it applies. Great criminals would no doubt brave its vain rigors; ordinary men see it as a decree which destroys their status, stains their honor, and condemns them to a disgraceful leisure worse than death.

Hence American political jurisdiction has all the more influence on the conduct of society just because it seems less formidable. It has no direct effect on the governed, but does make the majority complete masters of those who govern; it does not give the legislature some immense power which it could use only in a time of crisis, but allows it to claim a moderate and regulated power which it uses every day. While the force behind it is less, it is more convenient to use and easier to abuse.

In preventing political tribunals from pronouncing judicial penalties, the Americans seem to me to have provided against the more terrible consequences of legislative tyranny rather than against that tyranny itself. Everything considered, I wonder whether political

[3] Chapter I, section 2, subsection 8.
[4] See the constitutions of Illinois, Maine, Connecticut, and Georgia.

jurisdiction as understood in the United States is not the most formidable weapon ever put into the majority's hands.

Once the American republics begin to degenerate, I think one will
easily see that that is so; it will be enough to notice whether the
number of political judgments increases. (See Appendix I, N.)

Chapter 8

THE FEDERAL CONSTITUTION

So FAR I HAVE CONSIDERED each state as forming a complete whole and have shown the different springs which the people set in motion and the means of action they employ. But all these states which I have considered as independent are bound in certain cases to obey a superior authority, that of the Union. The time has now come to examine that portion of sovereignty which has been granted to the Union and to take a quick look at the federal Constitution.[1]

History of the Federal Constitution

Origin of the first Union. Its weakness. Congress appeals to the constituent power. Interval of two years between that moment and the promulgation of the new Constitution.

The thirteen colonies which simultaneously shook off the English yoke at the end of the last century had, as I have already said, the same religion, language, and mores, and almost the same laws; they fought against a common enemy; they must therefore have had strong reasons for uniting closely with each other and becoming absorbed in one and the same nation.

But each of them, having always had a separate existence and a government within its control, had created peculiar interests and usages and revolted against a solid and complete union which would have led to its individual importance being merged in the greatness of the Union. Hence there were two opposite tendencies: one drove the Anglo-Americans to unite, while the other induced them to divide.

As long as the war with the mother country continued, necessity made the principle of union prevail. And though the laws by which

[1] See the text of the federal Constitution. [The first edition of Tocqueville's *Democracy in America* reproduced the text of the American Constitution; the last edition in Tocqueville's lifetime, on which our edition is based, dispensed with this.]

this union was constituted were defective, the link subsisted in spite of them.[2]

But as soon as peace was concluded, the defects of this legislation stood revealed: the state seemed to dissolve all at once. Each colony, become an independent republic, assumed an absolute sovereignty. The federal government, condemned to weakness by its own Constitution and no longer sustained by the sense of public danger, witnessed the outrages offered to its flag by the great nations of Europe, while it could not even find resources sufficient to stand up to the Indian tribes or to pay the interest on the debts contracted during the War of Independence. On the verge of destruction, it officially declared itself powerless and appealed to the constituent power.[3]

If ever there was a short moment when America did rise to that climax of glory where the proud imagination of her inhabitants would constantly like us to see her, it was at that supreme crisis when the national authority had in some sort abdicated its dominion.

The spectacle of a nation struggling energetically to obtain its independence is one which every century has seen. Moreover, the efforts made by the Americans to throw off the English yoke have been much exaggerated. With twenty-eight hundred miles of ocean between them and their enemies, aided by a powerful ally, the United States owed their victory much more to their position than to the valor of their armies or the patriotism of their citizens. Who would dare to compare the American war to those of the French Revolution or the efforts of the Americans to ours, when France, a prey to the attacks of all Europe, without money, credit, or allies, threw a twentieth of her population in the face of her enemies, with one hand stifling the devouring flames within her and with the other brandishing the torch around her? But that which is new in the history of societies is to see a great people, warned by its lawgivers that the wheels of government are stopping, turn its attention on itself without haste or fear, sound the depth of the ill, and then wait for two years to find the remedy at leisure, and then finally, when the remedy has been indicated, submit to it voluntarily without its costing humanity a single tear or drop of blood.

[2] See the Articles of the first Confederation, formed in 1778. This federal Constitution was not adopted by all the states until 1781.

See also the analysis of this Constitution in Nos. 15 to 22, inclusive, of *The Federalist* and that of Mr. Story in his *Commentaries on the Constitution of the United States,* pp. 85–115. [Tocqueville refers here to the abridged edition of Story's *Commentaries* (Boston, 1833).]

[3] Congress made this declaration on February 21, 1787. [Cf. Story, *Commentaries,* p. 107.]

When the inadequacy of the first federal Constitution was first felt, that outburst of political passions which gave birth to the Revolution had somewhat calmed down, but all the great men then thrown to the front were still alive. That proved a double blessing for America. The assembly responsible for drafting the second Constitution was not numerous,[4] and it included the men of greatest intelligence and noblest character ever to have appeared in the New World. George Washington presided over it.

After long and mature deliberation, this national commission finally offered for the people's acceptance that body of organic laws which is still in force in the Union now. All the states adopted it in turn.[5] The new federal government took up its duties in 1789, after an interregnum of two years. So the American Revolution ended exactly when ours began.

Summary of the Federal Constitution

Division of sovereign powers between federal and state authority.
State authority is the rule and federal government the exception.

The first difficulty which the Americans had to face was how to divide sovereignty so that the various states of the Union continued to govern themselves in everything to do with internal prosperity but so that the whole nation, represented by the Union, should still be a unit and should provide for all general needs. That was a complicated question and hard to resolve.

It was impossible to define in advance, completely and exactly, the share of authority which should go to each of these governments dividing the sovereignty.

Who could foresee every detail of a nation's life?

The duties and rights of the federal government were simple and easy to define because the Union had been formed with the object of providing for certain great general needs. But the rights and duties of the governments of the states were many and complicated, for such a government was involved in all the details of social life.

Therefore the attributes of the federal government were carefully defined, and it was declared that everything not contained within that definition returned to the jurisdiction of state governments.

[4] It had only fifty-five members, including Washington, Madison, Hamilton, and the two Morrises.

[5] It was not the legislators who adopted it. The people appointed deputies for this sole purpose. There were searching debates about the new Constitution in each of these assemblies.

Hence state authority remained the rule and the federal government the exception.⁶

It was foreseen that in practice questions would arise about the exact limits of this exceptional authority and that it would be dangerous to leave the solution of these questions to the ordinary courts established in the different states by the states themselves. So they created a federal Supreme Court,⁷ a unique tribunal one of whose prerogatives was to maintain the division of powers appointed by the Constitution between these rival governments.⁸

Prerogatives of the Federal Government

Power granted to the federal government to make war and peace and to levy general taxes. Internal political matters within its sphere. Government of the Union more centralized in certain respects than the royal government under the old monarchy in France.

⁶ See amendments to the federal Constitution; *The Federalist*, No. 32. Story, p. 711; Kent's *Commentaries on American Law*, Vol. I, p. 364. [Tocqueville has used the first edition of James Kent's *Commentaries on American Law*.]

Note, too, that every time the Constitution has not reserved for Congress the *exclusive* right to regulate certain matters, the states may do it before Congress sees fit to begin. Example: Congress has the right to make a general law about bankruptcy, but does not do so; each state drafts one of its own. Moreover, that point was established only after argument before the courts. It is no more than a legal decision. [As late as 1898 Congress passed a federal bankruptcy act.]

⁷ The action of this court is indirect, as we shall see later.

⁸ No. 45 of *The Federalist* explains the division of sovereignty between the Union and each state as follows: "The powers delegated by the proposed Constitution to the federal government are few and defined. Those which are to remain in the state governments are numerous and indefinite. The former will be exercised principally on external objects, as war, peace, negotiation, and foreign commerce, with which last the power of taxation will, for the most part, be connected. The powers reserved for the several states will extend to all the objects which, in the ordinary course of affairs, concern the lives, liberties, and properties of the people, and the internal order, improvement, and prosperity of the state."

I shall often have occasion to quote *The Federalist* in this work. When the draft law, which has since become the Constitution of the United States, was still before the people and submitted for their adoption, three men, already famous and later to become even more celebrated—John Jay, Hamilton, and Madison—associated together with the object of pointing out to the nation the advantages of the plan submitted to it. With this intention they published in a journal a series of articles which together form a complete treatise. They gave their journal the name of *The Federalist*, and that name is used for the book.

The Federalist is a fine book, and though it especially concerns America, it should be familiar to statesmen of all countries.

Among nations, each nation is but a single unit. It is especially in order to face foreigners with advantage that a nation needs a single government.

Therefore the Union was granted the exclusive right of making war and peace, concluding commercial treaties, levying armies and equipping fleets.[9]

The necessity for a national government was not so imperiously felt in the direction of the internal affairs of society.

Nevertheless, there are some general interests for which a general authority alone can usefully provide.

The right to regulate everything relating to the value of money was left to the Union; it was responsible for the postal service; it was given the right to open the main lines of communications uniting the different parts of the country.[10]

In general, the government of each state was considered free within its sphere; however, it might abuse that independence and by imprudent measures compromise the security of the whole Union; in these rare cases, defined in advance, the federal government was allowed to intervene in the internal affairs of the states.[11] Thus, while allowing the confederated republics to modify and alter their legislation, they were forbidden to make laws retroactive or to create a body of nobles in the state.[12]

Finally, as the federal government had to have the means to fulfill the obligations imposed on it, it was given the unlimited right to levy taxes.[13]

If one examines the division of powers settled by the federal Constitution, noting which portions of sovereignty have been reserved for the several states and what share of power has been assumed by the Union, it is easy to see that the federal lawgivers had formed very clear and just ideas concerning what I have previously called governmental centralization.

The United States is not only a republic but also a confederation. Nevertheless, in some respects national authority was more centralized

[9] See Article I, section 8, of the Constitution; Nos. 41 and 42 of *The Federalist;* Kent's *Commentaries,* Vol. I, pp. 207 ff.; Story, pp. 358–382, 409–426.

[10] It also has several other rights of the same sort, such as bankruptcy legislation and the granting of patents. It is easy to see what made it necessary for the Union as a whole to intervene in such matters.

[11] Even in this eventuality its intervention is indirect. The Union intervenes through the courts, as we shall see later.

[12] Federal Constitution, Article I, section 19.

[13] Constitution, Article I, sections 8, 9, and 10; *The Federalist,* Nos. 30–36, inclusive; *ibid.,* 41, 42, 43, and 44; Kent's *Commentaries,* Vol. I, pp. 207 and 381; Story, pp. 329 and 514.

there than in several of the European absolute monarchies at that date. I will quote just two examples.

In France one could count thirteen sovereign courts which, most often, had the right to interpret the law without appeal. There were also certain provinces, called *pays d'État,* which, when the sovereign authority responsible to represent the nation had ordered a tax to be levied, could refuse their cooperation.

The Union has only one tribunal to interpret the law, as it has but one legislature to make it; the tax voted by the nation's representatives is obligatory for all citizens. Therefore, in these two essential respects the Union is more centralized than was the old monarchy in France; nevertheless, the Union is only an assemblage of confederated republics.

In Spain certain provinces had the power to establish a customs system of their own, a power which, by its very essence, is part of national sovereignty.

In America Congress alone has the right to regulate the commercial relations of the states among themselves. Therefore the government of the confederation was, in that matter, more centralized than the kingdom of Spain.

It is true that in France and Spain the crown was always in a position to carry out, by force if necessary, things which the constitution of the kingdom refused it the right to do; so the practical result was just the same. But here I am discussing the theory.

Federal Powers

The federal government being enclosed within a clearly defined sphere of action, the next problem was how to set it working.

Legislative Powers

Division of the legislative body into two branches. Differences in the way the two houses are formed. The principle of the independence of the states prevails in the formation of the Senate. The dogma of the sovereignty of the nation dictates the composition of the House of Representatives. Singular effects resulting from the fact that constitutions are logical only when nations are young.

In many respects the organization of the Union's powers followed plans previously worked out in the particular constitutions of each state.

The federal legislative body of the Union was composed of a Senate and a House of Representatives.

The spirit of conciliation caused diverse rules to be followed in the formation of each of these assemblies.

I have made it plain earlier that when a federal constitution was desired, two opposing interests were brought face to face. These two interests had given rise to two views.

One party wanted to make the Union a league of independent states, a sort of congress where representatives of distinct peoples came to discuss certain matters of common interest.

The other party wished to unite all the inhabitants of the former colonies in a single people and to give them a government which, though its sphere would be limited, could act within that sphere as the one and only representative of the nation. The practical consequences of these two theories were widely divergent.

If a league, and not a national government, was to be organized, it would be the majority of the states which would make the law, not the majority of the inhabitants of the Union. For each state, great or small, would then keep its character as an independent nation and enter into the Union on a footing of perfect equality.

But once the inhabitants of the United States were considered as forming one and the same people, then it would be natural that only the majority of the citizens should make the law.

One appreciates that the small states could not consent to the application of this doctrine without completely abdicating their existence as far as federal sovereignty was concerned; from being a coequal authority, they would become an insignificant fraction of a great people. The first system would have granted them unreasonable power; the second would annul it.

In these circumstances there occurred what almost always does happen when interests and theory are opposed: the rules of logic were bent. The lawgivers adopted a middle path which forcibly reconciled two theoretically irreconcilable systems.

The principle of state independence prevailed in the shaping of the Senate, the dogma of national sovereignty in the composition of the House of Representatives.

Each state was to send to Congress two senators and a number of representatives in proportion to its population.[14]

[14] Every ten years Congress decides anew how many deputies each state should send to the House of Representatives. In 1789 the total was 65; in 1833 it was 240. (*American Almanac*, 1834, p. 100.)

The Constitution provided that there should not be more than one representative for every 30,000, but no minimum was fixed. Congress has not thought it

As a result of this arrangement the state of New York has now forty representatives in Congress and only two senators; the state of Delaware has two senators and only one representative. So in the Senate the state of Delaware is the equal of the state of New York, whereas in the House of Representatives the latter has forty times as much influence. In this way it could happen that a minority of the nation dominating the Senate could completely paralyze the will of the majority represented in the other house, and that is contrary to the spirit of constitutional government.

All this clearly shows how rare and difficult it is rationally and logically to fit together all the machinery of legislation.

Within the same people in the long run time always generates different interests and consecrates different rights. When it comes to settling a general constitution, these interests and rights form so many natural obstacles preventing any political principle from being followed through to all its conclusions. It is therefore only at the birth of societies that lawmaking can be completely logical. When you see a people enjoying that advantage, do not hasten to conclude that it is wise; think rather that it is young.

At the time when the federal Constitution was shaped, there were still only two interests among the Anglo-Americans positively opposed one to the other: interests in its individuality for each particular state and interest in union for the whole nation; and it was necessary to come to a compromise.

In any case one must recognize that this part of the Constitution has not so far produced the evil consequences one might have feared.

All the states are young; they are close to one another; their mores, ideas, and needs are homogeneous; the difference resulting from their greater or smaller size is not enough to give them strongly opposed interests. So the small states have never been found leaguing together in the Senate against the plans of the great ones. Moreover, there is such an irresistible force in the legal expression of the will of a whole people that the Senate is very weak when

---

obligatory to increase the number of representatives in proportion to increased population. By the first law passed on this subject, that of April 14, 1792 (see Story's *Laws of the United States,* Vol. I, p. 235) [The exact title of the work referred to by Tocqueville is *The Public and General Statutes Passed by the Congress of the United States of America from 1789 to 1827 Inclusive,* published under the inspection of Joseph Story, 3 vols., Boston, 1827.], it was decided that there should be one representative for every 33,000 inhabitants. The last law, brought in in 1832, fixed the number of one representative for every 48,000 inhabitants. The population, for this purpose, was calculated as all free men and three fifths of the number of slaves.

faced by the will of the majority expressed in the House of Representatives.

One should also remember that it was not the task of the American lawgivers to make one single nation out of the people for whom they wanted to provide laws. The object of the federal Constitution was not to destroy the existence of the states but only to restrain them. As soon, therefore, as real power was left in the hands of these secondary bodies (and they could not be deprived of it), the habitual use of constraint to bend them to the will of the majority had been renounced in advance. This granted, there was nothing extraordinary in introducing the influence of the individual states into the machinery of government. It only acknowledged the existence of a recognized power which had to be humored and not constrained.

Another Difference Between the Senate and the House of Representatives

The Senate appointed by the state legislatures. The representatives by the people. Two stages of election for the former, one for the latter. Different terms of office. Functions.

There is a difference between the Senate and the other house not only in the principle of representation but also in the mode of election, length of the term of office, and diversity of prerogatives.

The House of Representatives is appointed by the people, the Senate by the legislatures of each state.

One results from direct election, the other from election in two stages.

The representatives' term of office only lasts two years, that of the senators six.

The House of Representatives has only legislative functions; its only share in judicial power is the right to impeach public officials. The Senate shares in making the laws; it judges the political offenders brought before it by the House of Representatives; it is also the great executive council of the nation. Treaties concluded by the President must be ratified by the Senate; his appointments are not final till they have been approved by that body.[15]

[15] See *The Federalist*, Nos. 52–66, inclusive; Story, pp. 199–314; Constitution, Article I, sections 2 and 3.

The Executive Power[16]

Dependence of the President. Elective and responsible. Free within his own sphere; the Senate supervises, but does not control him. The President's salary at his entry into office. Suspensive veto.

The American lawgivers had a difficult task to fulfill; they wanted to create an executive power dependent on the majority that yet should be sufficiently strong to act freely on its own within its proper sphere.

Maintenance of the republican form of government required that the representative of executive power should be subject to the national will.

The President is an elective magistrate. His honor, property, freedom, and life are a perpetual pledge to the people for the good use he will make of his power. Moreover, in exercising that power he is not completely independent; the Senate supervises him in his relations with foreign powers and in his appointments to offices so that he can neither corrupt nor be corrupted.

The lawgivers of the Union appreciated that the executive power could not worthily and profitably carry out its task unless it was given more stability and strength than were granted in the individual states.

The President was appointed for four years and could be reelected. With his future to consider, he should have the courage to work in the public interest and the means to do so.

The President was made the one and only representative of the executive power of the Union. Care was taken not to subordinate his will to that of a council, a dangerous expedient which both clogs government action and lessens the ruler's responsibility. The Senate has the right to annul certain of the President's acts, but it cannot force him to act or share executive power with him.

Some legislatures can act directly on the executive power, and we have seen that the Americans were careful to prevent that. But their action may be indirect.

The power of the two houses to deprive a public official of his salary takes away some of his independence; with the making of laws at their command, there is always a danger that they will gradually

[16] *The Federalist*, Nos. 67–77, inclusive; Constitution, Article II; Story, pp. 315, 518–580; Kent's *Commentaries*, p. 255.

encroach on that share of power which the Constitution intended the President to preserve.

This dependence of the executive power is one of the inherent vices of republican constitutions. The Americans could not eliminate that tendency which leads legislative assemblies to take over the government, but they did make it less irresistible.

The President's salary is fixed on his entry into office for the whole term thereof. Moreover, the President has a suspensive veto which allows him to check the passage of laws which might destroy that portion of independence which the Constitution entrusted to him. But a struggle between President and legislature is bound to be unequal, for the latter, if it sticks to its plans, is always able to overcome any resistance he can put up; but the suspensive veto at least forces it to go over the ground again; the matter must be reconsidered, and this time it requires a two-thirds majority to carry it. Moreover, the veto is a sort of appeal to the people. The executive power, which without that guarantee might be oppressed in secret, can then argue its case and make its reasons heard. But if the legislature persists in its plans, is it not always able to overcome any resistance put up against it? My answer to that is that in the constitution of any people whatsoever, one reaches some point at which the lawgiver is bound to rely on the good sense and virtue of the citizens. That point is nearer and more obvious in republics, further and more carefully hidden in monarchies; but it is always there somewhere. There is no country where the law can foresee everything or where institutions should take the place of reason and mores.

How the Position of the President of the United States Differs from That of a Constitutional King in France

In the United States the executive power is limited and exceptional, as also is the power in whose name it acts. In France both extend over everything. The king is one of the authors of the law. The President is only an executor of the law. Other differences resulting from the length of term of office. The President is checked in the exercise of executive power. The king is free therein. In spite of these differences, France is more like a republic than is America to a monarchy. Comparison of the number of officials dependent on the executive power in the two countries.

Executive power plays such an important part in the destiny of nations that I should like to linger a moment to make the place it occupies in the American system better understood.

To get a clear and precise idea of the position of the President in the United States, it is useful to compare him to a king in one of the constitutional monarchies of Europe.

In this comparison I shall take little notice of the external signs of power, for they deceive rather than guide an observer.

When a monarchy gradually transforms itself into a republic, the executive power there preserves titles, honors, respect, and even money long after it has lost the reality of power. The English, having cut off the head of one of their kings and chased another off the throne, still go on their knees to address the successors of those princes.

On the other hand, when a republic falls under one man's yoke, the ruler's demeanor remains simple, unaffected, and modest, as if he had not already been raised above everybody. Emperors who despotically disposed of the fortunes and lives of their fellow citizens were still addressed as Caesar, and dined familiarly with their friends.

Therefore one must disregard superficialities and look deeper.

Sovereignty in the United States is divided between the Union and the states, whereas with us it is unified and compact; that is the first and greatest difference which I see between a king of France and a President of the United States.

In the United States executive power is limited and exceptional, as is the sovereignty in whose name it acts; in France, like sovereignty, it extends to everything.

The Americans have a federal government and we a national one.

Therein lies the principle cause of inferiority, resulting from the very nature of things; but it is not the only such cause. The second in importance is this: sovereignty, properly speaking, can be defined as the right to make the laws.

In France the king forms a real part of sovereignty, for the laws cannot exist if he refuses to sanction them; and he is also the executor of the laws.

The President is also the executor of the laws, but he has no real part in making them, for by refusing his assent he cannot prevent them existing. Thus he is not part of the sovereign power, but its agent only.

The French king not only is himself a part of the sovereign power but also has a hand in forming the legislature, which is the other part. He does this by nominating the members of one chamber and by terminating at will the mandate of the other. The President of the United States has no part in the composition of the legislative body, and he cannot dissolve it.

The king shares with the chambers the right of introducing a law. The President has no similar initiative.

The king is represented in the chambers by a number of agents who explain his intentions, support his opinions, and make his maxims of government prevail.

The President has no entry into Congress; his ministers also are excluded, and it is only by indirect means that he can insinuate his influence and advice into that great body.

The king of France, therefore, is on an equal footing with the legislature, which cannot act without him, nor can he without it.

Beside the legislature, the President is an inferior and dependent power.

In the exercise of executive power properly so called, the matter in which his position seems most like that of the king of France, the President still suffers from several very substantial causes of inferiority.

In the first place the power of the king of France has an advantage over that of the President by its duration. Now, duration is one of the basic elements of power. One loves or fears only that which exists for a long time.

The President of the United States is a magistrate elected for four years. In France the king is a hereditary leader.

In the exercise of executive power the President is constantly subject to jealous supervision. He prepares treaties, but he does not make them; he suggests officials for appointments, but he does not appoint them.[17]

The king of France is absolute master in the sphere of executive power.

The President of the United States is answerable for his acts. French law states that the person of the king is inviolable.

Nevertheless, over the one as over the other, there is a directing power, that of public opinion. That power is less defined in France than in the United States, less recognized and less formulated in the laws, but it does in fact exist there. In America it works through elections and decrees, in France by revolutions. So France and the United States, in spite of their different constitutions, have this point in common, that, in practice, public opinion is the dominant power. In truth the generating principle behind the laws is the same in both nations, although its development may be more or less

[17] The Constitution had left it doubtful whether the President was bound to take the advice of the Senate concerning the dismissal as well as the appointment of a federal officer. *The Federalist*, in No. 77, seemed to establish the affirmative; but in 1789 Congress formally decided that, as the President was responsible, he ought not to be forced to employ agents who did not enjoy his confidence. See Kent's *Commentaries*, Vol. I, p. 289.

free, and the consequences deriving therefrom are often different. That principle is, by its nature, essentially republican. For this reason I think that France, with its king, has more resemblance to a republic than has the Union, with its President, to a monarchy.

In all these preceding remarks I have been at pains only to point out the main points of difference. If I had chosen to go into details, the picture would have been even more striking. But, having so much to say, I want to be brief.

I have remarked that the power of the President of the United States is exercised only within the sphere of a restricted authority, whereas that of the king of France is exercised within an undivided sphere of sovereignty.

I could have shown that the governmental power of the king in France goes even beyond these natural limits, extended though they be, and penetrates in a thousand ways into the administration of private interests.

To this cause of influence I could add that resulting from the great number of public officials, almost all of whom owe their mandate to the executive power. With us this number has gone beyond all known bounds; it amounts to 138,000.[18] Each of these 138,000 appointments should be considered as an element of power. The President has no absolute right to make public appointments, and those appointments hardly number more than 12,000.[19]

Accidental Causes That May Increase the Influence of the Executive Power

External security enjoyed by the Union. Waiting policy. Army of six thousand soldiers. Only a few ships. The President possesses great prerogatives which he has no occasion to use. In those which he has occasion to use, he is weak.

If executive power is weaker in America than in France, the reason for this lies perhaps more in circumstances than in the laws.

[18] The sums paid by the state to these various officials total two hundred million francs a year.

[19] An almanac, called *The National Calendar* [*The National Calendar and Annals of the United States for 1833*, Vol. XI, Washington, 1833], is published every year in America; one can find the names of all federal officials there. It is *The National Calendar* for 1833 which provided the figure I give here.

It would result from the foregoing that the king of France disposes of eleven times as many places as the President of the United States, although the population of France is only one and a half times as great as that of the Union.

It is generally in its relations with foreign powers that the executive power of a nation has the chance to display skill and strength.

If the Union's existence were constantly menaced, and if its great interests were continually interwoven with those of other powerful nations, one would see the prestige of the executive growing, because of what was expected from it and of what it did.

It is true that the President of the United States is commander-in-chief of the army, but that army consists of six thousand soldiers; he commands the navy, but the navy has only a few ships; he conducts the Union's relations with foreign nations, but the Union has no neighbors. Separated by the ocean from the rest of the world, still too weak to want to rule the sea, it has no enemies and its interests are seldom in contact with those of the other nations of the globe.

This makes it clear that we should not judge the practice of the government by the theory.

The President of the United States possesses almost royal prerogatives which he has no occasion to use, and the rights of which he has been able to make use so far are very circumscribed; the laws allow him to be strong, but circumstances have made him weak.

But it is circumstances, even more than laws, which give French royal authority its greatest strength.

The French executive is constantly striving against obstacles, and disposes of immense resources to overcome them. It is enlarged by the size of the things it does and the importance of the events it controls, without the need to modify its constitution.

Had the laws made it as weak and circumscribed as that of the Union, its influence would soon have become much greater.

Why the President of the United States Has No Need, in Order to Direct Affairs, of a Majority in the Two Houses

It is an accepted maxim in Europe that a constitutional king cannot govern when opinion in the legislative chambers is not in accord with his.

Several Presidents of the United States have been seen to lose the support of the majority in the legislative body without being obliged to surrender power and without any great evil resulting to society therefrom.

I have heard that fact quoted to prove the independence and strength of the American executive power. But a few moments' reflection will show that it rather proves its impotence.

A European king needs the support of the legislative body to fulfill the task which the constitution has imposed on him, for it is an immense task. A European constitutional king is not only the executor of the law; the task of its execution devolves so completely upon him that he could paralyze its strength if it opposed him. To make the law, he needs the chambers; to execute it, the chambers need him. They are two powers which cannot exist one without the other; the machinery of government would stop the moment there is discord between them.

In America the President cannot prevent the making of laws; he cannot escape from his obligation to execute them. His zealous and sincere aid is no doubt useful, but it is not necessary in order that the government should function. In everything important which he does, he is directly or indirectly subject to the legislature; where he is entirely independent of it, he can do almost nothing. It is, therefore, his weakness, not his strength, which allows him to carry on in opposition to the legislative power.

In Europe there must be agreement between king and chambers, because the fight between them might be serious. In America agreement is not obligatory because there such a fight is impossible.

Election of the President

The danger of the system of election increases in proportion to the extent of the prerogatives of the executive power. The Americans can adopt this system because they can manage without a strong executive power. How circumstances favor the establishment of the elective system. Why the election of the President does not change the principles of government. Influence exerted by the election of the President on the fate of secondary functionaries.

The system of election, applied to the head of the executive power of a great people, presents dangers which experience and historians have sufficiently indicated.

I only wish to speak of them in reference to America.

These dangers may be more or less formidable according to the position occupied by the executive power and its importance in the state, and they may vary according to the mode of election and the circumstances of the people taking part therein.

There is reason for criticizing the elective system, when applied to the head of state, in that it offers so great an attraction to private ambition and so inflames passions in the pursuit of power that often legal means do not suffice them, and men appeal to force when they do not have right on their side.

Clearly, the greater the prerogatives of the executive power, the greater is this attraction. The more the ambitions of the candidates are excited, the more warmly is their cause espoused by a crowd of partisans with lesser ambitions who hope for a share of power when their man has triumphed.

For this reason the dangers of the elective system increase in direct proportion to the influence exercised by the executive power over affairs of state.

The revolutions in Poland should not be attributed exclusively to the elective system as such, but partly to the fact that the election was for the head of a great monarchy.

Therefore, before discussing the absolute goodness of the elective system, a preliminary question must be answered, namely, whether the geographical position, laws, habits, mores, and opinions of the nation into which one wishes to introduce it allow it to establish a weak and dependent executive power; for often to desire both that the head of state should be armed with great power and that he should be elected is, in my view, to express two contradictory wishes. The only means I know of by which hereditary royalty can be reduced to the condition of an elective authority is to circumscribe its sphere of action beforehand, gradually to diminish its prerogatives, and to accustom the people by degrees to live without its protection. But European republicans never think of doing that. As many of them hate tyranny only because they are exposed to its severities, it is oppression, and not the extent of executive power, that chafes them. They only attack the source of power, not perceiving the close link between these two things.

No one has yet come forward willing to risk his honor and his life in order to become President of the United States, because the President has only temporary, restricted, and dependent power. Fortune must put a huge prize at stake if such desperate players are to present themselves in the lists. So far no candidate has been able to arouse ardent sympathies and dangerous popular passions in his favor. The reason for this is simple: when he gets to the head of the government, he has little power or wealth or glory to distribute among his friends, and his influence in the state is too small for any faction to feel that its success or its ruin depends on his elevation to power.

Hereditary monarchies have one great advantage: the private interest of a family is always intimately connected with the interest of the state, and therefore state interests are never for a moment left to look after themselves. I do not know whether business is better conducted in monarchies than elsewhere, but at least there is always someone who, well or ill, according to his capacity, does concern himself therewith.

Whereas in elective states, when an election approaches and long before it arrives, the machinery of government, in a sense, only goes on functioning by itself. No doubt suitably contrived laws could provide that the election take place rapidly and in one bout, so that the seat of executive power would never remain vacant; but whatever one might do, the void would remain in the minds of men despite the legislators' efforts.

When an election draws near, the head of the executive power only thinks of the coming struggle; he has no future; he can undertake nothing new and only feebly pursues matters which, perhaps, another will bring to completion. "I am so near the time of my retirement from office," wrote President Jefferson on January 21, 1809 (six weeks before the election), that I feel no passion, I take no part, I express no sentiment. It appears to me just to leave my successor the commencement of those measures which he will have to prosecute, and for which he will be responsible." [The passage to which Tocqueville refers is to be found in a letter from Jefferson to James Monroe, and reads accurately thus: "I am now so near the moment of retiring, ·that I take no part in affairs beyond the expression of an opinion. I think it fair that my successor should now originate those measures of which he will be charged with the execution and responsibility and that it is my duty to clothe them with the forms of authority." *The Writings of Thomas Jefferson,* ed. P. L. Ford, Vol. IX, New York, 1898, p. 243 f.]

As for the nation, it has all eyes turned to one single point, it is only concerned to watch the birthpangs in progress.

The more extensive the place occupied by the executive in the direction of affairs, and the wider and the more necessary its habitual activity, the greater is the danger from such a state of things. Among a people which has grown used to being governed by the executive power, and *a fortiori* to be administered by it, an election cannot fail to cause profound disturbance.

In the United States the activity of the executive power can safely slow down, for that activity is weak and circumscribed.

When the head of government is elected, there is almost always a resulting lack of stability in the internal and external policies of the state. That is one of the principal defects of this system.

But that defect is more or less felt in proportion to the power granted to the elected magistrate. At Rome the principles of the government remained unaltered, although the consuls were changed every year, because the Senate was the directing power, and the Senate was a hereditary body. In most of the monarchies of Europe, if the king were elected, the kingdom would change face with each new choice.

In America the President exercises very substantial influence on affairs of state, but he does not conduct them; the preponderant power resides in the representatives of the nation as a whole. So the whole people would have to be changed, and not only the President, for the maxims of politics to be altered. Hence in America the elective system, applied to the head of the executive power, does not shake government stability to any very noticeable extent.

But lack of stability is an evil so inherent in the elective system that it does make itself acutely felt in the sphere of the President's activity, restricted though that is.

The Americans have rightly considered that the head of the executive power, in order to fulfill his mission and bear the whole load of his responsibilities, ought to be as free as possible to choose his own agents and to dismiss them at will. The legislative body supervises the President rather than directs him. It follows from that that at each new election the fate of all federal employees is in suspense.

It is sometimes made a subject of complaint in European constitutional monarchies that the fate of humble agents of the administration often depends on that of the ministers. But things are much worse still in states where the head of government is elected. The reason is simple: in constitutional monarchies ministers succeed one another rapidly, but the chief representative of executive power never changes, and that keeps the spirit of innovation within bounds; the changes that take place in administrative systems there are matters of detail, not of principle; one set of principles cannot be abruptly substituted for another without causing a sort of revolution. In America such a revolution takes place every four years in the name of the law.

As for the suffering of individuals naturally resulting from such a system, it must be allowed that the uncertain tenure of public offices does not produce in America such ill consequences as might be anticipated elsewhere. In the United States it is so easy to establish an independent position that the official who loses his place may be deprived of the comforts of life but not of the means of subsistence.

I said at the beginning of this chapter that the extent of the dangers of this mode of election, applied to the head of the executive power, depended on the particular circumstances of the nation who elects him.

No matter what efforts are made to restrict its role and what position it legally occupies, in foreign affairs the influence of the executive is bound to be great; a negotiation cannot be initiated and brought to a fruitful conclusion except by one man.

The more precarious and perilous a nation's position, and the more the need for continuity and stability in the conduct of foreign policy is felt, the more dangerous does the practice of electing the head of state become.

American policy toward the world at large is simple; one might almost say that no one needs them, and they do not need anybody. Their independence is never threatened.

With them therefore the role of the executive power is restrained as much by circumstances as by the laws. The President can frequently change his views without the state perishing or suffering.

Whatever prerogatives are vested in the executive power, one must always consider the time immediately before and during an election as a period of national crisis.

The more embarrassed the internal position of a country, and the greater its external perils, the more dangerous is that moment of crisis for it. There are very few nations in Europe that would not have reason to fear conquest or anarchy every time they provided themselves with a new leader.

In America society is so constituted that it can carry on by itself without help: there are never external dangers there. The election of a President causes agitation, not ruin.

Mode of Election

Skill of American lawgivers in choosing the mode of election. Creation of a special electoral body. Separate vote of these special electors. In what circumstances the House of Representatives may be called on to choose the President. Results of the twelve elections which have taken place since the Constitution has been in force.

Besides the dangers inherent in the principle, there are many others arising from the actual methods of election, and these can be avoided by care on the lawgivers' part.

When a people in arms meets in the marketplace to choose its leaders, it is exposed not only to those dangers which spring from the elective system itself but also to all the risks of civil war which such a mode of election entails.

The laws of Poland which made the choice of a king turn on the veto of a single man, were an invitation to murder that man or a preparation for anarchy.

As one studies the institutions of the United States and looks more closely at the political and social state of that country, one discovers a wonderful harmony between fortune's favors and man's endeavors. America was a new country, but the people living there had already a long experience of liberty elsewhere: two circumstances most favorable to internal order. Moreover, America stood in no fear of conquest. The lawgivers of America, profiting by these happy circumstances, found no difficulty in establishing a weak and dependent executive power; having shaped it in that way, they could without danger make it elective.

They had then only to choose the least dangerous of the various modes of election; the rules they laid down in this respect admirably complete the guarantees already provided by the physical and political structure of the country.

The problem was to find that mode of election which, while expressing the real will of the people, would least arouse their passions and leave them least in suspense. It was first of all agreed that a *simple* majority should decide the point. But it was still a matter of great difficulty to ascertain that majority without fear of those delays which were most important to avoid.

In practice it seldom happens that one man can win a majority of the votes of a great nation at the first attempt. That is even more difficult in a republic of confederated states, where local influences are particularly well developed and strong.

To get around this second trouble, the following method was devised: the electoral powers of the nation were delegated to a body representing it.

This mode of election increased the chances of a majority, for the fewer the electors, the easier it is for them to come to an understanding. This method also made it more likely that their choice would be good.

But should the right of election be entrusted to the legislative body itself, the normal representatives of the nation, or should it rather be entrusted to an electoral college whose sole function would be the appointment of the President?

The Americans preferred the second alternative. They considered that the men sent to make the ordinary laws but incompletely represented the wishes of the people concerning the choice of their chief magistrate. Moreover, being elected for more than a year, they might represent a will which had already changed. They judged that if the legislature were responsible for choosing the head of the executive, the members of that body would, long before the election, be exposed to corrupting maneuvers and become the plaything of intrigues; whereas special electors would, like a jury, remain unrecognized in the crowd until the day when they had to act, and would then appear for one moment on the scene to pronounce their decision.

It was settled then that each state should nominate a certain number of electors,[20] who in turn would elect the President. As it had been noticed that assemblies responsible for choosing heads of government in countries with elective systems inevitably became centers of passion and of intrigue, that they sometimes took over powers not belonging to them, and that often their proceedings, with the uncertainty resulting therefrom, could drag on so long that they put the state in danger—for all these reasons it was settled that all the electors should vote on a fixed day, but without assembling together.[21]

The mode of election in two stages made a majority probable, but not assured, for the electors might differ among themselves just as much as their constituents might have done.

In that eventuality, a choice had to be made between one of three possible measures: either new electors had to be appointed, or those already nominated had to be consulted again, or finally the choice had to be handed over to a new authority.

The first two of these alternatives, apart from their uncertainty, entailed delays and would prolong a potentially dangerous excitement.

The third was therefore chosen, and it was arranged that the votes should be sent under seal to the president of the Senate; he was to break the seals on the appointed day in the presence of the two houses. If none of the candidates had obtained a majority, then the House of Representatives itself was to proceed immediately to elect a President; but this right of election was carefully limited. The representatives could choose only one of the three candidates who had received most votes.[22]

[20] Equal to the number of members it sent to Congress. There were 288 electors in the election of 1833 (*The National Calendar*).

[21] The electors from each state assemble, but they send in to the central government the list of individual votes, and not the result of a majority vote.

[22] In this context it was the majority of states, not the majority of members, which was decisive. As a result New York has no more influence in the matter than Rhode Island. Thus the citizens of the Union are first consulted as members of one united nation; when they cannot agree, the division into states

It is therefore only a rare event, and one hard to foresee, that the election is entrusted to the normal representatives of the nation, and moreover, they can choose only a citizen who has already been designated by a strong minority of the special electors; that is a happy combination which reconciles respect for the will of the people with celerity of execution and with precautions demanded by the interest of the state. However, to let the House of Representatives decide in case of a split does not completely solve all problems, for there may be no decided majority in the House of Representatives, and in that case the Constitution offers no remedy. Nevertheless, by fixing a limit of three possible candidates and by entrusting the choice to an enlightened body, it had smoothed out all those difficulties[23] over which it could have some control; the remaining difficulties were inherent in the elective system itself.

In the forty-four years during which the federal Constitution has been in force, the United States has twelve times chosen their President.

Ten elections were instantly decided by the simultaneous votes of the special electors scattered around the country.

The House of Representatives has only twice used the exceptional right given to it in case of a split: first in 1801 for the election of Mr. Jefferson, and for the second time in 1825, when Mr. Quincy Adams was appointed.

Crisis of the Election

The Presidential election may be considered as a moment of national crisis. Why? Passions of the people. Preoccupation of the President. Calm which follows the turmoil of the election.

I have spoken of the conditions favorable to the adoption of an elective system in which the Americans were situated, and I have pointed out the precautions taken by the lawgivers to minimize its dangers. The Americans are used to all sorts of elections. Experience has taught them what degree of agitation can be permitted and where they should stop. The vast extent of the territory over which the inhabitants spread makes collisions between the various parties

---

is brought back into play, and each of the latter is given a separate and independent vote.

That is just one more of the oddities found in the federal Constitution, oddities which can only be explained by the clash of contrary interests.

[23] However, in 1801 Jefferson was not elected until the thirty-sixth ballot.

less probable and less dangerous there than elsewhere. Up to the present the political circumstances of the nation at election time have presented no real danger.

Nevertheless, one may consider the time of the Presidential election as a moment of national crisis.

No doubt the influence exercised by the President on the conduct of affairs is weak and indirect, but it affects the whole nation; the choice of a President is of but moderate concern to each citizen, but it does concern them all. And any interest, however slight, takes on great importance when it is general.

Compared to a European king, no doubt the President has few opportunities of enlisting partisans; nevertheless, the places at his disposal are numerous enough for several thousand electors to be directly or indirectly interested in his cause.

Moreover, in the United States as elsewhere, parties feel the need to rally around one man in order more easily to make themselves understood by the crowd. Generally, therefore, they use the Presidential candidate's name as a symbol; in him they personify their theories. Hence the parties have a great interest in winning the election, not so much in order to make their doctrines triumph by the President-elect's help, as to show, by his election, that their doctrines have gained a majority.

Long before the appointed day arrives, the election becomes the greatest, and one might say the only, affair occupying men's minds. At this time factions redouble their ardor; then every forced passion that imagination can create in a happy and peaceful country spreads excitement in broad daylight.

The President, for his part, is absorbed in the task of defending himself. He no longer rules in the interest of the state, but in that of his own reelection; he prostrates himself before the majority, and often, instead of resisting their passions as duty requires, he hastens to anticipate their caprices.

As the election draws near, intrigues grow more active and agitation is more lively and wider spread. The citizens divide up into several camps, each of which takes its name from its candidate. The whole nation gets into a feverish state, the election is the daily theme of comment in the newspapers and private conversation, the object of every action and the subject of every thought, and the sole interest for the moment.

It is true that as soon as fortune has pronounced, the ardor is dissipated, everything calms down, and the river which momentarily overflowed its banks falls back to its bed. But was it not astonishing that such a storm could have arisen?

Concerning the Reelection of the President

*When the head of the executive power is reeligible, it is the state
itself which intrigues and corrupts. The desire to be reelected dominates all the thoughts of the President of the United States. The
disadvantages of reelection are something peculiar to the United
States. The natural vice of all democracies is the gradual subordination of all powers to the slightest wish of the majority. The
reelection of the President encourages this vice.*

Were the lawgivers of the United States right or wrong to allow
the reelection of the President?

To refuse the head of the executive the chance of reelection seems,
at first sight, contrary to reason. One knows what influence the talents
or character of a single man exercise over the fate of a whole people,
especially in times of difficulty or crisis. Laws forbidding the citizens
from reelecting their first magistrate would deprive them of their
best means of bringing prosperity to the state or of saving it. In that
way one would reach this odd result that a man would be excluded
from the government just at the moment when he had succeeded
in proving his capacity to rule well.

No doubt those are powerful arguments, but can one not bring
up even stronger ones against them?

Intrigue and corruption are natural vices of elective governments;
but when the head of state can be reelected, these vices spread
beyond bounds and compromise the very existence of the country.
When a simple candidate forces himself forward by intrigue, his
maneuvers can only take place within a restricted sphere. But when
the head of state himself is in the lists, he can borrow all the power
of the government for his private use.

In the first case it is a question of a man with feeble resources;
in the second, it is the state itself with all its immense resources
which intrigues and which corrupts.

The simple citizen guilty of disreputable maneuvers to gain power
can harm public prosperity only in some indirect way; but if the
representative of the executive power descends to compete, the
cares of government become for him a secondary consideration; his
main concern is for his election. For him negotiations, like laws, are
nothing but electoral combinations; places become the reward for
services rendered, not to the nation, but to its head. Even if the
government's action is not always contrary to the nation's interest,

at least it no longer serves it. But the function of government is solely to serve the country.

It is impossible to observe the normal course of affairs in the United States without noticing that desire for reelection dominates the President's thoughts, that the whole policy of his administration is bent toward that aim, that his slightest actions are subordinate to that aim, and that, particularly as the moment of crisis draws nearer, his private interest takes the place of the general interest in his mind.

Therefore the principle of reelection makes the corrupting influence of elective governments wider spread and more dangerous. It tends to degrade the political morality of the nation and to substitute craft for patriotism.

In America it attacks the very sources of national existence at still closer range.

Each type of government harbors one natural vice which seems inherent in the very nature of its being; the genius of a lawgiver consists in discerning that clearly. A state may stand triumphant over many bad laws, and the harm they do is often exaggerated. But any law having the effect of nourishing this mortal germ cannot fail, in the long run, to prove fatal, even though its ill effects may not be immediately apparent.

In absolute monarchies the ruinous principle is the unlimited and unreasonable extension of the royal power. Any measure, therefore, which takes away the counterweights left by the constitution to balance this power, is radically bad, even though its effects may long seem negligible.

In the same way, in a country where democracy holds sway and a people constantly attracts everything to itself, laws which make its action ever prompter and more irresistible are a direct attack on the existence of the government.

The greatest merit of the lawgivers of America was to have seen this truth clearly and to have had the courage to act accordingly.

They agreed that, besides the people, there must be a certain number of authorities which, though not entirely independent of it, nevertheless enjoyed within their sphere a fairly wide degree of freedom; by this means, though forced to obey the permanent directions of the majority, they could still struggle against its caprices and refuse to be the tools of its dangerous exigencies.

With this object, they concentrated the whole executive power of the nation in the hands of one man; they gave wide prerogatives to the President and armed him with the veto with which to resist the encroachments of the legislature.

But by introducing the principle of relection they destroyed a part of their work. They gave the President much power, but took away from him the will to use it.

Had he not been reeligible, the President would still not have been independent of the people, or his responsibility toward it never ceased; but the people's favor would not have been so necessary to him that he must in everything bend to its will.

Reeligible (and this is especially true in our day, when political morality is growing lax and men of great character are vanishing from the scene), the President of the United States is only a docile instrument in the hands of the majority. He loves what it loves and hates what it hates; he sails ahead of its desires, anticipating its complaints and bending to its slightest wishes; the lawgivers wished him to guide it, but it is he who follows.

In this way, intending not to deprive the state of one man's talents, they have rendered those talents almost useless, and to preserve a resource against extraordinary eventualities, they have exposed the country to dangers every day.

The Federal Courts[24]

Political importance of judicial power in the United States. Difficulty of dealing with this subject. Usefulness of justice in confederations. What courts are available in the Union? Necessity of establishing federal courts. Organization of federal justice. The Supreme Court. In what it differs from all courts of justice known to us.

I have dealt with the legislative and executive power of the Union. The judicial power remains to be considered.

Here I must be frank to my readers about my fears.

Judicial institutions exercise a great influence on the fate of the Anglo-Americans; they have a very important place among their political institutions properly so called. From that point of view they particularly deserve our attention.

But how can one make the political action of American tribunals

[24] See Chapter VI, entitled "Judicial Power in the United States." This chapter states the general principles of the Americans in the matter of justice. See also Article III of the federal Constitution. See *The Federalist*, Nos. 78–83, inclusive; *Constitutional Law, Being a View of the Practice and Jurisdiction of the Courts of the United States, by Thomas Sergeant* [Boston 1830]; Story, pp. 134–162, 489–511, 581, 688. See the organic law of September 24, 1789, in the collection entitled *Laws of the United States*, by Story, Vol. I, p. 53.

understandable without entering into some technical details of their constitution and procedures? And how can one plunge into these details of a naturally arid subject, rebuffing the reader's curiosity? How can one remain clear and still be brief?

I do not flatter myself that I have avoided these different perils. Lay readers will find me too lengthy, and lawyers too brief. But that is an inevitable disadvantage of my whole subject, and of this specialized part of it in particular.

The greatest difficulty was not to know how the federal government was constituted, but how its laws are enforced.

Governments in general have only two methods of overcoming the resistance of the governed: their own physical force and the moral force supplied to them by the decisions of courts.

A government for whom war was the only means of enforcing obedience to its laws would be on the verge of ruin. One of two things would probably happen to it: either, if it were feeble and moderate, it would use force only in the last extremity and would connive at many partial acts of insubordination; in that case the state would gradually fall into anarchy.

Or if it were audacious and powerful, it would have recourse to violence every day and would soon degenerate into a pure military despotism. Either its inaction or its activity would be equally fatal for the governed.

The great object of justice is to substitute the idea of right for that of violence, to put intermediaries between the government and the use of its physical force.

It is something astonishing what authority is accorded to the intervention of a court of justice by the general opinion of mankind. That power is so great that it clings even to judicial formalities when the substance is no longer there; it gives body to a shadow.

The moral force in which tribunals are clothed makes the use of physical force infinitely rarer, for in most cases it takes its place; and when finally physical force is required, its power is doubled by this moral authority.

A federal government more than any other should desire this support of justice, for by its nature it is feeble and resistance can more easily be organized against it.[25] If it had always and as its first move to use force, it would not be adequate to its task.

The Union therefore had a particular need for tribunals to make

[25] Federal laws need tribunals most, and yet they have made least use of them. The reason for this is that most confederations were formed by independent states who had no real intention of obeying the central government and who, while giving it the right to command, carefully reserved the capacity to disobey.

the citizens obey its laws and to repel the attacks that might be launched against it.

But what tribunals should it employ? Each state already had its own organized judicial authority. Should it turn to those courts? Or should it organize a federal judiciary? It is easy to show that the Union could not adapt the established state courts to its use.

The separation of the judiciary from all other powers in the state is certainly important for the security of each and the liberty of all, but it was equally necessary for national existence that the different powers of the state should have the same origin, follow the same principles, and act within the same sphere—in a word, that they should be correlative and homogeneous. No one, I imagine, has ever thought that crimes committed in France should be tried by foreign courts so as to be more sure of the impartiality of the judges.

In their relations with the federal government, the Americans are one single people, but within this nation they have allowed political bodies to remain which in some respects are dependent on the national government but are independent in all others; each has a distinct origin, maxims peculiar to itself, and special means of carrying on its affairs. To entrust the execution of the Union's laws to courts established by these political parties would be handing over the nations to foreign judges.

Furthermore, each state is not only foreign to the Union at large but is its perpetual adversary, since whatever authority the Union loses turns to the advantage of the states.

Thus, to make the state courts enforce the laws of the Union would be handing the nation over to judges who are prejudiced as well as foreign.

Besides this, it was not only their character which made the state courts incapable of serving the national end, but even more their number.

When the federal Constitution was formed, there were already thirteen courts of justice in the United States, judging cases without appeal. Today there are twenty-four. How could a state carry on if its fundamental laws could be interpreted and applied in twenty-four different ways at the same time? Such a system would be equally contrary to reason and to the lessons of experience.

The American lawgivers therefore agreed to create a federal judicial authority to apply the laws of the Union and decide certain questions of general interest which were carefully defined in advance.

The whole judicial power of the Union was concentrated in a single tribunal called the Supreme Court of the United States, but in order to facilitate the dispatch of business, inferior courts were added to it which were empowered to decide cases of small importance without appeal and to act as courts of first instance in more serious disputes. The members of the Supreme Court were not elected by the people or by the legislature. The President of the United States had to choose them after taking the advice of the Senate.

In order to render them independent of the other authorities, they were made irremovable, and it was decided that their salaries, once fixed, would be out of the control of the legislature.[26]

It is easy enough to proclaim the establishment of a federal judiciary in principle, but a mass of difficulties arose when it was a question of determining its prerogatives.

Means of Determining the Competence of the Federal Courts

Difficulty of defining the jurisdiction of the various tribunals in confederations. The courts of the Union obtained the right of deciding their own competence. Why that rule encroaches on the portion of sovereignty reserved for the individual states. The sovereignty of the states restricted by the laws and by the interpretation of the laws. The danger of this for the several states is more apparent than real.

An initial question arises: the Constitution of the United States established two distinct sovereignties facing each other, represented

---

[26] The Union was divided into districts, each with a resident federal judge. The court over which he presided was called a district court.

In addition, each judge of the Supreme Court had to tour a certain part of the territory of the republic annually in order to try the most important cases on the spot; the court over which he presided was called the circuit court.

Finally, the most serious cases had to be brought, either directly or on appeal, before the Supreme Court. For this purpose all the circuit judges assembled annually to hold a solemn session.

The jury system was introduced into the federal courts in the same form as in the state courts and for similar cases.

Obviously there is hardly any analogy between the Supreme Court of the United States and our *cour de cassation*. A case can be brought before the Supreme Court in the first instance, but before the *cour de cassation* only as a second or third stage. The Supreme Court does indeed, like the *cour de cassation*, form a unique tribunal responsible for establishing uniform jurisprudence; but the Supreme Court judges fact as well as law, and *itself* pronounces, without sending the case back before another tribunal—two things which the *cour de cassation* cannot do.

See the organic law of September 24, 1789, *Laws of the United States*, by Story, Vol. I, p. 53.

in the realm of justice by two different systems of tribunals; however much care was taken to define the jurisdiction of each of these systems, frequent collisions between the two could not be prevented. So, in such a case, who had the right to decide competence?

In nations that form one and the same political society, when a question of competence arises between two courts of justice, it is generally brought before a third court, which serves as arbitrator.

That is easily done, because in such nations questions of judicial competence have no relation with questions of national sovereignty.

But above a high court of a particular state and a high court of the United States it was impossible to establish any tribunal which would not belong to one or the other.

It was therefore necessary to give one of these courts the right to judge its own case and to accept or refuse competence in the matter disputed. One could not grant that privilege to the various courts of the states; that would have destroyed the sovereignty of the Union, in fact, when it had been established in law; for interpretation of the Constitution would soon have given the particular states that portion of independence which the terms of the Constitution had taken from them.

The intention in creating a federal tribunal was to deprive the state courts of the right to decide, each in its own way, questions of national interest, and in that manner to form a uniform body of jurisprudence interpreting the laws of the Union. That aim would not have been achieved if the courts of the particular states, while abstaining from judging cases as federal, had been able to judge them by pretending that they were not federal.

The Supreme Court of the United States was therefore entrusted with the right to decide all questions of competence.[27]

That was the most dangerous blow dealt against the sovereignty of the states. It was now restricted not only by the laws but also by the interpretation of the laws, by a known boundary and by another that was not known, by a fixed rule and by an arbitrary one. It is true that the Constitution had fixed precise limits to federal

---

[27] Furthermore, to make disputes of competence less frequent, it was decided that in a very large number of federal cases the tribunals of the particular states would have the right to pronounce concurrently with the tribunals of the Union; but then the unsuccessful party always had the right of appeal to the Supreme Court of the United States. The Supreme Court of Virginia disputed the right of the Supreme Court of the United States to judge an appeal from its decisions, but in vain. See Kent's *Commentaries*, Vol. I, pp. 300, 370, *et seq.;* Story's *Commentaries*, p. 646; and the organic law of 1789, *Laws of the United States*, Vol. I, p. 53 [*Story, The Public and General Statutes*, I, p. 53 f.].

sovereignty, but each time that that sovereignty is in competition with that of the states, it is a federal tribunal that must decide.

However, the dangers with which this method of procedure seemed to threaten the sovereignty of the states were not in reality as great as they appeared to be.

We shall see later that in America real power resided in the provincial governments rather than in the federal government. The federal judges feel the relative weakness of the power in whose name they act, and they are more ready to give up a right to jurisdiction in cases where the law has given it to them than to claim one illegitimately.

Different Cases of Jurisdiction

The matter and the party, bases of federal jurisdiction. Cases involving ambassadors, or the Union, or a particular state. Who judges them. Cases arising from the laws of the Union. Why judged by the federal tribunals. Cases relating to the nonperformance of contracts tried by the federal courts. Consequences of this.

When they had decided on the means of establishing federal competence, the lawgivers of the Union fixed the sphere of jurisdiction within which it should operate.

It was agreed that certain parties must always be brought before the federal courts, without regard to the subject of the suit.

It was then established that certain cases could only be decided by those same courts, whatever the standing of the parties.

So the party and the subject matter became the two bases of federal competence.

Ambassadors represent nations friendly to the Union; everything concerning ambassadors in some degree concerns the Union as a whole. When an ambassador is party to a suit, the case becomes a matter touching the well-being of the nation; it is natural that a federal court should pronounce on it.

The Union itself may be involved in a case: in that event it would be against reason and the custom of nations to appeal to a tribunal representing any other sovereignty but its own. It is for the federal courts alone to pronounce.

When two individuals belonging to different states go to law, one could not without inconvenience have the matter judged by the courts of one or other party's state. It is safer to choose a tribunal not suspect of partiality to either party, and the natural tribunal to select is that of the Union.

When the two parties in a case are not isolated individuals, but states, the same reasons of equity apply, and there is also a political consideration of first importance. Here the standing of the parties gives national importance to all cases; the slightest litigation between two states concerns the peace of the whole Union.[28]

Often the very nature of the case prescribes the rule of competence. Thus all cases concerning maritime trade have to be dealt with by Federal tribunals.[29]

The reason is easily indicated: almost all such questions turn on interpretations of international law. In that respect they are of essential interest to the whole Union in its relations with foreigners. Moreover, as the sea is not contained within one judicial sphere more than another, only a national court could have a claim to jurisdiction in maritime affairs.

The Constitution included under a single category almost all the cases that must by their very nature come before the federal courts.

The rule that it lays down is simple, but it comprises a vast system of ideas and a multitude of facts.

The federal courts, it states, "shall extend to all cases *in law and equity*" arising under the Constitution, laws, and treaties of the United States.[30]

Two examples will make the legislators' thought perfectly understood.

The Constitution forbids the states the right to make laws concerning the circulation of money. In spite of this prohibition, a state makes such a law. The interested parties refuse to obey it, claiming that it is contrary to the Constitution. They must go before a federal court because the basis of complaint arises from the laws of the United States.

Congress imposes an import duty. Difficulties arise in the collection

[28] The Constitution also provided that cases between a state and citizens of another state should be tried before the federal courts. The question was soon raised whether the Constitution intended to cover all cases that might arise between a state and the citizens of another state, regardless of which of the two was the *plaintiff*. The Supreme Court decided in the affirmative, but this decision alarmed the individual states, who were afraid of being dragged against their will into the federal courts at every turn. An amendment to the Constitution was therefore introduced, by virtue of which the judicial power of the Union does not extend to trying cases *brought against* one of the states by the citizens of another. See Story's *Commentaries,* p. 624.

[29] Example: all acts of piracy.

[30] [Cf. Story, *Commentaries,* p. 608.]

of this tax. Again the case must go before the federal courts because it turns on the interpretation of a law of the United States.

This rule is in perfect accord with the bases adopted for the federal Constitution.

It is true that the Union, as constituted in 1789, has only restricted sovereignty, but it was intended that within this sphere it should form one and the same people.[81] Within this sphere it is sovereign. Once that point has been put and agreed, all the rest becomes easy, for if you recognize that the United States, within the limits imposed by the Constitution, forms a single people, you must grant it the rights belonging to all peoples.

Now, from the origins of societies this point has been agreed: that each people has the right to have all questions relating to the execution of its own laws judged before its own courts. But to this there is the reply that the Union is in the peculiar position that it only forms one people in relation to certain aims; for all other purposes it is no such thing. What is the result? That, at least as far as all the laws relative to those aims are concerned, it has those rights which one would grant to complete sovereignty. The real point of difficulty is to know what those aims are. Once that point has been decided (and we have seen above, when dealing with competence, how that was settled), there is, in truth, no further question; for once it has been decided that a suit is federal—that is to say, that it comes within the sphere reserved for the Union by the Constitution—it naturally follows that only a federal court can pronounce on it.

Every time, therefore, that a man wishes to attack the laws of the United States or to invoke them in his defense, he must turn to the federal courts.

Thus the jurisdiction of the Union's courts expands or contracts as the Union's sovereignty itself contrasts or expands.

We have seen that the principal aim of the lawgivers of 1789 was to divide sovereignty into two distinct parts. In the one they put the direction of all the general interest of the Union, in the other the direction of all the interests special to some of its parts.

Their main care was to arm the federal government with enough power, within its sphere, to resist the encroachments of the separate states.

As for the states, the general principle was adopted of leaving

[81] Some restrictions to this principle were certainly introduced by treating each state as an independent power in the Senate and by making them vote separately in the House of Representatives for the election of the President; but those are exceptions. The opposite principle is the dominant one.

them free in their sphere. The central government could neither direct nor even supervise their conduct.

I have indicated in the chapter dealing with the division of powers that that principle was not always respected. There was some laws which a state cannot make, although, apparently, they are only of interest to itself.

When one state of the Union does enact such a law, the citizens injured by its application can appeal to the federal courts.

Thus the jurisdiction of the federal courts extends not only to all cases arising from the laws of the Union but also to all those which arise from laws of the separate states made contrary to the Constitution.

The states are forbidden to promulgate retroactive laws in criminal matters; a man condemned under such a law can appeal to federal justice.

The Constitution also forbids the states to make laws "impairing the obligations of contracts."[32]

As soon as a private person thinks that a law of his state impairs a right of that sort, he can refuse to obey it and appeal to federal justice.[33]

---

[32] It is perfectly clear, says Mr. Story on page 503 [*Commentaries*, Boston, 1833], that any law which extends, abridges, or in any way changes the intention of the parties, insofar as it results from the stipulations of a contract, impairs the contract. In the same place the author carefully defines what federal jurisprudence means by a contract. The definition is very broad. A concession made by the state to an individual and accepted by him is a contract and cannot be removed by the effect of a new law. A charter granted by the state to a company is a contract and is law to the state as well as to the grantee. The said article of the Constitution therefore assures the position of a large proportion of *acquired rights*, but not of all of them. I may be in very legitimate possession of a property without its having passed into my hands through a contract. For me its possession is an acquired right, but that right is not guaranteed by the federal Constitution. [Tocqueville summarizes Story's text.]

[33] Here is a remarkable example quoted by Story on page 508 [f.]. Dartmouth College, in New Hampshire, had been founded by virtue of a charter granted to certain individuals before the American Revolution. By virtue of this charter its administrators formed a constituted body or, using the American expression, a corporation. The legislature of New Hampshire thought it could change the terms of the original charter and transferred to new administrators all the rights, privileges, and franchises derived from this charter. The former administrators resisted and appealed to the federal court, which found in their favor since the original charter was a veritable contract between the state and the grantees, and the new law could not change the provisions of this charter without violating the rights acquired by virtue of a contract and consequently violating Article I, section 10, of the Constitution of the United States. [Tocqueville refers here to Story's *Commentaries*.]

This provision, more than any other, seems to me a profound attack on state sovereignty.

The rights granted to the federal government, with obviously national aims in view, are definite and easy to understand. Those granted to it indirectly by the article in question are not easy to understand, and their limits are not clearly defined. In fact, there is a whole multitude of political laws which have an effect on contracts and could thus be made a pretext for encroachment by the central power.

Procedure of the Federal Courts

Natural weakness of the judiciary in confederations. Efforts which lawgivers should make, as far as possible, only to bring isolated individuals, and not states, before federal tribunals. How the Americans achieved that. Direct action by the federal courts against single individuals. Indirect attack against those states that violate the laws of the Union. A decision of the federal judiciary does not destroy a state law, but enervates it.

I have described the rights of the federal courts; it is no less important to know how they exercise them.

The irresistible force of justice, in a country where sovereignty is in no way shared, derives from the fact that the courts in that country represent the whole nation in a struggle with the single individual against whom the judgment is directed. To the idea of right is joined the idea of the force which supports the right.

But in countries where sovereignty is divided, it is not always like that. There justice is most often faced, not with an isolated individual, but with a fraction of the nation. Its moral power and its physical force are both thereby diminished.

Therefore in federal states justice is by nature weaker and its victim stronger.

The lawgiver in a confederation must constantly strive to give the courts a standing analogous to that of those in nations which have not divided sovereignty; in other words, his constant efforts must be bent toward making federal justice represent the nation and its victim represent a particular interest.

A government, whatever its nature in other respects, needs to act on the governed to force them to render what is due to it: it needs to act against them in order to defend itself against their attacks.

As regards direct action of the government on the governed in

order to force them to obey its laws, the Constitution of the United
States so contrived things (and this was its master stroke) that the
federal courts, acting in the name of the laws, should never have to
deal with any but individuals. In fact, as it had been declared that
the confederation formed one and the same people within the limits
traced by the Constitution, it resulted that the government created
by this Constitution and acting within its limits was invested with all
the rights of a national government, of which the principal is that its
injunctions reach the single citizen without intermediary. Thus, for
example, when the Union imposed a tax, it did not have to turn
to the states to collect it, but to each American citizen, according to
his quota. Federal justice in turn, entrusted with the duty of seeing
that the Union's law is carried out, had to condemn, not a recalcitrant state, but the taxpayer. Like the justice of other nations, it
found itself faced only by an individual.

Note that here the Union itself chose its adversary. It chose a
weak one, so naturally he is worsted.

But when, instead of attacking, the Union is driven to defend itself, the difficulty grows greater. The Constitution recognizes the
states' power to make some laws. Those laws may violate the rights
of the Union. This is bound to lead to a clash with the sovereignty
of the state that has made the law. It only remains to choose the
least dangerous of the possible means of action. The general principles which I have previously stated[34] indicate what this means
should be.

In this hypothetical case, the Union might have summoned the
state before a federal court which would have declared the law void;
to do this would have been following the most natural train of
thought. But in that event federal justice would have faced a state
directly, a situation which it was desirable to avoid as much as possible.

The Americans reflected that it was almost impossible that the
execution of a new law should not injure some private interest.

The makers of the federal Constitution relied on that private interest to attack the legislative measure of which the Union might
have complained. It is to that interest that they offer protection.

A state sells some land to a company. A year later a new law disposes of that same land in some other way and thereby violates
the provision in the Constitution forbidding interference with rights
acquired under a contract. When the purchaser under the new law
claims possession, the owner, whose rights derive from the former
law, brings the case before the courts of the Union and has the

[34] See the chapter entitled "Judicial Power in the United States."

purchaser's title declared void.[35] Thus, in substance, federal justice is at odds with state sovereignty; but it attacks only indirectly, and with reference to an application of detail. In this way it strikes at the consequences of the law, not at its principle; it does not abolish but enervates it.

One last hypothesis remained.

Each state formed a corporation with a separate existence and civil rights; consequently it could sue or be sued in the courts. One state could, for instance, bring a case against another.

In that event it was not a question of the Union contesting a provincial law, but one of judging a case in which a state was a party. It was a suit like any other, only the standing of the parties being different. Here the danger pointed out at the beginning of this chapter was again present, but this time there was no way of avoiding it; it was inherent in the very essence of federal constitutions, the result of which is bound to be the creation within the nation of entities powerful enough for it to be difficult to make them amenable to justice.

High Standing of the Supreme Court Among the Great Authorities in the State

No other nation every constituted so powerful a judiciary as the Americans. Extent of its prerogatives. Its political influence. The peace and the very existence of the Union depend on the wisdom of the seven federal judges.

When, after a detailed examination of the organization of the Supreme Court, we come to consider the whole body of prerogatives granted to it, it soon becomes clear that a mightier judicial authority has never been constituted in any land.

The Supreme Court has been given higher standing than any known tribunal, both by the *nature* of its rights and by the *categories* subject to its jurisdiction.

In all the properly administered countries of Europe the government has always shown great repugnance to allowing the ordinary courts to deal with matters affecting itself. Naturally this repugnance is all the greater when the government is absolute. Contrariwise, as liberty increases, the prerogatives of the courts are continually enlarged; but no European nation has ever thought that all judicial

[35] See Kent's *Commentaries*, Vol. I, p. 387.

questions, whatever their origin, could be left to judges of common law.

But that is just the theory which has been put in practice in America. The Supreme Court of the United States is the sole and unique tribunal of the nation.

It is responsible for the interpretation of laws and of treaties; questions to do with overseas trade or in any way involving international law come within its exclusive competence. One might even say that its prerogatives are entirely political, although its constitution is purely judicial. Its sole object is to see that the laws of the Union are carried out; and the Union only controls relations between the government and the governed and between the nation and foreigners; relations between the citizens themselves are almost all regulated by state sovereignty.

To this first cause of its importance is added another even greater one. In the European nations only private persons come under the jurisdiction of the courts, but the Supreme Court of the United States may be said to summon sovereigns to its bar. When the court crier, mounting the steps of the tribunal, pronounces these few words: "The state of New York versus the state of Ohio," one feels that this is no ordinary court of justice. And when one considers that one of these parties represents a million men and the other two million, one is amazed at the responsibility weighing on the seven men whose decision will please or grieve so many of their fellow citizens.

The peace, prosperity, and very existence of the Union rest continually in the hands of these seven federal judges. Without them the Constitution would be a dead letter; it is to them that the executive appeals to resist the encroachments of the legislative body, the legislature to defend itself against the assaults of the executive, the Union to make the states obey it, the States to rebuff the exaggerated pretensions of the Union, public interest against private interest, the spirit of conservation against democratic instability. Their power is immense, but it is power springing from opinion. They are all-powerful so long as the people consent to obey the law; they can do nothing when they scorn it. Now, of all powers, that of opinion is the hardest to use, for it is impossible to say exactly where its limits come. Often it is as dangerous to lag behind as to outstrip it.

The federal judges therefore must not only be good citizens and men of education and integrity, qualities necessary for all magistrates, but must also be statesmen; they must know how to understand the spirit of the age, to confront those obstacles that can be overcome, and to steer out of the current when the tide threatens to carry them away, and with them the sovereignty of the Union and obedience to its laws.

The President may slip without the state suffering, for his duties are limited. Congress may slip without the Union perishing, for above Congress there is the electoral body which can change its spirit by changing its members.

But if ever the Supreme Court came to be composed of rash or corrupt men, the confederation would be threatened by anarchy or civil war.

However, we must not make a mistake; the original cause of the danger does not lie in the constitution of the tribunal, but in the very nature of the federal government. We have seen that nowhere is it more necessary to establish a strong judicial authority than in confederated nations, because nowhere else are there individual entities able to struggle against the body social that are stronger and in better state to resist the use of physical force by the government.

Now, the more necessary it is for an authority to be strong, the more scope and independence it must be given. The more scope and independence an authority has, the more dangerous will any abuse of its power prove. Hence, the origin of the evil is not in the constitution of that authority, but in the very constitution of the state which makes the existence of such a power necessary.

The Superiority of the Federal Constitution over That of the States

How the Constitution of the Union can be compared with that of the individual states. The superiority of the Constitution of the Union must be attributed particularly to the wisdom of the federal legislators. The legislature of the Union is less dependent on the people than is that of each state. The executive power is freer in its sphere. The judicial power is less subject to the will of the majority. Practical consequences of this. The federal legislators have lessened the dangers inherent in government by democracy; the state legislators have increased those dangers.

The federal Constitution differs essentially from that of the states in its intended aims, but it is very similar in the means of attaining those aims. The government's objective is different, but the forms of government are the same. From this special point of view one can profitably compare them.

I consider that the federal Constitution is superior to all the state constitutions. There are several reasons for that superiority.

The present Constitution of the Union was drafted later than those of most of the states and could therefore take advantage of the experience acquired.

But we shall be convinced that this is only a secondary cause of its superiority when we recollect that eleven states have been added to the American Union since the adoption of the federal Constitution and that these have almost always exaggerated rather than diminished the defects in the earlier constitutions.

The great cause of the superiority of the federal Constitution lies in the actual character of the lawgivers.

At the time when it was drafted, the ruin of the Confederation appeared imminent: that, one may say, was a consideration present before all eyes. In that extremity the people chose, not perhaps the men it loved best, but those it held in highest esteem.

I have already noted above that the lawgivers of the Union were almost all remarkable for their enlightenment, and even more remarkable for their patriotism.

They had all grown up at a time of social crisis, when the spirit of liberty had been in constant conflict with a strong and dominating authority. When the struggle was over, and when, as is usual, the passions aroused in the crowd were still directed against dangers which had long ceased to exist, these men called a halt; they looked at their country more calmly and with greater penetration; they were aware that a final revolution had been accomplished and that henceforth the perils threatening the people could only spring from abuses of liberty. What they thought, they had the courage to say; because they felt in the bottom of their hearts a sincere and ardent love for that same liberty, they dared to speak about restraining it, because they were sure they did not want to destroy it.[36]

[36] At this time the celebrated Alexander Hamilton, one of the most influential draftsmen of the Constitution, was not afraid to publish the following in No. 71 of *The Federalist:*

"There are some who would be inclined to regard the servile pliancy of the Executive to a prevailing current, either in the community or in the legislature, as its best recommendation. But such men entertain very crude notions, as well of the purpose for which government was instituted, as of the true means by which the public happiness may be promoted. The republican principle demands that the deliberate sense of the community should govern the conduct of those to whom they entrust the management of their affairs; but it does not require an unqualified complaisance to every sudden breeze of passion, or to every transient impulse which the people may receive from the arts of men who flatter their prejudices to betray their interests. It is a just observation, that the people commonly *intend* the PUBLIC GOOD.

Most of the state constitutions give only a one-year term to the mandate of the House of Representatives, and two years to that of the Senate. In this way the members of the legislature are constantly and most closely tied by the slightest wishes of their constituents.

The lawgivers of the Union thought that this extreme dependence of the legislature marred the main results of the representative system by making the actual government, and not just the source of powers, lie with the people.

They lengthened the duration of the electoral mandate to allow the deputy a fuller use of his free judgment.

Like the various state constitutions, the federal Constitution divided the legislature into two branches.

But in the states these two parts of the legislature were composed of the same elements elected in the same manner. As a result the passions and the whims of the majority came into the open with equal ease and found tools as ready and prompt to their hands in one house as in the other. This gave a violent and precipitate character to the laws drafted.

The federal Constitution also made the two houses depend on a popular vote, but it altered the conditions of eligibility and the manner of election; they intended that, even if one of the branches of the legislature did not, as in some other nations, represent interests different from those of the other, it should at least represent superior wisdom.

To be elected as a senator a man had to have reached mature years, and the assembly responsible for electing him was itself previously elected and not numerous.

This often applies to their very errors. But their good sense would despise the adulator who should pretend that they always *reason right* about the *means* of promoting it. They know from experience that they sometimes err; and the wonder is that they so seldom err as they do, beset, as they continually are, by the wiles of parasites and sycophants, by the snares of the ambitious, the avaricious, the desperate, by the artifices of men who possess their confidence more than they deserve it, and of those who seek to possess rather than to deserve it. When occasions present themselves, in which the interests of the people are at variance with their inclinations, it is the duty of the persons whom they have appointed to be the guardians of those interests, to withstand the temporary delusion, in order to give them time and opportunity for more cool and sedate reflection. Instances might be cited in which a conduct of this kind has saved the people from very fatal consequences of their own mistakes, and has procured lasting monuments of their gratitude to the men who had courage and magnanimity enough to serve them at the peril of their displeasure." [Everyman edition, p. 365.]

Democracies are naturally inclined to concentrate all the power of society in the hands of the legislative body. That being the authority which springs most directly from the people, it is also that which shares its all-embracing power most.

Hence one notes its habitual tendency to gather every kind of authority into its hands.

This concentration of powers, while it is singularly harmful to the proper conduct of business, also establishes the despotism of the majority.

The lawgivers of the states frequently yielded to these democratic propensities; those of the Union have always courageously fought against them.

In the states the executive power is put into the hands of a magistrate who is in appearance placed on a level with the legislature but who in reality is just a blind and passive tool of its will. Whence should he derive his strength? From the duration of his term of office? Generally he is appointed for only one year. From his prerogatives? He has, so to say, none. The legislature can reduce him to impotence by entrusting the execution of its laws to special commissions composed of its own members. If it wanted to, it could in some degree annul his appointment by retrenching his salary.

The federal Constitution has concentrated all the rights of the executive and all its responsibilities in the hands of one man. The Presidential term of office is made to last four years; throughout this term he is assured of the enjoyment of his salary; he has been provided with a following of appointees and armed with a suspensive veto. In a word, the Constitution, having carefully traced the sphere of the executive power, has striven to give it as strong and free a position within that sphere as possible.

In the constitutions of the states the judicial power is that among all others which has remained least dependent on the legislature.

Nevertheless, in all the states the legislature has kept the power of fixing the emoluments of the judges, which of necessity subjects the latter to its immediate influence.

In some states the judges are appointed for a limited time, which takes away a great part of their power and freedom.

In others legislative and judicial powers are entirely mingled. For instance, in certain cases the New York Senate functions as the high court of the state.

But the federal Constitution has been careful to separate the judicial power from all others. It has also made the judges independent by declaring their salary and their office irrevocable.

The practical consequences of these differences are easy to see. Any attentive observer notices that the business of the Union is infinitely better conducted than that of any individual state.

The federal government is more just and moderate in its proceedings than those of the states. There is more wisdom in its views; its projects are planned further ahead and more knowledgeably combined; there is more skill, consistency, and firmness in the execution of its measures.

A few words are enough to summarize this chapter.

Two main dangers threaten the existence of democracies:

Complete subjection of the legislative power to the will of the electoral body.

Concentration of all the other powers of government in the hands of the legislative power.

The lawgivers of the states favored the growth of these dangers. The lawgivers of the Union did what they could to render them less formidable.

What Distinguishes the Federal Constitution of the United States of America from All Other Federal Constitutions

The American confederation apparently resembles all other confederations. However, its effects are different. Why is this? How this confederation does differ from all others. The American government is not a federal government, but an incomplete national government.

The United States has not provided the first and only example of a confederation. Without speaking of antiquity, modern Europe furnishes several examples. Switzerland, the German Empire, and the republic of the Netherlands have been, or still are, confederations.

When one studies the constitutions of these various countries, one notes with surprise that the powers granted to the federal governments are nearly the same as those accorded to the government of the United States. Like the latter, they give the central authority the right to make war and peace, to raise men and money, to provide for the general needs, and to regulate the common interests of the nation.

Nevertheless, federal government in these various countries has always remained weak and impotent, whereas that of the Union conducts affairs with vigor and with ease.

Furthermore, the first American Union could not survive because of the excessive weakness of its government, but that government which proved so feeble had been granted rights as broad as those of the present federal government. One may even say that in certain respects its privileges were greater.

There must therefore be in the present Constitution of the United States some new principles which do not strike one at first glance but which have a profound influence.

This Constitution, which at first sight one is tempted to confuse with previous federal constitutions, in fact rests on an entirely new theory, a theory that should be hailed as one of the great discoveries of political science in our age.

In all confederations previous to that of 1789 in America, the peoples who allied themselves for a common purpose agreed to obey the injunctions of the federal government, but they kept the right to direct and supervise the execution of the union's laws in their territory.

The Americans who united in 1789 agreed not only that the federal government should dictate the laws but that it should itself see to their execution.

In both cases the right is the same, and only the application thereof different. But that one difference produces immense results.

In all confederations previous to that of contemporary America, a federal government appealed to the particular governments to provide its needs. Whenever one of these disliked the measure prescribed, it could always avoid the necessity of obedience. If it was strong, it could appeal to arms; if it was weak, it could tolerate resistance to laws of the union, though accepted as its own, giving its impotence as an excuse and relying on the force of inertia.

Consequently, one of two things has always happened: either the most powerful of the combined states assumed the prerogatives of the federal authority and dominated all the others in its name[37] or the federal government has been left to its own resources, anarchy has reigned among the confederates, and the union has lost its power to act.[38]

In America the Union's subjects are not states but private citizens.

[37] This happened in Greece, under Philip, when that prince took on himself the execution of the decrees of the Amphictyonic League. It is what happened in the Netherlands republic where the province of Holland has always made the law. The same thing is taking place now within the Germanic confederation. Austria and Prussia make themselves the agents of the Diet and dominate the whole confederation in its name.

[38] It has always been like this in the Swiss confederation. Switzerland would have ceased to exist centuries ago were it not for the jealousies of her neighbors.

When it wants to levy a tax, it does not turn to the government of Massachusetts, but to each inhabitant of Massachusetts. Former federal governments had to confront peoples, individuals of the Union. It does not borrow its power, but draws it from within. It has its own administrators, courts, officers of justice, and army.

No doubt the spirit of the nation, the collective passions, and the provincial prejudices of each state still singularly tend to diminish the power of the federal authority thus constituted and to create centers of resistance to its wishes; restricted in its sovereignty, it cannot be as strong as if it possessed complete sovereignty; but that is an evil inherent in the federative system.

In America each state has comparatively few opportunities or temptations to resist; if it does think of doing so, it cannot carry this out without openly violating the laws of the Union, interrupting the ordinary course of justice, and raising the standard of revolt; in a word, it would have directly to take up an extreme position, and men hesitate for a long time before doing that.

In previous confederations the rights accorded to the union furnished more elements of discord than of power, for they multiplied the nation's claims without augmenting its means of enforcing them. For this reason the real weakness of federal governments has almost always increased in direct proportion to their nominal powers.

That is not so in the American Union; like most ordinary governments, the federal government can do what it has been given the right to do.

The human mind invents things more easily than words; that is why many improper terms and inadequate expressions gain currency.

Some nations form a permanent league and establish a supreme authority which, though it cannot act directly in dealings with individual citizens as a national government would do, nevertheless acts directly on each of the confederate peoples taken as a body.

Such a government, so different from all others, is called federal.

A form of society is then discovered in which several peoples really fused into one in respect of certain common interests but remained separate and no more than confederate in all else.

Here the central power acts without intermediary on the governed, administering and judging them itself, as do national governments, but it only acts thus within a restricted circle. Clearly here we have not a federal government but an incomplete national government. Hence a form of government has been found which is neither precisely national nor federal; but things have halted there, and the new word to express this new thing does not yet exist.

It is because they have not understood this new type of confederation that all unions have come to civil war, subjection, or inertia. The peoples composing them have all lacked either enlightenment to see the remedies for their ills or courage to apply them.

The first American Union, too, suffered from the same defects.

But in America the confederated states, before gaining independence, had long been part of the same empire; they had, therefore, not yet formed the habit of governing themselves completely, and national prejudices had not been able to put down deep roots; more enlightened than the rest of the world, and with that enlightenment equally spread among them, they felt only in a mild degree those passions which ordinarily make people oppose the extension of federal power, and their greatest citizens strove against those passions. As soon as they felt the ill, the Americans firmly thought out the remedy. They amended their laws and saved their country.

Advantages of the Federal System in General and Its Special Usefulness in America

Happiness and freedom enjoyed by small nations. Power of great nations. Great empires favor developments in civilization. Force is often the first element in the prosperity of nations. The aim of the federal system is to unite the advantages derived from a small and from a great territory. Advantages of this system for the United States. The law adapted to the people's needs, and not people made to fit the necessities of the law. Activity, progress, and the tastes and habits of freedom among the American peoples. Public spirit in the Union is but the aggregate of provincial patriotism. Things and ideas circulate freely throughout the United States. The Union is free and happy like a small nation and respected like a great one.

In small nations the watchfulness of society penetrates everywhere and attention is paid to the improvement of the smallest details; national ambition is greatly tempered by weakness, and their efforts and resources are almost entirely directed toward internal well-being and are not liable to be dissipated in vain dreams of glory. Furthermore, each man's abilities being generally limited, his desires are limited also. Moderate fortunes make conditions roughly equal; mores are simple and quiet. Thus, all things considered and allowance made for various degrees of morality and enlightenment, we shall generally find more persons in easy circumstances, denser population, and more contentment in small nations than in large.

When tyranny is established in a small nation, it is more galling than elsewhere because, operating within a comparatively restricted sphere, it affects everything within that sphere. Unable to engage in any great design, it turns to a multitude of little ones; it is both violent and petty. From the political world which is properly its domain, it penetrates into private life. After actions, it aspires to regiment tastes; after the state, it wants to rule families. But this happens seldom; in truth, freedom is the natural condition of small societies. Government there offers too little attraction to ambition, and the resources of private people are too limited for sovereign power easily to be concentrated in the hands of one man. If that does happen, it is not difficult for the governed to unite and by common effort overthrow both tyrant and tyranny.

Hence at all times small nations have been the cradle of political liberty. It has happened that most of them have lost this liberty in growing larger, a fact which clearly shows that their freedom was more a consequence of their small size than of the character of the people.

World history provides no example of a large nation long remaining a republic,[89] and so it has been said that such a thing is impracticable. For my part, I think it very imprudent for man, who is commonly deceived in actual and immediate everyday affairs and who is constantly surprised by the unexpected in things most familiar, to seek to limit the possible and judge the future. What can be said with certainty is that the existence of a great republic will always be more exposed than that of a small one.

All passions fatal to a republic grow with the increase of its territory, but the virtues which should support it do not grow at the same rate.

The ambition of individuals grows with the power of the state; the strength of parties grow with the importance of the aim proposed; but love of country, which should combat these destructive passions, is no stronger in a vast republic than in a small one. It is even easy to demonstrate that it is less developed and less strong there. Great wealth and dire poverty, huge cities, depraved morals, individual egoism, and complication of interests are so many perils which almost always arise from the large size of the state. Several of these things are no threat to the existence of a monarchy, and some of them may even help it to endure. In monarchies the government has its own forces; it may use the people but does not depend thereon;

---

[89] I do not speak here of a confederation of small republics, but of a great consolidated republic.

the greater the people, the stronger the prince; but a republican government can rely only on the support of the majority against these dangers. Now, that element of force is not proportionately more powerful in a vast than in a small republic. Thus, while the means of attack constantly increase in number and in strength, the power of resistance remains the same. One may even say that it diminishes, for the more numerous a people is and the more varied its attitudes and interests, the harder it becomes to form a compact majority.

One may also remark that human passions grow in intensity, not only with the greatness of the aim proposed but also with the multitude of individuals feeling them at the same time. There is no one who does not find himself more moved in the midst of an excited crowd sharing his emotion than if he had experienced it alone. In a great republic political passions become irresistible not only because the aims pursued are immense but also because millions feel them in the same way at the same time.

It is therefore permissible to say in general terms that nothing is more inimical to human prosperity and freedom than great empires.

However, great states have their peculiar advantages, which must be recognized.

Just as the craving for power is fiercer there among the common sort, so love of glory is also more developed in certain persons, who find the applause of a great people both a worthy object for their efforts and one which can in a sense raise them above themselves. In a large state thought on all subjects is stimulated and accelerated; ideas circulate more freely; the capitals are vast intellectual centers concentrating all the rays of thought in one bright glow; that is why great nations contribute more and faster to the increase of knowledge and the general progress of civilization than small ones. One must add that important discoveries often require a concentration of national resources of which small nations are incapable; in great nations the government has more general ideas and is more effectively detached from the routine of precedent and from provincial selfishness. There is more of genius in its conceptions and more boldness in its approach.

Internal well-being is more complete and more widespread in little nations, so long as they remain at peace; but a state of war harms them more than the great ones. In the latter, distant frontiers sometimes allow the mass of the people to stay far from danger for centuries on end. For such a nation war is more a matter of discomfort than of ruin.

But in this matter, as in so many others, one consideration dominates all the rest: that of necessity.

If there were only small nations and no large ones, humanity would most certainly be more free and happier; but there is no way of providing that there should not be large nations.

The latter bring into the world a new element of national prosperity, that is, force. What does comfort or freedom profit a nation if it is in daily danger of being ravaged or conquered? What good are its industries and trade if another rules the seas and lays down the law in all markets? Small nations are often wretched not because they are small but because they are weak; the great ones prosper not because they are large but because they are strong. Therefore force is often for nations one of the primary conditions of happiness and even of existence. As a result of this, except in peculiar circumstances, small nations always end up by being forcibly united with great ones or by combining among themselves. I know nothing more deplorable than the state of a nation which can neither defend itself nor provide for itself.

The federal system was devised to combine the various advantages of large and small size for nations.

A glance at the United States of America will show all the advantages derived from adopting that system.

In large centralized nations the lawgiver is bound to give the laws a uniform character which does not fit the diversity of places and of mores; having never studied particular cases, he can only proceed by general rules; so men must bend to the needs of legislation, for the legislation has no skill to adapt itself to the needs and mores of men; and from this, much trouble and unhappiness results.

That inconvenience does not exist in confederations: the congress regulates the main features of social behavior, and all the details are left to the provincial legislatures.

One can hardly imagine how much this division of sovereignty contributes to the well-being of each of the states of the Union. In these little societies, unpreoccupied with cares of defense or aggrandizement, all the strength of society and all individual efforts are turned toward internal improvements. The central government of each state, being close to the governed, is continually informed of the needs that arise; every year new plans are put forward and discussed in the municipal assemblies or in the state legislature and then published in the press, exciting universal interest and eagerness among the citizens. Need for improvement constantly stirs, but does not trouble, the American republics; there ambition for power gives place to love of well-being, a more vulgar but less dangerous passion.

It is an opinion generally current throughout America that the existence and survival of republican forms in the New World depend on the federal system. Many of the misfortunes into which the new states of South America have plunged are attributed to the desire to establish great republics there instead of breaking sovereignty up.

It is indeed incontestable that in the United States the taste for and practice in republican government were born in the townships and provincial assemblies. In a little country such as Connecticut, for example, where the opening of a canal or the cutting of a road is the main political business, where there is no army to pay or war to finance, and where the country cannot give much wealth or glory to its rulers, nothing could be more natural or appropriate to the nature of things than a republic. Now, it is that same republican spirit, those same mores and habits of liberty, which, having come to birth and grown in the various states, are then applied without any trouble in the nation as a whole. Public spirit in the Union is, in a sense, only a summing up of provincial patriotism. Every citizen of the United States may be said to transfer the concern inspired in him by his little republic into his love of the common motherland. In defending the Union, he is defending the increasing prosperity of his district, the right to direct its affairs, and the hope of pressing through plans for improvements there which should enrich himself —all things which, in the normal run, touch men more than the general interests of the country and national glory.

Equally, while the turn of mind and mores of the inhabitants made them better fitted than others to bring prosperity to a great republic, the federal system has made that task much less difficult. The confederation of all the American states does not suffer from those disadvantages usual to large conglomerations. The Union is a great republic in extent, but it can in some fashion be likened to a small one because there are so few matters with which the government is concerned. Its acts are important but rare. As the Union's sovereignty is hampered and incomplete, its use is not at all dangerous to freedom. Moreover, it does not arouse that inordinate craving for power and renown which are so fatal to great republics. As there is no necessity for everything to end at one common center, one finds neither vast metropolises, nor immense wealth, nor extreme poverty, nor sudden revolutions. Political passions, instead of spreading like a sheet of fire instantaneously over the whole land, break up in conflict with individual passions of each state.

But things and ideas circulate freely throughout the Union as through one and the same people. Nothing restrains the soaring spirit of enterprise. Its government attracts men of talent and enlightenment. Within the frontiers of the Union profound peace reigns, as within a country subject to the same empire; outside it takes rank among the most powerful countries in the world; two thousand miles of coast are open to foreign trade; and, holding in its hands the keys to the New World, its flag is respected in the farthest seas.

The Union is free and happy like a small nation, glorious and strong like a great one.

Why the Federal System Is Not Within the Reach of All Nations and Why the Anglo-Americans Have Been Able to Adopt It

In all federal systems there are inherent vices which the lawgiver cannot combat. Complication of every federal system. It demands a daily exercise of intelligence on the part of the governed. Practical knowledge of the Americans in government business. Comparative weakness of the government of the Union, another vice inherent in the federal system. The Americans have reduced its seriousness but have not been able to eliminate it. In appearance the sovereignty of each state is weaker, but in reality it is stronger than that of the Union. Why? Apart from the laws, there must exist natural causes of union among confederated peoples. What are these causes in the case of the Anglo-Americans? Maine and Georgia, separated by a thousand miles, are more naturally united than Normandy and Brittany. That war is the main peril for confederations. This is proved by the example of the United States. The Union has no great wars to fear. Why? Risks which the peoples of Europe would run if they adopted the American federal system.

Sometimes, after a thousand efforts, a lawgiver succeeds in exercising some indirect influence over the destiny of nations, and then his genius is praised, whereas it is often the geographical position of the country, over which he has no influence, a social state which has been created without his aid, mores and ideas whose origin he does not know, and a point of departure of which he is unaware that give to society impetuses of irresistible force against which he struggles in vain and which sweep him, too, along.

A lawgiver is like a man steering his route over the sea. He, too, can control the ship that bears him, but he cannot change its structure, create winds, or prevent the ocean stirring beneath him.

I have shown what advantages the Americans derived from the federal system. It remains for me to make plain what allowed them to adopt this system, for it is not given to all peoples to enjoy its benefits.

In the federal system one finds some accidental defects deriving from the laws; these can be put right by the lawgivers. There are others, inherent in the system, which cannot be eliminated by the peoples who have adopted it. Therefore these peoples must find within themselves the strength necessary to support the natural imperfections of their government.

Among the inherent defects of every federal system, the most obvious of all is the complication of the means it employs. This system necessarily brings two sovereignties face to face. The lawgiver may succeed in making the operations of these two sovereignties as simple and balanced as possible and may enclose them both within precisely defined spheres of action, but he cannot contrive that they shall be but one or prevent their touching somewhere.

Whatever one does, therefore, the federal system rests on a complicated theory which, in application, demands that the governed should use the lights of their reason every day.

Generally speaking, it is only simple conceptions which take hold of a people's mind. A false but clear and precise idea always has more power in the world than one which is true but complex. That is the reason why parties, which are like small nations within the great one, always hasten to take as a symbol some name or principle, though it often only very imperfectly represents the aim proposed and the means employed but is something without which they could neither exist nor move. Governments which rely on a single idea or easily defined feeling are perhaps not the best, but they are certainly strongest and most enduring.

But when one examines the Constitution of the United States, the best of all known federal constitutions, it is frightening to see how much diverse knowledge and discernment it assumes on the part of the governed. The government of the Union rests almost entirely on legal fictions. The Union is an ideal nation which exists, so to say, only in men's minds and whose extent and limits can only be discerned by the understanding.

When the general theory is well understood, there remain difficulties of application; these are innumerable, for the sovereignty of the Union is so involved with that of the states that it is impossible at first glance to see their limits. Everything in such a government depends on artificially contrived conventions, and it is only suited to a people long accustomed to manage its affairs, and one in which even the lowest ranks of society have an appreciation of political science. Nothing has made me admire the good sense and practical intelligence of the Americans more than the way they avoid the innumerable difficulties deriving from their federal Constitution. I have hardly ever met one of the common people in America who did not surprisingly and easily perceive which obligations derived from a law of Congress and which were based on the laws of his state and who, having distinguished the matters falling within the general prerogatives of the Union from those suitable to the local legislature, could not indicate the point where the competence of the federal courts commences and that of the state courts ends.

The Constitution of the United States is like one of those beautiful creations of human diligence which give their inventors glory and riches but remains sterile in other hands.

Contemporary Mexico has shown that.

The Mexicans, wishing to establish a federal system, took the federal Constitution of their Anglo-American neighbors as a model and copied it almost completely.[40] But when they borrowed the letter of the law, they could not at the same time transfer the spirit that gave it life. As a result, one sees them constantly entangled in the mechanism of their double government. The sovereignty of the states and that of the union, going beyond the spheres assigned to them by the constitution, trespass continually on each other's territory. In fact, at present Mexico is constantly shifting from anarchy to military despotism and back from military despotism to anarchy.

The second and most fatal of all the defects which I regard as inherent in the federal system as such is the comparative weakness of the government of the union.

The principle on which all confederations rest is the breaking up of sovereignty. Lawgivers may make this division less noticeable and may even for a time conceal it from view, but they cannot prevent its existence. And a divided sovereignty must always be weaker than a complete one.

In our account of the Constitution of the United States, we saw with what art the Americans, while enclosing the power of the Union within the restricted sphere of federal governments, did succeed in the appearance and to some extent the strength of a national government.

By this means the lawgivers of the Union did diminish the natural danger of confederation, but they could not make it vanish entirely.

It is said that the American government does not address itself

40 See the Mexican Constitution of 1824.

to the states but transmits its injunction directly to the citizens and forces them individually to comply with the common will.

But if a federal law clashed violently with the interests and prejudices of a state, might there not be room to fear that each citizen of that state would believe himself interested in the cause of anyone who refused to obey it? Then, all the citizens of the state finding themselves injured by the authority of the Union at the same time and in the same way, the federal government would seek in vain to isolate them in order to combat them; they would instinctively feel that they must unite to defend themselves and would find a ready-made organization for that purpose in the portion of sovereignty which their state was allowed to enjoy. Then fiction would give place to reality and one might see the organized power of one part of the country in contest with the central authority.

I would say the same concerning federal justice. If in a particular case the courts of the Union violated an important law of one state, the struggle, in reality if not in appearance, would be between the injured state, represented by one citizen, and the Union, represented by its courts.[41]

A man must have had very little experience of the ways of this world if he can imagine that, when a means has been left for the satisfaction of men's passions, they can always be prevented by legal fictions from seeing and using that means.

Therefore, in making a conflict between the two sovereignties less probable, the lawgivers of America did not destroy the causes of conflict.

One might go further and even say that in case of conflict they could not assure the preponderance of the federal power.

They give the Union money and soldiers, but the states retained the love and the prejudices of the peoples.

The sovereignty of the Union is an abstract entity connected with a small number of external concerns. The sovereignty of the states strikes every sense; it is easily understood and is seen in action constantly. The former is an innovation, but the latter was born with the people themselves.

[41] Example: the Constitution has given the Union power to sell unoccupied land for its own profit. Suppose that Ohio claims the same right over lands within its territory, on the plea that the Constitution refers only to lands which do not come under the jurisdiction of any particular state, and consequently wishes to sell them itself. It is true that the question at issue in the courts would be between purchasers deriving their title from the Union and those deriving theirs from the state, and not between the Union and Ohio. But what would become of this legal fiction if the courts of the United States ordered the federal purchaser to be put in possession, while the courts of Ohio continued to support his rival's claim to the land?

The sovereignty of the Union is a work of art. That of the states is natural; it exists on its own, without striving, like the authority of the father in a family.

Men are affected by the sovereignty of the Union only in connection with a few great interests; it represents a huge and distant motherland and a vague, ill-defined sentiment. But state sovereignty enfolds every citizen and in one way or another affects every detail of daily life. To it falls the duty of guaranteeing his property, liberty, and life; it has a constant influence on his well-being or the reverse. State sovereignty is supported by memories, customs, local prejudices, and provincial and family selfishness; in a word, it is supported by all those things which make the instinct of patriotism so powerful in the hearts of men. How can one question its advantages?

As lawgivers cannot prevent dangerous collisions between the two sovereignties confronting each other in a federal system, their efforts to divert the confederated peoples from war must be accompanied by dispositions particularly designed to lead to peace.

It results from this that no federal pact can be of long duration unless in the peoples concerned there are a certain number of conditions of union making common life easy for them and facilitating the task of government.

Thus, for success the federal system requires not only good laws but also circumstances favorable to it.

All peoples who have formed confederations have had a certain number of common interests which served as the intellectual ties of the association.

But apart from material interests, men have ideas and feelings. For a confederation to last for long, the diverse peoples forming it, must share a homogeneous civilization as well as common needs. The difference between the Canton de Vaud and the Canton de Uri is like that between the nineteenth and fifteenth centuries, as Switzerland has never, in truth, had a federal government. The union between its various cantons exists on the map only, as one would clearly see, if a central authority wanted to apply the same laws throughout the territory.

In the United States one fact wonderfully smooths the existence of the federal government, namely, that the different states have not only more or less the same interests but also the same level of civilization, so it is almost always an easy matter for them to agree. I doubt whether there is any nation in Europe, however small, whose different parts are not less homogeneous than those of the United States with an area half the size of Europe.

From the state of Maine to that of Georgia is a distance of some thousand miles, but the difference in civilization between Maine and Georgia is less than that between Normandy and Brittany. Maine and Georgia, at the farthest ends of a vast land, have by nature better real opportunities of forming a confederation than Normandy and Brittany, separated only by a brook.

The geographical position of the country added further advantages to the American lawgivers beyond those derived from the mores and customs of the people. And the adoption and survival of the federal system is chiefly due to it.

War is the most important of all the events which can mark the life of a nation. In war a nation acts like a single individual toward foreign nations; it fights for its very existence.

Skill on the part of the government and good sense on that of the governed, combined with a natural attachment men almost always feel for their country, may easily be enough so long as it is only a question of maintaining internal order and favoring prosperity; but for a nation to be ready to face a great war, the citizens must impose great and painful sacrifices on themselves. To believe that a large number of men will be capable of submitting themselves to such social exigencies is to have a poor knowledge of humanity.

For that reason all nations that have had to engage in great wars have been led, almost in spite of themselves, to increase the powers of the government. Those which have not succeeded in this have been conquered. A long war almost always faces nations with this sad choice: either defeat will lead them to destruction or victory will bring them to despotism.

Generally speaking, then, it is war which most obviously and dangerously reveals the weakness of a government, and I have shown that the inherent defect of federal governments is to be very weak.

Under a federal system, not only is there no centralized administration or anything like it, but even governmental centralization is incomplete, and that is always a great cause of weakness when a nation must defend itself against other completely centralized nations.

Even in the federal Constitution of the United States, where the central government is invested with more real powers than in any other federal constitution, this evil is still strongly felt.

A single example will enable the reader to judge.

The Constitution gives Congress the right to call up the militia of the various states for active service when it is a question of suppressing a rebellion or repulsing an invasion; another article of the Constitution provides that in that case the President of the republic is the commander of the militia.

In the War of 1812 the President ordered the militias of the North to move toward the frontiers; Connecticut and Massachusetts, whose interests were harmed by the war, refused to send their contingents.

The Constitution, they maintained, authorized the federal government to make use of the militias in case of *rebellion* or *invasion*, but up to that moment there was neither rebellion nor invasion. They added that the same Constitution which gave the Union the right to call up the militias for active service left the states the right of appointing the officers; it followed, in their view, that no officer of the Union had the right to command the militias except the President in person. But this was a question of serving in an army commanded by someone other than he.

These absurd and noxious doctrines were supported not only by the governors and legislatures but also by the courts of these two states; and the federal government was constrained to look elsewhere for the troops it lacked.[42]

How, then, does it come about that the American Union, protected though it be by the comparative perfection of its laws, does not dissolve in the midst of a great war? The reason is that it has no great wars to fear.

Placed in the middle of a huge continent with limitless room for the expansion of human endeavor, the Union is almost as isolated from the world as if it were surrounded on all sides by the ocean.

The population of Canada is no more than a million and is divided into two hostile nations. The rigors of the climate limit the expansion of its territory and shut its ports for six months of the year.

From Canada to the Gulf of Mexico there are only some half-destroyed savage tribes, which six thousand soldiers drive before them.

To the south, at one point the Union touches the Mexican Empire; it is there that one day great wars will probably come. But for a long time to come the backward state of civilization, corruption of mores, and poverty will prevent Mexico from taking

[42] Kent's *Commentaries*, Vol. I, p. 244. Note that I have chosen this example from a date subsequent to the establishment of the existing Constitution. Had I chosen to go back to the time of the first Confederation, I could have cited even more conclusive facts. Then real enthusiasm prevailed in the nation; the Revolution was led by an eminently popular man, but nonetheless at that time Congress, strictly speaking, had no resources at its disposal. The whole time it lacked both men and money; its best-contrived plans failed in execution, and the Union, always on the verge of ruin, was saved much more by the weakness of its enemies than by its own strength.

high rank among the nations. As for the European powers, distance makes them little to be feared. (See Appendix I, O.)

The great good fortune of the United States is not to have found a federal Constitution enabling them to conduct great wars, but to be so situated that there is nothing for them to fear.

No one can appreciate the advantages of a federal system more than I. I hold it to be one of the most powerful combinations favoring human prosperity and freedom. I envy the lot of the nations that have been allowed to adopt it. But yet I refuse to believe that, with equal force on either side, a confederated nation can long fight against a nation with centralized government power.

A nation that divided its sovereignty when faced by the great military monarchies of Europe would seem to me, by that single act, to be abdicating its power, and perhaps its existence and its name.

How wonderful is the position of the New World, where man has as yet no enemies but himself. To be happy and to be free, it is enough to will it to be so.

PART II

So FAR I HAVE EXAMINED the institutions, reviewed the written laws, and described the present shape of political society in the United States.

But above all the institutions and beyond all the forms there is a sovereign power, that of the people, which can abolish or change them as it pleases.

It remains for me to show how this power that dominates the laws acts; what are its instincts and its passions; what secret springs urge on, retard, or direct its irresistible course; what are the effects of its almighty power; and what destiny is in store for it.

Chapter 1

WHY IT CAN STRICTLY BE SAID THAT
THE PEOPLE GOVERN IN THE
UNITED STATES

IN AMERICA THE PEOPLE appoint both those who make the laws and those who execute them; the people form the jury which punishes breaches of the law. The institutions are democratic not only in principle but also in all their developments; thus the people *directly* nominate their representatives and generally choose them *annually* so as to hold them more completely dependent. So direction really comes from the people, and though the form of government is representative, it is clear that the opinions, prejudices, interests, and even passions of the people can find no lasting obstacles preventing them from being manifest in the daily conduct of society.

In the United States, as in all countries where the people reign, the majority rules in the name of the people.

This majority is chiefly composed of peaceful citizens who by taste or interest sincerely desire the well-being of the country. They are surrounded by the constant agitation of parties seeking to draw them in and to enlist their support.

Chapter 2

PARTIES IN THE UNITED STATES

An important distinction must be made between parties. Parties
which behave to each other like rival nations. Parties properly
so called. Difference between great and small parties. When
they arise. Their different characteristics. America has had
great parties. It has none now. Federalists. Republicans.
Defeat of the Federalists. Difficulty of creating parties in the
United States. What is done to achieve this. Aristocratic or
democratic characteristics found in all parties. Struggle of
General Jackson against the bank.

I MUST FIRST DEFINE an important distinction between parties.

There are some countries so huge that the different populations
inhabiting them, although united under the same sovereignty, have
them. In such cases the various factions of the same people do not,
strictly speaking, form parties, but distinct nations; were civil war to
break out, it would be a conflict between rival peoples rather than between factions.

But when there are differences between the citizens concerning
matters of equal importance to all parts of the country, such for
instance as the general principles of government, then what I really
call parties take shape.

Parties are an evil inherent in free governments, but they do not
always have the same character and the same instincts.

There are times when nations are tormented by such great ills
that the idea of a total change in their political constitution comes
into their minds. There are other times when the disease is deeper
still and the whole social fabric is compromised. That is the time
of great revolutions and of great parties.

Between these centuries of disorder and of misery there are others
in which societies rest and the human race seems to take breath.
That is in truth only apparently so: time does not halt its progress
for peoples any more than for men; both men and peoples are daily
advancing into an unknown future, and when we think that they are

stationary, that is because we do not see their movements. Men may be walking and seem stationary to those who are running.

However that may be, there are times when the changes taking place in the political constitution and social structure of peoples are so slow and imperceptible that men think they have reached a final state; then the human spirit believes itself firmly settled on certain fundamentals and does not seek to look beyond a fixed horizon.

That is the time for intrigues and small parties.

What I call great political parties are those more attached to principles than to consequences, to generalities rather than to particular cases, to ideas rather than to personalities. Such parties generally have nobler features, more generous passions, more real convictions, and a bolder and more open look than others. Private interest, which always plays the greatest part in political passions, is there more skillfully concealed beneath the veil of public interest; sometimes it even passes unobserved by those whom it prompts and stirs to action.

On the other hand, small parties are generally without political faith. As they are not elevated and sustained by lofty purposes, the selfishness of their character is openly displayed in all their actions. They glow with a factitious zeal; their language is violent, but their progress is timid and uncertain. The means they employ are as disreputable as the aim sought. That is why, when a time of calm succeeds a great revolution, great men seem to disappear suddenly and minds withdraw into themselves.

Great parties convulse society; small ones agitate it; the former rend and the latter corrupt it; the first may sometimes save it by overthrowing it, but the second always create unprofitable trouble.

America has had great parties; now they no longer exist. This has been a great gain in happiness but not in morality.

When the War of Independence came to an end and a new government had to be established, the nation was divided between two opinions. Those opinions were as old as the world itself and are found under different forms and with various names in all free societies. One party wanted to restrict popular power and the other to extend it indefinitely.

With the Americans the struggle between these two opinions never took on the violent character that has often marked it elsewhere. In America the two parties agreed on the most essential points. Neither of the two had, to succeed, to destroy an ancient order or to overthrow the whole of a social structure. Consequently, in neither case did the private existence of a great number of people depend on the triumph of its principles. But immaterial interests of the first importance, such as love of equality and of independence, were affected. That was enough to rouse violent passions.

The party which wished to restrict popular power sought especially to have its ideas applied in the federal Constitution, from which it gained the name of Federal.

The other, which claimed to be the exclusive lover of liberty, called itself Republican.

America is the land of democracy. Consequently, the Federalists were always in a minority, but they included almost all the great men thrown up by the War of Independence, and their moral authority was very far-reaching. Moreover, circumstances favored them. The ruin of the first Confederation made the people afraid of falling into anarchy, and the Federalists profited from this passing tendency. For ten or twelve years they directed affairs and were able to apply some but not all of their principles, for the current running in the opposite direction became daily stronger and they could not fight against it.

In 1801 the Republicans finally got control of the government. Thomas Jefferson was elected President; he brought them the support of a famous name, great talents, and immense popularity.

There had always been something artificial in the means and temporary in the resources which maintained the Federalists; it was the virtues and talents of their leaders, combined with lucky circumstances, which had brought them to power. When the Republicans came in turn to power, the opposing party seemed to be engulfed by a sudden flood. A huge majority declared against it, and suddenly finding itself so small a minority, it at once fell into despair. Thenceforth the Republican, or Democratic, party has gone on from strength to strength and taken possession of the whole of society.

The Federalists, feeling themselves defeated, without resources, and isolated within the nation, divided up; some of them joined the victors; the others lowered their flag and changed their name. For many years now they have entirely ceased to exist as a party.

The period of Federalist power was, in my view, one of the luckiest circumstances attending the birth of the great American Union. The Federalists struggled against the irresistible tendency of their age and country. Whatever the virtues or defects of their theories, they had the disadvantage of being inapplicable in their entirety to the society they wished to control, so what happened under Jefferson would have come about sooner or later. But their rule at least gave the new republic time to settle down and afterwards to face without ill consequences the rapid development of the very doctrines they had opposed. Moreover, in the end many of their principles were introduced under their adversaries' slogans, and the still-extant federal Constitution is a lasting memorial to their patriotism and wisdom.

Thus today there is no sign of great political parties in the United States. There are many parties threatening the future of the Union, but none which seem to attack the actual form of government and the general course of society. The parties that threaten the Union rely not on principles but on material interests. In so vast a land these interests make the provinces into rival nations rather than parties. Thus recently we have seen the North contending for tariffs and the South taking up arms for free trade, simply because the North is industrial and the South agricultural, so that restrictions would profit the former and harm the latter.

Lacking great parties, the United States is creeping with small ones and public opinion is broken up ad infinitum about questions of detail. It is impossible to imagine the trouble they take to create parties; it is not an easy matter now. In the United States there is no religious hatred because religion is universally respected and no sect is predominant; there is no class hatred because the people is everything, and nobody dares to struggle against it; and finally, there is no public distress to exploit because the physical state of the country offers such an immense scope to industry that man has only to be left to himself to work marvels. Nevertheless, the ambitious are bound to create parties, for it is difficult to turn the man in power out simply for the reason that one would like to take his place. Hence all the skill of politicians consists in forming parties; in the United States a politician first tries to see what his own interest is and who have analogous interests which can be grouped around his own; he is next concerned to discover whether by chance there may not be somewhere in the world a doctrine or a principle that could conveniently be placed at the head of the new association to give it the right to put itself forward and circulate freely. It is like the royal imprimatur which our ancestors printed on the first page of their works and incorporated into the book even though it was no part of it.

This done, the new power is introduced into the political world. To a foreigner almost all the Americans' domestic quarrels seem at the first glance either incomprehensible or puerile, and one does not know whether to pity a people that takes such wretched trifles seriously or to envy the luck enabling it to do so.

But when one comes to study carefully the secret instincts governing American factions, one easily finds out that most of them are more or less connected with one or other of the two great parties which have divided mankind since free societies came into existence. As one comes to penetrate deeper into the intimate thought of these parties, one sees that some parties are working to restrict the use of public power and the others to extend it.

I am certainly not saying that American parties always have as their open or even their concealed aim to make aristocracy or democracy prevail in the country. I am saying that aristocratic or democratic passions can easily be found at the bottom of all parties and that though they may slip out of sight there, they are, as it were, the nerve and soul of the matter.

I will quote a recent example: the President attacks the Bank of the United States; the country gets excited and parties are formed; the educated classes in general line up behind the bank, while the people are for the President. Do you suppose that the people could understand the reason for their opinion amid the pitfalls of such a difficult question about which men of experience hesitate? Not at all? But the bank is a great establishment with an independent existence; the people, who destroy or elevate all authorities, could do nothing against it, and that was a surprise. With all the rest of society in motion, the sight of that stable point jars, and the people want to see if they can shake it, like everything else.

Remains of the Aristocratic Party in the United States

Secret opposition of the wealthy to democracy. They withdraw into private life. Taste shown at Rome for exclusive pleasures and for luxury. Their outward simplicity. Their affected condescension toward the people.

It sometimes happens in a nation where opinions are divided that the balance between parties breaks down and one of them acquires an irresistible preponderance. It breaks all obstacles, crushes its adversary, and exploits the whole of society for its own benefit. The vanquished, then despairing of success, go into hiding or keep quiet, universal stillness and silence prevails, the nation seems united in single thought. The victorious party arises and announces: "I have given the country peace, and I deserve to be thanked."

But beneath this apparent unanimity deep divisions and real opposition still lie hidden.

That is what has happened in America. When the Democratic

party gained preponderance it took exclusive control of affairs. Since then it has not ceased to mold both mores and laws to its desires.

Nowadays one may say that the wealthy classes in the United States are almost entirely outside politics and that wealth, so far from being an advantage there, is a real cause of disfavor and an obstacle to gaining power.

The wealthy, therefore, prefer to leave the lists rather than to engage in an often unequal struggle against the poorest of their fellow citizens. Being unable to assume a rank in public life analogous to that which they occupy in private life, they abandon the former and concentrate upon the latter. They form, within the state, a private society with its own tastes and enjoyments.

The wealthy man submits to this state of affairs as to an irremediable evil; he is even careful to avoid showing that he is hurt by it; thus one may hear him boasting in public of the blessings of republican government and the advantages of democratic forms. For apart from hating one's enemies, what is more natural to man than flattering them?

Take a look at this opulent citizen. Might one not think him a medieval Jew afraid that his wealth should be suspected? His clothes are simple and his manners modest; within the four walls of his house luxury is worshiped; he allows only a few chosen guests, whom he insolently calls his equals, into that sanctuary. There is no nobleman in Europe more exclusive in his pleasures or more jealous of the slightest advantages assured by a privileged position. But he goes out to work in a dusty den in the middle of a busy town, where everyone is free to accost him. He meets his shoemaker passing in the street and they stop to talk to each other. What can they be saying? These two citizens are concerned with affairs of state, and they do not part without shaking hands.

For all this conventional enthusiasm and obsequious formality toward the dominant power, it is easy to see that the rich have a great distaste for their country's democratic institutions. The people are a power whom they fear and scorn. If some day the bad government of democracy were to lead to a political crisis or if ever monarchy appeared as a practical possibility in the United States, one would see the truth of what I am saying.

The two main weapons used by the parties to assure success are newspapers and associations.

Chapter 3

FREEDOM OF THE PRESS IN THE UNITED STATES

Difficulty of restricting the freedom of the press. Particular reasons certain nations have for holding on to this freedom. The freedom of the press is a necessary consequence of the sovereignty of the people as understood in America. Violent language of the periodical press in the United States. The periodical press has instincts peculiar to itself, as the example of the United States proves. American view of judicial repression of offenses by the press. Why the press is less powerful in the United States than in France.

It is not political opinions only, but all the views of men which are influenced by freedom of the press. It modifies mores as well as laws. Elsewhere in this work I shall try to estimate the extent of the influence of freedom of the press on civil society in the United States; I shall try to discern the direction it has given to ideas and the habits which have infiltrated through it into the minds and feelings of the Americans. For the moment I wish only to examine the effects of freedom of the press in the political sphere.

I admit that I do not feel toward freedom of the press that complete and instantaneous love which one accords to things by their nature supremely good. I love it more from considering the evils it prevents than on account of the good it does.

If someone showed me an intermediate position I could hope to hold between complete independence and entire servitude of thought, perhaps I would adopt that position; but who can discover any such position? Starting from license of the press and wishing to move to something more orderly, what do you do? First you bring writers before juries; but the juries acquit, and what had been the opinion of only an isolated man becomes that of the country. You have therefore done both too much and too little and must try again. You hand the authors over to permanent magistrates, but judges have to listen before they can condemn, and things which men fear to avow in a book can be proclaimed with impunity in pleadings; and what would have been obscurely said in one written work is then repeated in a thousand others. Its expression is the external form and, if I may put it so, the body of the thought, but it is not the thought itself. Your courts may arrest the body, but the soul escapes and subtly slips between their fingers. Once more you have done too little and too much and must try again. Finally you hand writers over to censors; fine! We are getting close. But is not the political hustings free? So you have still done nothing; no, I am wrong, you have increased the evil. Do you perchance suppose that thought is one of those physical forces whose strength increases with numbers? Do you think that writers are like soldiers in an army? Unlike all physical forces, the power of thought is often actually increased by the small number of those expressing it. The word of a strong-minded man which alone reaches to the passions of a mute assembly has more power than the confused cries of a thousand orators; and so long as there is just one public place where one speaks freely, it is as if one had spoken publicly in each village. Therefore you must abolish freedom of speech as well as of writing; this time you have reached harbor; everyone is silent. But where have you arrived? You started from an abuse of liberty, and I find you beneath a despot's feet.

You have gone from extreme independence to extreme servitude without finding a single spot where it was possible to rest on that long journey.

There are peoples who, apart from the general reasons I have just stated, have particular motives for being attached to the liberty of the press.

In some nations which pretend to be free any agent of authority can break the law with impunity, and the country's constitution gives the person aggrieved no right to complain before the courts. In such nations the independence of the press is not just one of the guarantees, but the only guarantee remaining for the freedom and safety of the citizens.

So if the men ruling such nations speak of taking away the independence of the press, the whole people could answer them: "Let us punish your crimes in the ordinary courts, and then perhaps we shall agree not to appeal to the tribunal of public opinion."

In a country where the dogma of the sovereignty of the people openly prevails, censorship is not only a danger but even more a great absurdity.

When each man is given a right to rule society, clearly one must recognize his capacity to choose between the different opinions debated among his contemporaries and to appreciate the various facts which may guide his judgment.

The sovereignty of the people and the freedom of the press are therefore two entirely correlative things, whereas censorship and universal suffrage contradict each other and cannot long remain in the political institutions of the same people. Among the twelve million people living in the territory of the United States, there is not *one single man* who has dared to suggest restricting the freedom of the press.

The first newspaper I saw on arrival in America contained the following article, which I translate faithfully:

"In this whole affair the language used by Jackson [the President] was that of a heartless despot exclusively concerned with preserving his own power. Ambition is his crime, and that will be his punishment. Intrigue is his vocation, and intrigue will confound his plans and snatch his power from him. He governs by corruption, and his guilty maneuvers will turn to his shame and confusion. He has shown himself in the political arena as a gambler without shame or restraint. He has succeeded, but the hour of justice draws near; soon he will have to give up what he has won, throw his false dice away, and end his days in some retreat where he will be free to blaspheme against his folly, for repentance is not a virtue that it has ever been given to his heart to know." (Vincenne's *Gazette*.)[1]

Many people in France suppose that the violence of our press is due to the instability of the social state, to our political passions, and to the general uneasiness resulting therefrom. So they are ever waiting for a time when society will settle down quietly and the press too will become calm. For my part, I freely agree that its extreme ascendancy over us is due to the reasons above mentioned, but I do not think that these have much influence on its language. The periodical press seems to me to have instincts and passions of its own independent of the circumstances in which it is operating. What happens in America has proved that to me.

At this moment perhaps there is no country in the world harboring fewer germs of revolution than America. But in America the press has the same destructive tastes as in France and the same violence without the same reasons for anger. In America, as in France, it is the same extraordinary power, strange mixture of good and evil, without which freedom could not survive but with which order can hardly be maintained.

What needs saying is that the press has much less power in the United States than with us. Nothing, however, is rarer than to see

[1] [There was a Vincennes (Indiana) *Gazette* of this period, but we failed to trace the quotation. The Indiana State librarian doubts very much the correctness of Tocqueville's date.]

judicial proceedings taken against it. The reason is simple: the Americans, having accepted the dogma of the sovereignty of the people, apply it with perfect sincerity. They never had any idea of founding, with elements that change every day, constitutions that should last eternally. To attack the existing laws is therefore not a crime, provided that no violent infraction of them is intended.

They also think that courts are powerless to check the press, and that as the subtlety of human language perpetually eludes judicial analysis, offenses of this nature somehow slip through the fingers of those who try to grasp them. They think that to have effective influence over the press, one would have to find a court that was not only devoted to the existing order but also able to rise above the ferment of public opinion around it, a court which would judge without allowing publicity or giving reasons for its decisions and which would punish intention even more than words. Anyone who had the power to create and maintain such a tribunal would be wasting his time harassing the freedom of the press, for he would be absolute master of society itself and could get rid of the writers as well as their writings. So, where the press is concerned, there is not in reality any middle path between license and servitude. To cull the inestimable benefits assured by freedom of the press, it is necessary to put up with the inevitable evils springing therefrom. The wish to enjoy the former and avoid the latter is to indulge in one of those illusions with which sick nations soothe themselves when, weary of struggle and exhausted by exertion, they seek means to allow hostile opinions and contradictory principles to exist together at the same time—in the same land.

That the newspapers in America have little power is due to many reasons, of which these are the chief:

Freedom to write, like other forms of freedom, is the more formidable the newer it is; a people which has never heard affairs of state discussed in its presence believes the first tribune of the people who comes forward. For the Anglo-Americans this freedom dates back to the foundation of the colonies. Moreover, the press, so skilled to inflame human passions, can yet not create them all on its own. American political life is active, varied, and even agitated, but it is seldom disturbed by deep passions; such passions are not often roused unless material interests are compromised, and in the United States such interests prosper. A glance at our papers and at theirs is enough to show the difference between the two nations in this respect. In France little space is given over to trade advertisements, and even news items are few; the vital part of the newspaper is that devoted to political discussion. In America three quarters of the bulky newspaper put before you will be full of advertisements and the rest will usually contain political news or just anecdotes; only at long intervals and in some obscure corner will one find one of those burning arguments which for us are the readers' daily food.

The effective force of any power is increased in proportion to the centralization of its control; that is a general law of nature confirmed by observation, and one which the surest instinct has always revealed even to the least of despots.

The French press combines two distinct types of centralization.

Almost all its power is concentrated in the same place and, so to say, in the same hands, for the number of papers is very small.

In a skeptical nation the power of a press so constituted should be almost limitless. The government can make truces of more or less long duration with such an enemy, but it is hard for it to survive for long in opposition thereto.

Neither of these two types of centralization exists in America.

The United States has no capital; both enlightenment and power are dispersed throughout this vast land; therefore the rays of human intelligence, instead of radiating from one center, cross each other in every direction; there is no place in which the Americans have located the general control of thought, any more than that of affairs.

All that depends on local circumstances independent of human volition, but this is how the laws play a part:

In the United States printers need no licenses, and newspapers no stamps or registration; moreover, the system of giving securities is unknown.

For these reasons it is a simple and easy matter to start a paper; a few subscribers are enough to cover expenses, so the number of periodical or semiperiodical productions in the United States surpasses all belief. The most enlightened Americans attribute the slightness of the power of the press to this incredible dispersion; it is an axiom of political science there that the only way to neutralize the effect of newspapers is to multiply their numbers. I cannot imagine why such a self-evident truth has not been more commonly accepted among us. I can easily see why those bent on revolution through the press try to see that it should have only a few powerful organs; but that the official partisans of the established order and the natural supporters of existing laws should think that they are reducing the effectiveness of the press by concentrating it—that is something I just cannot understand. Faced by the press, the governments of Europe seem to me to behave as did the knights of old toward their enemies; they observed from their own experience that centralization was a powerful weapon, and they want to provide their enemy therewith, no doubt to win greater glory by resisting him.

There is hardly a hamlet in America without its newspaper. Of course, with so many combatants, neither discipline nor unity of action is possible, and so each fights under his own flag. It is not the case that all the political newspapers in the Union are lined up to support or oppose the administration, but they use a hundred different means to attack or defend it. Therefore American papers cannot raise those powerful currents of opinion which sweep away or sweep over the most powerful dikes. There are other equally noteworthy effects of this division of the forces of the press; starting a paper being easy, anybody may take to it; but competition prevents any newspaper from hoping for large profits, and that discourages anybody with great business ability from bothering with such undertakings. Even if the papers were a source of wealth, as there is such an excessive number of them, there would not be enough talented journalists to edit them all. So generally American journalists have a low social status, their education is only sketchy, and their thoughts are often vulgarly expressed. In all things the majority makes the law; it establishes certain ways to which all must afterward conform; the sum total of these common ways is called a spirit; there is the spirit of the bar, the spirit of the court. In France the hallmark of the spirit of journalism is a violent but lofty and often eloquent way of arguing about great interests of state; that may not always be so, but all laws have their exceptions; the hallmark of the American journalist is a direct and coarse attack, without any subtleties, on the passions of his readers; he disregards principles to seize on people, following them into their private lives and laying bare their weaknesses and their vices.

That is a deplorable abuse of the powers of thought. Later I shall go into the question of the influence of newspapers on the taste and morality of the American people, but here, I repeat, I am concerned only with the world of politics. One must admit that this license of the press, in its political effect, does indirectly contribute to the maintenance of public tranquillity. Because of it, men who already hold a high position in the regard of their fellow citizens do not dare to write in the papers and thus lose the most formidable weapon which they might have used to rouse popular passions for their own ends.[2] Above all, the result is that the

[2] They write in the papers only on the rare occasions when they want to address the people and speak in their own name: when, for example, slanderous imputations against them have been spread around and they wish to re-establish the true facts.

personal views expressed by journalists carry, so to speak, no weight with the readers. What they look for in a newspaper is knowledge of facts, and it is only by altering or distorting those facts that the journalist can gain some influence for his views.

However, with their sources thus restricted, the power of the American press is still immense. It makes political life circulate in every corner of that vast land. Its eyes are never shut, and it lays bare the secret shifts of politics, forcing public figures in turn to appear before the tribunal of opinion. The press rallies interest around certain doctrines and gives shape to party slogans; through the press the parties, without actually meeting, listen and argue with one another. When many organs of the press do come to take the same line, their influence in the long run is almost irresistible, and public opinion, continually struck in the same spot, ends by giving way under the blows.

Each individual American newspaper has little power, but after the people, the press is nonetheless the first of powers. (See Appendix I, P.)

Opinions established in America under the influence of its free press are often more firmly rooted than those formed elsewhere under censorship.

American democracy constantly brings new men forward to direct affairs; consequently there is little consistency or order in government measures. But the general principles of government are more stable there than in many other countries, and the opinions which rule society have proved more lasting there. Once the American people have got an idea into their head, be it correct or unreasonable, nothing is harder than to get it out again.

The same can be noticed in England, which for a century has been the European country with the greatest freedom of thought and with the most invincible prejudices.

I think this is due to that very fact that at first glance one would have thought bound to prevent it, namely, the freedom of the press. People enjoying that freedom become attached to their opinions as much from pride as from conviction. They love them because they think them correct, but also because they have chosen them; and they stick to them, not only as something true but also as something of their very own.

There are several other reasons too.

A great man has said that *ignorance lies at both ends of knowl-*

edge. Perhaps it would have been truer to say that deep convictions lie at the two ends, with doubt in the middle. In fact, one can distinguish three distinct and often successive states of human understanding.

A man may hold a firm belief which he has adopted without plumbing it. He doubts when objections strike him. Often he succeeds in resolving these doubts, and then he again begins to believe. This time he does not grasp the truth by chance or in the dark, but sees it face to face and is guided forward by its light.[3]

When freedom of the press finds men in this first condition, for a long time it does not disturb this habit of firm belief without reflection, but it does daily change the object of their implicit belief. The human mind continues to discern only one point at a time on the whole intellectual horizon, but that point is constantly changing. That is the time for sudden revolutions. Woe to these generations which first suddenly allow freedom to the press!

But soon almost the whole range of new ideas has been canvassed. Experience plunges mankind into universal doubt and distrust.

One may count on it that the majority of mankind will always stop short in one of these two conditions: they will either believe without knowing why or will not know precisely what to believe.

But only a few persevering people will ever attain to that deliberate and self-justified type of conviction born of knowledge and springing up in the very midst of doubt.

It has been noted that in ages of religious fervor men sometimes changed their beliefs, whereas in skeptical centuries each man held obstinately to his own faith. In politics the same thing happens under the reign of a free press. All social theories having been contested and opposed in turn, people who fixed on one of them stick to it, not because they are sure it is good but because they are not sure that there is a better one.

In such ages people are not so ready to die for their opinions, but they do not change them; and there are to be found both martyrs and fewer apostates.

This further and still more powerful motive must be added. When opinions are in doubt, men end by clinging only to instincts and material interests, which by nature are more visible, tangible, and permanent than opinions.

It is a very difficult question to decide whether aristocracy or

[3] Nevertheless, I doubt whether this deliberate and self-justified conviction ever inspires the same degree of ardor and devotion in man as do dogmatic beliefs.

democracy governs best. But it is clear that democracy constrains some and aristocracy oppresses others.

This is a self-established truth which it is needless to discuss: you are rich and I am poor.

Chapter 4

POLITICAL ASSOCIATION IN
THE UNITED STATES

Everyday use that the Anglo-Americans make of the right of association. Three types of political associations. How the Americans apply the representative system to associations. Dangers resulting therefrom to the state. Great convention of 1831 concerned with tariffs. Legislative character of that convention. Why the unlimited exercise of the right of association is not as dangerous in the United States as elsewhere. Why it may be considered necessary. Utility of associations in democratic nations.

BETTER USE HAS BEEN MADE OF association and this powerful instrument of action has been applied to more varied aims in America than anywhere else in the world.

Apart from permanent associations such as townships, cities, and counties created by law, there are a quantity of others whose existence and growth are solely due to the initiative of individuals.

The inhabitant of the United States learns from birth that he must rely on himself to combat the ills and trials of life; he is restless and defiant in his outlook toward the authority of society and appeals to its power only when he cannot do without it. The beginnings of this attitude first appear at school, where the children, even in their games, submit to rules settled by themselves and punish offenses which they have defined themselves. The same attitude turns up again in all the affairs of social life. If some obstacle blocks the public road halting the circulation of traffic, the neighbors at once form a deliberative body; this improvised assembly produces an executive authority which remedies the trouble before anyone has thought of the possibility of some previously constituted authority beyond that of those concerned. Where enjoyment is concerned, people associate to make festivities grander and more orderly. Finally, associations are formed to combat exclusively moral troubles: intemperance is fought in common. Public security, trade and industry, and morals and religion all provide the aims for associations in the United States. There is no end which the human will despairs of attaining by the free action of the collective power of individuals.

Later I shall have occasion to speak of the effects of association on civil life. For the moment I must stick to the world of politics.

The right of association being recognized, citizens can use it in different ways. An association simply consists in the public and formal support of specific doctrines by a certain number of individuals who have undertaken to cooperate in a stated way in order to make these doctrines prevail. Thus the right of association can almost be identified with freedom to write, but already associations are more powerful than the press. When some view is represented by an association, it must take clearer and more precise shape. It counts its supporters and involves them in its cause; these supporters get to know one another, and numbers increase zeal. An association unites the energies of divergent minds and vigorously directs them toward a clearly indicated goal.

Freedom of assembly marks the second stage in the use made of the right of association. When a political association is allowed to form centers of action at certain important places in the country, its activity becomes greater and its influence more widespread. There men meet, active measures are planned, and opinions are expressed with that strength and warmth which the written word can never attain.

But the final stage is the use of association in the sphere of politics. The supporters of an agreed view may meet in electoral colleges and appoint mandatories to represent them in a central assembly. That is, properly speaking, the application of the representative system to one party.

So, in the first of these cases, men sharing one opinion are held together by a purely intellectual tie; in the second case, they meet together in small assemblies representing only a fraction of the party; finally, in the third case, they form something like a separate nation within the nation and a government within the government. Their mandatories, like those of the majority, represent by themselves all the collective power of their supporters, and, like them in this too, they appear as national representatives with all the moral prestige derived therefrom. It is true that, unlike the others, they have no right to make laws, but they do have the power to attack existing laws and to formulate, by anticipation, laws which should take the place of the present ones.

Imagine some people not perfectly accustomed to the use of freedom, or one in which profound political passions are seething. Suppose that, besides the majority that makes the laws, there is a minority which only deliberates and which gets laws ready for adoption; I cannot help but think that then public order would be exposed to great risks.

There is certainly a great gap between proving that one law is in itself better than another and establishing that it ought to be substituted for it. But where trained minds may still see a wide gap, the hasty imagination of the crowd may be unaware of this. Moreover, there are times when the nation is divided into two almost equal parties, each claiming to represent the majority. If, besides the ruling power, another power is established with almost equal moral authority, can one suppose that in the long run it will just talk and not act?

Will it always stop short in front of the metaphysical consideration that the object of associations is to direct opinions and not to constrain them, and to give advice about the law but not to make it?

The more I observe the main effects of a free press, the more convinced am I that, in the modern world, freedom of the press is the principal and, so to say, the constitutive element in freedom. A nation bent on remaining free is therefore right to insist, at whatever cost, on respect for this freedom. But *unlimited* freedom of association must not be entirely identified with freedom to write. The former is both less necessary and more dangerous than the latter. A nation may set limits there without ceasing to be its own master; indeed, in order to remain its own master, it is sometimes necessary to do so.

In America there is no limit to freedom of association for political ends.

One example will show better than anything I could say just how far it is tolerated.

One remembers how excited the Americans were by the free-trade-tariff controversy. Not opinions only, but very powerful material interests stood to gain or lose by a tariff. The North thought that some of its prosperity was due thereto, while the South blamed it for almost all its woes. One may say that over a long period the tariff question gave rise to the only political passions disturbing the Union.

In 1831, when the quarrel was most envenomed, an obscure citizen of Massachusetts thought of suggesting through the newspapers that all opponents of the tariff should send deputies to Philadelphia to concert together measures to make trade free. Thanks to the invention of printing, this suggestion passed in but a few days from Maine to New Orleans. The opponents of the tariff took it up ardently. They assembled from all sides and appointed deputies. Most of the latter were known men, and some of them had risen to celebrity. South Carolina, which was later to take up arms in this cause, sent sixty-three people as its delegates. On October 1, 1831, the assembly, which in American fashion styled itself a convention, was constituted at Philadelphia; it counted more than two hundred members. The discussions were public, and from the very first day it took on an altogether legislative character; discussion covered the extent of the powers of Congress, theories of free trade, and finally the various provisions of the tariff. After ten days the assembly broke up, having issued an address to the American people. In that address it declared first that Congress had not the right to impose a tariff and that the existing tariff was unconstitutional, and second that it was against the interest of any people, in particular the American people, that trade should not be free.

It must be admitted that unlimited freedom of association in the political sphere has not yet produced in America the fatal results that one might anticipate from it elsewhere. The right of association is of English origin and always existed in America. Use of this right is now an accepted part of customs and of mores.

In our own day freedom of association has become a necessary guarantee against the tyranny of the majority. In the United States, once a party has become predominant, all public power passes into its hands; its close supporters occupy all offices and have control of all organized forces. The most distinguished men of the opposite party, unable to cross the barrier keeping them from power, must be able to establish themselves outside it; the minority must use the whole of its moral authority to oppose the physical power oppressing it. Thus the one danger has to be balanced against a more formidable one.

The omnipotence of the majority seems to me such a danger to the American republics that the dangerous expedient used to curb it is actually something good.

Here I would repeat something which I have put in other words when speaking of municipal freedom: no countries need associations more—to prevent either despotism of parties or the arbitrary rule of a prince—than those with a democratic social state. In aristocratic nations secondary bodies form natural associations which hold abuses of power in check. In countries where such associations do not exist, if private people did not artificially and temporarily create something like them, I see no other dike to hold back tyranny of whatever sort, and a great nation might with impunity be oppressed by some tiny faction or by a single man.

The meeting of a great political convention (for conventions are of all kinds), though it may often be a necessary measure, is always, even in America, a serious event and one that good patriots cannot envisage without alarm.

That came out clearly during the convention of 1831, when all the men of distinction taking part therein tried to moderate its language and limit its objective. Probably the convention of 1831 did greatly influence the attitude of the malcontents and prepared them for the open revolt of 1832 against the commercial laws of the Union.

One must not shut one's eyes to the fact that unlimited freedom of association for political ends is, of all forms of liberty, the last that a nation can sustain. While it may not actually lead it into anarchy, it does constantly bring it to the verge thereof. But this form of freedom, howsoever dangerous, does provide guarantees in one direction; in countries where associations are free, secret societies are unknown. There are factions in America, but no conspirators.

Concerning the different ways in which the right of association is understood in Europe and in America, and the different uses made of it.

The most natural right of man, after that of acting on his own, is that of combining his efforts with those of his fellows and acting together. Therefore the right of association seems to me by nature almost as inalienable as individual liberty. Short of attacking society itself, no lawgiver can wish to abolish it. However, though for some nations freedom to unite is purely beneficial and a source of prosperity, there are other nations who pervert it by their excesses and turn a fount of life into a cause of destruction. So I think it will be thoroughly useful both for governments and for political parties if I make a comparison between the different ways in which associations are used in those nations that understand what freedom is and in those where this freedom turns into license.

Most Europeans still regard association as a weapon of war to be hastily improvised and used at once on the field of battle.

An association may be formed for the purpose of discussion, but everybody's mind is preoccupied by the thought of impending action. An association is an army; talk is needed to count numbers and build up courage, but after that they march against the enemy. Its members regard legal measures as possible means, but they are never the only possible means of success.

The right of association is not understood like that in the United States. In America the citizens who form the minority associate in the first place to show their numbers and to lessen the moral authority of the majority, and secondly, by stimulating competition, to discover the arguments most likely to make an impression on the majority, for they always hope to draw the majority over to their side and then to exercise power in its name.

Political associations in the United States are therefore peaceful in their objects and legal in the means used; and when they say that they only wish to prevail legally, in general they are telling the truth.

There are several reasons for this difference between the Americans and ourselves. In Europe there are parties differing so much from the majority that they can never hope to win its support, and yet these parties believe themselves strong enough to struggle against it on their own. When such a party forms an association it intends not to convince but to fight. In America those whose opinions make a wide gap between them and the majority can do nothing to oppose its power; all others hope to win it over.

So the exercise of the right of association becomes dangerous when great parties see no possibility of becoming the majority. In a country like the United States, where differences of view are only matters of nuance, the right of association can remain, so to say, without limits.

It is our inexperience of liberty in action which still leads us to regard freedom of association as no more than a right to make war on the government. The first idea which comes into a party's mind, as into that of an individual, when it gains some strength is that of violence; the thought of persuasion only comes later, for it is born of experience.

The English, though the divisions between them are so deep, seldom abuse the right of associations, because they have had long experience of it.

Furthermore, we have such a passionate taste for war that there is no enterprise so reckless or dangerous to the state, but it is thought glorious to die for it with arms in one's hand.

But perhaps universal suffrage is the most powerful of all the elements tending to moderate the violence of political associations in the United States. In a country with universal suffrage the majority is never in doubt, because no party can reasonably claim to represent those who have not voted at all. Therefore associations know, and everyone knows, that they do not represent the majority. The very fact of their existence proves this, for if they did represent the majority, they themselves would change the law instead of demanding reforms.

Thereby the moral strength of the government they attack is greatly increased and their own correspondingly weakened.

Almost all associations in Europe believe or claim that they represent the wishes of the majority. This belief or claim greatly increases their strength and wonderfully serves to legitimize their acts. For what is more excusable than violence to bring about the triumph of the oppressed cause of right?

Thus in the immense complication of human laws it sometimes comes about that extreme freedom corrects the abuse of freedom, and extreme democracy forestalls the dangers of democracy.

In Europe associations regard themselves in a way as the legislature and executive council of the nation which cannot raise its own voice; starting from this conception, they act and they command. In America, where everyone sees that they represent only a minority in the nation, they talk and petition.

The means used by associations in Europe are in accord with the aim proposed.

The main aim of these associations being to act and not to talk, to fight and not to convince, there is naturally nothing civilian about their organization, and indeed military ways and maxims are introduced therein; one also finds them centralizing control of their forces as much as they can and placing the whole authority in very few hands.

Members of these associations answer to a word of command like soldiers on active service; they profess the dogma of passive obedience, or rather, by the single act of uniting, have made a complete sacrifice of their judgment and free will; hence within associations, there often prevails a tyranny more intolerant than that exercised over society in the name of the government they attack.

This greatly diminishes their moral strength. They lose the sacred character belonging to the struggle of the oppressed against the oppressor. For how can a man claim that he wants to be free when in certain cases he consents servilely to obey some of his fellow men, yielding up his will and submitting his very thoughts to them?

The Americans too have provided a form of government within their associations, but it is, if I may put it so, a civil government. There is a place for individual independence there; as in society, all the members are advancing at the same time toward the same goal, but they are not obliged to follow exactly the same path. There has been no sacrifice of will or of reason, but rather will and reason are applied to bring success to a common enterprise.

Chapter 5

GOVERNMENT BY DEMOCRACY IN AMERICA

I KNOW THAT I AM NOW treading on live cinders. Every word in this chapter must in some respect offend the various parties dividing my country. Nevertheless, I shall say all I think.

In Europe it is hard for us to judge the true character and permanent instincts of democracy, for in Europe two contrary principles are contending, and one cannot precisely know what is due to the principles themselves and what to the passions engendered by the fight.

That is not the case in America. There the people prevail without impediment; there are neither dangers to fear nor injuries to revenge.

Therefore in America democracy follows its own inclinations. Its features are natural and its movements free. It is there that it must be judged. And such a study should be interesting and profitable for nobody more than ourselves, for we are being daily carried along by an irresistible movement, walking like blind men toward—what? Despotism perhaps, perhaps a republic, but certainly toward a democratic social state.

Universal Suffrage

I have previously mentioned that all the states of the Union have adopted universal suffrage; consequently it functions among communities at very different stages on the social ladder. I have had the chance to see its effects in diverse places and among men who by race, language, religion, or mores are almost total strangers one to another, in Louisiana as well as New England and in Georgia as well as Canada. I noted that in America universal suffrage was far from producing all the blessings or all the ills expected from it in Europe and that, generally speaking, its effects are other than is supposed.

The People's Choice and the Instincts
of American Democracy in Such Choices

*In the United States the most outstanding men are seldom called
on to direct public affairs. Reasons therefor. The envy of the
lower classes toward their superiors in France is not a specifically
French feeling, but a democratic one. Why, in America, men of
distinction often deliberately avoid a political career.*

In Europe many people either believe without saying or say without believing that one of the great advantages of universal suffrage
is to summon men worthy of public confidence to the direction of
affairs. The people, men say, do not know how themselves to rule
but always sincerely desire the good of the state, and their instinct
unfailingly tells them who are filled with the same desire and most
capable of wielding power.

For my part, I am bound to say that what I saw in America gives
me no cause to think that so. When I arrived in the United States
I discovered with astonishment that good qualities were common
among the governed but rare among the rulers. In our day it is a
constant fact that the most outstanding Americans are seldom summoned to public office, and it must be recognized that this tendency
has increased as democracy has gone beyond its previous limits. It
is clear that during the last fifty years the race of American statesmen has strangely shrunk.

One can point to several reasons for this phenomenon.

Whatever one does, it is impossible to raise the standard of enlightenment in a nation above a certain level. Whatever facilities
are made available for acquiring information and whatever improvements in teaching technique make knowledge available cheaply, men
will never educate and develop their intelligence without devoting
time to the matter.

Therefore the greater or less ease with which people can live without working sets inevitable limits to their intellectual progress. That
limit is further off in some countries and closer in others, but for
it not to exist at all, the people would have to have no more trouble
with the material cares of life and so would no longer be "the people". It is therefore as difficult to conceive a society in which all
men are very enlightened as one in which all are rich; these two
difficulties are correlative. I freely admit that the mass of the
citizens very sincerely desires the country's good; I would go further

and say that the lower classes of society generally confuse their personal interests with this desire less than the upper classes do; but what they always lack to some extent is skill to judge the means to attain this sincerely desired end. Consider the manifold considerations and the prolonged study involved in forming an exact notion of the character of a single man. There, where the greatest geniuses go astray, are the masses to succeed? The people never can find time or means to devote themselves to such work. They are bound always to make hasty judgments and to seize on the most prominent characteristics. That is why charlatans of every sort so well understand the secret of pleasing them, whereas for the most part their real friends fail in this.

Furthermore, it is not always ability to choose men of merit which democracy lacks; sometimes it has neither desire nor taste to do so.

One must not blind oneself to the fact that democratic institutions most successfully develop sentiments of envy in the human heart. This is not because they provide the means for everybody to rise to the level of everybody else but because these means are constantly proving inadequate in the hands of those using them. Democratic institutions awaken and flatter the passion for equality without ever being able to satisfy it entirely. This complete equality is always slipping through the people's fingers at the moment when they think to grasp it, fleeing, as Pascal says, in an eternal flight; the people grow heated in search of this blessing, all the more precious because it is near enough to be seen but too far off to be tasted. They are excited by the chance and irritated by the uncertainty of success; the excitement is followed by weariness and then by bitterness. In that state anything which in any way transcends the people seems an obstacle to their desires, and they are tired by the sight of any superiority, however legitimate.

Many people suppose that this secret instinct leading the lower classes to keep their superiors as far as possible from the direction of affairs is found only in France; that is a mistake; the instinct of which I speak is not French, but democratic; political circumstances may give it a particularly bitter taste, but they do not create it.

In the United States the people have no hatred toward the higher classes of society; but they have little goodwill toward them and are careful to keep them from power; they are not afraid of great talents but have little taste for them. In general one notices that anyone who has risen without the people's support has difficulty in winning their favor.

While the natural instincts of democracy lead the people to keep

men of distinction from power, an equally strong instinct diverts
the latter from a political career, in which it would be difficult to
remain completely themselves or to make any progress without
cheapening themselves. Chancellor Kent gives very ingenuous expression to this feeling. For this famous author, after singing the
praises of the part of the Constitution which gives the executive
the right to appoint the judges, adds: "The fittest men would probably have too much reservedness of manners and severity of morals
to secure an election resting on universal suffrage." (Kent's *Commentaries*, Vol. I, p. 273.) That was printed, and not contradicted,
in America in the year 1830.

I take it as proved that those who consider universal suffrage as
a guarantee of the excellence of the resulting choice suffer under
a complete delusion. Universal suffrage has other advantages, but
not that one.

Elements Which May Provide a Partial Corrective to These Instincts of Democracy

*Contrary effects, on nations as on men, of great dangers. Why
there were so many outstanding men at the head of affairs in
America fifty years ago. Influence of enlightenment and mores on
the people's choices. Example of New England. States of the
Southwest. How certain laws influence the people's choices. Election by two stages. Its effect on the composition of the Senate.*

When great perils threaten the state, the people often make a
happy choice of those citizens best suited to save it.

It has been noticed that a man in imminent danger hardly ever
remains at his normal level; he rises above or falls below it. The
same thing happens to nations too. Sometimes extreme dangers, instead of elevating a nation, bring it low; they may arouse its passions without giving them direction, and bewilder, not clarify, its
thoughts. The Jews were still killing one another amid the smoking
ruins of the temple. But just as frequently, with nations as with men,
the very imminence of danger calls forth extraordinary virtues. At
such times great characters stand out in relief like monuments at
night illuminated by the sudden glare of a conflagration. Then genius no longer hesitates to come forward, and the people in their
fright forget their envious passions for a time. Then it is no rare
event to see famous names come out of the electoral urn. I have said
above that the statesmen of modern America seem greatly inferior

to those at the head of affairs fifty years ago. Circumstances, as well as laws, were responsible for that. When America was engaged in the most just of struggles, that of a people escaping from another people's yoke, and when it was a question of creating a new nation in the world, the spirits of all rose to the height of their efforts' goal. In this general excitement outstanding men anticipated the people's call, and the people welcomed them with open arms and put them at their head. But such events are rare, and one must judge by the ordinary aspect of things.

While passing events sometimes serve to quell the passions of democracy, enlightenment, and above all mores, exercise a no less powerful and more lasting influence over its inclinations. This can be seen well in the United States.

In New England, where education and liberty spring from morality and religion and where an already old and long-settled society has been able to shape its own maxims and habits, the people, though rid of all forms of superiority ever created by wealth or birth among men, are accustomed to respect intellectual and moral superiority and to submit thereto without displeasure; and so we find New England democracy making choices better than those made elsewhere.

But as one goes farther south to those states where the social tie is less old and less strong, where education is less widespread, and where principles of morality, religion, and liberty are less happily combined, one finds both talents and virtues becoming rarer among those in authority.

But when one gets right down to the new states of the Southwest, where the body of society, formed yesterday, is nothing but an agglomeration of speculators and adventurers, one is appalled to see into what hands public authority has been entrusted, and one wonders by what power, independent of legislation and of men, the state has been able to grow and society to prosper.

There are some laws, democratic in their nature, which nonetheless succeed in partially correcting democracy's dangerous instincts.

When one enters the House of Representatives at Washington, one is struck by the vulgar demeanor of that great assembly. One can often look in vain for a single famous man. Almost all the members are obscure people whose names form no picture in one's mind. They are mostly village lawyers, tradesmen, or even men of the lowest classes. In a country where education is spread almost universally, it is said that the people's representatives do not always know how to write correctly.

A couple of paces away is the entrance to the Senate, whose narrow precincts contain a large proportion of the famous men of

America. There is scarcely a man to be seen there whose name does not recall some recent claim to fame. They are eloquent advocates, distinguished generals, wise magistrates, and noted statesmen. Every word uttered in this assembly would add luster to the greatest parliamentary debates in Europe.

What is the reason for this bizarre contrast? Why are the elite of the nation in one room and not in the other? Why does the former assembly attract such vulgar elements, whereas the latter has a monopoly of talents and enlightenment? Both spring from the people, both are the result of universal suffrage, and as yet no voice has been raised in America declaring that the Senate is hostile to popular interests. Whence, then, comes this vast difference? I can see only one fact to explain it: the election which produces the House of Representatives is direct, whereas the Senate is subject to election in two stages. All citizens together appoint the legislature of each state, and then the federal Constitution turns each of these legislatures into electoral bodies that return the members of the Senate. The senators therefore do represent the result, albeit the indirect result, of universal suffrage, for the legislature which appoints the senators is no aristocratic or privileged body deriving its electoral right from itself; it essentially depends on the totality of citizens; it is generally annually elected by them, and they can always control its choice by giving it new members. But it is enough that the popular will has passed through this elected assembly for it to have become in some sense refined and to come out clothed in nobler and more beautiful shape. Thus the men elected always represent exactly the ruling majority of the nation, but they represent only the lofty thoughts current there and the generous instincts animating it, not the petty passions which often trouble or the vices that disgrace it.

It is easy to see a time coming when the American republics will be bound to make more frequent use of election in two stages, unless they are to be miserably lost among the shoals of democracy.

I have no objection to avowing that I see this system of election by two stages[1] as the only means of putting the use of political freedom within the reach of all classes of the people. Those who hope to make it the exclusive weapon of one party, and those who fear it, seem to me to be making equal mistakes.

[1] [In 1913 the Seventh Amendment, passed by both houses of Congress in 1912, was put in force. Under this new arrangement senators are elected directly by the people of the states after having been nominated in primaries or conventions, and as in the case of the House of Representatives, all persons are qualified to vote who are allowed to vote for the House of Representatives.]

Influence of American Democracy Upon Electoral Laws

When elections are rare they expose the state to violent crises. When they are frequent they keep it in feverish agitation. The Americans have preferred the second of these disadvantages. Mutability of the laws. Views of Hamilton, Madison, and Jefferson on this subject.

When elections come only at long intervals, the state risks overthrow each time.

Then the parties make prodigious efforts to grasp a chance so seldom within their reach, and since there is hardly any remedy for the lot of the unsuccessful candidate, there is everything to fear from their ambitions driven to despair. But if an equal struggle is soon to be renewed, then the defeated are patient.

When elections quickly follow one another, they keep society in feverish activity, with endless mutability in public affairs. Under one system there is a danger of malaise, and under the other a chance of revolution; in the first case the quality of government suffers, but in the second its existence is at stake.

The Americans chose to risk the former ill rather than the latter. In this they were guided by instinct much more than by reason, for democracy has a taste amounting to passion for variety. A strange mutability in their legislation is the result.

Many Americans consider the instability of their laws as a necessary consequence of a system whose general effects are useful. But there is, I think, nobody in the United States who denies the existence of this instability or regards it as anything but a great ill.

Hamilton, after demonstrating the usefulness of an authority which could prevent or at least retard the promulgation of bad laws, adds: "It may perhaps be said that the power of preventing bad laws includes that of preventing good ones, and may be used to the one purpose as well as to the other. But this objection will have little weight with those who can properly estimate the mischiefs of that inconstancy and mutability in the laws, which *form the greatest blemish in the character and genius of our governments.*" (*The Federalist*, No. 73.) [Everyman edition, p. 375. The italics are Tocqueville's.]

". . . the facility and excess of law-making seem to be the diseases to which our governments are most liable," says Madison. (*The Federalist*, No. 62.) [Everyman edition, p. 316.]

Jefferson himself, the greatest democrat ever to spring from American democracy, has pointed out the same perils:

"The instability of our laws is really an immense evil. I think it would be well to provide in our constitutions that there shall always be a twelve-month between engrossing a bill and passing it; that it should then be offered to its passage without changing a word; and that if circumstances should be thought to require a speedier passage, it should take two thirds of both Houses instead of a bare majority."[2]

Public Officers Under the Rule of American Democracy

Simplicity of American officials. Absence of uniforms. All officials are paid. Political consequences of this fact. There is no public career in America. Results of that.

American public officials blend with the mass of citizens; they have neither palaces nor guards nor ceremonial clothes. This external simplicity of persons in authority is not due to some peculiar twist in the American character but derives from the fundamental principles of their society.

In democratic eyes government is not a blessing but a necessary evil. Officials must be given certain powers, for without them how could they be of any use? But the external pomps of power are by no means essential to the conduct of business; the sight of them would offend the public uselessly.

The officials themselves are perfectly aware that they have won the right to place themselves above others by their power, only on condition that their manners keep them on a level with everybody else.

I can imagine no one more straightforward in his manners, accessible to all, attentive to requests, and civil in his answers than an American public official.

I like this natural demeanor of democratic government and the inner authority which goes more with the office than with the official, and more with the man than with external symbols of power, for there is something admirably virile therein.

I believe that in such an age as ours the importance attached to uniforms has been much exaggerated. I have not noticed American

[2] Letter of December 20, 1787, to Madison. [Cf. *The Writings of Thomas Jefferson* (Washington, 1905), Vol. VI, p. 393.]

officials in the exercise of their duties treated with less respect or regard because they rely on merit alone.

I also doubt whether a particular dress makes public men respect themselves if they are not naturally disposed to do so, for I cannot think that they will have more respect for their clothes than for themselves.

When I see some of our magistrates being sharp with the parties or witty at their expense, shrugging their shoulders at the pleas of the defense or smiling complacently when the charges are enumerated, I wish someone would try taking their robes away to see if, dressed as simple citizens, they might not be recalled to some of the natural dignity of the human race.

No American public official has a uniform, but all receive salaries.

This too, and even more naturally, is the result of democratic principles. A democracy could surround its magistrates with pomp, covering them in silk and gold, without making any direct attack on the principle of its existence. Such privileges are ephemeral, going with the place rather than with the man. But to establish unpaid official positions is to create a class of rich and independent functionaries and to shape the core of an aristocracy. Even if the people still retain the right of choice, the exercise of that right comes to have inevitable limitations.

When a democratic republic converts salaried appointments into unpaid ones, I think one may conclude that it is steering toward monarchy. And when a monarchy begins paying its unsalaried officials, that is a sure sign that it is working either toward a despotic or toward a republican condition.

I therefore think that the change from salaried to unpaid appointments by itself constitutes a real revolution.

I regard the complete absence of unpaid duties as one of the clearest indications of democracy's absolute sway in America. The public pays for all services of whatever sort performed in its interest; hence any man has the chance as well as the right to perform them.

Although in democratic states all citizens can hold office, not all are disposed to seek it. It is the number and capacities of the candidates, not the qualifications for candidature, which there often limits the electors' choice.

There is, properly speaking, no public career in a nation where the principle of election is universally applied. There is an element of chance about who is chosen, and no one can be sure of remaining in office. This is particularly the case where elections are annual. Consequently in calm times public office offers little attraction to ambition. In the United States it is men of moderate pretensions who engage in the twists and turns of politics. Men of parts and vaulting ambition generally avoid power to pursue wealth; the frequent result is that men undertake to direct the fortunes of the state only when they doubt their capacity to manage their private affairs.

These causes, quite as much as the ill choices of democracy, are responsible for the large number of vulgar men holding public positions. Should men of parts compete for their votes, I am sure that the American people would choose them, but it is certain that they do not so compete.

The Arbitrary Power of Magistrates[3] Under the Sway of American Democracy

Why the arbitrary powers of magistrates is greater under absolute monarchies and democratic republics than under limited monarchies. Arbitrary power of the magistrates in New England.

Under two types of government, magistrates exercise considerable arbitrary power, namely, under the absolute government of one man and under that of democracy.

Almost analogous causes produce the same effect.

In despotic states nobody's fate is certain, whether they be public officials or private individuals. As the sovereign always holds in his hands the life, fortune, and sometimes honor of those he employs, he thinks he has nothing to fear from them and leaves them wide freedom of action because he is sure they will never abuse it against himself.

In despotic states the sovereign is so enamored of his own power that he fears the constraint of his own regulations, and he is glad to see his agents behave almost at random, in order to be sure that he will never discover in them tendencies contrary to his own desires.

In democracies the majority, having an annual opportunity of taking power back from the hands to which it has entrusted it, also has no fear of its abuse against itself. With the power at any moment to make its will known to the rulers, it prefers to let them follow their own devices rather than to bind them with invariable rules which, in restraining them, would also in a sense control itself.

When one looks closely into the matter, one actually finds that the

[3] I here use the word "magistrates" in its most extended meaning, to include all whose duty it is to see to the execution of laws.

arbitrary power of democratic magistrates is even greater than that
of their counterparts in despotic states.

In those states the sovereign can punish immediately any faults
he discovers, but he cannot flatter himself into supposing that he
sees all the faults he should punish. But the sovereign power in
democracies is both all-powerful and omnipresent; as a result American officials are much freer within the sphere of action by law al-
lotted to them than is any corresponding European official. Often
only the goal to be aimed at is indicated to them, and they are
left to choose their own means. In New England, for instance, the
selectmen of each township are entrusted with the duty of forming
the jury list; the only rule laid down for them is this: they must
choose the juries from citizens enjoying electoral rights and of good
reputation.[4]

In France we should consider men's life and liberty in danger if
we entrusted any official, whoever he might be, with the exercise of
so formidable a right.

In New England these same magistrates can post the names of
drunkards in the taverns and, under penalty of a fine, prevent the
landlord from selling them wine.[5]

A people under the most absolute of monarchies would object
to such a censorial power, but here people readily submit to it.

Nowhere has the law left greater scope to arbitrary power than in
democratic republics, because there they feel they have nothing to
fear from it. It can even be said that magistrates become freer as
voting rights are wider spread and the duration of office shortened.

That is why it is so difficult to convert a democratic republic into
a monarchy. The magistrates, though they cease to be elected, usually retain both the rights and the habits of an elected magistrate.
That leads to despotism. It is only in limited monarchies that the
law, while assigning a sphere of action to public officials, is still at

---

[4] See the law of February 27, 1813, in the *General Collection of the Laws
of Massachusetts,* Vol. II, p. 331. It must be added that the jurors are
subsequently drawn by lot from the lists.

[5] Law of February 28, 1787, *ibid.,* Vol. I, p. 302. Here is the text: "That
the selectmen in each town shall cause to be posted up in the houses and
shops of all taverners, innholders, and retailers . . . within such towns or
districts, a list of the names of all persons reputed common drunkards, or
common tipplers, or common gamesters, misspending their time and estate
in such houses. And every keeper of such house or shop, after notice given
him, as aforesaid, that shall be convicted, before one or more Justices of
the Peace, of entertaining or suffering any of the persons, in such list, to
drink or tipple or game, in his or her house, or any of the dependencies
thereof, or of selling them spirituous liquor . . . shall forfeit and pay the
sum of sixty shillings."

pains to guide them therein at every step. It is easy to explain the causes of this.

In limited monarchies power is divided between people and prince. Both have an interest in the stability of the position of the magistrates.

The prince does not wish to place the fate of public officials in the people's hands for fear that they may betray his authority, whereas the people are also afraid that magistrates completely dependent on the prince might be used against their freedom. Thus, in a sense, they are left depending on nobody.

The same cause which leads prince and people to make officials independent induces them to look for guarantees against the abuse of this independence, so that it cannot be turned against the authority of the one or the liberty of the other. Hence both agree on the necessity of restricting officials to a line of conduct laid down in advance, and both find it to their interests to impose upon him rules that he cannot disregard.

Administrative Instability in the United States

American society often leaves fewer records of its proceedings than are left by a family. Newspapers are the only historical records. How extreme administrative instability injures the art of government.

After one brief moment of power, officials are lost again amid the everchanging crowd, and as a result, the proceedings of American society often leave fewer traces than do events in a private family. There is a sense in which public administration is oral and traditional. Nothing is written, or if it is, the slightest gust of wind carries it off, like Sibylline leaves to vanish without recall.

Newspapers are the only historical records in the United States. If one number is missing, it is as if the link of time was broken: present and past cannot be joined together again. I have no doubt that in fifty years' time it will be harder to collect authentic documents about the details of social life in modern America than about French medieval administration; and if some barbarian invasion caught the United States by surprise, in order to find out anything about the people who lived there one would have to turn to the history of other nations.

Administrative instability has begun to become a habit; I might almost say that by now everyone has developed a taste for it. Nobody bothers about what was done before his time. No method is adopted; no archives are formed; no documents are brought together, even when it would be easy to do so. When by chance someone has them, he is casual about preserving them. Among my papers I have original documents given to me by public officials to answer some of my questions. American society seems to live from day to day, like an army on active service. Nevertheless, the art of administration is certainly a science, and all sciences, to make progress, need to link the discoveries of succeeding generations. One man in the short space of life notices a fact and another conceives an idea; one man finds a means and another discovers a formula; as life goes on, humanity collects various fruits of individual experience and builds up knowledge. It is very difficult for American administrators to learn anything from each other. Thus the lights that guide them in the direction of society are those to be found widespread throughout that society, and not any particular administrative techniques. So democracy, pressed to its ultimate limits, harms the progress of the art of government. In this respect it is better adapted to a people whose administrative education is already finished than to a nation which is a novice in the experience of public affairs.

Moreover, this does not apply only to the science of administration. Democratic government, founded on such a simple and natural idea, nevertheless always assumes the existence of a very civilized and knowledgeable society.[6] At first glance it might be supposed to belong to the earliest ages of the world, but looking closer, one soon discovers that it could only have come last.

Public Expenses Under the Rule of American Democracy

The citizens of all societies are divided into a certain number of classes. The instinct guiding each of these classes in the control of state finances. Why public expenses must tend to increase when the people rule. Why there is comparatively little fear of democratic extravagance in America. Use of public funds under a democracy.

Is democratic government economical? First we must know with what we are comparing it.

The question could easily be answered if we wanted to compare a democratic republic with an absolute monarchy. One would find

[6] Needless to say, I am speaking here of democratic government applied to a people and not a small tribe.

public expenses in the former considerably greater than in the latter. But that is so of all free states compared with those not free. It is certain that despotism brings men to ruin more by preventing them from producing than by taking away the fruits of their labors; it dries up the fount of wealth while often respecting acquired riches. But liberty engenders a thousandfold more goods than it destroys, and in nations where it is understood, the people's resources always increase faster than the taxes.

At present I am concerned to make comparisons between free peoples and to discover what effect democracy there has on state finances.

Societies, like other organized bodies, are shaped according to certain fixed rules from which they cannot escape. They are made up of certain elements which are found at all times and in all places.

It will always be easy theoretically to divide each people up into three classes.

The first class is composed of the rich. The second of those who, without being rich, are in all respects comfortably off. The third class includes those with little or no property, who live primarily from the work which the other two classes provide for them.

The individuals in these various categories may be more or less numerous according to the state of society, but no contrivance will prevent these classes from existing.

It is clear that each of these classes will introduce certain instincts peculiar to itself into the management of state finances.

Suppose that the first class alone makes the laws; it probably will not take much trouble to economize public money, for a tax on a substantial fortune takes away only some of what is superfluous, with barely perceptible effect.

But suppose it is the middle classes alone who make the laws. Then one can be sure that they will not raise extravagant taxes, for there is nothing as disastrous as a heavy levy on a small fortune.

I think that among free governments middle-class rule is, I do not say the most enlightened and certainly not the most generous, but the most economical.

Finally, suppose that the last class has exclusive control of law-making. Then I see every chance of public expenditure growing rather than decreasing, and that for two reasons:

As most of the voters then have no taxable property, apparently all money spent in the interests of society can only profit and never harm them; and those who do have a little property easily find ways of imposing a tax so that it will weigh only on the rich and bring nothing but profit to the poor, and that is something the like of which the rich cannot do when they are masters of the government.

Countries, therefore, where lawmaking falls exclusively to the lot of the poor[7] cannot hope for much economy in public expenditure; expenses will always be considerable, either because taxes cannot touch those who vote for them or because they are assessed in a way to prevent that. In other words, a democratic government is the only one in which those who vote for a tax can escape the obligation to pay it.

It is vain to object that the people's interest properly understood should lead it to be careful with the fortunes of the wealthy, because it is bound at no long delay to feel the effects of the trouble it has caused. Is it not also the interest of kings to make their subjects happy and of nobles to know when to open their ranks? If remote advantages could prevail over the passions and needs of the moment, there would have been no tyrannical sovereigns or exclusive aristocracies.

Again, someone may stop me and say: "Who has ever thought of entrusting lawmaking to the poor alone?" Who? Those who introduced universal suffrage. Is it the majority or the minority who make the law? The majority certainly, and if I show that the poor always compose the majority, have I not reason to add that in countries where all are called to vote, the poor alone make the law?

Now, it is certain that up to the present in all countries of the world those without property or those whose property was so modest that they could not live comfortably without working have always formed the largest number. So universal suffrage really does hand the government of society over to the poor.

Some democratic republics of antiquity provide examples of the untoward influence of popular power on state finances, the public treasury being exhausted to support indigent citizens or to provide the people with games and spectacles.

True to say, the representative system was almost unknown in antiquity. In our day popular passions find less easy expression in public affairs; nevertheless, in the long run one can count on it that the delegate will always end by conforming to the spirit of his

[7] It will be understood that the word "poor" here and in the rest of this chapter has a relative and not an absolute meaning. The poor of America, compared to those of Europe, might often seem rich; nevertheless, they can rightly be called poor when compared to their richer fellow citizens.

constituents and will enable their inclinations as well as their interests to prevail.

There will, however, be less danger of extravagance in an increasingly property-owning democracy, both because the people will less need the wealthy's money and because it will become ever more difficult to contrive a tax which will not touch the people themselves. In this respect universal suffrage should be less dangerous in France than in England, where almost all taxable property is accumulated in but few hands. Since the great majority of American citizens possess something, that country is in a better position than France.

There are other causes too that may increase the total budget in democracies.

Those in charge of affairs of state under an aristocracy are naturally free of all wants; content with their lot, it is especially power and glory that they ask of society; and, placed above the obscure crowd of citizens, they do not always see clearly how general prosperity should augment their own greatness. It is not that they have no pity for the sufferings of the poor, but they cannot feel their distress as if they shared it themselves; so long as the people seem to put up with their lot, they assume that they are satisfied and expect nothing from the government. An aristocracy thinks more about preservation than about improvement.

But the people, when sovereign, feeling discontented, seek everywhere for something better.

The thirst for improvement, then, is concerned with thousands of different matters; it goes into infinite detail and is especially bent on those types of improvement that require expenditure, for it is a question of bettering the lot of the poor, who cannot help themselves.

There is also in democratic societies a stirring without precise aim; some sort of prevailing feverish excitement finds expression in innovations of all sorts, and innovations are almost always expensive.

In monarchies and in aristocracies men of ambition flatter the sovereign's natural taste for renown and power and thereby often drive him into great expenditures.

In democracies, where the sovereign power belongs to the needy, only an increase of its prosperity will win that master's goodwill; almost never can that be done without money.

Moreover, when the people begin to reflect on their position, they notice a mass of hitherto unfelt wants, which cannot be satisfied without recourse to the resources of the state. For that reason public expenditure increases with civilization, and as enlightenment spreads, taxes rise.

There is one other, final reason which makes democratic government more expensive than others. Sometimes a democracy wishes to economize its outlay, but does not succeed in doing so, because it has not learned the art of being economical.

As it changes its mind often and its agents even more frequently, its enterprises may be ill-conducted or remain uncompleted. In the first case, the state makes expenditures disproportionate to the size of the intended aim, and in the second its expenditure is unproductive.

The Instincts of American Democracy in Fixing the Salaries of Officials

In democracies those who authorize high salaries have no chance of profiting from them. Tendency of American democracy to raise the salaries of secondary officials and to reduce those of the principal ones. Why that is so. Comparative table of salaries of public officials in the United States and in France.

There is one important reason which generally leads democracies to economize on the salaries of public officials.

In democracies those who fix the salaries, being very numerous, have little chance of ever drawing them themselves.

But in aristocracies those who fix high salaries almost always have a vague hope of profiting from them themselves. They are creating capital for themselves, or at least preparing resources for their children.

Nevertheless, it must be admitted that democracy is excessively parsimonious only toward its principal agents.

In America officials of secondary rank are better paid than elsewhere, but high officials are much less well paid.

The same cause is responsible for these contradictory effects; in both cases the people fix the salaries of public officials, and the scale of remuneration is determined by a comparison with their own wants. Living in great comfort themselves, it seems natural to them that their servants should share therein.[8] But when it comes to fixing the sala-

[8] There is yet another reason for the comfort in which secondary American officials live; this has nothing to do with the general instincts of democracy; every sort of private career is very profitable; the state would find no secondary officials if it did not agree to pay them well. It is therefore in the same position as a commercial enterprise, forced, whatever taste it may have for economy, to face heavy competition.

ries of high officials of the state, such a rule gives no guidance, and things are decided at random.

A poor man has no distinct idea of the needs which the upper classes of society may feel. What seems a moderate sum to a rich man strikes the man accustomed to be satisfied with necessities as prodigious, and he supposes that a state governor with his six thousand francs must feel himself lucky and the object of envy.[9]

If you try to make him understand that the representative of a great nation ought to appear with some splendor in the eyes of foreigners, he will at first see the point; but when he comes to think of his simple home and the modest fruits of his hard work, he will dream of all that he could do with that salary which you consider inadequate, and he will be astonished and almost shocked at the contemplation of such wealth.

Remember also that the secondary official is almost on a level with the people, whereas the higher one dominates it. Thus the former may still excite its sympathy, whereas the latter rouses envy.

This is clearly seen in the United States, where salaries seem to diminish as the power of the recipients increases.[10]

But under aristocratic rule high functionaries receive very large emoluments, whereas inferior ones often have hardly enough to live on. Causes analogous to those mentioned above are obviously responsible for this.

If democracy either cannot conceive the pleasures of the rich or envies them, the aristocracy conversely has no understanding of the

[9] The state of Ohio, with a million inhabitants, gives its governor a salary of only 1,200 dollars, or 6,504 francs.

[10] To make the truth of this obvious, it is enough to set out the salaries of some of the federal government's agents. I have added the salaries of the corresponding French officials to give the reader a basis of comparison:

United States Treasury Department		France Ministry of Finance	
Messenger	3,734 fr.	Minister's messenger	1,500 fr.
Lowest-paid clerk	5,420	Lowest-paid clerk	1,000–1,800
Highest-paid clerk	8,672	Highest-paid clerk	3,200–3,600
Chief clerk	10,840	Secretary General	20,000
Secretary of State	32,520	Minister	80,000
President	135,000	Head of the government (King)	12,000,000

Perhaps I was wrong to take France as the basis of comparison. In France, where democratic instincts are daily penetrating further into the government, one already notices a strong tendency inducing the chambers to raise small salaries and especially to lower high ones. Thus the Minister of Finance, who in 1834 received 80,000 francs, received 160,000 under the Empire; the Directors General of Finance, who now receive 20,000, used to get 50,000.

wretchedness of the poor, or rather ignores it. The poor man is not, properly speaking, the rich man's "like", but a being of another species. Therefore an aristocracy is little worried about the lot of its inferior agents. It raises their salaries only when they refuse to work for it at too low a rate.

The parsimony of democracy toward its chief functionaries has caused it to be credited with very economical inclinations, which it does not possess.

It is true that democracy hardly provides its rulers with a decent living, but it spends huge sums to succor the needs or facilitate the pleasures of the people.[11] That is a better use of taxes, not an economy.

In general, democracy gives little to the rulers and much to the ruled. The opposite occurs in aristocracies, where the state's money especially benefits the class in control of affairs.

Difficulty of Discerning the Reasons That Incline the American Government Toward Economy

He who tries to uncover facts illustrating the real influence of the laws on the fate of humanity is liable to great mistakes, for nothing is so hard to appreciate as facts.

One nation may be naturally fickle and enthusiastic and another sober and calculating. This is due to their physical constitution itself or to remote causes of which I am ignorant.

One sees people who love show, bustle, and festivity and who do not regret a million vanished in smoke. One sees others with a taste for none but solitary pleasures, who seem ashamed of appearing happy.

In some countries beautiful buildings are highly prized. In others no value is attached to works of art, and nothing which does not make a profit is scorned. And finally, some countries love renown and others put money above all else.

Apart from the laws, all these causes have a very strong influence on the conduct of state finances.

---

[11] See *inter alia* in American budgets what maintenance of the needy and free education cost.

In 1831 the state of New York spent 245,433 dollars on the care of paupers. And the sum devoted to public education is estimated to rise to at least 1,080,698 dollars. (Williams' *New York Annual Register,* 1832, pp. 205 and 243.)

The state of New York had only 1,900,000 inhabitants in 1830, which is less than twice the population of the Department du Nord.

If the Americans have never spent the people's money on public festivities, that is not only because there the people vote the taxes but also because the people have no taste for enjoying themselves.

If they reject ornament in architecture and value only its material and positive advantages, that is not only because they are a democratic nation but also because they are a trading people.

The habits of private life are carried over into public life, and it is important there to distinguish between the economies that depend on their institutions and those that derive from habits and mores.

Can the Public Expenditure of the United States Be Compared with That of France?

Two points to ascertain in order to appreciate the extent of public expenses: national wealth and taxation. Neither the wealth of France nor her expenses are exactly known. Why one cannot hope to know the wealth and the expenses of the Union. The author's researches to discover the total amount of taxes in Pennsylvania. General indications by which the extent of a nation's wealth can be estimated. Result of such an examination for the Union.

There has been much preoccupation lately with comparisons between the public expenditure of the United States and our own. All such labors have been fruitless, and I think the reason why this must be so can briefly be explained.

To be in a position to appreciate the extent of public expenditure in a nation, two operations are necessary: first one must discover the amount of the national wealth, and then what proportion thereof is devoted to state expenses. Anyone who tries to discover the total of taxes without showing what resources are available to provide for them has undertaken a profitless task, for it is not the expenditure but the proportion which that bears to the revenue that it is interesting to know.

The same tax which can easily be borne by a rich taxpayer may reduce a poor one to misery.

The wealth of nations is composed of several elements: real property first, and secondly personal property.

It is hard to know the extent of the cultivable land in a nation and its natural or acquired value. It is even harder to estimate all the personal property at a people's disposal. The diversity and the quantity of such property eludes almost all efforts at analysis.

Thus we see that the European nations with the most ancient civilization, including even those with a centralized administration, have as yet failed to establish exactly the state of their fortune.

In America the idea of attempting that has not even been conceived. And how can one hope to succeed in this new country where society has not yet taken settled and definite shape, where the national government has not at its disposal, as our has, a crowd of agents whose efforts can be commanded and directed simultaneously, and finally, where the art of statistics is not cultivated, since no one has the chance of collecting documents or time to go through them?

Therefore the constituent elements for our calculations are not to be obtained. We do not know the comparative wealth of France and of the Union. The wealth of the former is still unknown and the means of discovering that of the latter do not exist.

But for the moment I am prepared to dispense with this necessary element in the comparison; giving up hope of knowing the relation between tax and income, I restrict myself to an attempt to discover the amount of the tax.

The reader will understand that by narrowing my sphere of investigation I have not made my task easier.

No doubt the French central administration, with the help of all its officials, could discover the exact total of direct and indirect taxes imposed on the citizens. But the French government itself has not accomplished this task, which is one no individual could undertake, or has at least not published the results. We know the total of state taxes; we also know the sum of departmental expenditure; we do not know what happens in the communes; therefore, no one yet knows the total of all French public expenditure.

Turning again to America, one is faced with more numerous and more insurmountable difficulties. The Union publishes an exact return of the amount of its taxes; I can get copies of the budgets of the four and twenty component states; but who can tell me what the citizens spend in the administrations of county and township?[12]

---

[12] There are, as we see, four types of budget in America; the Union, the states, the counties, and the townships each have their own. During my stay in America I made extensive investigations to discover the amount of public expenses in the townships and counties of the principal states of the Union. I could easily obtain the budgets of the largest townships, but it was impossible to get those of the smaller ones. I have documents concerning the expenditure of the counties, which, though incomplete, are perhaps worth the reader's attention. Mr. Richards, a former mayor of Philadelphia, was kind enough to provide me with the budgets of the thirteen counties of

Federal authority can not be stretched to oblige the provincial governments to enlighten us on this point, and even should those governments themselves simultaneously wish to help us in this matter, I doubt if they would be in a position to satisfy us. Apart from the inherent difficulty of the task, the political organization of the country would make success even harder. The magistrates of township and county are not appointed by those who administer the state and are in no way dependent on them. It is therefore not unfair to assume that if the state wanted to obtain the information we need, it would encounter great obstacles from the negligence of the inferior officials whose services it would have to use.[18]

Pennsylvania for the year 1830, namely, Lebanon, Centre, Franklin, La Fayette, Montgomery, La Luzerne, Dauphin, Butler, Allegheny, Columbia, Northumberland, Northampton, and Philadelphia. In 1830 there were 495,207 inhabitants. A glance at a map of Pennsylvania shows that these thirteen counties are scattered in all directions and subject to all the general causes influencing the state of the country; there, therefore, seems no reason to doubt that they give an accurate impression of the financial condition of the counties of Pennsylvania. Now, in 1830 these counties spent 1,800,221 francs, which comes to 3 francs, 64 centimes, per inhabitant. I have calculated that in the same year these inhabitants contributed 12 francs, 70 centimes, to the federal budget and 3 francs, 80 centimes, to that of Pennsylvania; consequently, in that year the contribution of each citizen to all public expenditure (except that of the townships) was 20 francs, 14 centimes. Obviously this figure is doubly incomplete, applying to one year only and only to a part of public expenditure, but it has the advantage of being certain.

[18] Those who have tried to establish a parallel between American expenditure and our own have clearly seen that they could not compare the total of French public expenditure with a similar total for the Union, but have sought to compare detached portions of these expenditures with one another. It is easy to prove that this second approach is as defective as the first.

To what, for instance, should our national budget be compared? To the budget of the Union? But the Union is concerned with far fewer matters than is our central government, and of course its expenditure should be much less. Could our departmental budgets be equated with those of the component states of the Union? But generally the states are in control of more numerous and more important interests than are our departmental administrations, so of course their expenses are more considerable. When it comes to county budgets, there is nothing like them in our financial system. Should their expenditure be included in the state budget or in that of the townships: There are expenditures for the townships in both countries, but they are not always analogous. The American township takes care of many matters which in France are left to the department or the state. Besides, what do we mean by township expenditure in America? The organization of the township is different in the various states. Shall we take what is done in New England as our standard, or in Georgia, in Pennsylvania, or in the state of Illinois?

It is easy to see a sort of analogy between certain budgets in the two countries, but there is always more or less difference in the elements composing them, and one cannot establish a serious comparison between them.

Moreover, it is useless to inquire what the Americans might do in such a matter, for it is certain that up till now they have done nothing.

So there is no single man in America or in Europe who can tell us what each citizen of the Union contributes annually to the expenses of society.[14]

Hence we must conclude that it is as difficult to compare social expenditure as it is to estimate the relative wealth of the Union and of France. I would add that it would even be dangerous to attempt it. When statistics are not based on strictly accurate calculations, they mislead instead of guide. The mind easily lets itself be taken in by the false appearance of exactitude which statistics retain even in their mistakes, and confidently adopts errors clothed in the forms of mathematical truth.

Let us abandon figures, then, and try to find our proofs elsewhere.

Does a country give the appearance of material prosperity? Having paid his dues to the state, does the poor man retain some resources and the rich some superfluity? Do they both seem satisfied with their lot and continually seek to improve it further, so that there is always capital to invest in industry, and industry is never short of capital?

[14] Even if one did succeed in discovering the precise sum paid by each French or American citizen into the public treasury, one would still have only part of the truth.

Governments do not demand only money from the taxpayers, but also personal efforts that can be valued in money. The state raises an army; apart from the pay which the whole nation undertakes to provide, the soldier must give his time, which is of greater or less value according to the use he could make of it if he were free. One can say the same about militia service. A man who serves in the militia sacrifices some valuable time to public security and really does give the state what he might have earned in that time. I could have quoted many other examples besides these. The governments of France and of America impose duties of this type; these duties are a burden on the citizens, but who can exactly estimate how much they amount to in each country?

That is not the last difficulty that holds you up when you want to compare the public expenditure of the Union with ours. In France the state imposes certain obligations not imposed in America, and vice versa. The French government pays the clergy; the American government leaves that to the care of the faithful. In America the state looks after the poor; in France they are left dependent on public charity. We give all our officials a fixed salary; the Americans allow them to collect certain dues. In France there are contributions in labor for the upkeep of very few roads, but in America this is so for almost all roads. Our roads are open to all travelers without payment, but in the United States there are many toll roads. All these differences in the way in which the taxpayer discharges the expenses of society make the comparison between these two countries very difficult. For there are certain expenses to which the citizens would not be subject, or which would at any rate be less considerable, if the state did not undertake to act in their name.

Where definite information is lacking, one can infer from such indications whether the public charges borne by a people are proportionate to its wealth.

An observer relying on such testimony would certainly conclude that the American of the United States gives a smaller proportion of his income to the state than the Frenchman does.

But how could one suppose that it should be otherwise?

Part of the French debt is the result of two invasions; the Union has nothing of that sort to fear. Our position compels us habitually to maintain a large army under arms; the isolation of the Union allows it to have no more than six thousand soldiers. We maintain nearly three hundred ships. The Americans have only fifty-two.[15] Why should the American pay the state as much as the Frenchman does?

Hence there is no parallel to be established between the finances of countries so differently situated.

It is by examining what actually happens in the Union, and not by comparing the Union with France, that we can judge whether the American government is in truth economical.

Glancing at the various republics of which the confederation is composed, I find that their government often lacks perseverance in its plans and that it exercises no continuous supervision over the people employed. I naturally draw the conclusion that it must often spend the taxpayers' money uselessly or devote more than is necessary to its undertakings. I see that, faithful to its popular origin, the government makes prodigious efforts to satisfy the needs of the lower classes of society, to open the way to power for them, and to diffuse prosperity and enlightenment among them. It looks after the poor, distributes annually millions to schools, pays for all services, and rewards its humblest agents liberally. Though such a way of governing seems useful and reasonable to me, I am bound to admit that it is expensive.

Seeing the poor man directing public affairs and disposing of national resources, I cannot believe that, profiting from state expenditure, he does not often lead the state into new expenses.

So, without relying on incomplete figures or trying to establish hazardous comparisons, I conclude that the democratic government of the Americans is not, as is sometimes claimed, a cheap government; and I am not afraid to predict that if the people of the United States are ever involved in serious difficulties, taxes there will soon be found to rise as high as in most of the aristocracies or monarchies of Europe.

[15] See the detailed budgets of the Ministry of Marine in France, and for America, the *National Calendar of 1833*, p. 228.

Corruption and Vices of the Rulers in a Democracy and Consequent Effect on Public Morality

Sometimes in aristocracies the rulers seek to corrupt. In democracies they are themselves often corrupted. In the former their vices make a direct attack on public morality. In the latter their influence is indirect but still more formidable.

Aristocracy and democracy mutually reproach each other for making corruption easy: a distinction must be made.

In aristocratic governments those who get to the head of affairs are rich men desiring power only. The statesmen in democracies are poor, with their fortunes to make.

As a result, the rulers in aristocratic states are little open to corruption and have only a very moderate taste for money, whereas the opposite occurs in democracies.

But in aristocracies those who wish to get to the head of affairs have great wealth at their disposal, and as the number of those by whose assistance they may rise is comparatively small, the government is in a sense up for auction. In democracies those who intrigue for power are hardly ever rich, and the number of those who help to give it to them is very great. Perhaps there are just as many men for sale in democracies, but there are hardly any buyers; besides, one would have to buy too many men at the same time to attain one's end.

Among those who have held power in France during the last forty years, several have been accused of making their fortunes at the expense of the state of its allies, a reproach seldom made against public men under the old monarchy. But in France there is hardly a case of votes bought at an election, whereas that is notoriously and publicly done in England.

I have never heard it said in the United States that a man used his wealth to bribe the governed, but I have often heard the integrity of public officials put in doubt. More often still, I have heard their success attributed to base intrigues or culpable maneuvers.

So while the rulers of aristocracies sometimes seek to corrupt, those of democracies prove corruptible. The first directly attack the morality of the people, whereas the others exercise on the public conscience an indirect effect which is even more to be feared.

As the men at the head of the state in democracies are almost always subject to untoward suspicions, in some sense they give government support to the crimes of which they are accused. They thus provide dangerous examples to still-struggling virtue and furnish glorious comparisons for hidden vice.

It is useless to say that dishonest passions are found among all ranks, that they often ascend the throne by right of birth, and that one may find very despicable men at the head of aristocratic nations as well as in democracies.

Such an answer does not satisfy me at all; there is in the corruption of those who reach power by chance something coarse and vulgar which makes it contagious to the crowd, but even in the very depravity of great noblemen there is often a certain aristocratic refinement and an air of grandeur which prevents it from being communicated.

The people never penetrate the obscure labyrinth of the spirit of a court; it is always painful for them to discover the baseness hidden under elegant manners, refined tastes, and graceful phrases. But stealing from the public purse or selling the favors of the state for money —those are matters any wretch can understand and hope to emulate in turn.

Moreover, there is less reason to fear the sight of the immorality of the great than that of immorality leading to greatness. In democracies private citizens see men rising from their ranks and attaining wealth and power in a few years; that spectacle excites their astonishment and their envy; they wonder how he who was their equal yesterday has today won the right to command them. To attribute his rise to his talents or his virtues is inconvenient, for it means admitting that they are less virtuous or capable than he. They therefore regard some of his vices as the main cause thereof, and often they are correct in this view. In this way there comes about an odious mingling of the conceptions of baseness and power, of unworthiness and success, and of profit and dishonor.

The Efforts of Which Democracy Is Capable

The Union has only once fought for its existence. Enthusiasm at the beginning of the war. Indifference at the end. Difficulty of establishing conscription or impressment of seamen in America. Why a democratic nation is less capable than any other of great continuous efforts.

I warn the reader that I am here speaking of a government that follows the real wishes of the people and not of one that simply issues its commands in their name.

There is nothing as irresistible as a tyrannical power commanding in the name of the people, for while being clothed in the moral strength derived from the will of the greatest number, it also acts with the decision, speed, and tenacity of a single man.

It is rather hard to say how great are the efforts a democratic government might make in time of national crisis.

No great democratic republic has yet existed. It would be an insult to republics to use that name for the oligarchy which ruled France in 1793. Only the United States presents this new phenomenon.

Now, in the half century since the Union took shape, its existence has only once been threatened, during the War of Independence. At the beginning of that long war there were extraordinary signs of enthusiasm for the country's service.[16] But as the struggle was prolonged, habitual selfishness reappeared: money no longer reached the public treasury, men no longer volunteered for the army, the people still wanted independence but recoiled before the measures necessary to gain it. "Tax laws have in vain been multiplied; new methods to enforce the collection have in vain been tried," wrote Hamilton in *The Federalist* (No. 12); "the public expectation has been uniformly disappointed, and the treasuries of the states have remained empty. The popular system of administration inherent in the nature of popular government, coinciding with the real scarcity of money incident to a languid and mutilated state of trade, has hitherto defeated every experiment for extensive collections and has at length taught the different legislatures the folly of attempting them."[17]

Since that time the United States has not had a single serious war to sustain.

To judge what sacrifices democracies are capable of imposing on themselves, we must await a time when the American nation will be forced to put half its income into the hands of the government, as England has done, or is bound to throw a twentieth of its population onto the battlefield, as has been done by France.

In America conscription is unknown; men are induced to enlist for pay. Compulsory recruitment is so contrary to the conceptions and alien to the habits of the people of the United States that I doubt whether anyone would ever dare to bring in such a law. In France conscription is certainly the heaviest of all state impositions,

[16] One of the most singular, to my mind, was the resolution by which the Americans temporarily gave up drinking tea. Those who know that men generally stick more tenaciously to their habits than to their lives will certainly be astonished at this great though unpretentious sacrifice made by a whole nation.

[17] [Everyman edition, p. 55.]

but without conscription, how could we sustain a great Continental war?

The Americans have not adopted the English practice of impressing seamen, and they have nothing corresponding to the French system of *inscription maritime*. The national navy, as well as the merchant service, is recruited from volunteers.

But it is hard to conceive that a nation could sustain a great sea war without recourse to one of the measures mentioned above; moreover, the Union, though it has already fought and won glory on the sea, has never had many ships, and the equipment of what few vessels it has, has always been very expensive.

I have heard American statesmen aver that the Union will scarcely hold its rank on the seas if it does not adopt impressment or *inscription maritime;* but the difficulty is to force the people, who rule, to tolerate either one or the other.

It is incontestable that in times of danger a free people generally displays infinitely more energy than one which is not so, but I am inclined to believe that this is especially true of a free people in which the aristocratic element is dominant. Democracy seems to me much better suited to directing a peaceful society, or if necessary, to making some sudden and violent effort rather than to braving over a long period the great storms that beset a nation's political existence. The reason for this is simple: enthusiasm leads men to face dangers and privations, but only reflection will induce them to continue to brave them over a long period. Even in what is called instinctive courage there is more of calculation than is usually supposed; and though it is generally passions alone which cause the first efforts to be made, it is with a view to the outcome that they are continued. One risks a part of what one holds dear to save the rest.

Now, it is this clear perception of the future, based on judgment and experience, which must often be lacking in a democracy. The people feel more strongly than they reason; and if present ills are great, it is to be feared that they will forget the greater evils that perhaps await them in case of defeat.

There is another reason which is bound to make the efforts of a democratic government less enduring than those of an aristocracy.

The people not only see less clearly than the upper classes what can be hoped or feared for the future, but they also suffer the ills of the present in quite another way. The noble who risks his life has equal chances of glory and of danger. In handing over to the state the greater part of his income, he temporarily deprives himself of some of the pleasures of wealth; but there is no glamour in the poor man's death, and that tax which is merely irksome to the rich often threatens the basis of his livelihood.

This relative weakness of democratic republics in time of crisis is perhaps the greatest obstacle preventing the foundation of such a republic in Europe. For a democratic republic to survive without trouble in a European nation, it would be necessary for republics to be established in all the others at the same time.

I think that in the long run government by democracy should increase the real strength of society, but it cannot immediately assemble, at one point and at a given time, forces as great as those at the disposal of an aristocratic government or an absolute monarchy. If for a century a democratic country were to remain under a republican government, one can believe that at the end of that time it would be richer, more populated, and more prosperous than neighboring despotic states; but during that century it would often have run the risk of being conquered by them.

American Democracy's Power of Self-Control

The American people are slow to accept, and sometimes refuse to accept, things beneficial to their prosperity. The American capacity for making mistakes that can be retrieved.

Democracy's difficulty in conquering the passions and silencing momentary requirements in the interest of the future can be observed in the United States in the most trivial things.

The people, surrounded by flatterers, find it hard to master themselves. Whenever anyone tries to persuade them to accept a privation or a discomfort, even for an aim that their reason approves, they always begin by refusing. The Americans rightly boast of their obedience to the laws. But one must add that in America legislation is made by the people and for the people. Therefore law in the United States patently favors those who everywhere else have the greatest interest in violating it. It is therefore fair to suppose that an irksome law of which the majority did not see the immediate utility either would not be passed or would not be obeyed.

There is no American legislation against fraudulent bankruptcies. Is that because there are no bankrupts? No, on the contrary, it is because there are many. In the mind of the majority the fear of being prosecuted as a bankrupt is greater than the apprehension of being ruined by other bankrupts, and so the public conscience has a sort of guilty tolerance for an offense which everyone individually condemns.

In the new states of the Southwest the citizens almost always take justice into their own hands, and murders are of frequent occurrence. That is because the people's habits are too rough and because enlightenment is not sufficiently widespread in that wilderness for people to see the advantage of giving strength to the law; duels are still preferred to lawsuits there.

Someone once told me in Philadelphia that almost all crimes in America are due to the abuse of strong drink, which, being sold cheaply, the lowest classes could consume at will. "How comes it," I asked, "that you do not put a duty on brandy?" "Our legislators have often thought about it," he answered, "but that is a difficult undertaking. There is fear of a revolt, and those who voted for such a law could be certain not to be reelected." "So," I replied, "with you, drunkards are in a majority and temperance is unpopular."

When one points out matters such as these to statesmen, the only answer they give is: "Let time do its work; a sense of the evil will enlighten the people and show them what they need." That is often the truth; a democracy may be more likely to be deceived than a king or a body of nobles, but it also has a better chance of returning to the truth when light does break through, because generally within it there are no interests opposed to the majority and ready to fight against reason. But a democracy cannot get at the truth without experience, and many nations may perish for lack of the time to discover their mistakes.

Therefore the great privilege enjoyed by the Americans is not only to be more enlightened than other nations but also to have the chance to make mistakes that can be retrieved.

One must add that in order to profit by past experience, a democracy must already have reached a certain degree of civilization and enlightenment.

There are peoples whose early education has been so vicious and whose character presents such a strange mixture of passions, ignorance, and mistaken notions on all subjects that they cannot by themselves see the cause of their afflictions; they succumb beneath unrecognized ills.

I have passed through vast lands once inhabited by powerful Indian tribes who now no longer exist; I have passed some time among the remnants of tribes which see their numbers daily decreasing and the brilliance of their savage glories vanishing; and I have heard these Indians themselves foretell the final destiny in store for their race. But every European can see what needs doing to preserve these unlucky people from otherwise inevitable destruction. However, they themselves do not see it; they feel the annually increasing woes that weight them down, and they will perish to the last man rejecting the remedy. Force would be needed to compel them to live.

People are astonished to see the new nations of South America convulsed by one revolution after another throughout the last quarter of a century, and daily expect them to return to what is called their *natural state*. But nowadays who can be sure? May not revolution be the most natural state for the Spaniards of South America? In that country society is floundering at the bottom of an abyss from which its own efforts cannot drag it.

The people dwelling in this beautiful half continent seem obdurately determined to tear out each other's guts; nothing can divert them from that objective. Exhaustion may induce momentary repose, repose the prelude to fresh frenzies. Contemplating their state of wretchedness alternating with bouts of crime, I am tempted to believe that for them despotism would be a blessing.

But those words "despotism" and "blessing" can never join together in my thoughts.

How American Democracy Conducts the External Affairs of the State

Direction given to American foreign policy by Washington and Jefferson. Almost all the natural defects of democracy are to the fore in the conduct of foreign policy, whereas its good qualities are hardly to be seen.

We have noted that the federal Constitution put the permanent control of the nation's foreign interests in the hands of the President and the Senate,[18] which to some extent frees the Union's general policy from direct and daily popular control. One should not therefore assert without qualification that American democracy controls the state's external affairs.

Two men have set a direction for American policy which is still followed today; the first is Washington and the second Jefferson.

[18] The Constitution (Article II, section 2, subsection 2) states that the President "shall have power, by and with the advice and consent of the Senate, to make treaties. . . ." The reader should not forget that senators are elected for a term of six years by the legislatures of each state and they are the result of election by two stages.

Washington, in that admirable letter addressed to his fellow citizens which was that great man's political testament, says:

"The great rule of conduct for us, in regard to foreign nations, is, in extending our commercial relations, to have with them as little *political* connection as possible. So far as we have already formed engagements, let them be fulfilled with perfect good faith. Here let us stop.

"Europe has a set of primary interests which to us have none, or a very remote relation. Hence she must be engaged in frequent controversies, the causes of which are essentially foreign to our concerns. Hence, therefore, it must be unwise in us to implicate ourselves, by artificial ties, in the ordinary vicissitudes of her politics or in the ordinary combinations and the collisions of her friendships or enmities.

"Our detached and distant situation invites and enables us to pursue a different course. If we remain one people, under an efficient government, the period is not far off when we may defy material injury from external annoyance; when we may take such an attitude as will cause the neutrality we may at any time resolve upon to be scrupulously respected; when belligerent nations, under the impossibility of making acquisitions upon us, will not lightly hazard the giving us provocation; when we may choose peace or war, as our interest, guided by justice, shall counsel.

"Why forgo the advantages of so peculiar a situation? Why quit our own to stand upon foreign ground? Why, by interweaving our destiny with that of any part of Europe, entangle our peace and prosperity in the toils of European ambition, rivalship, interest, humor, or caprice?

"It is our true policy to steer clear of permanent alliances with any portion of the foreign world; so far, I mean, as we are now at liberty to do it; for let me not be understood as capable of patronizing infidelity to existing engagements. I hold the maxim no less applicable to public than to private affairs, that honesty is always the best policy. I repeat it, therefore, let those engagements be observed in their genuine sense; but, in my opinion, it is unnecessary and would be unwise to extend them.

"Taking care always to keep ourselves, by suitable establishments, in a respectable defensive posture, we may safely trust to temporary alliances for extraordinary emergencies."[19]

Earlier Washington had expressed this beautiful and true idea: "The nation which indulges towards another an habitual hatred, or an habitual fondness, is in some degree a slave. It is a slave to its animosity or to its affection. . . ."[20]

Washington's political conduct was always guided by these maxims. He succeeded in keeping his country at peace while all the rest of the world was at war, and he established it as a fundamental doctrine that the true interest of the Americans was never to take part in the internal quarrels of Europe.

Jefferson went still further and introduced another maxim into American politics: "that the Americans should never ask for privileges from foreign nations, in order not to be obliged to grant any in return."

These two principles, whose evident truth makes them easily grasped by the multitudes, have greatly simplified the foreign policy of the United States.

As the Union does not meddle in the affairs of Europe, it has, so to say, no external interests at stake, for as yet it has no powerful neighbors in America. Detached by geography as well as by choice from the passions of the Old World, it neither needs to protect itself against them nor to espouse them. As for those of the New World, they are still hidden in the future.

The Union is free from preexisting obligations; it can therefore profit from the experience of Europe without being obliged, as European nations are, to take the past into account and adapt it to the present; nor need it, like them, accept a vast heritage of mixed glory and shame, national friendships and national hatreds, bequeathed by its ancestors. Expectancy is the keynote of American foreign policy; it consists much more in abstaining than in doing.

It is therefore hard as yet to know what talents American democracy might develop in conducting the state's foreign affairs. Both friends and enemies should suspend judgment on that point.

For my part, I have no hesitation in saying that in the control of society's foreign affairs democratic governments do appear decidedly inferior to others. Experience, mores, and education almost always do give a democracy that sort of practical everyday wisdom and understanding of the petty business of life which we call common sense. Common sense is enough for society's current needs, and in a nation whose education has been completed, democratic liberty applied to the state's internal affairs brings blessings greater than the ills resulting from a democratic government's mistakes. But that is not always true of relations between nation and nation.

Foreign policy does not require the use of any of the good qualities peculiar to democracy but does demand the cultivation of almost

20 [*Ibid.,* p. 775.]

all those which it lacks. Democracy favors the growth of the state's internal resources; it extends comfort and develops public spirit, strengthens respect for law in the various classes of society, all of which things have no more than an indirect influence on the standing of one nation in respect to another. But a democracy finds it difficult to coordinate the details of a great undertaking and to fix on some plan and carry it through with determination in spite of obstacles. It has little capacity for combining measures in secret and waiting patiently for the result. Such qualities are more likely to belong to a single man or to an aristocracy. But these are just the qualities which, in the long run, make a nation, and a man too, prevail.

But if you turn your attention to the natural defects of aristocracy, you find that their possible effects are hardly noticeable in the conduct of the state's external affairs. The main vice for which aristocracy is reproached is that of working for itself alone and not for the whole community. However, in foreign policy it very seldom happens that an aristocracy has an interest distinct from that of the people.

In politics the tendency of a democracy to obey its feelings rather than its calculations and to abandon a long-matured plan to satisfy a momentary passion was well seen in America at the time when the French Revolution broke out. The simplest lights of reason were enough then, as they are now, to make the Americans see that they had no interest in joining the struggle which was to lead to such bloodshed in Europe, but from which the United States could suffer no damage.

Nevertheless, the people's sympathies for France declared themselves with such violence that nothing less than the inflexible character of Washington and the immense popularity he enjoyed sufficed to prevent them from declaring war on England. Moreover, the austere arguments used by that great man to combat the generous but ill-considered passions of his fellow citizens came near to depriving him of the only reward he ever claimed, the love of his country. The majority pronounced against his policy; now the whole nation approves it.[21]

21 See the fifth volume of Marshall's *Life of Washington*, p. 314: "The chief magistrate, whatever his firmness, cannot oppose the torrent of popular opinion for long; and the opinion prevailing then seemed to lead to war. In fact, in the session of Congress held at that period, it was frequently noticed that Washington had lost the majority in the House of Representatives." Furthermore, the violence of the language used against him was extreme: at a political meeting someone was not afraid to compare him indirectly to the traitor Arnold (p. 265). On page 353 Marshall says that "those who held to the opposition party claimed that the partisans of the administration composed an

If the Constitution and public favor had not given Washington control over the state's foreign policy, it is certain that the nation would then have done exactly what it now condemns.

Almost all the nations that have exercised a powerful influence on the world's destiny by conceiving, following up, and carrying to completion great designs, from the Romans down to the English, were controlled by an aristocracy, and how can one be surprised at that?

Nothing in the world is so fixed in its views as an aristocracy. The mass of the people may be seduced by its ignorance or its passions; a king may be taken off his guard and induced to vacillate in his plans; and moreover, a king is not immortal. But an aristocratic body is too numerous to be caught, and yet so small that it does not easily yield to the intoxication of thoughtless passions. An aristocratic body is a firm and enlightened man who never dies.

---

aristocratic faction which was subject to England and which, wanting to establish monarchy, was consequently the enemy of France, a faction whose members constituted a sort of nobility, which had the actions of the bank as titles, and which had such a great fear of any measure which could influence funds that it was insensitive to the affronts which the honor and interest of the nation also command it to repel." [These three references to Marshall's work paraphrase and summarize to some extent; Tocqueville refers here to the French edition of his work, Vol. I, Paris, 1807. With regard to the last reference, we have again corrected Tocqueville: the quotation is to be found on p. 353, not on p. 355.]

Chapter 6

THE REAL ADVANTAGES DERIVED
BY AMERICAN SOCIETY FROM
DEMOCRATIC GOVERNMENT

BEFORE BEGINNING THIS CHAPTER I must remind the reader of something already mentioned several times in the course of this book.

The political constitution of the United States seems to me to be one of the forms that democracy can give to its government, but I do not think that American institutions are the only ones, or the best, that a democratic nation might adopt.

So in pointing out the blessings which the Americans derive from democratic government, I am far from claiming or from thinking that such advantages can only be obtained by the same laws.

The General Tendency of Laws Under the Sway of American Democracy and the Instincts of Those Who Apply Them

The vices of democracy are immediately apparent. Its advantages only become clear in the long run. American democracy is often clumsy, but the general tendency of its laws is advantageous. Under American democracy public officials have no permanent interests differing from those of the majority. The results of this.

The vices and weaknesses of democratic government are easy to see; they can be proved by obvious facts, whereas its salutary influence is exercised in an imperceptible and almost secret way. Its defects strike one at first glance, but its good qualities are revealed only in the long run.

The laws of American democracy are often defective or incomplete; they sometimes violate acquired rights or sanction dangerous ones; even if they were good, their frequent changes would be a great evil. All this is seen at first glance.

How, then, do the American republics maintain themselves and prosper?

In laws one should make a careful distinction between the aim sought and the way in which they progress toward that aim, and between their absolute and their relative excellence.

Suppose that the lawgiver's aim is to favor the interests of the few at the expense of the many; his measures are so combined as to accomplish the proposed aim in the shortest time and with least possible effort. The law will be well contrived, but its object bad; its very efficiency will make it the more dangerous.

In general, the laws of a democracy tend toward the good of the greatest number, for they spring from the majority of all the citizens, which may be mistaken but which cannot have an interest contrary to its own.

But those of an aristocracy do tend to monopolize power and wealth in the hands of a few, because in the nature of things an aristocracy is a minority.

One can therefore say in general terms that democracy's aim in its legislation is more beneficial to humanity than that of aristocracy in its lawmaking.

But there its advantages end.

An aristocracy is infinitely more skillful in the science of legislation than democracy can ever be. Being master of itself, it is not subject to transitory impulses; it has far-sighted plans and knows how to let them mature until the favorable opportunity offers. An aristocracy moves forward intelligently; it knows how to make the collective force of all its laws converge on one point at one time.

A democracy is not like that; its laws are almost always defective or untimely.

Therefore the measures of democracy are more imperfect than those of an aristocracy; it often unintentionally works against itself; but its aim is more beneficial.

Suppose a society so organized by nature or by its constitution that it can tolerate the passing effect of bad laws and can without disaster await the result of the *general tendency* of its laws, and in such a case you will appreciate that democratic government, for all its faults, is yet the best suited of all to make society prosper.

That is just what does happen in the United States; I here repeat what I have described elsewhere: the great privilege of the Americans is to be able to make retrievable mistakes.

I would say something similar about the public officials.

It is easy to see that American democracy often makes mistakes in the choice of men to whom it entrusts power, but it is not so easy to say why the state prospers in their hands.

Notice first that in a democratic state, though the rulers be less honest or less capable, the governed are more enlightened and more alert.

In democracies the people, constantly occupied as they are with their affairs and jealous of their rights, prevent their representatives from deviating from a general line indicated by their interests.

Note also that although a democratic magistrate may use his power worse than another, he generally holds it for a shorter time.

But there is a more general and satisfactory reason than any of these.

No doubt it is important for nations that their rulers should possess virtues and talents, but perhaps it is even more important for them that the rulers should not have interests contrary to those of the mass of the governed, for in that case their virtues might become almost useless and their talents disastrous.

I have said that it was important for the rulers not to have interests contrary or different from those of the mass of the ruled. I do not say that they should have interests similar to those of *all* the governed, for I don't suppose that such a thing has ever happened.

No one has yet found a political structure that equally favors the growth and prosperity of all the classes composing society. These classes have formed something like distinct nations within the same nation, and experience has proved it almost as dangerous completely to entrust the fate of all to one of these as it is to make one nation arbiter of the destiny of another. When the rich alone rule, the interests of the poor are always in danger; and when the poor make the law, the interests of the rich run great risks. What, then, is the advantage of democracy? The real advantage of democracy is not, as some have said, to favor the prosperity of all, but only to serve the well-being of the greatest number.

In the United States those who are entrusted with the direction of public affairs are often inferior both in capacity and in morality to those whom an aristocracy might bring to power; but their interest is mingled and identified with that of the majority of their fellow citizens. Hence they may often prove untrustworthy and make great mistakes, but they will never systematically follow a tendency hostile to the majority; they will never turn the government into something exclusive and dangerous.

The bad administration of one magistrate under a democracy is, moreover, an isolated fact that has an influence only during the short period of his tenure of office. Corruption and incapacity are not common interests capable of linking men in any permanent fashion.

A corrupt or incapable magistrate will not combine his efforts with another magistrate's simply because the latter is corrupt or incapable too, and these two men will never work in concert so that corruption or incapacity may flourish among their posterity. Quite the contrary, the ambition and intrigues of the one will help to unmask the other. Generally speaking, in a democracy the vices of a magistrate are altogether personal.

But under aristocratic rule public men have a class interest which, though it sometimes agrees with that of the majority, is more often distinct therefrom. That interest forms a lasting common link between them; it invites them to unite and combine their endeavors toward an aim which is not always the happiness of the greatest number. It not only forms a link between the actual rulers but also unites them with a considerable section of the ruled, for many of the citizens, without having any office, form part of the aristocracy.

The aristocratic magistrate therefore finds constant support within society, as well as from the government.

This common objective which in aristocracies unites the magistrates with the interests of one portion of their contemporaries identifies them also, so to say, with that of future generations. They work for the future as well as for the present. Hence the aristocratic magistrate is impelled at the same time and in the same direction by the passions of the ruled, by his own, and, I might almost say, by the passions of those who come after him.

How can we be surprised if he puts up no resistance? So in aristocracies one often sees class spirit carrying away even those who are not corrupted by it and finds that they are unconsciously shaping society gradually to their convenience and that of their descendants.

I do not know if there has ever been another aristocracy as liberal as that of England or one that has uninterruptedly furnished the government with men so worthy and so enlightened.

Nevertheless, it is easy to see that in English legislation the poor man's welfare has in the end often been sacrificed to that of the rich, and the rights of the greatest number have been sacrificed to the privileges of the few; and so England now contains within herself every extreme of human fate, and one there finds wretchedness almost as great as the greatness of her power and glory.

In the United States, where public officials have no class interest to promote, the general and continuous course of the government is beneficial, although the rulers are often inept and sometimes contemptible.

There is therefore at the bottom of democratic institutions some hidden tendency which often makes men promote the general prosperity, in spite of their vices and their mistakes, whereas in aristocratic institutions there is sometimes a secret bias which, in spite of talents and virtues, leads men to contribute to the afflictions of their fellows. In this way it may come about that under aristocratic governments public men do evil without intending it, and in democracies they bring about good results of which they have never thought.

Public Spirit in the United States

Instinctive patriotism. Well-considered patriotism. Their different characteristics. Why nations must strive with all their strength toward the second when the first has disappeared. The efforts of the Americans to achieve this. Individual interest intimately linked to that of the country.

There is a patriotism which mainly springs from the disinterested, undefinable, and unpondered feeling that ties a man's heart to the place where he was born. This instinctive love is mingled with a taste for old habits, respect for ancestors, and memories of the past; those who feel it love their country as one loves one's father's house. They love the peace they enjoy there; they are attached to the quiet habits they have formed; they are attached to the memories it recalls; and they even find a certain attraction in living there in obedience. This same patriotism is often also exalted by religious zeal, and then it works wonders. It is itself a sort of religion; it does not reason, but believes, feels, and acts. Some nations have in a sense personified their country and see the monarch as standing for it. Hence they have transferred some of the feelings of patriotism to him, and they boast of his triumphs and are proud of his power. There was a time under the old monarchy when the French experienced a sort of joy in surrendering themselves irrevocably to the arbitrary will of their monarch and said with pride: "We live under the most powerful king in the world."

Like all unpondered passions, this patriotism impels men to great ephemeral efforts, but not to continuous endeavor. Having saved the state in time of crisis, it often lets it decay in time of peace.

When peoples are still simple in their mores and firm in their belief, when society gently rests on an ancient order of things whose legitimacy is not contested, then that instinctive patriotism prevails.

There is also another sort of patriotism more rational than that; less generous, perhaps less ardent, but more creative and more lasting, it is engendered by enlightenment, grows by the aid of laws and the exercise of rights, and in the end becomes, in a sense, mingled with personal interest. A man understands the influence which his country's well-being has on his own; he knows the law allows him to contribute to the production of this well-being, and he takes an interest in his country's prosperity, first as a thing useful to him and then as something he has created.

But sometimes there comes a time in the life of nations when old customs are changed, mores destroyed, beliefs shaken, and the prestige of memories has vanished, but when nonetheless enlightenment has remained incomplete and political rights are ill-assured or restricted. Then men see their country only by a weak and doubtful light; their patriotism is not centered on the soil, which in their eyes is just inanimate earth, nor on the customs of their ancestors, which they have been taught to regard as a yoke, nor on religion, which they doubt, nor on the laws, which they do not make, nor on the lawgiver, whom they fear and scorn. So they find their country nowhere, recognizing neither its own nor any borrowed features, and they retreat into a narrow and unenlightened egoism. Such men escape from prejudices without recognizing the rule of reason; they have neither the instinctive patriotism of a monarchy nor the reflective patriotism of a republic, but have come to a halt between the two amid confusion and misery.

What can be done in such a condition? Retreat. But nations do not return to the feelings of their youth any more than men return to the innocent tastes of their infancy; they may regret them, but they cannot bring them back to life. Therefore it is essential to march forward and hasten to make the people see that individual interest is linked to that of the country, for disinterested patriotism has fled beyond recall.

Certainly I am far from claiming that in order to reach this result the exercise of political rights must immediately be granted to every man; but I do say that the most powerful way, and perhaps the only remaining way, in which to interest men in their country's fate is to make them take a share in its government. In our day it seems to me that civic spirit is inseparable from the exercise of political rights, and I think that henceforward in Europe the numbers of the citizens will be found to increase or diminish in proportion to the extension of those rights.

How is it that in the United States, where the inhabitants arrived but yesterday in the land they occupy, whither they brought with them neither customs nor memories, where they meet for the first time without knowing each other, where, to say it in one word, the instinct of country can hardly exist—how does it come about that each man is as interested in the affairs of his township, of his canton, and of the whole state as he is in his own affairs? It is because each man in his sphere takes an active part in the government of society.

The common man in the United States has understood the influence of the general prosperity on his own happiness, an idea so simple but nevertheless so little understood by the people. Moreover, he is accustomed to regard that prosperity as his own work. So he sees the public fortune as his own, and he works for the good of the state, not only from duty or from pride, but, I dare almost say, from greed.

There is no need to study the institutions or the history of the Americans to recognize the truth of what has just been said, for their mores are sufficient evidence of it. The American, taking part in everything that is done in his country, feels a duty to defend anything criticized there, for it is not only his country that is being attacked, but himself; hence one finds that his national pride has recourse to every artifice and descends to every childishness of personal vanity.

Nothing is more annoying in the ordinary intercourse of life than this irritable patriotism of the Americans. A foreigner will gladly agree to praise much in their country, but he would like to be allowed to criticize something, and that he is absolutely refused.

So America is the land of freedom where, in order not to offend anybody, the foreigner may speak freely neither about individuals nor about the state, neither about the ruled nor about the rulers, neither about public undertakings nor about private ones—indeed, about nothing that one comes across, except perhaps the climate and the soil, but yet one meets Americans ready to defend both of these, as if they had a share in forming them.

In our day we must make up our minds and dare to choose between the patriotism of all and the government of the few, for one cannot combine at the same time the social strength and activity given by the first with the guarantees of tranquillity sometimes provided by the second.

The Idea of Rights in the United States

No great people is without an idea of rights. How such a conception can be imparted to a nation. Respect for rights in the United States. Source of that respect.

Next to virtue as a general idea, nothing, I think, is so beautiful as that of rights, and indeed the two ideas are mingled. The idea of rights is nothing but the conception of virtue applied to the world of politics.

By means of the idea of rights men have defined the nature of license and of tyranny. Guided by its light, we can each of us be independent without arrogance and obedient without servility. When a man submits to force, that surrender debases him; but when he accepts the recognized right of a fellow mortal to give him orders, there is a sense in which he rises above the giver of the commands. No man can be great without virtue, nor any nation great without respect for rights; one might almost say that without it there can be no society, for what is a combination of rational and intelligent beings held together by force alone?

I keep asking myself how, in our day, this conception may be taught to mankind and made, so to say, palpable to their senses; and I find one only, namely, to give them all the peaceful use of certain rights. One can see how this works among children, who are men except in strength and in experience; when a baby first begins to move among things outside himself, instinct leads him to make use of anything his hands can grasp; he has no idea of other people's property, not even that it exists; but as he is instructed in the value of things and discovers that he too may be despoiled, he becomes more circumspect, and in the end is led to respect for others that which he wishes to be respected for himself.

As for a child with his toys, so is it later for a man with all his belongings. Why is it that in America, the land par excellence of democracy, no one makes that outcry against property in general that often echoes through Europe? Is there any need to explain? It is because there are no proletarians in America. Everyone, having some possession to defend, recognizes the right to property in principle.

It is the same in the world of politics. The American man of the people has conceived a high idea of political rights because he has some; he does not attack those of others, in order that his own may not be violated. Whereas the corresponding man in Europe would be prejudiced against all authority, even the highest, the American uncomplainingly obeys the lowest of his officials.

This truth is illustrated even in the smallest details of a nation's life. In France there are few pleasures exclusively reserved for the higher classes of society; the poor man is admitted almost everywhere where the rich can go, so one finds him behaving decently and with proper consideration for pleasures in which he shares. In England, where enjoyment is the privilege of the rich, who also monopolize power, people complain that when a poor man does furtively steal into the exclusive haunts of the rich he has a taste for causing pointless damage there. Why be surprised at that? Trouble has been taken to see that he has nothing to lose.

Democratic government makes the idea of political rights penetrate right down to the least of citizens, just as the division of property puts the general idea of property rights within reach of all. That, in my view, is one of its greatest merits.

I am not asserting it to be an easy matter to teach all men to make use of political rights; I only say that when that can happen, the results are important.

And I would add that if ever there was a century in which such an attempt should be made, that century is ours.

Do you not see that religions are growing weak and that the conception of the sanctity of rights is vanishing? Do you not see that mores are changing and that the moral conception of rights is being obliterated with them?

Do you not notice how on all sides beliefs are giving way to arguments, and feelings to calculations? If amid this universal collapse you do not succeed in linking the idea of rights to personal interest, which provides the only stable point in the human heart, what other means will be left to you to govern the world, if not fear?

So, then, when I am told that laws are feeble and the governed turbulent, that passions are lively and virtue powerless, and that in this situation one must not dream of increasing the rights of democracy, I answer that it is for these very reasons that one must consider doing so, and in truth, I think the governments have an even greater interest in doing this than has society, for governments perish but society cannot die. However, I do not wish to press the example of America too far.

In America the people were invested with political rights at a time when it was difficult for them to make ill use of them because the citizens were few and their mores simple. As they have grown more powerful, the Americans have not appreciably increased the powers of democracy; rather they have extended its domain.

There can be no doubt that the moment when political rights are granted to a people who have till then been deprived of them is a time of crisis, a crisis which is often necessary but always dangerous.

A child may kill when he does not understand the value of life; he carries off other people's property before he knows that his own may be snatched from him. The man of the people, at the moment when political rights are granted to him, is much in the same position with respect to those rights as is a child faced by the whole of nature, and it is then that famous phrase applies: *homo puer robustus.*

This truth can be tested even in America. Those states in which the citizens have longest enjoyed their rights are those in which they still best know how to use them.

It cannot be repeated too often: nothing is more fertile in marvels than the art of being free, but nothing is harder than freedom's apprenticeship. The same is not true of despotism. Despotism often presents itself as the repairer of all the ills suffered, the support of just rights, defender of the oppressed, and founder of order. Peoples are lulled to sleep by the temporary prosperity it engenders, and when they do wake up, they are wretched. But liberty is generally born in stormy weather, growing with difficulty amid civil discords, and only when it is already old does one see the blessings it has brought.

Respect for Law in the United States

American respect for law. Paternal affection they feel for it. Personal interest of everybody in increasing the law's strength.

It is not always feasible to call on the whole people, either directly or indirectly, to take its part in lawmaking, but no one can deny that when that can be done the law derives great authority therefrom. This popular origin, though often damaging to the wisdom and quality of legislation, gives it peculiar strength.

There is prodigious force in the expression of the wills of a whole people. When it stands out in broad daylight, even the imagination of those who would like to contest it is somehow smothered.

Parties are well aware of this truth.

For that reason, whenever possible they cast doubts on the majority's validity. Having failed to gain a majority from those who voted, they claim it among those who abstained from voting, and if that fails them, they claim a majority among those who have no right to vote.

In the United States, except for slaves, servants, and paupers fed by the township, no one is without a vote and, hence, an indirect share in lawmaking. Therefore those who would like to attack the laws are forced to adopt ostensibly one of two courses: they must either change the nation's opinion or trample its wishes under foot.

There is a second reason, too, more direct and powerful in its effect, namely, that every American feels a sort of personal interest in obeying the laws, for a man who is not today one of the majority party may be so tomorrow, and so he may soon be demanding for laws of his choosing that respect which he now professes for the lawgiver's will. Therefore, however annoying a law may be, the American will submit to it, not only as the work of the majority but also as his own doing; he regards it as a contract to which he is one of the parties.

So in the United States there is no numerous and perpetually turbulent crowd regarding the law as a natural enemy to fear and to suspect. On the contrary, one is bound to notice that all classes show great confidence in their country's legislation, feeling a sort of paternal love for it.

I am wrong in saying all classes. As in America, the European ladder of power has been turned upside down; the wealthy find themselves in a position analogous to that of the poor in Europe: it is they who often mistrust the law. As I have said elsewhere, the real advantage of democratic government is not that it guarantees the interests of all, as is sometimes claimed, but just that it does protect those of the greatest number. In the United States, where the poor man rules, the rich have always some fear that he may abuse his power against them.

This state of mind among the wealthy may produce a silent discontent, but it creates no violent trouble for society, for the same reason which prevents the rich man from trusting the lawgiver also prevents him from defying his commands. Because he is rich he does not make the law, and because of his wealth he does not dare to break it. Among civilized nations it is generally only those with nothing to lose who revolt. Hence, though democratic laws may not always deserve respect, they are almost always respected, for those who usually break the laws cannot fail to obey those they have made and from which they profit, and those citizens who might have an interest in infringing them are impelled both by character and by circumstance to submit to the lawgiver's will, whatever it may be. Moreover, in America the people obey the law not only because it is their work but also because they can change it if by any chance it does injure them; they submit to it primarily as a self-imposed evil, and secondly as a passing one.

Activity Prevailing in All Parts of the Political Body in the United States; the Influence Thereby Exerted on Society

The political activity prevailing in the United States is harder to conceive than the freedom and equality found there. The continual feverish activity of the legislatures is only an episode and an extension of a movement that is universal. How difficult an Amer-

*ican finds it to be occupied with his own business only. Political
agitation spills over into civil society. The industrial activity of
the Americans is in part due to this. Indirect advantages derived by
society from democratic government.*

When one passes from a free country into another which is not so,
the contrast is very striking: there, all is activity and bustle; here all
seems calm and immobile. In the former, betterment and progress
are the questions of the day; in the latter, one might suppose that
society, having acquired every blessing, longs for nothing but repose
in which to enjoy them. Nevertheless, the country which is in such a
rush to attain happiness is generally richer and more prosperous than
the one that seems contented with its lot. And considering them one
by one, it is hard to understand how this one daily discovers so many
new needs, while the other seems conscious of so few.

While this remark applies to free countries that have preserved the
forms of monarchy and to those dominated by an aristocracy, it is
even more true of democratic republics. In them it is not only one
section of the people that undertakes to better the state of society, for
the whole nation is concerned therewith. It is not just the necessities
and comforts of one class that must be provided for, but those of
all classes at once.

It is not impossible to conceive the immense freedom enjoyed by
the Americans, and one can also form an idea of their extreme
equality, but the political activity prevailing in the United States is
something one could never understand unless one had seen it.

No sooner do you set foot on American soil than you find yourself
in a sort of tumult; a confused clamor rises on every side, and a
thousand voices are heard at once, each expressing some social requirements. All around you everything is on the move: here the people of a district are assembled to discuss the possibility of building a
church; there they are busy choosing a representative; further on,
the delegates of a district are hurrying to town to consult about some
local improvements; elsewhere it's the village farmers who have left
their furrows to discuss the plan for a road or a school. One group
of citizens assembles for the sole object of announcing that they disapprove of the government's course, while others unite to proclaim
that the men in office are the fathers of their country. And here
is yet another gathering which regards drunkenness as the main
source of ills in the state and has come to enter into a solemn undertaking to give an example of temperance.[1]

[1] Temperance societies are associations whose members undertake to abstain
from strong drink. At the time of my visit temperance societies already counted

The great political movement which keeps American legislatures in a state of continual agitation, and which alone is noticed from outside, is only an episode and a sort of extension of the universal movement, which begins in the lowest ranks of the people and thence spreads successively through all classes of citizens. No one could work harder to be happy.

It is hard to explain the place filled by political concerns in the life of an American. To take a hand in the government of society and to talk about it is his most important business and, so to say, the only pleasure he knows. That is obvious even in the most trivial habits of his life; even the women often go to public meetings and forget household cares while they listen to political speeches. For them clubs to some extent take the place of theaters. An American does not know how to converse, but he argues; he does not talk, but expatiates. He always speaks to you as if addressing a meeting, and if he happens to get excited, he will say "Gentlemen" when addressing an audience of one.

The inhabitant in some countries shows a sort of repugnance in accepting the political rights granted to him by the law; it strikes him as a waste of time to spend it on communal interests, and he likes to shut himself up in a narrow egoism, of which four ditches with hedges on top define the precise limits.

But if an American should be reduced to occupying himself with his own affairs, at that moment half his existence would be snatched from him; he would feel it as a vast void in his life and would become incredibly unhappy.[2]

I am convinced that if despotism ever came to be established in the United States it would find it even more difficult to overcome the habits that have sprung from freedom than to conquer the love of freedom itself.

That constantly renewed agitation introduced by democratic government into political life passes, then, into civil society. Perhaps, taking everything into consideration, that is the greatest advantage of democratic government, and I praise it much more on account of what it causes to be done than for what it does.

It is incontestible that the people often manage public affairs very badly, but their concern therewith is bound to extend their

more than 270,000 members, and consequently, in the state of Pennsylvania alone the consumption of strong liquors had fallen by 500,000 gallons a year.

[2] The same fact was already noted at Rome under the first Caesars. Montesquieu remarks somewhere that nothing equals the despair of certain Roman citizens who after the excitements of a political existence suddenly return to the calm of private life.

mental horizon and shake them out of the rut of ordinary routine. A man of the people, when asked to share the task of governing society, acquires a certain self-esteem. Since he then has power, the brains of very enlightened people are put at his disposal. Constant efforts are made to enlist his support, and he learns from a thousand different efforts to deceive him. In politics he takes a part in under-takings he has not thought of, and they give him a general taste for enterprise. Daily new improvements to communal property are suggested to him, and that starts him wishing to improve his own. He may not be more virtuous or happier than his forebears, but he is more enlightened and active. I have no doubt that democratic institutions, combined with the physical nature of the land, are the indirect reason, and not, as is often claimed, the direct one, for the prodigious industrial expansion seen in the United States. It is not the laws' creation, but the people have learned to achieve it by mak-ing the laws.

When the enemies of democracy claim that a single man does his appointed task better than the government of all, I think they are right. There is more consistency in one man's rule than in that of a multitude, assuming equal enlightenment on either side; one man is more persevering, has more idea of the whole problem, at-tends more closely to details, and is a better judge of men. Anyone who denies that either has never seen a democratic republic or bases his view on too few examples. Democracy, even when local circum-stances and the character of the people allow it to maintain itself, does not display a regular or methodical form of government. That is true. Democratic freedom does not carry its undertakings through as perfectly as an intelligent despotism would; it often abandons them before it has reaped the profit, or embarks on perilous ones; but in the long run it produces more; each thing is less well done, but more things are done. Under its sway it is not especially the things accom-plished by the public administration that are great, but rather those things done without its help and beyond its sphere. Democracy does not provide a people with the most skillful of governments, but it does that which the most skillful government often cannot do: it spreads throughout the body social a restless activity, superabundant force, and energy never found elsewhere, which, however little favored by cir-cumstance, can do wonders. Those are its true advantages.

In this century, when the destinies of the Christian world seem in suspense, some hasten to assail democracy as a hostile power while it is still growing; others already worship this new deity emerging from chaos. But both parties have an imperfect knowledge of the object of their hate or their desire; they fight in the dark and strike at random.

What do you expect from society and its government? We must be clear about that.

Do you wish to raise mankind to an elevated and generous view of the things of this world? Do you want to inspire men with a certain scorn of material goods? Do you hope to engender deep convictions and prepare the way for acts of profound devotion?

Are you concerned with refining mores, elevating manners, and causing the arts to blossom? Do you desire poetry, renown, and glory?

Do you set out to organize a nation so that it will have a powerful influence over all others? Do you expect it to attempt great enterprises and, whatever be the result of its efforts, to leave a great mark on history?

If in your view that should be the main object of men in society, do not support democratic government; it surely will not lead you to that goal.

But if you think it profitable to turn man's intellectual and moral activity toward the necessities of physical life and use them to produce well-being, if you think that reason is more use to men than genius, if your object is not to create heroic virtues but rather tranquil habits, if you would rather contemplate vices than crimes and prefer fewer transgressions at the cost of fewer splendid deeds, if in place of a brilliant society you are content to live in one that is prosperous, and finally, if in your view the main object of government is not to achieve the greatest strength or glory for the nation as a whole but to provide for every individual therein the utmost well-being, protecting him as far as possible from all afflictions, then it is good to make conditions equal and to establish a democratic government.

But if there is no time left to make a choice, and if a force beyond human control is already carrying you along regardless of your desires toward one of these types of government, then at least seek to derive from it all the good that it can do; understanding its good instincts as well as its evil inclinations, try to restrain the latter and promote the former.

Chapter 7

THE OMNIPOTENCE OF THE MAJORITY IN THE UNITED STATES AND ITS EFFECTS

The natural strength of the majority in democracies. Most of the American constitutions have artificially increased this natural strength. How? Pledged delegates. Moral power of the majority. View of its infallibility. Respects for its rights. What increases it in the United States.

THE ABSOLUTE SOVEREIGNTY of the will of the majority is the essence of democratic government, for in democracies there is nothing outside the majority capable of resisting it.

Most American constitutions have sought further artificially to increase this natural strength of the majority.[1]

Of all political powers, the legislature is the one most ready to obey the wishes of the majority. The Americans wanted the members of the legislatures to be appointed *directly* by the people and for a *very short* term of office so that they should be obliged to submit not only to the general views but also to the passing passions of their constituents.

The members of both houses have been chosen from the same class and appointed in the same way, so that the activity of the legislative body is almost as quick and just as irresistible as that of a single assembly.

Having constituted the legislature in this way, almost all the powers of government were concentrated in its hands.

At the same time as the law increased the strength of naturally powerful authorities, it increasingly weakened those that were by nature feeble. It gave the representatives of the executive neither

[1] In examining the federal Constitution we have seen that the lawgivers of the Union strove in the opposite direction. The result of their efforts has been to make the federal government more independent in its sphere than are the states in theirs. But the federal government is hardly concerned with anything except foreign affairs; it is the state governments which really control American society.

stability nor independence, and by subjecting them completely to the caprices of the legislature, deprived them of what little influence the nature of democratic government might have allowed them to enjoy.

In several states the majority elected the judges, and in all they depended in a way on the legislature, whose members had the right annually to fix their salaries.

Custom has gone even beyond the laws.

A custom is spreading more and more in the United States which will end by making the guarantees of representative government vain; it frequently happens that the electors, when they nominate a deputy, lay down a plan of conduct for him and impose some positive obligations on him which he cannot avoid. It is as if, with tumult threatening, the majority were deliberating in the market-place.

In America several particular circumstances also tend to make the power of the majority not only predominant but irresistible.

The moral authority of the majority is partly based on the notion that there is more enlightenment and wisdom in a numerous assembly than in a single man, and the number of the legislators is more important than how they are chosen. It is the theory of equality applied to brains. This doctrine attacks the last asylum of human pride; for that reason the minority is reluctant in admitting it and takes a long time to get used to it. Like all powers, and perhaps more than any other of them, the power of the majority needs to have proved lasting to appear legitimate. When it is beginning to establish itself, it enforces obedience by constraint; it is only when men have long lived under its laws that they begin to respect it.

The idea that the majority has a right based on enlightenment to govern society was brought to the United States by its first inhabitants; and this idea, which would of itself be enough to create a free nation, has by now passed into mores and affects even the smallest habits of life.

Under the old monarchy the French took it as a maxim that the king could do no wrong, and when he did do wrong, they thought the fault lay with his advisers. This made obedience wonderfully much easier. One could grumble against the law without ceasing to love and respect the lawgiver. The Americans take the same view of the majority.

The moral authority of the majority is also founded on the principle that the interest of the greatest number should be preferred to that of those who are fewer. Now, it is easy to understand that the respect professed for this right of the greatest number naturally grows or shrinks according to the state of the parties. When a nation is divided between several great irreconcilable interests, the privilege of the majority is often disregarded, for it would be too unpleasant to submit to it.

If there existed in America one class of citizens whom the legislators were trying to deprive of certain exclusive privileges possessed for centuries and wanted to force them down from a high station to join the ranks of the crowd, it is probable that that minority would not easily submit to its laws.

But as men equal among themselves came to people the United States, there is as yet no natural or permanent antagonism between the interests of the various inhabitants.

There are states of society in which those who are in the minority cannot hope to win the majority over, for to do so would involve abandoning the very aim of the struggle in which they are engaged against it. An aristocracy, for instance, could not become a majority without giving up its exclusive privileges, and if it did let them go, it would no longer be an aristocracy.

In the United States, political questions cannot arise in such general and absolute fashion, and all the parties are ready to recognize the rights of the majority because they all hope one day to profit themselves by them.

Hence the majority in the United States has immense actual power and a power of opinion which is almost as great. When once its mind is made up on any question, there are, so to say, no obstacles which can retard, much less halt, its progress and give it time to hear the wails of those it crushes as it passes.

The consequences of this state of affairs are fate-laden and dangerous for the future.

How in America the Omnipotence of the Majority Increases the Legislative and Administrative Instability Natural to Democracies

How the Americans increase the legislative instability natural to democracies by changing their legislators every year and by giving them almost limitless power. The same effect on the administration. In America the drive toward social improvements is infinitely greater but less continuous than in Europe.

I have spoken before of the vices natural to democratic government, and every single one of them increases with the growing power of the majority.

To begin with the most obvious of all:

Legislative instability is an ill inherent in democratic government because it is the nature of democracies to bring new men to power. But this ill is greater or less according to the power and means of action accorded to the legislator.

In America the lawmaking authority has been given sovereign power. This authority can carry out anything it desires quickly and irresistibly, and its representatives change annually. That it is to say, just that combination has been chosen which most encourages democratic instability and allows the changing wishes of democracy to be applied to the most important matters.

Thus American laws have a shorter duration than those of any other country in the world today. Almost all American constitutions have been amended within the last thirty years, and so there is no American state which has not modified the basis of its laws within that period.

As for the laws themselves, it is enough to glance at the archives of the various states of the Union to realize that in America the legislator's activity never slows down. Not that American democracy is by nature more unstable than any other, but it has been given the means to carry the natural instability of its inclinations into the making of laws.[2]

The omnipotence of the majority and the rapid as well as absolute manner in which its decisions are executed in the United States not only make the law unstable but have a like effect on the execution of the law and on public administrative activity.

As the majority is the only power whom it is important to please, all its projects are taken up with great ardor; but as soon as its attention is turned elsewhere, all these efforts cease; whereas in free European states, where the administrative authority has an independent existence and an assured position, the legislator's wishes continue to be executed even when he is occupied by other matters.

Much more zeal and energy are brought to bear in America on certain improvements than anywhere else.

In Europe an infinitely smaller social force is employed, but more continuously.

A few years ago some pious people undertook to make the state

[2] The legislative acts promulgated by the state of Massachusetts alone between 1780 and the present day already fill three large volumes. Moreover, one must note that the collection to which I refer was revised in 1823, and that many outdated laws and those that had become irrelevant were omitted. Now, the state of Massachusetts, which has a population no greater than one of our departments, might be taken as the most stable in the whole Union and the one which shows most continuity and wisdom in its undertakings.

of the prisons better. The public was roused by their exhortations, and the reform of criminals became a popular cause.

New prisons were then built. For the first time the idea of reforming offenders as well as punishing them penetrated into the prisons. But that happy revolution in which the public cooperated with such eagerness and which the simultaneous efforts of the citizens rendered irresistible could not be accomplished in a moment.

Alongside the new penitentiaries, built quickly in response to the public's desire, the old prisons remained and housed a great number of the guilty. These seemed to become more unhealthy and more corrupting at the same rate as the new ones became healthy and devoted to reform. This double effect is easily understood: the majority, preoccupied with the idea of founding a new establishment, had forgotten the already existing ones. Everybody's attention was turned away from the matter that no longer held their master's, and supervision ceased. The salutary bonds of discipline were first stretched and then soon broken. And beside some prison that stood as a durable monument to the gentleness and enlightenment of our age, there was a dungeon recalling the barbarities of the Middle Ages.

Tyranny of the Majority

How the principle of the sovereignty of the people should be understood. Impossibility of conceiving a mixed government. Sovereign power must be placed somewhere. Precautions which one should take to moderate its action. These precautions have not been taken in the United States. Result thereof.

I regard it as an impious and detestable maxim that in matters of government the majority of a people has the right to do everything, and nevertheless I place the origin of all powers in the will of the majority. Am I in contradiction with myself?

There is one law which has been made, or at least adopted, not by the majority of this or that people, but by the majority of all men. That law is justice.

Justice therefore forms the boundary to each people's right.

A nation is like a jury entrusted to represent universal society and to apply the justice which is its law. Should the jury representing society have greater power than that very society whose laws it applies?

Consequently, when I refuse to obey an unjust law, I by no

means deny the majority's right to give orders; I only appeal from the sovereignty of the people to the sovereignty of the human race.

There are those not afraid to say that in matters which only concern itself a nation cannot go completely beyond the bounds of justice and reason and that there is therefore no need to fear giving total power to the majority representing it. But that is the language of a slave.

What is a majority, in its collective capacity, if not an individual with opinions, and usually with interests, contrary to those of another individual, called the minority? Now, if you admit that a man vested with omnipotence can abuse it against his adversaries, why not admit the same concerning a majority? Have men, by joining together, changed their character? By becoming stronger, have they become more patient of obstacles?[3] For my part, I cannot believe that, and I will never grant to several that power to do everything which I refuse to a single man.

It is not that I think that in order to preserve liberty one can mix several principles within the same government in such a way that they will be really opposed to one another.

I have always considered what is called a mixed government to be a chimera. There is in truth no such thing as a mixed government (in the sense usually given to the words), since in any society one finds in the end some principle of action that dominates all the others.

Eighteenth-century England, which has been especially cited as an example of this type of government, was an essentially aristocratic state, although it contained within itself great elements of democracy, for laws and mores were so designed that the aristocracy could always prevail in the long run and manage public affairs as it wished.

The mistake is due to those who, constantly seeing the interests of the great in conflict with those of the people, have thought only about the struggle and have not paid attention to the result thereof, which was more important. When a society really does have a mixed government, that is to say, one equally shared between contrary principles, either a revolution breaks out or that society breaks up.

I therefore think it always necessary to place somewhere one social power superior to all others, but I believe that freedom is

[3] No one would wish to maintain that a nation cannot abuse its power against another nation. But parties form something like little nations within the nation, and the relations between them are like those of strangers.

If it is agreed that a nation can be tyrannical toward another nation, how can one deny that a party can be so toward another party?

in danger when that power finds no obstacle that can restrain its course and give it time to moderate itself.

Omnipotence in itself seems a bad and dangerous thing. I think that its exercise is beyond man's strength, whoever he be, and that only God can be omnipotent without danger because His wisdom and justice are always equal to His power. So there is no power on earth in itself so worthy of respect or vested with such a sacred right that I would wish to let it act without control and dominate without obstacles. So when I see the right and capacity to do all given to any authority whatsoever, whether it be called people or king, democracy or aristocracy, and whether the scene of action is a monarchy or a republic, I say: the germ of tyranny is there, and I will go look for other laws under which to live.

My greatest complaint against democratic government as organized in the United States is not, as many Europeans make out, its weakness, but rather its irresistible strength. What I find most repulsive in America is not the extreme freedom reigning there but the shortage of guarantees against tyranny.

When a man or a party suffers an injustice in the United States, to whom can he turn? To public opinion? That is what forms the majority. To the legislative body? It represents the majority and obeys it blindly. To the executive power? It is appointed by the majority and serves as its passive instrument. To the police? They are nothing but the majority under arms. A jury? The jury is the majority vested with the right to pronounce judgment; even the judges in certain states are elected by the majority. So, however iniquitous or unreasonable the measure which hurts you, you must submit.[4]

---

[4] At Baltimore during the War of 1812 there was a striking example of the excesses to which despotism of the majority may lead. At that time the war was very popular at Baltimore. A newspaper which came out in strong opposition to it aroused the indignation of the inhabitants. The people assembled, broke the presses, and attacked the house of the editors. An attempt was made to summon the militia, but it did not answer the appeal. Finally, to save the lives of these wretched men threatened by the fury of the public, they were taken to prison like criminals. This precaution was useless. During the night the people assembled again; the magistrates having failed to bring up the militia, the prison was broken open; one of the journalists was killed on the spot and the others left for dead; the guilty were brought before a jury and acquitted.

I once said to a Pennsylvanian: "Please explain to me why in a state founded by Quakers and renowned for its tolerance, freed Negroes are not allowed to use their rights as citizens? They pay taxes; is it not right that they should vote?"

"Do not insult us," he replied, "by supposing that our legislators would commit an act of such gross injustice and intolerance."

But suppose you were to have a legislative body so composed that it represented the majority without being necessarily the slave of its passions, an executive power having a strength of its own, and a judicial power independent of the other two authorities; then you would still have a democratic government, but there would be hardly any remaining risk of tyranny.

I am not asserting that at the present time in America there are frequent acts of tyranny. I do say that one can find no guarantee against it there and that the reasons for the government's gentleness must be sought in circumstances and in mores rather than in the laws.

Effect of the Omnipotence of the Majority on the Arbitrary Power of American Public Officials

The freedom which American law leaves to functionaries within the sphere marked out for them. Their power.

It is important to make the distinction between arbitrary power and tyranny. Tyranny can use even the law as its instrument, and then it is no longer arbitrary; arbitrary power may be used in the interest of the ruled, and then it is not tyrannical.

Tyranny ordinarily makes use of arbitrariness, but it can at need do without it.

In the United States that omnipotence of the majority which favors the legal despotism of the legislator also smiles on the arbitrary power of the magistrate. The majority, being in absolute command both of lawmaking and of the execution of the laws, and equally controlling both rulers and ruled, regards public functionaries as its

---

"So, with you, Negroes do have the right to vote?"

"Certainly."

"Then how was it that at the electoral college this morning I did not see a single one of them in the meeting?"

"That is not the fault of the law," said the American. "It is true that Negroes have the right to be present at elections, but they voluntarily abstain from appearing."

"That is extraordinarily modest of them."

"Oh! It is not that they are reluctant to go there, but they are afraid they may be maltreated. With us it sometimes happens that the law lacks force when the majority does not support it. Now, the majority is filled with the strongest prejudices against Negroes, and the magistrates do not feel strong enough to guarantee the rights granted to them by the lawmakers."

"What! The majority, privileged to make the law, wishes also to have the privilege of disobeying the law?"

passive agents and is glad to leave them the trouble of carrying out its plans. It therefore does not enter by anticipation into the details of their duties and hardly takes the trouble to define their rights. It treats them as a master might treat his servants if, always seeing them act under his eyes, he could direct or correct them at any moment.

In general, the law leaves American officials much freer than ours within the sphere marked out for them. Sometimes the majority may even allow them to go beyond that. Assured of the views and strengthened by the support of the greatest number, they then dare to do things which astonish a European, accustomed though he be to the spectacle of arbitrary power. Thus habits form in freedom that may one day become fatal to that freedom.

The Power Exercised by the Majority in America over Thought

In the United States, when the majority has irrevocably decided about any question, it is no longer discussed. Why? Moral authority exercised by the majority over thought. Democratic republics have turned despotism into something immaterial.

It is when one comes to look into the use made of thought in the United States that one most clearly sees how far the power of the majority goes beyond all powers known to us in Europe.

Thought is an invisible power and one almost impossible to lay hands on, which makes sport of all tyrannies. In our day the most absolute sovereigns in Europe cannot prevent certain thoughts hostile to their power from silently circulating in their states and even in their own courts. It is not like that in America; while the majority is in doubt, one talks; but when it has irrevocably pronounced, everyone is silent, and friends and enemies alike seem to make for its bandwagon. The reason is simple: no monarch is so absolute that he can hold all the forces of society in his hands, and overcome all resistance, as a majority invested with the right to make the laws and to execute them, can do.

Moreover, a king's power is physical only, controlling actions but not influencing desires, whereas the majority is invested with both physical and moral authority, which acts as much upon the will as upon behavior and at the same moment prevents both the act and the desire to do it.

I know no country in which, speaking generally, there is less independence of mind and true freedom of discussion than in America.

There is no religious or political theory which one cannot preach freely in the constitutional states of Europe or which does not penetrate into the others, for there is no country in Europe so subject to a single power that he who wishes to speak the truth cannot find support enough to protect him against the consequences of his independence. If he is unlucky enough to live under an absolute government, he often has the people with him; if he lives in a free country, he may at need find shelter behind the royal authority. In democratic countries the aristocracy may support him, and in other lands the democracy. But in a democracy organized on the model of the United States there is only one authority, one source of strength and of success, and nothing outside it.

In America the majority has enclosed thought within a formidable fence. A writer is free inside that area, but woe to the man who goes beyond it. Not that he stands in fear of an *auto-da-fé,* but he must face all kinds of unpleasantness and everyday persecution. A career in politics is closed to him, for he has offended the only power that holds the keys. He is denied everything, including renown. Before he goes into print, he believes he has supporters; but he feels that he has them no more once he stands revealed to all, for those who condemn him express their views loudly, while those who think as he does, but without his courage, retreat into silence as if ashamed of having told the truth.

Formerly tyranny used the clumsy weapons of chains and hangmen; nowadays even despotism, though it seemed to have nothing more to learn, has been perfected by civilization.

Princes made violence a physical thing, but our contemporary democratic republics have turned it into something as intellectual as the human will it is intended to constrain. Under the absolute government of a single man, despotism, to reach the soul, clumsily struck at the body, and the soul, escaping from such blows, rose gloriously above it; but in democratic republics that is not at all how tyranny behaves; it leaves the body alone and goes straight for the soul. The master no longer says: "Think like me or you die." He does say: "You are free not to think as I do; you can keep your life and property and all; but from this day you are a stranger among us. You can keep your privileges in the township, but they will be useless to you, for if you solicit your fellow citizens' votes, they will not give them to you, and if you only ask for their esteem, they will make excuses for refusing that. You will remain among men, but you will lose your rights to count as one. When you approach your fellows, they will shun you as an impure being, and even those who believe in your innocence will abandon you too, lest they in turn be shunned. Go in peace. I have given you your life, but it is a life worse than death."

Absolute monarchies brought despotism into dishonor; we must beware lest democratic republics rehabilitate it, and that while they make it more oppressive toward some, they do not rid it of its detestable and degrading character in the eyes of the greatest number.

In the proudest nations of the Old World works were published which faithfully portrayed the vices and absurdities of contemporaries; La Bruyère[5] lived in Louis XIV's palace while he wrote his chapter on the great, and Molière criticized the court in plays acted before the courtiers. But the power which dominates in the United States does not understand being mocked like that. The least reproach offends it, and the slightest sting of truth turns it fierce; and one must praise everything, from the turn of its phrases to its most robust virtues. No writer, no matter how famous, can escape from this obligation to sprinkle incense over his fellow citizens. Hence the majority lives in a state of perpetual self-adoration; only strangers or experience may be able to bring certain truths to the Americans' attention.

We need seek no other reason for the absence of great writers in America so far; literary genius cannot exist without freedom of the spirit, and there is no freedom of the spirit in America.

In Spain the Inquisition was never able to prevent the circulation of books contrary to the majority religion. The American majority's sway extends further and has rid itself even of the thought of publishing such books. One finds unbelievers in America, but unbelief has, so to say, no organ.

One finds governments striving to protect mores by condemning the authors of licentious books. No one in the United States is condemned for works of that sort, but no one is tempted to write them. Not that all the citizens are chaste in their mores, but those of the majority are regular.

In this, no doubt, power is well used, but my point is the nature of the power in itself. This irresistible power is a continuous fact and its good use only an accident.

[5] [La Bruyère, *Caractères ou Les Moeurs du Siècle,* first edition (Paris, 1688); cf. the chapter "Les Grands," to which Tocqueville refers: La Bruyère, *Œuvres Complètes,* Pléiade edition, Paris, 1951, pp. 268 ff.]

Effects of the Majority's Tyranny on American National Character; the Courtier Spirit in the United States

Up to now the tyranny of the majority has had more effect on the mores than on the behavior of society. The growth of great characters is halted. Democratic republics organized on American lines put the courtier spirit within the reach of great numbers. Evidence of this spirit in the United States. Why the people are more patriotic than those who govern.

The influence of what I have been talking about is as yet only weakly felt in political society, but its ill effects on the national character are already apparent. I think that the rareness now of outstanding men on the political scene is due to the ever-increasing despotism of the American majority.

When the Revolution broke out, a crowd of them appeared; at that time public opinion gave direction to men's wills but did not tyrannize over them. The famous men of that time, while they freely took part in the intellectual movement of the age, had a greatness all their own; their renown brought honor to the nation, not vice versa.

The great men close to the throne of an absolute monarch flatter their master's passions and willingly bow to his caprices. But the mass of the nation does not countenance servitude; its submission is often from weakness, habit, or ignorance and sometimes from love of the throne or of the king. Some nations have taken a kind of pleasure and pride in sacrificing their wills to that of the prince, and by this means introducing a sort of independence of mind into the very heart of obedience. In such nations there is much less degradation than misery. Moreover, there is a great difference between doing something of which you do not approve and pretending to approve of what you are doing; the first is the part of a weak man, but the second fits only the manners of a valet.

In free countries, where everyone is more or less called on to give his opinion about affairs of state, and in democratic republics, where there is a constant mingling of public with private life and where the sovereign is approachable from every side, to raise one's voice being enough to attract his attention, one finds many more people seeking to gamble on his weaknesses and live off his passions than would be found under absolute monarchies. It is not that men are naturally worse there than elsewhere, but the temptation is greater and offered to more men at the same time. Consequently there is a much more general lowering of standards.

Democratic republics put the spirit of a court within reach of the multitude and let it penetrate through all classes at once. That is one of the main reproaches to be made against them.

This is particularly true of democratic states organized after the fashion of the American republics, where the majority has such absolute and irresistible sway that one must in a sense renounce one's rights as a citizen and, so to say, one's status as a man when one wants to diverge from the path it has marked out.

Among the immense thrusting crowd of American political aspirants I saw very few men who showed that virile candor and manly independence of thought which often marked the Americans of an earlier generation and which, wherever found, is the most salient feature in men of great character. At first glance one might suppose that all American minds had been fashioned after the same model, so exactly do they follow along the same paths. A foreigner does, it is true, sometimes meet Americans who are not strict slaves of slogans; such men may deplore the defects of the laws and the unenlightened mutability of democracy; often they even go as far as to point out the defects which are changing the national character and suggest means by which this tendency could be corrected, but no one, except yourself, listens to them, and you, to whom they confide these secret thoughts, are only a stranger and will pass on. To you they will disclose truths that have no use for you, but when they go down into the marketplace they use quite different language.

If these lines ever come to be read in America, I am sure of two things; first, that all readers will raise their voices to condemn me; secondly, that in the depths of their conscience many will hold me innocent.

I have heard talk of the motherland in the United States, and I have come across real patriotism among the people but have often looked in vain for any such thing among their rulers. An analogy will make this easily understandable: despotism corrupts the man who submits to it much more than the man who imposes it. In absolute monarchies the king may often have great virtues, but the courtiers are always vile.

It is true that American courtiers never say "Sire" or "Your Majesty," as if the difference mattered; but they are constantly talking of their master's natural brilliance; they do not raise the question which of all the prince's virtues is most to be admired, for they assure him that he possesses all virtues, without having acquired them and, so to say, without desiring them; they do not give him their wives or their daughters hoping that he will raise them to the rank of his mistresses, but they do sacrifice their opinions to him and so prostitute themselves.

American moralists and philosophers are not obliged to wrap their views in veils of allegory, but before hazarding an unpleasant truth they say: "We know that we are addressing a people so far above human weaknesses that they will always be masters of themselves. We would not use such language unless we knew that we were speaking to men whose virtues and enlightenment make them alone among all others worthy to remain free."

How could the flatterers of Louis XIV improve on that?

For my part, I think that in all governments whatsoever meanness will cling to strength, and flattery to power. And I know of only one way of preventing men from degrading themselves, namely, not to give anybody that omnipotence which carries with it sovereign power to debase them.

The Greatest Danger to the American Republics Comes from the Omnipotence of the Majority

It is not impotence but the ill use of power that threatens the existence of democratic republics. The government of the American republics is more centralized and more energetic than that of European monarchies. Consequential dangers. Views of Madison and Jefferson on the matter.

Governments ordinarily break down either through impotence or through tyranny. In the first case power slips from their grasp, whereas in the second it is taken from them.

Many people, seeing democratic states fall into anarchy, have supposed that government in such states was by nature weak and impotent. The truth is that once war has broken out between the parties, government influence over society ceases. But I do not think a lack of strength or resources is part of the nature of democratic authority; on the contrary, I believe that it is almost always the abuse of that strength and the ill use of those resources which bring it down. Anarchy is almost always a consequence either of the tyranny or of the inability of democracy, but not of its impotence.

One must not confuse stability with strength or a thing's size with its duration. In democratic republics the power directing[6] society is not stable, for both its personnel and its aims change often. But wherever it is brought to bear, its strength is almost irresistible.

The government of the American republics seems to me as centralized and more energetic than the absolute monarchies of Europe. So I do not think that it will collapse from weakness.[7]

If ever freedom is lost in America, that will be due to the omnipotence of the majority driving the minorities to desperation and forcing them to appeal to physical force. We may then see anarchy, but it will have come as the result of despotism.

President James Madison has given expression to just these thoughts. (*The Federalist*, No. 51.) [Everyman edition, pp. 266 f.]

"It is of great importance in a republic not only to guard the society against the oppression of its rulers, but to guard one part of the society against the injustice of the other part. . . . Justice is the end of government. It is the end of civil society. It ever has been and ever will be pursued until it be obtained, or until liberty be lost in the pursuit. In a society under the forms of which the stronger faction can readily unite and oppress the weaker, anarchy may as truly be said to reign as in a state of nature, where the weaker individual is not secured against the violence of the stronger; and as, in the latter state, even the stronger individuals are prompted, by the uncertainty of their condition, to submit to a government which may protect the weak as well as themselves; so, in the former state, will the more powerful factions or parties be gradually induced, by a like motive, to wish for a government which will protect all parties, the weaker as well as the more powerful. It can be little doubted that if the state of Rhode Island was separated from the Confederacy and left to itself, the insecurity of rights under the popular form of government within such narrow limits would be displayed by such reiterated oppressions of factious majorities that some power altogether independent of the people would soon be called for by the voice of the very factions whose misrule had proved the necessity of it."

Jefferson also said: "The executive, in our government is not the sole, it is scarcely the principal, object of my jealousy. The tyranny of the legislature is the most formidable dread at present and will

[6] Authority may be centralized in an assembly, and in that case it is strong but not stable. Or it may be centralized in one man, and in that case it is less strong but more stable.

[7] There is no need to remind the reader that here, and throughout this chapter, I am speaking not of the federal government but of the governments of each state, where a despotic majority is in control.

be for many years. That of the executive will come in its turn, but it will be at a remote period."[8]

I prefer to quote Jefferson rather than anybody else on this topic, regarding him as the most powerful apostle of democracy there has ever been.

[8] Letter from Jefferson to Madison, March 15, 1789. [Cf. *The Writings of Thomas Jefferson* (Washington, 1905), Vol. VII, p. 312.]

Chapter 8

WHAT TEMPERS THE TYRANNY OF THE MAJORITY IN THE UNITED STATES

Absence of Administrative Centralization

The national majority does not pretend to do everything. It is obliged to use the magistrates of the townships and counties to execute its sovereign wishes.

I HAVE PREVIOUSLY made the distinction between two types of centralization, calling one governmental and the other administrative.

Only the first exists in America, the second being almost unknown.

If the directing power in American societies had both these means of government at its disposal and combined the right to command with the faculty and habit to perform everything itself, if having established the general principles of the government, it entered into the details of their application, and having regulated the great interests of the country, it came down to consider even individual interests, then freedom would soon be banished from the New World.

But in the United States the majority, though it often has a despot's tastes and instincts, still lacks the most improved instruments of tyranny.

In all the American republics the central government is only occupied with a small number of matters important enough to attract its attention. It does not undertake to regulate society's secondary concerns, and there is no indication that it has even conceived the desire to do so. The majority, though ever increasingly absolute, has not enlarged the prerogatives of the central authority; it has only made it omnipotent within its own sphere. Thus despotism, though very oppressive on one point, cannot cover all.

Besides, however far the national majority may be carried away by its passions in its ardor for its projects, it cannot make all the citizens everywhere bow to its will in the same way and at the same time. The sovereign commands of its representative, the central government, have to be carried out by agents who often do not depend upon it and cannot be given directions every minute. Municipal bodies and county administrations are like so many hidden reefs retarding or dividing the flood of the popular will. If the law were oppressive, liberty would still find some shelter from the way the law is carried into execution, and the majority would not know how to enter into the details and, if I dare call them so, the puerilities of administrative tyranny. Indeed it does not even imagine that it could do so, for it is not entirely conscious of its own power. It is only aware of its natural strength, ignorant of how art might increase its scope.

It is worth thinking about this point. If ever a democratic republic similar to that of the United States came to be established in a country in which earlier a single man's power had introduced administrative centralization and had made it something accepted by custom and by law, I have no hesitation in saying that in such a republic despotism would become more intolerable than in any of the absolute monarchies of Europe. One would have to go over into Asia to find anything with which to compare it.

The Temper of the American Legal Profession and How It Serves to Counterbalance Democracy

Usefulness of inquiring what are the natural instincts of the legal temperament. Lawyers play a great part in a society struggling into existence. How the type of work in which they are engaged gives an aristocratic turn to their ideas. Chance circumstances that may prevent the development of these ideas. Ease with which the aristocracy joins forces with the lawyers. How a despot could make use of lawyers. How lawyers provide the only aristocratic element naturally able to combine with elements natural to democracy. Particular causes which tend to give an aristocratic turn to English and American legal thought. The American aristocracy is found at the bar and on the bench. Lawyers' influence on American society. How their spirit penetrates the legislatures and the administration and in the end gives the people themselves some of the instincts of magistrates.

Visiting Americans and studying their laws, one discovers that the prestige accorded to lawyers and their permitted influence in the government are now the strongest barriers against the faults of democracy. I think this result can be traced back to a general cause worth examining, because it might recur elsewhere.

For five hundred years lawyers have taken part in all the movements of political society in Europe. Sometimes they have been the tools of the political authorities, and sometimes they have made those authorities their tools. In the Middle Ages the lawyers' cooperation was invaluable in extending the domination of the kings; they have since striven hard to restrict that same power. In England they have become closely united with the aristocracy; in France they have proved its most dangerous enemies. Do lawyers, then, yield to sudden and temporary impulses, or are they more or less obedient, according to circumstances, to constantly recurring instincts natural to them? I should like to get this matter clear, for it may be that lawyers are called on to play the leading part in the political society which is striving to be born.

Men who have made a special study of the laws and have derived therefrom habits of order, something of a taste for formalities, and an instinctive love for a regular concatenation of ideas are naturally strongly opposed to the revolutionary spirit and to the ill-considered passions of democracy.

Study and specialized knowledge of the law give a man a rank apart in society and make of lawyers a somewhat privileged intellectual class. The exercise of their profession daily reminds them of this superiority; they are the masters of a necessary and not widely understood science; they serve as arbiters between the citizens; and the habit of directing the blind passions of the litigants toward the objective gives them a certain scorn for the judgment of the crowd. Add that they naturally form *a body*. It is not that they have come to an understanding among themselves and direct their combined energies toward one objective, but common studies and like methods link their intellects, as common interest may link their desires.

So, hidden at the bottom of a lawyer's soul one finds some of the tastes and habits of an aristocracy. They share its instinctive preference for order and its natural love of formalities; like it, they conceive a great distaste for the behavior of the multitude and secretly scorn the government of the people.

I have no intention of saying that these natural inclinations of lawyers are strong enough to bind them in any irresistible fashion. With lawyers, as with all men, it is particular interest, especially the interest of the moment, which prevails.

There are societies in which men of law cannot take a position in the world of politics analogous to that which they hold in private life; one can be sure that in such a society lawyers will be very active agents of revolution. But we need to inquire whether it is some permanent disposition or an accident which then leads them to destroy or to change. It is true that lawyers played a prominent part in overthrowing the French monarchy in 1789. We still need to discover whether they acted so because they had studied the laws or because they could not have a share in making them.

For five hundred years the English aristocracy put itself at the head of the people and spoke in its name; nowadays they support the throne and are the champions of royal authority. But the aristocracy still has instincts and inclinations peculiar to itself.

It is, moreover, important to be careful not to mistake isolated members of that body for the body itself.

Under all free governments, of whatever sort, one finds lawyers in the leading ranks of all the parties. The same remark also applies to the aristocracy. Almost all the democratic movements that have shaken the world have been directed by noblemen.

An elite body can never satisfy all the ambitions of all its members; if talents and ambitions are always more numerous than places, there are bound to be many who cannot rise quickly enough by making use of the body's privileges and who seek fast promotion by attacking them.

Hence, I do not claim that *all* lawyers will ever, or that most of them will *always,* prove supporters of order and enemies of change.

I do say that in a community in which lawyers hold without question that high rank in society which is naturally their due, their temper will be eminently conservative and will prove antidemocratic.

When an aristocracy closes its ranks against the lawyers, it finds them to be enemies all the more dangerous, because although beneath it in wealth and power, their work makes them independent of it and they feel that their enlightenment raises them to its level.

Every time that the nobles have wished the lawyers to share some of their privileges, these two classes have found many things that make it easy for them to combine and, so to say, they find that they belong to the same family.

Equally I am led to believe that it will always be easy for a king to make the lawyers the most useful instruments of his power.

By nature there is much more affinity between lawyers and executive officials than between the former and the people, although lawyers have often overthrown the executive. In the same way, there is more natural affinity between nobles and the king than between nobles and people, although the upper classes of society have often combined with the others to fight against the royal power.

What lawyers love above all things is an ordered life, and authority is the greatest guarantee of order. Moreover, one must not forget that although they value liberty, they generally rate legality as far more precious; they are less afraid of tyranny than of arbitrariness, and provided that it is the lawgiver himself who is responsible for taking away men's independence, they are more or less content.

I therefore think that when a prince is faced by an encroaching democracy and he seeks to impair the power of the judges in his states and diminish the political influence of the lawyers, he is making a great mistake. He would injure the substance of authority by grasping at the shadow.

I have no doubt that he would have done better to bring lawyers into his government. Having entrusted to them a despotism taking its shape from violence, perhaps he might receive it back from their hands with features of justice and law.

Democratic government favors the political power of lawyers. When the rich, the noble, and the prince are excluded from the government, the lawyers then step into their full rights, for they are then the only men both enlightened and skillful, but not of the people, whom the people can choose.

If their tastes naturally draw lawyers toward the aristocracy and the prince, their interest as naturally pulls them toward the people.

Therefore lawyers like democratic government without sharing its inclinations or imitating its weaknesses, a double cause for their power through it and over it.

The people in a democracy do not distrust lawyers, knowing that it is to their interest to serve the democratic cause; and they listen to them without getting angry, for they do not imagine them to have any *arrière pensée*. In actual fact, the lawyers do not want to overthrow democracy's chosen government, but they do constantly try to guide it along lines to which it is not inclined by methods foreign to it. By birth and interest a lawyer is one of the people, but he is an aristocrat in his habits and tastes; so he is the natural liaison officer between aristocracy and people, and the link that joins them.

The legal body is the only aristocratic element which can unforcedly mingle with elements natural to democracy and combine with them on comfortable and lasting terms. I am aware of the inherent defects of the legal mind; nevertheless, I doubt whether democracy could rule society for long without this mixture of the legal and democratic minds, and I hardly believe that nowadays a republic can hope to survive unless the lawyers' influence over its affairs grows in proportion to the power of the people.

This aristocratic character which I detect in the legal mind is much more pronounced still in the United States and in England than in any other land. This is not only due to English and American legal studies, but also to the very nature of the legislation and the position of lawyers as interpreters thereof in both these countries.

Both English and Americans have kept the law of precedents; that is to say, they still derive their opinions in legal matters and the judgments they should pronounce from the opinions and legal judgments of their fathers.

An English or American lawyer almost always combines a taste and respect for what is old with a liking for regularity and legality.

This influences in yet another way the turn of lawyers' minds, and so the course of society.

The first thing an English or American lawyer looks for is what has been done, whereas a French one inquires what one should wish to do; one looks for judgments and the other for reasons.

If you listen to an English or American lawyer, you are surprised to hear him quoting the opinions of others so often and saying so little about his own, whereas the opposite is the case with us.

A French lawyer will deal with no matter, however trivial, without bringing in his own whole system of ideas, and he will carry the argument right back to the constituent principles of the laws in order to persuade the court to move the boundary of the contested inheritance back a couple of yards.

The English or American lawyer who thus, in a sense, denies his own reasoning powers in order to return to those of his fathers, maintaining his thought in a kind of servitude, must contract more timid habits and conservative inclinations than his opposite number in France.

Our written laws are often hard to understand, but everyone can read them, whereas nothing could be more obscure and out of reach of the common man than a law founded on precedent. Where lawyers are absolutely needed, as in England and the United States, and their professional knowledge is held in high esteem, they become increasingly separated from the people, forming a class apart. A French lawyer is just a man of learning, but an English or an American one is somewhat like the Egyptian priests, being, as they were, the only interpreter of an occult science.

The social position of English and American lawyers also has an equally great influence on their habits and opinions. The English aristocracy, always anxious to absorb all elements bearing any likeness to itself, has given lawyers a very large share of consideration and of power. Lawyers are not in the first rank of English society, but they are content with their standing. They are like a cadet branch of the aristocracy, and they like and respect the elder line without sharing all its privileges. So English lawyers unite the aristocratic interests of the legal profession with the tastes and ways of the aristocrats with whom they consort.

Thus it is England above all that supplies the most striking portrait of the type of lawyer I am trying to depict; the English lawyer values laws not because they are good but because they are old; and if he is reduced to modifying them in some respect, to adapt them to the changes which time brings to any society, he has recourse to the most incredible subtleties in order to persuade himself that in adding something to the work of his fathers he has only developed their thought and completed their work. Do not hope to make him recognize that he is an innovator; he will be prepared to go to absurd lengths rather than to admit himself guilty of so great a crime. It is in England that this legal spirit was born, which seems indifferent to the substance of things, paying attention only to the letter, and which would rather part company with reason and humanity than with the law.

English law may be compared to the trunk of an old tree on which lawyers have continually grafted the strangest shoots, hoping that though the fruit will be different, the leaves at least will match those of the venerable tree that supports them.

In America there are neither nobles nor men of letters, and the people distrust the wealthy. Therefore the lawyers form the political upper class and the most intellectual section of society. Consequently they only stand to lose from any innovation; this adds an interest in conservation to their natural taste for order.

If you ask me where the American aristocracy is found, I have no hesitation in answering that it is not among the rich, who have no common link uniting them. It is at the bar or the bench that the America aristocracy is found.

The more one reflects on what happens in the United States, the more one feels convinced that the legal body forms the most powerful and, so today, the only counterbalance to democracy in that country.

In the United States it is easy to discover how well adapted the legal spirit is, both by its qualities and, I would say, even by its defects, to neutralize the vices inherent in popular government.

When the American people let themselves get intoxicated by their passions or carried away by their ideas, the lawyers apply an almost invisible brake which slows them down and halts them. Their aristocratic inclinations are secretly opposed to the instincts of democracy, their superstitious respect for all that is old to its love of novelty, their narrow views to its grandiose designs, their taste for formalities to its scorn of regulations, and their habit of advancing slowly to its impetuosity.

The courts are the most obvious organs through which the legal body influences democracy.

The judge is a lawyer who, apart from the taste for order and for rules imparted by his legal studies, is given a liking for stability by the permanence of his own tenure of office. His knowledge of the law in itself has assured him already high social standing among his equals, and his political power as a judge puts him in a rank apart with all the instincts of the privileged classes.

An American judge, armed with the right to declare laws unconstitutional, is constantly intervening in political affairs.[1] He cannot compel the people to make laws, but at least he can constrain them to be faithful to their own laws and remain in harmony with themselves.

I am aware of a hidden tendency in the United States leading the people to diminish judicial power; under most of the state constitutions the government can, at the request of both houses, remove a judge from office. Under some constitutions the *judges* are *elected* and subject to frequent reelection. I venture to predict that sooner or later these innovations will have dire results and that one day it will be seen that by diminishing the magistrates' independence, not judicial power only but the democratic republic itself has been attacked.

Besides, no one should imagine that in the United States a legalistic spirit is confined strictly to the precincts of the courts; it extends far beyond them.

Lawyers, forming the only enlightened class not distrusted by the people, are naturally called on to fill most public functions. The legislatures are full of them, and they head administrations; in this way they greatly influence both the shaping of the law and its execution. Though the lawyers are obliged to yield to the current of public opinion carrying them along, it is easy to see indications of what they would do if they were free. While their political laws are full of innovations, the Americans have only very reluctantly introduced slight changes into their civil laws, although many of these laws are utterly out of keeping with their social state. This is because the majority always has to turn to the lawyers concerning matters of

[1] See what I have said about judicial power in Part I.

270 *Democracy in America*

civil law, and American lawyers, when free to choose, make no innovations.

It is an odd experience for a Frenchman to hear American complaints about the conservative spirit of the lawyers and their prejudices in favor of everything established.

The influence of the spirit of the law spreads yet further beyond the precise limits I have indicated.

There is hardly a political question in the United States which does not sooner or later turn into a judicial one. Consequently the language of everyday party-political controversy has to be borrowed from legal phraseology and conceptions. As most public men are or have been lawyers, they apply their legal habits and turn of mind to the conduct of affairs. Juries make all classes familiar with this. So legal language is pretty well adopted into common speech; the spirit of the law, born within schools and courts, spreads little by little beyond them; it infiltrates through society right down to the lowest ranks, till finally the whole people have contracted some of the ways and tastes of a magistrate.

In the United States the lawyers constitute a power which is little dreaded and hardly noticed; it has no banner of its own; it adapts itself flexibly to the exigencies of the moment and lets itself be carried along unresistingly by every movement of the body social; but it enwraps the whole of society, penetrating each component class and constantly working in secret upon its unconscious patient, till in the end it has molded it to its desire.

The Jury in the United States Considered as a Political Institution

Trial by jury, which is one of the forms of sovereignty of the people, must be seen in relation to the other laws establishing that sovereignty. Composition of the jury in the United States. Effect of the jury system on the national character. Education it gives to the people. How it tends to establish the magistrates' influence and spread the spirit of the law.

My subject having led me to discuss the administration of justice in the United States, I shall not leave it without speaking of the jury.

One must make a distinction between the jury as a judicial institution and a political one.

If it were a question of deciding how far the jury, especially the jury in civil cases, facilitates the good administration of justice, I admit that its usefulness can be contested.

The jury system arose in the infancy of society, at a time when only simple questions of fact were submitted to the courts; and it is no easy task to adapt it to the needs of a highly civilized nation, where the relations between men have multiplied exceedingly and have been thoughtfully elaborated in a learned manner.[2]

At the moment my main object is to deal with the political aspect of the jury, since any other course would divert me too far from my subject. But I will just say a couple of words about the judicial use of the jury. The English adopted that institution when they were a semibarbarian people; they have since become one of the most enlightened nations in the world, and their attachment to the jury system seems to have grown with their enlightenment. They have left their native land to spread all over the globe; in some places they have formed colonies and in others independent states; the main body of the nation has kept its king; several groups of settlers have founded powerful republics; but everywhere alike the English have extolled the institution of the jury.[3] They have established it everywhere or have hastened to reestablish it. A judicial institution which has thus throughout long centuries been chosen by

[2] It would be both profitable and interesting to consider the jury as a judicial institution, evaluating its effects in the United States and discovering what use the Americans have made of it. The subject would fill a whole book, and one of interest for the French. One could, for instance, inquire how and by what stages American institutions connected with the jury might be introduced into our system. Louisiana would throw more light on this point than any other state, for its population is a mixture of French and English. The two legal systems face each other there and are slowly amalgamating, as the peoples also are doing. The best books to consult would be the two volumes of the *Digest of the Laws of Louisiana* [*A General Digest of the Acts of the Legislature of Louisiana Passed from the Year 1804, to 1827, Inclusive*, by L. Moreau Lislet, 2 vols., New Orleans, 1828], and better still, perhaps, a bilingual textbook on civil procedure entitled *Traité sur les Règles des Actions civiles*, published by Buisson at New Orleans in 1830. [See Library of Congress: Louisiana. Laws, Statutes, etc. *Code of practice in civil cases for the state of Louisiana*. New Orleans, printed by B. Buisson, 1830, 96 pp.] That work has one special advantage in that it provides a Frenchman with an exact and authoritative glossary of English legal terms. In all countries legal language is a thing apart, nowhere more so than in England.

[3] All English and American lawyers are unanimous on this point. Mr. Story, a judge of the Supreme Court of the United States, in his *Commentaries on the Constitution of the United States*, harps on the excellence of the institution of the jury in civil cases: "the inestimable privilege of a trial by jury in civil cases," he says, "a privilege scarcely inferior to that in criminal cases, which is conceded by all persons to be essential to political and civil liberty." (Story, Book III, chapter 38.) [*Commentaries on the Constitution of the United States* (Boston, 1834), p. 654.]

a great nation and which has been zealously reproduced at every stage of civilization in every climate and under every form of government cannot be contrary to the spirit of justice.[4]

But let us leave this subject. To regard the jury simply as a judicial institution would be taking a very narrow view of the matter, for great though its influence on the outcome of lawsuits is, its influence on the fate of society itself is much greater still. The jury is therefore above all a political institution, and it is from that point of view that it must always be judged.

By a "jury" I mean a certain number of citizens selected by chance and temporarily invested with the right to judge.

To use a jury to suppress crimes seems to me to introduce an eminently republican element into the government, for the following reasons:

The jury may be an aristocratic or a democratic institution, according to the class from which the jurors are selected; but there is always a republican character in it, inasmuch as it puts the real control of affairs into the hands of the ruled, or some of them, rather than into those of the rulers.

Force is never more than a passing element in success; the idea of right follows immediately after it. Any government which could only reach its enemies on a battlefield would soon be destroyed. Therefore the true sanction for political laws lies in the penal ones, and where that sanction is lacking, the law sooner or later loses its power. For that reason the man who is judge in *criminal* trial is the real master of society. Now, a jury puts the people themselves or at least one

---

[4] If one wanted to establish the usefulness of the jury as a judicial institution, many other arguments could be advanced, among them the following:

As more juries are used, the number of judges can be reduced without inconvenience, which is a great advantage. When there are a great number of judges, death is continually opening gaps in the judicial hierarchy and so offering new positions to those who survive. Thereby the judges' ambition is continually excited, and that, of course, makes them dependent on the majority or on the man who makes the appointments to the empty places, and so promotion in the courts comes to resemble that in the army. Such a state of things militates against the good administration of justice and the intentions of the legislator. One wants judges to be irremovable in order that they may be free; but how does it help that no one can snatch their independence from them if they voluntarily sacrifice it themselves?

When there are very many judges, many of them are bound to be incompetent, for a great judge is no ordinary man. Now, a half-enlightened court is perhaps the worst possible means of attaining the end in view when courts are established.

For my part, I would rather have a case decided by an ignorant jury guided by a skilled judge than hand it over to judges, most of whom have an incomplete knowledge both of jurisprudence and of the laws.

class of citizen on the judge's bench. Therefore the jury as an institution really puts control of society into the hands of the people or of that class.[5]

In England jurors are taken from the aristocratic part of the nation. The aristocracy makes the laws, applies them, and judges breaches of them. (See Appendix I, Q.) The whole thing is consistent, and England can properly be called an aristocratic state. In the United States the same system is applied to the whole people. Every American citizen can vote or be voted for and may be a juror. (See Appendix I, R.) The jury system as understood in America seems to me as direct and extreme a consequence of the dogma of the sovereignty of the people as universal suffrage. They are both equally powerful means of making the majority prevail.

All sovereigns who have wished to derive the sources of their power from themselves and to direct society instead of letting it direct them have destroyed the jury system or weakened it. The Tudors sent to prison jurors unwilling to convict, and Napoleon had them chosen by his agents.

Obvious though these truths are, they are not universally appreciated, and one often finds Frenchmen still with only a muddled conception of the jury system. When the question is from what elements the list of jurors should be composed, discussion is limited to the enlightenment and capacities of those to be chosen, as if one was concerned with a purely judicial institution. But, in my view, that is really the least important aspect of the matter; the jury is above all a political institution; it should be regarded as one form of the sovereignty of the people; when the sovereignty of the people is discarded, it too should be completely rejected; otherwise it should be made to harmonize with the other laws establishing that sovereignty. The jury is the part of the nation responsible for the execution of the laws, as the legislature assemblies are the part with the duty of making them; for society to be governed in a settled and uniform manner, it is essential that the jury lists should expand or shrink with the lists of voters. This aspect of the matter, in my opinion, should always be the lawgivers' main preoccupation. All the rest is, so to say, frills.

[5] However, one important qualification should be made:

It is true that the jury system gives the people a general right of control over the citizens' actions, but it does not supply means of exercising that control in all cases, nor do the people always exercise that control tyrannically.

When an absolute monarch can have crimes judged by his delegates, the accused's fate is, so to say, decided in advance. But even if the people were bent on conviction, the composition of the jury and the fact that it cannot be called to account would give an innocent man some chance.

So convinced am I that the jury is above all a political institution that I even look at it from that point of view when it is used in civil cases.

Laws are always unsteady when unsupported by mores; mores are the only tough and durable power in a nation.

When juries are reserved to criminal cases, the people only see them in action at long intervals and in a particular context; they do not form the habit of using them in the ordinary business of life and look on them as just a means, and not the only means, of obtaining justice.[6]

But juries used in civil cases too are constantly attracting some attention; they then impinge on all interests and everyone serves on them; in that way the system infiltrates into the business of life, thought follows the pattern of its procedures, and it is hardly too much to say that the idea of justice becomes identified with it.

For that reason, when juries are used only in criminal trials, the system is always in danger, but once introduced into civil cases, it defies both time and the assaults of men. If juries could have been wiped out from English mores as easily as from English laws, they would have succumbed entirely under the Tudors. Therefore it is the civil jury which really saved the liberties of England.

In whatever manner juries are used, they are bound to have a great influence on national character. But that influence is immeasurably increased the more they are used in civil cases.

Juries, especially civil juries, instill some of the habits of the judicial mind into every citizen, and just those habits are the very best way of preparing people to be free.

It spreads respect for the courts' decisions and for the idea of right throughout all classes. With those two elements gone, love of independence is merely a destructive passion.

Juries teach men equity in practice. Each man, when judging his neighbor, thinks that he may be judged himself. That is especially true of juries in civil suits; hardly anyone is afraid that he will have to face a criminal trial, but anybody may have a lawsuit.

Juries teach each individual not to shirk responsibility for his own acts, and without that manly characteristic no political virtue is possible.

Juries invest each citizen with a sort of magisterial office; they make all men feel that they have duties toward society and that they take a share in its government. By making men pay attention to things other than their own affairs, they combat that individual selfishness which is like rust in society.

[6] *A fortiori* this is true when juries are only used in certain criminal cases.

Juries are wonderfully effective in shaping a nation's judgment and increasing its natural lights. That, in my view, is its greatest advantage. It should be regarded as a free school which is always open and in which each juror learns his rights, comes into daily contact with the best-educated and most-enlightened members of the upper classes, and is given practical lessons in the law, lessons which the advocate's efforts, the judge's advice, and also the very passions of the litigants bring within his mental grasp. I think that the main reason for the practical intelligence and the political good sense of the Americans is their long experience with juries in civil cases.

I do not know whether a jury is useful to the litigants, but I am sure it is very good for those who have to decide the case. I regard it as one of the most effective means of popular education at society's disposal.

The foregoing applies to all nations, but what follows especially concerns the Americans and democratic peoples in general.

I have said above that in democracies the lawyers, and the judges in particular, are the only aristocratic body that can check the people's movements. This aristocracy has no physical power but exercises its influence over men's minds. It follows that civil juries are the main source of its power. In criminal trials, when society is fighting a single man, the jury is apt to look on the judge as the passive instrument of social authority and to mistrust his advice. Moreover, criminal cases turn entirely on simple facts easily within the range of common sense. On such ground judge and jury are equals.

But that is not the case in civil suits; there the judge appears as a disinterested arbitrator between the litigants' passions. The jurors feel confidence in him and listen to him with respect, for here his intelligence completely dominates theirs. It is he who unravels the various arguments they are finding it so hard to remember and takes them by the hand to guide them through procedural intricacies; it is he who limits their task to the question of fact and tells them what answer to give on questions of law. He has almost unlimited influence over them.

Is it still necessary to explain why arguments based on the incompetence of jurors in civil suits carry little weight with me?

In civil cases, at least when matters of fact are not at issue, the jury is a judicial body in appearance only.

The jurors pronounce the decision made by the judge. They give that judgment the authority of the society they represent, as he gives it that of reason and of law. (See Appendix I, S.)

The judges of England and of America have an influence over the outcome of criminal trials such as French judges have never possessed. The reason for this difference is easily understood: civil cases have established the authority of the English or American judge, and he is merely exercising it in another field, not the one in which he acquired it.

There are cases, and they are often the most important ones, in which the American judge has the right to pronounce alone.[7] He is, then, for the time being in the position which is usual for a French judge, but his moral authority is much greater; memories of the jury still cling to him, and his voice has almost as much authority as that of the society represented by them.

Moreover, his influence extends far beyond the precincts of the courts; the American judge is constantly surrounded by men accustomed to respect his intelligence as superior to their own, whether he is at some private entertainment or in the turmoil of politics, in the marketplace, or in one of the legislatures; and apart from its use in deciding cases, his authority influences the habits of mind and even the very soul of all who have cooperated with him in judging them.

Thus the jury, though seeming to diminish the magistrate's rights, in reality enlarges his sway, and in no other country are judges so powerful as in those where the people have a share in their privileges.

Above all, it is the jury in civil cases that enables the American bench to make what I have called the legal spirit penetrate right down into the lowest ranks of society.

The jury is both the most effective way of establishing the people's rule and the most efficient way of teaching them how to rule.

[7] Federal judges almost always alone decide those questions that touch the government of the country most closely.

Chapter 9

THE MAIN CAUSES TENDING TO MAINTAIN A DEMOCRATIC REPUBLIC IN THE UNITED STATES

THE UNITED STATES goes on being a democratic republic, and the main object of this book is to make clear the reasons for this phenomenon.

Several of these reasons have only been touched on in passing, as the train of my argument led me unintentionally close to their sphere. There are others with which I have not been able to deal. Also, those with which I have dealt at length have been left behind almost buried in detail.

So I feel that before going on to speak of the future I should make a short summary of everything that explains the present.

I shall make this summary very brief, only hastily reminding the reader of what he already knows, and just selecting the most important of the matters with which I have not yet dealt.

I have come to the conclusion that all the causes tending to maintain a democratic republic in the United States fall into three categories:

The first is the peculiar and accidental situation in which Providence has placed the Americans. Their laws are the second. Their habits and mores are the third.

Accidental or Providential Causes Helping to Maintain a Democratic Republic in the United States

The Union has no neighbors. No great capital. The chances of birth have favored the Americans. America is an empty land. How this circumstance is a great help toward maintaining a democratic republic. How the wildernesses of America are peopled. Avidity with which the Anglo-Americans take possession of the solitudes of the New World. Influence of material prosperity on the political opinions of the Americans.

There are very many circumstances unconnected with human volition which make things easy for a democratic republic in the United States. Some are well known and the others are easily pointed out. I will confine myself to the main ones.

The Americans have no neighbors and consequently no great wars, financial crises, invasions, or conquests to fear; they need neither heavy taxes nor a numerous army nor great generals; they have also hardly anything to fear from something else which is a greater scourge for democratic republics than all these others put together, namely, military glory.

How can one deny the incredible influence military glory has over a nation's spirit? General Jackson, whom the Americans have for the second time chosen to be at their head, is a man of violent character and middling capacities; nothing in the whole of his career indicated him to have the qualities needed for governing a free people; moreover, a majority of the enlightened classes in the Union have always been against him. Who, then, put him on the President's chair and keeps him there still? It is all due to the memory of a victory he won twenty years ago under the walls of New Orleans. But that New Orleans victory was a very commonplace feat of arms which could attract prolonged attention only in a country where there are no battles; and the nation who thus let itself be carried away by the prestige of glory is, most assuredly, the coldest, most calculating, the least militaristic, and if one may put it so, the most prosaic in all the world.

America has not yet any great capital[1] whose direct or indirect

[1] There is not yet any great capital in America, but there are already very large towns. In 1830 the population of Philadelphia was 160,000 and of New York, 202,000. The lowest classes in these vast cities are a rabble more dangerous even than that of European towns. The very lowest are the freed Negroes condemned by law and opinion to a hereditary state of degradation and wretchedness. Then, there is a crowd of Europeans driven by misfortune or misbehavior to the shores of the New World; such men carry our worst vices to the United States without any of those interests which might counteract their influence. Living in the land without being citizens, they are ready to profit from all the passions that agitate it; thus quite recently there have been serious riots in Philadelphia and New York. Such disorders are unknown in the rest of the country, which does not get excited because the populations of the towns do not at present exercise any authority or influence over the country people.

Nevertheless, I regard the size of some American cities and especially the nature of their inhabitants as a real danger threatening the future of the democratic republics of the New World, and I should not hesitate to predict that it is through them that they will perish, unless their government succeeds in creating an armed force which, while remaining subject to the wishes of the national majority, is independent of the peoples of the towns and capable of suppressing their excesses.

influence is felt through the length and breadth of the land, and I believe that that is one of the primary reasons why republican institutions are maintained in the United States. In towns it is impossible to prevent men assembling, getting excited together, and forming sudden passionate resolves. Towns are like great meeting houses with all the inhabitants as members. In them the people wield immense influence over their magistrates and often carry their desires into execution without intermediaries.

Therefore, to subject the provinces to the capital is to place the destinies of the whole empire not only into the hands of a section of the people, which is unfair, but also into the hands of the people acting on their own, which is very dangerous. Therefore the preponderance of capitals is a great threat to the representative system; it makes modern republics share this defect with those of antiquity, all of which perished because they did not know this system.

I could easily enumerate here a large number of secondary causes favoring the establishment and assuring the maintenance of the democratic republic in the United States. But among this mass of lucky circumstances there are two main features which I am anxious to point out now.

I have said before that I regarded the origin of the Americans, what I have called their point of departure, as the first and most effective of all the elements leading to their present prosperity. The chances of birth favored the Americans; their fathers of old brought to the land in which they live that equality both of conditions and of mental endowments from which, as from its natural source, a democratic republic was one day to arise. But that is not all; with a republican social state they bequeathed to their descendants the habits, ideas, and mores best fitted to make a republic flourish. When I consider all that has resulted from this first fact, I think I can see the whole destiny of America contained in the first Puritan who landed on those shores, as that of the whole human race in the first man.

Among the lucky circumstances that favored the establishment and assured the maintenance of a democratic republic in the United States, the most important was the choice of the land itself in which the Americans live. Their fathers gave them a love of equality and liberty, but it was God who, by handing a limitless continent over to them, gave them the means of long remaining equal and free.

General prosperity favors stability in all governments, but particularly in a democratic one, for it depends on the moods of the greatest number, and especially on the moods of those most exposed to want. When the people rule, they must be happy, if they are not to overthrow the state. With them wretchedness has the same effect as ambition has on kings. Now, the physical causes, unconnected with laws, which can lead to prosperity are more numerous in America than in any other country at any other time in history.

In the United States not legislation alone is democratic, for Nature herself seems to work for the people.

Where, among all that man can remember, can we find anything like what is taking place before our eyes in North America?

The famous societies of antiquity were all founded in the midst of enemy peoples who had to be conquered in order to take their place. Modern nations have found in some parts of South America vast lands inhabited by peoples less enlighted than themselves, but those peoples had already taken possession of the soil and were cultivating it. The newcomers, to found their states, had to destroy or enslave numerous populations, and civilization blushes at their triumphs.

But North America was only inhabited by wandering tribes who had not thought of exploiting the natural wealth of the soil. One could still properly call North America an empty continent, a deserted land waiting for inhabitants.

Everything about the Americans, from their social condition to their laws, is extraordinary; but the most extraordinary thing of all is the land that supports them.

When the Creator handed the earth over to men, it was young and inexhaustible, but they were weak and ignorant; and by the time that they had learned to take advantage of the treasures it contained, they already covered its face, and soon they were having to fight for the right to an asylum where they could rest in freedom.

It was then that North America was discovered, as if God had held it in reserve and it had only just arisen above the waters of the flood.

There, there are still, as on the first days of creation, rivers whose founts never run dry, green and watery solitudes, and limitless fields never yet turned by the plowshare. In this condition it offers itself not to the isolated, ignorant, and barbarous man of the first ages, but to man who has already mastered the most important secrets of nature, united to his fellows, and taught by the experience of fifty centuries.

Now, at the time of writing, thirteen million civilized Europeans are quietly spreading over these fertile wildernesses whose exact resources and extent they themselves do not yet know. Three or four thousand soldiers drive the wandering native tribes before them; behind the armed men woodcutters advance, penetrating the forests, scaring off the wild beasts, exploring the course of rivers, and preparing the triumphal progress of civilization across the wilderness.

In the course of this book I have often mentioned the material prosperity enjoyed by the Americans and have pointed it out as one of the great reasons for the success of their laws. Very many others before me have attributed it to the same cause, and as it is the only one that strikes the attention of Europeans, it has become familiar to us. I will not therefore expatiate on a subject so often dealt with and so well understood, but only wish to add a few new facts.

It is generally supposed that the wildernesses of America are peopled by European immigrants arriving annually on the shores of the New World, while the American population grows and multiplies on the soil occupied by their fathers; that is a great mistake. The European arriving in the United States comes without friends and often without resources; in order to live he is obliged to hire out his services, and he seldom goes beyond the great industrial zone stretching along the ocean. One cannot clear the wilderness without either capital or credit, and before a man ventures into the forest his body must be accustomed to the rigors of a new climate. It is therefore Americans who are continually leaving their birthplace and going forth to win vast far-off domains. So the European quits his hovel to go and dwell on the transatlantic coast, while the American who was born there moves off in turn into the central solitudes of America. This double movement of immigration never halts; it starts from the depths of Europe, continues across the great ocean, and then goes on through the solitudes of the New World. Millions of men are all marching together toward the same point on the horizon; their languages, religions, and mores are different, but they have one common aim. They have been told that fortune is to be found somewhere toward the west, and they hasten to seek it.

Nothing in history is comparable to this continuous movement of mankind except perhaps that which followed the fall of the Roman Empire. Then as now, men in crowds converged on the same point, jostling together in the same places; but the designs of Providence were different then. Then each newcomer brought death and destruction in his train, but now it is the seed of life and of prosperity that he bears.

The ultimate results of American migration to the west are still hidden in the future, but its immediate consequences are easily seen. As some of the old inhabitants annually leave the states in which they were born, the population of these aging states grows but slowly; thus in Connecticut, which still has only fifty-nine people to the square mile, the population has not increased by more than a quarter in the last forty years, whereas in England it has grown by a third within the same time. Hence the European immigrant always lands in a half-filled country where industry is perpetually short of manpower; he becomes a comfortably off workman; his son goes to seek his fortune in an empty land and turns into a rich landowner. The former accumulates the capital which the latter puts to good use, and neither foreigner nor native suffers poverty.

American legislation favors the division of property as much as possible, but something more powerful than legislation prevents it being divided up to excess.[2] The states which are at last beginning to be filled up illustrate this clearly. Massachusetts, the most densely populated part of the Union, has eighty inhabitants to the square mile, which is much less than the one hundred and sixty-two found in France.

But already it is a rare occurrence in Massachusetts for small properties to be divided up; generally the eldest keeps the land, while the younger sons go to seek their fortunes in the wilds.

The law has abolished primogeniture, but one may say that Providence has reestablished it without complaint from anybody, and just for once it does not offend equity.

A single fact will give an idea of the vast number of individuals who leave New England to make homes in the wilds. I am told that in 1830 thirty-six of the members of Congress had been born in the small state of Connecticut. Therefore Connecticut, with one forty-third of the population of the United States, furnished one eighth of the representatives.

But Connecticut itself only sends five members to Congress, while the other thirty-one came in the capacity of representatives of the new states to the west. If those thirty-one had stayed in Connecticut, in all probability they would have remained humble laborers, not rich landowners, and would have passed their lives in obscurity, not able to venture on a political career, and instead of becoming useful legislators, they would have been dangerous citizens.

The Americans are as aware of this point as we are.

In his *Commentaries on American Law* (Vol. IV, p. 385), Chancellor Kent says that "it would be very unfounded to suppose that the evils of the equal partition of estates have been seriously felt in these United States, or that they have borne any proportion to the great advantages of policy, or that such evils are to be anticipated for generations to come. The extraordinary extent of our unsettled territories, the abundance of uncultivated land in the market, and the constant stream of emigration from the Atlantic to the interior

[2] In New England the land is divided up into very small holdings, but it is not being further subdivided.

states, operates sufficiently to keep paternal inheritances unbroken." [Fourth edition (New York, 1840).]

It is hard to give an impression of the avidity with which the American throws himself on the vast prey offered him by fortune. To pursue it he fearlessly braves the arrows of the Indian and the diseases of the wilderness; he goes prepared to face the silence of the forest and is not afraid of the presence of wild beasts. A passion stronger than love of life goads him on. An almost limitless continent stretches before him, and he seems in such a hurry not to arrive too late that one might think him afraid of finding no room left.

I have spoken about emigration from the older states, but what should one say about that from the new? Ohio was only founded fifty years ago, most of its inhabitants were not born there, its capital is not thirty years old, and an immense stretch of unclaimed wilderness still covers its territory; nevertheless, the population of Ohio has already started to move west; most of those who come down to the fertile prairies of Illinois were inhabitants of Ohio. These men had left their first fatherland to better themselves; they leave the second to do better still; they find prosperity almost everywhere, but not happiness. For them desire for well-being has become a restless, burning passion which increases with satisfaction. They broke the ties of attachment to their native soil long ago and have not formed new ones since. To start with, emigration was a necessity for them; now it is a sort of gamble, and they enjoy the sensations as much as the profit.

Sometimes man advances so quickly that the wilderness closes in again behind him. The forest has only bent beneath his feet and springs up again when he has passed. Traveling through the new states of the West, one often finds abandoned houses in the middle of the forest, ruined cabins in the remotest solitude, and, to one's astonishment, attempts at clearings, bearing witness alike to the power and the fickleness of man. The ancient forest is not slow to push out new shoots over these abandoned fields and day-old ruins; animals again claim possession of their domain; smiling Nature covers the traces of man with green branches and flowers, obliterating all sign of his ephemeral passage.

I remember, when passing through one of the still-wild districts remaining in New York State, coming to the shore of a lake surrounded by forest, as at the beginning of the world. A little island rose from the water, its banks completely hidden by the foliage of the trees that covered it. Nothing on the lake shore suggested the presence of man; only on the horizon could one see a column of smoke stretching perpendicularly above the treetops to the clouds, as if hung from the sky instead of rising thither.

An Indian canoe was drawn up on the sand, and by its means I soon arrived at the island which had attracted my attention. The whole island was one of those delightful New World solitudes that almost make civilized man regret the savage life. The marvels of a vigorous vegetation told of the incomparable wealth of the soil. The deep silence of the North American wilderness was only broken by the monotonous cooing of wood pigeons or the tapping of green woodpeckers on the trees' bark. Nature seemed completely left to herself, and it was far from my thoughts to suppose that the place had once been inhabited. But when I got to the middle of the island I suddenly thought I noticed traces of man. Then, looking closely at everything around, I was soon convinced that a European had come to seek a refuge in this place. But how greatly his work had changed appearance! The logs he had hastily cut to build a shelter had sprouted afresh; his fences had become live hedges, and his cabin had been turned into a grove. Among the bushes were a few stones blackened by fire around a little heap of ashes; no doubt that was his hearth, covered with the ruins of a fallen chimney. For some little time I silently contemplated the resources of nature and the feebleness of man; and when I did leave the enchanted spot, I kept saying sadly: "What! Ruins so soon!"

In Europe we habitually regard a restless spirit, immoderate desire for wealth, and an extreme love of independence as great social dangers. But precisely those things assure a long and peaceful future for the American republics. Without such restless passions the population would be concentrated around a few places and would soon experience, as we do, needs which are hard to satisfy. What a happy land the New World is, where man's vices are almost as useful to society as his virtues!

This exercises a great influence over the way human actions are judged in the two hemispheres. What we call love of gain is praiseworthy industry to the Americans, and they see something of a cowardly spirit in what we consider moderation of desires.

In France we regard simple tastes, quiet mores, family feeling, and love of one's birthplace as great guarantees for the tranquillity and happiness of the state. But in America nothing seems more prejudicial to society than virtues of that sort. The French of Canada, who loyally preserve the tradition of their ancient mores, are already finding it difficult to live on their land, and this small nation which has only just come to birth will soon be a prey to all the afflictions of old nations. The most enlightened, patriotic, and humane men in Canada make extraordinary efforts to render people dissatisfied with the simple happiness that still contents them. They extol the advantages of wealth in much the same way as, perhaps, in France they would have praised the charms of a moderate competence, and are at greater pains to goad human passions than others elsewhere to calm them. To change the pure and quiet pleasures which his homeland offers even to the poor man for the sterile enjoyments of prosperity under an alien sky, to flee from the paternal hearth and the fields where his ancestors rest, and to leave both living and dead to chase after fortune are all things most praiseworthy in their eyes.

In our day no human industry could fully exploit all the vast opportunities America offers.

In America there cannot be enough of knowledge, for all knowledge benefits both those who possess it and those who do not. New wants are not to be feared, for there all wants can easily be satisfied; there is no need to dread the growth of excessive passions, for there is healthy food easily available to feed them all; men there cannot have too much freedom, for they are hardly ever tempted to make ill use thereof.

The present-day American republics are like companies of merchants formed to exploit the empty lands of the New World, and prosperous commerce is their occupation.

The passions that stir the Americans most deeply are commercial and not political ones, or rather they carry a trader's habits over into the business of politics. They like order, without which affairs do not prosper, and they set an especial value on regularity of mores, which are the foundation of a sound business; they prefer the good sense which creates fortunes to the genius which often dissipates them; their minds, accustomed to definite calculations, are frightened by general ideas; and they hold practice in greater honor than theory.

One must go to America to understand the power of material prosperity over political behavior, and even over opinions too, though those should be subject to reason alone. It is the foreigners who best illustrate the truth of this. Most European immigrants carry over to the New World that fierce love of independence and of change which often breeds amid our afflictions. Occasionally in the United States I met some of those Europeans who had been forced to leave their country on account of their political opinions. The conversation of all of them astonished me, but one most of all. As I was passing through one of the remotest parts of Pennsylvania, I was overtaken by night and went to ask for hospitality at the house of a rich planter. He was French. He welcomed me to his fireside, and we began to talk with the freedom suitable to people meeting in the depths of the forest two thousand leagues from their native land. I was aware that my host had been a great leveler and an ardent demagogue forty years before, for his name had left a mark on history.

It was therefore strange and astonishing to hear him talk like an economist—I almost said a landowner—about the rights of property; he spoke of the necessary hierarchy that wealth establishes among men, of obedience to the established law, of the influence of good mores in republics, and of the support to order and freedom afforded by religious ideas; and it even happened that he inadvertently quoted the authority of Jesus Christ in support of one of his political opinions.

I listened and marveled at the feebleness of human reason. A thing is true or false; but how can one find out amid the uncertainties of knowledge and the diverse lessons of experience? A new fact may come and remove all my doubts. I was poor, and now, look, I am rich; if only prosperity, while affecting my conduct, would leave my judgment free! In fact, my opinions do change with my fortune, and the lucky circumstances of which I take advantage really do provide that decisive argument I could not find before.

Prosperity's influence operates even more freely over Americans than over foreigners. The American has always seen order and public prosperity linked together and marching in step; it never strikes him that they could be separate; consequently he has nothing to forget and has no need to unlearn, as Europeans must, the lessons of his early education.

Influence of the Laws upon the Maintenance of a Democratic Republic in the United States

The three main factors which maintain the democratic republic.
Federal organization. Communal institutions. Judicial power.

The main object of this book has been to make American laws known; if this purpose has been accomplished, the reader can already judge for himself which of these laws in fact tend to support the democratic republic and which put it in danger. If my whole book has not achieved this, much less will this chapter do so.

I do not therefore want to go back over old ground, and a few lines of recapitulation will be enough.

Three factors seem to contribute more than all others to the maintenance of a democratic republic in the New World.

The first is the federal form adopted by the Americans, which allows the Union to enjoy the power of a great republic and the security of a small one.

The second are communal institutions which moderate the despotism of the majority and give the people both a taste for freedom and the skill to be free.

The third is the way the judicial power is organized. I have shown how the courts correct the aberrations of democracy and how, though they can never stop the movements of the majority, they do succeed in checking and directing them.

Influence of Mores upon the Maintenance of a Democratic Republic in the United States

I have said earlier that I considered mores to be one of the great general causes responsible for the maintenance of a democratic republic in the United States.

I here mean the term "mores" (*moeurs*) to have its original Latin meaning; I mean it to apply not only to *"moeurs"* in the strict sense, which might be called the habits of the heart, but also to the different notions possessed by men, the various opinions current among them, and the sum of ideas that shape mental habits.

So I use the word to cover the whole moral and intellectual state of a people. It is not my aim to describe American mores; just now I am only looking for the elements in them which help to support political institutions.

Religion Considered as a Political Institution and How it Powerfully Contributes to the Maintenance of a Democratic Republic Among the Americans

North America is peopled by men professing a democratic and republican Christianity. Arrival of the Catholics. Why the Catholics nowadays form the most democratic and republican class.

Every religion has some political opinion linked to it by affinity. The spirit of man, left to follow its bent, will regulate political society and the City of God in uniform fashion; it will, if I dare put it so, seek to *harmonize* earth with heaven.

Most of English America was peopled by men who, having shaken off the pope's authority, acknowledged no other religious supremacy; they therefore brought to the New World a Christianity which I can only describe as democratic and republican; this fact singularly favored the establishment of a temporal republic and democracy. From the start politics and religion agreed, and they have not since ceased to do so.

About fifty years ago Ireland began to pour a Catholic population into the United States. Also American Catholicism made converts. There are now in the United States more than a million Christians professing the truths of the Roman Church.

These Catholics are very loyal in the practice of their worship and full of zeal and ardor for their beliefs. Nevertheless, they form the most republican and democratic of all classes in the United States. At first glance this is astonishing, but reflection easily indicates the hidden causes therefore.

I think one is wrong in regarding the Catholic religion as a natural enemy of democracy. Rather, among the various Christian doctrines Catholicism seems one of those most favorable to equality of conditions. For Catholics religious society is composed of two elements: priest and people. The priest is raised above the faithful; all below him are equal.

In matters of dogma the Catholic faith places all intellects on the same level; the learned man and the ignorant, the genius and the common herd, must all subscribe to the same details of belief; rich and poor must follow the same observances, and it imposes the same austerities upon the strong and the weak; it makes no compromise with any mortal, but applying the same standard to every human being, it mingles all classes of society at the foot of the same altar, just as they are mingled in the sight of God.

Catholicism may dispose the faithful to obedience, but it does not prepare them for inequality. However, I would say that Protestantism in general orients men much less toward equality than toward independence.

Catholicism is like an absolute monarchy. The prince apart, conditions are more equal there than in republics.

It has often happened that a Catholic priest has left his sanctuary to become a power in society, taking his place in the social hierarchy; he has then sometimes used his religious influence to assure the duration of a political order of which he is part; then, too, one has found Catholic partisans of the aristocracy from religious motives.

But once priests are excluded or exclude themselves from the government, as happens in the United States, no men are more led by their beliefs than are Catholics to carry the idea of equality of conditions over into the political sphere.

So while the nature of their beliefs may not give the Catholics of the United States any strong impulsion toward democratic and republican opinions, they at least are not naturally contrary thereto, whereas their social position and small numbers constrain them to adopt them.

Most of the Catholics are poor, and unless all citizens govern, they will never attain to the government themselves. The Catholics are in a minority, and it is important for them that all rights should be respected so that they can be sure to enjoy their own in freedom. For these two reasons they are led, perhaps in spite of themselves, toward political doctrines which, maybe, they would adopt with less zeal were they rich and predominant.

The Catholic clergy in the United States has made no effort to strive against this political tendency but rather seeks to justify it. American Catholic priests have divided the world of the mind into two parts; in one are revealed dogmas to which they submit without discussion; political truth finds its place in the other half, which they think God has left to man's free investigation. Thus American Catholics are both the most obedient of the faithful and the most independent citizens.

Therefore one can say that there is not a single religious doctrine in the United States hostile to democratic and republican institutions. All the clergy there speak the same language; opinions are in harmony with the laws, and there is, so to say, only one mental current.

While I was temporarily living in one of America's great cities, I was invited to attend a political meeting designed to aid the Poles by helping them to get arms and money.

I found two or three thousand people in a vast hall prepared for their reception. Soon a priest dressed in his ecclesiastical habit came forward onto the platform. The audience took off their hats and stood in silence while he spoke as follows:

"Almighty God! Lord of Hosts! Thou who didst strengthen the hearts and guide the arms of our fathers when they fought for the sacred rights of their national independence! Thou who didst make them triumph over a hateful oppression and didst grant to our people the blessings of peace and of liberty, look with favor, Lord, upon the other hemisphere; have pity upon a heroic people fighting now as we fought before for the defense of these same rights! Lord, who hast created all men in the same image, do not allow despotism to deform Thy work and maintain inequality upon the earth. Almighty God! Watch over the destinies of the Poles and make them worthy to be free; may Thy wisdom prevail in their councils and Thy strength in their arms; spread terror among their enemies; divide the powers that contrive their ruin; and do not allow that injustice which the world has witnessed for fifty years to be consummated in our time. Lord, who holdest in Thy strong hand the hearts of peoples and of men, raise up allies to the sacred cause of true right; arouse at last the French nation, that, forgetting the apathy in which its leaders lull, it may fight once more for the freedom of the world.

"O Lord! Turn not Thou Thy face from us, and grant that we may always be the most religious and the most free nation upon earth.

"God Almighty, hear our supplications this day, and save the Poles. We beseech Thee in the name of Thy beloved son, our Lord Jesus Christ, who died upon the cross for the salvation of all men. Amen."

The whole assembly answered reverently, "Amen."

Indirect Influence of Religious Beliefs upon Political Society in the United States

Christian morality common to all sects. Influence of religion on American mores. Respect for the marriage tie. How religion keeps the imagination of the Americans within certain limits and moderates their passion for innovation. Opinion of the Americans concerning the political value of religion. Their efforts to extend and assure its sway.

I have just pointed out the direct action of religion on politics in the United States. Its indirect action seems to me much greater still, and it is just when it is not speaking of freedom at all that it best teaches the Americans the art of being free.

There is an innumerable multitude of sects in the United States. They are all different in the worship they offer to the Creator, but all agree concerning the duties of men to one another. Each sect worships God in its own fashion, but all preach the same morality in the name of God. Though it is very important for man as an individual that his religion should be true, that is not the case for society. Society has nothing to fear or hope from another life; what is most important for it is not that all citizens should profess the true religion but that they should profess religion. Moreover, all the sects in the United States belong to the great unity of Christendom, and Christian morality is everywhere the same.

One may suppose that a certain number of Americans, in the worship they offer to God, are following their habits rather than their convictions. Besides, in the United States the sovereign authority is religious, and consequently hypocrisy should be common. Nonetheless, America is still the place where the Christian religion has kept the greatest real power over men's souls; and nothing better demonstrates how useful and natural it is to man, since the country where it now has widest sway is both the most enlightened and the freest.

I have said that American priests proclaim themselves in general terms in favor of civil liberties without excepting even those who do not admit religious freedom; but none of them lend their support to any particular political system. They are at pains to keep out of affairs and not mix in the combinations of parties. One cannot therefore say that in the United States religion influences the laws or political opinions in detail, but it does direct mores, and by regulating domestic life it helps to regulate the state.

I do not doubt for an instant that the great severity of mores which one notices in the United States has its primary origin in beliefs. There religion is often powerless to restrain men in the midst of innumerable temptations which fortune offers. It cannot moderate their eagerness to enrich themselves, which everything contributes to arouse, but it reigns supreme in the souls of the women, and it is women who shape mores. Certainly of all countries in the world America is the one in which the marriage tie is most respected and where the highest and truest conception of conjugal happiness has been conceived.

In Europe almost all the disorders of society are born around the domestic hearth and not far from the nuptial bed. It is there that men come to feel scorn for natural ties and legitimate pleasures and develop a taste for disorder, restlessness of spirit, and instability of desires. Shaken by the tumultuous passions which have often troubled his own house, the European finds it hard to submit to the authority of the state's legislators. When the American returns from the turmoil of politics to the bosom of the family, he immediately finds a perfect picture of order and peace. There all his pleasures are simple and natural and his joys innocent and quiet, and as the regularity of life brings him happiness, he easily forms the habit of regulating his opinions as well as his tastes.

Whereas the European tries to escape his sorrows at home by

troubling society, the American derives from his home that love of order which he carries over into affairs of state.

In the United States it is not only mores that are controlled by religion, but its sway extends even over reason.

Among the Anglo-Americans there are some who profess Christian dogmas because they believe them and others who do so because they are afraid to look as though they did not believe in them. So Christianity reigns without obstacles, by universal consent; consequently, as I have said elsewhere, everything in the moral field is certain and fixed, although the world of politics seems given over to argument and experiment. So the human spirit never sees an unlimited field before itself; however bold it is, from time to time it feels that it must halt before insurmountable barriers. Before innovating, it is forced to accept certain primary assumptions and to submit its boldest conceptions to certain formalities which retard and check it.

The imagination of the Americans, therefore, even in its greatest aberrations, is circumspect and hesitant; it is embarrassed from the start and leaves its work unfinished. These habits of restraint are found again in political society and singularly favor the tranquillity of the people as well as the durability of the institutions they have adopted. Nature and circumstances have made the inhabitant of the United States a bold man, as is sufficiently attested by the enterprising spirit with which he seeks his fortune. If the spirit of the Americans were free of all impediment, one would soon find among them the boldest innovators and the most implacable logicians in the world. But American revolutionaries are obliged ostensibly to profess a certain respect for Christian morality and equity, and that does not allow them easily to break the laws when those are opposed to the executions of their designs; nor would they find it easy to surmount the scruples of their partisans even if they were able to get over their own. Up till now no one in the United States has dared to profess the maxim that everything is allowed in the interests of society, an impious maxim apparently invented in an age of freedom in order to legitimatize every future tyrant.

Thus, while the law allows the American people to do everything, there are things which religion prevents them from imagining and forbids them to dare.

Religion, which never intervenes directly in the government of American society, should therefore be considered as the first of their political institutions, for although it did not give them the taste for liberty, it singularly facilitates their use thereof.

The inhabitants of the United States themselves consider religious beliefs from this angle. I do not know if all Americans have faith in their religion—for who can read the secrets of the heart?—but I am sure that they think it necessary to the maintenance of republican institutions. That is not the view of one class or party among the citizens, but of the whole nation; it is found in all ranks.

In the United States, if a politician attacks a sect, that is no reason why the supporters of that very sect should not support him; but if he attacks all sects together, everyone shuns him, and he remains alone.

While I was in America, a witness called at assizes of the county of Chester (state of New York) declared that he did not believe in the existence of God and the immortality of the soul. The judge refused to allow him to be sworn in, on the ground that the witness had destroyed beforehand all possible confidence in his testimony.[3] Newspapers reported the fact without comment.

For the Americans the ideas of Christianity and liberty are so completely mingled that it is almost impossible to get them to conceive of the one without the other; it is not a question with them of sterile beliefs bequeathed by the past and vegetating rather than living in the depths of the soul.

I have known Americans to form associations to send priests out into the new states of the West and establish schools and churches there; they fear that religion might be lost in the depths of the forest and that the people growing up there might be less fitted for freedom than those from whom they sprang. I have met rich New Englanders who left their native land in order to establish the fundamentals of Christianity and of liberty by the banks of the Missouri or on the prairies of Illinois. In this way, in the United States, patriotism continually adds fuel to the fires of religious zeal. You will be mistaken if you think that such men are guided only by thoughts of the future life; eternity is only one of the things that concern them. If you talk to these missionaries of Christian civilization you will be surprised to hear them so often speaking of the goods of this world and to meet a politician where you expected to find a priest. "There is a solidarity between all the American

[3] This is how the New York *Spectator* of August 23, 1831, reported the matter: "The court of common pleas of Chester county (New York) a few days since, rejected a witness who declared his disbelief in the existence of God. The presiding judge remarked that he was not before aware that there was a man living who did not believe in the existence of God; that this belief constituted the sanction of all testimony in a court of justice; and that he knew of no cause in a Christian country, where a witness had been permitted to testify without such belief." [Tocqueville quotes this in English.]

republics," they will tell you; "if the republics of the West were to fall into anarchy or to be mastered by a despot, the republican institutions now flourishing on the Atlantic coast would be in great danger; we therefore have an interest in seeing that the new states are religious so that they may allow us to remain free."

That is what the Americans think, but our pedants find it an obvious mistake; constantly they prove to me that all is fine in America except just that religious spirit which I admire; I am informed that on the other side of the ocean freedom and human happiness lack nothing but Spinoza's belief in the eternity of the world and Cabanis' contention that thought is a secretion of the brain. To that I have really no answer to give, except that those who talk like that have never been in America and have never seen either religious peoples or free ones. So I shall wait till they come back from a visit to America.

There are people in France who look on republican institutions as a temporary expedient for their own aggrandizement. They mentally measure the immense gap separating their vices and their poverty from power and wealth, and they would like to fill this abyss with ruins in an attempt to bridge it. Such people stand toward liberty much as the medieval *condottieri* stood toward the kings; they make war on their own account, no matter whose colors they wear: the republic, they calculate, will at least last long enough to lift them from their present degradation. It is not to such as they that I speak, but there are others who look forward to a republican form of government as a permanent and tranquil state and as the required aim to which ideas and mores are constantly steering modern societies. Such men sincerely wish to prepare mankind for liberty. When such as these attack religious beliefs, they obey the dictates of their passions, not their interests. Despotism may be able to do without faith, but freedom cannot. Religion is much more needed in the republic they advocate than in the monarchy they attack, and in democratic republics most of all. How could society escape destruction if, when political ties are relaxed, moral ties are not tightened? And what can be done with a people master of itself if it is not subject to God?

The Main Causes That Make Religion Powerful in America

Care with which the Americans have separated church and state. The laws, public opinion, and the clergy's own endeavors all work

*toward this end. Religion's power over the souls of men in the
United States is due to this. Why? What is the natural state of
contemporary man in regard to religion? What peculiar and accidental causes in some countries prevent men from achieving this
state?*

Eighteenth-century philosophers had a very simple explanation for
the gradual weakening of beliefs. Religious zeal, they said, was
bound to die down as enlightenment and freedom spread. It is
tiresome that the facts do not fit this theory at all.

There are sections of the population in Europe where unbelief
goes hand in hand with brutishness and ignorance, whereas in
America the most free and enlightened people in the world zealously
perform all the external duties of religion.

The religious atmosphere of the country was the first thing that
struck me on arrival in the United States. The longer I stayed in
the country, the more conscious I became of the important political
consequences resulting from this novel situation.

In France I had seen the spirits of religion and of freedom almost
always marching in opposite directions. In America I found them
intimately linked together in joint reign over the same land.

My longing to understand the reason for this phenomenon increased daily.

To find this out, I questioned the faithful of all communions;
I particularly sought the society of clergymen, who are the deposi-
taries of the various creeds and have a personal interest in their
survival. As a practicing Catholic I was particularly close to the
Catholic priests, with some of whom I soon established a certain
intimacy. I expressed my astonishment and revealed my doubts to
each of them; I found that they all agreed with each other except
about details; all thought that the main reason for the quiet sway
of religion over their country was the complete separation of church
and state. I have no hesitation in stating that throughout my stay
in America I met nobody, lay or cleric, who did not agree about
that.

This led me to examine more closely than before the position
of American priests in political society. I was surprised to discover
that they held no public appointments.[4] There was not a single
one in the administration, and I found that they were not even
represented in the assemblies.

[4] Unless the phrase is taken to cover their work in the schools. The greater
part of education is entrusted to the clergy.

In several states the law,[5] and in all the rest public opinion, excludes them from a career in politics.

When I finally came to inquire into the attitudes of the clergy themselves, I found that most of them seemed voluntarily to steer clear of power and to take a sort of professional pride in claiming that it was no concern of theirs.

I heard them pronouncing anathemas against ambition and bad faith, under whatsoever political opinions those were at pains to hide. But I learned from their discourses that men are not guilty in the sight of God because of these very opinions, provided they are sincere, and that it is no more a sin to make a mistake in some question of government than it is a sin to go wrong in building one's house or plowing one's field.

I saw that they were careful to keep clear of all parties, shunning contact with them with all the anxiety attendant upon personal interest.

These facts convinced me that I had been told the truth. I then wished to trace the facts down to their causes. I wondered how it could come about that by diminishing the apparent power of religion one increased its real strength, and I thought it not impossible to discover the reason.

The short space of sixty years can never shut in the whole of man's imagination; the incomplete joys of this world will never satisfy his heart. Alone among all created beings, man shows a natural disgust for existence and an immense longing to exist; he scorns life and fears annihilation. These different instincts constantly drive his soul toward contemplation of the next world, and it is religion that leads him thither. Religion, therefore, is only one particular form of hope, and it is as natural to the human heart as

[5] See the Constitution of New York, Article VII, paragraph 4.

Idem of North Carolina, Article XXXI. [Tocqueville refers to the Constitution of 1776.]

Idem of Virginia.

Idem of South Carolina, Article I, section 23. [Constitution of 1790.]

Idem of Kentucky, Article II, section 26. [Tocqueville refers to the Constitution of 1799.]

Idem of Tennessee, Article VIII, section 1. [Constitution of 1796.]

Idem of Louisiana, Article II, section 22.

The article of the Constitution of New York is conceived thus:

"And whereas the ministers of the gospel are, by their profession, dedicated to the service of God and the cure of souls and ought not to be diverted from the great duties of their functions, therefore, no minister of the gospel or priest of any denomination whatever . . . be eligible to or capable of holding any civil or military office or place within this state." [Article VII, Section 4 of the Constitution of 1821.]

hope itself. It is by a sort of intellectual aberration, and in a way, by doing moral violence to their own nature, that men detach themselves from religious beliefs; an invincible inclination draws them back. Incredulity is an accident; faith is the only permanent state of mankind.

Considering religions from a purely human point of view, one can then say that all religions derive an element of strength which will never fail from man himself, because it is attached to one of the constituent principles of human nature.

I know that, apart from influence proper to itself, religion can at times rely on the artificial strength of laws and the support of the material powers that direct society. There have been religions intimately linked to earthly governments, dominating men's souls both by terror and by faith; but when a religion makes such an alliance, I am not afraid to say that it makes the same mistake as any man might; it sacrifices the future for the present, and by gaining a power to which it has no claim, it risks its legitimate authority.

When a religion seeks to found its sway only on the longing for immortality equally tormenting every human heart, it can aspire to universality; but when it comes to uniting itself with a government, it must adopt maxims which apply only to certain nations. Therefore, by allying itself with any political power, religion increases its strength over some but forfeits the hope of reigning over all.

As long as a religion relies only upon the sentiments which are the consolation of every affliction, it can draw the heart of mankind to itself. When it is mingled with the bitter passions of this world, it is sometimes constrained to defend allies who are such from interest rather than from love; and it has to repulse as adversaries men who still love religion, although they are fighting against religion's allies. Hence religion cannot share the material strength of the rulers without being burdened with some of the animosity roused against them.

Even those political powers that seem best established have no other guarantee of their permanence beyond the opinions of a generation, the interests of a century, or often the life of one man. A law can modify that social state which seems most fixed and assured, and everything changes with it.

Like our years upon earth, the powers of society are all more or less transitory; they follow one another quickly, like the various cares of life; and there has never been a government supported by some invariable disposition of the human heart or one founded upon some interest that is immortal.

So long as a religion derives its strength from sentiments, instincts, and passions, which are reborn in like fashion in all periods of history, it can brave the assaults of time, or at least it can only be destroyed by another religion. But when a religion chooses to rely on the interests of this world, it becomes almost as fragile as all earthly powers. Alone, it may hope for immortality; linked to ephemeral powers, it follows their fortunes and often falls together with the passions of a day sustaining them.

Hence any alliance with any political power whatsoever is bound to be burdensome for religion. It does not need their support in order to live, and in serving them it may die.

The danger I have just pointed out exists at all times but is not always equally obvious.

There are centuries when governments appear immortal and others when society's existence seems frailer than that of a man.

Some constitutions keep the citizens in a sort of lethargic slumber, while others force them into feverish agitation.

When governments seem so strong and laws so stable, men do not see the danger that religion may run by allying itself with power.

When governments are clearly feeble and laws changeable, the danger is obvious to all, but often then there is no longer time to avoid it. One must therefore learn to perceive it from afar.

When a nation adopts a democratic social state and communities show republican inclinations, it becomes increasingly dangerous for religion to ally itself with authority. For the time is coming when power will pass from hand to hand, political theories follow one another, and men, laws, and even constitutions vanish or alter daily, and that not for a limited time but continually. Agitation and instability are natural elements in democratic republics, just as immobility and somnolence are the rule in absolute monarchies.

If the Americans, who change the head of state every four years, elect new legislators every two years and replace provincial administrators every year, and if the Americans, who have handed over the world of politics to the experiments of innovators, had not placed religion beyond their reach, what could it hold on to in the ebb and flow of human opinions? Amid the struggle of parties, where would the respect due to it be? What would become of its immortality when everything around it was perishing?

The American clergy were the first to perceive this truth and to act in conformity with it. They saw that they would have to give up religious influence if they wanted to acquire political power, and they preferred to lose the support of authority rather than to share its vicissitudes.

In America religion is perhaps less powerful than it has been at certain times and among certain peoples, but its influence is more lasting. It restricts itself to its own resources, of which no one can deprive it; it functions in one sphere only, but it pervades it and dominates there without effort.

On every side in Europe we hear voices deploring the absence of beliefs and asking how religion can be given back some remnant of its former power.

I think we should first consider attentively what ought to be the *natural state* of man with regard to religion at the present day; then, knowing what we can hope and what we must fear, we can clearly see the aim to which our efforts should be directed.

Two great dangers threaten the existence of religion: schism and indifference.

In ages of fervor it sometimes happens that men abandon their religion, but they only escape from its yoke in order to submit to that of another. Faith changes its allegiance but does not die. Then the former religion rouses in all hearts ardent love or implacable hatred; some leave it in anger, others cling to it with renewed ardor: beliefs differ, but irreligion is unknown.

But this is not the case when a religious belief is silently undermined by doctrines which I shall call negative because they assert the falseness of one religion but do not establish the truth of any other.

Then vast revolutions take place in the human mind without the apparent cooperation of the passions of man and almost without his knowledge. One sees some men lose, as from forgetfulness, the object of their dearest hopes. Carried away by an imperceptible current against which they have not the courage to struggle but to which they yield with regret, they abandon the faith they love to follow the doubt that leads them to despair.

In such ages beliefs are forsaken through indifference rather than from hate; without being rejected, they fall away. The unbeliever, no longer thinking religion true, still considers it useful. Paying attention to the human side of religious beliefs, he recognizes their sway over mores and their influence over laws. He understands their power to lead men to live in peace and gently to prepare them for death. Therefore he regrets his faith after losing it, and deprived of a blessing whose value he fully appreciates, he fears to take it away from those who still have it.

On the other hand, he who still believes is not afraid openly to avow his faith. He looks on those who do not share his hopes as unfortunate rather than as hostile; he knows he can win their esteem without following their example; hence he is at war with no man; for him society is not an arena where religion has to fight a relentless battle against a thousand enemies, and he loves his contemporaries, while condemning their weaknesses and sorrowing over their mistakes.

With unbelievers hiding their incredulity and believers avowing their faith, a public opinion favorable to religion takes shape; religion is loved, supported, and honored, and only by looking into the depths of men's souls will one see what wounds it has suffered.

The mass of mankind, never left without religious feeling, sees no impediments to established beliefs. The instinctive sense of another life without difficulty leads them to the foot of the altar and opens their hearts to the precepts and consolations of faith.

Why does this picture not apply to us?

There are some among us who have ceased to believe in Christianity without adopting any other religion.

There are others in a permanent state of doubt who already pretend no longer to believe.

Yet others are still believing Christians but do not dare to say so.

Amid these tepid friends and ardent adversaries there are finally a very few faithful ready to brave all obstacles and scorn all dangers for their beliefs. These have triumphed over human weakness to rise above common opinion. Carried away by the very force of this effort, they no longer know precisely where to stop. Since they have seen in their country that the first use made of independence has been to attack religion, they dread their contemporaries and recoil in alarm from the freedom which they seek. Imagining unbelief to be something new, they comprise all that is new in one indiscriminate animosity. They are at war with their age and country and see each opinion professed as a necessary enemy of faith.

That should not now be the natural state of men with regard to religion.

Therefore with us there must be some accidental and particular cause preventing the human spirit from following its inclination and driving it beyond those limits within which it should naturally remain.

I am profoundly convinced that this accidental and particular cause is the close union of politics and religion.

Unbelievers in Europe attack Christians more as political than as religious enemies; they hate the faith as the opinion of a party much more than as a mistaken belief, and they reject the clergy less because they are the representatives of God than because they are the friends of authority.

European Christianity has allowed itself to be intimately united with the powers of this world. Now that these powers are falling, it is as if it were buried under their ruins. A living being has been tied to the dead; cut the bonds holding it and it will arise.

I do not know what is to be done to give back to European Christianity the energy of youth. God alone could do that, but at least it depends on men to leave faith the use of all the strength it still retains.

How the Enlightenment, Habits, and Practical Experience of the Americans Contribute to the Success of Democratic Institutions

What is to be understood by the enlightenment of the American people. American education is more superficial than European. But no one remains completely uneducated. Why? Speed with which thought circulates in the half-peopled states of the West. How practical experience serves the Americans even better than book-learning.

Throughout this book I have been reminding the reader of the influence of the enlightenment and habits of the Americans on the maintenance of their political institutions. So I have little new to add.

So far America has had only a very small number of noteworthy writers, no great historians, and not a single poet. The inhabitants have a sort of prejudice against anything really worthy of the name of literature, and there are towns of the third rank in Europe which yearly publish more literary works than all the twenty-four states of the Union put together.

The spirit of the Americans is averse to general ideas and does not seek theoretical discoveries. Neither politics nor industry leads that way. New laws are continually made in the United States, but there have not yet been great writers there inquiring into the general principles of the laws.

America has learned lawyers and commentators but no publicists, and in politics the world can learn from their example rather than from their teaching.

The same is true for the mechanical arts.

European inventions are sagaciously applied in America, improved, and wonderfully adapted to the country's needs. It is an industrial society but does not cultivate the science of industry. There are good workmen but few inventors. Fulton long hawked his genius in foreign lands before he was given a chance to devote it to his own.

Anyone trying to find out how enlightened the Anglo-Americans are is liable to see the same phenomenon from two different angles. If his attention is concentrated on the learned, he will be astonished how few they are; but if he counts the uneducated, he will think the Americans the most enlightened people in the world.

The whole population falls between these two extremes, as I have noted elsewhere.

In New England every citizen is instructed in the elements of human knowledge; he is also taught the doctrine and the evidences of his religion; he must know the history of his country and the main features of its Constitution. In Connecticut and Massachusetts you will very seldom find a man whose knowledge of all these things is only superficial, and anybody completely unaware of them is quite an oddity.

Comparing the republics of America to those of Greece and Rome, one thinks of the libraries full of manuscripts but the rude population of the former, and of the thousand newspapers which plow the latter land and the enlightened people who live there. When one comes to think of all the efforts made to judge the latter in the light of the former, and by studying what happened two thousand years ago to predict what will occur nowadays, I am tempted to burn my books in order to apply none but new ideas to such a new social state.

But what I have just said about New England should not be taken to apply to the whole of the rest of the Union indiscriminately. The farther one goes to the west or the south, the less public education is found. In the states bordering the Gulf of Mexico one may find, as with us, a certain number of individuals uninstructed in the rudiments of human knowledge, but one would search in vain through the United States for a single district sunk in complete ignorance. There is a simple reason for this: the peoples of Europe started from darkness and barbarism to advance toward civilization and enlightenment. Their progress has been unequal: some have run ahead, while others have done no more than walk; there are some who have halted and are still sleeping by the roadside.

Nothing like that happened in the United States.

The Anglo-Americans were completely civilized when they arrived in the land which their descendants occupy; they had no need to learn, it being enough that they should not forget. It is the children of these same Americans who yearly move forward into the wilderness, bringing, as well as their homes, the knowledge they have already acquired and a respect for learning. Education has made them realize the usefulness of enlightenment and put them in a position to pass this enlightenment on to their children. So in the United States, society had no infancy, being born adult.

The Americans never use the word "peasant"; the word is unused because the idea is unknown; the ignorance of primitive times, rural simplicity, and rustic villages have not been preserved with them, and they have no idea of the virtues or the vices or the rude habits and the naïve graces of a newborn civilization.

At the extreme borders of the confederated states, where organized society and the wilderness meet, there is a population of bold adventurers who to escape the poverty threatening them in their fathers' homes, have dared to plunge into the solitudes of America seeking a new homeland there. As soon as the pioneer reaches his place of refuge, he hastily fells a few trees and builds a log cabin in the forest. Nothing could look more wretched than these isolated dwellings. The traveler approaching one toward evening sees the hearth fire flicker through the chinks in the walls, and at night, when the wind rises, he hears the roof of boughs shake to and fro in the midst of the great forest trees. Who would not suppose that this poor hut sheltered some rude and ignorant folk? But one should not assume any connection between the pioneer and the place that shelters him. All his surroundings are primitive and wild, but he is the product of eighteen centuries of labor and experience. He wears the clothes and talks the language of a town; he is aware of the past, curious about the future, and ready to argue about the present; he is a very civilized man prepared for a time to face life in the forest, plunging into the wildernesses of the New World with his Bible, ax, and newspapers.

It is hard to imagine quite how incredibly quickly ideas circulate in these empty spaces.[6]

[6] I traveled through part of the frontier districts of the United States in a sort of open cart called the mail coach. We went at a great pace day and night along roads that had only just been cleared through immense forests of green trees; when the darkness became impenetrable, our driver set fire to branches of larch, by whose light we continued our way. From time to time we came to a hut in the forest; that was the post office. The mail dropped an enormous bundle of letters at the door of this isolated dwelling, and we went galloping on again, leaving each inhabitant of the neighborhood to come and fetch his share of that treasure.

I do not believe that there is so much intellectual activity in the most enlightened and populous districts of France.[7]

It cannot be doubted that in the United States the instruction of the people powerfully contributes to support the democratic republic. That will always be so, I think, where the instruction which teaches the mind is not separated from the education which is responsible for mores.

But I would not exaggerate this advantage and am very far from thinking, as many people in Europe do think, that to teach men to read and write is enough to make them good citizens immediately.

True enlightenment is in the main born of experience, and if the Americans had not gradually grown accustomed to rule themselves, their literary attainments would not now help them much toward success.

I have lived much among the people in the United States and cannot say how much I admire their experience and their good sense.

Do not lead an American on to talk about Europe; he will usually show great presumption and a rather foolish pride. He will stick to those general and undefined ideas which, in all countries, are such a comfort to the ignorant. But ask him about his own country and the mist clouding his mind will disperse at once; his thought and his language will become plain, clear, and precise. He will tell you what his rights are and what means he can use to exercise them; he knows the customs that obtain in the political world. You will find that he knows about administrative regulations and is familiar with the mechanism of the law. The citizen of the United States has not obtained his practical knowledge and his positive notions from books; his literary education has prepared him to receive them but has not furnished them.

It is by taking a share in legislation that the American learns to know the law; it is by governing that he becomes educated about the formalities of government. The great work of society is daily performed before his eyes, and so to say, under his hands.

In the United States, education as a whole is directed toward

---

[7] In 1832 the post-office revenue obtained 1 franc, 22 centimes, per head of population in Michigan and 1 franc, 5 centimes, in the Floridas. (See the *National Calendar,* 1833, p. 244.) In the same year the French post office received 1 franc, 4 centimes, per head in the Département du Nord. (See *Compte général de l'Administration des Finances,* 1833, p. 623.) Now, at that time Michigan had only 7 inhabitants per square league, and Florida, 5; education was less widespread and activity less in these two districts than in most other states of the Union, whereas the Département du Nord, with 3,400 inhabitants to the square league, is one of the most enlightened and industrialized parts of France.

political life; in Europe its main object is preparation for private life, as the citizens' participation in public affairs is too rare an event to be provided for in advance.

Looking at the two societies, one finds quite overt signs of these differences.

In Europe we often carry the ideas and habits of private life over into public life, and passing suddenly from the family circle to the government of the state, we may frequently be heard discussing the great interests of society in the same way that we talk with our friends.

But the Americans almost always carry the habits of public life over into their private lives. With them one finds the idea of a jury in children's games, and parliamentary formalities even in the organization of a banquet.

The Laws Contribute More to the Maintenance of the Democratic Republic in the United States Than Do the Physical Circumstances of the Country, and Mores Do More Than the Laws

A democratic social state is common to all the nations of America. But only the Anglo-Americans maintain democratic institutions. The Spaniards of South America, as favored by geography as the Anglo-Americans, are unable to maintain a democratic republic. Mexico, which has adopted the Constitution of the United States, cannot do it. The Anglo-Americans of the West find greater difficulty in maintaining it than those of the East. Reason for these differences.

I have said that the maintenance of democratic institutions in the United States must be attributed to circumstances, laws, and mores.[8]

Most Europeans are aware of the first of these three causes only and give it an undue, preponderating importance.

It is true that the Anglo-Americans brought equality of conditions with them to the New World. There were neither commoners nor nobles there, and professional prejudices were always as unknown as prejudices of birth. So with this democratic social state it was not hard for democracy to establish its sway.

But that fact was by no means peculiar to the United States;

[8] I would remind the reader of the general sense in which I use the word "mores": to cover the sum of the moral and intellectual dispositions of men in society.

almost all the colonies in America were founded by men who either started as equals among themselves or became so by living there. There is not a single place in the New World where the Europeans were able to create an aristocracy.

Nevertheless, democratic institutions prosper in the United States alone.

The American Union has no enemies to fight. It is as solitary amid the wildernesses as an island in the ocean.

But geography gave the Spaniards of South America equal isolation, and that isolation has not prevented them from maintaining great armies. They have made war on one another when there were no foreigners to fight. It is only the Anglo-American democracy which has so far been able to maintain itself in peace.

The territory of the Union offers unlimited scope to human activity; it provides inexhaustible supplies for industry and for labor. Love of wealth therefore takes the place of ambition, and prosperity quenches the fires of faction.

But where in the world can one find more fertile wildernesses, greater rivers, and more untouched and inexhaustible riches than in South America? Nevertheless, South America cannot maintain a democracy. If it was enough for the happiness of nations to be placed in a corner of the world where they can spread at will over uninhabited lands, the Spaniards of Central America would have no reason to complain of their lot. Even if they could not enjoy the same happiness as the dwellers in the United States, they ought at least to be the envy of European nations. Yet there are no nations on earth more miserable than those of South America.

Thus physical causes not only fail to produce analogous results in South and in North America, but in the former land they cannot even bring the population up to the European level, though in Europe geography is unfavorable.

Therefore physical causes do not influence the destiny of nations as much as is supposed.

I have met New Englanders ready to abandon their homeland, in which they could gain a comfortable living, to seek their fortunes in the wilderness. Nearby I saw the population of French Canada crowded into a space too narrow for them, although the same wilderness lay close at hand; and while the United States immigrant gained a large estate at the price of a few days' work, the French Canadian paid as high a price for his land as if he were still living in Europe.

Thus nature, in offering the solitudes of the New World to Europeans, offers something which they do not always know how to use.

Other nations in America have the same opportunities for prosperity as the Anglo-Americans, but not their laws or mores, and these nations are wretched. So the laws and mores of the Anglo-Americans are the particular and predominant causes, which I have been seeking, of their greatness.

I am far from claiming that there is absolute excellence in the American type of laws: I do not believe that they are applicable to all democratic peoples, and there are several of them that strike me as dangerous even in the United States.

But it cannot be denied that American legislation, taken as a whole, is well adapted to the genius of the people ruled thereby and to the nature of the country.

A great part of the success of democratic government must be attributed to these good American laws, but I do not think that they are the main cause. While I think that they have more influence on American social happiness even than the nature of the country, I still have reasons for thinking that mores are even more important.

Assuredly, federal laws are the most important part of United States legislation.

Mexico, as happily situated as the Anglo-American Union, has adopted these same laws but cannot get used to democratic government.

So there must be some other reason, apart from geography and laws, which makes it possible for democracy to rule the United States.

Another still more striking proof may be adduced. Almost everyone living within the Union is sprung from the same stock. They all speak the same language, pray to God in the same fashion, are subject to the same material conditions, and obey the same laws.

From what, then, do the obvious differences between them spring?

Why, in the East of the Union, is republican government strong and orderly, preceding with mature deliberation? What gives the wise and lasting character to all its acts?

On the other hand, in the West, why do the powers of society seem to proceed at random?

Why, in the conduct of public affairs, is there something so disorderly, passionate, and, one might almost say, feverish, by no means presaging a long future?

I am no longer comparing the Americans to foreign nations, but contrasting some Anglo-Americans with others and trying to find out why they are not alike. All arguments derived from the nature of the country and differences of laws are here irrelevant. There must be some other reason, and where can it be found if not in mores?

It is in the East that the Anglo-Americans have had the longest experience of democratic government and have formed the habits and conceived the ideas most favorable to its maintenance. Their customs, opinions, and forms of behavior have been gradually penetrated by democracy, and this shows in every detail of social life, as much as in the laws. It is in the East that both literary and practical education have been carried furthest, and it is there that religion and freedom are most closely linked. What name can one give to all these habits, opinions, usages, and beliefs except the one I have chosen, namely, mores?

But in the West some of these advantages are still lacking. Many of the Americans of the western states were born in the forest, and they mix the ideas and customs of savage life with the civilization of their fathers. Passions are more violent with them, religious morality has less authority, and their convictions are less decided. There men have no control over each other, for they hardly know each other. So, to some extent, the westerners display the inexperience and disorderly habits of a nation coming to birth. For though the elements from which their societies are formed are old, they are newly mixed together.

It is their mores, then, that make the Americans of the United States, alone among Americans, capable of maintaining the rule of democracy; and it is mores again that make the various Anglo-American democracies more or less orderly and prosperous.

Europeans exaggerate the influence of geography on the lasting powers of democratic institutions. Too much importance is attached to laws and too little to mores. Unquestionably those are the three great influences which regulate and direct American democracy, but if they are to be classed in order, I should say that the contribution of physical causes is less than that of the laws, and that of laws less than mores.

I am convinced that the luckiest of geographical circumstances and the best of laws cannot maintain a constitution in despite of mores, whereas the latter can turn even the most unfavorable circumstances and the worst laws to advantage. The importance of mores is a universal truth to which study and experience continually bring us back. I find it occupies the central position in my thoughts; all my ideas come back to it in the end.

I have only one more word to add on this subject.

If in the course of this book I have not succeeded in making the reader feel the importance I attach to the practical experience of the Americans, to their habits, opinions, and, in a word, their mores, in maintaining their laws, I have failed in the main object of my work.

Elsewhere Than in America, Would Laws and Mores Be Enough to Maintain Democratic Institutions?

If the Anglo-Americans were transported to Europe, they would have to modify their laws. One must make a distinction between democratic institutions and American ones. One can imagine democratic laws better than, or at least different from, those adopted by American democracy. The example of America only proves that one need not despair, with the help of laws and mores, of regulating democracy.

I have said that the success of democratic institutions in the United States was due more to their laws and mores than to the nature of the country.

But does it follow that these same causes, transported elsewhere, would by themselves have the same power, and if geography cannot take the place of laws and mores, can laws and mores take the place of geography?

Obviously there is no evidence to prove this; there are nations other than the Anglo-Americans in the New World, subjected to the same material conditions, and I have been able to make comparisons between them.

But outside America there are no nations which, deprived of the physical advantages of the Anglo-Americans, have nevertheless adopted their laws and mores.

Therefore we have no point of comparison in the matter and can only hazard opinions.

I think that first of all we should make a careful distinction between the institutions of the United States and democratic institutions in general.

When I consider the state of Europe, with its great nations, populous cities, formidable armies, and complicated politics, I cannot believe that even the Anglo-Americans, if they were transported with their ideas, religions, and mores onto our soil, could live there without considerably modifying their laws.

But one can imagine a democratic nation organized in a different way from the American people.

Is it, then, impossible to imagine a government founded on the genuine will of the majority, but a majority which, repressing its natural instincts for equality for the sake of order and stability of the state, would consent to invest one family or one man with all the attributes of executive power? Can one not imagine a democratic society in which national strength would be more centralized than in the United States and in which the people exercised a less direct and less irresistible sway over public affairs, but yet where each citizen, invested with certain rights, would take part within his sphere in the proceedings of the government?

What I have seen of the Anglo-Americans leads me to believe that democratic institutions of this nature, prudently introduced into society, so that they should little by little mingle with their habits and gradually become fused with the very opinions of the people, could subsist elsewhere than in America.

If the laws of the United States were the only imaginable democratic ones or the most perfect that could possibly be found, I should conclude that the success of the laws of the United States proved nothing for the success of democratic laws in general in a land less favored by nature.

But if American laws seem to me defective in many respects and I can easily imagine different ones, then the special nature of the country does not prove to me that democratic institutions could not succeed among a people who, while their physical circumstances were less favorable, had better laws.

If men turned out differently in America from what they are elsewhere or if the social condition of the Americans created habits and opinions among them different from those originating from the same social conditions in Europe, what happens in the American democracy would teach me nothing about what might happen in democracies elsewhere.

If the Americans displayed the same inclinations as all other democratic peoples, and their lawgivers had to rely on the nature of the country and the favor of circumstance to restrain these inclinations within just limits, one would have to attribute the prosperity of the United States to purely physical causes, and that would provide no encouragement to peoples wishing to follow their example without their natural advantages.

But the facts do not bear out either of those two suppositions.

In America I found passions like those familiar in Europe; some were due to the very nature of the human heart and others to the democratic state of society.

For example, I found in the United States that restlessness of heart natural to men when all conditions are almost equal and everyone sees the same chance of rising. I found too that the democratic sentiment of envy was expressed in a thousand different ways. I noticed that in the conduct of public affairs the people often displayed a great mixture of presumption and ignorance, and I concluded that, in America as here, men are subject to the same imperfections and exposed to the same afflictions.

But when I came to examine the state of society closely, I readily perceived that the Americans had made great and successful endeavors to combat these weaknesses of human nature and to correct the natural defects of democracy.

Their diverse municipal laws struck me as being so many barriers restraining the citizens' restless ambitions within a narrow sphere and turning to the township's profit those very passions which might have overthrown the state. American lawgivers seemed to have striven with some success to oppose the idea of rights to feelings of envy, the stability of religious morality to the constant changes in the world of politics, the people's experience to their ignorance of theory, and their practical knowledge of business to their impetuous desires.

The Americans have not relied on nature of their country to combat the dangers arising from their Constitution and political laws. They have applied remedies, of which so far they alone have thought, to the ills common to all democratic peoples; and though they were the first to attempt this, they have succeeded.

American laws and mores are not the only ones that would suit democratic peoples, but the Americans have shown that we need not despair of regulating democracy by means of laws and mores.

If other peoples, borrowing this general and creative idea from the Americans, but without wishing to imitate the particular way in which they have applied it, should try to adapt it to the social state which Providence has imposed on the men of our time and should seek by this means to escape the despotism of anarchy threatening them, what reasons have we to believe that they are bound to fail in their endeavor?

The great problem of our time is the organization and establishment of democracy in Christian lands. The Americans have certainly not solved this problem, but they have furnished useful lessons to those who wish to solve it.

The Importance of the Foregoing in Relation to Europe

It is easy to see why I have devoted such time to the foregoing investigations. The question I raise is of interest not to the United States only, but to the whole world; not to one nation, but to all mankind.

If peoples with a democratic social state could not remain free when they live in the wilderness, one would have to despair of the future of the human race, for men are progressing rapidly toward democracy, and the wildernesses are filling up.

If it were true that laws and mores were not enough to maintain democratic institutions, what refuge would remain open to the nations if not the despotism of one man?

I know that there are many worthy persons nowadays who are not afraid of this alternative and who, tired of liberty, would like finally to rest far from its storms.

But such people have little knowledge of the haven to which they are steering. Preoccupied by memories, they judge absolute power by what it was formerly and not by what it may be nowadays.

If absolute power were to be established again among the democratic nations of Europe, I have no doubt that it would take a new form and display features unknown to our fathers.

There was a time in Europe when the law and the people's consent invested kings with almost unlimited power, but they scarcely ever availed themselves of it.

I shall not speak of the prerogatives of the nobility, of the authority of sovereign courts, of the rights of corporations, or of provincial privileges, all things which softened the blows of authority and maintained a spirit of resistance in the nation.

Apart from these political institutions, which, though often opposed to the freedom of individuals, nevertheless served to keep the love of liberty alive in men's souls with obviously valuable results, opinion and mores surrounded the royal power with less-well-known but not less-powerful barriers.

Religion, the affections of the people, the prince's benevolence, honor, family spirit, provincial prejudices, custom, and public opinion all limited the king's power and kept their authority within an invisible boundary.

At that time national constitutions were despotic but mores free. Princes had the right but not the capacity or the desire to do everything.

But of the barriers that formerly held tyranny back, what remains with us today?

Religion having lost its sway over men's souls, the clearest line dividing good from ill has been obliterated; everything in the moral world seems doubtful and uncertain; kings and nations go forward at random, and none can say where are the natural limits of despotism and the bounds of license.

Prolonged revolutions have forever destroyed the respect surrounding heads of state. Unburdened by the weight of public esteem, princes may henceforth abandon themselves without fear to the intoxication of power.

When kings feel their people's hearts drawn toward them, they are merciful because they know they are strong; and they cultivate their subjects' love, for that is the bulwark of the throne. Then the reciprocal feelings of king and people resemble the gracious intercourse of domestic life. The subjects, though they may complain about the king, are yet sorry to displease him, and the sovereign strikes his subjects with a light hand, as a father chastises his children.

But when once the prestige of royalty has vanished in the tumult of revolutions, and when kings, succeeding one another on the throne, have taken turns to display the weakness of *right* and the harshness of *fact*, no one any longer sees the sovereign as father of the state, but each man sees him as his master. If he is weak, he is despised; if strong, hated. He himself is filled with anger and fear; consequently he feels a foreigner in his own country and treats his subjects as a conquered nation.

When towns and provinces form so many different nations within the common motherland, each of them has a particularist spirit opposed to the general spirit of servitude; but now that all parts of a single empire have lost their franchises, usages, prejudices, and even their memories and names and have grown accustomed to obey the same laws, it is no longer more difficult to oppress them all together than to do this to each separately.

While the nobility enjoyed its power, and for a long time, too, after it had lost it, aristocratic honor gave extraordinary strength to individual resistance.

Then there were men who, in spite of their impotence, still held a high idea of their individual worth and dared in isolation to resist the pressure of public authority.

But nowadays, with all classes jumbled together and the individual increasingly disappearing in the crowd, where he is readily lost in the common obscurity, and nowadays, when monarchic honor has almost lost its sway without being replaced by virtue, and there is nothing left which raises a man above himself, who can say where the exigencies of authority and the yielding of weakness will stop?

As long as family spirit endured, a man fighting against tyranny was never alone, for he had around him clients, hereditary friends, and relations. And even were this support lacking, he would still have felt sustained by his ancestors and by his descendants. But when patrimonies are divided up, and within a few years blood is mixed, where is there room for family spirit?

What strength can customs have among a people whose aspect has entirely changed and is still perpetually changing, where there is already some precedent for every act of tyranny, and every crime is following some example, where nothing ancient remains which men are afraid to destroy, and where they dare to do anything new that can be conceived?

What resistance can mores offer when they have so often been twisted before?

What can even public opinion do when not even a *score* of people are held together by any common bond, when there is no man, no family, no body, no class, and no free association which can represent public opinion and set it in motion?

When each citizen being equally impotent, poor, and isolated cannot oppose his individual weakness to the organized force of the government?

To find anything analogous to what might happen now with us, it is not in our own history that we must seek. Perhaps it is better to delve into the memorials of antiquity and carry our minds back to the terrible centuries of Roman tyranny, when mores had been corrupted, memories obliterated, customs destroyed; when opinions became changeable and freedom, driven out from the laws, was uncertain where it could find asylum; when nothing protected the citizens and when the citizens no longer protected themselves; when men made sport of human nature and princes exhausted heaven's mercy before their subjects' patience.

I find those very blind who think to rediscover the monarchy of Henry IV or Louis XIV. For my part, when I consider the state already reached by several European nations and that toward which all are tending, I am led to believe that there will soon be no room except for either democratic freedom or the tyranny of the Caesars.

Is not this worth thinking about? If men must, in fact, come to choose between all being free or all slaves, all having equal rights or all being deprived of them, if the rulers of societies are reduced to this alternative, either gradually to raise the crowd up to their own level or to let all citizens fall below the level of humanity, would not that be enough to overcome many doubts, to reassure many consciences, and to prepare each man readily to make great sacrifices?

Should we not, then, consider the gradual development of democratic institutions and mores not as the best but as the only means remaining to us in order to remain free? And, without loving democratic government, would one not, then, be disposed to adopt it as the readiest and most honorable remedy against the present ills of society?

It is hard to make the people take a share in government; it is even harder to provide them with the experience and to inspire them with the feelings they need to govern well.

The will of a democracy is changeable, its agents rough, its laws imperfect. I grant that. But if it is true that there will soon be nothing intermediate between the sway of democracy and the yoke of a single man, should we not rather steer toward the former than voluntarily submit to the latter? And if we must finally reach a state of complete equality, is it not better to let ourselves be leveled down by freedom rather than by a despot?

Those who, having read this book, should imagine that in writing it I am urging all nations with a democratic social state to imitate the laws and mores of the Anglo-Americans would be making a great mistake; they must have paid more attention to the form than to the substance of my thought. My aim has been to show, by the American example, that laws and more especially mores can allow a democratic people to remain free. But I am very far from thinking that we should follow the example of American democracy and imitate the means that it has used to attain this end, for I am well aware of the influence of the nature of a country and of antecedent events on political constitutions, and I should regard it as a great misfortune for mankind if liberty were bound always and in all places to have the same features.

But I do think that if we do not succeed in gradually introducing democratic institutions among us, and if we despair of imparting to all citizens those ideas and sentiments which first prepare them for freedom and then allow them to enjoy it, there will be no independence left for anybody, neither for the middle classes nor for the nobility, neither for the poor nor for the rich, but only an equal tyranny for all; and I foresee that if the peaceful dominion of the majority is not established among us in good time, we shall sooner or alter fall under the *unlimited* authority of a single man.

Chapter 10

SOME CONSIDERATIONS CONCERNING THE PRESENT STATE AND PROBABLE FUTURE OF THE THREE RACES THAT INHABIT THE TERRITORY OF THE UNITED STATES

I HAVE NOW FINISHED the main task that I set myself and have, to the best of my ability, described the laws and mores of American democracy. I could stop here, but perhaps the reader would feel that I had not satisfied his expectations.

There are other things in America besides an immense and complete democracy, and the inhabitants of the New World may be considered from more than one point of view.

In the course of this work I have been led to mention the Indians and the Negroes, but I have never had the time to stop and describe the position of these two races within the democratic nation I was bent on depicting; I have told in what spirit and by the aid of what laws the Anglo-American confederation was formed; I have only been able to indicate in passing, and in a very complete way, the dangers threatening that confederation, and I could not furnish a detailed account of its chances of survival, independently of laws and mores. When speaking of the united republics, I hazarded no conjecture concerning the permanence of republican forms in the New World, and though often referring to the commercial activity prevailing in the Union, I could not concern myself with the future of the Americans as a trading people.

These topics are like tangents to my subject, being American, but not democratic, and my main business has been to describe democracy. So at first I had to leave them on one side, but now at the end I must return to them.

The territory now occupied or claimed by the American Union extends from the Atlantic Ocean to the shores of the Pacific, its boundaries to east and west being those of the continent itself. To the south it stretches down to the edge of the tropics, and to the north it spreads up to the regions of ice.

The men scattered over it are not, as in Europe, shoots of the same stock. It is obvious that there are three naturally distinct, one might almost say hostile, races. Education, law, origin, and external features too have raised almost insurmountable barriers between them; chance has brought them together on the same soil, but they have mixed without combining, and each follows a separate destiny.

Among these widely different people, the first that attracts attention, and the first in enlightenment, power, and happiness, is the white man, the European, man par excellence; below him come the Negro and the Indian.

These two unlucky races have neither birth, physique, language, nor mores in common; only their misfortunes are alike. Both occupy an equally inferior position in the land where they dwell; both suffer the effects of tyranny, and, though their afflictions are different, they have the same people to blame for them.

Seeing what happens in the world, might one not say that the European is to men of other races what man is to the animals? He makes them serve his convenience, and when he cannot bend them to his will he destroys them.

In one blow oppression has deprived the descendants of the Africans of almost all the privileges of humanity. The United States Negro has lost even the memory of his homeland; he no longer understands the language his fathers spoke; he has abjured their religion and forgotten their mores. Ceasing to belong to Africa, he has acquired no right to the blessings of Europe; he is left in suspense between two societies and isolated between two peoples, sold by one and repudiated by the other; in the whole world there is nothing but his master's hearth to provide him with some semblance of a homeland.

The Negro has no family; for him a woman is no more than the passing companion of his pleasures, and from their birth his sons are his equals.

Should I call it a blessing of God, or a last malediction of His anger, this disposition of the soul that makes men insensible to extreme misery and often even gives them a sort of depraved taste for the cause of their afflictions?

Plunged in this abyss of wretchedness, the Negro hardly notices his ill fortune; he was reduced to slavery by violence, and the habit of servitude has given him the thoughts and ambitions of a slave; he admires his tyrants even more than he hates them and finds his joy and pride in a servile imitation of his oppressors.

His intelligence is degraded to the level of his soul.

The Negro is a slave from birth. What am I saying? He is often sold in his mother's belly and begins, so to say, to be a slave before he is born.

Devoid both of wants and of pleasures, useless to himself, his first notions of existence teach him that he is the property of another who has an interest in preserving his life; he sees that care for his own fate has not devolved on him; the very use of thought seems to him an unprofitable gift of Providence, and he peacefully enjoys all the privileges of his humiliation.

If he becomes free, he often feels independence as a heavier burden than slavery itself, for his life has taught him to submit to everything, except to the dictates of reason; and when reason becomes his only guide, he cannot hear its voice. A thousand new wants assail him, and he lacks the knowledge and the energy needed to resist them. Desires are masters against whom one must fight, and he has learned nothing but to submit and obey. So he has reached this climax of affliction in which slavery brutalizes him and freedom leads him to destruction.

Oppression has weighed as heavily upon the Indian tribes, but with different effects.

Before the white man's arrival in the New World, the inhabitants of North America lived tranquilly in the forests. Facing the normal vicissitudes of savage life, they displayed the vices and virtues of uncivilized peoples. The Europeans, having scattered the Indian tribes far into the wilderness, condemned them to a wandering vagabond life full of inexpressible afflictions.

Savage nations are governed by opinions and mores alone.

In its dealings with the North American Indians, the European tyranny weakened their feeling for their country, dispersed their families, obscured their traditions, and broke their chain of memories; it also changed their customs and increased their desires beyond reason, making them more disorderly and less civilized than they had been before. At the same time, the moral and physical condition of these peoples has constantly deteriorated, and in becoming more wretched, they have also become more barbarous. Nevertheless, the Europeans have not been able to change the character of the Indians entirely, and although they can destroy them, they have not been able to establish order or to subdue them.

The Negro has reached the ultimate limits of slavery, whereas the Indian lives on the extreme edge of freedom. The effect of slavery on the former is not more fatal than that of independence on the latter.

The Negro has lost even the ownership of his own body and cannot dispose of his own person without committing a sort of larceny.

But the savage is his own master as soon as he is capable of action.

Even his family had hardly any authority over him, and he has never bent his will to that of any of his fellows; no one has taught him to regard voluntary obedience as an honorable subjection, and law is unknown to him even as a word. He delights in this barbarous independence and would rather die than sacrifice any part of it. Civilization has little hold on such a man.

The Negro makes a thousand fruitless efforts to insinuate himself into a society that repulses him; he adapts himself to his oppressors' tastes, adopting their opinions and hoping by imitation to join their community. From birth he has been told that his race is naturally inferior to the white man and almost believing that, he holds himself in contempt. He sees a trace of slavery in his every feature, and if he could he would gladly repudiate himself entirely.

In contrast, the pretended nobility of his origin fills the whole imagination of the Indian. He lives and dies amid these proud dreams. Far from wishing to adapt his mores to ours, he regards barbarism as the distinctive emblem of his race, and in repulsing civilization he is perhaps less moved by hatred against it than by fear of resembling the Europeans.[1]

Having nothing but the resources of the wilderness with which to oppose our well-developed arts, undisciplined courage against our

[1] The North American native preserves his opinions and even the slightest details of his customs with an inflexibility otherwise unknown throughout history. In all the two centuries during which the wandering tribes of North America have been in daily contact with the white race, they have not, so to say, borrowed one idea or one custom from them. Nevertheless, the Europeans have had a very great influence over the savages. They have made the Indian character more disorderly but have not been able to make it more European.

In the summer of 1831 I happened to be on the far side of Lake Michigan, at a place called Green Bay, which marks the edge of the frontier between the United States and the Indians of the Northwest. There I became acquainted with an American officer, Major H., who, after talking at length about the inflexibility of the Indian character, told me the following story: "I once knew a young Indian who had been educated at a New England school, where he had greatly distinguished himself and acquired all the external aspect of a civilized man. When war broke out between us and the English in 1810 [*sic*], I saw this young man again; he was then serving in our army at the head of his tribe's warriors. The Americans had allowed the Indians into their ranks only on condition that they abstained from the horrible practice of scalping the defeated. On the evening after the battle of ——, C. came and sat down by our bivouac fire, and I asked what had happened to him that day; he told me, and gradually getting excited at the memory of his exploits, he ended by undoing his coat and saying: 'Don't betray me, but look!' And I actually beheld," said Major H., "between his coat and his shirt, the scalp of an Englishman still dripping with blood." [Cf. Tocqueville, *Journey to America*, ed. J. P. Mayer, New Haven, 1960, p. 37. Major "H." is here identified as Major Lamard.]

tactics, and the spontaneous instincts of his nature against our profound designs, he fails in the unequal contest.

The Negro would like to mingle with the European and cannot. The Indian might to some extent succeed in that, but he scorns to attempt it. The servility of the former delivers him over into slavery; the pride of the latter leads him to death.

I remember that, passing through the forests that still cover the state of Alabama, I came one day to the log cabin of a pioneer. I did not wish to enter the American's dwelling, but went to rest a little beside a spring not far off in the forest. While I was there, an Indian woman came up (we were in the neighborhood of the Creek territory); she was holding by the hand a little girl of five or six who was of the white race and who, I supposed, must be the pioneer's daughter. A Negro woman followed her. There was a sort of barbarous luxury in the Indian woman's dress; metal rings hung from her nostrils and ears; there were little glass beads in the hair that fell freely over her shoulders, and I saw that she was not married, for she was still wearing the bead necklace which it is the custom of virgins to lay down on the nuptial couch; the Negro was dressed in European clothes almost in shreds.

All three came and sat down by the edge of the spring, and the young savage, taking the child in her arms, lavished upon her such fond caresses as mothers give; the Negro, too, sought, by a thousand innocent wiles, to attract the little Creole's attention. The latter showed by her slightest movements a sense of superiority which contrasted strangely with her weakness and her age, as if she received the attentions of her companions with a sort of condescension.

Crouched down in front of her mistress, anticipating her every desire, the Negro woman seemed equally divided between almost maternal affection and servile fear, whereas even in the effusions of her tenderness, the savage woman looked free, proud, and almost fierce.

I had come close and was contemplating the sight in silence; no doubt my curiosity annoyed the Indian woman, for she got up abruptly, pushed the child away from her, almost roughly, and giving me an angry look, plunged into the forest.

I had often seen people of the three races inhabiting North America brought together in the same place; I had already noted very many different signs of white predominance, but there was something particularly touching in the scene I have just described; here a bond of affection united oppressors and oppressed, and nature bringing them close together made the immense gap formed by prejudices and by laws yet more striking.

The Present State and the Probable Future of the Indian Tribes Inhabiting the Territory of the Union

Gradual disappearance of the indigenous races. How it comes about. Miseries accompanying the forced migrations of the Indians. The savages of North America have only two means of escaping destruction: war or civilization. They can no longer make war. Why they refused to become civilized when it was in their power, and why they cannot become so when they have come to desire it. Example of the Creeks and Cherokees. Policy of the particular states toward these Indians. Policy of the federal government.

All the Indian tribes who once inhabited the territory of New England—the Narragansetts, the Mohicans, the Pequots—now live only in men's memories; the Lenapes, who received Penn one hundred and fifty years ago on the banks of the Delaware, have now vanished. I have met the last of the Iroquois; they were begging. All of the nations I have just named once reached to the shores of the ocean; now one must go more than a hundred leagues inland to meet an Indian. These savages have not just drawn back, they have been destroyed.[2] As the Indians have withdrawn and died, an immense nation is taking their place and constantly growing. Never has such a prodigious development been seen among the nations, nor a destruction so rapid.

It is easy to show how this destruction came about.

When the Indians alone dwelt in the wilderness from which now they are driven, their needs were few. They made their weapons themselves, the water of the rivers was their only drink, and the animals they hunted provided them with food and clothes.

The Europeans introduced firearms, iron, and brandy among the indigenous population of North America; they taught it to substitute our cloth for the barbaric clothes which had previously satisfied Indian simplicity. While contracting new tastes, the Indians did not learn the arts to gratify them, and they had to have recourse to the industry of the whites. In return for these goods, which they did not know how to make, the savages could offer nothing but the rich furs still abounding in their forests. From that time forward hunting had to provide not only for their own needs but also for the frivolous passions of Europe. They no longer hunted for forest animals simply

[2] In the thirteen original states there are only 6,373 Indians left. (See *Legislative Documents,* 20th Congress [Second Session], No. 117, p. 20 [?].)

for food, but in order to obtain the only things they could barter with us.[3]

While the needs of the natives were thus increasing, their resources were constantly diminishing.

As soon as a European settlement forms in the neighborhood of territory occupied by the Indians the wild game takes fright.[4] Thousands of savages wandering in the forest without fixed dwelling did not disturb it; but as soon as the continuous noise of European labor is heard in the vicinity, it begins to flee and retreat toward the west, where some instinct teaches it that it will still find limitless wildernesses. In their report to Congress of February 4, 1829, Messrs. Clark and Cass say: "The herds of bison are constantly retreating; several years ago they were approaching the foot of the Alleghenies; in a few years it will perhaps be difficult to see any of them in

[3] Mr. Clark and Mr. Cass, in their *Report to Congress* [Second Session, House of Representatives Document No. 117], February 4, 1829, p. 23 f., said that:

"The time is already far away from us when the Indians could produce the objects necessary for their nourishment and clothing without resorting to the industry of civilized men. Beyond the Mississippi, in a country where one still finds immense herds of buffalo, live Indian tribes which follow these wild animals in their migrations; the Indians of whom we are speaking still find the means of living in conforming to all the customs of their fathers; but the buffalo are constantly retreating. Now, only with guns or traps can one reach wild animals of a smaller species, such as the bear, the deer, the beaver, the muskrat, which particularly supply the Indian with what is necessary for the maintenance of life.

"It is principally in the Northwest that the Indians are obliged to resort to excessive labor in order to nourish their families. Often the hunter devotes several days in succession to pursuing the game without success; during this time his family must be nourished on bark and roots, or they will perish; and so there are many of them who die of hunger each winter." [Tocqueville paraphrases.]

The Indians do not want to live as the Europeans live; however, they cannot do without the Europeans, nor can they live entirely as their fathers did. One can judge this by this single fact, the knowledge of which I also drew from an official source. Men belonging to an Indian tribe on the shores of Lake Superior had killed a European; the American government forbade trading with the tribe of which the guilty men were members until the latter had been handed over, and this was done.

[4] "Five years ago," says Volney in his *Tableau des États-Unis*, p. 370, going from Vincennes to Kaskaskia, territory now included in the state of Illinois, but then completely wild (1797), "one could not cross the prairies without seeing herds of four or five hundred buffalo; but now there are none. They have swum across the Mississippi, disturbed by the hunters, but even more by the bells of the American cattle." [C.-F. Volney, *Tableau du Climat et du Sol des États-Unis d'Amérique* (Paris, 1822), p. 370; the copy Tocqueville used is to be found among his library at Château Tocqueville (La Manche).]

the immense plains that stretch the length of the Rocky Mountains." I have been assured that this effect of the approach of the white men is often felt at two hundred leagues distance from their frontier. So their influence is exerted over tribes whose names they hardly know and who suffer the ills of usurpation long before they see the authors of their distress.[5]

Hardy adventurers soon penetrate into the Indian country; they go fifteen or twenty leagues beyond the white man's extreme frontier, and there build a dwelling for a civilized man in the midst of barbarism. It is easy for them to do so: a hunting people's boundaries are ill-defined. Moreover, the land is the common property of the tribe and does not exactly belong to anybody in particular; therefore no one has an individual interest in defending any part of it.

A few European families occupying widely separated points succeed in chasing all the wild animals forever from the whole region stretching between these points. The Indians who used to live there in some sort of abundance find it difficult to subsist and still more difficult to obtain the needed articles of barter. To drive away their game is like making our farmers' fields sterile. Soon their means of subsistence has almost entirely gone, and these unlucky folk prowl their deserted forests like starving wolves. Instinctive love of country holds them to the soil where they were born,[6] but there is nothing but affliction and death there. At last they come to a decision; they depart, and following the tracks of elk, buffalo, and beaver, leave to these wild animals the choice of their new homeland. So, strictly speaking, it is not the Europeans who chase the natives of America away, but famine: a happy distinction which escaped our ancient casuists, but has been discovered by our learned contemporaries.

It is impossible to imagine the terrible afflictions involved in these forced migrations. The Indians leaving their ancestral fields are already worn down and exhausted. The country in which they intend to live is already occupied by tribes and who regard newcomers

[5] The truth of what I here state can easily be proved by consulting the general account of Indian tribes living within the boundaries claimed by the United States (*Legislative Documents,* 20th Congress, No. 117, pp. 90–105). It will be seen that the tribes in the center of America are rapidly decreasing, although the Europeans are still very far off from them.

[6] On page 15 of their *Report to Congress* Messrs. Clark and Cass say that the Indians are attached to their country by the same feelings of affection as we are to ours; and, moreover, they attach to the idea of alienating the land which the Great Spirit granted to their ancestors certain superstitious ideas which greatly influence the tribes who have still ceded nothing, or only a small portion of their territory, to the Europeans. "We will not sell the spot which contains the bones of our fathers"—that is the first answer they always make to anybody proposing to buy their land.

jealously. There is famine behind them, war in front, and misery everywhere. In the hope to escape so many enemies, they divide up. Each one of them in isolation tries furtively to find some means of subsistence, living in the immensity of the forest like some outlaw in civilized society. The long-weakened social bond then finally breaks. Their homeland has already been lost, and soon they will have no people; families hardly remain together; the common name is lost, the language forgotten, and traces of their origin vanish. The nation has ceased to exist. It barely survives in the memories of American antiquaries and is known to only a few learned men in Europe.

I would not like the reader to think this description too highly colored. With my own eyes I have seen some of the miseries just described; I have witnessed afflictions beyond my powers to portray.

At the end of the year 1831 I was on the left bank of the Mississippi, at the place the Europeans called Memphis. While I was there a numerous band of Choctaws (or Chactas as they are called by the French of Louisiana) arrived; these savages were leaving their country and seeking to pass over to the right bank of the Mississippi, where they hoped to find an asylum promised to them by the American government. It was then the depths of winter, and that year the cold was exceptionally severe; the snow was hard on the ground, and huge masses of ice drifted on the river. The Indians brought their families with them; there were among them the wounded, the sick, newborn babies, and the old men on the point of death. They had neither tents nor wagons, but only some provisions and weapons. I saw them embark to cross the great river, and the sight will never fade from my memory. Neither sob nor complaint rose from that silent assembly. Their afflictions were of long standing, and they felt them to be irremediable. All the Indians had already got into the boat that was to carry them across; their dogs were still on the bank; as soon as the animals finally realized that they were being left behind forever, they all together raised a terrible howl and plunged into the icy waters of the Mississippi to swim after their masters.

Nowadays the dispossession of the Indians is accomplished in a regular and, so to say, quite legal manner.

When the European population begins to approach the wilderness occupied by a savage nation, the United States government usually sends a solemn embassy to them; the white men assemble the Indians in a great plain, and after they have eaten and drunk with them, they say: "What have you to do in the land of your fathers? Soon you will have to dig up their bones in order to live. In what way is the country you dwell in better than another? Are there not forests and marshes and prairies elsewhere than where you live, and can you live nowhere but under your own sun? Beyond these mountains that you see on the horizon, and on the other side of the lake which skirts your land to the west, there are vast countries where wild beasts are still found in abundance; sell your lands to us and go and live happily in those lands." That speech finished, they spread before the Indians firearms, woolen clothes, kegs of brandy, glass necklaces, pewter bracelets, earrings, and mirrors.[7] If, after the sight of all these riches, they still hesitate, it is hinted that they cannot refuse to consent to what is asked of them and that soon the government itself will be powerless to guarantee them the enjoyment of their rights. What can they do? Half convinced, half constrained, the Indians go off to dwell in new wildernesses, where the white men will not let them remain in peace for ten years. In this way the Americans cheaply acquire whole provinces which the richest sovereigns in Europe could not afford to buy.[8]

[7] See *Legislative Documents,* 20th Congress, No. 117 [p. 15 f; Tocqueville summarizes], for an account of what happens in these circumstances. This curious record is found in the already cited *Report to Congress* of Messrs. Clarke and Lewis Cass of February 4, 1829. Mr. Cass is now Secretary of War. "When the Indians arrive in the place where the treaty is to take place, they are poor and almost naked. There they see and examine a large number of objects which are precious to them, which the American merchants have been careful to bring along. The women and children who wish to have their needs provided for then begin to torment the men with a thousand importunate demands and employ all their influence upon the latter to cause the sale of land to take place. The improvidence of the Indians is habitual and invincible. To provide for his immediate needs and gratify his present desires is the irresistible passion of the savage; the expectation of future advantages has only a feeble effect upon him; he easily forgets the past and is not concerned with the future. It would be useless to ask the Indians to cede part of their territory if one were not in a position to satisfy their needs on the spot. Upon considering impartially the situation of this unfortunate people one is not surprised at the fervor they put into obtaining some relief from their ills."

[8] On May 19, 1830, Mr. Edward Everett asserted before the House of Representatives that the Americans had already acquired by *treaty* 230,000,000 acres east and west of the Mississippi.

In 1808 the Osages ceded 48,000,000 acres for a rent of 1,000 dollars.

In 1818 the Quapaws ceded 20,000,000 acres for 4,000 dollars; a territory of 1,000,000 acres was reserved for them to hunt in. A solemn oath had been given to respect this, but it was not long before that too was invaded.

On February 24, 1830, Mr. Bell, in his report to Congress of the Committee on Indian Affairs, said: "The Indians are paid for their unimproved lands as much as the privilege of hunting and taking games upon them is supposed to be worth. . . . To pay an Indian tribe what their ancient hunting grounds are worth to them, after the game is fled or destroyed, as a mode of appropriating wild lands, claimed by Indians, has been found more convenient, and certainly it is more agreeable to the forms of Justice, as well as more

The ills I have just described are great, and I must add that they seem to me irremediable. I think that the Indian race is doomed to perish, and I cannot prevent myself from thinking that on the day when the Europeans shall be established on the coasts of the Pacific Ocean, it will cease to exist.[9]

There were only two roads to safety open to the North American Indians: war or civilization; in other words, they had either to destroy the Europeans or to become their equals.

At the first settlement of the colonies it would have been possible for them, by uniting their forces, to deliver themselves from the small number of foreigners who came to land on the coasts of the continent.[10] They more than once attempted this, and have been on the point of succeeding. Today the disproportion in resources is too great for them to contemplate such an undertaking. Nevertheless, men of genius do rise up among the Indian nations, who foresee the final fate that awaits the savage population and who seek to reunite all the tribes in common hatred against the Europeans; but their endeavors are unavailing. The tribes which are in the neighborhood of the white man are already too greatly weakened to offer effective resistance. The others, with the childish carelessness of the morrow characteristic of savage nature, wait for the danger to reach them before bothering about it. The former cannot and the latter will not act.

It is easy to foresee that the Indians will never want to become civilized, or when they do so desire, it will be too late.

---

merciful, than to assert the possession of them by the sword. Thus, the practice of buying Indian titles is but the substitute which humanity and expediency have imposed, in place of the sword in arriving at the actual enjoyment of property claimed by the right of discovery, and sanctioned by the natural superiority allowed to the claims of civilized communities over those of savage tribes. Up to the present time, so invariable has been the operation of certain causes, first in diminishing the value of forest lands to the Indians; and secondly in disposing them to sell readily; that the plan of buying their right of occupancy has never threatened to retard, in any perceptible degree, the prosperity of any of the States." (*Legislative Documents,* 21st Congress [First Session], No. 227, p. 6 [f.].)

[9] Furthermore, this opinion is shared by almost all American statesmen. Mr. Cass told Congress that "if one judges the future by the past, one can predict a progressive diminution in the number of Indians, and one can expect the final extinction of their race. In order that this event should not take place, it would be necessary that our frontiers cease to extend, and the savages settle beyond them, or that a complete change operate in our relations with them, which would be unreasonable to expect."

[10] See among others the war against New England colonies undertaken in 1675 by the Wampanoags and other confederated tribes under the leadership of Metacom, and that which the English had to sustain in 1622 in Virginia.

Civilization is the result of prolonged social endeavor taking place on the same spot, an endeavor which each generation bequeaths to the next. It is harder for civilization to establish its sway over a hunting people than over any other. Pastoral tribes move from place to place, but there is always a regular system in their migrations and they continually retrace their steps; the dwelling place of the hunter changes like that of the animals he hunts.

There have been several attempts to bring enlightenment to the Indians, leaving unchecked their vagabond mores; the Jesuits attempted it in Canada, and the Puritans in New England.[11] Neither achieved any durable result. Civilization was born in the hut and went to die in the forest. The great mistake of these lawgivers for the Indians was that they did not understand that to succeed in civilizing a people it is above all necessary to get them to take root, and that can only be done by cultivating the soil; therefore the first problem was to turn the Indians into cultivators.

Not only do the Indians not possess this indispensable preliminary for civilization, but it is very difficult for them to acquire it.

Once men have taken to the idle, adventurous life of hunting, they feel an almost insurmountable distaste for the constant and regular labor demanded by agriculture. This is noticeable even within our societies; but it is even more apparent when hunting has become a people's national habit.

Apart from this general cause, there is another equally powerful one applying to the Indians alone. I have already mentioned it but must now return to the subject.

The natives of North America consider labor not only an evil, but also a disgrace, and their pride fights against civilization almost as obstinately as does their laziness.[12]

No Indian in his bark hut is so wretched that he does not entertain a proud conception of his personal worth; he considers the cares of industry degrading occupations; he compares the cultivator to the

[11] See the different historians of New England. See also *Histoire de la Nouvelle France*, by Charlevoix, and *Lettres édifiantes*. [The first publication of the *Lettres édifiantes* is dated 1712. The collection begins in 1703 and continues to 1776 in 34 volumes. An augmented re-edition appeared in 1780. Cf. Gilbert Chinard, *L'Amérique et le Rêve exotique*, Paris, 1934, p. 438. On Charlevoix, see *ibid.*, p. 333 ff.]

[12] "In all the tribes," says Volney in his *Tableau des États-Unis*, p. 423, "there is still a generation of old warriors who, on seeing anybody using a hoe, keep crying out against the degeneration from ancient mores and attributing the decadence of the savages to these innovations, and saying that to regain their power and glory it is enough to return to primitive mores." [C.-F. Volney, *Tableau du Climat et du Sol des États-Unis d'Amérique* (Paris, 1822), p. 423; it is this edition which Tocqueville has used.]

ox plowing a furrow and regards all our crafts merely as the labor of slaves. Granted he has formed a very high opinion of the power and intelligence of the white man; but while admiring the results of our endeavors, he scorns the means to obtain them, and though he admits our ascendancy, he yet considers himself our superior. He thinks hunting and war the only cares worthy of a man.[13] Therefore the Indian in the miserable depths of his forests cherishes the same ideas and opinions as the medieval noble in his castle, and he only needs to become a conqueror to complete the resemblance. How odd it is that the ancient prejudices of Europe should reappear, not among the European population along the coast, but in the forests of the New World.

More than once in the course of this work I have tried to point out the prodigious influence which, I believe, the social state exercises over laws and mores. I beg leave to add one more word on that subject.

When I perceive the resemblance between the political institutions of our German ancestors and the wandering tribes of North America, between customs described by Tacitus and those I have witnessed myself, I cannot avoid the conclusion that in both hemispheres the same cause has produced the same effects and that amid the apparent diversity of human affairs it is possible to discover a few pregnant facts from which all others derive. In all that we call Germanic institutions I am tempted to see nothing but barbaric habits and to regard what we call feudal ideas as the opinions of savages.

Whatever the vices and prejudices preventing the North American Indians from becoming cultivators and civilized, necessity sometimes drives them to it.

Several considerable nations in the South, among others the Cherokees and the Creeks,[14] have found themselves practically surrounded

[13] The following description is taken from an official document:

"Until a young man has come to grips with an enemy and can boast some deeds of prowess, he is held in no consideration: he is almost regarded as a woman.

"In their great war dances all the warriors in turn strike the 'pole,' as it is called, and recount their exploits; the audience on this occasion is composed of the relatives, friends, and comrades of the narrator. The profound impression produced on them is manifest in the silence with which they listen and the loud applause with which they greet the end of the narration. The young man at such a meeting who has nothing to recount feels himself very unfortunate, and there have been instances of young warriors with their passions thus excited suddenly leaving the dance and going forth alone to seek for trophies that they can show and adventures of which they can boast."

[14] These nations are now contained within the states of Georgia, Tennessee, Alabama, and Mississippi.

all at once by Europeans who landed on the Atlantic coast and came simultaneously down the Ohio and up the Mississippi. These Indians were not chased from place to place, as were the Northern tribes, but had been gradually pressed within too narrow limits, as if by hunters encircling a copse before they finally break into it. The Indians, thus faced with the choice of civilization or death, found themselves reduced to living shamefully by their labor, like the white man. So they became cultivators, and not entirely giving up their habits and mores, sacrificed only as much of them as was absolutely necessary to survival.

The Cherokees went further; they created a written language and established a fairly stable form of government, and since everything goes forward at an impetuous rate in the New World, they had a newspaper[15] before they all had clothes.

The presence of half-castes[16] has especially favored the growth of European habits among these Indians. Sharing his father's enlightenment without entirely giving up the savage customs of his race on his mother's side, the half-caste forms the natural link between civilization and barbarism. Everywhere that half-castes have multiplied, the savages have gradually changed their social condition and their mores.[17]

In the South there were formerly four great nations (remnants of which still exist): the Choctaws, Chickasaws, Creeks, and Cherokees.

In 1830 the remnants of these four nations still numbered about 75,000 individuals. It is calculated that there are now about 300,000 Indians in the territory occupied or claimed by the Anglo-Americans. (See *Proceedings of the Indian Board in the City of New York*. [The following is the exact title of this publication: *Documents and Proceedings Relating to the Formation and Progress of a Board in the City of New York for the Emigration, Preservation, and Improvement of the Aborigines of America, July 22, 1829,* New York, 1829.]) Official documents furnished to Congress gave the number as 313,130. The reader curious to know the name and strength of all the tribes inhabiting Anglo-American territory should consult the documents I have just cited. (*Legislative Documents,* 20th Congress, No. 117 [Second Session], pp. 90–105.)

[15] I have brought back to France one or two copies of this singular publication.

[16] See the *Report of the Committee on Indian Affairs,* 21st Congress, No. 227 [First Session], p. 23, for the reason why the half-castes multiplied among the Cherokees. The main reason dates back to the War of Independence. Many Anglo-Americans from Georgia, having sided with England, were forced to withdraw among the Indians, and married there.

[17] Unfortunately the half-castes were fewer and exercised less influence in North America than anywhere else.

Two great European nations peopled this part of the American continent: the French and English.

The former were not slow in forming connections with the daughters of

The success of the Cherokees proves that the Indians have the capacity to become civilized, but it by no means proves that they will succeed in this.

This difficulty that the Indians find in submitting to civilization arises from a general cause almost impossible for them to avoid.

An attentive study of history shows that generally barbarous peoples have raised themselves gradually by their own efforts until they reach civilization.

When it happened that they did derive enlightenment from a foreign nation, then they were the conquerors, not the conquered.

When the conquered people are enlightened and the conquerors half savage, as when the nations of the North invaded the Roman Empire or the Mongols invaded China, the power which the barbarian has won by his victory enables him to keep on a level with the civilized man and to go forward as his equal, until he becomes his rival; one has force to support him and the other intelligence; the former admires the knowledge and arts of the conquered, and the latter envies the conquerors' power. In the end the barbarians invite the civilized people into their palaces, and the civilized open their schools to the barbarians. But when the side that has the physical force has intellectual superiority too, it is rare for the con-

---

the natives, but unfortunately there was some secret affinity between the Indian character and their own. Instead of giving the barbarians the tastes and habits of civilized life, they themselves often became passionately attached to the savage life. They became the most dangerous of the denizens of the wilderness, winning the Indian's friendship by exaggerating both his vices and his virtues. M. de Denonville, governor of Canada, writing to Louis XIV in 1685, says: "It has long been believed that in order to make the savages French we should draw them closer to us, but there is every reason to admit that this was a mistake. Those who have been brought into contact with us have not become French, and the French who frequented them changed into savages. They affected to dress and to live like them." (*Histoire de la Nouvelle France,* by Charlevoix, Vol. II, p. 325.) [We have corrected Tocqueville's page reference; Tocqueville has used the following edition of this work: *Histoire et Description Générale de la Nouvelle France . . .* par le P. de Charlevoix, 6 vols., Paris, 1744. There is also an American edition of this work: Charlevoix, *History and General Description of New France,* with Notes by J. G. Shea, New York, 1870, reprinted Chicago, 1962, 6 vols.]

The Englishman, on the other hand, being obstinately attached to the opinions, habits, and slightest customs of his fathers, has remained amid the solitudes of America just the same as he was in the towns of Europe; he therefore has not wished for any contact with the savages he scorns and has been careful not to mix his blood with that of the barbarians.

Hence, while the French exercised no healthy influence on the Indians, the English were always strangers to them.

quered to become civilized; they either withdraw or are destroyed.

For this reason one can say that, generally speaking, savages go forth in arms to seek enlightenment but do not accept it as a gift.

If the Indian tribes now dwelling in the middle of the continent could summon up energy enough to try to civilize themselves, perhaps they would succeed. For then, having become superior to the barbarous nations surrounding them, they would gradually gain strength and experience, and when the Europeans finally appeared on their borders, they would be in a position, if not to maintain their independence, at least to assert their right to the soil and to incorporate themselves with the conquerors. But the Indians' misfortune has been to come into contact with the most civilized nation in the world, and also, I would add, the greediest, at a time when they are themselves half barbarians, and to find masters in their instructors, having enlightenment and oppression brought to them together.

Living in freedom in the forest, the North American Indian was wretched but felt himself inferior to no man; as soon as he wants to penetrate the social hierarchy of the white men, he can only occupy the lowest rank therein, for he comes as a poor and ignorant man into a society where knowledge and wealth prevail. Having led an adventurous life, full of afflictions and dangers but also full of proud emotions,[18] he must submit to a monotonous, obscure, and degraded

[18] There is something in the adventurous life of a hunting people which seizes the heart of man and carries him away in spite of reason and experience. Anyone who has read Tanner's *Memoirs* must be convinced of this. [*A Narrative of the Captivity and Thirty Years' Residence Among the Indians in the Interior of North America,* New York, 1830. French edition: *Mémoires de John Tanner ou Trente Années dans les Déserts de l'Amérique du Nord,* Traduits sur l'édition originale, publiée à New York par Ernest de Blosseville, 2 vols., Paris, 1835.]

Tanner was a European who was carried off by the Indians at the age of six, and stayed for thirty years in the forests with them. Nothing can be more terrible than the afflictions he describes. He tells us of tribes without a chief, families without a nation, isolated men, the wrecks of powerful tribes, wandering at random through the ice and snow and desolate solitudes of Canada. Hunger and cold are their companions, and every day seems likely to be their last. Among such men mores have lost their sway, and traditions are powerless. Men become more and more barbarous. Tanner shares all these afflictions; he knows his European origin; it is not force that keeps him away from the white men; on the contrary, he goes every year to trade with them, enters their houses, and sees their comfort; he knows that any day that he wished to go back to civilized life he could easily do so, and he stays for thirty years in the wilderness. When he does in the end return to civilized society, he confesses that the existence whose afflictions he has described has secret charms which he cannot define; he returned to it again

existence. In his eyes the only result of this vaunted civilization is that he must earn his bread by hard and ignoble labor.

And even that result he cannot always be sure to obtain.

When the Indians undertake to imitate their European neighbors and to cultivate the soil as they do, they are immediately exposed to disastrous competition. The white man has mastered farming's secrets. The Indian is a clumsy beginner in an unknown art. The former easily grows abundant crops, while the latter has the greatest difficulty in making anything grow.

The European lives among a population whose wants he knows and shares.

The savage is isolated among a hostile people whose mores, language, and laws he does not completely understand, but whom he cannot do without. He can only gain comfort by exchanging his produce with those of the whites, for his compatriots are little help to him.

So when the Indian comes to sell the fruits of his labor, he does not always find a buyer, though the European finds one easily, and it has cost him much to produce what the latter can sell cheaply.

Thus the Indian has escaped the afflictions to which barbarous nations are exposed only to suffer worse miseries among civilized people, and he finds it almost as difficult to live amid our abundance as in the midst of his forests.

But he has not yet given up the passions of a wandering life. Traditions have not lost their sway over him, and his taste for hunting is not extinguished. The savage joys he once felt in the depths of the forest float back into his troubled imagination with enhanced colors, whereas his former privations seem less terrible and

---

and again after he had left it, and only with a thousand regrets could tear himself away from so many afflictions. And when he was finally settled among the white men, several of his children refused to share his tranquillity and comfort.

I myself met Tanner at the lower end of Lake Superior. He struck me as much more like a savage than a civilized man.

There is neither taste nor order in Tanner's work, but unconsciously he paints a vivid picture of the prejudices, passions, vices, and, above all, the miseries of those among whom he lived.

Vicomte Ernest de Blosseville, the author of an excellent book on the English penal colonies, has translated Tanner's *Memoirs*. The notes added by M. de Blosseville to his translation allow the reader to compare the facts related by Tanner with those previously recorded by many observers, both ancient and modern.

Anyone desiring to understand the present state and foresee the future destiny of the North American Indians should consult M. de Blosseville's book.

the dangers he faced less great. The independence he enjoyed among his equals contrasts with his servile position in civilized society.

But the solitudes in which he so long lived in freedom are still close to him, and a few hours' march will bring him back there. His neighbors, the white men, offer what he thinks a high price for the half-cleared field from which he hardly extracts enough to keep him alive. Perhaps the money that the Europeans offer him would enable him to live in peace and happiness far away from them. He quits the plow, takes up his weapons again, and goes back forever into the wilderness.[19]

The truth of this sad description can be judged by what is happening to the Creeks and Cherokees, to whom I have already alluded.

In the little that they have done, these Indians have assuredly displayed as much natural genius as the European peoples in their greatest undertakings; but nations, like men, need time to learn, whatever their intelligence or endeavors.

[19] This destructive influence of civilized nations on others less civilized can be observed among the Europeans themselves.

Nearly a century ago the French founded in the midst of the wilderness the town of Vincennes, on the Wabash. They lived there in great abundance until the American immigrants arrived. The latter immediately began to ruin the former inhabitants by their competition, and then bought up their lands cheaply. When M. de Volney, from whom I derive these details, passed through Vincennes, the numbers of the French had fallen to a hundred, most of whom intended to move to Louisiana or to Canada. These Frenchmen were worthy people, but neither educated nor industrious, and they had contracted some of the habits of savages. The Americans, who were perhaps morally inferior to them, had an immense intellectual superiority. They were industrious, educated, rich, and accustomed to govern themselves. [See C.-F. Volney, *Tableau du Climat et du Sol des États-Unis d'Amérique*, Paris, 1822, pp. 358 ff.]

I myself have noticed in Canada, where the intellectual difference between the two races is very much less pronounced, that the English, being in control of trade and industry in the country of the French Canadians, are spreading on all sides and restricting the French within very narrow limits.

In Louisiana, too, almost all commercial and industrial activity is concentrated in the hands of the Anglo-Americans.

But the case of the province of Texas is even more striking; the state of Texas is of course a part of Mexico and serves as its frontier on the United States side. [Tocqueville was writing this before 1835 when Texas was still part of Mexico.] For some years the Anglo-Americans had been penetrating as individuals into that still-underpopulated province, buying land, getting control of industry, and rapidly supplanting the original population. One can foresee that if Mexico does not hasten to halt this movement, Texas will soon be lost to her.

If comparatively imperceptible differences in European civilization lead to such results, it is easy to see what must happen when the most fully developed civilization of Europe comes into contact with Indian barbarism.

While these savages were laboring to civilize themselves, the Europeans continued to surround them on all sides and to hem them in more and more. Today the two races have finally met and come into contact. The Indian is already superior to his savage father but still very inferior to his white neighbor. With their resources and their knowledge, the Europeans have made no delay in appropriating most of the advantages the natives derived from possession of the soil; they have settled among them, having taken over the land or bought it cheaply, and have ruined the Indians by a competition which the latter were in no sort of position to face. Isolated within their own country, the Indians have come to form a little colony of unwelcome foreigners in the midst of a numerous and dominating people.[20]

In one of his messages to Congress Washington said: "We are more enlightened and more powerful than the Indian nations; it behooves our honor to treat them with kindness and even generosity."

The noble and virtuous policy has not been followed.

The tyranny of the government is usually added to the greed of the colonists. Although the Cherokees and Creeks were established on the land where they now live before the arrival of the Europeans and although the Americans have often treated with them as with foreign nations, the states in which they are found have not been willing to recognize them as independent peoples, and they have undertaken to make these men, who have scarcely left the forests,

[20] See *Legislative Documents*, 21st Congress, No. 89 [First Session], for the excesses of all sorts committed by the white population in Indian territory. Sometimes the Anglo-Americans establish themselves on part of the territory, as if land were lacking elsewhere, and troops sent by Congress have to drive them out; at other times they [the whites] carry off their [the Indians'] cattle, burn their houses, cut down the natives' crops, and do them personal violence.

All these documents prove that the natives are daily the victims of abuse of force. The Union habitually maintains an agent among the Indians with the duty of representing them; the report of the agent with the Cherokees is among the documents I have cited; this officer almost always expresses himself in terms favorable to the savages; on page 12 he says that "the intrusion of the whites into Cherokee territory would bring ruin to the inhabitants who lead a poor and inoffensive life." [Tocqueville summarizes; the sentence reads thus: "Because I fear (should that line be run) it would encourage and occasion a great number of white families to rush into, and settle on, the lands embraced within those lines, to the great annoyance, distress, and ruin of the poor, helpless, and inoffensive Cherokees who inhabit them."] Further on he remarks that the state of Georgia, wishing to restrict the boundaries of the Cherokees, proceeded to demarcate the frontier; the federal agent points out that the demarcation was carried out by the whites alone and consequently had no validity.

submit to their magistrates, their customs, and their laws.[21] Misery drove these unfortunate Indians toward civilization, and now oppression repulses them toward barbarism. Many of them leave their half-cleared fields and go back to the ways of savage life.

If one studies the tyrannous measures adopted by the legislators of the southern states, the conduct of their governors, and the decrees of their courts, one is readily convinced that the complete expulsion of the Indians is the final objective to which all their simultaneous endeavors are directed. The Americans in this part of the Union look jealously at the lands occupied by the natives;[22] they feel that the latter have not yet entirely lost the traditions of savage life, and before civilization has firmly attached them to the soil, they want to reduce them to despair and force them to go away.

Oppressed by the individual states, the Creeks and Cherokees appealed to the central government. The latter is far from insensible to their ills, sincerely wishing to preserve the remaining natives and to make them safe in the possession of their territory, which it has itself guaranteed;[23] but when it tries to carry this plan into execution, the individual states put up formidable resistance against it, and then it readily resolves to let a few already half-destroyed savage tribes perish rather than put the American Union in danger.

Unable to protect the Indians, the federal government wished at least to mitigate their fate; to that end it undertook to move them elsewhere at its expense.

[21] In 1829 the state of Alabama divided the territory of the Creeks into counties and made the Indian population subject to European magistrates.

In 1830 the state of Mississippi assimilated the Choctaws and the Chickasaws to the white population and declared that any of them who took the title of chief would be punished by a fine of 1,000 dollars and a year's imprisonment.

When the state of Mississippi thus extended its laws over the Choctaw Indians living within its boundaries, the latter met together; their chief informed them of the white men's claim and read to them some of the laws to which they were supposed to submit; the savages declared with one voice that it was better to plunge again into the wilderness. (*Mississippi Papers.*) [See also *Laws of the Colonial and State Governments Relating to Indians and Indian Affairs from 1633 to 1831 Inclusive,* Washington, 1832, p. 242 f.]

[22] The inhabitants of Georgia, who find the proximity of the Indians such an inconvenience, inhabit a territory which does not at present contain more than seven inhabitants to the square mile. In France the corresponding figure is one hundred and sixty-two.

[23] In 1818 Congress ordained that the territory of Arkansas should be visited by American commissioners, accompanied by a deputation from the Creeks, Choctaws, and Chickasaws. Messrs. Kennerly, McCoy, Wash Hood, and John Bell commanded this expedition. See the various reports of the commissioners and their journal in the *Documents of Congress,* No. 87, House of Representatives.

Between the thirty-third and thirty-seventh degrees of latitude north there is a vast territory which has been given the name of Arkansas, from the main river that waters it. It stretches from the Mexican border to the banks of the Mississippi. A great number of streams and rivers cut through it in all directions; the climate is mild and the soil fertile. In it there are only a few wandering bands of savages. The government of the Union wished to transport the remnants of the native populations in the South to the part of this territory nearest Mexico, and at a great distance from the American settlements.

At the end of 1831 we were assured that ten thousand Indians had already gone down to the banks of the Arkansas; more were arriving daily. But Congress has not yet been able to create a unanimous decision on the part of those whose fate it wishes to direct; some gladly consent to leave the abode of tyranny; the better educated refuse to leave their growing crops and new dwellings, for they think that if the process of civilization is once interrupted, it will never be resumed. They are afraid that sedentary habits, recently contracted, will be permanently lost in still-savage country, where nothing is prepared for the subsistence of an agricultural people. They know that they will find enemy bands in these new wildernesses and that to resist them they no longer have the energy of barbarism, while they have not yet acquired the strength of civilization. Moreover, the Indians readily perceive all that is provisional about the settlement proposed for them. Who can guarantee that they will be able to remain in peace in their new asylum? The United States pledges itself to maintain them there, but the territory they now occupy was formerly secured to them by the most solemn oaths.[24] Now, the American government does not, it is true, take their land from them, but it allows encroachments on it. No doubt within a few years that same white population which is now pressing around them will again be on their tracks in the solitudes of Arkansas; then they will suffer again from the same ills without the same remedies; and because sooner or later there will be no land left for them, their only refuge will be the grave.

[24] This clause is found in the treaty of 1790 with the Creeks: "The United States solemnly guarantees to the Creek nation all the land it owns in the territory of the Union."

The treaty concluded in July [2nd], 1791, with the Cherokees includes the following: "The United States solemnly guarantees to the Cherokee nation all their lands not hereby ceded [Article 7]. If any citizen of the United States or other person, not being an Indian, shall settle on any of the Cherokees' lands, such person shall forfeit the protection of the United States, and the Cherokees may punish him or not, as they please (Article 8). [Cf. *Indian Treaties and Laws and Regulations Relating to Indian Affairs*, p. 117, Washington, 1826.]

There is less of cupidity and violence in the Union's policy toward the Indians than in that of the individual states, but in both cases the governments are equally lacking in good faith.

The states, in extending what they are pleased to call the benefit of their laws over the Indians, calculate that the latter will sooner depart than submit; and the central government, when it promises these unlucky people a permanent asylum in the West, is well aware of its inability to guarantee this.[25]

The states' tyranny forces the savages to flee, and the Union's promises make flight easy. Both are means to the same end.[26]

In their petition to Congress[27] the Cherokees declare: "By the will of our heavenly Father, who rules the universe, the race of red men of America has become small; the white race has become large and renowned.

"When your ancestors arrived on our shores, the red man was strong, and although he was ignorant and savage, he allowed them to rest their numb feet on dry land. Our fathers and yours gave one another their hands as a sign of friendship and lived in peace.

"Everything the white man asked for to satisfy his needs, the In-

[25] That does not prevent it from expressing its promises in the most formal terms. See the letter of March 23, 1829, from the President to the Creeks (*Proceedings of the Indian Board in the City of New York*, p. 5): "Beyond the great river (the Mississippi) your Father has prepared a vast country to receive you. There your white brothers will not come to trouble you; they will have no rights on your land; you can live there with your children in peace and abundance as long as the grass grows and the streams flow; *it will belong to you forever*." [Tocqueville condenses the text. Here follows the original wording: "Beyond the great river Mississipi, where a part of your nation has gone, your father has provided a country large enough for all of you, but he advises you to remove to it. There your white brothers will not trouble you; they will have no claim to the land, and you can live upon it, you and all your children, as long as the grass grows or the water runs, in peace and plenty. It will be yours for ever."]
The Secretary of War, in a letter of April 18, 1829, to the Cherokees, declares that they must not hope to retain the land they now occupy, but he gives them the same positive assurance for the time when they shall have crossed to the other side of the Mississippi (*ibid.*, p. 6)—as if he would then have the power now lacking to keep his promise!
[26] To form an exact idea of the policy of the individual states and of the Union toward the Indians, one should consult: (1) the laws of the several states concerning the Indians (these are collected in *Legislative Documents*, 21st Congress, No. 319) [First Session, Report No. 319, House of Representatives]; (2) the Union's Laws on the same subject, and in particular that of March 30, 1802 (these laws can be found in Mr. Story's *Laws of the United States*) [cf. Vol. II, pp. 838 ff.]; (3) finally, to understand the present state of the Union's relations with the Indian tribes, see the report of November 29, 1823, by Mr. Cass, Secretary of War.
[27] November 19, 1829.

dian hastened to grant to him. Then the Indian was master, and
the white man was supplicant. Today the scene has changed: the
strength of the red man has become weakness. As his neighbors grew
in numbers, his power diminished more and more; and now, of
so many powerful tribes which once covered the surface of what you
call the United States, there barely remain a few that the universal
disaster has spared. The tribes of the North, so renowned in the past
among us for their power, have already almost disappeared. Such
has been the destiny of the red man of America.

"Here, we are the last of our race; must we also die?

"From time immemorial, our common Father, who is in heaven,
has given our ancestors the land we occupy; our ancestors have transmitted it to us as their heritage. We have preserved it with respect,
for it contains their ashes. Have we ever ceded or lost this heritage?
Permit us to ask you humbly what better right a nation can have
to a country than the right of inheritance and immemorial possession?
We know that the state of Georgia and the President of the United
States claim today that we have lost this right. But this seems to
us to be a gratuitous allegation. At what time have we lost it? What
crime have we committed which could deprive us of our homeland?
Are we being reproached for having fought under the flags of the
king of Great Britain in the War of Independence? If this is the
crime in question, why, in the first treaty following this war, did
you not declare that we had lost the ownership of our lands? Why
did you not insert an article thus conceived: 'The United States
wishes to grant peace to the Cherokees but to punish them for having
taken part in the war; it is declared that they shall no longer be
considered farmers of the soil and that they shall be subjected to
departing when their neighboring states demand that they shall do
so'? That was the moment to speak thus; but no one thought of it
then, and our fathers never consented to a treaty whose result was
to deprive them of their most sacred rights and to rob them of their
country." [Tocqueville slightly summarizes; for the full text see 21st
Congress, 1st Session, Report No. 311, House of Representatives,
p. 7 f.]

Such is the language of the Indians; what they say is true; what
they foresee seems to me inevitable.

From whatever angle one regards the destinies of the North American natives, one sees nothing but irremediable ills: if they remain
savages, they are driven along before the march of progress; if they
try to become civilized, contact with more-civilized people delivers
them over to oppression and misery. If they go on wandering in the
wilderness, they perish; if they attempt to settle, they perish just the

same. They cannot gain enlightenment except with European help, and the approach of the Europeans corrupts them and drives them back toward barbarism. So long as they are left in their solitudes, they refuse to change their mores, and there is no time left to do this, when at last they are constrained to desire it.

The Spaniards let their dogs loose on the Indians as if they were wild beasts; they pillaged the New World like a city taken by storm, without discrimination or mercy; but one cannot destroy everything, and frenzy has a limit; the remnant of the Indian population, which escaped the massacres, in the end mixed with the conquerors and adopted their religion and mores.[28]

On the other hand, the conduct of the United States Americans toward the natives was inspired by the most chaste affection for legal formalities. As long as the Indians remained in their savage state, the Americans did not interfere in their affairs at all and treated them as independent peoples; they did not allow their lands to be occupied unless they had been properly acquired by contract; and if by chance an Indian nation cannot live on its territory, they take them by the hand in brotherly fashion and lead them away to die far from the land of their fathers.

The Spaniards, by unparalleled atrocities which brand them with indelible shame, did not succeed in exterminating the Indian race and could not even prevent them from sharing their rights; the United States Americans have attained both these results with wonderful ease, quietly, legally, and philanthropically, without spilling blood and without violating a single one of the great principles of morality[29] in the eyes of the world. It is impossible to destroy men with more respect to the laws of humanity.

[28] But one should not give the Spaniards any credit for this result. If the Indian tribes had not been settled agriculturists when the Europeans arrived, no doubt in South America they would have been destroyed just as they were in the North.

[29] See *inter alia* the report of February 24, 1830, written by Mr. Bell on behalf of the Committee of Indian Affairs, in which on page 5 it is established by very logical arguments and most learnedly proved that: "The fundamental principle, that the Indians had no rights by virtue of their ancient possession either of soil or sovereignty, has never been abandoned either expressly or by implication."

Reading this report, written, moreover, by an able man, one is astonished at the facility and ease with which, from the very first words, the author disposes of arguments founded on natural right and reason, which he calls abstract and theoretical principles. The more I think about it, the more I feel that the only difference between civilized and uncivilized man with regard to justice is this: the former contests the justice of rights, the latter simply violates them.

Situation of the Black Race in the United States;[30] Dangers Entailed for the Whites by Its Presence

Why it is harder to abolish slavery and obliterate its traces in the modern than in the ancient world. In the United States prejudice of the whites against the blacks seems to increase in proportion as slavery is abolished. Situation of the Negro in the northern and in the southern states. Why the Americans abolish slavery. Servitude, which debases the slave, impoverishes the master. Contrast between the left and right banks of the Ohio. Reasons for this. The black race, as well as slavery, concentrated toward the South. Explanation of this. Difficulties preventing the southern states from abolishing slavery. Dangers in the future. General anxiety. Foundation of a black colony in Africa. Why the Americans of the South, although they feel a disgust for slavery, increase its rigors.

The Indians die as they have lived, in isolation; but the fate of the Negroes is in a sense linked with that of the Europeans. The two races are bound one to the other without mingling; it is equally difficult for them to separate completely or to unite.

The most formidable evil threatening the future of the United States is the presence of the blacks on their soil. From whatever angle one sets out to inquire into the present embarrassments or future dangers facing the United States, one is almost always brought up against this basic fact.

Generally speaking, it requires great and constant efforts for men to create lasting ills; but there is one evil which has percolated furtively into the world: at first it was hardly noticed among the usual abuses of power; it began with an individual whose name history does not record; it was cast like an accursed seed somewhere on the ground; it then nurtured itself, grew without effort, and spread with the society that accepted it; that evil was slavery.

[30] Before dealing with this matter, I would call the reader's attention to a book already mentioned, and soon to be published, by my traveling companion, M. Gustave de Beaumont, the main object of which is to make known in France the position of the Negroes among the white population of the United States. M. de Beaumont has plumbed the depths of a question which I need only touch upon.

His book, with notes containing a large number of very valuable and completely unknown legislative and historical documents, paints a picture as vivid as it is true. M. de Beaumont's book should be read by all those who want to know into what excesses men may be driven when once they abandon nature and humanity.

Christianity had destroyed servitude; the Christians of the sixteenth century reestablished it, but they never admitted it as anything more than an exception in their social system, and they were careful to restrict it to one of the races of man. In this way they inflicted a smaller wound on humanity but one much harder to cure.

It is important to make a careful distinction between slavery in itself and its consequences.

The immediate ills resulting from slavery were almost the same in the ancient as in the modern world, but the consequences of these ills were different. In antiquity the slave was of the same race as his master and was often his superior in education and enlightenment.[31] Only freedom kept them apart; freedom once granted, they mingled easily.

Therefore the ancients had a very simple means of delivering themselves from slavery and its consequences, namely, to free the slaves; and when they made a general use of this, they succeeded.

Admittedly the traces of servitude existed in antiquity for some time after slavery itself had been abolished.

A natural prejudice leads a man to scorn anybody who has been his inferior, long after he has become his equal; the real inequality, due to fortune or the law, is always followed by an imagined inequality rooted in mores; but with the ancients this secondary effect of slavery had a time limit, for the freedman was so completely like the man born free that it was soon impossible to distinguish between them.

In antiquity the most difficult thing was to change the law; in the modern world the hard thing is to alter mores, and our difficulty begins where theirs ended.

This is because in the modern world the insubstantial and ephemeral fact of servitude is most fatally combined with the physical and permanent fact of difference in race. Memories of slavery disgrace the race, and race perpetuates memories of slavery.

No African came in freedom to the shores of the New World; consequently all those found there now are slaves or freedmen. The Negro transmits to his descendants at birth the external mark of his ignominy. The law can abolish servitude, but only God can obliterate its traces.

The modern slave differs from his master not only in lacking freedom but also in his origin. You can make the Negro free, but you cannot prevent him facing the European as a stranger.

[31] It is known that several of the most celebrated authors of antiquity were or had been slaves: Aesop and Terence are among them. Slaves were not always captured from barbarian nations; war subjected very civilized men to servitude.

That is not all; this man born in degradation, this stranger brought by slavery into our midst, is hardly recognized as sharing the common features of humanity. His face appears to us hideous, his intelligence limited, and his tastes low; we almost take him for some being intermediate between beast and man.[32]

When they have abolished slavery, the moderns still have to eradicate three much more intangible and tenacious prejudices: the prejudice of the master, the prejudice of race, and the prejudice of the white.

Having had the luck to be born among men shaped by nature very like ourselves and equal before the law, it is very difficult for us to understand the insurmountable gap between the American Negro and the European. But we may form some remote idea of it by reasoning from analogy.

In the past there have been great inequalities among us, based only on legislation. What could be more fictitious than a purely legal inferiority! What more contrary to human instincts than permanent differences established between such obviously similar people! Nevertheless, these differences have lasted for centuries, and they still subsist in very many places; everywhere they have left traces which, though imaginary, time is hardly able to obliterate. If inequality created by the law alone is so hard to eradicate, how is one to destroy that which also seems to have immovable foundations in nature herself?

For my part, remembering the extreme difficulty with which aristocratic bodies, of whatsoever nature they be, mingle with the mass of the people, and the excessive care they take to preserve down the centuries the artificial barriers that keep them apart, I despair of seeing an aristocracy founded on visible and indelible signs vanish.

So, those who hope that the Europeans will one day mingle with the Negroes seem to me to be harboring a delusion. My reason does not lead me to expect that, and I see no evidence for it in the facts.

Hitherto, whenever the whites have been the more powerful, they have kept the Negroes down in degradation or in slavery. Everywhere where the Negroes have been the stronger, they have destroyed the whites; and that is the only reckoning there has ever been between the two races.

Turning my attention to the United States of our own day, I plainly see that in some parts of the country the legal barrier between the two races is tending to come down, but not that of mores:

[32] To induce the whites to abandon the opinion they have conceived of the intellectual and moral inferiority of their former slaves, the Negroes must change, but they cannot change so long as this opinion persists.

I see that slavery is in retreat, but the prejudice from which it arose is immovable.

In that part of the Union where the Negroes are no longer slaves, have they come closer to the whites? Everyone who has lived in the United States will have noticed just the opposite.

Race prejudice seems stronger in those states that have abolished slavery than in those where it still exists, and nowhere is it more intolerant than in those states where slavery was never known.

It is true that in the North of the Union the law allows legal marriages between Negroes and whites, but public opinion would regard a white man married to a Negro woman as disgraced, and it would be very difficult to quote an example of such an event.

In almost all the states where slavery has been abolished, the Negroes have been given electoral rights, but they would come forward to vote at the risk of their lives. When oppressed, they can bring an action at law, but they will find only white men among their judges. It is true that the laws make them eligible as jurors, but prejudice wards them off. The Negro's son is excluded from the school to which the European's child goes. In the theaters he cannot for good money buy the right to sit by his former master's side; in the hospitals he lies apart. He is allowed to worship the same God as the white man but must not pray at the same altars. He has his own clergy and churches. The gates of heaven are not closed against him, but his inequality stops only just short of the boundaries of the other world. When the Negro is no more, his bones are cast aside, and some difference in condition is found even in the equality of death.

So the Negro is free, but he cannot share the rights, pleasures, labors, griefs, or even the tomb of him whose equal he has been declared; there is nowhere where he can meet him, neither in life nor in death.

In the South, where slavery still exists, less trouble is taken to keep the Negro apart: they sometimes share the labors and the pleasures of the white men; people are prepared to mix with them to some extent; legislation is more harsh against them, but customs are more tolerant and gentle.

In the South the master has no fear of lifting the slave up to his level, for he knows that when he wants to he can always throw him down into the dust. In the North the white man no longer clearly sees the barrier that separates him from the degraded race, and he keeps the Negro at a distance all the more carefully because he fears lest one day they be confounded together.

Among the Americans of the South, Nature sometimes, reclaiming her rights, does for a moment establish equality between white and black. In the North pride silences even the most imperious of human passions. Perhaps the northern American might have allowed some Negro woman to be the passing companion of his pleasures, had the legislators declared that she could not hope to share his nuptial bed; but she can become his wife, and he recoils in horror from her.

Thus it is that in the United States the prejudice rejecting the Negroes seems to increase in proportion to their emancipation, and inequality cuts deep into mores as it is effaced from the laws.

But if the relative position of the two races inhabiting the United States is as I have described it, why is it that the Americans have abolished slavery in the North of the Union, and why have they kept it in the South and aggravated its rigors?

The answer is easy. In the United States people abolish slavery for the sake not of the Negroes but of the white men.

The first Negroes were imported into Virginia about the year 1621.[83] In America, as everywhere else in the world, slavery originated in the South. Thence it spread from one place to the next; but the numbers of the slaves grew less the farther one went north;[84] there have always been very few Negroes in New England.

When a century had passed since the foundation of the colonies, an extraordinary fact began to strike the attention of everybody. The population of those provinces that had practically no slaves increased in numbers, wealth, and well-being more rapidly than those that had slaves.

The inhabitants of the former had to cultivate the ground them-

[83] See Beverley's *History of Virginia*. [See Appendix I, F.] See also in Jefferson's *Memoirs* some curious details about the introduction of Negroes into Virginia, and the first act prohibiting this in 1778.

[84] There were fewer slaves in the North, but the advantages of slavery were not disputed there any more than in the South. In 1740 the legislature of the state of New York declared that the direct importation of slaves should be encouraged in every possible way and that smuggling should be severely punished, as it tended to discourage honest trade. (Kent's *Commentaries*, Vol. II, p. 206.) [Tocqueville refers to the first edition of Kent's second volume, published 1827 in New York.]

The *Historical Collection of Massachusetts*, Vol. IV, p. 193, gives Belknap's curious researches into slavery in New England. Apparently Negroes were introduced as early as 1630, but from that time onward legislation and mores were opposed to slavery. [Tocqueville refers to the following article: *Queries Respecting the Slavery and Emancipation of Negroes in Massachusetts, Proposed by the Hon. Judge Tucker of Virginia and Answered by the Rev. Dr. Belknap*, in *Collections of the Massachusetts Historical Society for the Year 1795*, Boston, 1795, pp. 191 ff.]

The same work also shows how first public opinion and then the law finally put a stop to slavery.

selves or hire another's services; in the latter they had laborers whom they did not need to pay. With labor and expense on the one side and leisure and economy on the other, nonetheless the advantage lay with the former.

This result seemed all the harder to explain since the immigrants all belonged to the same European stock, with the same habits, civilization, and laws, and there were only hardly perceptible nuances of difference between them.

As time went on, the Anglo-Americans left the Atlantic coast and plunged daily farther into the solitudes of the West; there they encountered soils and climates that were new; they had obstacles of various sorts to overcome; their races mingled, southerners going north, and northerners south. But in all these circumstances the same fact stood out time and again: in general, the colony that had no slaves was more populous and prosperous than the one where slavery was in force.

The farther they went, the clearer it became that slavery, so cruel to the slave, was fatal to the master.

But the banks of the Ohio provided the final demonstration of this truth.

The stream that the Indians had named the Ohio, or Beautiful River par excellence, waters one of the most magnificent valleys in which man has ever lived. On both banks of the Ohio stretched undulating ground with soil continually offering the cultivator inexhaustible treasures; on both banks the air is equally healthy and the climate temperate; they both form the frontier of a vast state: that which follows the innumerable windings of the Ohio on the left bank is called Kentucky; the other takes its name from the river itself. There is only one difference between the two states: Kentucky allows slaves, but Ohio refuses to have them.[85]

So the traveler who lets the current carry him down the Ohio till it joins the Mississippi sails, so to say, between freedom and slavery; and he has only to glance around him to see instantly which is best for mankind.

On the left bank of the river the population is sparse; from time to time one sees a troop of slaves loitering through half-deserted fields; the primeval forest is constantly reappearing; one might say that society had gone to sleep; it is nature that seems active and alive, whereas man is idle.

But on the right bank a confused hum proclaims from afar that

[85] Ohio not only refuses to allow slaves but also prohibits the entry of free Negroes into its territory and forbids them from owning anything there. See the statutes of Ohio.

346 *Democracy in America*

men are busily at work; fine crops cover the fields; elegant dwellings testify to the taste and industry of the workers; on all sides there is evidence of comfort; man appears rich and contented; he works.[36]

The state of Kentucky was founded in 1775 and that of Ohio as much as twelve years later; twelve years in America counts for as much as half a century in Europe. Now the population of Ohio is more than 250,000 greater than that of Kentucky.[37]

These contrasting effects of slavery and of freedom are easy to understand; they are enough to explain the differences between ancient civilization and modern.

On the left bank of the Ohio work is connected with the idea of slavery, but on the right with well-being and progress; on the one side it is degrading, but on the other honorable; on the left bank no white laborers are to be found, for they would be afraid of being like the slaves; for work people must rely on the Negroes; but one will never see a man of leisure on the right bank: the white man's intelligent activity is used for work of every sort.

Hence those whose task it is in Kentucky to exploit the natural wealth of the soil are neither eager nor instructed, for anyone who might possess those qualities either does nothing or crosses over into Ohio so that he can profit by his industry, and do so without shame.

In Kentucky, of course, the masters make the slaves work without any obligation to pay them, but they get little return from their work, whereas money paid to free workers comes back with interest from the sale of what they produce.

The free laborer is paid, but he works faster than the slave, and the speed with which work is done is a matter of great economic importance. The white man sells his assistance, but it is bought only when needed; the black can claim no money for his services, but he must be fed the whole time; he must be supported in old age as well as in the vigor of his years, in his useless childhood as well as in his productive youth, and in sickness as well as in health. So in both cases it is only by paying that one can get service; the free worker receives wages, the slave receives an upbringing, food,

[36] It is not only man as an individual who is active in Ohio; the state itself undertakes immense enterprises; the state of Ohio has constructed between Lake Erie and the Ohio a canal which connects the Mississippi valley with the river of the North. Thanks to this canal, European merchandise arriving at New York can go by water to New Orleans, across more than five hundred leagues of the continent.

[37] The exact figures from the 1830 census are Kentucky, 688,844; Ohio, 937,669. [Cf. *Fifth Census or Enumeration of the Inhabitants of the United States, 1830,* Washington, 1832, pp. 117, 143. The exact figure for Ohio is 937,679.]

medicine, and clothes; the master spends his money little by little in small sums to support the slave; he scarcely notices it. The workman's wages are paid all at once and seem only to enrich the man who receives them; but in fact the slave has cost more than the free man, and his labor is less productive.[38]

The influence of slavery extends even further, penetrating the master's soul and giving a particular turn to his ideas and tastes.

On both banks of the Ohio live people with characters by nature enterprising and energetic, but these common characteristics are turned to different use on one side and the other.

The white man on the right bank, forced to live by his own endeavors, has made material well-being the main object of his existence; as he lives in a country offering inexhaustible resources to his industry and continual inducements to activity, his eagerness to possess things goes beyond the ordinary limits of human cupidity; tormented by a longing for wealth, he boldly follows every path to fortune that is open to him; he is equally prepared to turn into a sailor, pioneer, artisan, or cultivator, facing the labors or dangers of these various ways of life with even constancy; there is something wonderful in his resourcefulness and a sort of heroism in his greed for gain.

The American on the left bank scorns not only work itself but also enterprises in which work is necessary to success; living in idle ease, he has the tastes of idle men; money has lost some of its value in his eyes; he is less interested in wealth than in excitement and pleasure and expends in that direction the energy which his neighbor puts to other use; he is passionately fond of hunting and war; he enjoys all the most strenuous forms of bodily exercise; he is accustomed to the use of weapons and from childhood has been ready to risk his life in single combat. Slavery therefore not only prevents

[38] Apart from these reasons which, wherever there are plenty of free laborers, make their work more productive and economical than that of slaves, there is another reason peculiar to the United States: there is as yet only one place in the whole Union where sugar cane has been successfully cultivated, and that is on the banks of the Mississippi near its mouth on the Gulf of Mexico. In Louisiana sugar is a very profitable crop; nowhere else does labor earn so high a return; and since there is always some relation between production expenses and produce, the price of slaves is very high in Louisiana. As Louisiana is one of the confederated states, slaves can be transported there from all parts of the Union; therefore the price paid for a slave in New Orleans raises their cost in all other markets. Consequently, where the land bears little, the expense of cultivation by slave labor continues to be very considerable, giving a great advantage to free laborers.

the white men from making their fortunes but even diverts them from wishing to do so.

The constant operation of these opposite influences throughout two centuries in the English North American colonies has in the end brought about a vast difference in the commercial capabilities of southerners and northerners. Today the North alone has ships, manufactures, railways, and canals.

Such differences can be noticed not only between South and North but also between different people living in the South. Almost all those in the most southern states who have gone in for commercial undertakings and try to make a profit out of slavery have come from the North; northerners are daily spreading over that part of the country, where they have less competition to fear; there they discover resources which the inhabitants have not noticed, and complying with a system of which they disapprove, they turn it to better advantage than those who founded and maintain it still.

Were I inclined to continue the parallel, I could easily demonstrate that almost all the marked differences in character between northerners and southerners have their roots in slavery, but at the moment I am not concerned with all the effects of slavery, but only with those that affect the material prosperity of those adopting that system.

Antiquity could only have a very imperfect understanding of this effect of slavery on the production of wealth. Then slavery existed throughout the whole civilized world, only some barbarian peoples being without it.

Christianity destroyed slavery by insisting on the slave's rights; nowadays it can be attacked from the master's point of view; in this respect interest and morality are in harmony.

As these truths become clear in the United States, one finds slavery retreating in face of education and experience.

Slavery, first introduced in the South, spread to the North, but now it is in retreat. Freedom, starting from the North, is spreading without interruption toward the South. Of all the great states Pennsylvania is now the extreme limit of slavery toward the North, but even within those limits the system is shaken; Maryland, immediately to the south of Pennsylvania, is just on the point of abolishing it, and in Virginia, which comes next to Maryland, its profitability and dangers are under discussion.[39]

[39] There is a particular reason tending to detach these two last-mentioned states from slavery's cause.

Formerly the wealth of this part of the Union was derived mainly from growing tobacco. Slaves are especially well suited to working on that crop;

Whenever there is a great change in human institutions, one always finds that one of the causes thereof is the laws of inheritance.

When primogeniture was the rule in the South, each family was represented by a rich man with neither need nor taste to work; the other members of his family, excluded by law from the common inheritance, lived around him like parasitic plants sharing the same way of life; the position then in all southern families was the same as is still found in noble families in certain parts of Europe, where the younger members, though they do not have the eldest son's wealth, live a life as idle as his. Entirely similar causes produced this same effect both in America and in Europe. In the South of the United States the whole white race formed an aristocratic body having at its head a certain number of privileged persons whose wealth was permanent and leisure hereditary. These leaders of the American nobility perpetuated the traditional prejudices of the white race in the body they represented, making idleness honorable. There were poor men within this aristocracy, but no workers; poverty seemed preferable to industry, so there was no competition with Negro workers and slaves, and whatever might be thought about the usefulness of the Negroes' efforts, they had to be employed for lack of anybody else.

As soon as primogeniture was abolished, fortunes began to diminish, and all the families in the country were simultaneously reduced to a state in which work became necessary to existence; many families completely disappeared; all became half aware that a moment would come when everyone had to provide for his own needs. Nowadays there are still wealthy men, but they no longer form part of a compact hereditary body; they cannot adopt an attitude, stick to it, and make it the fashion throughout all ranks of society. So the stigma against work begins by common consent to be forgotten; there are more poor people, and the poor have been able to set about earning their livings without blushing about it. Thus one of the most immediate effects of the equal sharing of inheritances has been to create a class of free laborers. As soon as the free worker begins to compete with the slave, the latter's inferiority begins to be felt, and the very basis of slavery, namely, the master's interest, is attacked.

---

it happens that for a good many years now the price of tobacco has been falling, whereas the cost of slaves remains the same. So the balance between cost of production and value of the crop has changed. And the inhabitants of Maryland and Virginia are more disposed than they would have been thirty years ago to give up the use of slaves in the tobacco fields or to give up both slavery and the cultivation of tobacco.

As slavery retreats, the black race retreats too, returning to the tropics from which it originally came.

That may seem extraordinary at first glance, but one soon sees why.

By abolishing the principle of servitude, the Americans do not make the slaves free.

Perhaps what follows would be hard to understand unless I quote an example, and I will choose that of New York. In 1788 the state of New York forbade the sale of slaves in its territory. That was a roundabout way of prohibiting importation. Henceforth only the birth rate increased the Negro population. Eight years later a more decisive measure was taken, and it was declared that from July 4, 1799, all children born of slave parents should be free. That closed all means of increase; though there are still some slaves, one may say that slavery does not exist.

As soon as a northern state took this measure against the importation of slaves, no more blacks were brought thither from the South.

As soon as a northern state forbade the sale of slaves, the master unable to part with his slave found him a troublesome possession and had an interest in transporting him to the South.

As soon as a northern state declared that the slave's son was born free, the former lost much of his value to sell, since his children could not be put on the market, and again it was a great advantage to transport him to the South.

Hence the same law prevents slaves coming from the South to the North and drives those in the North toward the South.

But there is one more cause even more powerful than those already mentioned.

As soon as the number of slaves in a state falls, the need for free workers is felt. But as work comes to be done by free hands, since a slave's labor is less productive, the slave becomes a possession of little or no value, and again there is great advantage in exporting him south, where there is no competition to fear.

Consequently the abolition of slavery does not make the slave free but just changes his master to a southerner instead of a northerner.

Freed Negroes and those born after the abolition of slavery do not leave the North to go south, but in face of the Europeans, they find themselves in much the same position as the natives; they remain half civilized and deprived of rights amid a population that is infinitely superior to them in wealth and enlightenment; they are exposed to the tyranny of laws[40] and the intolerance of mores. In

[40] Usually the states that have abolished slavery make life troublesome for any free Negroes residing in them; as there comes to be a sort of

some respects they are more unfortunate than the Indians, having memories of slavery against them and not having a single spot of land to call their own; many die[41] in misery; the rest crowd into the towns, where they perform the roughest work, leading a precarious and wretched existence.

Moreover, even if the numbers of the Negroes were to continue to increase as fast as before the time they had their freedom, yet, with the whites increasing twice as fast after the abolition of slavery, they would soon be engulfed in waves of alien population.

Generally speaking, land cultivated by slaves is less populous than that cultivated by free labor; moreover, America is a new country; therefore a state at the time it abolishes slavery is still only half full. As soon as servitude is destroyed, the need for free laborers is felt, and a crowd of bold adventurers presses thither from all parts of the country; they come to take advantage of the new opportunities for industry opening before them. The land is divided up among them; a white family settles on each bit and takes possession. Consequently European emigration is directed toward the free states. What would the impoverished European do if, coming to seek comfort and happiness in the New World, he went to live in a land where work is stained with ignominy?

So the white population grows both by natural increase and by the influx of immense numbers of immigrants, whereas the black population is in decline and receives no immigrants. Soon the present proportion between the races will be reversed. Then the Negroes will be no more than unlucky remnants, a poor little wandering tribe lost amid the huge nation that is master of the land; nothing but the injustices and hardships to which they are subjected will call attention to their presence.

In many states of the West the Negro race never made its appearance, and in all the northern states it is disappearing. So the great question of its future concerns a limited area, which makes it less frightening but not easier to solve.

---

rivalry between the various states in the matter, the unfortunate Negroes have only a choice of evils.

[41] There is a great difference between white and black mortality rates in the states in which slavery has been abolished: from 1820 to 1831 only 1 white in 42 died, whereas the figure for blacks was 1 in 20. The mortality rate is not nearly so high among Negro slaves. (See Emerson's *Medical Statistics*, p. 28.) [*Medical Statistics Consisting of Estimates Relating to the Population of Philadelphia with Its Changes as Influenced by the Deaths and Births during Ten Years, viz. from 1821 to 1830 Inclusive*, by Gouverneur Emerson, Philadelphia, 1831, p. 28; the exact figures are 42.3 for the whites, 21.7 for the blacks.]

The farther south one goes, the less profitable it becomes to abolish slavery. There are several physical reasons for this which need to be explained.

The first is the climate: certainly the closer they get to the tropics, the harder Europeans find it to work; many Americans maintain that below a certain latitude it is fatal for them, whereas Negroes can work there without danger;[42] but I do not think that this idea, with its welcome support for the southerner's laziness, is based on experience. The south of the Union is not hotter than the south of Spain or of Italy.[43] Why cannot the European do the same work there? And if slavery has been abolished in Italy and Spain without the masters perishing, why should not the same happen in the Union? I do not think that Nature has forbidden the Europeans of Georgia and the Floridas themselves, on pain of death, to draw their sustenance from the soil; but they would certainly be doing more troublesome[44] work for less return than the New Englanders. Therefore, in the South free labor loses some of its superiority over the slaves and there is less advantage in abolishing slavery.

All European plants grow in the North of the Union, but the South has its own specialities.

It has been noticed that it is expensive to grow cereals with slave labor. In countries where slavery is unknown, any farmer growing corn usually has only a few hands working for him; it is true that he calls in a great many more at harvest time and for sowing, but those only stay temporarily in his house.

To fill his granaries and sow his fields, a farmer living in a slave state has to feed many servants throughout the year, though he only needs them for a few days, for unlike free laborers, slaves cannot work on their own behalf while they are waiting for the moment when their services will be hired. To have them at all, they must be bought.

Therefore, apart from its general disadvantages, slavery is by nature

[42] This is true where rice is cultivated. Paddy fields are unhealthy the world over, and especially so under a burning tropical sun. Europeans would find it very troublesome to cultivate the ground in that part of the New World if they were obstinately determined to grow rice. But could one not manage without paddy fields?

[43] These states are nearer to the equator than Spain or Italy is, but the American continent is very much cooler than Europe.

[44] There was a time when the Spaniards brought some peasants from the Azores to a district of Louisiana called Attakapas. It was an experiment, and slavery was not introduced among them. Those people are still today cultivating the land without slaves, but they work so languidly that they hardly provide for their own necessities.

less well suited to lands where cereals are grown than to those with other crops.

On the other hand, tobacco, cotton, and especially sugar cane need continual attention. Women and children, who are of no use for corn, can be used there. So slavery is by nature better suited to lands growing those crops.

Tobacco, cotton, and sugar cane grow in the South only and are there the main sources of the country's wealth. If they abolished slavery, the southerners would be faced with one of these two alternatives: either they must change their system of cultivation, in which case they would find themselves in competition with the more active and experienced northerners, or they must grow the same crops without slaves in competition with other southern states still keeping theirs.

Therefore the South has particular reasons for preserving slavery, which the North has not.

But there is yet another motive more powerful than all the rest. The South could, at a pinch, abolish slavery, but how could it dispose of the blacks? The North rids itself of slavery and of the slaves in one move. In the South there is no hope of attaining this double result at the same time.

In proving that servitude is more natural and more advantageous in the South than in the North, I have given sufficient indication that the number of slaves should be much greater there. Africans were brought to the South first, and ever since then the largest numbers have been imported there. The farther south one goes, the stronger is the prejudice glorifying idleness. In the states nearest the tropics, not one white man works. So of course the Negroes are more numerous in the South than in the North. As mentioned before, this difference becomes daily greater, for as slavery is abolished at one end of the Union, the Negroes crowd into the other. So the black population grows not only by natural increase but also on account of forced emigration from the North. Much the same type of reason makes the African race increase there as makes the European population grow in the North at such a rate.

In the state of Maine there is one Negro to every three hundred of the population; in Massachusetts, one in a hundred; in the state of New York, two in a hundred; in Pennsylvania, three; in Maryland, thirty-four; in Virginia, forty-two; and finally in South Carolina, fifty-five.[45] Those were the comparative figures for the year 1830.

[45] An American book, Carey's *Letters on the Colonization Society,* published in 1833, states that "in South Carolina, for forty years, the black race has grown faster than the white race. Taking together the population of the five

But the proportions are continually changing, getting less in the North and higher in the South.

It is clear that the most southern states of the Union could not abolish slavery, as has been done in the northern state, without running very great risks which did not face the latter.

We have pointed out how the northern states managed the transition from slavery to freedom. They keep the present generation in chains, emancipating those of the future; by this means Negroes are introduced only slowly into society, and while that man who might make ill use of his independence is retained in servitude, the one who is emancipated before he is master of himself has still time to learn the art of being free.

It would be hard to apply that method in the South. Once one had declared that from a certain date the Negro's son would be free, the principle and the idea of liberty would have been introduced into the very core of slavery; the blacks, who see that the legislator keeps them in slavery, while their sons escape therefrom, are astonished at their unequal fates and grow restless and irritated. Thenceforth slavery has lost for them the sort of moral power it derived from time and custom, and it is reduced to no more than an obvious abuse of strength. There was nothing to fear from this contrast in the North, where the Negroes were few and the whites very many. But if this first dawn of freedom shone on two million people at the same moment, the oppressors would have reason to tremble.

Having freed the sons of their slaves, the Europeans in the South would soon be forced to extend that benefit to the whole black race.

In the North, as I have said above, as soon as slavery is abolished, and even from the moment when it begins to look likely that abolition is coming sometime, a double movement sets in: the slaves quit the country, being transported South; whites from the North and immigrants from Europe flow in to replace them.

---

states of the South which first had slaves, Maryland, Virginia, North Carolina, South Carolina, and Georgia, we discover from 1790 to 1830 the whites increased in a ratio of 80 to 100 in these states, and the blacks in a ratio of 112 to 100." [Tocqueville summarizes Carey. Cf. M. Carey, *Letters on the Colonization Society and on Its Probable Results,* Philadelphia, April 15, 1833, p. 12 f.]

In the United States in 1830 the two races were distributed as follows: states in which slavery was abolished, 6,565,434 whites, 120,520 Negroes; states in which slavery still exists, 3,960,814 whites, 2,208,102 Negroes.

These two causes cannot operate in the same way in the states farthest south. In the first place, with so many slaves it is impossible that they will leave the country; and secondly, Europeans and Anglo-Americans from the North are afraid to come and live in a country where work has not yet regained its proper prestige. Moreover, they rightly feel that states in which the Negro population equals or surpasses the white are threatened with great misfortunes, and they refrain from turning their activity in that direction.

So by abolishing slavery the southerners could not succeed, as their brothers in the North have done, in advancing the Negroes gradually toward freedom; they would not be able to diminish the numbers of the blacks appreciably, and they would be left alone to keep them in check. In the course of a few years one would have a large free Negro population among an approximately equal white population.

Those same abuses of power which now maintain slavery would then become the sources of the greatest dangers facing the southern whites. Nowadays only descendants of Europeans own the land and are absolute masters of the whole labor force; they alone are rich, educated, and armed. The black man has none of these advantages, but being a slave, he can manage without them. When he has become free and responsible for his own fate, can he be deprived of all these things and not die? What gave the white man his strength in times of slavery would expose him to a thousand dangers once slavery is abolished.

As long as the Negro is kept as a slave, he can be held in a condition not far removed from that of a beast; once free, he cannot be prevented from learning enough to see the extent of his ills and to catch a glimpse of the remedy. There is, moreover, a curious principle of relative justice very deeply rooted in the human heart. Men are much more struck by inequalities within the same class than by inequalities between classes. Slavery is understood, but how can one allow several million citizens to live under a burden of eternal infamy and hereditary wretchedness? The free Negro population in the North feels these ills and resents these injustices, but it is weak and in decline; in the South it would be numerous and strong.

Once one admits that whites and emancipated Negroes face each other like two foreign peoples on the same soil, it can easily be understood that there are only two possibilities for the future: the Negroes and the whites must either mingle completely or they must part.

I have already expressed my conviction concerning the first possibility.[46] I do not think that the white and black races will ever be brought anywhere to live on a footing of equality.

But I think that the matter will be still harder in the United States than anywhere else. It can happen that a man will rise above prejudices of religion, country, and race, and if that man is a king, he can bring about astonishing transformations in society; but it is not possible for a whole people to rise, as it were, above itself.

Some despot subjecting the Americans and their former slaves beneath the same yoke might perhaps force the races to mingle; while American democracy remains at the head of affairs, no one would dare attempt any such thing, and it is possible to foresee that the freer the whites in America are, the more they will seek to isolate themselves.[47]

I have said before that the real link between the European and the Indian was the half-breed; in the same way, it is the mulatto who forms the bridge between black and white; everywhere where there are a great number of mulattoes, the fusion of the two races is not impossible.

There are parts of the United States where European and Negro blood are so crossed that one cannot find a man who is either completely white or completely black; when that point has been reached, one can really say that the races are mixed, or rather that there is a third race derived from those two, but not precisely one or the other.

Of all Europeans, the English have least mingled their blood with that of Negroes. There are more mulattoes in the South of the Union than in the North, but infinitely fewer than in any other European colony; there are very few mulattoes in the United States; they have no strength by themselves, and in racial disputes they generally make common cause with the whites. One finds much

[46] This opinion is moreover supported by authorities much more weighty than I. For instance, in Jefferson's *Memoirs* one reads: "Nothing is more certainly written in the book of fate than that these people are to be free; nor is it less certain that the two races, equally free, cannot live in the same government. Nature, habit, opinion, have drawn indelible lines of distinction between them." (See *Extracts from Jefferson's Memoirs*, by M. Conseil.) [This was Tocqueville's source; cf. *Mélanges politiques et Philosophiques: Extraits des Mémoires et de la Correspondance de Thomas Jefferson*, par L.-P. Conseil, 2 vols., Paris, 1833; see also *The Writings of Thomas Jefferson* (Washington, 1853), Vol. I, p. 49.]

[47] If the English in the Antilles had governed themselves, one can be sure that they would not have granted the act of emancipation which was imposed by the motherland.

the same in Europe when the lackeys of great lords behave haughtily to the people.

This pride of origin, which is natural to the English, is most remarkably increased in the American by the personal pride derived from democratic liberty. The white man in the United States is proud of his race and proud of himself.

Furthermore, if whites and Negroes do not mingle in the North of the Union, how should they do so in the South? Can one for a moment suppose that the southern American, situated as he will always be between the white man, with all his physical and moral superiority, and the black, would ever dream of mingling with the latter? The southern American has two active passions which will always lead him to isolate himself: he is afraid of resembling the Negro, once his slave, and he is afraid of falling below the level of his white neighbor.

If I absolutely had to make some guess about the future, I should say that in the probable course of things the abolition of slavery in the South would increase the repugnance felt by the white population toward the Negroes. I base this opinion on analogy with what I have previously noticed in the North. I have mentioned that the white northerners shun Negroes with all the greater care, the more legislation has abolished any legal distinction between them; why should it not be the same in the South? In the North the white man afraid of mingling with the black is frightened by an imaginary danger. In the South, where the danger would be real, I do not think the fear would be less.

If, on the one hand, one admits (and the fact is not in doubt) that Negroes are constantly crowding into the far South and increasing faster than the whites and if, on the other hand, one agrees that it is impossible to foresee a time when blacks and whites will come to mingle and derive the same benefits from society, must one conclude that sooner or later in the southern states whites and blacks must come to blows?

What would be the final result of such a struggle?

Obviously one cannot go beyond vague guesses about that. It is difficult enough for the human mind to trace some sort of great circle around the future, but within that circle chance plays a part that can never be grasped. In any vision of the future, chance always forms a blind spot which the mind's eye can never penetrate. All that one can say is this: in the Antilles the white race seems destined to succumb, but on the continent, the black.

In the Antilles the whites are isolated within a vast black population; on the continent the blacks are situated between the sea and an innumerable people who already extend above them in a compact mass from the icy boundaries of Canada to the frontiers of Virginia and from the banks of the Missouri to the Atlantic coast. If the whites of North America remain united, it is difficult to believe that the Negroes will escape the destruction threatening them; the sword or misery will bring them down. But the black populations crowding along the Gulf of Mexico have a chance of salvation if the struggle between the two races comes at a time when the American confederation has been dissolved. Once the federal link has been broken, the southerners would be wrong to count on lasting support from their brothers in the North. The latter know that the danger can never reach them; if no positive duty compelled them to march to the help of the South, one may anticipate that racial sympathy would be powerless.

However, whenever the struggle should come, the southern whites would enter the arena with an immense superiority in education and resources, but the blacks would have on their side numbers and the energy of despair. Those are great resources once a man has arms in his hands. Perhaps then the white race in the South will suffer the fate of the Moors in Spain. Having occupied the country for some centuries, they will in the end retreat gradually to the country from which their ancestors came long ago, leaving the Negroes in possession of a country which Providence seems to have destined for them, since they have no trouble in living there and can work the ground more easily than the whites can.

The more or less distant but inevitable danger of a conflict between the blacks and whites of the South of the Union is a nightmare constantly haunting the American imagination. The northerners make it a common topic of conversation, though they have nothing directly to fear from it. They seek in vain for some means of obviating the misfortunes they foresee.

In the southern states there is silence; one does not speak of the future before strangers; one avoids discussing it with one's friends; each man, so to say, hides it from himself. There is something more frightening about the silence of the South than about the North's noisy fears.

This general disquietude has resulted in an enterprise which, though few are aware of it, may change the fate of a portion of the human race.

Fearing the dangers which I have just described, some American citizens combined in a society with the object of transporting to the Guinea coast at their expense such free Negroes as wished to escape the tyranny weighing down upon them.[48]

In 1820 this society succeeded in founding a settlement, which it called Liberia, in Africa on the seventh degree of latitude north. The latest information is that twenty-five hundred Negroes have already gathered there. Transported to their old country, the blacks have introduced American institutions there. Liberia has a representative system, Negro juries, Negro magistrates, and Negro clergy; there are churches and newspapers there, and by a singular reversal of fortune, whites are forbidden to settle within its walls.[49]

This is certainly a strange caprice of fortune! Two centuries have passed since Europe first began to snatch Negroes from their families and country to transport them to the North Atlantic coast. Now the European is again busy carrying the descendants of these same Negroes across the Atlantic to settle them on that very soil from which his fathers had seized them. Barbarians have in servitude acquired the enlightenment of civilization and learned through slavery the art of being free.

Up to the present time Africa has been shut to the arts and sciences of the whites. Now perhaps European enlightenment, brought by Africans, will penetrate there. The foundation of Liberia is based on a fine and grand idea, but that idea, which may prove so creative for the Old World, is sterile for the New.

In twelve years the Colonization Society has transported twenty-five hundred Negroes to Africa. Within the same space of time about seven hundred thousand were born in the United States.

Were the colony of Liberia in a position to receive thousands of new inhabitants every year and if there were Negroes ready to be sent there with advantage, if the Union took the place of the society and annually devoted its wealth[50] and its ships to sending the

[48] This society took the name of the Society for the Colonization of the Blacks.

See its annual reports, especially the fifteenth. See also the pamphlet entitled *Letters on the Colonization Society and Its Probable Results,* by M. Carey (Philadelphia, April [15], 1833).

[49] The last rule was drafted by the founders of the settlement themselves. They were afraid of something similar happening in Africa as on the frontiers of the United States, and that the Negroes, like the Indians, by coming into contact with a race more enlightened than themselves, might be destroyed before they could civilize themselves.

[50] There are many other difficulties besides in such an undertaking. If, in order to send the American Negroes to Africa, the Union started buying them from their masters, the price of Negroes, growing in proportion to their rarity, would soon reach enormous sums, and it is unbelievable that the northern states would agree to such an expense from which they

Negroes to Africa, it would still not be possible to counterbalance the natural increase of the black population; being unable each year to carry away as many as were born into the world, it would not even be able to halt the growth of this constantly increasing internal malady.[51]

The Negro race will never again leave the American continent, to which the passions and vices of Europe brought it; it will not disappear from the New World except by ceasing to exist. The inhabitants of the United States may postpone the misfortunes they dread, but they cannot now remove their cause.

I am obliged to confess that I do not consider the abolition of slavery as a means of delaying the struggle between the two races in the southern states.

The Negroes might remain slaves for a long time without complaining, but as soon as they join the ranks of free men, they will soon be indignant at being deprived of almost all the rights of citizens; and being unable to become the equals of the whites, they will not be slow to show themselves their enemies.

In the North there was every advantage in freeing the slaves; in that way one is rid of slavery without having anything to fear from the free Negroes. They were too few ever to claim their rights. But it is not the same in the South.

For the masters in the North slavery was a commercial and industrial question; in the South it is a question of life and death. Therefore one must not confuse slavery in the North and in the South.

God protect me from trying, as certain American writers do try, to justify the principle of Negro slavery; I am only saying that all those who formerly accepted this terrible principle are not now equally free to get rid of it.

I confess that in considering the South I see only two alternatives for the white people living there: to free the Negroes and to mingle with them or to remain isolated from them and keep them as long as possible in slavery. Any intermediate measures seem to me likely to terminate, and that shortly, in the most horrible of civil wars, and perhaps in the extermination of one or other of the two races.

---

would reap no benefit. If the Union seized the southern slaves by force or bought them at a low price fixed by itself, it would come up against insurmountable resistance from the states of that part of the Union. In both cases the matter would become impossible.

[51] In the United States in 1830 there were 2,010,327 slaves and 319,439 emancipated blacks; in all, 2,329,766 Negroes, which is a little more than one fifth of the total population of the United States at that time.

The southern Americans see the question from the point of view and act accordingly. Not wishing to mingle with the Negroes, they do not want to set them free.

It is not that all the inhabitants of the South think slavery necessary to the master's wealth; on that point many of them agree with the northerners and readily admit that slavery is an evil; but they think that they have to preserve that evil in order to live.

Increasing enlightenment in the South makes the people there see that slavery is harmful to the master, and the same enlightenment makes them see, more clearly than they had seen before, that it is almost impossible to abolish it. A strange contrast results from this: slavery is more and more entrenched in the laws just when its utility is most contested; and while this principle is gradually being abolished in the North, in the South increasingly harsh consequences are derived therefrom.

Present-day legislation concerning slaves in the southern states is of unprecedented atrocity, which by itself indicates some profound disturbance in humanity's laws. To judge the desperate position of the two races living there, it is enough to read the legislation of the southern states.

Not that the Americans living in that part of the Union have actually increased the hardships of slavery; on the contrary, they have bettered the physical condition of the slaves. The ancients only knew of fetters and death as means to maintain slavery; the Americans of the South of the Union have found guarantees of a more intellectual nature to assure the permanence of their power. They have, if I may put it in this way, spiritualized despotism and violence. In antiquity men sought to prevent the slave from breaking his bonds; nowadays the attempt is made to stop him wishing to do so.

The ancients bound the slave's body but left his spirit free and allowed him to educate himself. In this they were acting consistently; at that time there was a natural way out of slavery: from one day to the next the slave could become free and equal to his master.

The Americans of the South, who do not think that at any time the Negroes can mingle with them, have forbidden teaching them to read or write under severe penalties. Not wishing to raise them to their own level, they keep them as close to the beasts as possible.

At all times some hope of liberty had softened the hardships of slavery.

The Americans of the South have realized that emancipation

always presented dangers, when the freed slave could not succeed in assimilating himself to his master. To give a man liberty but to leave him in ignominious misery, what was that but to prepare a leader for some future slave rebellion? Moreover, it had long been noticed that the presence of a free Negro vaguely disturbs the minds of those not free, infecting them with some glimmering notion of their rights. In most cases the Americans of the South have deprived the masters of the right to emancipate.[52]

Once in the South of the Union I chanced to meet an old man who had lived in illicit intercourse with one of his Negro women. He had several children by her, who became their father's slaves as soon as they entered the world. He had several times thought of giving them at least their liberty, but years flowed by and he was still unable to remove the obstacles to emancipation put there by the legislators. Meanwhile he had grown old and was on the point of death. He imagined his sons dragged from market to market, exchanging a stranger's rod for a father's authority. Such horrible visions threw the dying man's imagination into delirium. I saw him a prey to the agony of despair, and then I understood how nature can revenge the wounds made by the laws.

There is no doubt that these evils are terrible, but are they not the foreseen and necessary consequence of the very principle of slavery in modern times?

From the moment when the Europeans took their slaves from a race different from their own, which many of them considered inferior to the other human races, and assimilation with whom they all regarded with horror, they assumed that slavery would be eternal, for there is no intermediate state that can be durable between the excessive inequality created by slavery and the complete equality which is the natural result of independence. The Europeans have vaguely sensed this truth but have not admitted it. In everything concerning the Negroes, either interest and pride or pity has dictated their behavior. They first violated every right of humanity by their treatment of the Negro and then taught him the value and inviolability of those rights. They have opened their ranks to their slaves, but when they tried to come in, they drove them out again with ignominy. Wishing to have servitude, they have nevertheless been drawn against their will or unconsciously toward liberty, without the courage to be either completely wicked or entirely just.

If it is impossible to foresee a time when the Americans of the

[52] Emancipation is not actually forbidden, but it is subjected to formalities which make it difficult.

South will mix their blood with that of the Negroes, can they, without exposing themselves to peril, allow the latter to attain freedom? And if, to save their own race, they are bound to keep the other race in chains, should one not pardon them for using the most effective means to that end?

What is happening in the South of the Union seems to me both the most horrible and the most natural consequence of slavery. When I see the order of nature overthrown and hear the cry of humanity complaining in vain against the laws, I confess that my indignation is not directed against the men of our own day who are the authors of these outrages; all my hatred is concentrated against those who, after a thousand years of equality, introduced slavery into the world again.

Whatever efforts the Americans of the South make to maintain slavery, they will not forever succeed. Slavery is limited to one point on the globe and attacked by Christianity as unjust and by political economy as fatal; slavery, amid the democratic liberty and enlightenment of our age, is not an institution that can last. Either the slave or the master will put an end to it. In either case great misfortunes are to be anticipated.

If freedom is refused to the Negroes in the South, in the end they will seize it themselves; if it is granted to them, they will not be slow to abuse it.

What Are the Chances That the American Union Will Last? What Dangers Threaten It?

Why preponderant power resides in the states rather than in the Union. The confederation will last only as long as all the states composing it wish to remain in it. Reasons that should lead them to stay united. Value of unity for resisting foreigners and seeing that there are none in America. Providence has raised no natural barriers between the different states. There are no material interests dividing them. The North's interest in the prosperity and unity of the South and West, the South's in that of the North and West, and the West's in that of the two others. Immaterial interests which unite the Americans. Uniformity of opinions. The dangers to the confederation arise from the difference in character of the men composing it and from their passions. Characteristics of southerners and of northerners. Rapid growth of the Union is one of its greatest dangers. Movement of the population toward the Northwest. Shift of power in that direction. Passions arising from

these rapid changes of fortune. If the Union survives, will its gov-
ernment tend to grow stronger or weaker? Various signs of weak-
ening. Internal improvements. Empty lands. Indians. The
bank. The tariff. General Jackson.

The maintenance of the existing conditions in the various component states partly depends on the existence of the Union. So we
must first examine the probable fate of the Union. But first of
all it is as well to be clear about one point: if the present confederation should break up, it seems to me incontestable that the
component states would not return to their original separateness.
Instead of one union, they would form several. I do not intend to
inquire into the possible bases for such new unions; I only want
to show what causes might lead to the dismemberment of the present
confederation.

To do this, I must go again over some ground that I have already
covered. I must call attention to several matters which are already
known. I know that I risk the reader's reproaches for doing this,
but the importance of the matter in question must be my excuse.
I prefer to repeat myself sometimes rather than not be understood,
and I would rather the author suffered than the subject.

The lawgivers who drafted the Constitution of 1789 were at
pains to give federal authority a separate existence and preponderant
strength.

But they were limited by the actual conditions they had to solve.
They were not appointed to shape the government of a single
people but to regulate the association of several peoples, and whatever
they may have desired, they were always bound to divide the exercise
of sovereignty.

To understand the consequences of this division properly, one
must make a rough distinction between various acts of sovereignty.

Some matters are by their very nature national, that is to say,
they concern only the nation as a whole and cannot be entrusted
to a man or to an assembly which does not represent the entire
nation as completely as possible. War and diplomacy come into
this category.

There are others which are by nature provincial; they concern
only certain localities and can be conveniently dealt with only in
the locality itself. The budget of a township is of that sort.

There are other matters which are of a naturally mixed character;
they are national insofar as they concern all the individuals composing
the nation; they are provincial insofar as there is no necessity for
the nation itself to provide for them. Such, for example, are the

rights which regulate the civil and political status of the citizens. There can be no social state without political and civil rights. Therefore all the citizens are equally concerned in such rights; but it is not always necessary for the existence and prosperity of the nation that such rights should be uniform and consequently regulated by the central power.

There are therefore bound to be two categories in the matters with which sovereignty is concerned; they are found in all well-constituted societies, whatever may be the basis on which the social contract has been established.

Between these two extremes one finds a floating mass of questions which are general but not national and which I have called mixed. These matters being neither exclusively national nor entirely provincial, responsibility for seeing to them may be attributed either to the national or to the provincial government, as those associating may decide, without affecting the object of the association.

In most cases plain individuals unite to form a sovereign authority and their reunion creates a people. In such case there is nothing below the general government which they have adopted, except the strength of individuals or collective powers which each represent a very minute particle of sovereignty. In such case too it is most natural to call on the general government to regulate not only questions which are essentially national but also most of those which I have called mixed. The localities are restricted to that portion of sovereignty indispensable to their well-being.

Sometimes, owing to some event previous to the association, the sovereign authority is composed of preorganized political bodies; then it happens that the provincial government is responsible not only for matters which are exclusively provincial in their nature but also for all or most of the mixed affairs which come in question. For confederated nations, which were sovereign authorities before their union and which continued to represent a very considerable portion of that sovereignty after unification, have only intended to cede to the general government the exercise of rights indispensable to the union.

When the national government is entrusted not only with the prerogatives inherent in its nature but also with the regulation of questions of mixed sovereignty, it has the preponderant power. Not only does it have many rights, but all rights will be at its mercy, and there is a danger that it may come to take away from the provincial governments their natural and necessary prerogatives.

But when it is a provincial government which has the right to regulate the mixed questions, then the opposite tendency prevails in society. Preponderant power resides in the province, not in the nation, and one may fear that the national government may in the end be despoiled of privileges necessary to its existence.

Therefore single nations are naturally led toward centralization, and confederation toward dismemberment.

Now we have only to apply these general ideas to the American Union.

The particular states were bound to have the right to regulate purely provincial matters.

Moreover, these same states preserved their power to settle the civil and political status of the citizens, to regulate the relations between one man and another, and to dispense justice, all of which are rights of a general nature but ones which need not necessarily belong to the national government.

We have seen that the government of the Union is invested with authority to act in the name of the whole nation when it has to act as a single and undivided power. It represents it in relations with foreigners, and it directs the common forces against the common enemy. In a word, it is concerned with those questions I have called exclusively national.

In this division of the rights of sovereignty, at first the Union's share appears larger than that of the states, but a deeper examination shows that in fact it is less.

The government of the Union does carry out some vast undertakings, but such activity is rare. The provincial government does small things, but it never rests and there is continual evidence of its activity.

The government of the Union looks after the general interests of the country, but the general interests of a nation have no more than a questionable influence over individual happiness.

However, provincial matters visibly influence the well-being of the inhabitants.

The Union secures the independence and greatness of the nation, matters which do not affect private persons directly. The state preserves liberty, regulates rights, guarantees property, and makes the life and whole future of each citizen safe.

The federal government stands at a great distance from its subjects; the provincial government is within reach of all. One has only to raise his voice to be heard by it. The central government is supported by the zeal of a few outstanding men who aspire to direct it; the provincial government is supported by the interest of men of the second rank who only hope for power in their own state; and it is men of that sort who, being close to the people, have the most influence over them.

Americans therefore have much more to expect and to fear from the state than from the Union and, in view of the natural inclinations of the human heart, are bound to feel a more lively attachment to the former than to the latter.

In this respect habits and feelings are in harmony with interests.

When a compact nation breaks up its sovereignty and turns into a confederation, memories, habits, and customs for a long while struggle against the laws and give the central government a strength refused by the law. But when confederated peoples unite under one sovereignty, the same causes act in the opposite direction. I have no doubt that if France became a confederated republic like the United States, at first the government there would display much more energy than that of the Union; and if the Union turned into a monarchy like France, I think that the American government would long remain feebler than ours. When the Anglo-Americans created their national life, the existence of the provinces was already of long standing, and the required links had been formed with the townships and with the individuals of each state; people were accustomed to see some questions from a communal point of view and to conduct other affairs as exclusively relating to their own special interests.

The Union is a vast body and somewhat vague as the object of patriotism. But the state has precise shape and circumscribed boundaries; it represents a define number of familiar things which are dear to those living there. It is identified with the soil, with the right of property, the family, memories of the past, activities of the present, and dreams for the future. Patriotism, which is most often nothing but an extension of individual egoism, therefore remains attached to the state and has not yet, so to say, been passed on to the Union.

Thus interest, custom, and feelings are united in concentrating real political life in the state, and not in the Union.

It is easy to estimate the difference in the strength of these two governments by watching them at work within their spheres.

Whenever the government of a state addresses a man or an association of men, its language is clear and imperative; it is the same with the federal government when it is addressing individuals; but when it is faced by a state, it begins to parley; it explains its motives and justifies its conduct; it argues and advises but does not command. If doubts arise about the constitutional powers of either government, the provincial government claims its rights boldly and takes prompt and energetic measures to support them. Meanwhile, the government of the Union reasons; it appeals to the good sense, the interests, and the glory of the nation; it temporizes, negotiates, and only consents to act in the last extremity. At first sight one might suppose that it was the state government that was armed with all the forces of the nation and that Congress represented a state.

The federal government therefore, in spite of the efforts of its founders, is, as I have said before, one of such naturally feeble sort that it requires, more than any other, the free support of the governed in order to survive.

It is easy to see that its object is to facilitate the desire of the states to remain united. As long as this preliminary condition is fulfilled, it is wise, strong, and flexible. It is so organized that it is generally faced by individuals only and can easily overcome any resistance put up against the common will; but in forming the federal government it was not anticipated that the states, or several among them, would cease to wish to be united. If today the sovereignty of the Union was to come into conflict with one of the states, one can readily foresee that it would succumb; I even doubt whether such a struggle would ever be seriously undertaken. Each time that determined resistance has been offered to the federal government, it has yielded. Experience has proven that up till now, when a state has been obstinately determined on anything and demanded it resolutely, it has never failed to get it; and when it has flatly refused to act,[53] it has been allowed to refuse.

If the government of the Union had a force of its own, the physical nature of the country would make it very hard to use.[54]

The United States covers an immense territory with long distances separating its parts, and the population is scattered over a country still half wilderness. If the Union attempted to enforce by arms the allegiance of the confederated states, it would be in very much the same position as that of England in the War of Independence.

Moreover, a government, even if it is strong, cannot easily escape

---

[53] See the conduct of the northern states in the War of 1812. Jefferson, in a letter of May 14, 1817, to General La Fayette, says: ". . . with four eastern states tied to us, as dead to living bodies, all doubt was removed as to the achievements of the war, had it continued." (*Correspondence of Jefferson*, published by M. Conseil.) [Cf. *The Writings of Thomas Jefferson* (Washington, 1905), Vol. XV, p. 115.]

[54] The present state of peace enjoyed by the Union gives it no pretext for having a permanent army. Without a permanent army, a government has nothing prepared in advance to take advantage of a favorable opportunity, overcome resistance, and take over sovereign power by surprise.

from the consequences of a principle once admitted as the foundation of the public right which ought to rule it. The confederation was formed by the free will of the states; these, by uniting, did not lose their nationality or become fused in one single nation. If today one of those same states wished to withdraw its name from the contract, it would be hard to prove that it could not do so. In resisting it the federal government would have no obvious source of support either in strength or in right. To enable the federal government easily to overcome the resistance offered to it by any one of its subjects, it would be essential that the particular interest of one or more of them should be intimately involved in the existence of the Union, a thing that has often happened in the history of confederations.

Suppose that among the states united by the federal tie there are some which exclusively enjoy the principal advantages of union or whose prosperity entirely depends on the continued existence of the Union; it is clear that then the central power would find great support from them in maintaining the others in obedience. But in that case it would derive its strength not from itself but from a principle that is contrary to its nature. Peoples only join a confederation in order to derive equal advantages from the union, and in the case quoted above, it is because inequality prevails among the nations united that the federal government is strong.

Again, suppose that one of the confederated states had acquired sufficient preponderance to be able to take exclusive possession of the central power; it would regard the other states as its subjects and would enforce respect for its own sovereignty under cover of the sovereignty of the Union. Then great things might be done in the federal government's name, but in truth the Union would have ceased to exist.[55]

In both these cases the power acting in the name of the confederation becomes stronger the more it abandons the natural state and acknowledged principles of confederations.

In America the present Union is useful to all the states but is not essential to any of them. Several states could break the federal bond without compromising the fate of the others, although their sum of happiness would be less. As neither the existence nor the prosperity of any state is entirely bound up with the present confederation, none of them would be prepared to make very great sacrifices to preserve it.

[55] It was in this way that the province of Holland in the republic of the Netherlands and the emperor in the German confederation have sometimes taken the place of the union and have exploited the federal power in their particular interest.

On the other hand, there has not yet been any state which seems to have motives of high ambition for desiring the preservation of the confederation in its present form. Certainly they do not all have the same influence in federal councils, but there is none that imagines it is dominant there or can treat the others as inferiors or as subjects.

I therefore think it certain that if some part of the Union wished to separate from the rest, not only would it be able to do so, but there would be no one to prevent this. The present Union will only last so long as all the states composing it continue to wish to remain a part thereof.

With that point decided, the matter is easier; it is not a question of finding out whether the states at present confederated can separate, but whether they wish to remain united.

Among all the reasons that tend to render the existing Union useful to the Americans, two main ones are particularly obvious to any observer.

Although, in a sense, the Americans are alone on their continent, trade makes neighbors of all the nations of the world with whom they have commerce. In spite of their apparent isolation, the Americans need to be strong, and they can only be strong if they all remain united.

If the states broke up their unity, they not only would diminish their power in the face of foreign nations, but would create such nations on their own soil. A system of internal customs would then be established, the valleys would be divided by imaginary lines, the free flow of traffic down the rivers would be impeded, and there would be all manner of hindrances to the exploitation of the immense continent which God has given them as their domain.

They have now no invasion to fear and so no army to supply or any taxes to levy; once the Union were dissolved, they would soon feel the need for all these things.

Therefore the Americans have an immense interest in remaining united.

On the other hand, it is almost impossible to discover what sort of material interest any part of the Union would at present have in separating from the rest.

Glancing at a map of the United States and seeing the chain of the Alleghenies running from northeast to southwest and stretching across the country for nearly a thousand miles, one is tempted to believe that Providence intended to raise between the basin of the Mississippi and the Atlantic coast one of those natural barriers which interrupt the mutual intercourse of men and make the inevitable boundaries between different nations.

But the average height of the Alleghenies is not above eight hundred meters.[56] There are a thousand easy approaches to their rounded peaks and the wide valleys enclosed within them. Moreover, all the main rivers that flow into the Atlantic—the Hudson, the Susquehanna, and the Potomac—all have their sources on the far side of the Alleghenies in the wide plain bordering the basin of the Mississippi. Starting from this region,[57] they make their way through the rampart, which apparently ought to drive them back westward, and trace through the mountains natural roads open all the year.

There is, then, no barrier between the various parts of the country now occupied by the Anglo-Americans. The Alleghenies, far from being the boundaries of nations, are not even the frontiers of states. Parts of them are included in New York, Pennsylvania, and Virginia, states which extend as far to the west as to the east of them.[58]

The land now occupied by the twenty-four states of the Union and the three great districts which do not yet count as states, although already populated, covers an area of 131,144 square[59] leagues, or nearly five times that of France. Within this area there is a variety of soils and climate and a great variety of crops.

This great extent of the territory occupied by the Anglo-American republics has given rise to doubts about the maintenance of their Union. There is a distinction to make: contrary interests developing in different parts of a vast empire may finally lead to conflict between them; in such a case it is the size of a state that most compromises its lasting power. But if there are no contrary interests among the inhabitants of this vast territory, their prosperity is advanced by its very size, for unity of government makes it extraordinarily much easier to exchange the various products of the soil, and by making the flow of trade smoother, unity increases the value of these products.

[56] According to Volney (*Tableau des États-Unis,* p. 33), the average height of the Alleghenies is 700 to 800 meters; 5,000 to 6,000 feet, according to Darby; the highest point in the Vosges is 1,400 meters above sea level.

[57] See Darby's *View of the United States,* pp. 64 and 79. [William Darby, *View of the United States, Historical, Geographical and Statistical,* Philadelphia, 1828; it is this edition which Tocqueville used.]

[58] The chain of the Alleghenies is not as high as the Vosges and offers less impediment to human activity. The country to the east of the Alleghenies is as naturally linked to the Mississippi valley as Franche-Comté, Upper Burgundy, and Alsace are to France.

[59] 1,002,600 square miles. See Darby's *View of the United States,* p. 435.

I can see plainly enough that the different parts of the Union have different interests, but I cannot discover any interests in which they are opposed to one another.

The states of the South are almost exclusively agricultural; those of the North specialize more in trade and manufacture; those of the West go in both for manufacture and for agriculture. Tobacco, rice, cotton, and sugar are grown in the South; in the North and the West there is corn and wheat. These are varied sources of wealth, but to draw the benefit from them there is one common method equally advantageous to all, and that is union.

The North, which conveys the wealth of the Anglo-Americans to all parts of the world and brings back the world's wealth to the Union, has an obvious interest in the confederation continuing as it now is: so that it may have the greatest possible number of American producers and consumers to serve. The North is the most natural intermediary, both between the South and West of the Union and between the whole Union and the rest of the world; therefore the North wishes the South and West to be united and prosperous so that they can supply its manufactures with raw materials and its ships with freight.

On their side the South and West have an even more direct interest in the preservation of the Union and the prosperity of the North. Southern crops are, for the most part, exported overseas; therefore the South and West need the commercial resources of the North. They are bound to wish the Union to have a strong fleet to protect them efficiently. The South and the West should be ready to contribute toward the cost of the fleet, although they have no ships, for if the fleets of Europe should blockade the southern ports and the Mississippi delta, what would become of the Carolinas' rice, Virginia's tobacco, and the sugar and cotton that grow in the Mississippi valley? Consequently there is no part of the federal budget which is not applied to preserve some material interest common to all the confederates.

Apart from this commercial interest, the South and the West see great political advantage in their union with the North.

The South has a large slave population, which is a menace now and will be a greater menace in the future.

All the states of the West are in a single valley. The rivers that irrigate their territory rise in the Rocky Mountains or in the Alleghenies, flowing into the Mississippi and down into the Gulf of Mexico. By their position the western states are entirely isolated from the traditions of Europe and the civilization of the Old World.

So the southerners must wish to preserve the Union so that they should not face the blacks alone, and the westerners must desire it so that they should not be shut up within central America without free communication with the outside world.

The North, too, does not want the Union broken up, for it wishes to remain the connecting link between this great body and the rest of the world.

Consequently there is a close link between the material interests of all parts of the Union.

I would say the same about opinions and feelings, which may be called man's immaterial interests.

The inhabitants of the United States talk a great deal about their love for their country; I confess that I have no confidence in that calculated patriotism which is founded on interest and which a change of interests may destroy.

Nor do I attach very great importance to what the Americans say when they constantly proclaim their intention to preserve the federal system adopted by their fathers.

What keeps a great number of citizens under the same government is much less a reasoned desire to remain united than the instinctive and, in a sense, involuntary accord which springs from like feelings and similar opinions.

I would never admit that men form a society simply by recognizing the same leader and obeying the same laws; only when certain men consider a great many questions from the same point of view and have the same opinions on a great many subjects and when the same events give rise to like thoughts and impressions is there a society.

Anyone taking the matter up from that angle, who studies what happens in the United States, will readily discover that the inhabitants, though divided under twenty-four distinct sovereign authorities, nevertheless constitute a single nation; and perhaps he will even come to think that the Anglo-American Union is in reality more of a united society than some European nations living under the same laws and the same prince.

Although there are many sects among the Anglo-Americans, they all look at religion from the same point of view.

They do not always agree about the best means of governing well, and they have varied views about some of the forms of government expedient to adopt, but they agree about the general principles which should rule human societies. From Maine to the Floridas, from Missouri to the Atlantic Ocean, it is believed that all legitimate powers have their origin in the people. Men have the same ideas concerning freedom and equality; they profess the same opinions about the press, the right of association, juries, and the responsibilities of agents of authority.

If we turn from political and religious ideas to philosophical and moral opinions controlling the daily actions of life and the general lines of behavior, we find the same agreement.

The Anglo-Americans[60] regard universal reason as the source of moral authority, just as the universality of the citizens is the source of political power, and they consider that one must refer to the understanding of everybody in order to discover what is permitted or forbidden, true or false. Most of them think that knowledge of his own interest properly understood is enough to lead a man to what is just and honest. They believe that each man at birth receives the faculty to rule himself and that nobody has the right to force his fellow man to be happy. All have a lively faith in human perfectibility; they think that the spread of enlightenment must necessarily produce useful results and that ignorance must have fatal effects; all think of society as a body progressing; they see humanity as a changing picture in which nothing either is or ought to be fixed forever; and they admit that what seems good to them today may be replaced tomorrow by something better that is still hidden.

I do not assert that all these opinions are correct, but they are American.

While the Americans are thus united together by common ideas, they are separated from everybody else by one sentiment, namely, pride.

For fifty years the inhabitants of the United States have been repeatedly and constantly told that they are the only religious, enlightened, and free people. They see that democratic institutions flourish among them, whereas they come to grief in the rest of the world; consequently they have an immensely high opinion of themselves and are not far from believing that they form a species apart from the rest of the human race.

Hence the dangers threatening the American Union spring no more from diversity of opinions than from diversity of interests. They must be sought in the variety of American characteristics and passions.

Almost all the dwellers in the immense territory of the United States have sprung from the same stock, but over the years the climate and, more especially, slavery have introduced marked dif-

[60] It is hardly necessary to explain that when I say "the Anglo-Americans" I am speaking of the great majority of them. There are always some isolated individuals outside that majority.

ferences of character between the English in the southern states and the English in the northern ones.

It is generally believed among us that slavery gives one part of the Union some interests opposed to those of the other part. I have not noticed that this was so. In the South slavery has not created interests opposed to those of the North, but it has modified the character of the southerners and given them different customs.

I have elsewhere pointed out the influence of slavery on the commercial capacity of the Americans of the South; the same influence extends equally to their mores.

The slave is a servant who does not argue and submits to everything without a murmur. Sometimes he assassinates his master, but he never resists him. No family in the South is so poor that it does not have some slaves. From his birth the American of the South is invested with a sort of domestic dictatorship; the first notions he receives in life teach him that he is born to command, and the first habit he contracts is that of effortless domination. So education has a powerful influence in making the southerner a haughty, hasty, irascible man, ardent in his desires and impatient of obstacles; but he is easy to discourage if he cannot triumph at the first effort.

The American of the North does not see slaves hurrying around his cradle. He does not even meet free servants, for most often he is reduced to seeing to his requirements for himself. He has hardly arrived in the world before he is confronted on all sides with the idea of necessity, so he learns in good time to recognize for himself the natural limits of his power; he does not expect by force to bend the wills of those opposed to his, and he knows that if he wants to get others to help him he must win their favor. He is therefore patient, calculating, tolerant, slow to act, but persevering in his designs.

In the southern states man's most pressing wants are always satisfied. Hence the southern American is not preoccupied with the material cares of life; someone else can look after that for him. Free on that score, his imagination turns to wider and less-defined objectives. The southerner loves greatness, luxury, renown, excitement, enjoyment, and, above all, idleness; nothing forces him to make an effort in order to live, and having no necessary work, he slumbers, not even attempting anything useful.

In the North, where there are no slaves and wealth is evenly distributed, men are absorbed in just those material cares which the southerner scorns. From infancy he has been fighting against poverty, and he places comfort above every other enjoyment of mind or heart. Concentration on the trivial details of life suffocates his imagination, and his ideas are comparatively few and generalized but practical, clear, and precise. As all the endeavors of his mind are directed to attaining prosperity, he soon excels in that; he wonderfully understands how to take advantage of nature and of men so as to gain wealth; he is also wonderfully skilled in the art of making society advance the prosperity of each of its members and of extracting the happiness of all from the selfishness of each.

The northerner has knowledge as well as experience; nevertheless, he does not value knowledge as a pleasure, but only as a means, and he is only greedy to seize on its useful applications.

The southerner is more spontaneous, witty, open, generous, intellectual, and brilliant.

The northerner is more active, has more common sense, and is better informed and more skillful.

The former has the tastes, prejudices, weaknesses, and grandeur of every aristocracy.

The latter has the good and bad qualities characteristic of the middle classes.

If two men belonging to the same society have the same interests and, to some extent, the same opinions, but their characters, education, and style of civilization are different, it is highly probable that the two will not be harmonious. The same observation applies to a society of nations.

Slavery therefore does not attack the American confederation directly, through interests, but indirectly, through mores.

Thirteen states adhered to the federal pact of 1790, but there are now twenty-four in the confederation. The population, which was nearly four million in 1790, has quadrupled in forty years; in 1830 it was nearly thirteen million.[61]

Such changes cannot take place without danger.

For a society of nations, just as for one of individuals, there are three main elements which give it lasting power: the wisdom of those associating, their individual weakness, and the smallness of their numbers.

Those Americans who go out far away from the Atlantic Ocean, plunging into the West, are adventurers impatient of any sort of yoke, greedy for wealth, and often outcasts from the states in which they were born. They arrive in the depths of the wilderness without knowing one another. There is nothing of tradition, family feeling, or example to restrain them. Laws have little sway over them, and mores still less. Therefore the men who are continually pouring in

[61] Census of 1790, 3,929,328; census of 1830, 12,856,163.

to increase the population of the Mississippi valley are in every respect inferior to the Americans living within the former limits of the Union. Nevertheless, they already have great influence over its counsels, and they are taking their place in the government of public affairs before they have learned to rule themselves.[62]

The weaker the members of a society are individually, the better are that society's chances of lasting, for in that case their only security lies in remaining united. In 1790, when the most populous of the American republics had no more than five hundred thousand inhabitants,[63] each of them felt its insignificance as an independent nation, and this feeling made obedience to the federal authority easier. But when one of the confederate states—as New York now—has two million inhabitants and covers an area equal to a quarter of France,[64] it feels strong in itself, and if it continues to want union as something useful to its well-being, it no longer regards it as necessary to its existence; it can do without it, and although consenting to remain united, it soon wants to be preponderant.

The increase in the number of the state members of the Union by itself puts a heavy strain on the federal bond. All men, when seeing things from the same point of view, still do not see the same things in the same way. When the point of view is different, this is more emphatically the case. So as the number of the American republics increases, the less chance will there be for all of them to agree on the same laws.

At present the interests of the different parts of the Union are not opposed to one another, but who can foresee the various changes of the near future in a country where new towns spring up every day and new nations every five years?

Since the time of the English settlements the population has been doubling about every twenty-two years; I see no reason why this rate of increase should be halted during the next hundred years. I think that before that time has run out, the land now occupied or claimed by the United States will have a population of over one hundred million and be divided into forty states.[65]

---

[62] It is true that this is only a passing danger. I have no doubt that society will in time settle down and learn to control itself in the West, just as has happened on the Atlantic coast.

[63] The population of Pennsylvania was 431,373 in 1790.

[64] The area of the state of New York is about 6,213 square leagues (500 [*sic;* about 50,000] square miles). See Darby's *View of the United States,* p. 435.

[65] If the population of the United States continues to double every twenty-two years, as it has done for the last two hundred years, by 1852 it would be twenty-four million; by 1874, forty-eight; and by 1896, ninety-six. This would be so even if the land on the eastern slopes of the Rocky Moun-

I am ready to admit that these hundred million men will have no opposing interests, and I am even ready to suppose that, on the contrary, they will have an equal interest in maintaining the Union; but I do say that the very fact of their being one hundred million divided into forty distinct and not equally powerful nations would make the maintenance of the federal government no more than a happy accident.

I would like to believe in human perfectibility, but until men have changed their nature and been completely transformed, I shall refuse to believe in the duration of a government which is called upon to hold together forty different nations covering an area half that of Europe,[66] to avoid all rivalry, ambition, and struggles between them, and to unite all their independent wills in the accomplishment of common designs.

But the greatest risk which growth makes the Union run arises from the continual shift of its internal forces.

As the crow flies, it is about four hundred French leagues from Lake Superior to the Gulf of Mexico. The frontier of the United States winds along the whole of this immense line, sometimes retreating back from it but more often extending well out into the wilds beyond it. It has been calculated that on the average the whites advance seven leagues annually along this vast front.[67] From time to time some impediment stands in the way: it may be an unproductive region, or a lake, or an Indian nation met unexpectedly on the way. In that case the column halts for a moment; its two extremities bend inward, and when they have joined, the march goes on. This continual, gradual advance of the European race toward the Rocky Mountains has something providential in it: it is like some flood of humanity rising constantly and driven on by the hand of God.

Within this front line held by conquering settlers, towns are built and vast states founded. In 1790 there were only a few thousand

---

tains proved unsuitable for cultivation. The land already occupied can easily contain that number of inhabitants. One hundred million spread over the existing twenty-four states and three territories would only give a population of 762 to the square league, a figure far below the average French population of 1,006 to the square league or England's 1,457, and would even be less than that for Switzerland. In spite of its lakes and mountains, there are 783 inhabitants to the square league in Switzerland. See Malte-Brun, Vol. VI, p. 92. [Tocqueville has used the edition of 1826.]

[66] The area of the United States is 295,000 square leagues, and that of Europe, according to Malte-Brun, Vol. VI, p. 4, is 500,000.

[67] See *Legislative Documents,* 20th Congress [Second Session], No. 117, p. 105.

pioneers scattered over the valleys of the Mississippi; today the
population of these same valleys is as great as that of the whole
Union in 1790. It is nearly four million.[68] The town of Washington
was founded in 1800, in the very center of the American confederation; it is now situated at one of its extremities. The deputies from
the farthest western states,[69] in order to take their place in Congress,
have to make a journey as long as that from Vienna to Paris.

All the states of the Union are simultaneously growing rich, but
they cannot all grow and prosper at the same rate.

In the North of the Union detached offshoots of the Alleghenies
stretch right down to the Atlantic, forming spacious anchorages
and ports open the whole year to the largest ships. But down past
the Potomac, all along the American coast as far as the mouth
of the Mississippi, there is nothing but level, sandy ground. In that
part of the Union the mouths of almost all the rivers are obstructed,
and the few ports that are found at long intervals in these lagoons
are not so deep for shipping and offer much less satisfactory facilities
for trade than those of the North.

Nature is responsible for this first disadvantage, but there is
another, due to the laws.

We have seen that slavery, which is abolished in the North, still
exists in the South, and I have traced its fatal influence on the
well-being of the master himself.

Trade[70] and industry are bound to flourish more in the North

[68] 3,672,371, census of 1830.

[69] From Jefferson, capital of the state of Missouri, to Washington, it is
1,019 miles, or 420 postal leagues. (*American Almanac,* 1831, p. 43.)

[70] A glance at the following statistics is enough to show the difference
between commercial activity in South and North:

In 1829 the total tonnage of ocean-going and coastal shipping belonging
to the four great states of the South—Virginia, the two Carolinas, and
Georgia—was only 5,234 tons.

In the same year that of the state of Massachusetts alone amounted to
17,322 tons. (See *Legislature Documents,* 21st Congress, 2nd session, No. 140,
p. 244.) So the state of Massachusetts alone had three times as much
shipping as those four states put together.

However, the state of Massachusetts has an area of only 959 square
leagues (7,335 square miles) and 610,014 inhabitants, whereas the area and
population of the four states of which I am speaking are 27,204 square
leagues (210,000 square miles) and 3,047,767 inhabitants. Thus the area of
the state of Massachusetts forms only one thirtieth of the area of the
four states, and its population is only one fifth. (See Darby's *View of the
United States.*) There are several ways in which slavery damages the commercial prosperity of the South: it reduces the spirit of enterprise among
the whites and it prevents their finding sailors available when they want
them. In general, sailors are only recruited from the lowest class of the
population. Now, in the South, slaves form that class, and it is difficult

than in the South. It is natural that both population and wealth should pile up there more quickly.

The states bordering the Atlantic are already half peopled. Most of the land there has some owner; they therefore cannot receive the same number of immigrants as the western states, who offer an unlimited free field to enterprise. But the Mississippi basin is infinitely more fertile than the Atlantic coast. This reason, added to all the others, is a powerful incentive driving the Europeans toward the West. Statistics emphatically prove this.

If one takes the whole United States together, the population has roughly tripled in the last forty years. But that of the Mississippi basin[71] taken alone has multiplied thirty-one times over in the same period.[72]

The center of federal power is constantly shifting. Forty years ago most of the Union's citizens lived near the coast in the neighborhood where Washington has now been built; now the majority have spread farther inland and farther to the north; there is no doubt that within twenty years the majority will be living west of the Alleghenies. If the Union lasts, the extent and fertility of the Mississippi basin make it inevitable that it will become the permanent center of federal power. Within thirty or forty years the Mississippi basin will have assumed its natural rank. It is easy to calculate that by then its population will stand roughly in a ratio of forty to eleven compared to that of the Atlantic coast states. So in a few years' time control of the Union will have slipped completely out of the hands of the states which founded it, and the population of the Mississippi valley will dominate federal councils.

This constant shift of federal power and influence toward the northwest is revealed every ten years, when a general census of the population is made and the number of representatives which each state should send to Congress is fixed.[73]

---

to use them at sea. They would be less efficient than the whites, and there would always be the danger that they might rebel in mid-ocean and take flight on landing at some foreign coast.

[71] Darby's *View of the United States,* p. 444.

[72] Note that in speaking of the Mississippi basin I am not including those parts of the states of New York, Pennsylvania, and Virginia which lie to the west of the Alleghenies and which should therefore strictly be included therein.

[73] It will be seen that within the last ten years one state, e.g., Delaware, may have increased its population by 5 percent, whereas somewhere else, e.g., the territory of Michigan, has increased 250 percent. Within the same period the population of Virginia has grown by 13 percent, whereas that

In 1790 Virginia had nineteen representatives in Congress, and this number continued to increase till 1813, when it was twenty-three. From that time onward it has begun to decrease. In 1833 it was only twenty-one.[74] During the same period the state of New York followed a contrary direction: in 1790 it sent ten representatives to Congress; in 1813, twenty-seven; in 1823, thirty-four; in 1833, forty. Ohio had only one representative in 1803; in 1833 it had nineteen.

It is difficult to conceive of a lasting relation between two peoples, one of whom is poor and weak, the other rich and strong, even if it is proved that the strength and wealth of the one are in no way the cause of the weakness and poverty of the other. The Union is even harder to maintain at a time when the one is gaining the strength which the other is losing.

The disproportionately rapid growth of some states threatens the independence of the others. If New York, with its two million inhabitants and forty representatives, tried to lay down the law in Congress, perhaps it might succeed. But even if the most powerful states did not seek to oppress the lesser ones, the danger would still be there, for it lies as much in the possibility of such action as in any actual act.

The weak seldom have confidence in the justice and reasonableness of the strong. States which are growing comparatively slowly therefore look with jealous distrust on fortune's favorites. That is the reason for the deep uneasiness and vague restlessness which one

---

of the neighboring state of Ohio has increased by 61 percent. The general table printed in the *National Calendar* gives a striking impression of the varied fortunes of different states [49 ff.].

[74] It has been mentioned previously that during that same period the population of Virginia went up by thirteen percent. It is as well to explain how the number of a state's representatives can decrease although its population is not decreasing at all but actually increasing.

I will quote Virginia, already mentioned, as an instance. In 1823 the number of the representatives from Virginia, compared to those from the whole Union, was calculated on the basis of the ratio between the population of Virginia and the total population of the Union. In 1833 the calculation was made on the same basis, comparing the increased population of Virginia with the increased population of the whole Union over ten years. The relation between the number of deputies from Virginia in 1833 as compared with 1823 depends: (1) on the relation between the new total number of deputies and the old, (2) the ratio of increase in population between Virginia and the whole Union. Thus if the (1) and (2) are in exact inverse ratio, the number of Virginia deputies will be the same. But if the second ratio is in the least smaller than the first, then the number of Virginian representatives will be less.

notices in one part of the Union, in contrast to the well-being
and confidence prevailing in the other. I think there are no other
reasons for the hostile attitude of the South.

Of all Americans the southerners are those who ought to be
most attached to the Union, for it is they who would suffer most
if left to themselves; nevertheless, they alone threaten to break
the federal bond. Why is that so? The answer is easy: the South,
which provided the Union with four Presidents,[75] which now knows
that federal power is slipping from it, which yearly sees its number
of representatives in Congress falling and that of the North and
West rising—the South, whose men are ardent and irascible, is
getting angry and restless. It turns its melancholy gaze inward and
back to the past, perpetually fancying that it may be suffering oppression. Noticing that a law of the Union is not obviously favorable
to itself, it cries out against this abuse of power, and when no
one listens to its ardent remonstrances, it grows indignant and
threatens to leave an association whose burdens it bears without
share of the profits.

In 1832 the inhabitants of Carolina declared: "The tariff laws
are enriching the North and ruining the South; for without them,
how could it be imagined that the North, with its inhospitable
climate and its arid soil, could constantly increase its wealth and
power, while the South, which is like the garden of America, is
rapidly falling into decay?"[76]

If the changes just described happened gradually so that there
was at least time for each generation to pass away together with
the order of things to which it was accustomed, the danger would
be less; but there is something precipitate, one might almost say
revolutionary, in the progress of American society. The same citizen
may have seen his state march at the head of the Union and then
become impotent in federal councils. An American republic may
grow as fast as a man, being born, waxing, and reaching maturity
within thirty years.

Nevertheless, one should not fancy that the states which are losing
power are also losing population or fading away; there is no halt

[75] Washington, Jefferson, Madison, and Monroe.

[76] See the report of the committee to the convention which proclaimed
nullification in South Carolina. [Cf. *The Statutes at Large of South Carolina*,
by Thomas Cooper, Vol. I, Columbia, S.C., 1836, p. 316. Tocqueville
summarizes. The passage reads in the original document thus: "Can it excite
any surprise, that under the operation of the Protecting System, the manufacturing states should be constantly increasing in riches, and growing in
strength, with an inhospitable climate and barren soil, while the Southern
States, the natural garden of America, should be rapidly falling into decay?"]

to their prosperity; they are even growing faster than any kingdom in Europe.[77] But they feel that they are getting poor because they are not getting rich as quickly as their neighbors, and they think they are losing their power because they have suddenly come in contact with a power greater than theirs.[78] So it is their feelings and passions that are wounded rather than their interests. But is not that enough to put the confederation in danger? If from the beginning of the world nations and kings had kept nothing but their real advantage in view, we should hardly know what war between men was.

Hence the greatest danger threatening the United States springs from its very prosperity, for in some of the confederate states it brings that intoxication which goes with sudden access of fortune, and in others it brings the envy, distrust, and regrets which most often follow where it is lost.

The Americans rejoice at this extraordinary change, but I think they should regard it with sorrow and fear. Whatever they do, the Americans of the United States will become one of the greatest nations in the world; their offshoots will cover almost the whole of North America; the continent in which they dwell is their domain and will not slip from them. Why need they hurry, then, to take possession of it today? Wealth, power, and glory cannot fail to be theirs one day, but they rush at this immense fortune as if they had only one moment in which to seize it.

I think I have proved that the existence of the present confederation entirely depends on the agreement of all the confederates in wishing to remain united, and starting from that premise, I have investigated the various causes that might lead the different states to wish to separate. But there are two ways in which the Union might perish: one of the united states might wish to withdraw from the contract and use force to break the common bond; most of the observations I have made so far concern that possibility; but the federal government might progressively lose its power owing to

[77] A country's population is certainly the first element in its wealth. Over the period between 1820 and 1832, in which Virginia lost two representatives in Congress, its population grew by 13.7 percent, that of the Carolinas by 15 percent, and that of Georgia by 51.5 percent. (See the *American Almanac*, 1832, p. 162.) Now, the Russian population, which grows faster than that of any other European country, only increases by 9.5 percent over ten years, that of France by 7 percent, and Europe in general by 4.7 percent. (See Malte-Brun, Vol. VI, p. 95 [Edition of 1826].)

[78] One must, however, admit that the fall in the price of tobacco over the last fifty years has substantially diminished the affluence of southern planters, but that fact depends as little on the northerners' wishes as on their own.

a simultaneous tendency on the part of all the united republics to reclaim the use of their independence. The central power, deprived of all its prerogatives in turn and reduced to impotence by a tacit agreement, would become incompetent to fulfill its purpose, and the second Union, like the first, would die of a sort of senile debility.

Furthermore, the gradual weakening of the federal bond, which could lead ultimately to the annulment of the Union, is a distinct circumstance which may lead to a variety of less-drastic consequences before that final result. The confederation could still go on existing when the feebleness of its government might have reduced the nation to impotence, causing internal anarchy and a check to the country's general prosperity.

So, having investigated all that strains Anglo-American unity, it is also important to see, if the Union subsists, whether the sphere of government action will expand or retract and whether it is becoming more energetic or weaker.

The Americans are obviously preoccupied by one great fear. They see that in most nations of the world the exercise of the rights of sovereignty tends to be concentrated in few hands, and they are frightened by the thought that it may be so with them in the end. The statesmen, too, feel this alarm, or at least pretend to feel it, for in America centralization is not popular, and there is no subtler way of flattering the majority than to protest against the encroachments of the central power. The Americans refuse to see that in the countries where this alarming centralizing tendency is manifest, there is one single nation, whereas the Union is a confederation of different peoples, a fact which is enough to upset all prophecies based on analogy.

I confess that many Americans' fears seem to me entirely fanciful. Far from sharing their fears about the consolidation of sovereignty in the hands of the Union, I believe the federal government is getting visibly weaker.

To prove my point, I shall not refer back to distant events, but only to things I have seen myself or things that have occurred in our time.

When one examines what is happening in the United States closely, one soon discovers two contrary tendencies; they are like two currents flowing in the same bed in opposite directions.

In the forty-five years of the Union's existence time has mellowed a mass of provincial prejudices which at first strove against its authority. The patriotism attaching each American to his state has become less exclusive. By getting to know each other better, the various parts of the Union have drawn closer. The post, that great link between minds, now penetrates into the heart of the wilderness,[79] and steamships provide daily connections between all points on the coast. Trade flows up and down the rivers of the interior with unexampled rapidity.[80] To these facilities due to nature and to art may be added the instability of desires, cravings of a restless mind, and the love of wealth which constantly drive the American from his home and put him in contact with many of his fellow citizens. He travels through his country in all directions and visits all its various populations. There is no French province where the inhabitants know each other as well as do the thirteen million men spread over the extent of the United States.

As they mingle, the Americans become assimilated; the differences which climate, origin, and institutions had created among them become less great. They all get closer and closer to one common type. Yearly thousands of northerners spread out through all parts of the Union; they bring with them their beliefs, opinions, and mores, and as they are more enlightened than the men among whom they come to dwell, they soon rise to the head of affairs and change society to their advantage. This continual emigration from the North to the South singularly favors the fusion of all provincial characteristics into one national character. So the civilization of the North appears destined to be the norm to which all the rest must one day conform.

In step with the progress of American industry, all the commercial links uniting the confederated states are tightened, and the Union, which at first was the child of their imagination, is now a part of their habits. The march of time has dissipated a crowd of fantastic alarms that tormented the imagination of the men of 1789. Federal authority has not become oppressive; it has not destroyed the independence of the states; it has not led the confederates toward monarchy; and since the Union, the small states have not fallen into dependence on the great ones. The confederation has continuously grown in population, wealth, and power.

Therefore I am convinced that the natural obstacles to the con-

[79] In 1832 the district of Michigan, with no more than 31,639 inhabitants and hardly more than clearings in the wilderness, constructed 940 miles of post road. There were already 1,938 miles of post road through the almost entirely wild territory of Arkansas. See the *Report of the Postmaster General,* November 30, 1833. The carriage of newspapers alone brought in 254,796 dollars annually.

[80] In the ten years from 1821 to 1831, 271 steamships have been launched on the rivers watering the Mississippi valley alone.

In 1829 there were only 256 steamships in the United States. See *Legislative Documents,* No. 140, p. 274.

tinuance of the American Union are not so great as they were in
1789 and that fewer men are hostile to the Union now than then.

Nevertheless, a careful study of the history of the United States
over the last forty-five years readily convinces one that federal power
is decreasing.

The reasons for this phenomenon are not hard to indicate.

When the Constitution of 1789 was promulgated, everything was
falling to pieces in anarchy; the Union which followed on this disorder aroused both fear and hate, but because it answered a deeply
felt need, it had ardent supporters. Although under heavier attack
then than now, the federal power quickly attained its maximum authority, as is usually the case when a government triumphs after
bracing its strength for the struggle. At that time interpretation of
the Constitution tended to extend rather than to restrict federal
sovereignty, and in several respects the Union appeared as one single
nation, directed both in foreign and in home policy by a single
government.

But to attain this the people had in a sense risen above themselves.

The Constitution had not destroyed the individuality of the states,
and all bodies, of whatsoever sort, have a secret instinct leading them
toward independence. That instinct is especially pronounced in such
a country as America, where every village is a sort of republic accustomed to rule itself.

It therefore required an effort for the states to submit to federal
preponderance, and every effort, even when crowned with success,
is bound to relax when the original cause for it has passed.

As the federal government consolidated its power, America again
took her due place among the nations, peace returned to her frontiers,
and confidence in public credit was restored; a settled state of affairs
followed the confusion, and each man's industry could find its natural
outlet and develop in freedom.

The consequent prosperity itself made men forget the cause that
had produced it, and with the danger passed, the Americans could
no longer summon the energy or the patriotism which had enabled
them to get rid of it. Their anxious preoccupations gone, they readily
returned to their normal everyday habits, letting their usual inclinations have their head. As soon as a strong government did not seem
necessary, people began to think it troublesome. Everything in the
Union was prospering, and no one wanted to break away from it;
but people would be glad if they could hardly feel the action of the
authority representing it. There was a general desire to remain united,
but in each particular case the tendency was to reclaim independence. It was ever increasingly easy to subscribe to the principle of

federation and to apply it less and less; in this way the peace and order brought about by the federal government led to its own decline.

As soon as this tendency in public opinion began to be obvious, the party hacks, for whom the people's passions are meat and drink, began to exploit it to their own advantage.

Thenceforward the federal government found itself in a very critical position; its enemies enjoyed popular favor, and it was by promising to weaken it that one won the right to control it.

From then onward, every time the federal government has gone into the ring against those of the states it has almost invariably been obliged to retreat. When it has been a question of interpreting the terms of the Constitution, that interpretation has generally been against the Union and in favor of the states.

The Constitution entrusted the federal government with the duty of looking after national interests; it was thought that it was for it to carry out or to encourage those great internal improvements such as canals that added to the prosperity of the whole Union.

The states became frightened at the thought of some authority other than themselves thus disposing of a portion of their territory. They were afraid that by that means the central power would acquire formidable patronage within their sphere and would come to exercise an influence which they wanted to keep for their agents alone.

Therefore the Democratic party, which has always opposed any extension of federal power, raised its voice; Congress was accused of usurpation; the head of state, of ambition. Intimidated by this outcry, the central government in the end admitted its mistake and confined its activity precisely within the prescribed sphere.

The Constitution gave the Union the privilege of treating with foreign peoples. The Union had generally considered the Indian tribes bordering its territory from this point of view. So long as the savages agreed to fly before civilization, this federal right was not contested; but as soon as an Indian tribe attempted to fix its residence on any given spot, the adjacent states claimed possession of the land and a right of sovereignty over the people living there. The central government hurriedly recognized both claims, and whereas it used to treat with the Indians as with independent peoples, it then handed them over as subjects to the legislative tyranny of the states.[81]

[81] See, in the legislative documents already cited in the chapter about the Indians, the letter from the President of the United States to the Cherokees, his correspondence on the subject with his agents, and his messages to Congress.

Some of the states of the Atlantic coast extended indefinitely to the west, into wild country where no European had yet penetrated. The states whose boundaries were irrevocably fixed looked with a jealous eye on the unbounded regions thus open to their neighbors. The latter, in a spirit of conciliation and to help the Union to function smoothly, agreed to delimit their frontiers and to hand over the lands beyond them to the Union as a whole.[82]

Since this period the federal government has become the owner of all uncultivated land beyond the borders of the original thirteen states. It has the duty of dividing it up and selling it, and the money so raised goes exclusively into the federal treasury. With this revenue the federal government buys their lands from the Indians, opens up roads through the new districts, and does all it can to facilitate the rapid development of society there.

In the course of time new states have been formed in those lands formerly ceded by the Atlantic states. Congress has continued to sell, on behalf of the nation at large, the yet uncultivated lands included within those states. But the latter are now claiming that once they have been constituted, they should have the exclusive right to apply the sums so raised to their own use. With these complaints becoming more and more threatening, Congress decided to take part of the privileges, previously enjoyed, away from the Union, and at the end of 1832 it passed a law which, without giving the republics of the West the ownership over their uncultivated lands, applied to their sole benefit the larger part of the money raised therefrom.[83]

It is enough to travel through the United States in order to appreciate the advantages derived from the bank. These advantages are of several kinds, but there is one that especially strikes the foreigner: the Bank of the United States' notes are accepted for the same value upon the border of the wilderness as at Philadelphia, which is the seat of its operations.[84]

The Bank of the United States is, nevertheless, the object of great

[82] The first act of cession was made by the state of New York in 1780; Virginia, Massachusetts, Connecticut, and South and North Carolina followed this example at different times; the last was Georgia, whose act of cession did not come till 1802.

[83] It is true that the President refused to sanction that law, but he completely accepted the principle of it. See the message of December 8, 1833. [President Jackson's message concerning the land bill is dated December 4, 1833.]

[84] The present Bank of the United States was created in 1816, with a capital of 35,000,000 dollars; its privilege expires in 1836. Last year Congress passed a law to renew it, but the President refused his sanction. The struggle is now on and is conducted by both sides with extreme violence; it is easy to predict the approaching collapse of the bank.

animosity. Its directors have declared themselves against the President, and they are accused, with some probability, of abusing their influence to thwart his election. The President therefore throws all the ardor of personal hostility into his attack on the institution represented by the latter. The President has been encouraged thus to pursue his vengeance because he feels that he is supported by the secret instincts of the majority.

The bank forms the great monetary link of the Union, just as Congress is the great legislative link, and the same passions which tend to make the states independent of the central power tend toward the destruction of the bank.

The Bank of the United States always has in its hands a large number of the notes of provincial banks; any day it could force the latter to repay these notes in cash. But it has no fear of a similar danger to itself; the extent of its available resources enables it to face all demands. With their existence thus threatened, the provincial banks are obliged to exercise restraint and to keep their notes in circulation proportionate to their capital. The provincial banks are impatient at this salutary control. The newspapers that they have brought up, and the President, whose interest makes him their mouthpiece, therefore attack the bank with the greatest vehemence. They rouse local passions and the blind democratic instinct of the country against it. According to them, the directors of the bank constitute a permanent aristocratic body whose influence is bound to make itself felt on the government and will sooner or later change the principles of equality on which American society rests.

The bank's battle against its enemies is only one incident in the great American fight between the provinces and the central power, between the spirit of independence and democracy, and the spirit of hierarchy and subordination. I am not making out that the enemies of the Bank of the United States are precisely the same individuals who attack the federal government in other matters, but I do say that the attacks against the Bank of the United States are the result of the same instincts that militate against the federal government, and the great number of the enemies of the first is a disturbing symptom of the weakening of the second.

But the Union has never shown so much weakness as in the famous tariff affair.[85]

The French revolutionary wars and the War of 1812, by preventing free communication between America and Europe, brought into being manufacturing establishments in the North of the Union. When

[85] The main source for the details of this affair is *Legislative Documents*, 22nd Congress, 2nd session, No. 30.

peace allowed European products to reach the New World again, the Americans felt that they should establish a customs system both to protect their nascent industry and to pay all the debts contracted in the war.

The southern states, who have no manufactures to encourage, being exclusively agricultural, were quick to complain about this measure.

I will not here examine how far these complaints were imaginary and how far real. I just recount the facts.

In the year 1820, in a petition to Congress, South Carolina declared that the tariff law was *unconstitutional, oppressive, and unjust.* Later on, Georgia, Virginia, North Carolina, Alabama, and Mississippi all made more or less energetic complaints in the same sense.

Far from taking these murmurs into account, Congress in the years 1824 and 1828 raised the customs levels higher and freshly reasserted the principle.

A famous doctrine was then proclaimed, or rather revived, in the South, which took the name of nullification.

I have shown in its proper place that the aim of the federal Constitution was not to establish a league but to create a national government. In all matters anticipated by their Constitution the Americans of the United States form one and the same people. On all such points, the national will is expressed, as in all constitutional nations, through a majority. Once the majority has spoken, it is the duty of the minorities to submit.

Such is the legal doctrine, and the only one which agrees with the text of the Constitution and the known intention of its founders.

The nullifiers of the South claimed, on the contrary, that the Americans when they united did not intend to fuse themselves into one united people, but that they only wished to form a league of independent peoples; from which it follows that each state, having preserved its complete sovereignty, if not in fact, at least in principle, has the right to interpret the laws of Congress and to suspend within its boundaries the execution of those which seem to it opposed to the Constitution or to justice.

The whole doctrine of nullification is summed up in a statement made in 1833 before the United States Senate by Mr. Calhoun, the recognized leader of the southern nullifiers, who said: "The Constitution is a contract in which the states appear as sovereigns. Now, every time there is a contract between parties having no common arbitrator, each of them retains the right to judge the extent of its obligation by itself."

It is clear that such a doctrine would in principle destroy the federal bond and actually bring back that anarchy from which the Constitution of 1789 delivered the Americans.

When South Carolina saw that Congress was deaf to its complaints, it threatened to apply the nullifiers' doctrine to the federal tariff law. Congress persisted in its course and finally the storm broke.

In the course of 1832 the people of South Carolina[86] appointed a national convention to advise on the extraordinary measures to be taken; on November 24 of that year this convention published, under the name of an ordinance, a law that nullified the federal tariff law, forbade raising the duties imposed by it, and forbade recognition of any appeal that might be made to the federal courts.[87] This decree

[86] That is to say, a majority of the people, for the opposition party, called Union party, always claimed a very strong and active minority in its favor. Carolina must have had about 47,000 voters; 30,000 were in favor of nullification and 17,000 against it.

[87] This decree was preceded by a report from the committee appointed to draft it; this report contains an explanation of the motive and object of the law. On page 34 it states that "when the rights reserved to the different states by the Constitution are deliberately violated, the right and the duty of these states is to intervene in order to stop the progress of the evil, to oppose itself to the usurpation, and to maintain within their respective limits the powers and privileges that belong to them as *independent sovereigns.* If the states do not possess this right, it would be in vain for them to claim themselves sovereign. South Carolina declares that it does not recognize any tribunal on earth placed above it. It is true that it has, with other sovereign states like itself, passed a solemn contract of union, but it claims and will exercise the right to explain the sense of this contract in its eyes, and when this contract is violated by its associates and by the government they have created, it wants to use the unquestionable right to judge the extent of the infraction and the measures to be taken to obtain justice."

[Here again Tocqueville summarizes. Cf. *op. cit.,* p. 326 f.: "We believe that the redeeming spirit of our system is STATE SOVEREIGNTY, but that it results from the very form and structure of the Federal Government—that when the rights reserved to the several states are deliberately invaded, it is their right and their duty to 'interpose for the purpose of arresting the progress of the evil of usurpation, and to maintain, within their respective limits, the authorities and privileges belonging to them as independent sovereignties.' (Virginia Resolutions of '98.) If the several states do not possess this right, it is vain that they claim to be sovereign. They are at once reduced to the degrading condition of humble dependents on the will of the Federal Government. South Carolina claims to be a Sovereign State. She recognizes no tribunal upon earth as above her authority. It is true, she has entered into a solemn compact of union with other Sovereign States—but she claims, and will exercise, the right to determine the extent of her obligations under that compact, nor will she consent that any other power shall exercise the right of judging for her. And when that compact is violated by her co-states, or by the Government which they have created, she asserts her unquestionable right *'to judge of the infractions,* as well as of the *mode* and *measure of redress.'* (Kentucky Resolutions of '98.)"]

was not to come into force until the following February, and it was intimated that if Congress modified the tariff before that time South Carolina might agree not to follow its threats further. Later on a vague and indeterminate desire was expressed to submit the question to an extraordinary assembly of all the confederated states.

Meanwhile, South Carolina armed its militia and prepared for war.

What did Congress do? Congress, which had been deaf to the complaints of its suppliant subjects, listened to them when they had arms in their hands.[88] A law was passed[89] by which the tariff duties were to be reduced by stages over ten years until they should be brought so low as not to exceed the supplies necessary to the government. Thus Congress completely abandoned the principle of the tariff. In the place of protective duties for industry it substituted a purely fiscal measure.[90] The Union government, to conceal its defeat, had recourse to an expedient much in vogue with feeble governments: while it yielded the point *de facto,* it remained inflexible in principle. At the same time as it altered the tariff law, it passed another law investing the President with extraordinary power to use force to overcome a resistance no longer to be feared.

South Carolina did not even consent to leave the Union with this feeble appearance of victory; the same national convention that nullified the tariff law assembled again and accepted the offered concession, but at the same time it declared its intention to persevere in the doctrine of nullification with increased emphasis and, to prove this, nullified the law giving the President extraordinary powers, though it was quite certain that they would not be used.

Almost all these events took place during General Jackson's Presidency. There is no denying that in the tariff affair the latter was both skillful and energetic in upholding the Union's rights. Nevertheless, I think that one risk now facing the federal authority is the actual conduct of the man representing it.

There are some in Europe who formed an opinion about General Jackson's influence over his country's affairs that appears much exaggerated to those who have seen things at close hand.

One hears it said that General Jackson was a man who had won

[88] What finally made Congress decide to adopt this measure was a demonstration by the powerful state of Virginia, whose legislature offered to act as arbitrator between the Union and South Carolina. Up to then the latter had seemed entirely abandoned, even by the states that had joined in its protest.

[89] Law of March 2, 1833.

[90] This law was proposed by Mr. Clay and passed within four days by both houses of Congress by an immense majority.

battles, that he is an energetic man, prone by nature and habit to the use of force, covetous of power, and a despot by inclination. All this may be true, but the inferences derived from these truths are profoundly mistaken.

General Jackson is supposed to wish to establish a dictatorship in the United States, bringing a militaristic spirit to the fore and extending central-government powers in a way dangerous to provincial liberties. But in America the time for such attempts and the age suited to men of this type have not come yet. If General Jackson had wished to assert himself in that way, he would certainly have lost his political position and put his life in hazard, so he was not so rash as to attempt it.

Far from wishing to extend federal power, the present President belongs to the party which wishes to limit that power to the clear and precise terms of the Constitution and never to allow it to be interpreted in a way favorable to the Union's government; far from standing as the champion of centralization, General Jackson is the spokesman of provincial jealousies; it was *decentralizing* passions (if I may put it so) that brought him to sovereign power. He keeps his position and his popularity by daily flattery of those passions. General Jackson is the majority's slave; he yields to its intentions, desires, and half-revealed instincts, or rather he anticipates and forestalls them.

Whenever there is some dispute between the Union and a state government, the President is almost always the first to express doubts about his rights; in this he almost always is ahead of the legislature; when it is a case of interpreting the extent of federal power, in a sense he takes sides against himself; he tries to look small, to hide and efface himself. Not that he is by nature either weak or hostile to the Union; once the majority had pronounced against the pretensions of the southern nullifiers, we have seen him put himself at its head, clearly and energetically formulating the doctrines it professed and being the first to appeal to force. General Jackson, if I may use terms borrowed from the vocabulary of American parties, seems to me *federal* by taste and *republican* by calculation.

After bowing before the majority to gain its favor, General Jackson rises again; he advances toward the objectives approved by the majority or those that do not arouse its jealousy, overthrowing all obstacles in its path. Strong in the support which his predecessors did not have, he tramples his personal enemies underfoot wherever he finds them, with an ease impossible to any previous President; on his own responsibility he adopts measures which no one else would have dared to attempt; sometimes he even treats the national rep-

resentatives with a sort of disdain that is almost insulting; he refuses
to sanction laws of Congress and often fails to answer that important
body. He is a favorite who is sometimes rude to his master. Hence
General Jackson's power is constantly increasing, but that of the
President grows less. The federal government is strong in his hands;
it will pass to his successor enfeebled.

Unless I am strangely mistaken, the federal government of the
United States is tending to get daily weaker; stage by stage it with-
draws from public affairs, continually narrowing its sphere of action.
Being naturally weak, it gives up even the appearance of strength.
On the other hand, I think I have seen the feeling of independence
becoming more and more lively in the states, and affection for the
provincial government more and more pronounced.

The Americans want their Union, but one reduced to a shadow;
they want it strong in some cases and weak in all others; in time
of war it must unite in its hands the national forces and all the
resources of the country, while in time of peace it ceases, so to say,
to exist at all, as if such alternating weakness and vigor were a possibility of nature.

At present I can see nothing to stop this general tendency of
opinion; the causes which have brought it about still operate in the
same way. So it will continue, and barring some extraordinary circumstance, one can foresee that the government of the Union will
go on getting daily weaker.

Nevertheless, I think that the day is still far off when the federal
power, unable to protect itself or to keep the country at peace, will,
in a sense, extinguish itself of its own accord. The Union is a part of
American mores and is desired; its results are obvious and its benefits visible. When men come to notice that the weakness of the federal
government hazards the Union's existence, I have no doubt that one
will see a reaction spring up in favor of strength.

Of all the federal governments established in our time, that of the
United States is the one most naturally destined to act; provided
it is not indirectly attacked by the interpretation of its laws and
provided there is no profound aberration in its basic structure, a
change of opinion, an internal crisis, or a war could all at once
restore the vigor it needs.

The point I want to make is simply this: many of us think that
there is a trend of American public opinion favoring centralization
of power in the hands of the President and of Congress. I hold that
a contrary tendency can be distinctly observed. So far from the
federal government increasing its strength with age and threatening
the sovereignty of the states, I say that it tends to grow daily weaker
and that it is only the sovereignty of the Union which is in danger.

That is what one now sees. What will the final result of this tendency be, and what events may halt, slow down, or accelerate the movement I have described? That is hidden in the future, and I cannot pretend to be able to lift the veil.

Concerning the Republican Institutions of the United States and Their Chances of Survival

The Union is only an accident. Republican institutions have more permanence. A republic is at present the natural state for the Anglo-Americans. Why? In order to destroy it, it would be necessary to destroy all the laws and make great changes in all mores at the same time. Difficulties for the Americans in creating an aristocracy.

The dismemberment of the Union, bringing with it war between the now confederate states, standing armies, dictatorship, and taxes, might in the long run compromise the fate of republican institutions.

Nevertheless, the future of the republic should not be confused with that of the Union.

The Union is an accident and will last only as long as circumstances favor it, but a republic seems to me the natural state for the Americans, and nothing but the continued action of hostile causes always pressing in the same direction could change it into a monarchy.

The Union principally exists in the law that created it. A revolution or a change in public opinion could shatter it forever. The republic has deeper roots.

What is meant by "republic" in the United States is the slow and quiet action of society upon itself. It is an orderly state really founded on the enlightened will of the people. It is a conciliatory government under which resolutions have time to ripen, being discussed with deliberation and executed only when mature.

In the United States republicans value mores, respect beliefs, and recognize rights. They hold the view that a nation must be moral, religious, and moderate all the more because it is free. In the United States "republic" means the tranquil reign of the majority. The majority, when it has had time to examine itself and to prove its standing, is the common source of every power. But even then the majority is not all-powerful. Humanity, justice, and reason stand above it in the moral order; and in the world of politics, acquired rights take precedence over it. The majority recognizes these limits, and if it does break through them, that is because, like any man, it has its passions and, like him, may do evil knowing what is good.

But we in Europe have made some strange discoveries.

According to some among us, a republic does not mean the reign of the majority, as conceived hitherto, but the rule of its strenuous partisans. In governments of this type it is not the people who control affairs, but those who know what is best for the people: a happy distinction which allows rulers to act in the nation's name without consulting it and to claim its gratitude while trampling it under foot. Moreover, a republican government is the only one whose right must be recognized to do whatever it chooses and which is allowed to scorn everything that men have hitherto respected, from the highest moral laws to the common conventions of accepted opinion.

Until our day it had been thought that despotism was odious, whatever form it took. But now it has been discovered that there are legitimate tyrannies in this world and holy injustices, provided that it is all done in the people's name.

The Americans' conception of a republic is singularly easy to apply and has lasting qualities. With them, though in practice a republican government often behaves badly, the theory is always good, and in the end the people's actions always conform to it.

In the beginning it was impossible, and it would still be very difficult in America to establish a centralized administration. Men are scattered over too wide an area and separated by too great natural obstacles for it to be possible for any single authority to direct all the details of their existence. Therefore America is par excellence the land of provincial and township government.

That was something that affected all Europeans in the New World equally, but other elements are peculiar to the Anglo-Americans.

When the North American colonies were founded, municipal freedom had already sunk deep into English laws and mores, so the English emigrants adopted it not only as something necessary but also as a blessing whose full value they understood.

We have already seen how the colonies were founded: each province and, so to say, each district was separately peopled by men who were strangers to one another or who had associated for aims that were different.

From the beginning the English in the United States found themselves divided into a great number of small, distinct societies which could not be attached to any common center, and each of these small societies was bound to look after its own affairs, for there was no central authority anywhere which could naturally or easily take charge of them.

Thus the nature of the country, the very manner in which the colonies had been founded, and the habits of the first immigrants all united to develop township and provincial liberties to an extraordinary degree.

Hence in the United States the sum of all institutions is essentially republican; in order permanently to destroy the laws which form the basis of the republic, one would almost have to abolish all the laws at once.

At the present day it would be even more difficult for a party to set up a monarchy in the United States than for a French party to proclaim a republic. The Crown would not find a system of legislation prepared in advance for it, and it really would be a case of a monarchy surrounded by republican institutions.

It would be equally difficult for the principle of monarchy to sink into American mores.

In the United States the dogma of the sovereignty of the people is not an isolated doctrine, bearing no relation to the people's habits and prevailing ideas; on the contrary, one should see it as the last link in a chain of opinions which binds around the whole Anglo-American world. Providence has given each individual the amount of reason necessary for him to look after himself in matters of his own exclusive concern. That is the great maxim on which civil and political society in the United States rests; the father of a family applies it to his children, a master to his servants, a township to those under its administration, a province to the townships, a state to the provinces, and the Union to the states. Extended to the nation as a whole, it becomes the dogma of the sovereignty of the people.

Thus in the United States the creative principle underlying the republic is the same as that which controls the greater part of human actions. Hence the republic penetrates, if I may put it so, into the ideas, the opinions, and all the habits of the Americans at the same time that it becomes established in their laws; and in order to change their laws, they would in a sense have to change the whole of themselves. For most people in the United States religion, too, is republican, for the truths of the other world are held subject to private judgment, just as in politics the care for men's temporal interests is left to the good sense of all. Each man is allowed to choose freely the path that will lead him to heaven, just as the law recognizes each citizen's right to choose his own government.

It is obvious that nothing but a long series of events all tending in the same direction could substitute for this combination of laws, opinions, and mores an opposite set of opinions and laws.

If republican principles are to perish in the United States, they will do so only after long social travail, frequently interrupted and as often resumed; they will have many apparent revivals and will vanish beyond recall only when an entirely new people has taken the place of the one there now. There is no reason to foresee such a revolution, and no symptom indicates its approach.

What strikes one most on arrival in the United States is the kind of tumultuous agitation in which one finds political society. Laws are constantly changing, and at first glance it seems inevitable that a people so uncertain of its intentions will soon come to substitute some entirely new form of government for the one it has at present. But such fears are premature. In political institutions there are two kinds of instability which should not be confused: one kind concerns secondary laws, and it can prevail for a long time within a very settled society; the other kind is constantly undermining the very basis of the Constitution and attacks the creative principles on which the laws are founded; that kind always leads to troubles and revolutions, and the nation that suffers from it is in a state of violent transition. Experience shows that there is no necessary connection between these two kinds of legislative instability, for they occur together or separately at different times and in different places. The first is present in the United States, but not the second. The Americans often change their laws, but the basis of the Constitution is respected.

Nowadays the republican principle is as dominant in America as that of monarchy was in the France of Louis XIV. At that time the French not only loved their monarchy, but could not imagine the possibility of putting anything else in its place; they accepted it as one accepts the sun's course and the succession of the seasons. With them there were neither advocates nor adversaries of the royal power.

In America the republic is in just that position, existing without contention, opposition, argument, or proof, being based on a tacit agreement and a sort of *consensus universalis.*

Nevertheless, I do think that by changing their administrative procedures as frequently as they do, the Americans compromise the future of republican government.

Having their plans constantly thwarted by continual changes in the law, there is a danger that men come to consider the republic as an inconvenient form of social organization; the ill effects of instability in secondary laws may then put fundamental laws in question and indirectly lead to a revolution; but such a time is still far distant from us.

What can be foreseen now is that if the Americans do give up republican government, they will pass rapidly on to despotism, without any very long interval of limited monarchy. Montesquieu has noted that nothing is more absolute than the authority of a prince who immediately succeeds a republic, since the undefined powers that had been fearlessly entrusted to an elected magistrate then pass into the hands of a hereditary sovereign. This is true in general but applies more particularly to a democratic republic. In the United States the magistrates are not elected by any particular class of the citizens but by the majority of the nation; they directly represent the passions of the crowd and depend entirely on its will; consequently they inspire neither hatred nor fear; I have previously pointed out how little care has been taken to limit their authority, leaving them in possession of a great deal of arbitrary power. This state of things has created habits which will survive it. The American magistrate would keep his undefined power while ceasing to be accountable, and in that case it is impossible to say where tyranny would end.

There are some among us who expect to see an aristocracy arise in America and already predict the exact period when it will take over power.

I repeat what I have said before, that the present tendency of American society seems to me to be toward ever-increasing democracy.

But I do not deny that at some future date the Americans may restrict the sphere of political rights, taking some of them away in order to entrust them to a single man; but I do not believe that they will ever entrust exclusive control of them to one particular class of citizen, or in other words, that they will establish an aristocracy.

An aristocratic body is composed of a certain number of citizens who, without being elevated very far above the mass of the citizens, are nevertheless permanently stationed above them—a body which one can touch but never strike, one with which the people are in daily contact but with which they can never mingle.

One can conceive of nothing more contrary to nature and to the secret instincts of the human heart than subjection of this sort; left to themselves, men will always prefer the arbitrary power of a king to the regular administration of an aristocracy.

An aristocracy cannot last unless it is founded on an accepted principle of inequality, legalized in advance, and introduced into the family as well as into the rest of society—all things so violently repugnant to natural equity that only constraint will make men submit to them.

I do not think that a single example can be cited, since human societies first began to take shape, of a people which of its own free will and by its own exertions created an aristocracy in its midst. All the aristocracies of the Middle Ages sprang from conquest. The conqueror was the noble, and the conquered the serf. Force then imposed an inequality which, once it had passed into mores, maintained itself and took a natural place in laws.

There have been cases of societies which, as a result of events before they took shape, have, so to say, been born aristocratic and which each succeeding century then led closer to democracy. That is what happened to the Romans and to the barbarians who followed after them. But a nation which, starting from a basis of civilization and democracy, should gradually establish inequality of condition, until it arrived at inviolable privileges and exclusive castes, would be a novelty in the world.

There is no indication that America is destined to provide the first example of such a spectacle.

Some Considerations Concerning the Causes of the Commercial Greatness of the United States

Nature destines the Americans to be a great seagoing people. Extent of their coasts. Depth of their harbors. Size of their rivers. However, the commercial superiority of the Anglo-Americans should be attributed much less to physical causes than to intellectual and moral ones. Reasons for this opinion. Future of the Anglo-Americans as a commercial nation. The dissolution of the Union would not put a stop to the seagoing enterprise of the people composing it. Why? The Anglo-Americans are naturally called on to serve the needs of the inhabitants of South America. Like the English, they will become the commercial agents for a great part of the world.

From the Bay of Fundy to the Sabine River, in the Gulf of Mexico, the coast of the United States stretches for the length of nearly nine hundred leagues.

The coast forms one long, uninterrupted line, all under the same domination.

No other nation in the world possesses vaster, deeper, or more secure ports for commerce than the Americans.

The inhabitants of the United States form a great civilized nation, placed by fortune in the midst of wildernesses, twelve hundred leagues from the main heart of civilization. Hence America stands in daily need of Europe. In time, no doubt, the Americans will come themselves to grow or to manufacture most of the things they need, but the two continents will never be able to live entirely independently of each other. There are too many natural links between their needs, ideas, habits, and mores.

The Union grows some things that have become necessary to us and that our soil entirely refuses to provide or can grow only at great expense. The Americans consume only a very small part of these products; they sell us the rest.

Consequently Europe is the market for America, as America is the market for Europe. And sea trade is as necessary to the inhabitants of the United States to bring their raw materials to our harbors as to bring our manufactures to them.

The United States would either provide a great deal of business to other maritime nations, if they were to give up trade themselves, as up till now the Spaniards in Mexico have done, or must become one of the leading maritime powers of the world; that alternative is inevitable.

At all times the Anglo-Americans have shown a decided taste for the sea. Independence, by breaking their commercial links with England, gave a new and powerful stimulus to their maritime genius. Since that time the number of the Union's ships has grown at almost as quick a rate as the number of its inhabitants. Today it is the Americans themselves who carry to their shores nine tenths of the products of Europe.[91] It is the Americans too who carry three quarters of the exports of the New World to European consumers.[92]

American ships fill the docks of Le Havre and Liverpool, while the number of English and French vessels in New York harbor is comparatively small.[93]

Thus American commerce cannot only face competition on its own ground, but can even compete to advantage with foreigners on their own.

[91] The total value of imports for the year ending September 30, 1832, was 101,129,266 dollars. The imports made on foreign ships accounted for a sum of only 10,731,039 dollars, about one tenth of the total.

[92] The total value of exports during the same year was 87,176,945 dollars; the value exported on foreign vessels was 21,036,183 dollars, or about one quarter of the total. (Williams's *Register*, 1833, p. 398.)

[93] During the years 1829, 1830, and 1831 ships drawing a total of 3,307,719 tons entered the Union's ports. Foreign shipping amounted to only 544,571 tons out of this total. So they were in a proportion of about 16 to 100. (*National Calendar*, 1833, p. 305.)

During the years 1820, 1826, and 1831 the total tonnage of English vessels entering the ports of London, Liverpool, and Hull was 443,800. In the same years in these ports the total of foreign shipping was 159,431 tons. So the proportion between the two is about 36 to 100. (*Companion to the Almanac*, 1834, p. 169.)

In the year 1832 the proportion of foreign to English ships entering the ports of Great Britain was 29 to 100.

The reason is simple: of all the world's shipping, American vessels cross the sea most cheaply. As long as the American merchant marine keeps this advantage, it will not only keep what it has won but it will also make further conquests continually.

But it is hard to discover why the Americans can navigate more cheaply than other nations; one is at first tempted to attribute this superiority to certain material advantages not shared by others, but that is not the case.

American ships are almost as expensive to build as ours;[94] they are not better constructed and generally do not last as long.

An American sailor's wages are higher than those of a European; the large number of European sailors in the American merchant navy proves that.

Why, then, is it that the Americans sail their ships with less cost than we do?

I think it is no good looking for physical advantages as the reason for this superiority; it depends on purely intellectual and moral qualities.

Perhaps this comparison will make my meaning clear:

During the wars of the Revolution, the French introduced new tactics into the art of war which perplexed the most experienced generals and nearly overthrew the most ancient monarchies of Europe. For the first time they undertook to do without a lot of things previously regarded as indispensable in warfare; they demanded novel exertions from their troops that no civilized nation had ever required from theirs before; they did everything at the double and had no hesitation in risking men's lives to attain the aim in view.

The French were less numerous and less wealthy than their enemies; they had infinitely fewer resources; nevertheless, they were constantly victorious until the latter decided to imitate them.

The Americans have introduced a similar system into commerce. What the French did for the sake of victory, they are doing for the sake of economy.

The European navigator is prudent about venturing out to sea; he only does so when the weather is suitable; if any unexpected accident happens, he returns to port; at night he furls some of his sails; and when the whitening billows indicate the approach of land, he checks his course and takes an observation of the sun.

The American, neglecting such precautions, braves these dangers; he sets sail while the storm is still rumbling; by night as well as by day he spreads full sails to the wind; he repairs storm damage as

[94] In general, raw materials cost less in America than in Europe, but labor is much more expensive.

he goes; and when at last he draws near the end of his voyage, he flies toward the coast as if he could already see the port.

The American is often shipwrecked, but no other sailor crosses the sea as fast as he. Doing what others do but in less time, he can do it at less expense.

In the course of a long voyage the European navigator will touch at several ports. He loses precious time in seeking a port to rest in or in waiting for a chance to leave it, and every day he is paying for the right to stay there.

An American navigator leaves Boston to go and buy tea in China. He arrives at Canton, stays a few days there, and comes back. In less than two years he has gone around the whole globe, and only once has he seen land. Throughout a voyage of eight or ten months he has drunk brackish water and eaten salted meat; he has striven continually against the sea, disease, and boredom; but on his return he can sell tea a farthing cheaper than an English merchant can: he has attained his aim.

I cannot express my thoughts better than by saying that the Americans put something heroic into their way of trading.

It will always be very difficult for a European merchant to imitate his American competitor in this. In acting in the way just described, the American is not just working by calculation but is rather obeying an impulse of his nature.

The inhabitant of the United States experiences all the wants and all the desires to which a high civilization can give rise, but, unlike the European, he does not find himself part of a society expertly organized to satisfy them; consequently he often has to provide for himself the various things that education and habit have made necessary for him. In America it sometimes happens that one and the same man will till his fields, build his house, make his tools, cobble his shoes, and with his own hands weave the coarse cloth that covers him. This is bad for improving craftsmanship but greatly serves to develop the worker's intelligence. An extreme division of labor, more than anything else whatsoever, tends to turn men into machines and to deprive the things made of any trace of soul. In such a country as America, where specialists are very rare, it is impossible to insist on a long apprenticeship before a man enters a profession. Consequently an American finds it very easy to change his trade, suiting his occupation to the needs of the moment. One comes across those who have been in turn lawyers, farmers, merchants, ministers of the Gospel, and doctors. Though the American may be less skilled than a European in each particular craft, there is hardly any skill to which he is a complete stranger.

His capacities are more general and the sphere of his intelligence wider. No craftsman's axiom ever makes an American pause; all professional prejudices pass him by; he is not attached more to one way of working than to another; he has no preference for old methods compared to a new one; he has created no habits of his own, and he can easily rid himself of any influence foreign habits might have over his mind, for he knows that his country is like no other and that his situation is something new in the world.

The American lives in a land of wonders; everything around him is in constant movement, and every movement seems an advance. Consequently, in his mind the idea of newness is closely linked with that of improvement. Nowhere does he see any limit placed by nature to human endeavor; in his eyes something which does not exist is just something that has not been tried yet.

The universal movement prevailing in the United States, the frequent reversals of fortune, and the unexpected shifts in public and private wealth all unite to keep the mind in a sort of feverish agitation which wonderfully disposes it toward every type of exertion and keeps it, so to say, above the common level of humanity. For an American the whole of life is treated like a game of chance, a time of revolution, or the day of a battle.

These same causes working simultaneously on every individual finally give an irresistible impulse to the national character. Choose any American at random, and he should be a man of burning desires, enterprising, adventurous, and, above all, an innovator. The same bent affects all he does; it plays a part in his politics, his religious doctrines, his theories of social economy, and his domestic occupations; he carries it with him into the depths of the backwoods as well as into the city's business. This same spirit applied to maritime commerce makes the American cross the sea faster and sell his goods cheaper than any other trader in the whole world.

As long as American sailors keep these intellectual advantages and the practical superiority derived from them, they will not only continue to provide for the needs of producers and consumers in their own country, but they will increasingly tend to become, like the English,[95] the commercial agents of other nations.

This is already beginning to happen before our eyes. Already we find American navigators acting as intermediary agents in the trade

[95] It must not be supposed that English ships are solely occupied in transporting foreign goods to England or English goods abroad; nowadays the English merchant navy is like some great public transport enterprise, ready to serve all the producers of the world and to enable all nations to communicate with one another. The maritime genius of the Americans prompts them to start a rival concern to the English.

of several European nations[96]; America offers them an even greater future.

The Spaniards and the Portuguese founded great colonies in South America, which have since become empires. Civil war and despotism are now desolating these huge countries. The movement of population is stopping, and the few men who live there, absorbed by the cares of defending themselves, hardly feel the need to better their lot.

But it cannot always be like that. Europe, left to itself, succeeded in piercing the darkness of the Middle Ages; South America is Christian like ourselves, with the same laws and usages; it holds all the seeds of the civilization which has since come to flower among the European nations and their offshoots; unlike ourselves, South America also has the benefit of our example: why should it always remain barbarous?

In this case it is clearly just a question of time: at some more or less distant time the South Americans will form flourishing and enlightened nations.

But when the Spaniards and Portuguese of South America begin to feel the needs of civilized peoples, they will still be far from able to satisfy them themselves; the last born of civilization, they will have to accept the superiority already attained by their elders. They will be farmers long before they are manufacturers and traders, and they will need the mediation of foreigners to see their produce overseas and to get in exchange those things newly felt to be necessities.

One cannot doubt that the North Americans will one day be called on to provide for the wants of the South Americans. Nature has placed them close together and has furnished the former with every means of knowing and appreciating the latter's needs in order to establish permanent relations and gradually gain control of that market. American merchants could not lose those natural advantages unless they were decidedly inferior to the merchants of Europe, whereas in fact they are superior to them in several respects. The Americans of the United States already have great moral influence over all the peoples of the New World. Enlightenment comes from them. All the nations inhabiting the same continent are already accustomed to consider them as the most enlightened, the most powerful, and the richest member of the great American family. Consequently all eyes are turned toward the United States, and as far as they can, they imitate the peoples dwelling there. They are

[96] Part of the Mediterranean trade is already carried in American ships.

continually deriving political doctrines from the United States and borrowing their laws.

The Americans of the United States stand in just the same position toward the nations of South America as their fathers, the English, stand toward the Italians, Spaniards, Portuguese, and all the other nations of Europe, who, being less advanced in civilization and in industry, receive most articles of consumption from them.

England is now the natural commercial center for all neighboring nations; the American Union is destined to fill the same role in the other hemisphere. So every nation that comes to birth or grows up in the New World does so, in a sense, for the benefit of the Anglo-Americans.

Should the Union be dissolved, the trade of the states forming it would no doubt for a time be checked in its growth, but less than is generally supposed. It is clear that whatever may happen, the trading states will remain united. They all are both contiguous and share the same opinions, interests, and mores, and they are capable of forming a very great maritime power. Even if the South of the Union did become independent of the North, it still could not manage without it. I have said that the South is not a land of commerce, and there is nothing at present to indicate that it will become so. Therefore for a long while ahead the Americans of the southern states will be obliged to rely on foreigners to export their produce and to bring them the things they need. Of all possible intermediaries, their northern neighbors are most certainly those able to serve them most cheaply. So they will serve them, for low cost is the supreme law of trade. There is no sovereign will or national prejudice that can fight for long against cheapness. There could not be hate more venomous than that between the Americans of the United States and the English. But despite these hostile sentiments, the English provide the Americans with most of their manufactured commodities because she can supply them at a cheaper rate than any other nation. Hence the growing prosperity of America turns, against the Americans' wishes, to the profit of English manufacturers.

Reason suggests and experience proves that there is no lasting commercial greatness unless it can, at need, combine with military power.

That truth is as well understood in the United States as anywhere else. Already the Americans can enforce respect for their flag; soon they will be able to make it feared.

I am convinced that dismemberment of the Union, far from reducing American naval strength, would have a strong tendency to increase it. At present the trading states are linked to others that do not trade and that therefore are often reluctant to increase a maritime power from which they benefit only indirectly.

But if all the trading states of the Union were combined in one coherent nation, then for them trade would become a national interest of the first importance; they would then be disposed to make great sacrifices to protect their ships, and there would be nothing to stop their following their inclinations in this respect.

I think that nations, like men, in their youth almost always give indications of the main features of their destiny. Seeing how energetically the Anglo-Americans trade, their natural advantages, and their success, I cannot help believing that one day they will become the leading naval power on the globe. They are born to rule the seas, as the Romans were to conquer the world.

CONCLUSION

Now I AM APPROACHING the end. Up to now, in discussing the future destiny of the United States, I have tried to divide my subject into various parts so as to study each of them more carefully.

It is time to take a general look at the whole from a single point of view. What I am going to say will be less detailed but more certain. Each object will stand out less distinctly, but the general lines will be clearer. I shall be like a traveler who has gone out beyond the walls of some vast city and gone up a neighboring hill; as he goes farther off, he loses sight of the men he has just left behind; the houses merge and the public squares cannot be seen; the roads are hard to distinguish; but the city's outline is easier to see, and for the first time he grasps its shape. Like that, I fancy I can see the whole future of the English race in the New World spread before me. The details of this huge picture are in shadow, but I can see the whole and form a clear idea of it.

The territory now occupied or owned by the United States of America forms about one twentieth of the habitable globe.

But wide though these bounds are, it would be a mistake to suppose that the Anglo-American race will always remain within them; it is already spreading far beyond them.

There was a time when we too might have created a great French nation in the wilds of America and might have shared the destinies of the New World with the English. There was a time when France possessed in North America a territory almost as vast as the whole of Europe. Then the three greatest rivers of the continent all flowed for their whole course within our dominions. The Indian nations dwelling between the mouth of the St. Lawrence and the Mississippi delta heard no language spoken but ours; all the European settlements scattered over that immense area echoed memories of our motherland: Louisbourg, Montmorency, Duquesne, Saint-Louis, Vincennes, and Nouvelle-Orléans, all names dear to France and familiar in our ears.

But a combination of circumstances too long to enumerate[1] deprived us of the magnificent heritage. In all places where the French were few and weakly established, they disappeared. The rest crowded into a narrow area and passed under other laws. The four hundred thousand French inhabitants of lower Canada now constitute the remnants of an ancient people lost in the flood of a new nation. The foreign population around them is constantly increasing and spreading out on all sides; it even penetrates into the ranks of the former owners of the soil, dominating their cities and corrupting their language. That population is identical with that of the United States. I am right, therefore, to say that the English race does not stop at the boundaries of the Union but advances far beyond toward the northwest.

To the northwest there is nothing but a few Russian settlements of no importance, but to the southwest Mexico presents a barrier to the Anglo-Americans.

In truth, therefore, there are only two rival races sharing the New World today: the Spaniards and the English.

The boundaries between these two races have been fixed by a treaty. But however favorable that treaty may have been to the Anglo-Americans, I have no doubt that they will soon infringe it.

Vast provinces extending beyond the frontiers of the Union toward Mexico are still empty of inhabitants. The people of the United States will penetrate into these solitary regions even sooner than those who have a right to occupy them. They will appropriate the soil and establish a society, so that when the legitimate owner finally arrives, he will find the wilderness cultivated and strangers quietly settled in his heritage.

The lands of the New World belong to the first man to occupy them, and dominion is the prize in that race.

Even the lands already peopled will have some difficulty in warding off invasion.

I have previously referred to what is happening in the province of Texas. Daily, little by little, the inhabitants of the United States are infiltrating into Texas, acquiring land there, and, though submitting to the country's laws, establishing there the empire of their language and mores. The province of Texas is still under Mexican rule, but soon there will, so to say, be no more Mexicans there.

[1] The most important reason was this: free peoples accustomed to municipal government find it much easier than do others to establish flourishing colonies. The habit of thinking for oneself and governing oneself is indispensable in a new country, where success is bound to depend in great measure on the individual efforts of the colonists.

The same sort of thing happens in every place where the Anglo-Americans come into contact with populations of a different origin.

It is no good pretending that the English race has not established an immense preponderance over all the other Europeans in the New World. It is far superior to them in civilization, industry, and power. As long as there lie before it only empty lands or ones thinly inhabited, and it does not encounter crowded populations through which it is impossible to force a passage, the English race will go on spreading constantly. It will not halt at lines drawn in treaties, but will flow over such imaginary bounds in all directions.

Its geographical position in the New World is another powerful aid to the rapid spread of that race.

There is polar ice beyond its northern frontiers, and a few degrees below its southern boundaries one comes into the burning tropics. So the English in America occupy the most temperate and inhabitable zone in the continent.

It is supposed that the prodigious increase observed in the population of the United States dates only from independence, but that is a mistake. The population increased as fast under the old colonial system as in our day; it was doubling every twenty-two years or so just the same. But then it was a question of some thousands of inhabitants, whereas now it is a matter of millions. Something which passed unnoticed a century ago now strikes the attention of all.

The English in Canada, who are subjects of a king, increase almost as quickly as the English of the United States under a republican government.

Throughout the eight years of the War of Independence the population went on increasing at just this same rate.

Although at that time on their western frontiers there were great Indian nations allied to the English, the movement of migration toward the west was, so to say, never slowed down. While the enemy was ravaging the Atlantic coast, Kentucky, the western districts of Pennsylvania, and the states of Vermont and Maine were filling up with inhabitants. The disorders after that war did not prevent the population from growing or halt the continual advance into the wilderness. Thus different laws, a state of peace or of war, order or anarchy, have had no perceptible influence on the continuous expansion of the Anglo-Americans.

That is easy to understand: there is no cause sufficiently general to exercise a simultaneous influence over the whole of such an immense land. One part of the country always offers a refuge from the calamities afflicting some other part, and however great such ills may be, the remedy at hand is always greater still.

So, then, it must not be thought possible to halt the impetus of the English race in the New World. The dismemberment of the Union, bringing war into the continent, or the abolition of the republic, bringing tyranny, might slow expansion down, but cannot prevent the people ultimately fulfilling their inevitable destiny. No power on earth can shut out the immigrants from that fertile wilderness which on every side offers rewards to industry and a refuge from every affliction. Whatever the future may hold in store, it cannot deprive the Americans of their climate, their inland seas, their great rivers, or the fertility of their soil. Bad laws, revolutions, and anarchy cannot destroy their taste for well-being or that spirit of enterprise which seems the characteristic feature of their race; nor could such things utterly extinguish the lights of knowledge guiding them.

Thus, in all the uncertainty of the future, one event at least is sure. At a period which we may call near, for we are speaking of the life of nations, the Anglo-Americans alone will cover the whole of the immense area between the polar ice and the tropics, extending from the Atlantic to the Pacific coast.

I think the land over which the Anglo-American race will spread will be three quarters of the size of Europe.[2] The Union's climate is, on balance, better than that of Europe; its natural advantages are as great; it is clear that its population will one day be proportionate to our own.

Europe, divided into different nations, torn by constant renewal of warfare and held back by the barbarism of the Middle Ages, has come to have 410 inhabitants to the square league.[3] What cause is powerful enough to prevent the United States one day having as many?

Many centuries will pass by before the various offshoots of the English race in America cease to present a common physiognomy. One cannot foresee a time when permanent inequality of conditions could be established in the New World.

[2] The United States alone already covers an area equal to half Europe. The area of Europe is 500,000 square leagues; its population is 205,000,000. (Malte-Brun, Vol. VI, Book 114, p. 4.) [As a matter of fact, Malte-Brun gives here the figure as 200,000,000, but on p. 92 he estimates that this figure should be increased to 205,000,000. So Tocqueville uses, with his somewhat generous scholarship, this increased figure also for this reference. Cf. 1826 edition. We have also corrected the references to Book 114; Tocqueville's reference to Book 116 is inaccurate.]

[3] See Malte-Brun, Vol. VI, Book 116, p. 92 [1826 edition].

Whatever differences—peace or war, freedom or tyranny, prosperity or affliction—may one day arise between the various branches of the great Anglo-American family, at least they will all preserve a similar social state and will share the usages and ideas which derive therefrom.

In the Middle Ages the link of religion alone was enough to unite all the various races of Europe in one civilization. The English of the New World have a thousand other links between them, and they live at a time when there is a general tendency toward equality in human affairs.

The Middle Ages were a time of divisions. Each people, each province, each city, and each family had a strong urge to assert its individuality. In our day an opposite tendency is noticeable, and nations seem to steer toward unity. There are intellectual links between the most distant parts of the earth, and men cannot remain strangers to each other for a single day or fail to know what happens in any corner of the world. That is why one now notices less difference between contemporary Europeans and their descendants in the New World, in spite of the ocean that divides them, than there was in the thirteenth century between towns separated only by a river.

If this tendency toward assimilation brings foreign nations closer to each other, it must *a fortiori* prevent branches of the same people becoming strangers to one another.

Therefore, the time must come when there will be in North America one hundred and fifty million people[4] all equal one to the other, belonging to the same family, having the same point of departure, the same civilization, language, religion, habits, and mores, and among whom thought will circulate in similar forms and with like nuances. All else is doubtful, but that is sure. And this is something entirely new in the world, something, moreover, the significance of which the imagination cannot grasp.

There are now two great nations in the world which, starting from different points, seem to be advancing toward the same goal: the Russians and the Anglo-Americans.

Both have grown in obscurity, and while the world's attention was occupied elsewhere, they have suddenly taken their place among the leading nations, making the world take note of their birth and of their greatness almost at the same instant.

All other peoples seem to have nearly reached their natural limits

[4] This figure assumes a population density like that of Europe, namely, 410 people to the square league.

and to need nothing but to preserve them; but these two are growing.⁵ All the others have halted or advanced only through great exertions; they alone march easily and quickly forward along a path whose end no eye can yet see.

The American fights against natural obstacles; the Russian is at grips with men. The former combats the wilderness and barbarism; the latter, civilization with all its arms. America's conquests are made with the plowshare, Russia's with the sword.

To attain their aims, the former relies on personal interest and gives free scope to the unguided strength and common sense of individuals.

The latter in a sense concentrates the whole power of society in one man.

One has freedom as the principal means of action; the other has servitude.

Their point of departure is different and their paths diverse; nevertheless, each seems called by some secret design of Providence one day to hold in its hands the destinies of half the world.

⁵ The population of Russia, proportionately speaking, is increasing more rapidly than that of any other nation in the Old World.

Volume Two

AUTHOR'S PREFACE TO VOLUME TWO

THE DEMOCRATIC social order in America springs naturally from some of their laws and conceptions of public morality.

Moreover, a great many feelings and points of view that were unknown in the old established aristocratic societies of Europe have come into their world as the offspring of this social order. The links which formerly bound men together have been destroyed or altered, and new links have been formed. Changes in the pattern of civil society have been as great as those in the world of politics.

The book about American democracy which I published five years ago dealt with the first of these subjects. This book is concerned with the second. The two volumes are complementary and should be read as a single book.

I must at once warn the reader against a mistake through which I might be seriously misunderstood.

Noticing how many different effects I hold due to equality, he might suppose that I consider equality the sole cause of everything that is happening now. That would be a very narrow view to attribute to me.

There are nowadays a great number of opinions, feelings, and instincts due to circumstances strange, in some cases even antipathetic, to equality. Thus, basing myself on observation of the United States, I could easily show that ways of thinking and feeling have been and still are profoundly influenced by the nature of the country, the origin of the colonists, the religion of the founding fathers, the enlightenment they acquired, and their former habits, all things unconnected with democracy. In like manner a great deal of what is happening in Europe can be explained by various factors, different from those operative in America but equally untouched by the fact of equality.

I know that all these different elements exist and are powerful, but the theme of this book does not deal with them. I have not undertaken to account for all our inclinations and all our ideas, but only wish to demonstrate how equality has modified both.

As I am firmly convinced that the democratic revolution occurring before our eyes is an irresistible fact and that it would be neither desirable nor wise to try to combat it, it may seem surprising that this book expresses such severe criticisms of the democratic societies created by this revolution.

My answer is simply that, being no enemy of democracy, I want to treat it with sincerity.

Enemies never tell men the truth, and it is seldom that their friends do so. That is why I have done so.

It seems to me that many people are ready to advertise the new benefits which democracy promises to mankind, but that few are prepared to point out the distant perils with which it threatens them. So my attention has been directed principally against these dangers, and thinking that I have seen them clearly, I have not played the coward and kept silent.

I hope that the impartiality for which my first book was credited will be found again in this work.

In the midst of the contradictory opinions that divide us, I have tried to divest myself for the moment of sympathies in favor of or instincts against each of them. If my readers find a single phrase calculated to flatter one of the great parties that have shaken our land or one of the petty factions which are now bringing on us confusion and paralysis, then let my readers raise their voices in protest against me.

The ground I wish to cover is vast. It includes the greater part of the feelings and ideas which are responsible for the changed state of the world. Such a subject is certainly beyond my strength, and I am far from satisfied with my own achievement.

But if I have not succeeded in the task I set myself, I hope I shall be credited with conceiving and pursuing the undertaking in a spirit which could make me worthy of success.

CONTENTS OF VOLUME TWO

PART II
The Influence of Democracy on the
Sentiments of the Americans

PART III
Influence of Democracy on Mores
Properly So Called

PART IV
On the Influence of Democratic Ideas and
Feelings on Political Society

APPENDICES

PART I

Influence of Democracy on the Intellectual
Movements in the United States

Chapter 1

CONCERNING THE PHILOSOPHICAL
APPROACH OF THE AMERICANS

LESS ATTENTION, I suppose, is paid to philosophy in the United States than in any other country of the civilized world. The Americans have no school of philosophy peculiar to themselves, and they pay very little attention to the rival European schools. Indeed they hardly know their names. Nevertheless, it is noticeable that the people of the United States almost all have a uniform method and rules for the conduct of intellectual inquiries. So, though they have not taken the trouble to define the rules, they have a philosophical method shared by all.

To escape from imposed systems, the yoke of habit, family maxims, class prejudices, and to a certain extent national prejudices as well; to treat tradition as valuable for information only and to accept existing facts as no more than a useful sketch to show how things could be done differently and better; to seek by themselves and in themselves for the only reason for things, looking to results without getting entangled in the means toward them and looking through forms to the basis of things—such are the principal characteristics of what I would call the American philosophical method.

To carry the argument further and to select the chief among these various features, and the one which includes almost all the others within itself, I should say that in most mental operations each American relies on individual effort and judgment.

So, of all countries in the world, America is the one in which the precepts of Descartes are least studied and best followed. No one should be surprised at that.

The Americans never read Descartes's works because their state of society distracts them from speculative inquiries, and they follow his precepts because this same state of society naturally leads them to adopt them.

The continuous activity which prevails in a democratic society leads to the relaxation or the breaking of the links between generations. It is easy for a man to lose track of his ancestors' conceptions or not to bother about them.

Men living in such a society cannot base their beliefs on the opinions of the class to which they belong, for, one may almost say, there are no more classes, and such as do still exist are composed of such changing elements that they can never, as a body, exercise real power over their members.

When it comes to the influence of one man's mind over another's, that is necessarily very restricted in a country where the citizens have all become more or less similar, see each other at very close quarters, and since they do not recognize any signs of incontestable greatness or superiority in any of their fellows, are continually brought back to their own judgment as the most apparent and accessible test of truth. So it is not only confidence in any particular man which is destroyed. There is a general distaste for accepting any man's word as proof of anything.

So each man is narrowly shut up in himself, and from that basis makes the pretension to judge the world.

This American way of relying on themselves alone to control their judgment leads to other mental habits.

Seeing that they are successful in resolving unaided all the little difficulties they encounter in practical affairs, they are easily led to the conclusion that everything in the world can be explained and that nothing passes beyond the limits of intelligence.

Thus they are ready to deny anything which they cannot understand. Hence they have little faith in anything extraordinary and an almost invincible distaste for the supernatural.

Being accustomed to rely on the witness of their own eyes, they like to see the object before them very clearly. They therefore free it, as far as they can, from its wrappings and move anything in the way and anything that hides their view of it, so as to get the closest view they can in broad daylight. This turn of mind soon leads them to a scorn of forms, which they take as useless, hampering veils put between them and truth.

So the Americans have needed no books to teach them philosophic method, having found it in themselves. Much the same can be said of what has happened in Europe.

This same method has only become established and popular in Europe as conditions of life have become more equal and men more like one another.

Let us turn our attention for a moment to the chronological development.

The sixteenth-century reformers subjected some of the dogmas of the ancient faith to individual reason, but they still refused to allow all the others to be discussed by it. In the seventeenth century Bacon, in natural science, and Descartes, in philosophy strictly so called, abolished accepted formulas, destroyed the dominion of tradition, and upset the authority of masters.

The eighteenth-century philosopher turned this same principle into a general rule and undertook to submit the object of all his beliefs to each man's individual examination.

It is surely clear that Luther, Descartes, and Voltaire all used the same method, and they differed only in the greater or lesser extent to which they held it should be applied.

How did it happen that the reformers were shut in so narrowly within the circle of religious ideas? Why did Descartes, not wanting to use his method except for certain subjects, declare that one should judge philosophical questions for oneself, but not political ones? Why did men in the eighteenth century suddenly draw general conclusions from this same method, which Descartes and his forerunners had either not noticed or refused to observe? Finally, why was it at that time that this method suddenly came out of the schools, worked its way into society, and became the common coin of thought; moreover, when the French had spread its popularity, why was it openly adopted or secretly followed by all the peoples of Europe?

It was possible for this philosophic method to come into the world in the sixteenth century and to be defined and generalized in the seventeenth, but it could not be commonly accepted in either of those centuries. The political laws, the state of society, and habits of thought, all deriving from first causes of their own, were opposed to it.

It was discovered at a time when men were beginning to grow more equal and more like each other. It could not be generally followed except in centuries when conditions had become more or less similar and people like each other.

It follows that the eighteenth-century philosophic method is not just French, but democratic, and that explains its easy admission throughout Europe, which has been so greatly changed partly by its means. The reason the French turned the world upside down is not simply that they changed their ancient beliefs and modified their ancient morality. The reason is that they were the first to generalize and call attention to a philosophic method by which all ancient things could be attacked and the way opened for everything new.

If I am asked why nowadays that method is more often and more strictly applied by the French than by the Americans, though liberty is as complete and of longer date among the latter, I reply that that is partly due to two circumstances that must first be understood.

It was religion that gave birth to the English colonies in America. One must never forget that. In the United States religion is mingled with all the national customs and all those feelings which the word fatherland evokes. For that reason it has peculiar power.

There is another circumstance equally potent in its influence. In America religion has, if one may put it so, defined its own limits. There the structure of religious life has remained entirely distinct from the political organization. It has therefore been easy to change ancient laws without shaking the foundations of ancient beliefs.

In this way Christianity has kept a strong hold over the minds of Americans, and—this is the point I wish to emphasize—its power is not just that of a philosophy which has been examined and accepted, but that of a religion believed in without discussion.

In the United States there are an infinite variety of ceaselessly changing Christian sects. But Christianity itself is an established and irresistible fact which no one seeks to attack or to defend.

Since the Americans have accepted the main dogmas of the Christian religion without examination, they are bound to receive in like manner a great number of moral truths derived therefrom and attached thereto. This puts strict limits on the field of action left open to individual analysis and keeps out of this field many of the most important subjects about which men can have opinions.

The other circumstance which I referred to is this:

The state of society and the Constitution in America are democratic, but there has been no democratic revolution. They were pretty well as they now are when they first arrived in the land. That is a very important point.

Every revolution must shake ancient beliefs, sap authority, and cloud shared ideas. So any revolution, to a greater or lesser extent, throws men back on themselves and opens to each man's view an almost limitless empty space.

When standards of equality have resulted from a long struggle between the different classes of which the old society was composed, envy, hatred, and distrust of his neighbor, together with pride and exaggerated confidence in himself, invade the human heart and for some time hold dominion there. That fact, without reference to equality, works powerfully to divide men and to ensure that they be mistrustful of one another's judgment and look for enlightenment only in themselves.

Consequently each man undertakes to be sufficient to himself and glories in the fact that his beliefs about everything are peculiar to himself. No longer do ideas, but interests only, form the links between men, and it would seem that human opinions were no more than a sort of mental dust open to the wind on every side and unable to come together and take shape.

Thus the independence of mind which equality supposes to exist is never so great and never shows itself so excessive as at the moment when equality begins to be established and during the pangs of its birth. One must make a careful distinction between that type of intellectual liberty which can result from equality and the anarchy brought in by revolution. Each of these two elements must be considered separately if we are not to conceive exaggerated hopes and fears for the future.

I think that the men who live in the new societies will often make use of individual judgment, but I am far from believing that they will often abuse it.

The reason for this, which I reserve for the next chapter, is something of more general application to democratic countries, something which must in the long run hold the independence of individual thought within fixed, indeed sometimes narrow, bounds.

Chapter 2

CONCERNING THE PRINCIPAL SOURCE OF BELIEFS AMONG DEMOCRATIC PEOPLES

DOGMATIC BELIEFS are more or less numerous at different periods. They come into existence in various ways and can change both form and substance. But it can never happen that there are no dogmatic beliefs, that is to say, opinions which men take on trust without discussion. If each man undertook to make up his mind about everything himself and to pursue truth only along roads that he himself had cleared, it is unlikely that any large number of people would ever succeed in agreeing on any common belief.

However, it is easy to see that no society could prosper without such beliefs, or rather that there are no societies which manage in that way. For without ideas in common, no common action would be possible, and without common action, men might exist, but there could be no body social. So for society to exist and, even more, for society to prosper, it is essential that all the minds of the citizens should always be rallied and held together by some leading ideas; and that could never happen unless each of them sometimes came to draw his opinions from the same source and was ready to accept some beliefs ready made.

Moreover, considering each man by himself, dogmatic beliefs seem no less indispensable for living alone than for acting in common with his fellows.

If man had to prove for himself all the truths of which he makes use every day, he would never come to an end of it. He would wear himself out proving preliminary points and make no progress. Since life is too short for such a course and human faculties are too limited, man has to accept as certain a whole heap of facts and opinions which he has neither leisure nor power to examine and verify for himself, things which cleverer men than he have discovered and which the crowd accepts. On that foundation he then builds the house of his own thoughts. He does not act so from any conscious choice, for the inflexible laws of his existence compel him to behave like that.

No philosopher in the world, however great, can help believing a million things on trust from others or assuming the truth of many things besides those he has proved.

Such behavior is desirable as well as necessary. Anyone who undertook to go into everything himself could give but little time or attention to each question. He would keep his mental faculties in a state of perpetual excitement, which would prevent his going deeply into any truth or being firmly convinced of anything at all. His intelligence would be independent but weak. So a choice must be made among all the things about which men have opinions, and some beliefs must be accepted without discussion so that it is possible to go deeply into a few selected ones for examination.

It is true that any man accepting any opinion on trust from another puts his mind in bondage. But it is a salutary bondage, which allows him to make good use of freedom.

So somewhere and somehow authority is always bound to play a part in intellectual and moral life. The part may vary, but some part there must be. The independence of the individual may be greater or less but can never be unlimited. Therefore we need not inquire about the existence of intellectual authority in democratic ages, but only where it resides and what its limits are.

The last chapter showed how standards of equality give men a sort of instinctive incredulity about the supernatural and a very high and often thoroughly exaggerated conception of human reason.

Thus men who live in times of equality find it hard to place the intellectual authority to which they submit, beyond and outside humanity. Generally speaking, they look into themselves or into their fellows for the sources of truth. That is enough to prove that no new religion could become established in such periods and that any attempts to bring one into existence would be not only impious but also ridiculous and unreasonable. One can anticipate that democratic peoples will not easily believe in divine missions, that they will be quick to laugh at new prophets, and that they will wish to find the chief arbiter of their beliefs within, and not beyond, the limits of their kind.

When standards are unequal and men unalike, there are some very enlightened and learned individuals whose intelligence gives them great power, while the multitude is very ignorant and blinkered. As a result men living under an aristocracy are naturally inclined to be guided in their views by a more thoughtful man or class, and they have little inclination to suppose the masses infallible.

In times of equality the opposite happens.

The nearer men are to a common level of uniformity, the less are they inclined to believe blindly in any man or any class. But they are readier to trust the mass, and public opinion becomes more and more mistress of the world.

Not only is public opinion the only guide left to aid private judgment, but its power is infinitely greater in democracies than elsewhere. In times of equality men, being so like each other, have no confidence in others, but this same likeness leads them to place almost unlimited confidence in the judgment of the public. For they think it not unreasonable that, all having the same means of knowledge, truth will be found on the side of the majority.

The citizen of a democracy comparing himself with the others feels proud of his equality with each. But when he compares himself with all his fellows and measures himself against this vast entity, he is overwhelmed by a sense of his insignificance and weakness.

The same equality which makes him independent of each separate citizen leaves him isolated and defenseless in the face of the majority.

So in democracies public opinion has a strange power of which aristocratic nations can form no conception. It uses no persuasion to forward its beliefs, but by some mighty pressure of the mind of all upon the intelligence of each it imposes its ideas and makes them penetrate men's very souls.

The majority in the United States takes over the business of supplying the individual with a quantity of ready-made opinions and so relieves him of the necessity of forming his own. So there are many theories of philosophy, morality, and politics which everyone adopts unexamined on the faith of public opinion. And if one looks very closely into the matter, one finds that religion is strong less as a revealed doctrine than as part of common opinion.

I know that American political laws give the majority the sovereign right to rule society, and that considerably increases the dominion it has anyhow over men's minds. For nothing comes more natural to man than to recognize the superior wisdom of his oppressor.

So this political omnipotence simply augments the power which public opinion would have had without it over each citizen, but it is not the foundation thereof. One must look to equality itself for the source of that influence, and not to the more or less popular institutions which egalitarian men have created for themselves. One may suppose that the intellectual dominion of the greatest number would be less absolute among a democratic people subject to a king than in a pure democracy. But it will always be very nearly absolute in times of equality, and no matter what political laws men devise for themselves, it is safe to foresee that trust in common opinion will become a sort of religion, with the majority as its prophet.

Thus intellectual authority will be different, but it will not be less. Far from believing that it is likely to disappear, I anticipate that it may easily become too great and that possibly it will confine the activity of private judgment within limits too narrow for the dignity and happiness of mankind. I see clearly two tendencies in equality; one turns each man's attention to new thoughts, while the other would induce him freely to give up thinking at all. I can see how, abetted by certain laws, democracy might extinguish that freedom of the mind which a democratic social condition favors. Thus it might happen that, having broken down all the bonds which classes or men formerly imposed on it, the human spirit might bind itself in tight fetters to the general will of the greatest number.

If democratic peoples substituted the absolute power of a majority for all the various powers that used excessively to impede or hold back the upsurge of individual thought, the evil itself would only have changed its form. Men would by no means have found the way to live in independence; they would only have succeeded in the difficult task of giving slavery a new face. There is matter for deep reflection there. I cannot say this too often for all those who see freedom of the mind as something sacred and who hate not only despots but also despotism. For myself, if I feel the hand of power heavy on my brow, I am little concerned to know who it is that oppresses me; I am no better inclined to pass my head under the yoke because a million men hold it for me.

Chapter 3

WHY THE AMERICANS SHOW MORE APTITUDE AND TASTE FOR GENERAL IDEAS THAN THEIR ENGLISH FOREFATHERS

THE DEITY DOES NOT VIEW the human race collectively. With one glance He sees every human being separately and sees in each the resemblances that makes him like his fellows and the differences which isolate him from them.

It follows that God has no need of general ideas, that is to say, He never feels the necessity of giving the same label to a considerable number of analogous objects in order to think about them more conveniently.

It is not like that with man. If a human intelligence tried to examine and judge all the particular cases that came his way individually he would soon be lost in a wilderness of detail and not be able to see anything at all. In this pass he has recourse to an imperfect though necessary procedure which aids the weakness that makes it necessary.

After a superficial inspection of a certain number of objects he notes that they resemble each other and gives them all the same name. After that he puts them on one side and continues on his way.

General ideas do not bear witness to the power of human intelligence but rather to its inadequacy, for there are no beings exactly alike in nature, no identical facts, no laws which can be applied indiscriminately in the same way to several objects at once.

General ideas have this excellent quality, that they permit human minds to pass judgment quickly on a great number of things; but the conceptions they convey are always incomplete, and what is gained in extent is always lost in exactitude.

As societies grow older they learn new facts and daily take hold almost unconsciously of some particular truths.

The more truths of this kind a man apprehends, the more general ideas he is naturally led to entertain. One cannot see a multitude of particular facts separately without at last discovering the link which connects them. Several individuals lead to the notion of the species, several species to that of the genus. So the use of general ideas and the taste for them will always increase the older a people's culture is and the wider their knowledge.

But there are also other influences which lead a people to adopt general ideas or which distract them from them.

The Americans use general ideas much more than the English and have a greater relish for them. This seems very strange at first sight, considering that the two nations have a common origin, that for centuries they have lived under the same laws, and that there is still a continual give and take of ideas and moral standards between them. The contrast is even more striking if we turn our attention home to Europe and consider the two most enlightened nations there.

It seems to be pain and grief to the English to turn their attention away from particular facts in order to trace back their causes, and if they do make a generalization, it is in spite of themselves.

With us, on the other hand, there seems to have developed such an unrestrained passion for generalizations that it must, in whatever context, be satisfied. I wake every morning to be told that some general and eternal law of which I have never heard before has just been discovered. No writer, however second-rate, is satisfied with an essay revealing truths applicable to one great kingdom, and he remains dissatisfied with himself if his theme does not embrace the whole of mankind.

I am astonished at so great a difference between two highly cultivated peoples. Turning to England and considering especially the way things have gone in the last half century, I think I can point to an increased taste for generalization which goes hand in hand with a weakening of the old constitution.

So a more or less highly developed culture is clearly not by itself enough to account for a taste for or aversion from generalization.

When standards are very far from equal and the inequalities are permanent, individuals gradually become so dissimilar that one can almost talk of as many types of humanity as there are classes. Attention is never fixed on more than one of these at the same time, and losing sight of the connecting thread which links them all within the vast bosom of mankind, it is invariably not man but certain men who are observed. Members, therefore, of aristocratic societies never make grand generalizations about themselves, and that is enough to give them a habitual distrust and unconscious distaste for all generalizations.

Contrariwise, the democratic citizen sees nothing but people more or less like himself around him, and so he cannot think about one branch of mankind without widening his view until it includes the whole. Truths applicable to himself seem equally applicable, *mutatis mutandis,* to his fellow citizens and to all men. Having acquired a taste for generalizations in the matters which most closely take up his attention and touch his interests, he carries it with him when dealing with everything else. Hence it becomes an ardent and often blind passion of the human spirit to discover common rules for everything, to include a great number of objects under the same formula, and to explain a group of facts by one sole cause.

The views of the ancient world about slaves clearly demonstrate the truth of this proposition.

The profoundest and most wide-seeing minds of Greece and Rome never managed to grasp the very general but very simple conception of the likeness of all men and of the equal right of all at birth to liberty. They were at pains to show that slavery was natural and would always exist. Moreover, there is every indication that those of the ancients who had been slaves before they became free, several of whom wrote fine books which have been preserved, saw slavery in the same light.

All the great writers of antiquity were either members of the aristocracy of masters or, at the least, saw that aristocracy in undisputed possession before their eyes. Their minds roamed free in many directions but were blinkered there. Jesus Christ had to come down to earth to make all members of the human race understand that they were naturally similar and equal.

In ages of equality all men are independent of each other, isolated and weak. One finds no man whose will permanently directs the actions of the crowd. At such times humanity always seems to progress of its own accord. So to explain what happens in the world, one is reduced to looking for certain great causes which, acting in the same fashion on each of our fellow men, lead them all of their own accord to follow one and the same road. That too leads minds to conceive generalizations and acquire a taste for them.

I have shown before how equal standards induce each man to look for truth for himself. It is easy to see that such a method insensibly directs the human spirit toward generalizations. When traditions of class, of profession, and of family are repudiated and the dominion of precedent is left behind for the search by one's own unaided reason for the way to follow, one has a natural inclination to deduce the motives for one's views from the very nature of man, and that leads of necessity and almost in spite of oneself to a great number of very broad generalizations.

All this goes to show why the English have much less taste and aptitude for generalization than their American descendants, and more especially, than their French neighbors, and also why the English nowadays have more of this taste than had their fathers.

The English have long been a very cultivated people and a very aristocratic one. While their culture continually drew them toward broad generalizations, their aristocratic habits confined them to the particular. From this arose that brand of philosophy, both bold and timid, broad and narrow, which has dominated English thought up to our time and still hampers and immobilizes so many minds.

Apart from the preceding considerations, there are others, less obvious but equally potent, which give almost all democratic peoples a taste, and often a passion, for generalization.

It is important to make a distinction between different kinds of generalization. One kind results from the slow, detailed, and conscientious labor of the mind, and that kind widens the sphere of human knowledge.

The other kind springs up at once from the first quick exercise of the wits and begets only very superficial and uncertain notions.

Men living in times of equality have much curiosity and little leisure. Life is so practical, complicated, agitated, and active that they have little time for thinking. So democratic man likes generalizations because they save him the trouble of studying particular cases. They contain, if I may put it so, a lot in a small space and give a great return quickly. So when, after a cursory and casual glance, they think they can see a common link between certain things without looking into the matter further, and disregarding the details in which these various things may be like or unlike, they are in a hurry to class them all under the same formula so as to go on to something else.

One of the characteristics of democratic times is that all men have a taste for easy successes and immediate pleasures. This is true of intellectual pursuits as well as of all others. Most men who live in times of equality are full of lively yet indolent ambition. They want great success at once, but they want to do without great efforts. These contrary instincts lead them straight to looking for generalizations, by means of which they flatter themselves that they can paint vast canvases very cheaply and attract public attention without trouble.

I do not know that they are wrong in thinking so. For their

readers are just as afraid of profundity as they are themselves and generally look only for facile pleasures and effortless instruction in the works of the mind.

If aristocratic nations do not make enough use of generalizations and often show an ill-considered scorn of them, democratic peoples, on the contrary, are always ready to make bad use of that type of conception and espouse them with injudicious warmth.

Chapter 4

WHY THE AMERICANS HAVE NEVER BEEN AS EAGER AS THE FRENCH FOR GENERAL IDEAS ABOUT POLITICAL AFFAIRS

I HAVE SAID BEFORE THAT THE Americans have a less lively taste for general ideas than the French. That is especially true where politics are concerned.

Although the Americans bring general ideas to bear on their legislation much more than the English and make much more effort than they to adjust practice to theory, there have been no political bodies in the United States as much in love with general ideas as were our Constituent Assembly and Convention. Never has the whole American people shown such a passion for conceptions of this sort as did the French people in the eighteenth century, and they have never had such blind faith in the virtue and absolute truth of any theory.

There are several reasons for this difference between the Americans and ourselves, of which the following is the chief.

The Americans are a democratic people which has always managed its own political affairs, whereas we are a democratic people which for a long time could only speculate on the best way to manage them.

Our state of society led us to conceive broad general ideas about ways of government at a time when our Constitution prevented us from correcting them by experience and gradually finding out their deficiencies. Whereas in America the two things naturally and constantly balance and correct each other.

That may seem at first sight to contradict what I said before, that democratic nations derive the love they show for theories from the very excitement of their practical life. But looking at the matter more carefully, one sees that there is no contradiction.

Citizens of democracies are greedy for general ideas because they have little leisure, and such conceptions save them from wasting time considering particular cases. That is true, but it should not be understood to cover matters which are not the habitual and necessary subject of their thoughts. Merchants eagerly grasp all philosophic generalizations presented to them without looking closely into them, and the same is true about politics, science, and the arts. But only after examination will they accept those concerning trade, and even then they do so with reserve.

Statesmen behave just the same when it comes to political generalizations.

If, then, there is a subject concerning which a democracy is particularly liable to commit itself blindly and extravagantly to general ideas, the best possible corrective is to make the citizens pay daily, practical attention to it. That will force them to go into details, and the details will show them the weak points in the theory.

The remedy is often painful but always effective.

That is how democratic institutions which make each citizen take a practical part in government moderate the excessive taste for general political theories which is prompted by equality.

Chapter 5

HOW RELIGION IN THE UNITED STATES MAKES USE OF DEMOCRATIC INSTINCTS

AN EARLIER CHAPTER HAS SHOWN that men cannot do without dogmatic beliefs, and even that it is most desirable that they should have them. I would add here that religious dogmas seem to me the most desirable of all. That can clearly be deduced, even if one only considers the interests of this world.

There is hardly any human action, however private it may be, which does not result from some very general conception men have of God, of His relations with the human race, of the nature of their soul, and of their duties to their fellows. Nothing can prevent such ideas from being the common spring from which all else originates.

It is therefore of immense importance to men to have fixed ideas about God, their souls, and their duties toward their Creator and their fellows, for doubt about these first principles would leave all their actions to chance and condemn them, more or less, to anarchy and impotence.

That is therefore the most important question about which all of us need fixed ideas, and unfortunately it is the subject on which it is most difficult for each of us, left to his own unaided reason, to settle his ideas.

Only minds singularly free from the ordinary preoccupations of life, penetrating, subtle, and trained to think, can at the cost of much time and trouble sound the depths of these truths that are so necessary.

Indeed we see that philosophers themselves are almost always surrounded by uncertainties, that at each pace the natural light which guides them grows dimmer and threatens to go out, and that for all their efforts they have done no more than discover a small number of contradictory ideas on which the mind of man has been ceaselessly tossed for thousands of years without ever firmly grasping the truth or even finding mistakes that are new. Studies of this sort are far above the average capacities of men, and even if most men were capable of such inquiries, they clearly would not have time for them.

Fixed ideas about God and human nature are indispensable to men for the conduct of daily life, and it is daily life that prevents them from acquiring them.

The difficulty seems unparalleled. Among the sciences some that are useful to the crowd are also within its capacities; others can be mastered only by the few and are not cultivated by the majority, who need nothing beyond their more remote applications. But the sciences in question are essential to the daily life of all, though their study is out of reach of most.

General ideas respecting God and human nature are therefore the ideas above all others which ought to be withdrawn from the habitual action of private judgment and in which there is most to gain and least to lose by recognizing an authority.

The chief object and one of the principal advantages of religion is to provide answers to each of these primordial questions; these answers must be clear, precise, intelligible to the crowd, and very durable.

Some religions are very false and very ridiculous. Nevertheless, one can say that all those religions which remain within the circle of influence which I have just defined and do not claim to go beyond it (as many religions have tried to do, restraining the free flight of the human mind on every side) impose a salutary control on the intellect, and one must recognize, whether or not they save men's souls in the next world, that they greatly contribute to their happiness and dignity in this.

This is especially true of men living in free countries.

When a people's religion is destroyed, doubt invades the highest faculties of the mind and half paralyzes all the rest. Each man gets into the way of having nothing but confused and changing notions about the matters of greatest importance to himself and his fellows. Opinions are ill-defended or abandoned, and in despair of solving unaided the greatest problems of human destiny, men ignobly give up thinking about them.

Such a state inevitably enervates the soul, and relaxing the springs of the will, prepares a people for bondage.

Then not only will they let their freedom be taken from them, but often they actually hand it over themselves.

When there is no authority in religion or in politics, men are soon frightened by the limitless independence with which they are faced. They are worried and worn out by the constant restlessness of everything. With everything on the move in the realm of the mind, they want the material order at least to be firm and stable, and as they cannot accept their ancient beliefs again, they hand themselves over to a master.

For my part, I doubt whether man can support complete religious independence and entire political liberty at the same time. I am led to think that if he has no faith he must obey, and if he is free he must believe.

The great usefulness of religions is even more apparent among egalitarian peoples than elsewhere.

One must admit that equality, while it brings great benefits to mankind, opens the door, as I hope to show later, to very dangerous instincts. It tends to isolate men from each other so that each thinks only of himself.

It lays the soul open to an inordinate love of material pleasure.

The greatest advantage of religions is to inspire diametrically contrary urges. Every religion places the object of man's desires outside and beyond worldly goods and naturally lifts the soul into regions far above the realm of the senses. Every religion also imposes on each man some obligations toward mankind, to be performed in common with the rest of mankind, and so draws him away, from time to time, from thinking about himself. That is true even of the most false and dangerous religions.

Thus religious peoples are naturally strong just at the point where democratic peoples are weak. And that shows how important it is for people to keep their religion when they become equal.

I have neither the right nor the intention to examine the means by which God inspires a sense of religious belief into the heart of man. At the moment I am only looking at religions from a purely human point of view. I seek to discover how they can most easily preserve their power in the democratic centuries which lie before us.

I have pointed out how in times of enlightenment and democracy the human spirit is loath to accept dogmatic beliefs and has no lively sense of the need for them except in the matter of religion. This shows that, at such times above all, religions should be most careful to confine themselves to their proper sphere, for if they wish to extend their power beyond spiritual matters they run the risk of not being believed at all. They should therefore be at pains to define the sphere in which they claim to control the human spirit, and outside that sphere it should be left completely free to follow its own devices.

Muhammad brought down from heaven and put into the Koran not religious doctrines only, but political maxims, criminal and civil laws, and scientific theories. The Gospels, on the other hand, deal only with the general relations between man and God and between man and man. Beyond that, they teach nothing and do not oblige people to believe anything. That alone, among a thousand reasons, is enough to show that Islam will not be able to hold its power long in ages of enlightenment and democracy, while Christianity is destined to reign in such ages, as in all others.

Continuing this line of argument further, I find that, humanly speaking, if religions are to be capable of maintaining themselves in democratic ages, it is not enough that they should simply remain wthin the spiritual sphere. Their power also depends a great deal on the nature of the beliefs they profess, the external forms they adopt, and the duties they impose.

The preceding observation, that equality leads men to very general and very vast ideas, is especially applicable to religion. Men who are alike and on the same level in this world easily conceive the idea of a single God who imposes the same laws on each man and grants him future happiness at the same price. The conception of the unity of mankind ever brings them back to the idea of the unity of the Creator, whereas when men are isolated from one another by great differences, they easily discover as many divinities as there are nations,

castes, classes, and families, and they find a thousand private roads
to go to heaven.

One cannot deny that Christianity itself has in some degree been
affected by the influence of social and political conditions on religious beliefs.

At the time when Christianity appeared on earth, Providence, which
no doubt was preparing the world for its reception, had united a
great part of mankind, like an immense flock, under the scepter of the
Caesars. The men composing this multitude were of many different
sorts, but they all had this in common, that they obeyed the same
laws, and each of them was so small and weak compared to the
greatness of the emperor that they all seemed equal in comparison
to him.

One must recognize that this new and singular condition of humanity disposed men to receive the general truths preached by Christianity, and this serves to explain the quick and easy way in which
it then penetrated the human spirit.

The counterpart of this state of things was evident after the destruction of the empire.

The Roman world being then broken up into a thousand fragments, each nation reverted to its former individuality. There soon
developed within these nations an infinite hierarchy of ranks. Racial
differences became marked, and castes divided each nation into several peoples. In the midst of this communal effort, which seemed
bent on subdividing humanity into as many fragments as it is possible
to conceive, Christianity did not lose sight of the principal general
ideas which it had brought to light, but seemed nonetheless to lend
itself, as far as it could, to the new tendencies which came into
existence as humanity was broken up. Men continued to worship
one sole God, creator and preserver of all things, but each people,
each city, and, one may almost say, each man thought he could
obtain some particular privilege and win the favor of private pro-
tectors before the throne of grace. Unable to subdivide the Deity,
they could at least multiply and aggrandize His agents beyond measure. For most Christians the worship of angels and saints became an
almost idolatrous cult, and for a time there was room to fear that
the Christian religion might relapse into the religions it had conquered.

It seems clear that the more the barriers separating the nations
within the bosom of humanity and those separating citizen from
citizen within each people tended to disappear, by so much the more
did the spirit of humanity, as if of its own accord, turn toward the
idea of a unique and all-powerful Being who dispensed the same

laws equally and in the same way to all men. In democratic ages, therefore, it is particularly important not to confuse the honor due to secondary agents with the worship belonging to the Creator alone.

Another truth seems very clear to me, that religions should pay less attention to external practices in democratic times than in any others.

In speaking of the philosophical method of the Americans I have made clear that in a time of equality nothing is more repugnant to the human spirit than the idea of submitting to formalities. Men living at such times are impatient of figures of speech; symbols appear to them as childish artifices used to hide or dress up truths which could more naturally be shown to them naked and in broad daylight. Ceremonies leave them cold, and their natural tendency is to attach but secondary importance to the details of worship.

In democratic ages those whose duty is to regulate the external forms of worship should pay special attention to these natural propensities of the human mind in order not to run counter to them unnecessarily.

I believe firmly in the need for external ceremonies. I know that they fix the human spirit in the contemplation of abstract truths and help it to grasp them firmly and believe ardently in them. I do not imagine that it is possible to maintain a religion without external observances. Nevertheless, I think that in the coming centuries it would be particularly dangerous to multiply them beyond measure, indeed that they should be limited to such as are absolutely necessary to perpetuate dogma itself, which is the essence of religions,[1] whereas ritual is only the form. A religion which became more detailed, more inflexible, and more burdened with petty observances at a time when people were becoming more equal would soon find itself reduced to a band of fanatic zealots in the midst of a skeptical multitude.

I anticipate the objection that religions with general and eternal truths for their subject cannot thus trim their sails to the changing urges of each century without losing their reputation for certainty in men's eyes. My answer is that one must make a very careful distinction between the chief opinions which form a belief, and are what the theologians call articles of faith, and those secondary notions which are connected with it. Religions are bound to hold firmly to the first, whatever may be the spirit of the time. But they should be very careful not to bind themselves like that to the secondary ones at a time when everything is in flux and the mind, accustomed to

[1] In all religions there are ceremonies which are inherent in the very substance of belief, and one must take care not to change anything in them. That is especially seen in the Catholic religion, where form and substance are so closely united that they are one.

the moving pageant of human affairs, is reluctant to be held fixed. Things external and secondary, it would seem, have a chance of enduring only when society itself is static. In any other circumstances I am disposed to regard rigidity as dangerous.

A passion for well-being is, as we shall see, the most lively of all the emotions aroused or inflamed by equality, and it is a passion shared by all. So this taste for well-being is the most striking and unalterable characteristic of democratic ages.

It may be that, should any religion attempt to destroy this mother of all desires, it would itself be destroyed thereby. If it attempted to wean men entirely from thinking of the good things of this world in order to concentrate all their faculties on the contemplation of the next, sooner or later one may be sure that men's souls would slip through its fingers to plunge headlong into the delights of purely material and immediate satisfactions.

The main business of religions is to purify, control, and restrain that excessive and exclusive taste for well-being which men acquire in times of equality, but I think it would be a mistake for them to attempt to conquer it entirely and abolish it. They will never succeed in preventing men from loving wealth, but they may be able to induce them to use only honest means to enrich themselves.

This leads me to raise a final point, which in some degree includes all the others. The more people are assimilated to one another and brought to an equality, the more important it becomes that religions, while remaining studiously aloof from the daily turmoil of worldly business, should not needlessly run counter to prevailing ideas or the permanent interests of the mass of the people. For as public opinion becomes ever increasingly the first and more irresistible of powers, there is no force outside it to support a prolonged resistance. The same holds good of a democratic people either in a republic or subject to a despot. In times of equality kings may often command obedience, but it is always the majority that establishes belief. So in all matters not contrary to faith one must defer to the majority.

I have shown in the first part of this book how the American clergy stands aloof from public business. That is the most striking, but not the only, example of their self-restraint. Religion in America is a world apart in which the clergyman is supreme, but one which he is careful never to leave; within its limits he guides men's minds, while outside them he leaves men to themselves, to the freedom and instability natural to themselves and the times they live in. I have seen no country in which Christianity is less clothed in forms, symbols, and observances than it is in the United States, or where the mind is fed with clearer, simpler, or more comprehensive conceptions.

Though American Christians are divided into very many sects, they all see their religion in the same light. This is true of Roman Catholics as well as of other beliefs. Nowhere else do Catholic priests show so little taste for petty individual observances, for extraordinary and peculiar ways to salvation, and nowhere else do they care so much for the spirit and so little for the letter of the law. Nowhere else is that doctrine of the church which forbids offering to saints the worship due to God alone more clearly taught or more generally obeyed. Yet the Roman Catholics of America are very submissive and very sincere.

Another observation can be made which applies to the clergy of every communion. American priests do not try to divert and concentrate all of people's attention on the future life; they freely allow them to give some of their hearts' care to the needs of the present, apparently considering the good things of this world as objects of some, albeit secondary, importance. While they themselves do no productive work, they take an interest in the progress of industry and praise its achievements; while they are ever pointing to the other world as the great object of the hopes and fears of the faithful, they do not forbid the honest pursuit of prosperity in this. Far from trying to show that these two worlds are distinct and opposed to each other, they seek to discover the points of connection and alliance.

All the clergy of America are aware of the intellectual domination of the majority, and they treat it with respect. They never struggle against it unless the struggle is necessary. They keep aloof from party squabbles, but they freely adopt the general views of their time and country and let themselves go unresistingly with the tide of feeling and opinion which carries everything around them along with it. They try to improve their contemporaries but do not quit fellowship with them. Public opinion is therefore never hostile to them but rather supports and protects them. Faith thus derives its authority partly from its inherent strength and partly from the borrowed support of public opinion.

Thus, by respecting all democratic instincts which are not against it and making use of many favorable ones, religion succeeds in struggling successfully with that spirit of individual independence which is its most dangerous enemy.

Chapter 6

CONCERNING THE PROGRESS OF ROMAN CATHOLICISM IN THE UNITED STATES

AMERICA IS THE MOST democratic country in the world, and at the same time, according to reliable reports, it is the country in which the Roman Catholic religion is making most progress. That seems at first sight surprising.

We must here make a clear distinction between two things: equality makes men want to form their own opinions, but it also gives them a taste for and a conception of a power in society which is unique, simple, and the same for all. People in democracies are therefore very prone to shake off all religious authority, but if they do consent to submit to any such authority, they want it to be at least single and uniform. Religious authorities which do not all stem from one center naturally shock their intelligence, and they find it almost as easy to assume that there is no religion as that there are several.

At the present time, more than in any previous age, we find Catholics turning into unbelievers and Protestants turning Catholic. Catholicism seen from the inside seems to be losing, but seen from the outside, to be gaining. There is a reason for this.

Our contemporaries are naturally little disposed to belief, but once they accept religion at all, there is a hidden instinct within them which unconsciously urges them toward Catholicism. Many of the doctrines and customs of the Roman Church astonish them, but they feel a secret admiration for its discipline, and its extraordinary unity attracts them.

If Catholicism could ultimately escape from the political animosities to which it has given rise, I am almost certain that that same spirit of the age which now seems so contrary to it would turn into a powerful ally and that it would suddenly make great conquests.

One of the most familiar weaknesses of the human mind is to want to reconcile conflicting principles and to buy peace at the cost of logic. So there are now and always will be some people who, having submitted to authority in some of their religious beliefs, still seek to exempt some of their other beliefs from it and let their minds float at random between obedience and freedom. But I am disposed to believe that their number will be fewer in democratic ages than at other times and that our grandchildren will tend more and more to be divided clearly between those who have completely abandoned Christianity and those who have returned to the Church of Rome.

Chapter 7

WHAT CAUSES DEMOCRATIC NATIONS TO INCLINE TOWARD PANTHEISM

I WILL SHOW HEREAFTER how the predominating taste of democratic peoples for very general ideas manifests itself in politics, but for the moment I am concerned with its principal effect on philosophy.

It cannot be denied that pantheism has made great progress in our time. The writings in part of Europe bear visible marks of it. The Germans are introducing it into philosophy and the French into literature. Most works of fiction published in France contain some opinions or some descriptions deriving from pantheistic teaching or show some tendency toward such doctrines on their authors' part. This cannot, I think, be explained as an accident, but is due to some enduring reason.

As conditions become more equal, each individual becomes more like his fellows, weaker, and smaller, and the habit grows of ceasing to think about the citizens and considering only the people. Individuals are forgotten, and the species alone counts.

At such times the human mind seeks to embrace a multitude of different objects at once, and it constantly strives to link up a variety of consequences with a single cause.

The concept of unity becomes an obsession. Man looks for it everywhere, and when he thinks he has found it, he gladly reposes in that belief. Not content with the discovery that there is nothing in the world but one creation and one Creator, he is still embarrassed by this primary division of things and seeks to expand and simplify his conception by including God and the universe in one great whole. If one finds a philosophical system which teaches that all things material and immaterial, visible and invisible, which the world contains are only to be considered as the several parts of an immense

Being who alone remains eternal in the midst of the continual flux and transformation of all that composes Him, one may be sure that such a system, although it destroys human individuality, or rather just because it destroys it, will have secret charms for men living under democracies. All their habits of mind prepare them to conceive it and put them on the way toward adopting it. It naturally attracts their imagination and holds it fixed. It fosters the pride and soothes the laziness of their minds.

Of all the different philosophical systems used to explain the universe, I believe that pantheism is one of those most fitted to seduce the mind in democratic ages. All those who still appreciate the true nature of man's greatness should combine in the struggle against it.

Chapter 8

HOW EQUALITY SUGGESTS TO THE AMERICANS THE IDEA OF THE INDEFINITE PERFECTIBILITY OF MAN

EQUALITY PUTS many ideas into the human mind which would not have come there without it, and it changes almost all the ideas that were there before. I take the concept of human perfectibility as an example, for that is one of the chief ideas which the mind can conceive and which by itself constitutes a great philosophical theory, a theory whose effects can be seen at every moment in the conduct of affairs.

Though man resembles the animals in many respects, one characteristic is peculiar to him alone: he improves himself, and they do not. Mankind could not fail to discover this difference from the beginning. So the idea of perfectibility is as old as the world; equality had no share in bringing it to birth, but it has given it a new character.

When citizens are classified by rank, profession, or birth, and when all are obliged to follow the career which chance has opened before them, everyone thinks that he can see the ultimate limits of human endeavor quite close in front of him, and no one attempts to fight against an inevitable fate. It is not that aristocratic peoples absolutely deny man's capacity to improve himself, but they do not think it unlimited. They think in terms of amelioration, not change; they imagine that the conditions of the societies of the future will be better but not really different; while admitting that humanity has made great advances and may be able to go still further, they assume in advance certain impassable limits to such progress.

So they do not imagine that they have arrived at the supreme good or absolute truth (what man or what people has ever been so mad as to imagine that?), but they like to persuade themselves that they have pretty nearly reached the degree of greatness and knowledge which our imperfect nature allows; and as nothing around them is on the move, they gladly assume that everything is in its right place. At such times legislators presume to lay down eternal laws, nations and kings are bent on building none but enduring monuments, and the present generation undertakes to save generations to come the trouble of regulating their own destinies.

But when castes disappear and classes are brought together, when men are jumbled together and habits, customs, and laws are changing, when new facts impinge and new truths are discovered, when old conceptions vanish and new ones take their place, then the human mind imagines the possibility of an ideal but always fugitive perfection.

Every man sees changes continually taking place. Some make things worse, and he understands only too well that no people and no individual, however enlightened he be, is ever infallible. Others improve his lot, and he concludes that man in general is endowed with an indefinite capacity for improvement. His setbacks teach him that no one has discovered absolute good; his successes inspire him to seek it without slackening. Thus, searching always, falling, picking himself up again, often disappointed, never discouraged, he is ever striving toward that immense grandeur glimpsed indistinctly at the end of the long track humanity must follow.

It is hard to realize how much follows naturally from this philosophic theory of the indefinite perfectibility of man and what a prodigious influence it has even on those who, concentrating solely on action to the exclusion of thought, act according to this theory of which they know nothing.

I once met an American sailor and asked him why his country's ships are made so that they will not last long. He answered offhand that the art of navigation was making such quick progress that even the best of boats would be almost useless if it lasted more than a few years.

I recognized in these casual words of an uneducated man about a particular subject the general and systematic conception by which a great people conducts all its affairs.

Aristocratic nations are by their nature too much inclined to restrict the scope of human perfectibility; democratic nations sometimes stretch it beyond reason.

Chapter 9

WHY THE EXAMPLE OF THE AMERICANS DOES NOT PROVE THAT A DEMOCRATIC PEOPLE CAN HAVE NO APTITUDE OR TASTE FOR SCIENCE, LITERATURE, OR THE ARTS

IT MUST BE ADMITTED THAT few of the civilized nations of our time have made less progress than the United States in the higher sciences or had so few great artists, distinguished poets, or celebrated writers.

Some Europeans, struck by this fact, have considered it the natural and inevitable result of equality, and they have supposed that if a democratic state of society and democratic institutions were ever to prevail over the whole earth, the human mind would gradually find its beacon lights grow dim and men would fall back into darkness.

I think that those who argue in this way are confusing several ideas which it is important to divide and examine separately. Unintentionally they confuse what is democratic with what is only American.

The religion professed by the first immigrants and bequeathed by them to their descendants was simple in its forms, austere and almost harsh in its principles, and hostile to eternal symbols and ceremonial pomp. It was therefore naturally unfavorable to the fine arts and only reluctantly made room for the pleasures of literature.

The Americans are a very old and very cultivated people who have fallen on a new and unbounded country in which they could spread out at will and which they could make fertile without difficulty. That is something without parallel elsewhere in the world. In America everyone finds opportunities unknown anywhere else for making or increasing his fortune. A breathless cupidity perpetually distracts the mind of man from the pleasures of the imagination and the labors of the intellect and urges it on to nothing but the pursuit of wealth. Industrial and commercial classes are to be found in all other countries as well as in the United States, but only there is the whole community simultaneously engaged in productive industry and in trade.

However, I am convinced that if the Americans had been alone in the world, with the freedom and the knowledge inherited from their forefathers and with the passionate desires which are their own, they would not have been slow to discover that progress cannot long be made in the application of the sciences without studying the theory of them. They would have seen that one skill leads to improvements in another, and however absorbed they might have been in the pursuit of the principal object of their desires, they would soon have realized that it is necessary to turn aside from it occasionally in order the better to attain it in the end.

The taste for the pleasures of the mind, moreover, is so natural to the heart of civilized man that even among those highly civilized nations least disposed to indulge in these pursuits there are always a certain number of people who take to them. This intellectual craving, once felt, would very soon have been satisfied.

But just at the time when the Americans were naturally inclined to require nothing of science but its limited application to the useful arts and ways of making life comfortable, the learned and literary men of Europe were undertaking the search for the basic principles of truth, and at the same time improving everything that can minister to the pleasures or satisfy the wants of men.

The people of the United States were particularly closely linked by their origin and common habits to one of the leading nations in the cultural life of the Old World. They found distinguished men of science, able artists, and great writers among this people and so could gather the treasures of the mind without working to produce them themselves.

I do not think the intervening ocean really separates America from Europe. The people of the United States are that portion of the English people whose fate it is to explore the forests of the New World, while the rest of the nation, enjoying more leisure and being less preoccupied with the material needs of life, can devote its energies to thought and enlarge the empire of the mind in all directions.

Thus the Americans are in an exceptional situation, and it is unlikely that any other democratic people will be similarly placed. Their strictly Puritan origin; their exclusively commercial habits; even the country they inhabit, which seems to divert their minds from the study of science, literature, and the arts; the accessibility of Europe, which allows them to neglect these things without relapsing into barbarism—a thousand special causes, of which I have indicated only the most important, have singularly concurred to fix the mind of the American on purely practical objects. His desires, needs, education, and circumstances all seem united to draw the American's mind earthward. Only religion from time to time makes him turn a transient and distracted glance toward heaven.

We should therefore give up looking at all democratic peoples through American spectacles and try at last to see them as they actually are.

It is possible to conceive a people without castes, hierarchy, or classes, in which the law, recognizing no privileges, divides inheritances equally, and which, at the same time, has neither culture nor freedom. That is not an empty hypothesis; a despot might find it in his interest to make his subjects equal and leave them ignorant in order the more easily to keep them slaves.

Not only would a democratic people of that type fail to show any aptitude or taste for science, literature, or the arts, but it would probably never come into contact with them at all.

The law of inheritance by itself would break up large fortunes for each succeeding generation, and no one would amass new ones. The poor, without either culture or freedom, would not so much as conceive the idea of raising themselves, and the rich would let themselves be dragged down into poverty without knowing how to defend themselves. They would soon both be reduced to complete and permanent equality. Then no one would have time or taste for the labors and pleasures of the mind. They would all stay benumbed in a like ignorance and equal slavery.

When I conceive a democratic society of this kind, I fancy myself in some low, close, and gloomy abode where the light which breaks in from without soon faints and fades away. A sudden heaviness overpowers me, and I grope through the surrounding darkness to find an opening that will restore me to the air and to the light of day. But none of that would apply to men already enlightened who retain their freedom after abolishing those peculiar and hereditary rights which perpetuated the tenure of property by certain individuals or certain classes.

Enlightened men living in a democracy readily discover that nothing can confine them, hold them, or force them to be content with their present lot.

They all therefore conceive the idea of bettering themselves. Being free, they all attempt it, but all do not succeed in the same way. The law, it is true, no longer grants privileges, but nature does so. Natural inequality being very great, fortunes become unequal as soon as every man exerts all his faculties to get rich.

The law of inheritance still stands in the way of the foundation of rich families, but it does not stop individuals' getting rich. It continually brings the citizens back to a common level from which they are as continually escaping. The inequality of their fortunes augments as knowledge is diffused and liberty increases.

A sect[1] which arose in our time and was celebrated for its talents and its extravagance proposed to concentrate all property in the hands of a central power whose function it should be to parcel it out to individuals according to their merits. That would have been a way of escaping from the complete and eternal equality which seems to threaten democratic societies.

But there is another simpler and less dangerous method. That is to give privileges to none, but equal enlightenment and independence to all, and to leave each man to make a place for himself. Natural inequality will soon make itself felt, and wealth will pass spontaneously into the hands of the most capable.

Free democratic societies will then always include a number of people who are rich or comfortably off. There will not be the same close ties between these rich people as there was between the members of the old aristocracy; their temperaments will be different and they will hardly ever be assured of such complete leisure. But they will be infinitely more numerous than any aristocracy could be. These persons will not be strictly tied to the drudgery of practical life, and they will be able, in different degrees of course, to devote themselves to the labors and pleasures of the mind. In those pleasures they will indulge, for though one part of the human mind inclines to the banal, the material, and the useful, there is another side which is naturally drawn toward the infinite, the spiritual, and the beautiful. Physical needs hold it to the earth, but when these are relaxed it rises of its own accord.

Not only will the number of those who can take an interest in things of the mind be greater, but the taste for intellectual enjoyment will descend step by step even to those who in aristocratic societies seem to have neither time nor ability to enjoy them.

When there is no more hereditary wealth, class privilege, or prerogatives of birth, and when every man derives his strength from himself

---

[1] [No doubt Tocqueville refers here to Saint-Simon and his school. Cf. Frank E. Manuel, *The New World of Henri Saint-Simon* (Cambridge, Mass.: Harvard, 1956); and S. Charléty, *Histoire du Saint-Simonisme (1825–1864)* (Paris, 1931).]

alone, it becomes clear that the chief source of disparity between the fortunes of men lies in the mind. Whatever tends to invigorate, expand, or adorn the mind rises instantly to a high value.

Even the crowd can now plainly see the utility of knowledge, and those who have no taste for its charms set store by its results and make some effort to acquire it.

In times of freedom and enlightened democracy there is nothing to separate men from one another or to keep them in their place. They rise or fall extraordinarily quickly. They are so close to each other that men of different classes are continually meeting. Every day they mix and exchange ideas, imitating and emulating one another. So the people get many ideas, conceptions, and desires which they never would have had if distinctions of rank had been fixed and society static. In such nations a servant never considers himself an entire stranger to the pleasures and work of his master, nor the poor man to those of the rich. The countryman is at pains to be like the townsman, and the provinces to take after the metropolis.

Therefore no one easily allows himself to be confined to the mere material cares of life, and the humblest artisan occasionally casts an eager, furtive glance at the higher regions of the mind. The way of reading and the whole approach to it is quite different from that of aristocratic peoples, but the circle of readers continually increases and finally includes all the citizens.

As soon as the crowd begins to take an interest in the labors of the mind it finds out that to excel in some of them is a powerful aid to the acquisition of fame, power, or wealth. Restless ambition born of equality turns to this as to all other directions. The number of those studying science, literature, and the arts becomes immense. There is vast activity in the realms of the mind; everyone tries to blaze a trail for himself and attract public attention. Much the same happens as in the political life of the United States; what is done is often imperfect, but the attempts are innumerable; and though each individual achievement is generally very small, the total effect is always very great.

So it is not true that men living in democratic times are naturally indifferent to science, literature, and the arts; only it must be acknowledged that they cultivate them in their own fashion and bring their own peculiar qualities and defects to the task.

Chapter 10

WHY THE AMERICANS ARE MORE CONCERNED WITH THE APPLICATIONS THAN WITH THE THEORY OF SCIENCE

IF DEMOCRATIC SOCIETY AND ITS institutions do not curb the vigor of the human mind, they certainly do direct it in one direction rather than another. The efforts, thus circumscribed, are still exceedingly great, and I may be pardoned if I pause for a moment to consider them.

Several observations made earlier about the philosophical method of the Americans are applicable here.

Equality stimulates each man to want to judge everything for himself and gives him a taste in everything for the tangible and real and a contempt for tradition and formalities. These general tendencies are especially to the fore in the context of this chapter.

Those in democracies who study sciences are always afraid of getting lost in utopias. They mistrust systems and like to stick very close to the facts and study them for themselves. As they have little deference for the mere name of any fellow being, they are never inclined to take a master's word on trust, but ever tend to look for the weak side of his argument. Scientific traditions have little hold over them, and they never spend much time studying the subtleties of any school and will not accept big words as sterling coin. They penetrate, as far as they can, into the main parts of the subject that interests them, and they like to expound them in popular language. Scientific pursuits thus follow a freer and safer course but a less lofty one.

The mind, it appears to me, can divide science into three parts.

The first comprises the most theoretical principles and the most abstract conceptions whose application is either unknown or very remote.

The second comprises general truths which, though still based in theory, lead directly and immediately to practical application.

Methods of application and means of execution make up the third.

Each of these different aspects of science can be studied apart, although reason and experience teach us that none of them can prosper for long if entirely separated from the other two.

In America the purely practical side of science is cultivated admirably, and trouble is taken about the theoretical side immediately necessary to application. On this side the Americans always display a clear, free, original, and creative turn of mind. But hardly anyone in the United States devotes himself to the essentially theoretical and abstract side of human knowledge. In this the Americans carry to excess a trend which can, I think, be noticed, though in a less degree, among all democratic nations.

The higher sciences or the higher parts of all sciences require meditation above everything else. But nothing is less conducive to meditation than the setup of democratic society. There, in contrast to aristocratic societies, one finds no numerous class that remains at leisure because all is well with it, nor that other class which does not stir because it despairs of any improvement. Everyone is on the move, some in quest of power, others of gain. In the midst of this universal tumult, this incessant conflict of jarring interests, this endless chase for wealth, where is one to find the calm for the profound researches of the intellect? How can the mind dwell on any single subject when all around is on the move and when one is himself swept and buffeted along by the whirling current which carries all before it?

One must make a clear distinction between the sort of permanent agitation characteristic of a peaceful and well-established democracy, and the tumultuous revolutionary movements that almost always go with the birth and development of a democracy.

When a violent revolution occurs among a highly civilized people, it cannot fail to give a sudden impulse to their feelings and thoughts.

This is especially true of democratic revolutions, which stir up at the same time all the classes of which a people is composed and also give rise to vast ambitions in the heart of every citizen.

The French made wonderful advances in the exact sciences at the very moment when they were completing the destruction of the remains of their old feudal society, yet this sudden creative activity should be attributed not to democracy but to the unexampled revolution which attended its growth. What happened then was a special case, and it would be unwise to take it as indicating a general law.

Great revolutions are not more common among democratic peoples than among others; I even tend to think that they are less common. But within those nations there is always a slight but troublesome restlessness, a sort of continual jostling of men against each other, which disturbs and distracts the mind without stimulating or elevating it.

Not only is meditation difficult for men in democracies, but they naturally attach little importance to it. Democratic social conditions and institutions involve most people in continual activity, but habits of thought useful in action are not always helpful to thought. The man of action often has to make do with approximations, for he would never accomplish his purpose if he wanted to make every detail perfect. He must always be acting on the basis of ideas which he has not had time to plumb deeply, for the seasonableness of an idea is much more often useful to him than its strict accuracy. Moreover, by and large it is less risky for him to rely on some false principles than to waste his time establishing the truth of them all. It is not long and learned demonstrations which keep the world going. A quick glance at a particular fact, the daily study of the changing passions of the crowd, the chance of the moment, and skill to grasp it—such things decide all its affairs.

In democratic centuries when almost everyone is engaged in active life, the darting speed of a quick, superficial mind is at a premium, while slow, deep thought is excessively undervalued.

This public attitude influences the judgment of those who do study the sciences; they are persuaded that they can succeed without meditation or are diverted from those pursuits which require it.

There are many ways of studying the sciences. One finds a crowd of people with a selfish, commercial, and banal taste for the discoveries of the mind, but that is not to be confused with the disinterested passion which burns in the heart of a few. There is lust to make use of knowledge and a pure desire to know. I have no doubt but that, at long intervals, an inextinguishable, burning love of truth is born in a few souls and that for them this is the food on which their spirit feeds continually without satiety. It is this ardent, proud, disinterested love of truth which leads right to the abstract sources of truth with which their thought becomes pregnant.

If Pascal had had nothing in view beyond some great gain, or even if he had been stimulated by the love of fame alone, I cannot conceive that he would have been able, as able he was, to rally all the powers of his mind to discover the most hidden secrets of the Creator. When I see him, if one may put it so, tearing his soul free from the cares of this life so as to stake the whole of it on this quest, and prematurely breaking the ties which bound him to the flesh, so that he died of old age before he was forty, I stand amazed, and understand that no ordinary cause was at work in such an extraordinary effort.

The future will show whether such rare, creative passions come to birth and grow as easily in democracies as in aristocratic communities. For myself, I confess that I can hardly believe it.

In aristocratic societies the class which gives the tone to opinion and takes the lead in the conduct of affairs, being placed by heredity permanently above the crowd, naturally conceives a high idea of itself and of man. It comes natural to it to imagine glorious delights, and it sets ambitious targets for its desires. Aristocracies are often guilty of very tyrannical and inhuman acts, but they rarely entertain groveling thoughts, and they show a kind of haughty contempt for petty pleasures even when they indulge in them. This greatly raises the general tone. In aristocratic ages vast ideas are generally entertained of the dignity, the power, and the greatness of man. Such opinions influence those who cultivate the sciences, as they do all others. They facilitate the natural impulse of the mind toward the highest regions of thought, and they naturally prepare it to conceive a sublime, almost a divine love of truth.

At such times men of learning are consequently impelled toward theory, and it even happens that they frequently conceive an inconsiderate contempt for practice. "Archimedes," Plutarch tells us, "was of such a lofty spirit that he never condescended to write any treatise on the way to make all these engines of war. As he held this science of inventing and putting together machines, and all arts, generally speaking, which tended to any useful end in practice, to be vile, low, and mercenary, he spent his talents and his studious hours in writing only of those things whose beauty and subtlety had in them no admixture of necessity."[1] That is the aristocratic view of science.

It cannot be the same in democracies.

Most of the people in these nations are extremely eager in the pursuit of immediate material pleasures and are always discontented with the position they occupy and always free to leave it. They think about nothing but ways of changing their lot and bettering it. For people in this frame of mind every new way of getting wealth more quickly, every machine which lessens work, every means of diminishing the costs of production, every invention which makes pleasures easier or greater, seems the most magnificent accomplishment of the human mind. It is chiefly from this line of approach that democratic peoples come to study sciences, to understand them, and to value them. In aristocratic ages the chief function of science is to give pleasure to the mind, but in democratic ages to the body.

[1] [Cf. *Life of Marcellus*, Plutarch's *Lives*, Bohn's Edition, Vol. II, p. 47, London 1887. Tocqueville seems to quote rather freely.]

It may be assumed that the more democratic, enlightened, and free a people is, the greater will be the number of these selfish admirers of scientific genius, and the more profit will be made out of discoveries immediately applicable to industry, bringing renown and even power to their inventors. For in democracies the working class takes part in public affairs, and those who serve its interests can win honors as well as money.

It is easy to see how, in a society organized on these lines, men's minds are unconsciously led to neglect theory and devote an unparalleled amount of energy to the applications of science, or at least to that aspect of theory which is useful in practice.

The instinctive bent of the mind toward the higher spheres of the intelligence exercises its power in vain, for interest draws it down to the middle zone. That is where its strength and its restless activity are at work, and there it performs wonders. These same Americans who have never discovered a general law of mechanics have changed the face of the world by introducing a new machine for navigation.

I certainly do not mean to imply that the democratic nations of our time will witness the extinction of the transcendent lights of the mind, or even that they will not light new flames. At the stage the world has now reached, with so many cultivated nations in a fever of excited industry, the links connecting the various branches of science cannot fail to be noticed. The taste itself for practice, if it is enlightened, should lead men not to neglect theory. While so many things are being tried out, with new experiments every day, it is almost impossible that very general laws should not frequently be brought to light. Great discoveries are bound to be frequent, though great discoverers may be few.

Besides that, I believe that science is a high vocation. Democracy may not lead men to study science for its own sake, but it does immensely increase the number of those who do study it. Nor is it credible that among so great a multitude a speculative genius should not from time to time arise inspired by the love of truth alone. Such a one will surely penetrate the deepest mysteries of nature, whatever be the spirit of his time and place. His spirit's flight needs no help; it is enough if it is not impeded. All that I mean to say is this: permanent inequality of lot leads men to confine themselves to the proud and sterile search for abstract truths, while the institutions of democratic society tend to make them look only for the immediate practical applications of science.

This tendency is both natural and inevitable. It is interesting to note, and perhaps necessary to point out.

If those who are called on to direct the affairs of nations in our time can clearly and in good time understand these new tendencies which will soon be irresistible, they will see that, granted enlightenment and liberty, people living in a democratic age are quite certain to bring the industrial side of science to perfection anyhow and that henceforth the whole energy of organized society should be directed to the support of higher studies and the fostering of a passion for pure science.

Nowadays the need is to keep men interested in theory. They will look after the practical side of things for themselves. So, instead of perpetually concentrating attention on the minute examination of secondary effects, it is good to distract it therefrom sometimes and lift it to the contemplation of first causes.

Because Roman civilization perished through barbarian invasions, we are perhaps too much inclined to think that that is the only way a civilization can die.

If the lights that guide us ever go out, they will fade little by little, as if of their own accord. Confining ourselves to practice, we may lose sight of basic principles, and when these have been entirely forgotten, we may apply the methods derived from them badly; we might be left without the capacity to invent new methods, and only able to make a clumsy and an unintelligent use of wise procedures no longer understood.

Three hundred years ago, when the first Europeans came to China, they found that almost all the arts had reached a certain degree of improvement, and they were surprised that, having come so far, they had not gone further. Later on they found traces of profound knowledge that had been forgotten. The nation was a hive of industry; the greater part of its scientific methods were still in use, but science itself was dead. That made them understand the strange immobility of mind found among this people. The Chinese, following in their fathers' steps, had forgotten the reasons which guided them. They still used the formula without asking why. They kept the tool but had no skill to adapt or replace it. So the Chinese were unable to change anything. They had to drop the idea of improvement. They had to copy their ancestors the whole time in everything for fear of straying into impenetrable darkness if they deviated for a moment from their tracks. Human knowledge had almost dried up at the fount, and though the stream still flowed, it could neither increase nor change its course.

China nonetheless had existed in peace for centuries; her conquerors had adopted her mores; order prevailed. Material prosperity of a sort was visible everywhere. Revolutions were very rare and war, one might almost say, unknown.

We therefore should not console ourselves by thinking that the barbarians are still a long way off. Some peoples may let the torch be snatched from their hands, but others stamp it out themselves.

Chapter 11

IN WHAT SPIRIT THE AMERICANS CULTIVATE THE ARTS

IT WOULD BE A WASTE OF MY readers' time and of my own to explain how the general moderate standard of wealth, the absence of superfluity, and the universal desire for comfort, with the constant efforts made by all to procure it, encourage a taste for the useful more than the love of beauty. Naturally, therefore, democratic peoples with all these characteristics cultivate those arts which help to make life comfortable rather than those which adorn it. They habitually put use before beauty, and they want beauty itself to be useful.

But I want to carry the argument further, and having made this first point, to sketch several other characteristics.

It normally happens in ages of privilege that the practice of almost all the arts becomes a privilege, and every profession is a world apart into which all and sundry cannot enter. Even when industry is free the immobility natural to aristocratic peoples tends to form all those who practice the same craft into a distinct class, always composed of the same families who know one another and among whom a corporate public opinion and sense of corporate pride soon develop. Hence each craftsman belonging to this industrial class has not only his fortune to make but also his professional standing to preserve. Corporate interests count for more with him than either his own self-interest or even the purchaser's needs. So in aristocratic ages the emphasis is on doing things as well as possible, not as quickly or as cheaply as one can.

In contrast, when every profession is open to all, with a crowd of folk forever taking it up and dropping it again, when the craftsmen don't know or care about one another and indeed hardly ever meet, being so many, the social link between them is broken, and each, left to himself, only tries to make as much money as easily as possible. The customer's wishes are his only restraint, but he too is involved at the same time in an equally radical change of attitude.

Where wealth and power are permanently in the hands of a few, it is these people, always the same, who enjoy most of the good things of this world; necessity, convention, and their own modest desires keep the rest from such enjoyment.

This aristocracy, keeping its high place without contraction or enlargement, always has the same requirements felt in the same way. The heirs to this hereditary superiority naturally like things very well made and lasting.

This affects the whole way a people looks at the arts.

Among such nations it often happens that even a peasant will sooner do without the things he wants than get imperfect ones.

Craftsmen in aristocratic societies work for a strictly limited number of customers who are very hard to please. Perfect workmanship gives the best hope of profit.

The situation is very different when privileges have been abolished and classes intermingled and when men are continually rising and falling in the social scale.

There are always plenty of citizens in any democracy whose patrimonies are being divided up and diminished. These still have the tastes acquired in their time of prosperity without the means to indulge them, and they are anxiously on the lookout for some roundabout way of doing so.

There are, too, in any democracy men whose fortunes are on the increase but whose desires increase much more quickly than their wealth, so that their eyes devour the good things wealth will one day provide long before they can afford them. They are always on the lookout for shortcuts to these anticipated delights. These two elements always provide democracies with a crowd of citizens whose desires outrun their means and who will gladly agree to put up with an imperfect substitute rather than do without the object of their desire altogether.

The craftsman easily understands this feeling, for he shares it. In aristocracies he charged very high prices to a few. He sees that he can now get rich quicker by selling cheaply to all.

Now, there are only two ways of making a product cheaper.

The first is to find better, quicker, more skillful ways of making it. The second is to make a great number of objects which are more or less the same but not so good. In a democracy every workman applies his wits to both these points.

He seeks ways of working, not just better, but quicker and more cheaply, and if he cannot manage that, he economizes on the intrinsic quality of the thing he is making, without rendering it wholly unfit for its intended use. When only the rich wore watches, they were almost all excellent. Now few are made that are more than mediocre, but we all have one. In this way democracy, apart from diverting attention to the useful arts, induces workmen to make shoddy things very quickly and consumers to put up with them.

Admittedly artisans in a democracy can, if need be, produce wonders. That happens sometimes when there are clients ready to pay for their time and trouble. In this rivalry of every kind of industry accompanied by intense competition and innumerable experiments, some excellent workmen learn their craft down to its last refinements. But these seldom have the chance to show what they can do. They stick to standards of prudent and conscious mediocrity, and though they could go beyond the set objective, confine their attention to their intended aim. Whereas in aristocratic communities workmen always do the best of which they are capable, and when they stop short, it is because they have reached the limit of their skill.

To arrive in a country and find some things admirably made tells one nothing about the social conditions or political institutions of that country. But if one finds quantities of things generally shoddy and very cheap, one can be sure that in that country privilege is on the wane and classes are beginning to mix and will soon lose their identity.

Craftsmen in democratic ages do not seek only to bring the useful things they make within the reach of every citizen, but also try to give each object a look of brilliance unconnected with its true worth.

In the confusion of classes each man wants to appear as something he is not and is prepared to take much trouble to produce this effect. Such feelings are not born of democracy, for they are all too natural to the heart of man, but it is democracy which applies them to material products. The hypocrisy of virtue is of every age, but the hypocrisy of luxury is peculiar to democratic centuries.

To satisfy these new cravings of human vanity the arts have recourse to every kind of imposture, and these devices sometimes go so far that they defeat their own purpose. Diamonds are already so well imitated that it is easy to be taken in. As soon as sham diamonds can be made so well that they cannot be distinguished from real stones; it is probable that both will be disregarded and become mere pebbles again.

That leads me on to speak about the fine arts properly so called.

I do not think that it is a necessary result of the social conditions and institutions of democracy to diminish the number of those engaged in the fine arts, but they do exert a powerful influence on the

manner in which these arts are cultivated. Since most people who
had a taste for them have become poor, and many of those who
are not yet rich begin, by social imitation, to develop a taste for them,
amateurs in general become more numerous, but very rich and dis-
criminating amateurs become more rare. So much the same takes
place in the case of the fine arts as we have seen happening in the
case of the useful arts. Quantity increases; quality goes down.

Unable any longer to conceive greatness, they try for elegance and
prettiness. Appearance counts for more than reality.

Aristocracies produce a few great pictures, democracies a multitude
of little ones. The one makes statues of bronze, the other of plaster.

When I first arrived in New York by that part of the Atlantic
known as the East River, I was surprised to notice along the shore
at some distance out from the city a number of little white marble
palaces, some of them in classical architectural style. The next day,
when I looked more closely at one of those that had struck me most,
I found that it was built of whitewashed brick and that the columns
were of painted wood. All the buildings I had admired the day before
were the same.

The social conditions and institutions of democracy also impart
certain peculiar tendencies to all the imitative arts, and these are
easily pointed out. The soul is often left out of the picture which
portrays the body only; movement and sensation take the place of
feeling and thought; finally realism takes the place of the ideal.

I doubt if Raphael made such an elaborate study of the detailed
mechanism of the human body as do the draftsmen of our own day.
He did not think strict accuracy in this matter as important as they
do, for he claimed to surpass nature. He sought to make of man
something better than man and to add beauty to beauty.

In contrast, David and his pupils were as good anatomists as they
were painters. They copied the models before their eyes wonderfully
well, but imagination seldom added anything more. They followed
nature exactly, whereas Raphael tried to do better than nature.
They have given us an exact representation of man, but his works
sometimes show us glimpses of divinity.

The same tendencies influence choice of subject as well as its
treatment.

Renaissance painters generally looked for mighty subjects over
their heads and far away in time so that imagination could have
ample play. Our painters often employ their talents in the exact
delineation of everyday life whose details are always before their
eyes; they copy trivial objects from every angle, though nature
provides only too many originals.

Chapter 12

WHY THE AMERICANS ERECT SOME PETTY MONUMENTS AND OTHERS THAT ARE VERY GRAND

I HAVE JUST OBSERVED that in democratic ages artistic monuments tend to be more numerous and less important. I now hasten to point out the exception to this rule.

Individuals in democracies are very weak, but the state, which represents them all and holds them all in the palm of its hand, is very strong. Nowhere else do the citizens seem smaller than in a democratic nation, and nowhere else does the nation itself seem greater, so that it is easily conceived as a vast picture. Imagination shrinks at the thought of themselves as individuals and expands beyond all limits at the thought of the state. Hence people living cramped lives in tiny houses often conceive their public monuments on a gigantic scale.

When the Americans planned to build a capital, they marked out a vast extent of land for a huge city; that city, even today, has hardly more inhabitants than Pontoise, but according to them it should one day hold a population of a million. They have already rooted up trees for ten miles around, lest they should get in the way of the future citizens of this imagined capital. They have erected a magnificent palace for Congress in the center of the city and given it the pompous name of the Capitol.

The several states of the Union are daily planning and carrying out prodigious enterprises which would astonish the engineers of the great nations of Europe.

Thus democracy not only encourages the making of a lot of trivial things but also inspires the erection of a few very large monuments. However, there is nothing at all between these two extremes. A few scattered remains of enormous buildings can therefore tell us nothing about the social conditions and institutions of the people who put them up.

I may add, though this goes beyond my subject, that they tell us nothing about their greatness, civilization, and real prosperity.

At any time when any power is able to concentrate the efforts of a whole people on a single undertaking, it will be able, with little skill but lots of time, to make something huge from their accumulated efforts. But that does not justify the conclusion that that people are very happy, very enlightened, or even very strong. The Spaniards found Mexico City full of magnificent temples and vast palaces, but that did not prevent Cortes from conquering the Mexican Empire with six hundred infantry and sixteen horses.

If the Romans had understood the laws of hydraulic engineering a little better they would not have built all those aqueducts that surround the ruins of their cities and could have used their power and wealth to better purpose. If they had invented the steam engine, perhaps they would not have made those long artificial rocks, called Roman roads, extending to the uttermost limits of their empire.

Such things bear massive testimony to their ignorance as well as to their greatness.

A people who left nothing but a few lead pipes in the ground and some iron rails on top of it might have mastered nature better than the Romans.

Chapter 13

LITERARY CHARACTERISTICS OF DEMOCRATIC CENTURIES

WHEN ONE VISITS A BOOKSHOP in the United States and notes the American books crowding the shelves, one is struck by the great number of them, but the number of authors one has heard of seems, on the contrary, very small.

First of all there are a multitude of elementary treatises intended to teach the rudiments of human knowledge. Most of these books were written in Europe; the Americans reprint them, adapting them for their use. Next come an almost innumerable quantity of religious books, Bibles, sermons, pious stories, controversial tracts, and reports of charitable societies. Then there comes the long catalog of political pamphlets, for in America the parties do not publish books to refute each other, but pamphlets which circulate at an incredible rate, last a day, and die.

Among this host of dim productions appear the more remarkable works of only a small number of authors who are known in Europe or deserve to be known there.

Although America now pays perhaps less attention to literature than any other civilized country, there is nevertheless a large number of people who take an interest in things of the mind, and if they do not give their lives to such studies, at least entertain their leisure with them. But it is England which supplies them with most of the books they need. Almost all important English books are republished in the United States. The literary inspiration of Great Britain darts its beams into the depths of the forests of the New World. There is hardly a pioneer's hut which does not contain a few odd volumes of Shakespeare. I remember reading the feudal drama of *Henry V* for the first time in a log cabin.

Not only do the Americans constantly draw upon the treasures of English literature, but one can truly say that English literature flourishes on their own soil. Most of the small band of American men of letters are English in origin and, notably, in ways of thought. So they transplant into democracy thoughts and ways of writing current in the aristocratic nation which they have taken as their model. They paint with the borrowed colors of foreign manners, and as they hardly ever portray the country of their birth as it actually is, they are seldom popular there.

American citizens seem so convinced that books are not published for their benefit that before deciding on the merits of one of their own writers they usually wait till the English have had a chance to sample his work, just as a painter may be held entitled to judge the merit of a copy of his own work.

So the Americans have not yet, properly speaking, got any literature. Only the journalists strike me as truly American. They certainly are not great writers, but they speak their country's language and they make themselves heard. I should class the others as foreigners. They stand to the Americans much as the imitators of the Greeks and Romans stood to ourselves at the time of the Renaissance—objects of curiosity, but not of general sympathy. They are entertaining, but they do not affect mores.

I have already pointed out that all this is not due to democracy alone and that one must look to several peculiar and independent circumstances to find the reason for it.

If the Americans, with the same social condition and laws, had had a different origin and been transplanted into a different country, I do not doubt that they would have had a literature. As things are, I am sure that they will have one in the end. But it will have a character peculiarly its own, different from the American literature of today. No one can guess that character beforehand.

Take the case of an aristocratic people interested in literature; in that case the labors of the mind as well as the business of government are controlled by a ruling class. Literature as well as politics is almost entirely confined to that class or those nearest it. That gives the key to all the rest.

When a small, unchanging group of men are concerned at the same time with the same subject, they easily get together and agree on certain guiding principles to direct their efforts. If it is literature with which they are concerned, strict canons will soon prescribe rules that may not be broken.

If these men occupy a hereditary position in their country they will naturally be inclined not only to invent rules for themselves but also to follow those laid down by their ancestors. Their code will be both strict and traditional.

As neither they nor their fathers have ever needed to be engrossed in material drudgery, several generations will have cultivated things of the mind. They will have learned to understand literature as an art, to love it in the end for its own sake, and to take a scholarly pleasure in seeing that the rules are obeyed.

Nor is this all. Such men, beginning and ending their lives in comfortable circumstances, naturally conceive a taste for choice pleasures full of refinement and delicacy.

Moreover, the long and peaceful enjoyment of so much wealth will have induced a certain softness of thought and feeling, and even in their enjoyments they will avoid anything too unexpected or too lively. They would rather be amused than deeply moved; they want to be interested but not carried away.

Now let us fancy a great literary output produced by or for such people. Everything will be regular and carefully prepared. The slightest work will be polished in every detail; everything will bear witness to skill and care; each genre of writing will have its special rules which must not be broken and which distinguish it from every other genre.

Style will seem almost as important as thought, form as substance; style will be polished, measured, and sustained. There will be more dignity than vivacity. Writers will take more trouble to perfect what they write than to write much.

It will sometimes happen that men of letters, seeing none but themselves and only writing for themselves, will entirely lose sight of the rest of the world, and that will make their work farfetched and sham. They will impose petty literary rules for their exclusive use, and that will gradually make them lose first common sense and then contact with nature.

Wanting to talk a language different from the vulgar, they will end up with a brand of aristocratic jargon which is hardly less far from pure speech than is the dialect of the people.

Such are the natural perils for literature among aristocracies.

Even aristocracy that keeps entirely aloof from the people becomes impotent. That is as true in literature as in politics.[1]

Let us now consider the other side of the picture.

Imagine a democracy prepared by old tradition and present culture to enjoy the pleasures of the mind. Classes there are intermingled and confused; knowledge as well as power is infinitely divided up and, if I may put it so, scattered all around.

Here, then, is a motley multitude with intellectual wants to be supplied. These new votaries of the pleasure of the mind have not all had the same education; they are not guided by the same lights, do not resemble their own fathers; and they themselves are changing every moment with changing place of residence, feelings, and fortune. So there are no traditions, or common habits, to forge links between their minds, and they have neither the power nor the wish nor the time to come to a common understanding.

But it is from this heterogeneous, stirring crowd that authors spring, and from it they must win profit and renown.

In these circumstances one will not expect to find many of those strict conventions accepted by writers and readers in aristocracies. Even if a few conventions are accepted by one generation, it does not follow that the next will observe them too, for in a democracy each generation is a new people. So it is difficult to establish strict literary rules among them, and out of the question that they should be lasting.

In democracies it is by no means the case that all who cultivate literature have received a literary education, and most of those who have some acquaintance with good writing go into politics or adopt some profession which leaves only short, stolen hours for the pleasures of the mind. They therefore do not make such delights the principal joy of their existence, but think of them rather as a passing relaxation needed from the serious business of life. Such men will never have a deep enough understanding of literature to appreciate its refine-

[1] All this is especially true of aristocratic countries long peacefully ruled by a king.

When liberty prevails in an aristocracy the higher ranks are constantly obliged to make use of the lower classes, and by using them they draw close to them. This frequently infects them with something of the democratic spirit. Moreover, a privileged class which actually rules shows energy and enterprise and a taste for stir and excitement which are bound to influence all its literature.

ments. Fine nuances will pass them by. With but short time to spend on books, they want it all to be profitable. They like books which are easily got and quickly read, requiring no learned researches to understand them. They like facile forms of beauty, self-explanatory and immediately enjoyable; above all, they like things unexpected and new. Accustomed to the monotonous struggle of practical life, what they want is vivid, lively emotions, sudden revelations, brilliant truths, or errors able to rouse them up and plunge them, almost by violence, into the middle of the subject.

Need I say any more? Who does not guess what is coming before I say it?

By and large the literature of a democracy will never exhibit the order, regularity, skill, and art characteristic of aristocratic literature; formal qualities will be neglected or actually despised. The style will often be strange, incorrect, overburdened, and loose, and almost always strong and bold. Writers will be more anxious to work quickly than to perfect details. Short works will be commoner than long books, wit than erudition, imagination than depth. There will be a rude and untutored vigor of thought with great variety and singular fecundity. Authors will strive to astonish more than to please, and to stir passions rather than to charm taste.

No doubt there will occasionally be writers who want to follow a different path, and if their merit is great, in spite of their faults and also in spite of their good qualities, they will find readers. But these exceptions will be rare, and those writers whose works in general stand apart from the common usage will relapse into it in some details.

I have described two extreme examples. But nations do not jump suddenly from the first to the second. The transition is gradual, with infinite nuances. When a literate people is moving from one to the other, there is almost always a stage when the literary genius of democratic nations clashes with that of aristocracies, and both seek to hold their sway jointly over the human mind.

Such periods do not last long, but they are very brilliant; they are fertile without exuberance and animated without confusion. Eighteenth-century French literature is an example.

I should say more than I mean if I asserted that a nation's literature is always subordinated to its social state and political constitution. I know that, apart from these, there are other causes that give literature certain characteristics, but those do seem the most important to me.

There are always numerous connections between the social and political condition of a people and the inspiration of its writers. He who knows the one is never completely ignorant of the other.

Chapter 14

THE INDUSTRY OF LITERATURE

DEMOCRACY NOT ONLY GIVES the industrial classes a taste for letters but also brings an industrial spirit into literature.

In aristocracies readers are few and fastidious; in democracies they are immensely more numerous and easier to please. In consequence, among aristocratic nations no one can hope to succeed unless he takes a great deal of trouble, and even then, though he may win great renown, he will never gain much money, whereas in democracies a writer may hope to gain moderate renown and great wealth cheaply. For this purpose he does not need to be admired; it is enough if people have a taste for his work.

The ever growing crowd of readers always wanting something new ensures the sale of books that nobody esteems highly.

A democratic public often treats its authors much as kings usually behave toward their courtiers: it enriches and despises them. What more do the venal souls who are born in courts or deserve to live there merit?

Democratic literature is always crawling with writers who look upon letters simply as a trade, and for each of the few great writers you can count thousands of idea-mongers.

Chapter 15

WHY THE STUDY OF GREEK AND LATIN LITERATURE IS PECULIARLY USEFUL IN DEMOCRATIC SOCIETIES

WHAT MEN CALLED "THE PEOPLE" in the most democratic republics of antiquity was very unlike what we designate by that term. In Athens all the citizens played a part in public affairs, but there were only twenty thousand citizens in a population of over three hundred and fifty thousand. All the rest were slaves who performed most of the functions of our lower or even middle classes.

Athens, then, with her universal suffrage, was no more than an aristocratic republic in which all the nobles had an equal right to the government.

The struggle between patricians and plebeians at Rome must be seen in the same light as an internal quarrel between the elder and younger branches of the same family. They all belonged to the aristocracy and had an aristocratic spirit.

One must also remember that throughout antiquity books were scarce and expensive, very laborious to copy and circulate. Literary tastes and habits were thus concentrated in a small group forming a small literary aristocracy of the elite of a larger political aristocracy. Accordingly, there is nothing to show that literature was ever treated as an industry among the Greeks and Romans.

These peoples, who were not only aristocracies but also very well-organized and very free nations, were bound to show in their literature the qualities and defects characteristic of aristocratic literature.

A glance at writings left to us by the ancients is enough to show that those writers sometimes lacked variety and fertility in the choice of subjects and boldness, movement, and a power of generalization in their thought, but they were always admirably careful and skillful in detail. Nothing is written hurriedly or casually, but is always intended for connoisseurs and is always seeking an ideal beauty. No other literature puts in bolder relief just those qualities democratic writers tend to lack, and therefore no other literature is better to be studied at such times. This study is the best antidote against the inherent defects of the times, whereas the good qualities natural to the age will blossom untended.

This point should be clearly understood.

It may be good for the literature of one people to study that of another even though it has no bearing on their social and political needs.

An obstinate determination to teach nothing but the classics in a society always struggling to acquire or keep wealth would produce very well-educated but very dangerous citizens. For the state of politics and society would always make them want things which their education had not taught them how to earn, and they would perturb the state, in the name of the Greeks and Romans, instead of enriching it by their industry.

It is clear that in democracies individual interests and those of the state demand that education for most people should be scientific, commercial, and industrial rather than literary.

Greek and Latin should not be taught in all the schools. But it is important that those who are destined by nature or fate to adopt a literary career or to cultivate such tastes should be able to find schools where the classics are well taught and true scholars formed. A few excellent universities are a better means to this end than a multitude of bad schools in which the classics are an ill-taught extra, standing in the way of sound instruction in necessary studies.

All who have ambitions to literary excellence in democratic nations should ever refresh themselves at classical springs; that is the most wholesome medicine for the mind.

Not that I hold the classics beyond criticism, but I think that they have special merits well calculated to counterbalance our peculiar defects. They provide a prop just where we are most likely to fall.

Chapter 16

HOW AMERICAN DEMOCRACY HAS MODIFIED THE ENGLISH LANGUAGE

THE READER WHO HAS FOLLOWED my argument about literature in general will easily understand the sort of influence brought to bear on language itself, language which is the chief tool of thought, by democratic society and its institutions.

American authors may fairly be said to live more in England than in America, for they are continually studying English writers and invariably take them as models. But the general population is not like that, being much more immediately affected by the conditions peculiar to the United States. So we must take note of the spoken, not the written, language if we want to understand how the speech of an aristocracy is modified when it becomes the language of a democracy.

Educated Englishmen, better able to appreciate these fine nuances than I, have often told me that the language of well-educated Americans is decidedly different from that spoken by the same class in Great Britain.

Their complaint is not only that the Americans have introduced a lot of new words (the difference between the two countries and the distance between them would have been enough to account for that), but that these new words are generally taken from the jargon of parties, the mechanical arts, or trade. They also say that the Americans have given new meanings to old English words. Finally, they maintain that the Americans often mix their styles in an odd way, sometimes putting words together which, in the mother tongue, are carefully kept apart.

Often hearing these same comments from people who seemed to know what they were talking about set me thinking about the subject, and starting from a theoretical approach, I came to the same conclusions that they had reached empirically.

The language of an aristocracy ought to be as at rest as are all its other institutions. But few new words are needed, as few new things are made; and even when something new is made, people are at pains to describe it in familiar words whose meaning is fixed by tradition.

If it happens that there is an intellectual awakening, spontaneously or due to light from outside, the new expressions invented always have a learned, intellectual, and philosophic character, sure signs that they are not the children of democracy. When the fall of Constantinople drove learned men of letters to the West, the French language was invaded by a multitude of new words, all of Greek or Latin origin. Thus, then, in France these learned neologisms were peculiar to the educated classes, and common folk either remained perpetually unaware of them or discovered them only long afterward.

The same story repeated itself among all the European nations. Milton alone introduced over six hundred words into English, nearly all of them derived from Greek, Latin, or Hebrew.

But the continual restlessness of a democracy leads to endless change of language as of all else. In the general stir of intellectual competition a great many new ideas take shape; old ideas get lost or take new forms or are perhaps subdivided with an infinite variety of nuances.

So some words must go out of currency, while others come in.

Moreover, democracies like movement for its own sake. That applies to language as well as politics. Even when there is no need to change words, they do so because they want to.

The genius of democracies is seen not only in the great number of new words introduced but even more in the new ideas they express.

Among such peoples the majority lays down the law about language as about all else. Its prevailing spirit is manifest there as elsewhere. Now, the majority is more interested in business than study, in trade and politics than in philosophic speculation or fine writing. Most of the words coined or adopted for its use will bear the marks of these habits; they will chiefly serve to express the needs of industry, the passions of politics, or the details of public administration. Language will spread out endlessly in that direction, but metaphysics and theology will slowly lose ground.

It is easy to tell where democratic nations will find their new words and how they will shape them.

Citizens living in democratic countries are hardly aware of the languages spoken in Rome and Athens, and they will not be at pains to go back to the classics for the word they need. If they do sometimes make use of learned etymologies, it is generally vanity that sends them rooting among dead languages, and not learning that naturally suggests them to the mind. It can even happen that the most ignorant people among them use such derivations most. The very democratic wish to rise above their station often leads them to want to dignify a very mean occupation by a Greek or Latin word. The lower the calling and the more remote from learning, the more pompous and erudite the name found for it. Thus rope-dancers are turned into acrobats and funambulists.

Democratic peoples willingly borrow from living languages rather than from dead ones, for there is continual communication between them, and peoples of different nations gladly copy one another as they daily grow more like one another.

But democracies chiefly use their own languages when making their innovations. Occasionally they pick up forgotten words and put them back into use, or they will borrow a technical term from some particular group and put it into general currency with a figurative meaning. Many phrases originally limited to the trade slang of a craft or group have thus become part of the language.

However, the most common innovation is to give an unwonted meaning to an expression already in use. That method is simple, quick, and easy. No learning is needed to make use of it, and ignorance itself can make it easier. But it involves great dangers for the language. In thus giving double meanings to one word, democratic peoples often make both the old and the new signification ambiguous.

A writer begins by the slight deflection of a known expression from its original meaning, and he adapts it, thus modified, as best he can for his purpose. A second writer twists its meaning in a different direction. Then comes a third, taking it off down a new track. Then, since there is no accepted judge, no permanent court to decide the meaning of a word, the phrase is left to wander free.

As a result, writers hardly ever appear to stick to a single thought, but always seem to envisage a group of ideas, leaving the reader to guess which is intended.

This is an annoying feature of democracy. I would rather have the language decked out with Chinese, Tartar, or Huron words than let the meaning of French words become doubtful. To be harmonious and homogeneous is but a secondary beauty of language. Convention plays a great part in that sort of thing, and if need be, one can do without it. But you cannot have a good language without clear terms.

Equality necessarily changes language in other ways as well.

In aristocratic ages, when each nation likes to stand apart from the rest and have its own peculiar physiognomy, it often happens that several peoples of a common origin become much estranged from one another, so that although they can still make themselves understood, they do not speak in the same way.

At such times also, nations are divided into classes which see one another little and do not mix at all; invariably each of these classes develops and keeps intellectual habits peculiar to itself, and it adopts certain words and certain expressions which are passed on from generation to generation as an inheritance. So the same linguistic stem comes to comprise a language of the poor and a language of the rich, a language of the common people and one of the nobility, a learned and a vulgar language. The higher and more impassable are the class distinctions, the more will this be the case. I would gladly bet that speech varies immensely between the different Indian castes and that an untouchable differs as much in language as in habits from a Brahmin.

But when men are no longer held to a fixed social position, when they continually see one another and talk together, when castes are destroyed and classes change and merge, all of the words of a language get mixed up too. Those which cannot please the majority die; the rest form a common stock from which each man chooses at random. Almost all the dialects dividing up the languages of Europe are visibly tending to disappear; in the New World there are no dialects, and in the Old they are vanishing.

This social revolution affects style as much as language.

Not only does everyone use the same words, but they get into the habit of using them without discrimination. The rules of style are almost destroyed. Hardly any expressions seem, by their nature, vulgar, and hardly any seem refined. Individuals from different strata of society have brought along with them, to whatever station they may have risen, the expressions and phrases they were accustomed to use; the origin of words is as much forgotten as that of men, and language is in as much confusion as society.

I know that in the hierarchy of words there are some rules which do not depend on one form of society or another but derive from the very nature of things. Some expressions and some turns of phrase are vulgar because the feelings they express are really low, and others are elevated because they describe things which are, in their nature, above the ordinary.

Social change will never efface such distinctions. But equality is bound to destroy all that is purely conventional and arbitrary in forms of thought. Perhaps even the necessary distinction I have just made will always be less respected by democratic peoples than by others, because among them there will be no men whose education, understanding, and leisure incline them to make a systematic study of the natural laws of language and who make others respect them by observing them themselves.

I will not pass on from this subject without pointing out one last trait that is perhaps more characteristic of democratic languages than all the others.

I have noted before that democracies have a taste, and often a passion, for general ideas; that is because of their peculiar qualities, good and bad. The form this love of general ideas takes in language is a continual use of generic terms and abstract words and a particular way of using them. That is the great strength and the great weakness in such languages.

Democratic peoples have this passion for generic terms and abstract words because such phrases broaden the scope of thought and allow the mind to include much in few words.

A democratic writer will freely put "the capabilities," meaning capable men, without going into details as to what these capabilities are to be applied to. He will speak of "actualities," thereby including everything taking place before his eyes in one word, and he will use "eventualities" to cover all that can happen in the universe after the moment at which he is speaking.

Democratic writers are forever using abstract words of this sort, and using them in a more and more abstract sense.

They go further, and to make speech run quicker, personify these abstractions and make them act like real men. They will say, "The force of things wills that capacities govern."

I can best illustrate my meaning by my own example.

I have often used the word "equality" in an absolute sense, and several times have even personified it, so that I have found myself saying that equality did certain things or abstained from others.

Frenchmen in the reign of Louis XIV would never have spoken in that way; it would never have entered the head of any of them to use the word "equality" without applying it to some particular thing, and they would have preferred not to use the word at all rather than turn it into a living being.

This abundance of abstract terms in the language of democracy, used the whole time without reference to any particular facts, both widens the scope of thought and clouds it. They make expression quicker but conceptions less clear. However, in matters of language democracies prefer obscurity to hard work.

Besides, I wonder if vagueness may not have a secret charm for talkers and writers too in these lands.

As these people are often left to depend on the unaided powers of their own minds, they are almost always harassed by doubts. Besides this, in a continually changing situation they are never obliged by unchanging circumstances to stick firmly to any view once held.

Democratic citizens, then, will often have vacillating thoughts, and so language must be loose enough to leave them play. As they never know whether what they say today will fit the facts of tomorrow, they have a natural taste for abstract terms. An abstract word is like a box with a false bottom; you may put in it what ideas you please and take them out again unobserved.

The languages of all peoples have a base of generic and abstract terms, and I do not make out that they are only found among democracies. I only assert that the tendency of men in times of equality is to increase the number of words of this type and in particular to use them detachedly and with the most abstract possible meaning and to use them on every conceivable occasion, whether needed or not.

Chapter 17

ON SOME SOURCES OF POETIC INSPIRATION IN DEMOCRACIES

THE WORD "POETRY" HAS BEEN GIVEN very many different meanings, and I will not bore the reader by arguing which definition is best but will simply state which I am using.

For me poetry is the search for and representation of the ideal.

The poet is one who, by omitting parts of what is there, adding some imaginary touches, and putting together things actual but not found together, ennobles nature. It is, therefore, not the poet's function to portray reality but to beautify it and offer the mind some loftier image.

I take verse to be the fairest flower of language, and in that sense it will be eminently poetic, but verse does not of itself make poetry.

I want to find out whether among the activities, feelings, and ideas of democracies there are any which lead to a conception of the ideal and may for that reason be considered natural sources of poetry.

It must first of all be acknowledged that the taste for ideal beauty and the pleasure derived from seeing it expressed are never as lively or as widespread in democracies as in aristocracies.

In aristocratic societies it can happen that the needs of the body see to themselves, while the soul is burdened with abundance of leisure. In such nations even the lower classes often have a taste for poetry, the spirit rising beyond and above its surroundings.

But in democracies the love of physical pleasures, the hope to better one's lot, competition, and the lure of success anticipated all goad men to activity in their chosen careers and forbid them to stray one moment from the track. The soul's chief effort goes in that direction. Imagination is not dead, but its chief function is to conceive what may be useful and to portray what is actual.

Equality not only turns attention away from the description of the ideal but also provides less to be described.

Aristocracy, by keeping society fixed, favors the stability and endurance of positive religions as well as political institutions. Not only does it keep the human mind within a framework of belief, but disposes it to accept one faith rather than another. An aristocratic people will always be inclined to put intermediate powers between God and man.

In that respect aristocracy favors poetry. When the universe is peopled with supernatural beings, not palpable to sense, but discovered by the mind, imagination ranges free, and poets find a thousand subjects for poetry and a countless audience to appreciate them.

But in democracies it can happen that men's faith is as much afloat as their laws. Then doubt brings the poet's imagination back to earth and shuts it up in the actual, visible world.

Even when equality does not bring religions crashing down, it simplifies them and turns attention away from secondary beings to concentrate it chiefly on the Supreme Being.

Aristocracy naturally leads the mind back to the past and fixes it in the contemplation thereof. But democracy engenders a sort of instinctive distaste for what is old. In that, aristocracy is much more favorable to poetry than is democracy, for things commonly seem grander and more mysterious as they recede into the distance, and for both those reasons they are more suited to represent the ideal.

Having deprived poetry of the past, equality also takes away part of the present.

There are some privileged people in aristocracies whose existence is, so to say, beyond and above man's lot; power, wealth, renown, wit, refinement, and distinction in all things seem their natural prerogative. The crowd neither sees them very close nor follows them in detail. It is not hard to represent such men in poetic terms.

On the other hand, in the same society are classes so ignorant, debased, and ground down that they too, from the very excess of their uncouth misery, are fit subjects for poetry, as are the others because of their grandeur and refinement. Moreover, in view of the great distance separating the classes and the lack of understanding between them, imagination can always add or subtract something from reality in representing them.

In democratic societies where all are insignificant and very much alike, each man, as he looks at himself, sees all his fellows at the same time. So poets in democracies can never take a particular man as the subject of their poetry, for something of medium size, seen clearly from every angle, never has the making of the ideal.

Thus the spread of equality over the earth dries up the old springs of poetry.

We must try to show how other springs are revealed.

When skepticism had depopulated heaven, and equality had cut each man to a smaller and better known size, the poets, wondering what to substitute for the great themes lost with the aristocracy, first turned their eyes to inanimate nature. Gods and heroes gone, they began by painting rivers and mountains.

This gave rise in the eighteenth century to what is known, par excellence, as descriptive poetry.

Some have thought that this poetry embellishing the physical and inanimate things that cover the earth is the true poetry of democracy. But I think that is a mistake, regarding it only as a transitional phenomenon.

In the long run I am sure that democracy turns man's imagination away from externals to concentrate it on himself alone.

Democratic peoples may amuse themselves momentarily by looking at nature, but it is about themselves that they are really excited. Here, and here alone, are the true springs of poetry among them, and those poets, I believe, who will not draw inspiration from these springs will lose their hold over the audience they intend to charm and find that they are left with cold witnesses to their ecstasies.

I have before noted how attuned to democratic ages are the ideas of progress and the indefinite perfectibility of the human race.

Democratic peoples do not bother at all about the past, but they gladly start dreaming about the future, and in that direction their imagination knows no bounds, but spreads and grows beyond measure.

Here, then, are wide vistas open to poetic inspiration that give the chance of painting distant scenes. Democracy shuts the past to poetry but opens the future.

None of the single, nearly equal, roughly similar citizens of a democracy will do as a subject for poetry, but the nation itself calls for poetic treatment. The very likeness of individuals, which rules them out as subjects for poetry on their own, helps the poet to group them in imagination and make a coherent picture of the nation as a whole. Democracies see themselves more vividly than do other nations, thus imposing an aspect wonderfully suited to painters of the ideal.

I gladly agree that there are no American poets, but I could not admit that Americans have no poetic ideas.

Europeans think a lot about the wild, open spaces of America, but the Americans themselves hardly give them a thought. The wonders of inanimate nature leave them cold, and, one may almost say, they do not see the marvelous forests surrounding them until they begin to fall beneath the ax. What they see is something different. The American people see themselves marching through wildernesses, drying up marshes, diverting rivers, peopling the wilds, and subduing nature. It is not just occasionally that their imagination catches a glimpse of this magnificent vision. It is something which plays a real part in the least, as in the most important, actions of every man, and it is always flitting before his mind.

There is nothing more petty, insipid, crowded with paltry interests —in one word, antipoetic—than the daily life of an American. But among the thoughts that direct his life there is always one full of poetry, and that is like a hidden sinew giving strength to the whole frame.

In ages of aristocracy peoples as well as individuals are inclined to stay immobile and separated from one another.

In ages of democracy men are always on the move from place to place, trying to satisfy their impatient longings, and peoples of different countries mix, see one another, hear one another, and borrow from one another. So it is not only the members of a single nation that come to resemble each other; the nations themselves are assimilated, and one can form the picture of one vast democracy in which a nation counts as a single citizen. Thus for the first time all mankind can be seen together in broad daylight.

The existence of the entire human race, its vicissitudes and its future, thus becomes a fertile theme for poetry.

Incidents in the life of a man or people have made fine subjects for poetry in aristocratic ages, but none of their poets has ever attempted to include the destiny of the whole human race in the scope of his work. That is a task which poets writing in democratic ages may be able to undertake.

Just when every man, raising his eyes above his country, begins at last to see mankind at large, God shows himself more clearly to human perception in full and entire majesty.

In democratic ages faith in positive religions may waver and belief in intermediate agents, by whatever name they are called, may grow dim, yet men are disposed to conceive a much more vast conception of divinity itself, and God's intervention in human affairs appears in a new and brighter light.

Seeing the human race as one great whole, they easily conceive that its destinies are regulated by the same design and are led to recognize in the actions of each individual a trace of the universal and consistent plan by which God guides mankind.

This too may be a rich source for the poetry about to blossom in democratic times.

Democratic poets will always seem petty and cold if they try to give corporeal form to gods or demons or angels and if they attempt to bring them down from heaven to dispute the supremacy of the earth.

But if they strive to connect the events they commemorate with the general designs of God for the universe, and without showing the hand of the Supreme Governor, reveal His thought, they will be admired and understood, for the imagination of their contemporaries is following the same road.

One may also anticipate that these poets will depict passions and ideas rather than men and deeds.

The language, dress, and daily actions of democratic man are repugnant to conceptions of the ideal. Such things are not poetic in themselves, and anyhow, too great familiarity would spoil them for the audience. The poet therefore must look beyond external appearance and palpable fact to glimpse the soul itself. The hidden depths of man's spiritual nature are the fittest subject for the poet of the ideal.

There is no need to traverse earth and sky to find a wondrous object full of contrasts of infinite greatness and littleness, of deep gloom and amazing brightness, capable at the same time of arousing piety, wonder, scorn, and terror. I have only to contemplate myself; man comes from nothing, passes through time, and disappears forever in the bosom of God. He is seen but for a moment wandering on the verge of two abysses, and then is lost.

If man were wholly ignorant of himself he would have no poetry in him, for one cannot describe what one does not conceive. If he saw himself clearly, his imagination would remain idle and would have nothing to add to the picture. But the nature of man is sufficiently revealed for him to know something of himself and sufficiently veiled to leave much in impenetrable darkness, a darkness in which he ever gropes, forever in vain, trying to understand himself.

Among a democratic people poetry will not feed on legends or on traditions and memories of old days. The poet will not try to people the universe again with supernatural beings in whom neither his readers nor he himself any longer believes, nor will he coldly personify virtues and vices better seen in their natural state. All these resources fail him, but man remains, and the poet needs no more. Human destiny, man himself, not tied to time or place, but face to face with nature and with God, with his passions, his doubts, his unexpected good fortune, and his incomprehensible miseries, will for these peoples be the chief and almost the sole subject of poetry. One can already be sure that this will be so if one considers the greatest poets that have appeared in the world since it turned toward democracy.

The writers of our time who have so wonderfully portrayed the features of Childe Harold,[1] René,[2] and Jocelyn[3] have not sought to record the actions of an individual, but by exaggeration to illuminate certain dark corners of the human heart.

Such are the poems of democracy.

Equality, then, does not destroy all the subjects of poetry. It makes them fewer but more vast.

[1] [Byron.]
[2] [Chateaubriand.]
[3] [Lamartine.]

Chapter 18

WHY AMERICAN WRITERS AND SPEAKERS ARE OFTEN BOMBASTIC

I HAVE OFTEN NOTICED that the Americans, whose language when talking business is clear and dry, without the slightest ornament, and of such extreme simplicity as often to be vulgar, easily turn bombastic when they attempt a poetic style. They are then pompous, without stopping from beginning to end of a speech, and one would have supposed, seeing them thus prodigal of metaphors at every opportunity, that they could never say anything simply.

The English fall into the same mistake, but less often.

The reason is easily pointed out.

Each citizen of a democracy generally spends his time considering the interests of a very insignificant person, namely, himself. If he ever does raise his eyes higher, he sees nothing but the huge apparition of society or the even larger form of the human race. He has nothing between very limited and clear ideas and very general and very vague conceptions; the space between is empty.

When he is drawn out of himself, he always expects to have some prodigious subject put before him, and that is the only consideration which would induce him for one moment to tear himself away from the complicated little cares that are the excitement and joy of his life.

This appears to me to explain sufficiently why democratic citizens, whose concerns are in general so paltry, call on their poets for such vast conceptions and descriptions out of proportion.

Writers, for their part, almost always pander to this propensity, which they share; they inflate their imaginations and swell them out beyond bounds, so that they achieve gigantism, missing real grandeur.

By this means they hope to catch the eye of the crowd at once and easily keep it fixed on themselves, an object in which they often succeed. For the crowd seeks nothing in poetry but objects of vast dimensions; it has neither the time to measure the objects set before it accurately nor the trained taste to sense easily how they are out of proportion. Writer and public join in corrupting each other.

We have noted before that in democracies the springs of poetry are fine but few. They are soon exhausted. Finding no stuff for the ideal in what is real and true, poets, abandoning truth and reality, create monsters.

I have no fear that the poetry of democratic peoples will be found timid or that it will stick too close to the earth. I am much more afraid that it will spend its whole time getting lost in the clouds and may finish up by describing an entirely fictitious country. I am alarmed at the thought of too many immense, incoherent images, overdrawn descriptions, bizarre effects, and a whole fantastic breed of brainchildren who will make one long for the real world.

Chapter 19

SOME OBSERVATIONS ON THE THEATER AMONG DEMOCRATIC PEOPLES

OF ALL FORMS OF LITERATURE it is generally the drama that is first affected by the social and political revolution upsetting an aristocratic order, and its influence is always conspicuous there.

The audience in a theater is, to a certain extent, taken by surprise by the impression conveyed. There is no time to refer to memory or to consult expert critics. It does not occur to the audience to resist the charms of new literary tendencies which they are beginning to enjoy; they yield, not knowing what they yield to.

Authors are quick to see in what direction public taste secretly inclines, and they trim their sails accordingly. The drama, which first gave an indication of the literary revolution in store, soon brings it to completion. If you want advance knowledge of the literature of a people which is turning toward democracy, pay attention to the theater.

Moreover, even in aristocracies the drama represents the most democratic side of literature. The crowd can enjoy sights on the stage more easily than any other form of literature. No preparation and no study are needed to take them in. It is they that carry you off your feet, however preoccupied and however ignorant you may be. When the yet untutored love of the pleasure of the mind begins to affect any class of the community, it is to the theater that they turn. Even in aristocratic societies the theaters have always been full of spectators who were not aristocrats. Only in the theater have the upper classes mingled with the middle and lower classes, and if they have not actually agreed to receive the latters' advice, at least they have allowed it to be given. It has always been in the theater that the learned and the educated have had the greatest difficulty in making their tastes prevail over that of the people and preventing themselves from being carried away by them. The pit often lays down the law for the boxes.

If it is difficult for an aristocracy to stop the people's getting the upper hand in the theater, it is obvious that the people will be supreme when democratic principles have permeated laws and mores, when ranks are intermixed and thoughts as well as fortunes are brought in closer contact, and when the upper class has lost with its hereditary wealth its power, traditions, and leisure.

So the natural literary tastes and instincts of democracy are first seen in the theater, and one must expect them to break in vehemently there. In written works aristocratic canons will be modified little by little in a gradual and, so to say, legal way. In the theater they will be overthrown by revolts.

The theater makes most of the good qualities and almost all the defects inherent in democratic literature stand out clearly.

Democratic peoples have but little reverence for learning and scarcely bother at all about what happened in Rome or Athens. They want the talk to be about themselves and to see the present world mirrored.

So when the heroes of antiquity and their moral problems are frequent subjects in the theater and dramatists are carefully faithful to antique traditions, it is safe to conclude that the democratic classes do not yet rule the stage.

In the preface to Racine's *Britannicus*[1] he apologizes humbly for allowing Junia to become a vestal virgin, when, according to Aulus Gellius, he says, "they did not accept anyone under six years old or over ten." Had he been writing nowadays, he would surely not have accused or defended himself for a crime like that.

Such behavior illustrates not only the state of literature at that time but also the state of society. Democratic drama does not prove a nation democratic, for as already mentioned, democratic tastes can influence the stage even in an aristocracy. But when the spirit of aristocracy reigns alone on the stage, that is sure proof that the whole of society is aristocratic, and one can confidently conclude that the

[1] [Cf. *Britannicus* (Première) Préface, in Racine, *Œuvres Complètes*, I, édition de La Pléiade, Paris, 1950, p. 386.]

same learned and educated class which lays down the law for authors also rules the people and the country.

It almost always happens that the refined tastes and penchant to arrogance of an aristocracy, when it gives the law to the drama, lead it to choose out certain aspects of human nature. Certain social conditions chiefly interest aristocrats, and they like to see them represented on the stage. Certain virtues, certain vices too, seem to them particularly worth treatment. That is what pleases them, and the rest is banished from view. At the theater, as everywhere else, they want to meet only great nobles and to have their emotions touched only by the misfortunes of kings. The same is true of style. An aristocracy likes to insist on authors' maintaining a certain way of speaking; it wants everything to be said after this fashion.

Thus the theater is often limited to one side only of man, and sometimes it illustrates things never found in human nature, rising above and beyond nature.

Democratic audiences have no analogous preferences, and they seldom show similar antipathies. On the stage they like to see the same medley of conditions, feelings, and opinions that occur in life. The drama becomes more striking, more vulgar, and more true.

Sometimes, however, writers for the democratic stage do go beyond the limits of human nature, but it is in a different direction from their predecessors. Seeking to represent in minute detail the little singularities of the present and the peculiar characteristics of particular people, they forget to sketch the basic features of mankind.

When democratic audiences rule the stage they introduce as much license in the manner of treating subjects as in the choice of them.

As love of the drama is, of all literary tastes, that most natural to democratic peoples, the number of authors, spectators, and plays is constantly on the increase. Such a multitude, composed of such varied elements and scattered so widely over the land, cannot acknowledge the same rules or submit to the same laws. No agreement is possible among judges so numerous, who never know when they may meet again and who all like to judge for themselves. All literary rules and conventions are shaken by the impact of democracy, but in the drama they are entirely abolished, leaving only the caprice of each author and each audience.

The drama also supplies a specially pronounced example of what I have mentioned before in speaking generally about style and art in democratic literature. In reading dramatic criticism from the age of Louis XIV, one is surprised by the great importance the public attached to probability in the plot and consistency in the characterization, no one being allowed to do anything which cannot easily be explained and understood. It is equally astonishing what value was then put on forms of speech and with what petty linguistic criticisms dramatists were then assailed.

It seems that men of the age of Louis XIV attached very exaggerated importance to such details, which may be perceived in the study but pass unnoticed on the stage. For, after all, the main object of a drama is to be performed, and its greatest merit to touch the emotions. The reason is that the audience in that age were readers too; when they left the theater they read the drama at home, and it was there that they pronounced judgment.

A democratic audience listens in the theater but does not read plays. Most of the spectators are not looking for pleasures of the mind, but for lively emotions of the heart. They want to see a play, not to discover a fine work of literature, and provided the author writes his native tongue well enough to be understood, and his characters excite curiosity and arouse sympathy, the audience is satisfied. They ask no more of fiction, and go back immediately to real life. Style is therefore less necessary, for breaches of rules tend to pass unnoticed on the stage.

As for probability, it is incompatible with perpetual novelty, unexpectedness, and speed. So it is neglected, and the public does not mind. You may be sure that if you succeed in finding something that touches the audience, they will not mind by what road you reached this result. They will never blame you for having excited their emotions in spite of the rules.

The audience in an American theater displays all these instincts very clearly. But one must remember that as yet very few of them go to the theater at all. Although there are many more plays and playgoers in the United States now than there were forty years ago, the population still has great reserves about indulging in amusements of this sort.

This is due to particular causes of which the reader is already aware, so that few words will be enough to remind him of them.

The Puritan founders of the American republics were not only hostile to all pleasures but professed a special abhorrence for the stage. They thought it an abominable amusement, and so long as their principles prevailed without question, the drama was wholly unknown among them. These opinions of the founding fathers of the colonies have left deep traces on the minds of their descendants.

In America extreme regularity of habits and great strictness of morals have up to now told against the growth of the drama.

There are no subjects for drama in a country which has seen no great political catastrophes and in which love always leads by a direct and easy road to marriage. People who spend every weekday making money and Sunday in praying to God give no scope to the Muse of Comedy.

A single fact is enough to show that the stage is not very popular in America.

The Americans, whose laws allow the utmost freedom, and even license, of language in other respects, nevertheless subject the drama to a sort of censorship. Plays can only be performed by permission of the municipal authorities. This illustrates how like communities are to individuals: without a thought they give way to their chief passions, and then take great care not to be carried away by tastes they do not possess.

The drama, more than any other form of literature, is bound by many close links to the actual state of society.

The drama of one age will never suit the next if an important revolution has changed manners and laws.

The great writers of another age are still studied. But no one goes to see plays written for another public. Dramatists of the past live only in books.

An aristocratic theater may survive for some time in a democracy, sustained by the traditional tastes of some, by vanity, by fashion, or by the genius of an actor. But soon it will fall of its own accord, not overthrown, but abandoned.

Chapter 20

SOME CHARACTERISTICS PECULIAR TO HISTORIANS IN DEMOCRATIC CENTURIES

HISTORIANS WHO WRITE in aristocratic ages generally attribute everything that happens to the will and character of particular men, and they will unhesitatingly suppose slight accidents to be the cause of the greatest revolutions. With great sagacity they trace the smallest causes and often leave the greatest unnoticed.

Historians who live in democratic ages show contrary tendencies.

Most of them attribute hardly any influence over the destinies of mankind to individuals, or over the fate of a people to the citizens.

But they make great general causes responsible for the smallest particular events. There is a reason for these opposite tendencies.

Historians of aristocratic ages, looking at the world's theater, first see a few leading actors in control of the whole play. These great personages who hold the front of the stage strike their attention and hold it fixed. Bent on discovering the secret motives that make these men act and speak, they forget the rest.

Seeing some men do great things gives them an exaggerated idea of the influence one man can exercise and leads them to suppose that one must always explain the actions of the crowd by tracing the impulse back to one man's act.

But when all the citizens are independent of one another and each is weak, no one can be found exercising very great or, more particularly, very lasting influence over the masses. At first sight individuals appear to have no influence at all over them, and society would seem to progress on its own by the free and spontaneous action of all its members.

That naturally prompts the mind to look for the general reason which acts on so many men's faculties at once and turns them all simultaneously in the same direction.

I am firmly convinced that even in democratic nations the genius, vices, or virtues of individuals delay or hasten the course of the natural destiny of a people. But in periods of equality, as compared to ages of aristocracy, causes of this secondary and accidental nature are infinitely more various, better hidden, more complex, less powerful, and hence less easy to sort out and trace, whereas the historian of an aristocratic age has simply to analyze the particular action of one man or of a few men and amid the general mass of events.

In the former case the historian is soon tired of such a labor. Lost in a labyrinth, unable clearly to see or to explain individual influences, he ends by denying that they exist. He prefers to talk about the nature of races, the physical character of the country, or the spirit of civilization. That shortens his labors and satisfies the reader better at less cost.

M. de La Fayette says somewhere in his memoirs that an exaggerated belief in a system of general causes is wonderfully consoling for mediocre public men. I would add that it is the same for mediocre historians. It always provides them with a few mighty reasons to extricate them from the most difficult part of their task, and while indulging their incapacity or laziness, gives them a reputation for profundity.

For my part, I think that in all ages some of the happenings in this world are due to very general causes and others depend on very particular influences. These two kinds of causes are always in operation; only their proportion varies. General causes explain more, and particular influences less, in democratic than in aristocratic ages. In ages of aristocracy the opposite is true; particular influences are stronger and general causes weaker, unless one considers as a general cause the fact that inequality of condition makes it possible for some individuals to go against the natural inclinations of all the rest.

Therefore historians who describe the happenings in democratic societies are right in attaching much importance to general causes and in spending most of their time discovering them. They would, however, be wrong to deny entirely the importance of the actions of individuals just because that is hard to find and trace out.

Historians who live in democratic ages are not only prone to attribute each happening to a great cause but also are led to link facts together to make a system.

In aristocratic ages, as the attention of historians is constantly drawn to individuals, the connection of events escapes them, or rather they do not believe in such a connection. It seems to them that the thread of history is being constantly broken as a man crosses its path.

But the historian of democratic epochs, seeing the actors less and the events more, can easily string facts together in a methodical order.

Ancient literature, so rich in fine historical writing, has not left us one great historical system, whereas even the poorest of modern literatures is swarming with them. Apparently classical historians made too little use of general theories, whereas our own are always on the verge of using them too much.

Those who write in democratic ages have another tendency that is more dangerous.

Once the trace of the influence of individuals on the nations has been lost, we are often left with the sight of the world moving without anyone moving it. As it becomes extremely difficult to discern and analyze the reasons which, acting separately on the will of each citizen, concur in the end to produce movement in the whole mass, one is tempted to believe that this movement is not voluntary and that societies unconsciously obey some superior dominating force.

Even supposing that it is on earth that we must find the general law controlling the particular wills of all individuals, that does not serve to preserve human freedom. A cause so vast that it acts at the same time on millions of men, and so strong that it bends them all together in the same direction, may easily seem irresistible. Seeing that one does yield to it, one is very near believing that one cannot stand up to it.

Thus historians who live in democratic times do not only refuse to admit that some citizens may influence the destiny of a people, but also take away from the peoples themselves the faculty of modifying their own lot and make them depend either on an inflexible providence or on a kind of blind fatality. According to them each nation is inexorably bound by its position, origin, antecedents, and nature to a fixed destiny which no efforts can change. Generation is firmly bound to generation, and so going back from age to age, from necessity to necessity, they reach the origin of the world, forging a tight, enormous chain which girds and binds the human race.

Not content to show how events have occurred, they pride themselves on proving that they could not have happened differently. They see a nation which has reached a certain point in its history, and they assert that it was bound to have followed the path that led it there. That is easier than demonstrating how it might have taken a better road.

In reading historians of aristocratic ages, those of antiquity in particular, it would seem that in order to be master of his fate and to govern his fellows a man need only be master of himself. Perusing the histories written nowadays, one would suppose that man had no power, neither over himself nor over his surroundings. Classical historians taught how to command; those of our own time teach next to nothing but how to obey. In their writings the author often figures large, but humanity is always tiny.

If this doctrine of fatality, so attractive to those who write history in democratic periods, passes from authors to readers, infects the whole mass of the community, and takes possession of the public mind, it will soon paralyze the activities of modern society and bring Christians down to the level of Turks.

I would add that such a doctrine is particularly dangerous at the present moment. Our contemporaries are all too much inclined to doubts about free will, since each of them feels himself confined on every side by his own weakness. But they will freely admit the strength and independence of men united in a body social. It is important not to let this idea grow dim, for we need to raise men's souls, not to complete their prostration.

Chapter 21

OF PARLIAMENTARY ELOQUENCE
IN THE UNITED STATES

IN ARISTOCRATIC PEOPLES all the members of the community are connected with and dependent on one another. There is a link in the
hierarchy connecting them all that keeps each in his place and the
whole body in obedience. Something analogous always happens in
the political assemblies of such peoples. Parties naturally arrange
themselves under certain leaders, whom they obey by a sort of instinct which is only the result of habits contracted elsewhere. They
carry the habits of their social world into this smaller society.

In democratic countries it often happens that a great many citizens
make for the same point, but each goes, or at least flatters himself
that he goes, of his own accord. Accustomed to control his movements according to his personal wish, he finds it uncomfortable to
take orders from outside. He takes this taste and habit of independence with him into the councils of the nation. If he consents to
join with others in the pursuit of a common aim, he likes at least
to remain free to contribute to the common success after his own
fashion.

That is why parties in democratic countries are so impatient of
direction and show themselves obedient only when the danger is very
great. Even then, though in those circumstances the leaders' authority
may be enough to make them act and speak, it is hardly ever sufficient
to make them keep quiet.

Among aristocratic peoples the members of political assemblies are
also aristocrats. Each of them possesses on his own account a high
and secure rank, and the position which he occupies in the assembly
often seems, in his own eyes, less important than that which he occupies in the country. This consoles him if he plays no part in the discussion of public affairs and restrains him from too eagerly seeking to
play an unimportant one.

In America a deputy is generally a nobody apart from his position
in the assembly. He is therefore perpetually stung by the need to

acquire importance there, and he has a petulant longing to air his ideas in and out of season.

He is pushed in that direction not only by his own vanity but also by that of his electors, whom he is always bound to gratify.

The member of a legislature among aristocratic peoples is seldom closely dependent on his constituents; they often feel him to be in some way their only possible representative; sometimes they are themselves strictly dependent upon him, and if at length they do refuse to vote for him, he can easily get himself elected elsewhere, or giving up a public career, he can retire to a leisure not without its own magnificence.

In a democratic country such as the United States a deputy hardly ever has a lasting hold over the minds of his constituents. However small an electoral body may be, it is constantly changing shape with the fluctuations of democracy. It must therefore be courted unceasingly. He is never sure of them, and if they forsake him, he is left without resource, for natural position is too humble for him to be easily known to those not close to him; and in view of the complete independence enjoyed by all the citizens, he cannot hope that his friends or the government will find it easy to impose him on constituents who do not know him. The seeds of his fortune therefore are sown in the neighborhood he represents; it is from that corner of land that he must come out to raise himself to command the people and influence the destinies of the world.

So it is natural that democratic representatives think more about their constituents than about their party, while those of aristocracies think more of party than of constituents.

But what needs to be said to please constituents is not always the same as what needs to be done to help forward the political view they profess to support.

It is often to the general interest of a party that a deputy should never talk about great matters which he does not well understand, that he should speak little about the small matters that might interfere with great ones, and finally, for the most part, that he should keep quiet. His silence is the most useful service an indifferent speaker can render to the common good.

But this is not at all how his constituents see the matter.

The population of a neighborhood choose a citizen to take part in the government because they have a vast opinion of his merit. Since men always look bigger when surrounded by small objects, it may be assumed that the slighter the supply of talents among his constituents, the greater will be their admiration of him. So the frequent result is that the less it is reasonable to expect from him, the more they do expect; and however incapable he may be, they will expect the signal exertions appropriate to their belief in him.

The electors see their representative not only as a legislator for the state but also as the natural protector of local interests in the legislature; indeed, they almost seem to think that he has a power of attorney to represent each constituent, and they trust him to be as eager in their private interests as in those of the country.

The electors therefore take it for granted that their chosen deputy is an orator, that if he can he will speak often, and that in case he is forced to refrain, the few speeches which he does make will show what he can do and include both an examination of all the great affairs of state and a catalog of all their petty grievances, and that if he is not to be continually lavish of his oratory, he should from time to time condense all that he and his constituents stand for into a brilliant and complete résumé. On these terms they promise to vote for him again.

This drives to despair those honest mediocrities who, knowing their limitations, would never willingly have stepped forward. Thus goaded, the deputy gets up to speak, to the great distress of his friends, and rashly bursting in among the most celebrated orators, he confuses the debate and bores the assembly.

It follows that all laws making the deputy more dependent on his constituents affect not only the behavior of the legislators, as already noted, but also their language. The influence is both on the substance of business and on the way it is discussed.

There is hardly a congressman prepared to go home until he has at least one speech printed and sent to his constituents, and he won't let anybody interrupt his harangue until he has made all his useful suggestions about the twenty-four states of the Union, and especially the district he represents. So his audience has to listen to great general truths which he often does not understand himself and makes a muddle of exposing, and very minute particulars which he has not much chance of verifying or explaining. Consequently the debates of that great assembly are frequently vague and perplexed, seeming to be dragged, rather than to march, to the intended goal.

Something of this sort must, I think, always happen in public democratic assemblies.

Lucky circumstances and good laws might combine to provide a democratic legislature with much more remarkable men than those sent by the Americans to Congress. But nothing will ever stop the mediocrities who do get there from complacently airing all their views.

I do not think this ill can be entirely cured, for it is not solely due to rules of procedure, but to the constitution both of Congress and of the whole country.

Americans themselves seem to see the matter like that, and they bear witness to their long experience of parliamentary practice not by refraining from dull speeches but by summoning their courage to listen to them. They are resigned to them, as to an evil that they know by experience cannot be cured.

We have seen the petty side of democratic political debates; let us now consider their imposing aspects.

For a hundred and fifty years the proceedings of the English Parliament have never caused much stir outside that land; the speakers' views and feelings have never aroused much sympathy even in the countries nearest to that great theater of British liberty. But Europe was stirred by the first debates that took place in the little colonial assemblies of America at the time of the Revolution.

This was due not only to particular and accidental circumstances but also to general and lasting reasons.

There is nothing more wonderful or more impressive than a great orator discussing great affairs in a democratic assembly. As no particular class is ever represented there by men commissioned to defend its special interests, the orator always speaks to the whole nation, for the whole nation. This heightens both his thought and his power of expression.

As precedents have little force, and there are no more privileges attached to certain property or rights inherent in certain bodies or certain men, the argument, to deal with the particular matter at hand, must be carried back to general propositions derived from the nature of humanity. For this reason the political discussions of a democracy, no matter how small, have a general character which often attracts the interest of the human race. All men are interested because they treat of man, who is everywhere the same.

But among even the greatest aristocratic peoples questions of the widest general interest are almost always treated on the basis of arguments derived from the particular customs of an age or the rights of a class. Thus only the class in question is interested, or at most, the people among whom it exists.

It is as much due to this reason as to the greatness of France and the prejudice in her favor among the listening nations that our political debates sometimes have so much effect in the world.

Our orators often speak to all men, even when they are addressing only their fellow citizens.

PART II

The Influence of Democracy on the Sentiments of the Americans

Chapter 1

WHY DEMOCRATIC NATIONS SHOW A MORE ARDENT AND ENDURING LOVE FOR EQUALITY THAN FOR LIBERTY

THE FIRST AND LIVELIEST of the passions inspired by equality is, I need not say, love of that equality itself. My readers will therefore not be surprised if I speak of that before all the others.

Everybody has noticed that in our age, and especially in France, this passion for equality is daily acquiring a greater hold over the human heart. It has been said a hundred times that our contemporaries love equality much more ardently and tenaciously than liberty. But I do not think that anyone has yet adequately explained the reason for this fact. I will try to do so.

It is possible to imagine an extreme point at which freedom and equality would meet and blend.

Let us suppose that all the citizens take a part in the government and that each of them has an equal right to do so.

Then, no man is different from his fellows, and nobody can wield tyrannical power; men will be perfectly free because they are entirely equal, and they will be perfectly equal because they are entirely free. Democratic peoples are tending toward that ideal.

That is the completest possible form for equality on this earth. But there are a thousand other forms which, though less perfect, are no less cherished by those nations.

There can be established equality in civil society, though there is none in the world of politics. One can have the right to enjoy the same pleasures, to engage in the same professions, and to meet in the same places—in a word, to live in the same manner and seek wealth by the same means—without all taking the same part in the government.

There can even be a sort of equality in the world of politics without any political freedom. A man may be the equal of all his fellows save one, who is the master of all without distinction and chooses the agents of his power equally from among all.

One can easily invent several other hypotheses in which a great deal of equality is easily combined with institutions more or less free, or even not free at all.

Although men cannot be absolutely equal without being entirely free, and consequently equality, in its most extreme form, must merge with freedom, there is good reason to distinguish one from the other.

So men's taste for freedom and their taste for equality are in fact distinct, and, I have no hesitation in adding, among democracies they are two unequal elements.

On close inspection one finds in every age some peculiar and predominating element which controls all the rest. This element almost always engenders some seminal thought or ruling passion which in the end drags all other feelings and ideas along in its course. It is like a great river which seems to make all surrounding rivulets flow toward it.

Freedom is found at different times and in different forms; it is not exclusively dependent on one social state, and one finds it elsewhere than in democracies. It cannot therefore be taken as the distinctive characteristic of democratic ages.

The particular and predominating fact peculiar to those ages is equality of conditions, and the chief passion which stirs men at such times is the love of this same equality.

Do not ask what singular charm the men of democratic ages find in living as equals or what special reason they may have for clinging so tenaciously to equality rather than the other advantages society offers. Equality forms the distinctive characteristic of the age in which they live. That is enough to explain why they prefer it to all the rest.

But apart from that reason there are several others which at all times lead men to prefer equality to liberty.

If a people could ever succeed in destroying or even diminishing the equality prevailing in its body social, it could only do so by long and laborious efforts. They would have to modify their social condition, repeal their laws, supersede their opinions, change their habits, and alter their mores. But political liberty is easily lost; neglect to hold it fast, and it is gone.

Men therefore hold on to equality not only because it is precious to them; they are also attached to it because they think it will last forever.

Nobody is so limited and superficial as not to realize that political liberty can, if carried to excess, endanger the peace, property, and lives of individuals. But only perceptive and clearsighted men see the dangers with which equality threatens us, and they generally avoid pointing them out. They see that the troubles they fear are distant and console themselves that they will only fall on future generations, for which the present generation hardly cares. The ills which liberty brings may be immediate; all can see them and all, more or less, feel them. The ills produced by extreme equality only become apparent little by little; they gradually insinuate themselves into the body social; they are only occasionally noticed, and when they do become most excessive, habit has already made them pass unfelt.

The good things that freedom brings are seen only as time passes, and it is always easy to mistake the cause that brought them about.

The advantages of equality are felt immediately, and it is daily apparent where they come from.

Political liberty occasionally gives sublime pleasure to a few.

Equality daily gives each man in the crowd a host of small enjoyments. The charms of equality are felt the whole time and are within the reach of all; the noblest spirits appreciate them, and the commonest minds exult in them. The passion engendered by equality is therefore both strong and general.

Men cannot enjoy political liberty without some sacrifice, and they have never won it without great effort. But equality offers its pleasures free; each little incident in life occasions them, and to taste them one needs but to live.

Democratic peoples always like equality, but there are times when their passion for it turns to delirium. This happens when the old social hierarchy, long menaced, finally collapses after a severe internal struggle and the barriers of rank are at length thrown down. At such times men pounce on equality as their booty and cling to it as a precious treasure they fear to have snatched away. The passion for equality seeps into every corner of the human heart, expands, and fills the whole. It is no use telling them that by this blind surrender to an exclusive passion they are compromising their dearest interests; they are deaf. It is no use pointing out that freedom is slipping from their grasp while they look the other way; they are blind, or rather they can see but one thing to covet in the whole world.

The foregoing applies to all democratic nations, what follows only to the French.

Among most modern nations, especially those of Europe, the taste for freedom and the conception of it only began to take shape and grow at the time when social conditions were tending toward equality, and it was a consequence of that very equality. It was the absolute monarchs who worked hardest to level down ranks among their subjects. For the peoples equality had come before liberty, so equality was an established fact when freedom was still a novelty; the one had already shaped customs, opinions, and laws to its use when the other was first stepping lonely forward into broad daylight. Thus the latter was still only a matter of opinion and preference, whereas the former had already insinuated itself into popular habits, shaped mores, and given a particular twist to the slightest actions of life. Why, then, should we be surprised that our contemporaries prefer the one to the other?

I think democratic peoples have a natural taste for liberty; left to themselves, they will seek it, cherish it, and be sad if it is taken from them. But their passion for equality is ardent, insatiable, eternal, and invincible. They want equality in freedom, and if they cannot have that, they still want equality in slavery. They will put up with poverty, servitude, and barbarism, but they will not endure aristocracy.

This is true at all times, but especially in our own. All men and all powers who try to stand up against this irresistible passion will be overthrown and destroyed by it. In our day freedom cannot be established without it, and despotism itself cannot reign without its support.

Chapter 2

OF INDIVIDUALISM IN DEMOCRACIES

I HAVE SHOWN HOW, in ages of equality, every man finds his beliefs within himself, and I shall now go on to show that all his feelings are turned in on himself.

"Individualism" is a word recently coined to express a new idea. Our fathers only knew about egoism.

Egoism is a passionate and exaggerated love of self which leads a man to think of all things in terms of himself and to prefer himself to all.

Individualism is a calm and considered feeling which disposes each citizen to isolate himself from the mass of his fellows and withdraw into the circle of family and friends; with this little society formed to his taste, he gladly leaves the greater society to look after itself.

Egoism springs from a blind instinct; individualism is based on misguided judgment rather than depraved feeling. It is due more to inadequate understanding than to perversity of heart.

Egoism sterilizes the seeds of every virtue; individualism at first only dams the spring of public virtues, but in the long run it attacks and destroys all the others too and finally merges in egoism.

Egoism is a vice as old as the world. It is not peculiar to one form of society more than another.

Individualism is of democratic origin and threatens to grow as conditions get more equal.

Among aristocratic nations families maintain the same station for centuries and often live in the same place. So there is a sense in which all the generations are contemporaneous. A man almost always knows about his ancestors and respects them; his imagination extends to his great-grandchildren, and he loves them. He freely does his duty by both ancestors and descendants and often sacrifices personal pleasures for the sake of beings who are no longer alive or are not yet born.

Moreover, aristocratic institutions have the effect of linking each man closely with several of his fellows.

Each class in an aristocratic society, being clearly and permanently limited, forms, in a sense, a little fatherland for all its members, to which they are attached by more obvious and more precious ties than those linking them to the fatherland itself.

Each citizen of an aristocratic society has his fixed station, one above another, so that there is always someone above him whose protection he needs and someone below him whose help he may require.

So people living in an aristocratic age are almost always closely involved with something outside themselves, and they are often inclined to forget about themselves. It is true that in these ages the general conception of *human fellowship* is dim and that men hardly ever think of devoting themselves to the cause of humanity, but men do often make sacrifices for the sake of certain other men.

In democratic ages, on the contrary, the duties of each to all are much clearer but devoted service to any individual much rarer. The bonds of human affection are wider but more relaxed.

Among democratic peoples new families continually rise from nothing while others fall, and nobody's position is quite stable. The woof of time is ever being broken and the track of past generations lost. Those who have gone before are easily forgotten, and no one gives a thought to those who will follow. All a man's interests are limited to those near himself.

As each class catches up with the next and gets mixed with it, its members do not care about one another and treat one another as strangers. Aristocracy links everybody, from peasant to king, in one long chain. Democracy breaks the chain and frees each link.

As social equality spreads there are more and more people who, though neither rich nor powerful enough to have much hold over others, have gained or kept enough wealth and enough understanding to look after their own needs. Such folk owe no man anything and hardly expect anything from anybody. They form the habit of thinking of themselves in isolation and imagine that their whole destiny is in their own hands.

Thus, not only does democracy make men forget their ancestors, but also clouds their view of their descendants and isolates them from their contemporaries. Each man is forever thrown back on himself alone, and there is danger that he may be shut up in the solitude of his own heart.

Chapter 3

HOW INDIVIDUALISM IS MORE PRONOUNCED AT THE END OF A DEMOCRATIC REVOLUTION THAN AT ANY OTHER TIME

IT IS JUST AT THE MOMENT when a democratic society is establishing itself on the ruins of an aristocracy that this isolation of each man from the rest and the egoism resulting therefrom stand out clearest.

Not only are there many independent people in such a society, but their number is constantly increasing with more and more of those who have just attained independence and are drunk with their new power. These latter have a presumptuous confidence in their strength, and never imagining that they could ever need another's help again, they have no inhibition about showing that they care for nobody but themselves.

There is usually a prolonged struggle before an aristocracy gives way, and in the course of that struggle implacable hatreds have been engendered between the classes. Such passions last after victory, and one can see traces of them in the ensuing democratic confusion.

Those who once held the highest ranks in the subverted hierarchy cannot forget their ancient greatness at once and for a long time feel themselves strangers in the new society. They regard all those whom society now makes their equals as oppressors whose fate could not concern them; they have lost sight of their former equals and no longer feel tied by common interests to their lot; each of them, in his separate retreat, feels reduced to taking care of himself alone. But those formerly at the bottom of the social scale and now brought up to the common level by a sudden revolution cannot enjoy their new-found independence without some secret uneasiness: there is a look of fear mixed with triumph in their eyes if they do meet one of their former superiors, and they avoid them.

Therefore it is usually at the time when democratic societies are taking root that men are most disposed to isolate themselves.

There is a tendency in democracy not to draw men together, but democratic revolutions make them run away from each other and perpetuate, in the midst of equality, hatreds originating in inequality.

The Americans have this great advantage, that they attained democracy without the sufferings of a democratic revolution and that they were born equal instead of becoming so.

Chapter 4

HOW THE AMERICANS COMBAT THE EFFECTS OF INDIVIDUALISM BY FREE INSTITUTIONS

DESPOTISM, BY ITS VERY nature suspicious, sees the isolation of men as the best guarantee of its own permanence. So it usually does all it can to isolate them. Of all the vices of the human heart egoism is that which suits it best. A despot will lightly forgive his subjects for not loving him, provided they do not love one another. He does not ask them to help him guide the state; it is enough if they do not claim to manage it themselves. He calls those who try to unite their efforts to create a general prosperity "turbulent and restless spirits", and twisting the natural meaning of words, he calls those "good citizens" who care for none but themselves.

Thus vices originating in despotism are precisely those favored by equality. The two opposites fatally complete and support each other.

Equality puts men side by side without a common link to hold them firm. Despotism raises barriers to keep them apart. It disposes them not to think of their fellows and turns indifference into a sort of public virtue.

Despotism, dangerous at all times, is therefore particularly to be feared in ages of democracy.

It is easy to see that in such ages men have a peculiar need for freedom.

Citizens who are bound to take part in public affairs must turn from the private interests and occasionally take a look at something other than themselves.

As soon as common affairs are treated in common, each man notices that he is not as independent of his fellows as he used to suppose and that to get their help he must often offer his aid to them.

When the public governs, all men feel the value of public goodwill and all try to win it by gaining the esteem and affection of those among whom they must live.

Those frigid passions that keep hearts asunder must then retreat and hide at the back of consciousness. Pride must be disguised; contempt must not be seen. Egoism is afraid of itself.

Under a free government most public officials are elected, so men whose great gifts and aspirations are too closely circumscribed in private life daily feel that they cannot do without the people around them.

It thus happens that ambition makes a man care for his fellows, and, in a sense, he often finds his self-interest in forgetting about himself. I know that one can point to all the intrigues caused by an election, the dishonorable means often used by candidates, and the calumnies spread by their enemies. These do give rise to feelings of hatred, and the more frequent the elections, the worse they are.

Those are great ills, no doubt, but passing ones, whereas the benefits that attend them remain.

Eagerness to be elected may, for the moment, make particular men fight each other, but in the long run this same aspiration induces mutual helpfulness on the part of all; and while it may happen that the accident of an election estranges two friends, the electoral system forges permanent links between a great number of citizens who might otherwise have remained forever strangers to one another. Liberty engenders particular hatreds, but despotism is responsible for general indifference.

The Americans have used liberty to combat the individualism born of equality, and they have won.

The lawgivers of America did not suppose that a general representation of the whole nation would suffice to ward off a disorder at once so natural to the body social of a democracy and so fatal. They thought it also right to give each part of the land its own political life so that there should be an infinite number of occasions for the citizens to act together and so that every day they should feel that they depended on one another.

That was wise conduct.

The general business of a country keeps only the leading citizens occupied. It is only occasionally that they come together in the same places, and since they often lose sight of one another, no lasting bonds form between them. But when the people who live there have to look after the particular affairs of a district, the same people are always meeting, and they are forced, in a manner, to know and adapt themselves to one another.

It is difficult to force a man out of himself and get him to take an interest in the affairs of the whole state, for he has little understanding of the way in which the fate of the state can influence his own lot. But if it is a question of taking a road past his property, he sees at once that this small public matter has a bearing on his greatest private interests, and there is no need to point out to him the close connection between his private profit and the general interest.

Thus, far more may be done by entrusting citizens with the management of minor affairs than by handing over control of great matters, toward interesting them in the public welfare and convincing them that they constantly stand in need of one another in order to provide for it.

Some brilliant achievement may win a people's favor at one stroke. But to gain the affection and respect of your immediate neighbors, a long succession of little services rendered and of obscure good deeds, a constant habit of kindness and an established reputation for disinterestedness, are required.

Local liberties, then, which induce a great number of citizens to value the affection of their kindred and neighbors, bring men constantly into contact, despite the instincts which separate them, and force them to help one another.

In the United States the most opulent citizens are at pains not to get isolated from the people. On the contrary, they keep in constant contact, gladly listen and themselves talk any and every day. They know that the rich in democracies always need the poor and that good manners will draw them to them more than benefits conferred. For benefits by their very greatness spotlight the difference in conditions and arouse a secret annoyance in those who profit from them. But the charm of simple good manners is almost irresistible. Their affability carries men away, and even their vulgarity is not always unpleasant.

The rich do not immediately appreciate this truth. They generally stand out against it as long as a democratic revolution is in progress and do not admit it at once even after the revolution is accomplished. They will gladly do good to the people, but they still want carefully to keep their distance from them. They think that that is enough, but they are wrong. They could ruin themselves in that fashion without warming their neighbors' hearts. What is wanted is not the sacrifice of their money but of their pride.

It would seem as if in the United States every man's power of invention was on the stretch to find new ways of increasing the wealth and satisfying the needs of the public. The best brains in every neighborhood are constantly employed in searching for new secrets to increase the general prosperity, and any that they find are at once at the service of the crowd.

If one takes a close look at the weaknesses and vices of many of those who bear sway in America, one is surprised at the growing prosperity of the people, but it is a mistake to be surprised. It is certainly not the elected magistrate who makes the American democracy prosper, but the fact that the magistrates are elected.

It would not be fair to assume that American patriotism and the universal zeal for the common good have no solid basis. Though private interest, in the United States as elsewhere, is the driving force behind most of men's actions, it does not regulate them all.

I have often seen Americans make really great sacrifices for the common good, and I have noticed a hundred cases in which, when help was needed, they hardly ever failed to give each other trusty support.

The free institutions of the United States and the political rights enjoyed there provide a thousand continual reminders to every citizen that he lives in society. At every moment they bring his mind back to this idea, that it is the duty as well as the interest of men to be useful to their fellows. Having no particular reason to hate others, since he is neither their slave nor their master, the American's heart easily inclines toward benevolence. At first it is of necessity that men attend to the public interest, afterward by choice. What had been calculation becomes instinct. By dint of working for the good of his fellow citizens, he in the end acquires a habit and taste for serving them.

There are many men in France who regard equality of conditions as the first of evils and political liberty as the second. When forced to submit to the former, they strive at least to escape the latter. But for my part, I maintain that there is only one effective remedy against the evils which equality may cause, and that is political liberty.

Chapter 5

ON THE USE WHICH THE AMERICANS MAKE OF ASSOCIATIONS IN CIVIL LIFE

I DO NOT PROPOSE TO SPEAK OF THOSE political associations by means of which men seek to defend themselves against the despotic action of the majority or the encroachments of royal power. I have treated that subject elsewhere. It is clear that unless each citizen learned to combine with his fellows to preserve his freedom at a time when he individually is becoming weaker and so less able in isolation to defend it, tyranny would be bound to increase with equality. But here I am only concerned with those associations in civil life which have no political object.

In the United States, political associations are only one small part of the immense number of different types of associations found there.

Americans of all ages, all stations in life, and all types of disposition are forever forming associations. There are not only commercial and industrial associations in which all take part, but others of a thousand different types—religious, moral, serious, futile, very general and very limited, immensely large and very minute. Americans combine to give fêtes, found seminaries, build churches, distribute books, and send missionaries to the antipodes. Hospitals, prisons, and schools take shape in that way. Finally, if they want to proclaim a truth or propagate some feeling by the encouragement of a great example, they form an association. In every case, at the head of any new undertaking, where in France you would find the government or in England some territorial magnate, in the United States you are sure to find an association.

I have come across several types of association in America of which, I confess, I had not previously the slightest conception, and I have often admired the extreme skill they show in proposing a common object for the exertions of very many and in inducing them voluntarily to pursue it.

Since that time I have traveled in England, a country from which the Americans took some of their laws and many of their customs, but it seemed to me that the principle of association was not used nearly so constantly or so adroitly there.[1]

A single Englishman will often carry through some great undertaking, whereas Americans form associations for no matter how small a matter. Clearly the former regard association as a powerful means of action, but the latter seem to think of it as the only one.

Thus the most democratic country in the world now is that in which men have in our time carried to the highest perfection the art of pursuing in common the objects of common desires and have applied this new technique to the greatest number of purposes. Is that just an accident, or is there really some necessary connection between associations and equality?

In aristocratic societies, while there is a multitude of individuals who can do nothing on their own, there is also a small number of very rich and powerful men, each of whom can carry out great undertakings on his own.

In aristocratic societies men have no need to unite for action, since they are held firmly together.

Every rich and powerful citizen is in practice the head of a permanent and enforced association composed of all those whom he makes help in the execution of his designs.

But among democratic peoples all the citizens are independent and weak. They can do hardly anything for themselves, and none of them is in a position to force his fellows to help him. They would all therefore find themselves helpless if they did not learn to help each other voluntarily.

If the inhabitants of democratic countries had neither the right nor the taste for uniting for political objects, their independence would run great risks, but they could keep both their wealth and their knowledge for a long time. But if they did not learn some habits of acting together in the affairs of daily life, civilization itself would be in peril. A people in which individuals had lost the power of carrying through great enterprises by themselves, without acquir-

[1] [Cf. Alexis de Tocqueville, *Journeys to England and Ireland,* edited by J. P. Mayer, New Haven, Conn.: Yale, 1958.]

ing the faculty of doing them together, would soon fall back into barbarism.

Unhappily, the same social conditions that render associations so necessary to democratic nations also make their formation more difficult there than elsewhere.

When several aristocrats want to form an association, they can easily do so. As each of them carries great weight in society, a very small number of associates may be enough. So, being few, it is easy to get to know and understand one another and agree on rules.

But that is not so easy in democratic nations, where, if the association is to have any power, the associates must be very numerous.

I know that many of my contemporaries are not the least embarrassed by this difficulty. They claim that as the citizens become weaker and more helpless, the government must become proportionately more skillful and active, so that society should do what is no longer possible for individuals. They think that answers the whole problem, but I think they are mistaken.

A government could take the place of some of the largest associations in America, and some particular states of the Union have already attempted that. But what political power could ever carry on the vast multitude of lesser undertakings which associations daily enable American citizens to control?

It is easy to see the time coming in which men will be less and less able to produce, by each alone, the commonest bare necessities of life. The tasks of government must therefore perpetually increase, and its efforts to cope with them must spread its net ever wider. The more government takes the place of associations, the more will individuals lose the idea of forming associations and need the government to come to their help. That is a vicious circle of cause and effect. Must the public administration cope with every industrial undertaking beyond the competence of one individual citizen? And if ultimately, as a result of the minute subdivision of landed property, the land itself is so infinitely parceled out that it can only be cultivated by associations of laborers, must the head of the government leave the helm of state to guide the plow?

The morals and intelligence of a democratic people would be in as much danger as its commerce and industry if ever a government wholly usurped the place of private associations.

Feelings and ideas are renewed, the heart enlarged, and the understanding developed only by the reciprocal action of men one upon another.

I have shown how these influences are reduced almost to nothing in democratic countries; they must therefore be artificially created, and only associations can do that.

When aristocrats adopt a new idea or conceive a new sentiment, they lend it something of the conspicuous station they themselves occupy, and so the mass is bound to take notice of them, and they easily influence the minds and hearts of all around.

In democratic countries only the governing power is naturally in a position so to act, but it is easy to see that its action is always inadequate and often dangerous.

A government, by itself, is equally incapable of refreshing the circulation of feelings and ideas among a great people, as it is of controlling every industrial undertaking. Once it leaves the sphere of politics to launch out on this new track, it will, even without intending this, exercise an intolerable tyranny. For a government can only dictate precise rules. It imposes the sentiments and ideas which it favors, and it is never easy to tell the difference between its advice and its commands.

Things will be even worse if the government supposes that its real interest is to prevent the circulation of ideas. It will then stand motionless and let the weight of its deliberate somnolence lie heavy on all.

It is therefore necessary that it should not act alone.

Among democratic peoples associations must take the place of the powerful private persons whom equality of conditions has eliminated.

As soon as several Americans have conceived a sentiment or an idea that they want to produce before the world, they seek each other out, and when found, they unite. Thenceforth they are no longer isolated individuals, but a power conspicuous from the distance whose actions serve as an example; when it speaks, men listen.

The first time that I heard in America that one hundred thousand men had publicly promised never to drink alcoholic liquor, I thought it more of a joke than a serious matter and for the moment did not see why these very abstemious citizens could not content themselves with drinking water by their own firesides.

In the end I came to understand that these hundred thousand Americans, frightened by the progress of drunkenness around them, wanted to support sobriety by their patronage. They were acting in just the same way as some great territorial magnate who dresses very plainly to encourage a contempt of luxury among simple citizens. One may fancy that if they had lived in France each of these hundred thousand would have made individual representations to the government asking it to supervise all the public houses throughout the realm.

Nothing, in my view, more deserves attention than the intellectual and moral associations in America. American political and industrial associations easily catch our eyes, but the others tend not to be noticed. And even if we do notice them we tend to misunderstand them, hardly ever having seen anything similar before. However, we should recognize that the latter are as necessary as the former to the American people; perhaps more so.

In democratic countries knowledge of how to combine is the mother of all other forms of knowledge; on its progress depends that of all the others.

Among laws controlling human societies there is one more precise and clearer, it seems to me, than all the others. If men are to remain civilized or to become civilized, the art of association must develop and improve among them at the same speed as equality of conditions spreads.

Chapter 6

ON THE CONNECTION BETWEEN ASSOCIATIONS AND NEWSPAPERS

WHEN NO FIRM AND LASTING TIES any longer unite men, it is impossible to obtain the cooperation of any great number of them unless you can persuade every man whose help is required that he serves his private interests by voluntarily uniting his efforts to those of all the others.

That cannot be done habitually and conveniently without the help of a newspaper. Only a newspaper can put the same thought at the same time before a thousand readers.

A newspaper is an adviser that need not be sought out, but comes of its own accord and talks to you briefly every day about the commonweal without distracting you from your private affairs.

So the more equal men become and more individualism becomes a menace, the more necessary are newspapers. We should underrate their importance if we thought they just guaranteed liberty; they maintain civilization.

I am far from denying that newspapers in democratic countries lead citizens to do very ill-considered things in common; but without newspapers there would be hardly any common action at all. So they mend many more ills than they cause.

A newspaper is not only able to suggest a common plan to many men; it provides them with the means of carrying out in common the plans that they have thought of for themselves.

The leading citizens living in an aristocratic country can see each other from afar, and if they want to unite their forces they go to meet one another, bringing a crowd in their train.

But in democratic countries it often happens that a great many men who both want and need to get together cannot do so, for all being very small and lost in the crowd, they do not see one another at all and do not know where to find one another. Then a newspaper gives publicity to the feeling or idea that had occurred to them all simultaneously but separately. They all at once aim toward that light, and these wandering spirits, long seeking each other in the dark, at last meet and unite.

The newspaper brought them together and continues to be necessary to hold them together.

In a democracy an association cannot be powerful unless it is numerous. Those composing it must therefore be spread over a wide area, and each of them is anchored to the place in which he lives by the modesty of his fortune and a crowd of small necessary cares. They need some means of talking every day without seeing one another and of acting together without meeting. So hardly any democratic association can carry on without a newspaper.

There is therefore a necessary connection between associations and newspapers. Newspapers make associations, and associations make newspapers; and if it were true to say that associations must multiply as quickly as conditions become equal, it is equally certain that the number of papers increases in proportion as associations multiply.

Thus, of all countries on earth, it is in America that one finds both the most associations and the most newspapers.

This connection between the multiplicity of newspapers and associations leads on to the discovery of another relation between the state of the ephemeral press and the form of administration of the country. We find that the number of newspapers among a democratic people must diminish or increase according to the greater or lesser centralization of the administration. For in democracies it is not possible to entrust the exercise of local powers to the leading citizens as is done in aristocracies. Either such powers must be abolished or be placed in the hands of a very large number of men. The latter form a true association permanently established by law to administer a part of the country, and they feel the need for a newspaper which will reach them daily in the midst of their petty business and keep them informed about the state of public affairs. The more numerous these local authorities are, the greater the number of people legally required to exercise these powers, and so, the need for them being felt continually, the more profusely do newspapers abound.

The extraordinary subdivision of administrative power has much more to do with the enormous number of American newspapers than has the great political freedom of the country and the absolute independence of the press. If all the inhabitants of the Union were electors, but the suffrage only involved the choice of members of Congress, they would only need a few newspapers, for the occasions on which they had to act together, though important, would be very rare. But within the great association which is the nation, the law has established in each province, each city, and, one may almost say, each village little associations responsible for local administration. The legislature has thus compelled each American to cooperate every day of his life with some of his fellow citizens for a common purpose, and each one of them needs a newspaper to tell him what the others are doing.

I think that a democratic people[1] without any national representative assembly but with a great number of small local powers would in the end have more newspapers than would another people governed by a centralized administration and an elected legislature. I find the best explanation for the prodigious growth of the daily press in the United States in the fact that there the greatest national freedom is combined with all manner of local liberties.

It is generally believed in France and in England that to abolish the taxes weighing down the press would be enough to increase the number of newspapers indefinitely. That greatly exaggerates the effect of such a reform. Newspapers do not multiply simply because they are cheap, but according to the more or less frequent need felt by a great number of people to communicate with one another and to act together.

I should also attribute the increasing influence of the daily press to causes more general than those by which it is commonly explained.

A newspaper can only survive if it gives publicity to feelings or principles common to a large number of men. A newspaper therefore

[1] I say a "democratic people". The administration might be very much decentralized in an aristocracy without the need for newspapers being felt, since in that case the local powers are in the hands of a very small number of men who either act on their own or know one another and can easily meet and come to an understanding.

always represents an association whose members are its regular readers.

This association may be more or less strictly defined, more or less closed, more or less numerous, but there must at least be the seed of it in men's minds, for otherwise the paper would not survive.

That leads me to the final reflection with which I will end this chapter.

As equality spreads and men individually become less strong, they ever increasingly let themselves glide with the stream of the crowd and find it hard to maintain alone an opinion abandoned by the rest.

The newspaper represents the association; one might say that it speaks to each of its readers in the name of all the rest, and the feebler they are individually, the easier it is to sweep them along.

The power of newspapers must therefore grow as equality spreads.

Chapter 7

RELATIONSHIPS BETWEEN CIVIL AND POLITICAL ASSOCIATIONS

THERE IS ONE COUNTRY in the world which, day in, day out, makes use of an unlimited freedom of political association. And the citizens of this same nation, alone in the world, have thought of using the right of association continually in civil life, and by this means have come to enjoy all the advantages which civilization can offer.

In all countries where political associations are forbidden, civil associations are rare.

It is hardly likely that this is due to accident, and it is wiser to conclude that there must be some natural, perhaps inevitable connection between the two types of association.

Men chance to have a common interest in a certain matter. It may be a trading enterprise to direct or an industrial undertaking to bring to fruition; those concerned meet and combine; little by little in this way they get used to the idea of association.

The more there are of these little business concerns in common, the more do men, without conscious effort, acquire a capacity to pursue great aims in common.

Thus civil associations pave the way for political ones, but on the other hand, the art of political association singularly develops and improves this technique for civil purpose.

In civil life each man can, at a stretch, imagine that he is in a position to look after himself. In politics he could never fancy that. So when a people has a political life, the idea of associations and eagerness to form them are part of everybody's everyday life. Whatever natural distaste men may have for working in common, they are always ready to do so for the sake of a party.

In this way politics spread a general habit and taste for association. A whole crowd of people who might otherwise have lived on their own are taught both to want to combine and how to do so.

Politics not only brings many associations into being, it also creates extensive ones.

The common interests of civil life seldom naturally induce great numbers to act together. A great deal of artifice is required to produce such a result.

But in politics opportunities for this are continually offering themselves of their own accord. Moreover, it is only large associations which make the general value of this method plain. Individually weak citizens form no clear conception in advance of the power they might gain by combining; to understand that, they must be shown it. Hence it is often easier to get a multitude to work together than just a few people; where one thousand do not see the advantage in combining, ten thousand do see it. In politics men combine for great ends, and the advantages gained in important matters give them a practical lesson in the value of helping one another even in lesser affairs.

A political association draws a lot of people at the same time out of their own circle; however much differences in age, intelligence, or wealth may naturally keep them apart, it brings them together and puts them in contact. Once they have met, they always know how to meet again.

One cannot take part in most civil associations without risking some of one's property; this is the case with all manufacturing and trading companies. Men who have as yet little skill in the technique of association and do not understand the main rules thereof are afraid, the first time they combine in this way, that they may pay dearly for their experience. They may therefore prefer not to use a powerful means toward success because of the risks involved. But they have less hesitation in joining political associations, which do not strike them as dangerous because they do not risk losing their money. But they cannot belong to such associations for long without discovering how to maintain order among large numbers and what procedures enable men to advance in methodical agreement toward a common aim. They thus learn to submit their own will to that of all the rest and to make their own exertions subordinate to the common action, all things which are as necessary to know, whether the association be political or civil.

So one may think of political associations as great free schools to which all citizens come to be taught the general theory of association.

But even if political association did not directly contribute to the progress of civil association, to destroy the former would harm the latter.

When citizens can only combine for certain purposes, they regard association as a strange and unusual procedure and hardly consider the possibility thereof.

When they are allowed to combine freely for all purposes, they come in the end to think of association as the universal, one might almost say the only, means by which men can attain their various aims. Every new want at once revives that idea. Thus, as I have said before, the technique of association becomes the mother of every other technique; everyone studies and applies it.

When some types of association are forbidden and others allowed, it is hard to tell in advance the difference between the former and the latter. Being in doubt, people steer clear of them altogether, and in some vague way public opinion tends to consider any association whatsoever as a rash and almost illicit enterprise.[1]

It is therefore a delusion to suppose that the spirit of association, if suppressed in one place, will nevertheless display the same vigor in all other directions, and that if only men are allowed to prosecute

[1] This is more especially true when the executive power has the responsibility for allowing or forbidding associations by its arbitrary prerogative.

When the law forbids certain associations and leaves the courts to punish those who disobey, the ill is much less; in that case every citizen knows beforehand more or less how things stand; in a sense he can judge the matter for himself before it gets to the courts, and keeping clear of those forbidden, joins those permitted. All free peoples have always understood that limits may thus be set to the right of association. But if the legislature should entrust a man with the power of deciding beforehand which associations are dangerous and which are useful, and left him free either to destroy any and every association in the bud or to let it grow, because no one would be able to see beforehand in what cases associations would be permitted and in what other cases it was best to avoid them, the movement toward association would be completely paralyzed. Laws of the former type are directed only against certain associations; those of the latter type are directed against society itself and inflict damage on it. I can conceive that a just government might have recourse to the former, but I do not admit the right of any government to introduce the latter.

certain undertakings in common, that is enough to ensure that they will eagerly do so. When citizens have the faculty and habit of associating for everything, they will freely associate for little purposes as well as great. But if they are only allowed to associate for trivial purposes, they will have neither the will nor the power to do so. To leave them entire liberty to combine in matters of trade will be in vain; they will hardly feel the slightest interest in using the rights granted; and having exhausted your strength in keeping them from forbidden associations, you will be surprised to find that you cannot persuade them to form those that are allowed.

I do not assert that there can be no civil associations in a country in which political associations are forbidden, for men cannot live in society without undertaking some things in common. But I maintain that in such a country civil associations will always be few, feebly conceived, and unskillfully managed and either will never form any vast designs or will fail in the execution of them.

This naturally leads me to think that freedom of political association is not nearly as dangerous to public peace as is supposed and that it could happen that it might give stability to a state which for some time it had shaken.

In democratic countries political associations are, if one may put it so, the only powerful people who aspire to rule the state. Hence the governments of today look upon associations of this type much as medieval kings regarded the great vassals of the Crown; they feel a sort of instinctive abhorrence toward them and combat them whenever they meet.

But they bear a natural goodwill toward civil associations because they easily see that they, far from directing public attention to public affairs, serve to turn men's minds away therefrom, and getting them more and more occupied with projects for which public tranquillity is essential, discourage thoughts of revolution. But they do not take the point that the multiplication of political associations is an immense help for civil associations and that in avoiding one dangerous ill they deprive themselves of an efficacious remedy. When you see the Americans every day freely combining to make some political opinion triumph, to get some politician into the government, or to snatch power from another, it is hard to conceive that men of such independence will not often fall into the abuse of license.

But if, on the other hand, you come to think of the infinite number of industrial undertakings which are run in partnership in the United States, if you notice how on every side the Americans are working without relaxation on important and difficult designs which would be thrown into confusion by the slightest revolution, you will easily understand why these people who are so well occupied have no temptation to disturb the state or to upset the public calm by which they profit.

It is enough to see things separately, or should we discover the hidden link connecting them? It is through political associations that Americans of every station, outlook, and age day by day acquire a general taste for association and get familiar with the way to use the same. Through them large numbers see, speak, listen, and stimulate each other to carry out all sorts of undertakings in common. Then they carry these conceptions with them into the affairs of civil life and put them to a thousand uses.

In this way, by the enjoyment of a dangerous liberty, the Americans learn the art of rendering the dangers of freedom less formidable.

By picking on one moment in the history of a nation it is easy to prove that political associations disturb the state and paralyze industry. But if you take the life of a people as one complete whole it may prove easy to show that freedom of political association favors the welfare and even the tranquillity of the citizens.

I said in the first part of this book: "Unlimited freedom of association should not be confused with freedom to write; the one is both less necessary and more dangerous than the other. A country can set limits there without ceasing to be its own master; it must sometimes do so in order to continue to control its fate." And later on I added: "One must understand that unlimited political freedom of association is of all forms of liberty the last which a people can sustain. If it does not topple them over into anarchy, it brings them continually to the brink thereof."

For these reasons I certainly do not think that a nation is always in a position to allow its citizens an absolute right of political association, and I even doubt whether there has ever been at any time a nation in which it was wise not to put any limits to the freedom of association.

One hears it said that such and such a nation could not maintain internal peace, inspire respect for its laws, or establish a stable government if it did not set strict limits to the right of association. These are undoubtedly great benefits, and one can understand why, to gain or keep them, a nation may agree for a time to impose galling restrictions on itself; but still a nation should know what price it pays for these blessings.

To save a man's life, I can understand cutting off his arm. But I don't want anyone to tell me that he will be as dexterous without it.

Chapter 8

HOW THE AMERICANS COMBAT INDIVIDUALISM BY THE DOCTRINE OF SELF-INTEREST PROPERLY UNDERSTOOD

WHEN THE WORLD WAS UNDER the control of a few rich and powerful men, they liked to entertain a sublime conception of the duties of man. It gratified them to make out that it is a glorious thing to forget oneself and that one should do good without self-interest, as God himself does. That was the official doctrine of morality at that time.

I doubt whether men were better in times of aristocracy than at other times, but certainly they talked continually about the beauties of virtue. Only in secret did they study its utility. But since imagination has been taking less lofty flights, and every man's thoughts are centered on himself, moralists take fright at this idea of sacrifice and no longer venture to suggest it for consideration. So they are reduced to inquiring whether it is not to the individual advantage of each to work for the good of all, and when they have found one of those points where private advantage does meet and coincide with the general interest, they eagerly call attention thereto. Thus what was an isolated observation becomes a general doctrine, and in the end one comes to believe that one sees that by serving his fellows man serves himself and that doing good is to his private advantage.

I have already shown elsewhere in several places in this book how the inhabitants of the United States almost always know how to combine their own advantage with that of their fellow citizens. What I want to point out now is the general theory which helps them to this result.

In the United States there is hardly any talk of the beauty of virtue. But they maintain that virtue is useful and prove it every day. American moralists do not pretend that one must sacrifice himself for his fellows because it is a fine thing to do so. But they boldly assert that such sacrifice is as necessary for the man who makes it as for the beneficiaries.

They have seen that in their time and place the forces driving man in on himself are irresistible, and despairing of holding such forces back, they only consider how to control them.

They therefore do not raise objections to men pursuing their interests, but they do all they can to prove that it is in each man's interest to be good.

I do not want to follow their arguments in detail here, as that would lead too far from my subject. It is enough for my purpose to note that they have convinced their fellow citizens.

Montaigne said long ago: "If I did not follow the straight road for the sake of its straightness, I should follow it having found by experience that, all things considered, it is the happiest and the most convenient."[1]

So the doctrine of self-interest properly understood is not new, but it is among the Americans of our time that it has come to be universally accepted. It has become popular. One finds it at the root of all actions. It is interwoven in all they say. You hear it as much from the poor as from the rich.

The version of this doctrine current in Europe is much grosser but at the same time less widespread and, especially, less advertised. Every day men profess a zeal they no longer feel.

The Americans, on the other hand, enjoy explaining almost every act of their lives on the principle of self-interest properly understood. It gives them pleasure to point out how an enlightened self-love continually leads them to help one another and disposes them freely to give part of their time and wealth for the good of the state. I think that in this they often do themselves less than justice, for sometimes in the United States, as elsewhere, one sees people carried away by the disinterested, spontaneous impulses natural to man. But the Americans are hardly prepared to admit that they do give way to emotions of this sort. They prefer to give the credit to their philosophy rather than to themselves.

I might drop the argument at this point without attempting to pass judgment on what I have described. The extreme difficulty of the subject would be my excuse. But I do not want to plead that. I would rather that my readers, seeing clearly what I mean, refuse to agree with me than that I should leave them in suspense.

Self-interest properly understood is not at all a sublime doctrine, but it is clear and definite. It does not attempt to reach great aims, but it does, without too much trouble, achieve all it sets out to do. Being within the scope of everybody's understanding, everyone grasps it and has no trouble in bearing it in mind. It is wonderfully

[1] [Cf. Montaigne, *Essais*, Pléiade edition, p. 268; Tocqueville appears to paraphrase the first sentence of Chapter XLIV.]

agreeable to human weaknesses, and so easily wins great sway. It has no difficulty in keeping its power, for it turns private interest against itself and uses the same goad which excites them to direct passions.

The doctrine of self-interest properly understood does not inspire great sacrifices, but every day it prompts some small ones; by itself it cannot make a man virtuous, but its discipline shapes a lot of orderly, temperate, moderate, careful, and self-controlled citizens. If it does not lead the will directly to virtue, it establishes habits which unconsciously turn it that way.

If the doctrine of self-interest properly understood ever came to dominate all thought about morality, no doubt extraordinary virtues would be rarer. But I think that gross depravity would also be less common. Such teaching may stop some men from rising far above the common level of humanity, but many of those who fall below this standard grasp it and are restrained by it. Some individuals it lowers, but mankind it raises.

I am not afraid to say that the doctrine of self-interest properly understood appears to me the best suited of all philosophical theories to the wants of men in our time and that I see it as their strongest remaining guarantee against themselves. Contemporary moralists therefore should give most of their attention to it. Though they may well think it incomplete, they must nonetheless adopt it as necessary.

I do not think, by and large, that there is more egoism among us than in America; the only difference is that there it is enlightened, while here it is not. Every American has the sense to sacrifice some of his private interests to save the rest. We want to keep, and often lose, the lot.

I see around nothing but people bent publicly on proving, by word and deed, that what is useful is never wrong. Is there no chance of finding some who will make the public understand that what is right may be useful?

No power on earth can prevent increasing equality from turning men's minds to look for the useful or disposing each citizen to get wrapped up in himself.

One must therefore expect that private interest will more than ever become the chief if not the only driving force behind all behavior. But we have yet to see how each man will interpret his private interest.

If citizens, attaining equality, were to remain ignorant and coarse, it would be difficult to foresee any limit to the stupid excesses into which their selfishness might lead them, and no one could foretell into what shameful troubles they might plunge themselves for fear of sacrificing some of their own well-being for the prosperity of their fellow men.

I do not think that the doctrine of self-interest as preached in America is in all respects self-evident. But it does contain many truths so clear that for men to see them it is enough to educate them. Hence it is all-important for them to be educated, for the age of blind sacrifice and instinctive virtues is already long past, and I see a time approaching in which freedom, public peace, and social stability will not be able to last without education.

Chapter 9

HOW THE AMERICANS APPLY THE DOCTRINE OF SELF-INTEREST PROPERLY UNDERSTOOD TO RELIGION

IF THE DOCTRINE OF self-interest properly understood were concerned with this world only, that would not be nearly enough. For there are a great many sacrifices which can only be rewarded in the next. However hard one may try to prove that virtue is useful, it will always be difficult to make a man live well if he will not face death.

One therefore wants to know whether this doctrine can easily be reconciled with religious beliefs.

The philosophers who teach this doctrine tell men that to be happy in life they must watch their passions and be careful to restrain their excesses, that lasting happiness cannot be won except at the cost of a thousand ephemeral pleasures, and finally, that one must continually master oneself in order to serve oneself better.

The founders of almost all religions have used very much the same language. The way they point out to man is the same; only the goal is farther off; instead of putting in this world the reward for the sacrifices demanded, they transpose it to the next.

Nevertheless, I refuse to believe that all who practice virtue from religious motives do so only in hope of reward.

I have known zealous Christians who constantly forgot themselves to labor more ardently for the happiness of others, and I have heard them claim that they did this only for the sake of rewards in the next world. But I cannot get it out of my head that they were deceiving themselves. I respect them too much to believe them.

Christianity does, it is true, teach that we must prefer others to ourselves in order to gain heaven. But Christianity also teaches that we must do good to our fellows for love of God. That is a sublime utterance; man's mind filled with understanding of God's thought; he sees that order is God's plan, in freedom labors for this great design, ever sacrificing his private interests for this wondrous ordering of all that is, and expecting no other reward than the joy of contemplating it.

Hence I do not think that interest is the only driving force behind men of religion. But I do think that interest is the chief means used by religions themselves to guide men, and I have no doubt that that is how they work on the crowd and become popular.

I do not therefore see any plain reason why the doctrine of self-interest properly understood should drive men away from religious beliefs, but rather do I see how to unravel the ways in which it brings them close thereto.

Let us start from the assumption that in order to gain happiness in this world a man resists all his instinctive impulses and deliberately calculates every action of his life, that instead of yielding blindly to the first onrush of his passions he has learned the art of fighting them, and that he habitually and effortlessly sacrifices the pleasure of the moment for the lasting interests of his whole life.

If such a man believes in the religion that he professes, it will hardly cost him anything to submit to such restrictions as it imposes. Reason itself advises him to do so, and habits already formed make it easy.

Even if he does feel some doubt about the object of his hopes, he will not easily let that hold him back, and he will think it wise to risk some of the good things of this world to save his claims to the immense inheritance promised in the next.

"If we make a mistake by thinking the Christian religion true," Pascal has said, "we have no great thing to lose. But if we make a mistake by thinking it false, how dreadful is our case."[1]

The Americans affect no vulgar indifference to a future state, nor do they affect a childish pride in despising perils from which they hope to escape.

They practice their religion therefore without shame and without weakness. But in the very midst of their zeal one generally sees

[1] [Tocqueville quotes Pascal's *Pensées* rather freely. Cf. Brunschvicg's edition, Fragment 233.]

something so quiet, so methodical, so calculated that it would seem that the head rather than the heart leads them to the foot of the altar.

Not only do the Americans practice their religion out of self-interest, but they often even place in this world the interest which they have in practicing it. Priests in the Middle Ages spoke of nothing but the other life; they hardly took any trouble to prove that a sincere Christian might be happy here below.

But preachers in America are continually coming down to earth. Indeed they find it difficult to take their eyes off it. The better to touch their hearers, they are forever pointing out how religious beliefs favor freedom and public order, and it is often difficult to be sure when listening to them whether the main object of religion is to procure eternal felicity in the next world or prosperity in this.

Chapter 10

THE TASTE FOR PHYSICAL COMFORT IN AMERICA

IN AMERICA THE TASTE for physical well-being is not always exclusive, but it is general; and though all do not feel it in the same manner, yet it is felt by all. Everyone is preoccupied caring for the slightest needs of the body and the trivial conveniences of life.

Something of the same sort is more and more conspicuous in Europe.

Among the causes responsible for these similar results in the New and Old Worlds there are some so germane to my subject that they should be mentioned.

When wealth is fixed by heredity in the same families, one finds many people in the enjoyment of the comforts of life without their developing an exclusive taste for them.

That which most vividly stirs the human heart is certainly not the quiet possession of something precious but rather the imperfectly satisfied desire to have it and the continual fear of losing it again.

The rich in aristocratic societies, having never experienced a lot different from their own, have no fear of changing it; they can hardly imagine anything different. The comforts of life are by no means the aim of their existence; they are just a way of living. They take them as part of existence and enjoy them without thinking about them.

The universal, natural, and instinctive human taste for comfort being thus satisfied without trouble or anxiety, their faculties turn elsewhere and become involved in some grander and more difficult undertaking that inspires and engrosses them.

That is why aristocrats often show a haughty contempt for the physical comforts they are actually enjoying and show singular powers of endurance when ultimately deprived of them. Every revolution which has shaken or overthrown an aristocracy has proved how easily people accustomed to superfluity can manage without necessities, whereas those who have laboriously attained comfort can hardly survive when they have lost it.

Turning from the upper classes to the lower, I can discern analogous effects from different causes.

In nations where an aristocracy dominates society, the people finally get used to their poverty just as the rich do to their opulence. The latter are not preoccupied with physical comfort, enjoying it without trouble; the former do not think about it at all because they despair of getting it and because they do not know enough about it to want it.

In societies of that sort the poor are driven to dwell in imagination on the next world; it is closed in by the wretchedness of the actual world but escapes therefrom and seeks for joys beyond.

But when distinctions of rank are blurred and privileges abolished, when patrimonies are divided up and education and freedom spread, the poor conceive an eager desire to acquire comfort, and the rich think of the danger of losing it. A lot of middling fortunes are established. Their owners have enough physical enjoyments to get a taste for them, but not enough to content them. They never win them without effort or indulge in them without anxiety.

They are therefore continually engaged in pursuing or striving to retain these precious, incomplete, and fugitive delights.

If one tries to think what passion is most natural to men both stimulated and hemmed in by the obscurity of their birth and the mediocrity of their fortune, nothing seems to suit them better than the taste for comfort. The passion for physical comfort is essentially a middle-class affair; it grows and spreads with that class and becomes preponderant with it. Thence it works upward into the higher ranks of society and thence spreads downward to the people.

In America I never met a citizen too poor to cast a glance of hope and envy toward the pleasures of the rich or whose imagination did not snatch in anticipation good things that fate obstinately refused to him.

On the other hand, I never found among the wealthy Americans that lofty disdain for physical comfort which can sometimes be seen among even the most opulent and dissolute aristocracies.

Most of these rich men were once poor; they had felt the spur of need; they had long striven against hostile fate, and now that they had won their victory, the passions that accompanied the struggle survived. They seemed drunk on the petty delights it had taken forty years to gain.

Not but that in the United States, as elsewhere, there are a fairly large number of rich men who, having inherited their property, effortlessly possess a wealth they have not gained. But even these people appear to be no less attached to the delights of the material world. Love of comfort has become the dominant national taste. The main current of human passions running in that direction sweeps everything along with it.

Chapter 11

PARTICULAR EFFECTS OF THE LOVE OF PHYSICAL PLEASURES IN DEMOCRATIC TIMES

IT MIGHT BE SUPPOSED, from what has just been said, that the love of physical pleasures would continually lead the Americans into moral irregularities, disturb the peace of families, and finally threaten the stability of society itself.

But it does not happen like that. The passion for physical pleasures produces in democracies effects very different from those it occasions in aristocratic societies.

It sometimes happens that boredom with public affairs, excess of wealth, decay of belief, and national decadence little by little seduce an aristocracy to pursue nothing but sensual delights. At other times the power of a prince or the weakness of a people, without depriving the nobility of their wealth, forces them to avoid positions of power, and shutting the road to great undertakings, leaves them abandoned to restless desires. Then with heavy hearts they fall back on their own resources and seek in sensual joys oblivion of their former greatness.

When the members of an aristocratic society thus turn exclusively to sensual pleasures they usually force into that one direction all the energy accumulated by long experience of power.

Just to seek comfort is not enough for such men. What they require is sumptuous depravity and startling corruption. They worship material things magnificently and seem eager to excel in the art of besotting themselves.

The stronger, more glorious, and free an aristocracy once was, the more depraved will it appear, and whatever may have been the splendor of its virtues, I dare predict that its vices will always be more startling.

But love of physical pleasures never leads democratic peoples to such excesses. Among them love of comfort appears as a tenacious, exclusive, and universal passion, but always a restrained one. There is no question of building vast palaces, of conquering or excelling nature, or sucking the world dry to satisfy one man's greed. It is more a question of adding a few acres to one's fields, planting an orchard, enlarging a house, making life ever easier and more comfortable, keeping irritations away, and satisfying one's slightest needs without trouble and almost without expense. These are petty aims, but the soul cleaves to them; it dwells on them every day and in great detail; in the end they shut out the rest of the world and sometimes come between the soul and God.

This, it may be said, can only apply to men of middling fortune; the rich will display tastes akin to those which flourished in aristocratic periods. I contest that suggestion.

Where physical pleasures are concerned, the opulent citizens of a democracy do not display tastes very different from those of the people, either because, themselves originating from the people, they really do share them or because they think they ought to accept their standards. In democratic societies public sensuality has adopted a moderate and tranquil shape to which all are expected to conform. It is as hard for vices as for virtues to slip through the net of common standards.

Wealthy men living in democracies therefore think more of satisfying their slightest needs than seeking extraordinary delights. They indulge a quantity of little wants but do not let themselves give rein to any great disorderly passion. They are more prone to become enervated than debauched.

So in democracies the taste for physical pleasures takes special forms which are not opposed by their nature to good order; indeed they often require good order for their satisfaction. Nor is it hostile to moral regularity, for sound morals are good for public tranquillity and encourage industry. It may even, not infrequently, combine with a type of religious morality; people want to do as well as possible in this world without giving up their chances in the next.

Some physical delights cannot be indulged without crime; from these they abstain strictly. There are others allowed by religion and morality; the heart, imagination, and life itself are given up to these without reserve, until, snatching at these, men lose sight of those more precious goods which constitute the greatness and the glory of mankind.

I do not reproach equality for leading men astray with forbidden delights, but I do complain that it absorbs them in the quest of those permitted completely.

By such means a kind of decent materialism may come to be established on earth, which will not corrupt souls but soften and imperceptibly loosen the springs of action.

Chapter 12

WHY SOME AMERICANS DISPLAY ENTHUSIASTIC FORMS OF SPIRITUALITY

ALTHOUGH THE DESIRE TO acquire the good things of this world is the dominant passion among Americans, there are momentary respites when their souls seem suddenly to break the restraining bonds of matter and rush impetuously heavenward.

In every state of the Union, but especially in the half-peopled lands of the West, there are preachers hawking the word of God from place to place.

Whole families, old men, women, and children, cross difficult country and make their way through untamed forests to come great distances to hear them. When they do arrive and listen to them, for several days and several nights they neglect to look after their affairs and even forget the most pressing needs of the body.

Here and there throughout American society you meet men filled with an enthusiastic, almost fierce spirituality such as cannot be found in Europe. From time to time strange sects arise which strive to open extraordinary roads to eternal happiness. Forms of religious madness are very common there.

We should not be surprised at this.

It was not man who implanted in himself the taste for the infinite and love of what is immortal. These sublime instincts are not the offspring of some caprice of the will; their foundations are embedded in nature; they exist despite a man's efforts. Man may hinder and distort them, but he cannot destroy them.

The soul has needs which must be satisfied. Whatever pains are taken to distract it from itself, it soon grows bored, restless, and anxious amid the pleasures of the senses.

If ever the thoughts of the great majority of mankind came to be concentrated solely on the search for material blessings, one can anticipate that there would be a colossal reaction in the souls of men. They would distractedly launch out into the world of spirits for fear of being held too tightly bound by the body's fetters.

It is therefore no cause for astonishment that in a society thinking about nothing but the world a few individuals should want to look at nothing but heaven. I should be surprised if, among a people uniquely preoccupied with prosperity, mysticism did not soon make progress.

It is said that the emperors' persecutions and the massacres in the amphitheaters peopled the deserts of the Thebaid; I should rather hold Roman luxury and Greek Epicureanism responsible.

If their social condition, circumstances, and laws did not so closely confine the American mind to the search for physical comfort, it may well be that when they came to consider immaterial things they would show more experience and reserve and be able to keep themselves in check without difficulty. But they feel imprisoned within limits from which they are apparently not allowed to escape. Once they have broken through these limits, their minds do not know where to settle down, and they often rush without stopping far beyond the bounds of common sense.

Chapter 13

WHY THE AMERICANS ARE OFTEN SO RESTLESS IN THE MIDST OF THEIR PROSPERITY

IN CERTAIN REMOTE corners of the Old World you may sometimes stumble upon little places which seem to have been forgotten among the general tumult and which have stayed still while all around them moves. The inhabitants are mostly very ignorant and very poor; they take no part in affairs of government, and often governments oppress them. But yet they seem serene and often have a jovial disposition.

In America I have seen the freest and best educated of men in circumstances the happiest to be found in the world; yet it seemed to me that a cloud habitually hung on their brow, and they seemed serious and almost sad even in their pleasures.

The chief reason for this is that the former do not give a moment's thought to the ills they endure, whereas the latter never stop thinking of the good things they have not got.

It is odd to watch with what feverish ardor the Americans pursue prosperity and how they are ever tormented by the shadowy suspicion that they may not have chosen the shortest route to get it.

Americans cleave to the things of this world as if assured that they will never die, and yet are in such a rush to snatch any that come within their reach, as if expecting to stop living before they have relished them. They clutch everything but hold nothing fast, and so lose grip as they hurry after some new delight.

An American will build a house in which to pass his old age and sell it before the roof is on; he will plant a garden and rent it just as the trees are coming into bearing; he will clear a field and leave others to reap the harvest; he will take up a profession and leave it, settle in one place and soon go off elsewhere with his changing desires. If his private business allows him a moment's relaxation, he will plunge at once into the whirlpool of politics. Then, if at the end of a year crammed with work he has a little spare leisure, his restless curiosity goes with him traveling up and down the vast territories of the United States. Thus he will travel five hundred miles in a few days as a distraction from his happiness.

Death steps in in the end and stops him before he has grown tired of this futile pursuit of that complete felicity which always escapes him.

At first sight there is something astonishing in this spectacle of so many lucky men restless in the midst of abundance. But it is a spectacle as old as the world; all that is new is to see a whole people performing in it.

The taste for physical pleasures must be regarded as the first cause of this secret restlessness betrayed by the actions of the Americans, and of the inconstancy of which they give daily examples.

A man who has set his heart on nothing but the good things of this world is always in a hurry, for he has only a limited time in which to find them, get them, and enjoy them. Remembrance of the shortness of life continually goads him on. Apart from the goods he has, he thinks of a thousand others which death will prevent him from tasting if he does not hurry. This thought fills him with distress, fear, and regret and keeps his mind continually in agitation, so that he is always changing his plans and his abode.

Add to this taste for prosperity a social state in which neither law nor custom holds anyone in one place, and that is a great further stimulus to this restlessness of temper. One will then find people continually changing path for fear of missing the shortest cut leading to happiness.

It is, however, easy to understand that although those whose passions are bent on physical pleasures are eager in their desires, they are also easily discouraged. For as their ultimate object is enjoyment, the means to it must be prompt and easy, for otherwise the trouble of getting the pleasure would be greater than the pleasure when won. Hence the prevailing temper is at the same time ardent and soft, violent and enervated. Men are often less afraid of death than of enduring effort toward one goal.

Equality leads by a still shorter path to the various effects I have just described.

When all prerogatives of birth and fortune are abolished, when all professions are open to all and a man's own energies may bring him to the top of any of them, an ambitious man may think it easy to launch on a great career and feel that he is called to no common destiny. But that is a delusion which experience quickly corrects. The same equality which allows each man to entertain vast hopes makes each man by himself weak. His power is limited on every side, though his longings may wander where they will.

Not only are men powerless by themselves, but at every step they find immense obstacles which they had not at first noticed.

They have abolished the troublesome privileges of some of their fellows, but they come up against the competition of all. The barrier has changed shape rather than place. When men are more or less equal and are following the same path, it is very difficult for any of them to walk faster and get out beyond the uniform crowd surrounding and hemming them in.

This constant strife between the desires inspired by equality and the means it supplies to satisfy them harasses and wearies the mind.

One can imagine men who have found a degree of liberty completely satisfactory to them. In that case they will enjoy their independence without anxiety or excitement. But men will never establish an equality which will content them.

No matter how a people strives for it, all the conditions of life can never be perfectly equal. Even if, by misfortune, such an absolute dead level were attained, there would still be inequalities of intelligence which, coming directly from God, will ever escape the laws of man.

No matter, therefore, how democratic the social condition and political constitution of a people may be, one can be sure that each and every citizen will be aware of dominating positions near him, and it is a safe guess that he will always be looking doggedly just in that direction. When inequality is the general rule in society, the greatest inequalities attract no attention. When everything is more or less level, the slightest variation is noticed. Hence the more equal men are, the more insatiable will be their longing for equality.

Among democratic peoples men easily obtain a certain equality, but they will never get the sort of equality they long for. That is a quality which ever retreats before them without getting quite out of sight, and as it retreats it beckons them on to pursue. Every instant they think they will catch it, and each time it slips through their fingers. They see it close enough to know its charms, but they do not get near enough to enjoy it, and they will be dead before they have fully relished its delights.

That is the reason for the strange melancholy often haunting inhabitants of democracies in the midst of abundance, and of that disgust with life sometimes gripping them in calm and easy circumstances.

In France we are worried about the increasing rate of suicides; in America suicide is rare, but I am told that madness is commoner than anywhere else.

Those are different symptoms of the same malady.

The Americans do not kill themselves, however distressed they may be, because their religion forbids them to do so and because materialist philosophy is practically unknown to them, although the passion for prosperity is general.

Their will resists, but reason frequently gives way.

In democratic times enjoyments are more lively than in times of aristocracy, and more especially, immeasurably greater numbers taste them. But, on the other hand, one must admit that hopes and desires are much more often disappointed, minds are more anxious and on edge, and trouble is felt more keenly.

Chapter 14

HOW IN AMERICA THE TASTE FOR PHYSICAL PLEASURES IS COMBINED WITH LOVE OF FREEDOM AND ATTENTION TO PUBLIC AFFAIRS

WHEN A DEMOCRATIC state turns to absolute monarchy, the activity formerly directed toward public and private affairs is suddenly all concentrated on the latter. The result, for a limited time, is great material prosperity, but soon the impetus slackens and the growth of production stops.

I doubt if one can cite a single example of any people engaged in both manufacture and trade, from the men of Tyre to the Florentines and the English, who were not a free people. There must therefore be a close link and necessary relationship between these two things, that is, freedom and industry.

That is true in general about all nations, but especially about democratic ones.

I have already pointed out how men living in ages of equality continually need to form associations in order to get the things they long for, and have also shown how great political freedom improves and spreads the technique of association. Thus freedom in such ages is particularly favorable to the production of wealth. One can see too that despotism is particularly hostile thereto.

It is in the nature of absolute power in democratic ages not to be savage or cruel, but meddlesome in detail. Despotism of that type, though it does not trample men under foot, is directly opposed to the trading spirit and instincts of industry.

Men in democratic times always need to be free in order easily to provide themselves with the physical pleasures for which they ever hanker.

Nevertheless, it sometimes happens that their excessive taste for these same pleasures hands them over to the first master who offers himself. Greed for prosperity then turns against itself and unconsciously drives away the very thing it wants.

Indeed there is a very dangerous phase in the life of democratic peoples.

When the taste for physical pleasures has grown more rapidly than either education or experience of free institutions, the time comes when men are carried away and lose control of themselves at sight of the new good things they are ready to snatch. Intent only on getting rich, they do not notice the close connection between private fortunes and general prosperity. There is no need to drag their rights away from citizens of this type; they themselves voluntarily let them go. They find it a tiresome inconvenience to exercise political rights which distract them from industry. When required to elect representatives, to support authority by personal service, or to discuss public business together, they find they have no time. They cannot waste their precious time in unrewarding work. Such things are all right for idlers to play at, but they do not become men of weight occupied with the serious business of life. Such folk think they are following the doctrine of self-interest, but they have a very crude idea thereof, and the better to guard their interests, they neglect the chief of them, that is, to remain their own masters.

As those who work are unwilling to attend to public affairs, and the class which might have wished thus to fill its leisure no longer exists, the role of government is left unfilled.

If, at this critical moment, an able and ambitious man once gets power, he finds the way open for usurpations of every sort.

So long as he sees to it for a certain time that material interests flourish, he can easily get away with everything else. He must above all guarantee good order. People passionately bent on physical pleasures usually observe how agitation in favor of liberty threatens prosperity before they appreciate how liberty helps to procure the same. When the slightest rumor of public passions disturbs the trivial pleasures of their private lives, they wake up and feel worried. The fear of anarchy long haunts them, and they are always ready to jettison liberty in the slightest storm.

I freely agree that public tranquillity is a very good thing. Nevertheless, I do not want to forget that it is through good order that all peoples have reached tyranny. That is certainly no reason for nations to despise public peace, but they should not be satisfied with that alone. A nation which asks nothing from the government beyond the maintenance of order is already a slave in the bottom of its heart. It is a slave to its prosperity, and the road is free for the man to tie the fetters.

The despotism of a faction is as much to be feared as that of a man.

When the great mass of citizens does not want to bother about anything but private business, even the smallest party need not give up hope of becoming master of public affairs.

In such cases one often sees in the vast theater of the world a spectacle familiar on the stage, when a few actors represent a crowd. These few alone speak in the name of an absent or inattentive crowd; they alone are on the move while others rest; their caprice controls everything, changing laws and tyrannizing over moral standards; and one is left in astonishment at the small number of weak and unworthy hands into which a great people can fall.

Up to now the Americans have happily avoided all the reefs I have just charted, and one really must admire them for that.

There is perhaps no country in the world with fewer men of leisure than America, nor one in which all those who work are so keen on making themselves prosperous. But violent though the American passion for physical satisfactions may be, it is at least not blind, and reason, unable to restrain it, does direct it.

An American will attend to his private interests as if he were alone in the world; the moment afterward, he will be deep in public business as if he had forgotten his own. Sometimes he seems to be animated by the most selfish greed and sometimes by the most lively patriotism. But a human heart cannot really be divided in this way. Americans alternately display passions so strong and so similar first for their own welfare and then for liberty that one must suppose these urges to be united and mingled in some part of their being. Americans in fact do regard their freedom as the best tool of and the firmest guarantee for their prosperity. They love them both for the sake of each other. They are therefore by no means inclined to suppose that it is no business of theirs to meddle in public affairs. On the contrary, they think it their most important concern to secure a government which will allow them to get the good things they want and which will not stop their enjoying those they have in peace.

Chapter 15

HOW RELIGIOUS BELIEFS AT TIMES TURN THE THOUGHTS OF AMERICANS TOWARD SPIRITUAL THINGS

IN THE UNITED STATES, when the seventh day comes, trade and industry seem suspended throughout the nation. All noise stops. A deep repose, or rather solemn contemplation, takes its place. At last the soul comes into its own and meditates upon itself.

On this day places of business are deserted; every citizen, accompanied by his children, goes to a church; there he listens to strange language apparently hardly suited to his ear. He is told of the countless evils brought on by pride and covetousness. He is reminded of the need to check his desires and told of the finer delights which go with virtue alone, and the true happiness they bring.

When he gets home he does not hurry to his business ledgers. He opens the book of Holy Scripture and there finds sublime and touching accounts of the greatness and goodness of the Creator, of the infinite magnificence of the works of God, of the high destiny reserved for men, of their duties and of their claims to immortality.

Thus it is that the American in some degree from time to time escapes from himself, and for a moment free from the petty passions that trouble his life and the passing interests that fill it, he suddenly breaks into an ideal world where all is great, pure, and eternal.

Elsewhere in this book I have pointed to the causes helping to maintain American political insitutions, among which religion seemed one of the most important. Now, when speaking of individuals, religion again comes into the picture, and I think that it is just as much help to each man on his own as it is to the state.

By their practice Americans show that they feel the urgent necessity to instill morality into democracy by means of religion. What they think of themselves in this respect enshrines a truth which should penetrate deep into the consciousness of every democratic nation.

I have no doubt that the social and political structure of a nation predisposes people in favor of certain tastes and beliefs which then flourish carefree; and the same reason, without deliberate striving and indeed almost unconsciously, keeps other opinions and inclinations out of mind.

The essence of the lawgiver's art is by anticipation to appreciate these natural bents of human societies in order to know where the citizens' efforts need support and where there is more need to hold them back. For different times make different demands. The goal alone is fixed, to which humanity should press forward; the means of getting there ever change.

If I had been born in an aristocratic age, when both the hereditary wealth of some and the irremediable poverty of others diverted men from the thought of bettering their lot and held them in a state of torpor, fixed on the contemplation of another world, I should be glad to wake such a people to a sense of its needs; I should want to find the quickest and easiest means of satisfying these newly awakened longings and directing the best efforts of the best brains into physical studies; I should try to send them hunting for prosperity.

Should it happen that some people got too keen on the pursuit of riches and were altogether too enamored of physical delights, I should not be worried at all. Such particular characteristics would be soon lost in the general picture.

Legislators for democracies have other cares.

If you give democratic peoples education and freedom and leave them alone, they will easily extract from this world all the good things it has to offer. They will improve all useful techniques and make life daily more comfortable, smooth, and bland. Since their social condition by its nature urges them this way, there is no need to fear that they will stop.

But while man takes delight in this proper and legitimate quest for prosperity, there is a danger that in the end he may lose the use of his sublimest faculties and that, bent on improving everything around him, he may at length degrade himself. That, and nothing else, is the peril.

In a democracy therefore it is ever the duty of lawgivers and of all upright educated men to raise up the souls of their fellow citizens and turn their attention toward heaven. There is a need for all who are interested in the future of democratic societies to get together and with one accord to make continual efforts to propagate throughout society a taste for the infinite, an appreciation of greatness, and a love of spiritual pleasures.

When some of those pernicious theories are found in the intellectual climate of a democratic people which tend to suggest that everything perishes with the body, the men who profess them must be regarded as the natural enemies of the people.

There are many things that offend me about the materialists. I think their doctrines pernicious, and their pride revolts me. By giving man a modest conception of himself, it might seem that their system could be useful to him. But they give no reason to suppose that this is so; rather, when they think they have sufficiently established that they are no better than brutes, they seem as proud as if they had proved that they were gods.

In all nations materialism is a dangerous malady of the human spirit, but one must be particularly on guard against it among a democratic people, because it combines most marvelously well with that vice which is most familiar to the heart in such circumstances.

Democracy favors the taste for physical pleasures. This taste, if it becomes excessive, soon disposes men to believe that nothing but matter exists. Materialism, in its turn, spurs them on to such delights with mad impetuosity. Such is the vicious circle into which democratic nations are driven. It is good that they see the danger and hold back.

Most religions are only general, simple, and practical means of teaching men that the soul is immortal. That is the greatest advantage which a democratic people derives from beliefs, and it is that which make beliefs more necessary for them than for all others.

Thus, then, when any religion has taken deep root in a democracy, be very careful not to shake it, but rather guard it as the most precious heritage from aristocratic times. Do not try to detach men from their old religious opinions in order to establish new ones for fear lest in the passage from one belief to another the soul may for a moment be found empty of faith and love of physical pleasures come and spread and fill it all.

Certainly the doctrine of metempsychosis is not more reasonable than that of materialism, but if it were absolutely necessary for a democracy to make the choice between one or the other, I should not hesitate, and should think the citizens ran less danger of reducing themselves to the level of brutes by thinking that their soul would pass into a pig's body than by believing that it is nothing.

Belief in an immaterial and immortal principle, for a time united to matter, is so indispensable to man's greatness that it has fine effects even when it is not united to a conception of rewards and punishments and when one believes no more than that after death the divine principle embodied in man is absorbed in God or goes to animate some other creature.

Even such beliefs make men consider the body as the secondary and inferior part of our nature, and they will despise it even while they fall under its influence. Whereas they will have a natural regard and secret admiration for the immaterial part of man, even though they sometimes refuse to submit to its sway. That is enough to give a somewhat elevated tone to their ideas and tastes and make them turn, without selfishness and as if of their own accord, to pure feelings and majestic thoughts.

It is not certain that Socrates and his school had any very precise ideas about what should become of man in the future life. But the one belief of which they were sure, that the soul had nothing in common with the body and would survive it, was enough to give Platonic philosophy the sublime impetus which distinguishes it.

In reading Plato it is clear that many writers before him and in his own day had anticipated the doctrine of materialism. Such writers have not survived till our day, or are known only from fragments. The same is true of almost all other centuries. Most great literary reputations are based on spirituality. The instinct and taste of mankind support this doctrine and often preserve it in spite of men themselves, keeping the names of its defenders safe above the tide of time. So one must not suppose that at any time, no matter what the political conditions are, the passion for physical pleasures and the conceptions that go therewith can ever satisfy a whole people. The heart of man embraces much more than we suppose; it can at the same time contain a taste for the good things of this world and love of heavenly things; at times it seems madly intent on one of the two, but it is never long before it thinks of the other.

It is easy to see that it is particularly important in democratic times to make spiritual conceptions prevail, but it is far from easy to say what those who govern democratic peoples should do to make them prevail.

I have no belief in the virtue or the durability of official philosophies, and when it comes to state religions, I have always thought that, though they may perhaps sometimes momentarily serve the interests of political power, they are always sooner or later fatal for the church.

Nor am I one of those who think that to exalt religion in the eyes of the people and to do honor to the spirituality of religious teaching, it is good to give its ministers indirectly a political influence which the laws refuse.

I am so deeply convinced of the almost inevitable dangers which face beliefs when their interpreters take part in public affairs, and so firmly persuaded that at all costs Christianity must be maintained

among the new democracies that I would rather shut priests up
within their sanctuaries than allow them to leave them.

What means are then left to the authorities to lead men back
toward spiritual opinions or to hold them within the religion thereby
suggested?

What I am going to say will certainly do me harm in the eyes of
politicians. I think that the only effective means which governments
can use to make the doctrine of the immortality of the soul respected
is daily to act as if they believed it themselves. I think that it is
only by conforming scrupulously to religious morality in great affairs
that they can flatter themselves that they are teaching the citizens
to understand it and to love and respect it in little matters.

Chapter 16

HOW EXCESSIVE LOVE OF PROSPERITY
CAN DO HARM TO IT

THERE IS A CLOSER connection than is supposed between the soul's
improvement and the betterment of physical conditions. A man
can treat the two things as distinct and pay attention to each in
turn. But he cannot entirely separate them without in the end
losing sight of both.

Animals have the same senses as ourselves and much the same
appetites. There are no physical passions which are not possessed
in common with them and of which the seed is not found in a dog as
much as in ourselves.

Why is it, then, that animals only know how to satisfy their
primary and coarsest needs, whereas we can infinitely vary and
continually increase our delights?

That which makes us better than the brutes in this is that we employ our souls to find those material benefits to which instinct alone
directs them. In man an angel teaches a brute how to satisfy its desires. It is because man is able to raise himself above the things of
the body and even to scorn life itself, a matter of which the beasts
have not the least notion, that he can multiply these same good
things of the body to a degree of which they have no conception.

Whatever elevates, enlarges, and expands the soul makes it more able to succeed even in those undertakings which are not the soul's concern.

On the other hand, whatever enervates and lowers it weakens it for every purpose, the least as well as the greatest, and threatens to make it almost equally impotent in both. Therefore the soul must remain great and strong, if only that it may from time to time put its strength and greatness at the service of the body.

If men ever came to be content with physical things only, it seems likely that they would gradually lose the art of producing them and would end up by enjoying them without discernment and without improvement, like animals.

Chapter 17

WHY IN AGES OF EQUALITY AND SKEPTICISM IT IS IMPORTANT TO SET DISTANT GOALS FOR HUMAN ENDEAVOR

IN AGES OF FAITH the final aim of life is placed beyond life.

The men of those ages therefore naturally and almost involuntarily grow accustomed to fix their eyes for years together on some static object toward which their progress is ever directed, and they learn by imperceptible degrees to repress a crowd of petty passing desires in order ultimately best to satisfy the one great permanent longing which obsesses them. When these same men engage in worldly affairs, such habits influence their conduct. They gladly fix some general and definite aim as the object of their actions here below and direct all their efforts toward it. They do not shift from day to day, chasing some new object of desire, but have settled designs which they never tire of pursuing.

That is why religious nations have often accomplished such lasting achievements. For in thinking of the other world, they had found out the great secret of success in this.

Religions instill a general habit of behaving with the future in view. In this respect they work as much in favor of happiness in this world as of felicity in the next. That is one of their most salient political characteristics.

But as the light of faith grows dim, man's range of vision grows more circumscribed, and it would seem as if the object of human endeavors came daily closer.

When once they have grown accustomed not to think about what will happen after their life, they easily fall back into a complete and brutish indifference about the future, an attitude all too well suited to certain propensities of human nature. As soon as they have lost the way of relying chiefly on distant hopes, they are naturally led to want to satisfy their least desires at once; and it would seem that as soon as they despair of living forever, they are inclined to act as if they could not live for more than a day.

In skeptical ages, therefore, there is always a danger that men will give way to ephemeral and casual desires and that, wholly renouncing whatever cannot be acquired without protracted effort, they may never achieve anything great or calm or lasting.

If, with a people so disposed, social conditions become democratic, this danger is increased.

When everyone is constantly striving to change his position, when an immense field of competition is open to all, when wealth is amassed or dissipated in the shortest possible space of time in the turmoil of democracy, men think in terms of sudden and easy fortunes, of great possessions easily won and lost, and chance in every shape and form. Social instability favors the natural instability of desires. Amid all these perpetual fluctuations of fate the present looms large and hides the future, so that men do not want to think beyond tomorrow.

In such a country where unhappily skepticism and democracy exist together, philosophers and the men in power should always strive to set a distant aim as the object of human efforts; that is their most important business.

The moralist must learn to defend his position, adapting himself to his age and country. He must constantly endeavor to show his contemporaries that even in the midst of all the turmoil around them it is easier than they suppose to plan and execute long-term projects. He must make them see that although the aspect of humanity has changed, the means by which men can obtain prosperity in this world are still the same and that, in democracies as elsewhere, it is only by resisting a thousand daily petty urges that the fundamental anxious longing for happiness can be satisfied.

The duty of rulers is equally clear.

It is at all times important that the rulers of nations should act with the future in view. But this is even more necessary in ages of democracy and skepticism than in any others. By giving such a lead, the chief men in democracies not only bring prosperity in public affairs but also teach individuals by their example to conduct their private affairs properly.

They must especially strive to banish chance, as much as possible, from the world of politics.

The sudden and undeserved promotion of a courtier in an aristocratic country causes no more than an ephemeral impression, because the whole complex of institutions and beliefs forces men to progress slowly along paths they cannot leave.

But such events give the worst possible example to a democratic people, for they urge it on down in the direction whither all its emotions are anyhow leading. So it is chiefly in times of skepticism and equality that particular precautions are required to prevent the favor of prince or people, which comes and goes at random, from taking the place due to merit or duties performed. One must hope that all promotion will be seen as the reward of effort, so that no high position should be too easily acquired and men of ambition should be obliged to plan well ahead before they reach their goal.

Governments must study means to give men back that interest in the future which neither religion nor social conditions any longer inspire, and without specifically saying so, give daily practical examples to the citizens proving that wealth, renown, and power are the rewards of work, that great success comes when it has been long desired, and that nothing of lasting value is achieved without trouble.

Once men have become accustomed to foresee from afar what is likely to befall them in this world and to feed upon hopes, they can hardly keep their thoughts always confined within the precise limits of this life and will always be ready to break out through these limits and consider what is beyond.

I have therefore no doubt that, in accustoming the citizens to think of the future in this world, they will gradually be led without noticing it themselves toward religious beliefs.

Thus the same means that, up to a certain point, enable men to manage without religion are perhaps after all the only means we still possess for bringing mankind back, by a long and roundabout path, to a state of faith.

Chapter 18

WHY AMERICANS CONSIDER ALL
HONEST CALLINGS HONORABLE

AMONG DEMOCRATIC peoples where there is no hereditary wealth, every man works for his living, or has worked, or comes from parents who have worked. Everything therefore prompts the assumption that to work is the necessary, natural, and honest condition of all men.

Not only is no dishonor associated with work, but among such peoples it is regarded as positively honorable; the prejudice is for, not against, it. A wealthy American feels he owes it to public opinion to devote his leisure to some public duties. He would expect his reputation to suffer if he just spent his life in living. It is to escape this obligation to work that so many rich Americans come to Europe; there they find the relics of aristocratic societies in which leisure is still honorable.

Equality makes not only work itself, but work specifically to gain money, honorable.

In aristocracies it is not exactly work itself which is despised, but work with an eye to profit. Work is glorious when inspired by ambition or pure virtue. However, under an aristocracy it constantly happens that he who works for honor is not insensible to greed for gain. But these two desires only meet in the depths of his soul. He is very careful to hide the place where they meet from prying eyes. He will gladly hide it from himself too. In aristocratic countries there are hardly any public officials who do not claim to serve the state without interested motives. Their salary is a detail to which sometimes they give little thought and to which they always pretend to give none.

Thus the notion of profit remains distinct from that of work. The two may go together in fact, but tradition denies that.

But in democratic societies the two notions are always visibly united. As the desire for prosperity is universal, fortunes are middling and ephemeral, and everyone needs to increase his resources or create fresh ones for his children, all see quite clearly that it is profit which, if not wholly then at least partially, prompts them to work. Even those whose chief motive for action is love of fame cannot help knowing that that is not their only reason, and they realize that, whoever they are, they do want to live, as well as to make their lives worthy.

As soon as these two assumptions are made, that work is an honorable necessity of the human state and that it is always clearly done, at least in part, for pay, the immense difference separating different professions in aristocratic societies disappears. If they are not all just the same, at least they have one characteristic in common.

There is no profession at which a man works except for pay. This payment, enjoyed by all, gives them all a family resemblance.

This serves to explain the views of Americans about different callings.

American servants do not feel degraded because they work, for everyone around them is working. There is nothing humiliating about the idea of receiving a salary, for the President of the United States works for a salary. He is paid for giving orders, as they are for obeying them.

In the United States professions are more or less unpleasant, more or less lucrative, but they are never high or low. Every honest profession is honorable.

Chapter 19

WHAT GIVES ALMOST ALL AMERICANS A PREFERENCE FOR INDUSTRIAL CALLINGS

AGRICULTURE is perhaps, of all the useful arts, the one which improves most slowly in democratic nations. One is often inclined to suppose it stationary because some other techniques are improving at such a rate.

But almost all the tastes and habits born of equality naturally lead men in the direction of trade and industry.

Suppose a man to be active, educated, free, comfortably off, and full of desire. He is too poor to live in idleness; he is rich enough not to be in fear of immediate want and is anxious to improve his lot. Our man has formed a taste for physical pleasures; he sees thousands around him enjoying them; he himself has tasted some too, and he is very keen to acquire the means to enjoy them more. But life goes by, and time presses. What is he to do?

To cultivate the ground promises an almost certain reward for his efforts, but a slow one. In that way you only grow rich little by little and with toil. Agriculture only suits the wealthy, who already have a great superfluity, or the poor, who only want to live. His choice is made; he sells his field, moves from his house, and takes up some risky but lucrative profession.

Now, democratic societies are full of people of this type. As equality spreads, their crowd increases.

Democracy therefore not only multiplies the number of workers but also leads men to adopt one type of work rather than another. It gives them a distaste for agriculture and directs them into trade and industry.[1]

This turn of mind is manifest even among the wealthiest citizens.

In democratic countries, no matter how rich a man is, he is almost always dissatisfied with his fortune, because he finds that he is less wealthy than his father was and he is afraid that his son will be less wealthy than he. So most wealthy men in democracies are dreaming of ways to increase their riches, and naturally their eyes turn to trade and industry, for these seem the quickest and best means of getting rich. In this respect they share the poor man's instincts without his necessities, or rather they are driven by the most imperious of all necessities, that of not sinking.

In aristocracies the rich are also the ruling class. Constant attention to great affairs of state diverts them from the petty cares of trade and industry. Should one of them nonetheless feel a natural inclination toward business, corporate public opinion at once bars his path. For however men may declaim against the rule of numbers, they cannot wholly escape it; and even among those aristocratic bodies which most obstinately refuse to recognize the rights of the

[1] It has often been noted that industrialists and merchants have an inordinate taste for physical pleasures, and trade and industry have been held responsible for this. I think that is to mistake the effect for the cause.

It is not trade and industry that give men the taste for physical pleasures, but rather the taste for them which induces men to go into trade and industry, so as to satisfy this taste more completely and quickly.

If trade and industry do increase the desire for prosperity, that is because every passion grows stronger the more attention it gets and is swollen by every effort to satisfy it. Every cause which makes love of the things of this world predominate in the human heart also favors trade and industry. Equality is one of these causes. It favors commerce, not directly, by giving men a taste for trade, but indirectly, by strengthening and spreading in their consciousness a taste for well-being.

national majority, a private majority is formed which governs the rest. (See Appendix I, T.)

In democratic countries where money does not carry its possessor to power, but often rather bars him from it, rich men tend not to know what to do with their leisure. The restlessness and extent of their desires, the greatness of their resources, and that taste for the extraordinary which is almost always felt by men who rise, by whatever means, above the crowd all urge them to action. Trade is the only road open to them. In democracies nothing has brighter luster than commerce; it attracts the attention of the public and fills the imagination of the crowd; all passionate energies are directed that way. There is nothing to stop the rich going in for it, neither their own prejudices nor those of anyone else. The rich in democracies never form a body with its own mores and way of enforcing the same; no opinions peculiar to their class restrain them, and public opinion urges them on. Moreover, the great fortunes found in a democracy are almost always of commercial origin, and so it takes several generations for their possessors entirely to lose habits of business.

Thus, with but a narrow field of political action left to them, the rich men of democracies throw themselves on all sides into commercial undertakings. In that field they can expand and make use of their natural advantages. One can even guess, judging by the very extent and audacity of their industrial undertakings, what a contemptuous view they would have held of industry if they had been born members of an aristocracy.

The following observation applies to everyone in a democracy, rich or poor.

Chance is an element always present to the mind of those who live in the unstable conditions of a democracy, and in the end they come to love enterprises in which chance plays a part.

This draws them to trade not only for the sake of promised gain, but also because they love the emotions it provides.

It is only half a century since the United States has escaped from the position of colonial dependence in which England held it; there are few great fortunes there and capital is still scarce. But no other nation has made as rapid progress in trade and industry as the Americans. Today they are the second maritime nation in the world, and although their manufactures have to struggle against almost insurmountable natural obstacles, they are daily making new advances.

In the United States the greatest industrial undertakings are executed without trouble because the whole population is engaged in industry and because the poorest man as well as the most opulent gladly joins forces therein. One is therefore in daily astonishment at the immense works carried through without difficulty by a nation which, one may say, has no rich men. The Americans arrived but yesterday in the land where they live, and they have already turned the whole order of nature upside down to their profit. They have joined the Hudson to the Mississippi and linked the Atlantic Ocean with the Gulf of Mexico across a continent of more than five hundred leagues separating the two seas. The longest railways yet constructed are in the United States.

But in the United States I am even more struck by the innumerable multitude of little undertakings than by the extraordinary size of some of their industrial enterprises.

Almost all the farmers in the United States have combined some trade with agriculture; most of them have made agriculture itself a trade.

It is unusual for an American farmer to settle forever on the land he occupies; especially in the provinces of the West, fields are cleared to be sold again, not to be cultivated. A farm is built in the anticipation that, since the state of the country will soon be changing with the increase of population, one will be able to sell it for a good price.

Every year a swarm of people arrive from the North in the southern states and settle in the lands where cotton and sugar cane grow. These men cultivate the land in order to make it produce enough to enrich them within a few years, and they already look forward to the day when they will be able to return to their native land to enjoy the comfortable fortune thus acquired. In such fashion the Americans carry over into agriculture the spirit of a trading venture, and their passion for industry is manifest there as elsewhere.

The Americans make great advances in industry because they are all at the same time engaged in it, and for this same reason they are subject to very unexpected and formidable industrial crises.

As they are all engaged in trade, trade is affected by such various and complex causes that it is impossible to foresee what embarrassments may arise. As they are all more or less engaged in industry, at the least shock given to business activity all private fortunes are in jeopardy at the same time and the state is shaken.

I believe that the recurrence of these industrial crises is an endemic disease among all democratic nations in our day. It can be made less dangerous, but not cured, for it is not due to accident but to the essential temperament of these peoples.

Chapter 20

HOW AN ARISTOCRACY MAY
BE CREATED BY INDUSTRY

I HAVE SHOWN how democracy favors the development of industry by multiplying without limit the number of those engaged in it. We shall now see by what roundabout route industry may in turn lead men back to aristocracy.

It is acknowledged that when a workman spends every day on the same detail, the finished article is produced more easily, quickly, and economically.

It is likewise acknowledged that the larger the scale on which an industrial undertaking is conducted with great capital assets and extensive credit, the cheaper will its products be.

People had formed some inkling of these truths long ago, but it is in our day that they have been demonstrated. They have already been applied to several very important industries, and in due turn even the smallest will take advantage of them.

There is nothing in the world of politics that deserves the lawgivers' attention more than these two new axioms of industrial science.

When a workman is constantly and exclusively engaged in making one object, he ends by performing this work with singular dexterity. But at the same time, he loses the general faculty of applying his mind to the way he is working. Every day he becomes more adroit and less industrious, and one may say that in his case the man is degraded as the workman improves.

What is one to expect from a man who has spent twenty years of his life making heads for pins? And how can he employ that mighty human intelligence which has so often stirred the world, except in finding out the best way of making heads for pins?

When a workman has spent a considerable portion of his life in this fashion, his thought is permanently fixed on the object of his daily toil; his body has contracted certain fixed habits which it can never shake off. In a word, he no longer belongs to himself, but to his chosen calling. In vain are all the efforts of law and morality to break down the barriers surrounding such a man and open up a thousand different roads to fortune for him on every side. An industrial theory stronger than morality or law ties him to a trade, and often to a place, which he cannot leave. He has been assigned a certain position in society which he cannot quit. In the midst of universal movement, he is stuck immobile.

As the principle of the division of labor is ever more completely applied, the workman becomes weaker, more limited, and more dependent. The craft improves, the craftsman slips back. On the other hand, as it becomes ever clearer that the products of industry become better and cheaper as factories become vaster and capital greater, very rich and well-educated men come forward to exploit industries which, up to that time, had been left to ignorant and rough artisans. They are attracted by the scale of the efforts required and the importance of the results to be achieved.

Thus, at the same time that industrial science constantly lowers the standing of the working class, it raises that of the masters.

While the workman confines his intelligence more and more to studying one single detail, the master daily embraces a vast field in his vision, and his mind expands as fast as the other's contracts. Soon the latter will need no more than bodily strength without intelligence, while to succeed the former needs science and almost genius. The former becomes more and more like the administrator of a huge empire, and the latter more like a brute.

So there is no resemblance between master and workman, and daily they become more different. There is no connection except that between the first and last links in a long chain. Each occupies a place made for him, from which he does not move. One is in a state of constant, narrow, and necessary dependence on the other and seems to have been born to obey, as the other was to command.

What is this, if not an aristocracy?

As conditions become more and more equal in the body of the nation, the need for manufactured products becomes greater and more general, and the cheapness which brings these things within reach of men of moderate fortune becomes an ever greater element in success.

Thus there is a constant tendency for very rich and well-educated men to devote their wealth and knowledge to manufactures and to seek, by opening large establishments with a strict division of labor, to meet the fresh demands which are made on all sides.

Hence, just while the mass of the nation is turning toward democracy, that particular class which is engaged in industry becomes more aristocratic. Men appear more and more like in the one context and more and more different in the other, and inequality increases within the little society in proportion as it decreases in society at large.

It would thus appear, tracing things back to their source, that a natural impulse is throwing up an aristocracy out of the bosom of democracy.

But that aristocracy is not at all like those that have preceded it.

First, be it noted that because it only flourishes in industry and in some industrial callings, it is an exception, a monstrosity, within the general social condition.

The little aristocratic societies formed by certain industries in the midst of the vast democracy of our day contain, as did the great aristocratic societies of former days, some very opulent men and a multitude of wretchedly poor ones.

These poor men have few means of escaping from their condition and becoming rich, but the rich are constantly becoming poor or retiring from business when they have realized their profits. Hence the elements forming the poor class are more or less fixed, but that is not true of those forming the rich class. To be exact, although there are rich men, a class of the rich does not exist at all, for these rich men have neither corporate spirit nor objects in common, neither common traditions nor hopes. There are limbs, then, but no body.

Not only is there no solidarity among the rich, but one may say that there is no true link between rich and poor.

They are not forever fixed, one close to the other; at any moment interest, which brought them together, can pull them apart. The workman is dependent on masters in general, but not on a particular master. These two men see each other at the factory but do not know each other otherwise, and though there is one point of contact, in all other respects they stand far apart. The industrialist only asks the workman for his work, and the latter only asks him for his pay. The one contracts no obligation to protect, nor the other to defend, and they are not linked in any permanent fashion either by custom or by duty.

A business aristocracy seldom lives among the manufacturing population which it directs; its object is not to rule the latter but to make use of it.

An aristocracy so constituted cannot have a great hold over its employees, and even if it does for a moment hold them, they will soon escape. It does not know its own mind and cannot act.

The territorial aristocracy of past ages was obliged by law, or thought itself obliged by custom, to come to the help of its servants and relieve their distress. But the industrial aristocracy of our day, when it has impoverished and brutalized the men it uses, abandons them in time of crisis to public charity to feed them. This is the natural result of what has been said before. Between workman and master there are frequent relations but no true association.

I think that, generally speaking, the manufacturing aristocracy which we see rising before our eyes is one of the hardest that have appeared on earth. But at the same time, it is one of the most restrained and least dangerous.

In any event, the friends of democracy should keep their eyes anxiously fixed in that direction. For if ever again permanent inequality of conditions and aristocracy make their way into the world, it will have been by that door that they entered.

PART III

Influence of Democracy on Mores Properly So Called

Chapter 1

HOW MORES BECOME MORE GENTLE AS SOCIAL CONDITIONS BECOME MORE EQUAL

WE SEE that for several centuries social conditions have been getting more equal and notice that at the same time mores have become more gentle. Did these two things simply take place at the same time, or is there some secret connection between them, so that the one could not make headway without setting the other moving?

There are several causes which can concur in making a nation's mores less rough, but I think that the most potent of them all is equality of conditions. So equality of conditions and greater gentleness of mores are not, in my view, things happening just by chance at the same time, but correlative facts.

When the writers of fables want to get us interested in the behavior of animals, they attribute human ideas and passions to them. The poets do the same when they speak of spirits and angels. There is no misery so deep, nor happiness so pure, that it can touch our minds and move our hearts, unless we are shown ourselves under a different guise.

This is very relevant to the subject in question.

When all men are irrevocably marshaled in an aristocratic society according to their profession, property, and birth, the members of each class think of themselves as all children of the same family, feeling a constant sense of sympathy for one another, such as can never be found to the same degree among the citizens of a democracy.

But the same feeling toward one another does not exist between the several classes.

Among an aristocratic people each caste has its opinions, feelings, rights, mores, and whole separate existence. Hence its members are not at all like members of all the other castes. They have not at all the same way of thinking or feeling, and they hardly manage to think of themselves as forming part of the same humanity.

Hence they cannot well understand what the others suffer, nor judge them by themselves.

Nevertheless, they are sometimes eager to give each other mutual support, but that does not contradict what I have just said.

These same aristocratic institutions which have caused such differences between beings of the same race have yet linked them by a very tight political connection.

Although the serf had no natural interest in the fate of nobles, he would nonetheless feel obliged to devote himself to the service of the one who happened to be his lord. And though the noble might think himself of different nature from his serfs, he might still feel that duty and honor compelled him to defend those who lived on his land, at the risk of his own life.

It is clear that such obligations do not spring from natural right, but from political rights, and that society obtains what humanity by itself would not win. It was not to the man that one felt bound to render assistance, it was to the vassal or to the lord. Feudal institutions made people very sensible to the sufferings of certain men but not at all to the miseries of the human race. They inspired generosity in mores rather than gentleness, and though they prompted spectacular acts of devotion, they did not arouse real sympathies. For real sympathy can only exist between people of like sort, and in aristocratic ages only members of the same caste were thought of in that way.

When the chroniclers of the Middle Ages, who were all by birth or assimilation aristocrats, relate the tragic end of a noble, there is no end to their grief; but they mention all in a breath and without wincing massacres and tortures of the common people.

That is not because these writers entertained a habitual hatred or systematic contempt for the common people. War between the different classes in the state had not yet been declared. They obeyed an instinct rather than a passion; as they did not form a clear idea of the sufferings of the poor, they took but a feeble interest in their fate.

The same is true of the common people when the feudal link was broken. The same ages which witnessed so many acts of heroic devotion on the part of vassals for their lords saw unheard-of cruelties from time to time practiced by the lower classes on the upper.

It should not be supposed that this mutual insensibility was solely due to lack of public order and education, for one finds the trace of it in the following centuries, which, for all their good order and education, remained aristocratic.

In the year 1675 the lower classes in Brittany broke into revolt because of a new tax. These disturbances were put down with

unexampled severity. This is how Madame de Sévigné, a witness of
these horrors, tells her daughter about them:

> "Aux Rochers, October 30, 1675

"My word, dear daughter, how amusing your letter from Aix is!
At least read them over again before you send your letters. Let
yourself be surprised by how delightful they are, and console yourself
by that pleasure for the trouble of writing so many. So you have
kissed the whole of Provence? There would be no pleasure in
kissing the whole of Brittany, unless one liked the smell of wine. . . .
Do you want to hear the news from Rennes? A tax of one hundred
thousand crowns has been imposed on the citizens, and if that sum
is not found within twenty-four hours, it will be doubled and
collected by the soldiers. They have chased everyone out and banished
them from a whole main street, and forbidden anyone to receive
them on pain of death; so one saw all these wretched people,
women near their time, old men, and children, wandering in tears
out of the town, not knowing where to go, without food, without
bedding. The day before yesterday they broke on the wheel the
fiddler who had started the dance and the stealing of stamped
paper; he was quartered . . . and his limbs exposed at the four
corners of the town. . . . They have taken sixty townsmen and will
start hanging them tomorrow. This province is a good example
to the others, teaching them especially to respect the governors and
their wives . . . and never to throw stones into their gardens."[1]

". . . Mme. de Tarente was here yesterday in the woods in delightful weather. No question of a room or meal for her. She comes
in by the gate and goes out the same way. . . ."[2]

In another letter she adds:

"You talk very cheerily about our miseries; we are not so broken
on the wheel now; one in a week, to keep justice going; it is true
that hanging now seems quite a treat. I have got quite a new idea
of justice since I have been in this part of the country. Your galley
slaves seem to me a society of worthy folk who have retired from
the world to lead a quiet existence. . . ."[3]

It would be a mistake to suppose that Mme. de Sévigné, who
wrote these lines, was a selfish and barbarous person; she was pas-

[1] To appreciate the reference in this last joke, one must know that Mme.
de Grignan was the wife of the governor of Provence.
[2] [Cf. *Lettres de Madame de Sévigné*, edited by M. Monmerqué, Vol.
IV, p. 205 ff.]
[3] [*Ibid.*, p. 248; the letter is dated November 24.]

sionately fond of her children and showed herself very sensitive of
the sorrows of her friends; and one can even notice, in reading
her letters, that she treated her vassals and servants with kindness
and indulgence. But Mme. de Sévigné could not conceive clearly
what it was like to suffer if one were not of noble birth.

In our day the hardest-hearted man writing to the most im-
perceptive of correspondents would not venture to indulge in the
cruel jokes I have just quoted, for even if his personal morality
allowed him to do so, the general moral standards of the nation
would forbid it.

How does this come about? Have we more sensibility than our
fathers? I do not know, but it is certain that our sensibility embraces more objects.

When ranks are almost equal among a people, as all men think
and feel in nearly the same manner, each instantaneously can judge
the feelings of all the others; he just casts a rapid glance at himself,
and that is enough. So there is no misery that he cannot readily
understand, and a secret instinct tells him its extent. It makes no
difference if strangers or enemies are in question; his imagination
at once puts him in their place. Something of personal feeling is
mingled with his pity, and that makes him suffer himself when
another's body is torn.

In democratic ages men rarely sacrifice themselves for another, but
they show a general compassion for all the human race. One never
sees them inflict pointless suffering, and they are glad to relieve
the sorrows of others when they can do so without much trouble
to themselves. They are not disinterested, but they are gentle.

Although the Americans may be said to have reduced egoism to
a social and philosophic theory, they nonetheless show themselves
just as accessible to pity.

There is no country in which criminal justice is administered
with more kindness than in the United States. While the English
seem bent on carefully preserving in their penal legislation the bloody
traces of the Middle Ages, the Americans have almost eliminated
capital punishment from their codes.

North America is, I think, the only country on earth which has
not taken the life of a single citizen for political offenses during
the last fifty years.

There is a circumstance which conclusively shows that this singular
mildness of the Americans is chiefly due to their social condition,
and that is the way they treat their slaves.

It may be that, generally speaking, there is no European colony
in the New World where the physical conditions of the blacks are
less hard than in the United States. Nevertheless, slaves there suffer

terrible afflictions and are constantly subject to very cruel punishments.

It is easy to see that the lot of these unfortunates inspires very little compassion in their masters and that they look upon slavery not only as an institution profitable to them but also as an ill which scarcely touches them. Thus the same man who is full of humanity toward his fellows when they are also his equals becomes insensible to their sorrows when there is no more equality. It is therefore to this equality that we must attribute his gentleness, even more than to his civilization and education.

What I have just been saying about individuals applies to some extent to peoples too.

When each nation has its own opinions, beliefs, laws, and customs, it looks on itself as composing the whole of humanity and feels touched only by its own sorrows. If war breaks out between peoples of this disposition, it is sure to be conducted with barbarity.

At the time of their highest culture the Romans strangled the generals of their enemies when they had dragged them in triumph behind their chariots, and they delivered prisoners over to wild beasts for the amusement of the people. Cicero, who raised such a storm of complaint about the crucifixion of a Roman citizen, had nothing to say about this atrocious abuse of victory. It is evident that in his eyes a stranger is not of the same type of humanity as a Roman.

But as people become more like one another, they show themselves reciprocally more compassionate, and the law of nations becomes more gentle.

Chapter 2

HOW DEMOCRACY LEADS TO EASE AND SIMPLICITY IN THE ORDINARY RELATIONS BETWEEN AMERICANS

DEMOCRACY DOES NOT CREATE strong attachments between man and man, but it does put their ordinary relations on an easier footing.

Suppose two Englishmen meet by chance at the antipodes and are there surrounded by strangers whose language and manners they hardly understand.

First they will look at each other with great curiosity and a sort of secret anxiety; then they will turn away, or if they do address each other, they will take care to talk with a constrained and absent air about matters of little importance.

But there is no hostility between them; they have never met before, and each believes the other to be a perfectly respectable person. Why, then, do they take such trouble to avoid each other?

One must go back to England to find the reason.

When birth alone, independent of wealth, decides a man's class, each knows exactly where he stands on the social ladder. He neither seeks to rise nor fears to fall. In a society so organized, men of different castes have little communication with one another. But when chance does throw them together, they are ready to converse without hoping or fearing to change status. Their relations are not based on equality, but they are not constrained.

When an aristocracy of wealth takes the place of one of birth, this is no longer the case.

Some men still enjoy great privileges, but the possibility of acquiring them is open to all. From which it follows that those who possess them are constantly preoccupied with the fear of losing or sharing them. And those who have not got them want to get them at all costs, or if they cannot manage that, to seem to have them, something which is not at all impossible. As a man's social worth is not ostensibly and permanently fixed by his birth, but varies infinitely with his wealth, ranks still exist, but it cannot be seen clearly at first sight by whom they are represented.

The immediate result is an unspoken warfare between all the citizens. One side tries by a thousand dodges to infiltrate, in fact or in appearance, among those above them. The others are constantly trying to push back these usurpers of their rights. Or rather the same man plays both parts, and while he tries to insinuate himself into the sphere above him, he fights relentlessly against those working up from below.

Such is the state of England today, and I believe that to be the chief reason for what I have noted above.

Aristocratic pride still being a very strong force with the English, and the boundaries of the aristocracy having become doubtful, each man is constantly afraid lest advantage be taken of his familiarity. Not being able to judge at first sight the social position of the people he meets, he prudently avoids contact with them. He is afraid that some slight service rendered may draw him into an unsuitable friendship. He dreads civilities and is as much anxious to avoid the demonstrative gratitude of a stranger as his hostility.

Many people explain this strange unsociability and reserved and taciturn disposition of the English by purely physical causes. I freely admit that blood may count for something in the matter, but I think that social conditions count for much more. The example of the Americans serves to prove this.

In America, where privileges of birth never existed and where wealth brings its possessor no peculiar right, men unacquainted with one another readily frequent the same places and find neither danger nor advantage in telling each other freely what they think. Meeting by chance, they neither seek nor avoid each other. Their manner is therefore natural, frank, and open. One sees that there is practically nothing that they either hope or fear from each other and that they are not concerned to show or to hide their social position. They may often look cold and serious, but never haughty or constrained, and if they do not say a word to each other, it is because they do not want to talk, not that they think it to their interest to keep quiet.

In a foreign land two Americans are friends at once for the simple reason that they are Americans. There is no prejudice to hold them back, and their common fatherland draws them together. For two Englishmen the same blood is not enough; they must also have the same rank to bring them together.

The Americans notice this unsociable disposition of the English to one another as much as we do, and they are just as surprised by it as we are. Yet the Americans are close to the English in origin, religion, language, and partly also mores. Their social condition is the only difference. It therefore seems fair to assert that English reserve is due much more to the constitution of the country than of the citizens.

Chapter 3

WHY THE AMERICANS ARE SO HARD TO OFFEND IN THEIR OWN COUNTRY AND SO EASILY OFFENDED IN OURS

THE AMERICANS, in common with all serious and thoughtful nations, have a vindictive temperament. They hardly ever forget an offense, but it is not easy to offend them, and their resentment is as slow to kindle as to abate.

In aristocratic societies, in which a few individuals manage everything, the outward intercourse of men is settled by more or less fixed conventions. So everyone has a precise conception of how to show respect or affability, and everyone is assumed to be conversant with the principles of etiquette.

The customs of the highest class in society come to serve as models for all the others, and besides this, each of the others forms a code of its own to which all its members are expected to conform.

Thus rules of politeness form a complicated code which it is difficult to master completely but which nonetheless it is dangerous to contravene. As a result, men are in daily danger of suffering or inflicting unintended cruel wounds.

But as distinctions of rank are obliterated and men of different education and birth mix and mingle in the same places, it is almost impossible to agree upon the rules of good manners. The code being uncertain, to contravene it is no longer a crime in the eyes even of those who do know it. So the substance of behavior comes to count for more than the form, and men grow less polite but also less quarrelsome.

There is a mass of little attentions to which an American attaches no importance; he thinks that they are not his due, or he supposes that people do not know they are due to him. So he either does not notice that he has been slighted or forgives the slight; his formal behavior becomes less courteous but his manners simpler and more manly.

The mutual tolerance of the Americans and the virile confidence with which they treat one another are due to yet another more general and deeper reason.

I have already referred to it in the preceding chapter.

In the United States distinctions of rank are slight in civil society and do not exist at all in the world of politics. An American therefore feels no call to pay particular attention to any of his fellows, nor does he think of expecting anything of that sort himself. Not seeing that he has any interest in eagerly seeking the company of particular fellow citizens, he finds it hard to suppose that his own company is unwelcome. Scorning no man on account of his status, it does not occur to him that anyone scorns him for that reason, and unless the insult is clearly seen, he does not think that anyone wants to offend him.

Social conditions make the Americans slow to take offense in trivial matters, and further, democratic liberty infuses this forbearance into national manners.

The political institutions of the United States put citizens of all classes in constant contact and compel them to carry out great undertakings together. People busy in this way have hardly time to think about the details of etiquette, and they also have too great an interest in living in harmony to stop for that. They therefore easily acquire the habit of considering the feelings and opinions of those whom they meet rather than their formal behavior, and they do not allow themselves to be put out by trifles.

I have often noticed in the United States that it is not at all easy to make a man understand that his presence is unwelcome. To make that point, roundabout methods are by no means always enough.

If I contradict every word an American says to show him that his conversation bores me, he will constantly renew his efforts to convince me. If I remain obstinately silent, he thinks that I am reflecting deeply on the truths he has put to me. If finally I get up abruptly and go, he supposes that I have some urgent business which I have not mentioned. Unless I tell him plainly, the man will not understand that he exasperates me, and I cannot escape from him except by becoming his deadly enemy.

It therefore seems surprising at first sight that this same man, transported to Europe, becomes suddenly so sensitive and touchy that it is as hard now to avoid offending him as it once was to cause offense. Both these very different results are due to the same cause.

Democratic institutions generally give men a grandiose opinion of their country and themselves.

The American leaves his country with a heart swollen with pride. He comes to Europe and at once discovers that we are not nearly so interested as he had supposed in the United States and the great nation that lives there. This begins to annoy him.

He had heard it said that conditions are not equal on our side of the world. He does in fact notice that traces of rank have not been entirely effaced among European nations, that wealth and birth still preserve some uncertain privileges which are as difficult to ignore as to define. He is both surprised and disturbed by all this, it being an entirely new experience to him. Nothing that he has seen in his own country helps him to understand it. He therefore has not the faintest notion what status he ought to enjoy in this half-ruined hierarchy, among classes distinct enough to hate and despise each other but close enough to be always ready to get confused. He is afraid of claiming too high a status and even more afraid of being ranked too low. This double peril is a constant worry and embarrassment to his every act and word.

He knows about the European tradition and is aware that the ceremonials of politeness have infinite variations dependent on rank; he is bothered by this ghost from the past, and his fear of not receiving due attention is increased just because he does not know exactly what that attention should be. So he moves through a land full of traps; social intercourse is no recreation for him, but a serious business. He weighs your slightest move, questions every look, and carefully analyzes every word for fear of some hidden offensive allusion. I doubt if one could find any country nobleman more punctilious than he about every detail of politeness. He is at pains himself to observe every tiny rule of etiquette, and he will not let any neglect to himself pass; he is both extremely scrupulous and very demanding; he wants to do enough but is afraid of doing too much, and not knowing the limit of one or the other, falls back into an embarrassed and haughty reserve.

But that is not the whole story; here is another queer twist of human sensibility.

An American is constantly talking about the wonderful equality prevailing in the United States. As far as his country is concerned, he loudly proclaims his pride in this, but he has a secret anxiety about its bearing on himself, and he likes to show that, in his own case, he is an exception to the rule he has extolled.

One hardly ever meets an American who does not want to claim some connection by birth with the first founders of the colonies, and as for offshoots of great English families, I think America is simply full of them.

When an opulent American lands in Europe, his first care is to surround himself with all the luxuries of wealth, and he is so much afraid that you may take him for the simple citizen of a democracy that he thinks up a hundred roundabout ways of calling fresh attention to his wealth every day. He usually takes up his quarters in the most fashionable part of the town and is always surrounded by his numerous servants.

I have heard an American complain that one met mixed company in the best drawing rooms of Paris. The taste prevailing there did not strike him as sufficiently refined, and he subtly hinted that, in his view, there was a lack of distinction in manners there. He was not used to seeing fine sensibility thus obscured by vulgar behavior.

We should not be astonished at such contrasts.

If the traces of ancient aristocratic distinctions had not been so completely wiped away in America, the Americans would be less simple and tolerant in their own country, less pretentious and affected in ours.

Chapter 4

CONSEQUENCES DERIVING FROM THE THREE PRECEDING CHAPTERS

WHEN MEN FEEL a natural compassion for the sufferings of others, when they are brought together in easy and frequent intercourse and no susceptibilities keep them apart, it is easy to understand that they will give each other mutual support when needed. When an American needs the assistance of his fellows, it is very rare for that to be refused, and I have often seen it given spontaneously and eagerly.

Where there is an accident on the public road, people hurry from all sides to help the victim. When some unexpected disaster strikes a family, a thousand strangers willingly open their purses, and small but very numerous gifts relieve their distress.

It often happens in the most civilized countries of the world that a man in misfortune is almost as isolated in the crowd as a savage in the woods. That is hardly ever seen in the United States. The Americans, always cold in manner and often coarse, are hardly ever insensitive, and though they may be in no hurry to volunteer services, yet they do not refuse them.

All this does not contradict what I have said about individualism. Indeed the two aspects of things agree, and are not at variance.

Equality which makes men feel their freedom also shows them their weakness. They are free, but liable to a thousand accidents, and experience is not slow to teach them that although they may not usually need the help of others, a moment will almost always arrive when they cannot do without it.

It is a matter of daily observation in Europe that men of the same profession gladly help one another; they are all liable to the same ills; that is reason enough for seeking mutual guarantees against them, however hard and selfish they be in other respects.

When, therefore, one of them is in danger and the others can help, either by some slight temporary sacrifice or by a sudden effort, they do not fail to make the attempt. Not that they are profoundly interested in his fate, for if it be chance that their efforts to help are useless, they will forget him at once and return to their own affairs; but there is a sort of tacit and almost unintentional agreement between them which provides that each owes to the other a temporary assistance which he in turn can claim at need.

Take what I have said as applying to one class only as true of a whole nation, and you will grasp my meaning.

There does in fact exist between all the citizens of a democracy an understanding analogous to that which I have described. They all know themselves weak and subject to like dangers, and interest as well as sympathy prompts a code of lending each other mutual assistance at need.

The more similar conditions become, the more do people show this readiness of reciprocal obligation.

In democracies, though no one is presented with great benefits, constant acts of kindness are performed. A self-sacrificing man is rare, but all are obliging.

Chapter 5

HOW DEMOCRACY MODIFIES THE RELATIONS BETWEEN MASTER AND SERVANT

AN AMERICAN who had traveled a lot in Europe once said to me: "We find the haughtiness and imperiousness of the English toward their servants astonishing, but on the other hand, the French sometimes treat them with a friendliness and considerate politeness which we cannot understand. One would think they were afraid of giving orders. The position of superior and inferior is ill-maintained."

The observation is fair and I have often noticed it myself.

In the whole world in our time I have always considered England as the country in which the bonds of domestic service are most tight, and France as that in which they are most relaxed. The extremes of haughtiness and humility on the master's part are found in these two countries.

The Americans come somewhere between these two extremes.

Such are the superficial and apparent facts. One has to go a long way back to find their causes.

There has not yet been a society in which conditions were so equal that there was neither rich nor poor, and consequently neither masters nor servants.

Democracy in no way prevents the existence of these two classes, but it changes their attitudes and modifies their relations.

In aristocracies servants are a class apart, which changes no more than that of the masters. A fixed order is soon created; in both classes there is soon a hierarchy, with numerous classifications and defined ranks, and generation succeeds generation without positions changing. There are two societies imposed one on top of the other, always distinct, but with analogous principles.

This aristocratic constitution has as much influence on the opinions and manners of the servants as on those of the masters, and though the effects are different, one can easily see the same cause at work.

Both classes form little nations within the great one, and in the end certain permanent conceptions of right and wrong are established among them. Some aspects of human behavior come to be seen in a quite particular and unchanging light. Within the community of servants, as in that of masters, men exercise great influence over one another. They recognize fixed rules, and in default of law, come up against a directing public opinion; their ways are settled and controlled.

These men whose destiny is to obey certainly do not understand fame, virtue, honesty, and honor in the same way as their masters. But they have devised fame, virtues, and honesty suited to servants, and they conceive, if I may put it so, a sort of servile honor.[1]

Because a class is low, one must not suppose that all its members are mean-spirited; that would be a great mistake. However inferior the class may be, he who is first within it and has no thought of leaving it has an aristocratic position which prompts high thoughts, strong pride, and self-respect and makes him capable of heroism and actions out of the ordinary.

---

[1] If one makes a close and detailed examination of the chief opinions which guide men, the analogy is even more striking. One is astonished to find among them, as among the most highly placed members of the feudal hierarchy, pride of birth, respect for ancestors and descendants, scorn for inferiors, a fear of contact, and a taste for etiquette, precedents, and antiquity.

In the service of the great lords of an aristocratic society it was not rare to find men of noble and vigorous character who did not feel the servitude they bore and submitted to the will of their masters without fearing their wrath.

It has hardly ever been like that in the lower ranks of domestic servants. It may be imagined that he who occupies the lowest step in a hierarchy of valets is low indeed.

The French invented a word especially to designate this lowest of the servants of an aristocracy. They call him the lackey.

The term "lackey" served, when all other words were exhausted, as the ultimate designation of human meanness. Under the old monarchy, when one wanted a single exprression to denote a vile and degraded creature, one said he had "the soul of a lackey." That alone was enough. The full meaning was understood.

Permanent inequality not only gives servants certain particular virtues and vices but also places them in a particular position as against their masters.

In aristocratic societies the poor are trained from infancy to thoughts of obedience. All around, wherever they look, they see hierarchies of command.

Hence, in countries where permanent inequality prevails, the master easily obtains from his servants an obedience which is prompt, complete, respectful, and easy, because they honor him not only as the master, but as representing the class of masters. He brings the whole weight of the aristocracy to bear on their wills.

He commands their actions and also to some extent directs their thoughts. In aristocracies the master often exercises, even unconsciously, an immense power over the thoughts, habits, and mores of those who obey him, and his influence extends far beyond even his authority.

In aristocratic societies, not only are there hereditary families of valets, as there are of masters, but the same families of valets are settled for generations with the same families of masters (they are parallel lines which never meet and never separate); and that makes prodigious modifications in the mutual relations between the two orders.

Thus, though under an aristocracy there is no natural resemblance between master and servant, though fortune, education, opinion, and rights set them at great distance apart on the ladder of existence, yet time in the end binds them together. Long-shared memories unite them, and however different they be, yet they grow alike. But in democracies, where by nature they are almost alike, they always remain strangers one to the other.

In aristocracies the master comes to think of his servants as an inferior and secondary part of himself, and he often takes an interest in their fate by the extended scope of his selfishness.

The servants, for their part, see themselves in almost the same way, and they sometimes identify themselves so much with the master personally that they become an appendage to him in their own eyes as well as in his.

In aristocracies the servant occupies a subordinate position from which he cannot escape; close to him stands another man with a higher rank which he cannot lose. On the one side, obscurity, poverty, and obedience forever; on the other, fame, wealth, and power to command forever. Their lots are always different and always close, and the link between them is as lasting as life itself.

In this extreme case the servant ends by losing his sense of self-interest; he becomes detached from it; he deserts himself, as it were, or rather he transports the whole of himself into his master's character; he there creates an imaginary personality for himself. He takes pleasure in identifying himself with the wealth of those whom he obeys; he glories in their fame, exalts himself by their nobility, and constantly feeds on borrowed grandeur to which he often attaches more value than do those who possess it fully and in truth.

There is something both touching and ridiculous in this strange medley of two existences.

These emotions of masters, passed into the souls of valets, adopt the size appropriate to the place they occupy; they shrink and lower themselves. What had been pride in the former becomes childish vanity and wretched pretension in the latter. The servants of a great man are usually very punctilious about the attentions due to him, and they care more about his smallest privileges than he does himself.

One still sometimes meets among us one of these old servants of the aristocracy; they are survivals from a race which will soon vanish.

In the United States I have not seen anyone at all like them. The Americans not only have no knowledge of the type in question, but are very hard to convince of his existence. It is almost as difficult for them to form an idea thereof as for us to picture a Roman slave or a serf of the Middle Ages. All these men are in fact, though to different degrees, the result of the same cause. They are slipping from our sight and daily merging into the darkness of the past with the social state that bore them.

Equality makes new men of servant and of master and establishes new connections between them.

When conditions are almost equal, men are continually changing places. There is still a class of valets and a class of masters, but they are not forever composed of the same individuals, and more especially, not of the same families. Those who give the orders are no more permanent than those who obey.

As servants do not form a race apart, they have no customs, prejudices, or mores peculiar to themselves; one does not notice that they have any special ways of thought or modes of feeling; they know nothing of vices or virtues peculiar to their status, but share the education, opinions, feelings, virtues, and vices of their contemporaries; and they are honest or scoundrels in the same style as their masters.

The same equality prevails among servants as among masters.

As no fixed ranks or permanent hierarchies are found among them, one must not expect to find either the meanness or the distinction seen in the aristocracy of valets as in all other aristocracies.

Never in the United States have I seen anything to put one in mind of the trusted retainer whose memory still haunts us in Europe, but neither did I find the conception of the lackey. Both are lost without trace.

In democracies servants are not only equal among themselves, but one can say that in some fashion they are equal to their masters.

That needs some explanation to be fully understood.

The servant may at any time become the master, and he wants to do so. So the servant is not a different type of man from the master.

Why, then, has the latter the right to command, and what makes the former obey? A temporary and freely made agreement. By nature they are not at all inferior one to the other, and they only become so temporarily by contract. Within the terms of the contract, one is servant and the other master; beyond that, they are two citizens, two men.

I would like the reader to understand clearly that this is not just the way in which the servants see their position. The masters see domestic service in the same light, and the precise limits of command and obedience are as firmly fixed in the mind of the one as of the other.

When most of the citizens have long since attained a roughly similar status, and equality is an old and accepted fact, public opinion, which is never influenced by exceptions, broadly speaking, assigns certain limits to a man's worth, and it is difficult for any man long to rise above or fall below this level.

No matter how wealth or poverty, power or obedience, accidentally put great distances between two men, public opinion, based on the normal way of things, puts them near the common level and creates a sort of fancied equality between them, in spite of the actual inequality of their lives.

This all-powerful opinion finally infuses itself into the thoughts even of those whose interest it is to fight against it; it both modifies their judgment and subdues their will.

In the depths of their being neither master nor servant any longer sees a profound difference between them, and they neither hope nor fear ever to find such a difference. Hence they are neither scornful nor angry, and look at each other without pride or humility.

The master considers the contract the sole source of his power, and the servant thinks it the sole reason for his obedience. There is no dispute between them about their reciprocal position; each easily sees what is his and keeps to it.

In our army the soldier comes from much the same class as the officer and may reach the same ranks. In civil life he considers himself completely the equal of his commanders, and in fact is so. But in the army he does not hesitate to obey, and his obedience is no less prompt, precise, and ready for being freely given and defined.

That will give an idea of the relations between master and servant in a democracy.

It would be silly to suppose that there could ever be between these two men such warm and deep emotions as are sometimes kindled in the domestic service of aristocracy, nor should one expect striking examples of self-sacrifice.

In aristocracies servant and master see each other only occasionally, and often they talk only through an intermediary. Yet they usually stand firmly by each other.

In democracies servant and master are very close; their bodies constantly touch, but their souls remain apart; they have occupations together, but they hardly ever have common interests.

Among such peoples the servant always thinks of himself as a temporary inmate in his master's house. He has not known his ancestors and will not see his descendants; he has nothing lasting to expect from them. Why, then, should he identify his life with his master's, and what reason could there be for such a strange sacrifice of himself? The reciprocal position is changed; the relationship must be changed also.

I want to base all I have just said on the example of the Americans, but I cannot do so without making careful distinctions concerning persons and places.

In the South there is slavery, so all I have said cannot apply there.

In the North most of servants are freed slaves or the sons of these. Such men hold a doubtful position in public esteem. The law brings them up close to their master's level. Mores obstinately push them back. They cannot see their own status clearly and are almost always either insolent or cringing.

But in these northern states, especially in New England, one does find a fairly large number of white men who agree for wages temporarily to perform the wishes of others. I have heard it said that these servants usually carry out the duties of their status accurately and sensibly, and without thinking themselves naturally inferior to those who give the orders, they submit without reluctance to obey them.

It seems to me that such men carry into domestic service some of those manly habits which are born of freedom and equality. Having once chosen a hard lot, they do not strive by indirect means to escape from it, and they have enough self-respect not to refuse their masters the obedience which they have freely promised.

The masters, for their part, do not expect more from their servants than the faithful and strict performance of the contract; they do not ask for marks of respect; they do not claim their love or devotion; it is enough if they are punctual and honest.

It would not therefore be true to say that in a democracy the relationship between master and servant is unorganized; it is organized in another way; the rule is different, but there is a rule.

It is not my business here to discover whether the new state of affairs which I have described is worse than what went before or simply different. It is enough for me that it is fixed and regulated, for what is important to find among men is not any particular order but just order.

But what am I to say of those sad and troubled times when equality comes into its own in the midst of revolutionary tumult, when democracy, after it has been established in the social system, still fights painfully against prejudice and mores?

Already law and, in part, public opinion proclaim that there is no natural and permanent inferiority of servant compared to master. But this new belief has not yet penetrated right to the bottom of the latter's mind, or rather his heart rejects it. In the secret places of his soul the master still considers that he is of a different and superior race; he does not dare to say so, but he shudders at allowing himself to be dragged down to the same level. His commands become at once timid and harsh; already he no longer feels those protective and kindly sentiments toward his servants which are always the fruit of long and uncontested power, and, changed himself, he is surprised to find his servant changed; he wants a man who is, so to say, only passing through a phase of domestic service to contract regular, permanent habits; he wants him to appear satisfied and proud of the servile status from which, sooner or later, he should escape; that he should sacrifice himself for a man who can neither protect nor ruin him; and finally, that he should be attached by an eternal link to beings who are like himself and do not endure longer than he.

In aristocratic societies it often happens that a man's soul is not degraded by the fact that he is a domestic servant, because he neither knows nor thinks of any other status, and the immense inequality between him and his master seems the necessary and inevitable effect of some hidden law of Providence.

In a democracy there is nothing degrading about the status of a domestic servant, because it is freely adopted and temporary and because it is not stigmatized by public opinion and creates no permanent inequality between master and servant.

But in the journey from one social condition to the other, there is almost always a moment of hesitation between the aristocratic conception of subjection and the democratic conception of obedience.

Obedience, then, loses its moral basis in the eyes of him who obeys; he no longer considers it as some sort of divinely appointed duty, and he does not yet see its purely human aspect; in his eyes it is neither sacred nor just, and he submits to it as a degrading though useful fact.

It is at this moment that a confused and incomplete picture of equality forms itself in the servants' minds; they do not at once perceive whether this equality to which they have a right is to be found within or outside the scope of domestic service, and from the bottom of their hearts they revolt against an inferiority to which they have themselves submitted and from which they draw the profit. They agree to serve and are ashamed to obey; they are fond of the advantages of service but not of their master, or more accurately, they are not sure that they should not be the masters, and they are inclined to consider the man who gives them orders as an unjust usurper of their rights.

Then, every citizen's house shows the same sad spectacle as can be seen in the world of politics. There is an unspoken intestinal war between permanently suspicious rival powers; the master is malevolent and soft, the servant malevolent and intractable; the former constantly tries by unfair restrictions to evade his duty to protect and remunerate, and the latter shirks his duty to obey. The reins of domestic administration flap between them, each trying to grasp them. The lines between authority and tyranny, liberty and license, and right and might seem to them so jumbled and confused that no one knows exactly what he is, what he can do, and what he should do.

Such a condition is revolutionary, not democratic.

Chapter 6

HOW DEMOCRATIC INSTITUTIONS AND MORES TEND TO RAISE RENT AND SHORTEN THE TERMS OF LEASES

WHAT HAS BEEN SAID ABOUT masters and servants applies to some extent to landlords and tenants of farms, but the subject is worth treating by itself.

One may almost say that in America there are no tenant farmers; every man owns the field he cultivates.

It must be recognized that democratic laws have a strong tendency to increase the number of owners and diminish that of tenants. Nonetheless, what occurs in the United States is due less to the country's institutions than to the nature of the country itself. In America land costs little; anyone can easily become a landowner. The returns are low, and hardly enough to be divided between a landlord and a tenant.

America is therefore unique in that, as in other respects, and it would be a mistake to take it as typical.

In democracies, as in aristocracies, one will, I think, find both landlords and tenants, but the relations between them will be different.

In aristocracies rents are not paid in money only, but also by respect, attachment, and service. In democracies money only is paid. When patrimonies are divided up and change hands and the permanent connection between families and the land vanishes, only chance puts landlord and tenant in contact. They get together just for a moment to work out the conditions of the contract and then lose sight of each other. They are two strangers, brought together by interest, who discuss a rigid business arrangement only concerned with money.

As property is divided and wealth scattered here and there throughout the land, the country gets full of people whose ancient wealth is in decline and of new rich whose requirements grow faster than their resources. For men of both these types the slightest profit matters, and not a single one of them feels inclined to let any of his advantages slip or to lose any fraction of his income.

As ranks are intermingled and very large as well as very small fortunes become rare, the difference in social position between landlord and tenant becomes daily less. The former has no undisputed natural superiority over the latter. So, both men being equal and both unsure of themselves, what other basis than money could there be for the tenancy agreement between them?

A man who owns a whole neighborhood with a hundred farms knows that it is up to him to win the hearts of several thousand men all at the same time; that is a matter worth taking trouble about for him. To win so great an aim, he will gladly make some sacrifices.

But the owner of a hundred acres does not bother about such considerations and hardly cares to win the private regard of his tenant.

An aristocracy does not die, like a man, in one day. The principle on which it rests is slowly eroded in the depths of consciousness before it is legally attacked. Long, therefore, before war is declared against it, the binding links between the upper and lower classes have been loosened little by little. Scorn and callousness on one side, jealousy and hatred on the other; contacts between rich and poor become rare and less friendly; rents are raised. Still this is not the result of the democratic revolution, but it certainly is its harbinger. For an aristocracy which has definitely let the people's affection slip through its fingers is like a tree with dead roots, which is more easily blown over by the wind the higher it is.

In the last fifty years rents have risen prodigiously, not in France only, but throughout Europe. The remarkable progress of agriculture and industry during the same period does not, in my view, suffice to account for this phenomenon. One must look for some other reason, both more powerful and less obvious. I think that one should trace it to the democratic institutions adopted by several countries in Europe and to the democratic emotions which, to greater or lesser degree, stir all the rest.

I have often heard the great landed proprietors of England congratulate themselves on getting much more money from their lands than did their fathers.

Perhaps they are right to be pleased, but for certain they do not understand in what it is that they take pleasure. They think they are clearing a net profit, when they are only making an exchange. They are selling their influence for cash down, and what they gain in money they will soon lose in power.

There is yet another sign which clearly indicates that a great democratic revolution is in progress or about to start.

In the Middle Ages almost all land was leased in perpetuity, or at least for very long terms. When one studies the domestic economy of those times, one finds that leases of ninety-nine years were more common then than are leases of twelve years now.

At that time people thought of families as immortal, conditions seemed fixed forever, and the whole of society appeared so stable that no one imagined that anything could ever stir within it.

In times of equality thoughts take quite a different turn. It is easy to suppose that nothing stays still. The sense of instability is in the air.

In such a mental climate landlord and tenant too feel a sort of instinctive terror of long-term obligations; they are afraid that one day they will be hampered by the agreement which at the moment profits them. They are vaguely conscious of the possibility of a sudden and unexpected change in their condition. They are afraid of themselves, dreading that, their taste having changed, they will come to regret not being able to drop what once had formed the object of their lust. And they are right to feel this fear, for in ages of democracy all things are unstable, but the most unstable of all is the human heart.

Chapter 7

INFLUENCE OF DEMOCRACY ON WAGES

MOST OF WHAT HAS BEEN SAID above about masters and servants applies to masters and workmen.

As the rules of social hierarchy are less strictly observed, as great ones fall and the humble rise, as poverty as well as wealth ceases to be hereditary, the distance separating master from workman daily diminishes both in fact and in men's minds.

The workman conceives a higher idea of his rights, of his future, and of himself; new ambitions, new desires, fill his mind, and he is besieged by new wants. He constantly looks with covetous eyes at his master's profits, and in striving to share them, he aims to put up the price of his labor, and usually succeeds in this.

In democratic countries, as elsewhere, most of industry is carried on at small expense by men whose wealth and education do not raise them above the common level of those they employ. These industrial adventurers are very numerous, their interests differ, and so it is not easy for them to come to an understanding and unite their efforts.

On the other hand, the workers have almost all got some sure resources which allow them to refuse their work if they cannot get what they consider the fair reward for their labor.

In the constant struggle about wages between these two classes, power is thus divided, and success goes first to one, then to the other.

It even seems probable that in the long run the workers' interest should prevail. For the high wages they have already gained make them daily less dependent on their masters, and in proportion, as they are more independent, it is easier for them to obtain higher wages.

I take as my example that occupation which in our day is still the most commonly followed among us, as among almost all other nations—the cultivation of the land.

In France most agricultural wage earners themselves own some little plot of land which, at a pinch, will keep them alive without working for another man. When such as these offer to work for a great landlord or for a neighboring tenant farmer and are refused a certain wage, they go back to their little domain and wait for another opportunity.

I think that, taking the whole picture into consideration, one can assert that a slow, progressive rise in wages is one of the general laws characteristic of democratic societies. As conditions become more equal, wages rise; and as wages rise, conditions become more equal.

But in our time there is one great and unfortunate exception.

I have shown in a previous chapter how aristocracy, chased out of political society, has taken refuge in some parts of the world of industry and established its sway there in another shape.

That has a strong influence on the rate of wages.

As one must be very rich to embark on the great industrial undertakings of which I speak, the number of those engaged in them is very small. Being very few, they can easily league together and fix the rate of wages that pleases them.

Their workers, on the other hand, are very numerous, and their number is constantly on the increase, for from time to time there are periods of extraordinary prosperity in which wages rise disproportionately and attract the surrounding population into industry. But once men have adopted this calling, they cannot, as we have seen, get out of it, for they soon develop habits of body and mind which render them unsuited to any other work. Such men usually have little education, energy, or resources and are therefore at their master's mercy. When competition or any other chance circumstance reduces the master's profits, he can lower their wages at his pleasure and easily recover at their expense that of which fortune has deprived him.

If by common accord they withhold their work, the master, who is rich, can easily wait without ruining himself until necessity brings them back to him. But as for them, they must work every day if they are not to die, for they scarcely have any property beyond their arms. They have long been impoverished by oppression, and increasing poverty makes them easier to oppress. This is the vicious circle from which they cannot escape.

One must therefore not be surprised if wages, which have sometimes gone up suddenly, in this case fall permanently, whereas in other callings the reward of work, which generally rises only little by little, does rise constantly.

This state of dependence and poverty affecting part of the industrial population in our day is an exceptional fact running counter to conditions all around it. But for that very reason it is nonetheless serious and claims the particular attention of legislators. For it is hard when the whole of society is on the move to keep one class stationary, and when the greater number of men are constantly opening up new roads to fortune, to force some to bear in peace their needs and their desires.

Chapter 8

INFLUENCE OF DEMOCRACY ON THE FAMILY

I HAVE JUST BEEN CONSIDERING how among democratic peoples, particularly America, equality modifies the relations between one citizen and another.

I want to carry the argument further and consider what happens within the family. I am not trying to discover new truths, but to show how known facts have a bearing on my subject.

Everyone has noticed that in our time a new relationship has evolved between the different members of a family, that the distance formerly separating father and son has diminished, and that paternal authority, if not abolished, has at least changed form.

Something analogous, but even more striking, occurs in the United States.

In America the family, if one takes the word in its Roman and aristocratic sense, no longer exists. One only finds scattered traces thereof in the first years following the birth of children. The father then does, without opposition, exercise the domestic dictatorship which his sons' weakness makes necessary and which is justified by both their weakness and his unquestionable superiority.

But as soon as the young American begins to approach man's estate, the reins of filial obedience are daily slackened. Master of his thoughts, he soon becomes responsible for his own behavior. In America there is in truth no adolescence. At the close of boyhood he is a man and begins to trace out his own path.

It would be wrong to suppose that this results from some sort of domestic struggle, in which, by some kind of moral violence, the son had won the freedom which his father refused. The same habits and principles which lead the former to grasp at independence dispose the latter to consider its enjoyment as an incontestable right.

So in the former one sees none of those hateful, disorderly passions which disturb men long after they have shaken off an established yoke. The latter feels none of those bitter, angry regrets which usually accompany fallen power. The father has long anticipated the moment when his authority must come to an end, and when that time does come near, he abdicates without fuss. The son has known in advance exactly when he will be his own master and wins his liberty without haste or effort, as a possession which is his due and which no one seeks to snatch from him.[1]

---

[1] It has, however, never occurred to the Americans to do what we have done in France and take away from fathers one of the chief elements of their power by refusing them the right to dispose of their possessions after their death. In the United States testamentary powers are unlimited.

In this as in almost every other case, it is easy to see that while American political legislation is much more democratic than ours, our civil legislation is infinitely more democratic than theirs. That is easily understood.

Our civil code was written by a man who saw that it was to his interest to satisfy all the democratic yearnings of his contemporaries in everything that did not immediately and directly threaten his power. He gladly allowed certain popular principles to control property and the management

Perhaps it is useful to point out how the changes that have taken place within the family are closely connected with the social and political revolution taking place under our eyes.

There are certain great social principles which a people either introduces everywhere or tolerates nowhere.

In countries organized on the basis of an aristocratic hierarchy, authority never addresses the whole of the governed directly. Men are linked one to the other and confine themselves to controlling those next on the chain. The rest follows. This applies to the family as well as to all associations with a leader. In aristocracies society is, in truth, only concerned with the father. It only controls the sons through the father; it rules him, and he rules them. Hence the father has not only his natural right. He is given a political right to command. He is the author and support of the family; he is also its magistrate.

In democracies, where the long arm of government reaches each particular man among the crowd separately to bend him to obedience to the common laws, there is no need for such an intermediary. In the eyes of the law the father is only a citizen older and richer than his sons.

When conditions generally are very unequal and this inequality is permanent, the conception of superiority works on the imagination of men. Even if the law gave no parental prerogatives, custom and public opinion would supply them. But when men are little different from one another and such differences are not permanent, the general conception of superiority becomes weaker and less defined. It would be useless for a legislator to put the man who obeys in a position of great inferiority compared to him who gives the orders; mores bring these two men close to one another and daily put them more on a level.

So, then, if I do not see any particular privileges accorded to the head of a family in the legislation of an aristocratic people, I can nonetheless rest assured that his power is much respected there and of wider extent than in a democracy, for I know that, whatever the laws may be, the superior will always seem higher and the inferior lower in aristocracies than in democracies.

---

of family affairs, provided there was no pretension to apply them to the management of the state. While the torrent of democracy flooded over civil law, he hoped he could easily keep safe entrenched behind political laws. In this he was both very skillful and very selfish, but such a compromise could not be lasting. For in the long run political society cannot fail to become the expression and mirror of civil society. Indeed, it is in that sense that one can say that there is nothing more political about a people than its civil legislation.

When men are more concerned with memories of what has been than with what is, and when they are much more anxious to know what their ancestors thought than to think for themselves, the father is the natural and necessary link between the past and the present, the link where these two chains meet and join. In aristocracies, therefore, the father is not only the political head of the family but also the instrument of tradition, the interpreter of custom, and the arbiter of mores. He is heard with deference, he is addressed always with respect, and the affection felt for him is ever mingled with fear.

When the state of society turns to democracy and men adopt the general principle that it is good and right to judge everything for oneself, taking former beliefs as providing information but not rules, paternal opinions come to have less power over the sons, just as his legal power is less too.

Perhaps the division of patrimonies which follows from democracy does more than all the rest to alter the relations between father and children.

When the father of a family has little property, his son and he live constantly in the same place and carry on the same work together. Habit and necessity bring them together and force them all the time to communicate with each other. There is bound, then, to be a sort of intimate familiarity between them which makes power less absolute and goes ill with respectful formalities.

Moreover, in democracies those who possess these small fortunes are the very class which gives ideas their force and sets the tone of mores. Both its will and its thoughts prevail everywhere, and even those who are most disposed to disobey its orders end by being carried along by its example. I have known fiery opponents of democracy who allowed their children to call them "thou."

So at the same time as aristocracy loses its power, all that was austere, conventional, and legal in parental power also disappears and a sort of equality reigns around the domestic hearth.

I am not certain, generally speaking, whether society loses by the change, but I am inclined to think that the individual gains. I think that as mores and laws become more democratic the relations between father and sons become more intimate and gentle; there is less of rule and authority, often more of confidence and affection, and it would seem than the natural bond grows tighter as the social than that gladly given to the kindness and experience of an old link loosens.

In a democratic family the father scarcely exercises more power man. His orders might be ill-received, but his advice is usually weighty. He may not be surrounded with formal marks of respect, but at least his sons address him with confidence. There is no recognized formula of address, but they talk to him constantly and freely consult him every day. The master and magistrate have vanished; the father remains.

A perusal of the family correspondence surviving from aristocratic ages is enough to illustrate the difference between the two social states in this respect. The style is always correct, ceremonious, rigid, and cold, so that natural warmth of heart can hardly be felt through the words.

But among democratic nations every word a son addresses to his father has a tang of freedom, familiarity, and tenderness all at once, which gives an immediate impression of the new relationship prevailing in the family.

An analogous revolution changes the relations between the children.

As in aristocratic society, so in the aristocratic family, all positions are defined. Not only the father holds a rank apart and enjoys immense privileges; the children too are by no means equal among one another; age and sex irrevocably fix the rank for each and ensure certain prerogatives. Democracy overthrows or lowers all these barriers.

In the aristocratic family the eldest son, who will inherit most of the property and almost all the rights, becomes the chief and to a certain extent the master of his brothers. Greatness and power are his; for them there is mediocrity and dependence. But yet it would be a mistake to suppose that in aristocracies the privileges of the eldest are profitable to him alone and that they excite nothing but jealousy and hatred around him.

The eldest usually takes trouble to procure wealth and power for his brothers, the general reputation of the house reflecting credit on its head. And the younger sons try to help the eldest in all his undertakings, for the greatness and power of the head of the family increase his ability to promote all the branches of the family. So the various members of the aristocratic family are closely linked together; their interests are connected and their minds are in accord, but their hearts are seldom in harmony.

Democracy too draws brothers together, but in a different way.

Under democratic laws the children are perfectly equal, and consequently independent; nothing forcibly brings them together, but also nothing drives them apart. Having a common origin, brought up under the same roof, and treated with the same care, as no peculiar privilege distinguishes or divides them, the affectionate and frank intimacy of childhood easily takes root among them. Scarcely anything can occur to break the bond thus formed at the start of life, for brotherhood daily draws them together, and there is no cause for friction.

Not interest, then, but common memories and the unhampered sympathy of thoughts and tastes draw brothers, in a democracy, to one another. Their inheritance is divided, but their hearts are free to unite.

This gentleness of democratic manners is such that even the partisans of aristocracy are attracted by it, and when they have tasted it for some time, they are not at all tempted to return to the cold and respectful formalities of the aristocratic family. They gladly keep the family habits of democracy, provided they can reject its social state and laws. But these things hold together, and one cannot enjoy the one without putting up with the others.

What I have said about filial love and fraternal affection applies to all the spontaneous feelings rooted in nature itself.

If a certain way of thinking or feeling is the result of particular conditions of life, when the conditions change, nothing is left. Thus law may make a very close link between two citizens; if the law is repealed, they separate. Nothing could have been tighter than the bond uniting lord and vassal in the feudal world. Now those two men no longer know each other. The fear, gratitude, and affection which once joined them have vanished. One cannot find a trace of them.

But it is not like that with feelings natural to man. Whenever a law attempts to shape such feelings in any particular way, it almost always weakens them. By trying to add something, it almost always takes something away, and they are always stronger if left to themselves.

Democracy, which destroys or obscures almost all social conventions and which makes it harder for men to establish new ones, leads to the complete disappearance of almost all the feelings originating in such conventions. But it only modifies those of the other sort and often affords them an energy and gentleness which they had not before.

I think that I may be able to sum up in one phrase the whole sense of this chapter and of several others that preceded it. Democracy loosens social ties, but it tightens natural ones. At the same time as it separates citizens, it brings kindred closer together.

Chapter 9

EDUCATION OF GIRLS IN
THE UNITED STATES

THERE HAVE NEVER BEEN FREE societies without mores, and as I observed in the first part of this book, it is woman who shapes these mores. Therefore everything which has a bearing on the status of women, their habits, and their thoughts is, in my view, of great political importance.

In almost all Protestant nations girls are much more in control of their own behavior than among Catholics ones.

This independence is even greater in those Protestant countries, such as England, which have kept or gained the right of self-government. In such cases both political habits and religious beliefs infuse a spirit of liberty into the family.

In the United States, Protestant teaching is combined with a very free constitution and a very democratic society, and in no other country is a girl left so soon or so completely to look after herself.

Long before the young American woman has reached marriageable age, the process of freeing her from her mother's care has started stage by stage. Before she has completely left childhood behind she already thinks for herself, speaks freely, and acts on her own. All the doings of the world are ever plain for her to see; far from trying to keep this from her sight, she is continually shown more and more of it and taught to look thereon with firm and quiet gaze. So the vices and dangers of society are soon plain to her, and seeing them clearly, she judges them without illusion and faces them without fear, for she is full of confidence in her own powers, and it seems that this feeling is shared by all around her.

Thus you can hardly expect an American girl to show that virgin innocence amid burgeoning desires and those naïve and artless graces which in Europe generally go with the stage between childhood and youth. Seldom does an American girl, whatever her age, suffer from shyness or childish ignorance. She, like the European girl, wants to please, but she knows exactly what it costs. She may avoid evil, but at least she knows what it is; her morals are pure rather than her mind chaste.

I have often been surprised and almost frightened to see the singular skill and happy audacity with which young American women contrive to steer their thoughts and language through the traps of sprightly conversation; a philosopher would stumble at every step along the narrow path which they tread with assured facility.

It is easy to see that, even in the freedom of early youth, an American girl never quite loses control of herself; she enjoys all permitted pleasures without losing her head about any of them, and her reason never lets the reins go, though it may often seem to let them flap.

In France, where there is still such a strange mixture of thoughts and tastes, relics of all the ages, we often give girls a timid, withdrawn, almost cloistered education, as was done under the aristocracy, and then leave them unguided and unaided amid all the disorder inseparable from democratic society.

The Americans are more consistent.

They realize that there must be a great deal of individual freedom in a democracy; youth will be impatient, tastes ill-restrained, customs fleeting, public opinion often unsettled or feeble, paternal authority weak, and a husband's power contested.

In such circumstances they have calculated that there was little chance of repressing in woman the most tyrannical passions of the human heart and that it was a safer policy to teach her to control them herself. Unable to prevent her chastity from being often in danger, they want her to know how to defend herself, and they count on the strength of her free determination more than on safeguards which have been shaken or overthrown. Instead, therefore, of teaching her to distrust herself, they seek to increase her confidence in her own powers. Unable and unwilling to keep a girl in perpetual and complete ignorance, they are in a hurry to give her precocious knowledge of everything. Far from hiding the world's corruption from her, they want her to see it at once and take her own steps to avoid it, and they are more anxious to ensure her good conduct than to guard her innocence too carefully.

Although the Americans are a very religious people, they have not relied on religion alone to defend feminine chastity; they have tried to give arms to her reasoning powers. In this they are using the same approach that they have employed in many other circumstances. In the first place, they make incredible efforts to provide that individual freedom shall be able to control itself, and it is only when they have reached the utmost limits of human strength that they call in the aid of religion.

I know that such an education has its dangers; I know too that it tends to develop judgment at the cost of imagination and to make women chaste and cold rather than tender and loving companions of men. Society may thus be more peaceful and better ordered, but the charms of private life are often less. But that is a secondary evil, which should be faced for the sake of the greater good. At the point we have now reached, we no longer have a choice to make; a democratic education is necessary to protect women against the dangers with which the institutions and mores of democracy surround them.

Chapter 10

THE YOUNG WOMAN AS A WIFE

IN AMERICA a woman loses her independence forever in the bonds of matrimony. While there is less constraint on girls there than anywhere else, a wife submits to stricter obligations. For the former, her father's house is a home of freedom and pleasure; for the latter, her husband's is almost a cloister.

These two states are not perhaps as contradictory as one tends to think, and it is natural for Americans to pass through the one to reach the other.

Religious peoples and industrial nations take a particularly serious view of marriage. The former consider the regularity of a woman's life the best guarantee and surest sign of the purity of her morals. The latter see in it the surest safeguard of the order and prosperity of the house.

The Americans are both a Puritan and a trading nation. Therefore both their religious beliefs and their industrial habits lead them to demand much abnegation on the woman's part and a continual sacrifice of pleasure for the sake of business, which is seldom expected in Europe. Thus in America inexorable public opinion carefully keeps woman within the little sphere of domestic interests and duties and will not let her go beyond them.

When she is born into the world the young American girl finds these ideas firmly established; she sees the rules that spring therefrom; she is soon convinced that she cannot for a moment depart from the usages accepted by her contemporaries without immediately putting in danger her peace of mind, her reputation, and her very social existence, and she finds the strength required for such an act of submission in the firmness of her understanding and the manly habits inculcated by her education.

One may say that it is the very enjoyment of freedom that has given her the courage to sacrifice it without struggle or complaint when the time has come for that.

Moreover, the American woman never gets caught in the bonds of matrimony as in a snare set to catch her simplicity and ignorance. She knows beforehand what will be expected of her, and she herself has freely accepted the yoke. She suffers her new state bravely, for she has chosen it.

Because in America paternal discipline is very lax and the bonds of marriage very tight, a girl is cautious and wary in agreeing thereto. Precocious weddings hardly occur. So American women only marry when their minds are experienced and mature, whereas elsewhere women usually only begin to mature when they are married.

However, I am far from thinking that only the constraint of public opinion imposes this great change in the ways of women as soon as they are married. Often it is simply their own will which imposes this sacrifice on them.

When the time has come to choose a husband, her cold and austere powers of reasoning, which have been educated and strengthened by a free view of the world, teach the American woman that a light and free spirit within the bonds of marriage is an everlasting source of trouble, not of pleasure, that a girl's amusements cannot become the recreation of a wife, and that for a married woman the springs of happiness are inside the home. Seeing beforehand and clearly the only path that can lead to domestic felicity, from the first step she sets out in that direction and follows it to the end without seeking to turn back.

This same strength of will exhibited by the young married women of America in immediately submitting without complaint to the austere duties of their new state is no less manifest in all the great trials of their lives.

In no country of the world are private fortunes more unstable than in the United States. It is not exceptional for one man in his lifetime to work up through every stage from poverty to opulence and then come down again.

American women face such upheavals with quiet, indomitable

energy. Their desires seem to contract with their fortune as easily
as they expand.

Most of the adventurers who yearly go to people the empty spaces
of the West belong, as I have noted in my earlier book, to the old
Anglo-American stock of the North. Many of these who launch out
so boldly in search of wealth have already gained a comfortable
living in their own land. They take their wives with them and make
them share the dangers and innumerable privations that always go
with such undertakings. In the utmost confines of the wilderness
I have often met young wives, brought up in all the refinement
of life in the towns of New England, who have passed almost without
transition from their parents' prosperous houses to leaky cabins in
the depths of the forest. Fever, solitude, and boredom had not broken
the resilience of their courage. Their features were changed and faded,
but their looks were firm. They seemed both sad and resolute. (See
Appendix I, U.)

I am sure that it was the education of their early years which
built up that inner strength on which they were later to draw.

So, in America the wife is still the same person that she was
as a girl; her part in life has changed, and her ways are different,
but the spirit is the same. (See Appendix I, U.)

Chapter 11

HOW EQUALITY HELPS TO MAINTAIN
GOOD MORALS IN AMERICA

SOME PHILOSOPHERS and historians have stated or implied that
women's morals are more or less strict in accordance with the distance
at which they live from the equator. That is a cheap way of getting
out of the matter, and on that showing we should only need a
globe and a compass to solve in a moment one of the most difficult
problems of human behavior.

But I do not find this materialist theory by any means established
by the facts.

The same nations, in different periods of their history, have proved
chaste or dissolute. Therefore strictness and irregularity in morals

must depend on some causes that change, and not only the nature of the land, which does not change.

I am not denying that in certain climates the passions arising from the reciprocal attraction of the sexes may be particularly intense. But I think that this natural intensity may always be excited or restrained by social conditions and political institutions.

Although travelers who have visited North America differ on many points, they all agree that mores are infinitely stricter there than anywhere else.

It is evident that in that respect the Americans are greatly superior to their fathers, the English. A superficial glance at the two nations is enough to show that.

In England, as in all other European countries, malicious gossip constantly attacks the frailties of women. Philosophers and statesmen are frequently heard complaining that mores are not strict enough, and the country's literature constantly suggests that this is so.

In America all books, not excepting novels, suppose women to be chaste, and no one there boasts of amorous adventures.

No doubt this great strictness of American mores is due partly to the country, the race, and the religion. But all those causes, which can be found elsewhere, are still not enough to account for the matter. To do so one must discover some particular reason.

I think that reason is equality and institutions deriving therefrom. (See Appendix I, V.)

Equality of conditions does not by itself alone make mores strict, but there can be doubt that it aids and increases such a tendency.

Among aristocratic peoples birth and fortune often make a man and a woman such different creatures that they would never be able to unite with one another. Their passions draw them together, but social conditions and the thoughts that spring from them prevent them from uniting in a permanent and open way. The necessary result of that is a great number of ephemeral and clandestine connections. Nature secretly gets her own back for the restraint imposed by laws.

Things do not happen in the same way when equality of conditions has swept down all the real or imaginary barriers separating man and woman. No girl then feels that she cannot become the wife of the man who likes her best, and that makes irregular morals before marriage very difficult. For however credulous passion may make us, there is hardly a way of persuading a girl that you love her when you are perfectly free to marry her but will not do so.

The same cause is at work, though in a more indirect way, after marriage.

Nothing does more to make illegitimate love seem legitimate in the eyes both of those who experience it and of the watching crowd than forced marriages or ones entered into by chance.[1]

In a country where the woman can always choose freely and where education has taught her to choose well, public opinion is inexorable against her faults.

The severity of the Americans is in part due to this cause. They regard marriage as a contract which is often burdensome but every condition of which the parties are strictly bound to fulfill, because they knew them all beforehand and were at liberty not to bind themselves to anything at all.

The same cause which renders fidelity more obligatory also renders it easier.

The object of marriage in aristocratic lands is more to unite property than persons, so it can happen sometimes that the husband is chosen while at school and the wife at the breast. It is not surprising that the conjugal tie which unites the fortunes of the married couple leaves their hearts to rove at large. That is the natural result of the spirit of the contract.

But when each chooses his companion for himself without any external interference or even prompting, it is usually nothing but similar tastes and thoughts that bring a man and a woman together, and these similarities hold and keep them by each other's side.

Our ancestors conceived a singular opinion with regard to marriage.

As they had noticed that the few love matches which took place in their days almost always ended in tragedy, they came to the firm conclusion that in such matters it was very dangerous to rely on one's own heart. They thought that chance saw clearer than choice.

But it was not hard to see that the examples before their eyes proved nothing.

In the first place, I would say that while democratic peoples allow

[1] All European literature bears out the truth of this observation.

When a European wants to describe in fiction one of the great catastrophes in matrimony which are so frequent among us, he is careful to enlist the reader's sympathy beforehand by depicting an ill-assorted or compulsory marriage. Although long habits of tolerance have long since relaxed our moral standards, it is difficult for him to interest us in his characters' misfortunes if he does not begin by making excuses for their fault. This artifice seldom fails of success. The daily scenes we witness prepare us in advance to be indulgent.

American writers could never make such excuses seem probable to their readers; their customs and laws resist the attempt, and despairing of making irregular conduct seem pleasing, they do not describe it at all. That is in part the reason why so few novels are published in the United States.

women the right to choose their husbands freely, they have been careful to educate their understanding beforehand and to give their wills the strength necessary for such a choice; but the girls who in an aristocracy secretly escape from paternal authority to throw themselves into the arms of a man whom they have had neither time to know nor capacity to judge lack all these guarantees. One should not be surprised that they make ill use of their free choice the first time they avail themselves of it, nor that they make such cruel mistakes when, without receiving a democratic education, they wish, in marriage, to follow democratic customs.

But there is more to it than that.

When a man and a woman wish to come together in spite of the inequalities of an aristocratic social system, they have immense obstacles to overcome. After they have broken down or eloped from the ties of filial obedience, they must by a further effort escape the sway of custom and the tyranny of opinion; and then, when they have finally reached the end of this rough passage, they find themselves strangers among their natural friends and relations; the prejudice which they have defied separates them. This situation soon wears down their courage and embitters their hearts.

If, then, it happens that spouses united in this way are first unhappy and then guilty, one ought not to suppose that this is because they chose freely, but rather because they live in a society which does not allow such a choice.

One should also not forget that the same energy which makes a man break through a common error almost always drives him on beyond what is reasonable, that to enable him to dare to declare war, even legitimately, on the ideas of his country and age means that he must have something of violence and adventure in his character, and people of this type, whatever direction they take, seldom achieve happiness or virtue. That, one may say in passing, is the reason why, even in the case of the most necessary and hallowed revolutions, one seldom finds revolutionaries who are moderate and honest.

There is therefore no just ground for surprise if, in an age of aristocracy, a man who chooses to consult nothing but his taste and inclination in selecting a wife soon finds that irregular morals and wretchedness break into his home life. But when such behavior is part of the natural and usual order of things, when the social system makes it easy, when paternal authority supports it and public opinion recognizes it, one should not doubt that the internal peace of families will be increased thereby and conjugal faith better protected.

Almost all the men in a democracy either enter politics or practice some calling, whereas limited incomes oblige the wives to stay at home and watch in person very closely over the details of domestic economy.

All these separate and necessary occupations form as many natural barriers which, by keeping the sexes apart, make the solicitations of the one less frequent and less ardent and the resistance of the other easier.

Not that equality of conditions could ever make man chaste, but it gives the irregularity of his morals a less dangerous character. As no man any longer has leisure or opportunity to attack the virtue of those who wish to defend themselves, there are at the same time a great number of courtesans and a great many honest women.

Such a state of affairs leads to deplorable individual wretchedness, but it does not prevent the body social from being strong and alert; it does not break up families and does not weaken national morality. Society is endangered not by the great profligacy of a few but by the laxity of all. A lawgiver must fear prostitution much less than intrigues.

The disturbed and constantly harassed life which equality makes men lead not only diverts their attention from lovemaking by depriving them of leisure for its pursuit but also turns them away by a more secret but more certain path.

Everyone living in democratic times contracts, more or less, the mental habits of the industrial and trading classes; their thoughts take a serious turn, calculating and realistic; they gladly turn away from the ideal to pursue some visible and approachable aim which seems the natural and necessary object of their desires. Equality does not by this destroy the imagination, but clips its wings and only lets it fly touching the ground.

No men are less dreamers than the citizens of democracy; one hardly finds any who care to let themselves indulge in such leisurely and solitary moods of contemplation as generally precede and produce the great agitations of the heart.

They do, it is true, set great store on obtaining that type of deep, regular, and peaceful affection which makes life happy and secure. But they would not willingly chase violent and capricious emotions which disturb life and cut it short.

I realize that all I have just said applies, in its completeness, only to America and that up to now it is not generally applicable to Europe.

For half a century laws and habits have, with unparalleled violence, been driving several nations of Europe in the direction of democracy, and one certainly does not find there that relations between men and women have become more regular or more chaste. In some places the very opposite is true. Some classes are more orderly; general morality seems more lax. I am not afraid to note that, being no more disposed to flatter my contemporaries than to slander them.

It is a matter for regret but not surprise.

The beneficent influence which a democratic social system can exercise on the regularity of habits is something which requires a considerable time to take effect. While equality favors sound morals, the social upheaval leading to it has a very damaging influence on them.

During the last fifty years of transformation France has rarely known freedom, disorder always. In the universal confusion of thought undermining all established concepts, incoherently jumbling right and wrong, truth and falsehood, law and fact, public virtue has become unreliable and private morality shaken.

But all revolutions, whatever their aim or means, have always at first produced such results. Even those which in the end imposed stricter moral standards began by relaxing them.

I do not think the moral disorders of which we now see so much will prove a lasting state. There are already some odd pointers that way.

Nothing is quite so wretchedly corrupt as an aristocracy which has lost its power but kept its wealth and which still has endless leisure to devote to nothing but banal enjoyments. All its great thoughts and passionate energy are things of the past, and nothing but a host of petty, gnawing vices now cling to it like worms to a corpse.

No one denies that the eighteenth-century French aristocracy was very dissolute. But at that time ancient habits and old beliefs still maintained respect for moral standards among the other classes.

On the other hand, we can all agree that the relics of this same aristocracy now exhibit a marked austerity of principles, whereas lax morals have spread through the middle and lower classes. Thus those very families that were most lax fifty years ago now set the best example, and it would seem as if democracy had improved the moral standards only of the aristocracy.

The Revolution, which broke up the wealth of the nobles, forced them to pay attention to their affairs and to their families, compelled them to live under the same roof with their children, and finally gave a more rational and serious turn to their thoughts, thereby, without their being quite conscious of this themselves, putting into their heads thoughts of respect for religious belief, love of order, quiet pleasures, and happy domestic prosperity, whereas the rest of the nation, which used naturally to have such tastes, was swept into anarchy by the sheer effort required to overthrow laws and political customs.

The old French aristocracy has suffered the consequences of the Revolution without in any way feeling revolutionary passions and without sharing the often anarchical excitement which caused it. Hence one can easily understand how it came to experience the salutary influence of this revolution on moral standards even before those who were responsible for the Revolution.

One can therefore conclude, surprising though this seems at first sight, that in our day it is the most antidemocratic element in the nation which gives the best example of the moral standards one can rationally expect from democracy.

I cannot but think that when the democratic revolution has produced its full effect, and when we have escaped from the confusion in which it was born, that which is true now only of some will become gradually true of all.

Chapter 12

HOW THE AMERICAN VIEWS
THE EQUALITY OF THE SEXES

I HAVE SHOWN HOW democracy destroys or modifies those various inequalities which are in origin social. But is that the end of the matter? May it not ultimately come to change the great inequality between man and woman which has up till now seemed based on the eternal foundations of nature?

I think that the same social impetus which brings nearer to the same level father and son, master and servant, and generally every inferior to every superior does raise the status of women and should make them more and more nearly equal to men.

But in this I need more than ever to make myself clearly understood. For there is no subject on which the crude, disorderly fancy of our age has given itself freer rein.

In Europe there are people who, confusing the divergent attributes of the sexes, claim to make of man and woman creatures who are, not equal only, but actually similar. They would attribute the same functions to both, impose the same duties, and grant the same rights; they would have them share everything—work, pleasure, public affairs. It is easy to see that the sort of equality forced on both sexes degrades them both, and that so coarse a jumble of nature's works could produce nothing but feeble men and unseemly women.

That is far from being the American view of the sort of democratic equality which can be brought about between man and woman. They think that nature, which created such great differences between the physical and moral constitution of men and women, clearly intended to give their diverse faculties a diverse employment; and they consider that progress consists not in making dissimilar creatures do roughly the same things but in giving both a chance to do their job as well as possible. The Americans have applied to the sexes the great principle of political economy which now dominates industry. They have carefully separated the functions of man and of woman so that the great work of society may be better performed.

In America, more than anywhere else in the world, care has been taken constantly to trace clearly distinct spheres of action for the two sexes, and both are required to keep in step, but along paths that are never the same. You will never find American women in charge of the external relations of the family, managing a business, or interfering in politics; but they are also never obliged to undertake rough laborer's work or any task requiring hard physical exertion. No family is so poor that it makes an exception to this rule.

If the American woman is never allowed to leave the quiet sphere of domestic duties, she is also never forced to do so.

As a result, American women, who are often manly in their intelligence and in their energy, usually preserve great delicacy of personal appearance and always have the manners of women, though they sometimes show the minds and hearts of men.

Nor have the Americans ever supposed that democratic principles should undermine the husband's authority and make it doubtful who is in charge of the family. In their view, every association, to be effective, must have a head, and the natural head of the conjugal association is the husband. They therefore never deny him the right to direct his spouse. They think that in the little society composed of man and wife, just as in the great society of politics, the aim of democracy is to regulate and legitimatize necessary powers and not to destroy all power.

That is by no means an opinion maintained by one sex and opposed by the other.

I have never found American women regarding conjugal authority as a blessed usurpation of their rights or feeling that they degraded themselves by submitting to it. On the contrary, they seem to take pride in the free relinquishment of their will, and it is their boast to bear the yoke themselves rather than to escape from it. That, at least, is the feeling expressed by the best of them; the others keep quiet, and in the United States one never hears an adulterous wife noisily proclaiming the rights of women while stamping the most hallowed duties under foot.

In Europe one has often noted that a certain contempt lurks in the flattery men lavish on women; although a European may often make himself a woman's slave, one feels that he never sincerely thinks her his equal.

In the United States men seldom compliment women, but they daily show how much they esteem them.

Americans constantly display complete confidence in their spouses' judgment and deep respect for their freedom. They hold that woman's mind is just as capable as man's of discovering the naked truth, and her heart as firm to face it. They have never sought to place her virtue, any more than his, under the protection of prejudice, ignorance, or fear.

It would seem that in Europe, where men so easily submit to the despotic sway of women, they are nevertheless denied some of the greatest attributes of humanity, and they are regarded as seductive but incomplete beings. The most astonishing thing of all is that women themselves end by looking at themselves in the same light and that they almost think it a privilege to be able to appear futile, weak, and timid. The women of America never lay claim to rights of that sort.

It may, moreover, be said that our moral standards accord a strange immunity to man, so that virtue is one thing in his case and quite another for his spouse, and that the same act can be seen by public opinion as a crime in the one but only a fault in the other.

The Americans know nothing of this unfair division of duties and rights. With them the seducer is as much dishonored as his victim.

It is true that the Americans seldom lavish upon women the eager attentions which are often paid to them in Europe, but their conduct always shows that they assume them to be virtuous and refined; and they have such respect for their moral freedom that in their presence every man is careful to keep a watch on his tongue for fear that they should be forced to listen to language which offends them. In America a young woman can set out on a long journey alone and without fear.

American legislators, who have made almost every article in the criminal code less harsh, punish rape by death; and no other crime is judged with the same inexorable severity by public opinion. There is reason for this: as the Americans think nothing more precious than a woman's honor and nothing deserving more respect than her freedom, they think no punishment could be too severe for those who take both from her against her will.

In France, where the same crime is subject to much milder penalties, it is difficult to find a jury that will convict. Is the reason scorn of chastity or scorn of woman? I cannot rid myself of the feeling that it is both.

To sum up, the Americans do not think that man and woman have the duty or the right to do the same things, but they show an equal regard for the part played by both and think of them as beings of equal worth, though their fates are different. They do not expect courage of the same sort or for the same purposes from woman as from man, but they never question her courage. They do not think that a man and his wife should always use their intelligence and understanding in the same way, but they do at least consider that the one has as firm an understanding as the other and a mind as clear.

Thus, then, while they have allowed the social inferiority of woman to continue, they have done everything to raise her morally and intellectually to the level of man. In this I think they have wonderfully understood the true conception of democratic progress.

For my part, I have no hesitation in saying that although the American woman never leaves her domestic sphere and is in some respects very dependent within it, nowhere does she enjoy a higher station. And now that I come near the end of this book in which I have recorded so many considerable achievements of the Americans, if anyone asks me what I think the chief cause of the extraordinary prosperity and growing power of this nation, I should answer that it is due to the superiority of their women.

Chapter 13

HOW EQUALITY NATURALLY DIVIDES THE AMERICANS INTO A MULTITUDE OF SMALL PRIVATE CIRCLES

IT MIGHT BE SUPPOSED that the final and necessary result of democratic institutions would be to jumble all the citizens together in private as well as in public life and compel them all to lead a common existence.

That would be giving a very coarse and tyrannical interpretation to the nature of the equality produced by democracy.

No social system and no laws can ever make men so similar that education, fortune, and tastes can put no differences between them; and though men who are different may sometimes find it to their interest to do the same things and do them together, one must suppose that they will never make it their pleasure. So they will always slip through the legislator's fingers, whatever he does; somehow or other they will escape from the sphere in which he wishes to enclose them and establish, side by side with the great political society, little provate societies held together by similar conditions, habits, and mores.

In the United States the citizens have no sort of pre-eminence over one another; they owe one another neither obedience nor respect; they all help to administer justice and govern the state, and in general they all get together to deal with matters which affect the common destiny; but I have never heard anyone suggest that they should all be brought together to entertain themselves in the same way and take their pleasures jumbled together in the same places.

The Americans, who mix so easily in the sphere of law and politics are, on the contrary, very careful to break up into small and very distinct groups to taste the pleasures of private life. Each freely recognizes every other citizen as equal, but he only accepts a very small number as his friends or guests.

That strikes me as very natural. As the extent of political society expands, one must expect the sphere of private life to contact. Far from supposing that the members of our new societies will ultimately come to live in public, I am more afraid that they will in the end only form very small coteries.

The different classes in aristocracies resemble vast enclosures which one can neither leave nor enter. There is no communication between the classes, but within them men are bound to live in daily contact. Even though their natural characters are not in the least sympathetic, the expediencies of a similar status bring them together.

But when neither law nor custom is at pains to bring particular men into frequent and habitual contact, the chance coincidence of opinions and inclinations decides the matter, and that leads to an infinite variety of private societies.

In democracies, where there is never much difference between one citizen and another and where in the nature of things they are so close that there is always a chance of their all getting merged in a common mass, a multitude of artificial and arbitrary classifications are established to protect each man from the danger of being swept along in spite of himself with the crowd.

This will always be the case. For one can change human institutions, but not man. However energetically society in general may strive to make all the citizens equal and alike, the personal pride of each individual will always make him try to escape from the common level, and he will form some inequality somewhere to his own profit.

In aristocracies men are separated by high, immovable barriers. In democracies they are divided by a lot of almost invisible little threads, which are continually getting broken and moved from place to place.

Therefore, whatever the progress toward equality, in democracies a large number of little private associations will always be formed within the great political society. But none of these will resemble in manners the upper class which rules in aristocracies.

Chapter 14

SOME REFLECTIONS ON
AMERICAN MANNERS

NOTHING, AT FIRST SIGHT, seems less important than the external formalities of human behavior, yet there is nothing to which men attach more importance. They can get used to anything except living in a society which does not share their manners. The influence of the social and political system on manners is therefore worth serious examination.

Manners, speaking generally, have their roots in mores; they are also sometimes the result of an arbitrary convention agreed between certain men. They are both natural and acquired.

When some see that, without dispute or effort of their own, they stand first in society; when they daily have great aims in view which keep them occupied, leaving details to others; and when they live surrounded by wealth they have not acquired and do not fear to lose, one can see that they will feel a proud disdain for all the petty interests and material cares of life and that there will be a natural grandeur in their thoughts that will show in their words and manners.

In democracies there is generally little dignity of manner, as private life is very petty. Manners are often vulgar, as thoughts have small occasion to rise above preoccupation with domestic interests.

True dignity in manners consists in always taking one's proper place, not too high and not too low; that is as much within the reach of a peasant as of a prince. In democracies everybody's status seems doubtful; as a result, there is often pride but seldom dignity of manners. Moreover, manners are never well regulated or well thought out.

There is too much mobility in the population of a democracy for any definite group to be able to establish a code of behavior and see that it is observed. So everyone behaves more or less after his own fashion, and a certain incoherence of manners always prevails, because they conform to the feelings and ideas of each individual rather than to an ideal example provided for everyone to imitate.

In any case, this is much more noticeable when an aristocracy has just fallen than when it has long been destroyed.

New political institutions and new mores then bring together in the same places men still vastly different in education and habits and compel them to a life in common; this constantly leads to the most ill-assorted juxtapositions. There is still some memory of the former strict code of politeness, but no one now knows quite what it said or where to find it. Men have lost the common standard of manners but have not yet resolved to do without it, so each individual tries to shape, out of the ruins of former customs, some rule, however arbitrary and variable. Hence manners have neither the regularity and dignity frequent in aristocracies nor the qualities of simplicity and freedom which one sometimes finds in democracies; they are both constrained and casual.

But this is not a normal state of things.

When equality is complete and old-established, all men, having roughly the same ideas and doing roughly the same things, do not need to come to an understanding or to copy each other in order to behave and talk in the same way; one sees a lot of petty variations in their manners but no great differences. They are never exactly alike, since they do not copy one pattern; they are never very unlike, because they have the same social condition. At first sight one might be inclined to say that the manners of all Americans are exactly alike, and it is only on close inspection that one sees all the variations among them.

The English make game of American manners, but it is odd that most of those responsible for those comic descriptions belong themselves to the English middle classes, and the cap fits them very well too. So these ruthless critics generally themselves illustrate just what they criticize in America; they do not notice that they are abusing themselves, to the great delight of their own aristocracy.

Nothing does democracy more harm than its outward forms of behavior; many who could tolerate its vices cannot put up with its manners.

But I will not admit that there is nothing to praise in democratic manners.

In aristocracies, all within reach of the ruling class are at pains to imitate it, and very absurd and insipid imitations result. Democracies, with no models of high breeding before them, at least escape the necessity of daily looking at bad copies thereof.

In democracies manners are never so refined as among aristocracies, but they are also never so coarse. One misses both the crude words of the mob and the elegant and choice phrases of the high nobility. There is much triviality of manner, but nothing brutal or degraded.

I have already said that a precise code of behavior cannot take shape in democracies. That has its inconveniences and its advantages. In aristocracies rules of propriety impose the same demeanor on all, making every member of the same class seem alike in spite of personal characteristics; they bedizen and conceal nature. Democratic manners are neither so well thought out nor so regular, but they often are more sincere. They form, as it were, a thin, transparent veil through which the real feelings and personal thoughts of each man can be easily seen. Hence there is frequently an intimate connection between the form and the substance of behavior; we see a less decorative picture, but one truer to life. One may put the point this way: democracy imposes no particular manners, but in a sense prevents them from having manners at all.

Sometimes the feelings, passions, virtues, and vices of an aristocracy may reappear in a democracy, but its manners never. They are lost and vanish past return when the democratic revolution is completed. It would seem that nothing is more lasting than the manners of an aristocratic class, for it preserves them for some time after losing property and power, nor more fragile, for as soon as they have gone, no trace of them is left, and it is even difficult to discover what they once were when they have ceased to exist. A change in the state of society works this marvel, and a few generations are enough to bring it about.

The principal characteristics of the aristocracy remain engraved in history after its destruction, but the slight and delicate forms of its manners are lost to memory almost immediately after its fall. No one can imagine them when they are no longer seen. Their disappearance is unnoted and unfelt. For the heart needs an apprenticeship of custom and education to appreciate the refined pleasure derived from distinguished and fastidious manners; once the habit is lost, the taste for them easily goes too.

Thus, not only are democratic peoples unable to have aristocratic manners, but they cannot even conceive or desire them. As they cannot imagine them, from their point of view it is as if they had never existed.

One should not attach too much importance to this loss, but it is permissible to regret it.

I know it has happened that the same men have had very distinguished manners and very vulgar feelings; the inner life of courts has shown well enough that grand appearances may conceal the meanest hearts. But though the manners of an aristocracy by no means create virtue, they may add grace to virtue itself. It was no ordinary sight to see a numerous and powerful class whose every gesture seemed to show a constant and natural dignity of feeling and thought, an ordered refinement of taste and urbanity of manners.

The manners of the aristocracy created a fine illusion about human nature; though the picture was often deceptive, it was yet a noble satisfaction to look on it.

Chapter 15

ON THE GRAVITY OF THE AMERICANS
AND WHY IT OFTEN DOES NOT PREVENT
THEIR DOING ILL-CONSIDERED THINGS

THE INHABITANTS of democratic countries set no store by those sorts of naïve, unruly, coarse entertainments to which in aristocracies the people are addicted. They find them childish or stupid. But they have almost as little interest in the refined intellectual amusements of the aristocratic classes. They look for something solid and productive in their pleasures; they want profit as well as delight.

In aristocratic societies the people freely let themselves go in bursts of tumultuous, boisterous gaiety, which at once make them forget all the wretchedness of their lives. But in democracies people do not at all like to feel violently drawn out of themselves; to them it is always a cause of regret if they lose sight of themselves. To frivolous transports of delight they prefer those staid and quiet amusements which are more like business and which do not drive business entirely out of their minds.

Instead of dancing gaily in the public square as many people of the same social status in Europe still delight to do, an American may prefer to spend his leisure hours quietly drinking in his own house. Such a man enjoys two pleasures at once: he thinks about his business affairs and gets drunk decently at home.

I used to think that the English were the most serious-minded people on earth, but having seen the Americans, I have changed my mind.

I am not denying that temperament is an important element in the American character, but I think that political institutions count for even more.

I think that the gravity of Americans is partly due to pride. In democratic countries even a poor man has a high idea of his personal worth. They find it pleasant to think about themselves, and gladly suppose that others are looking at them too. This disposes them to measure their words and their behavior carefully and not to let themselves go, lest they should reveal their deficiencies. They imagine that to appear dignified they must remain solemn.

But I see another, more intimate and more powerful, cause from which this astonishing American gravity instinctively results.

Peoples under despotism burst out from time to time in mad fits of gaiety, but usually they are sad and constrained through fear.

Under those absolute monarchies which are tempered by custom and mores, men's spirits are often cheerful and even; having some freedom and much security, they are untroubled by the major cares of life. But all free peoples are serious-minded because they are habitually preoccupied with some dangerous or difficult project.

This is more especially true of those free nations which have formed democracies. In those cases there are an infinite number of people of all classes constantly concerned with serious questions of government, and those who are not ambitious to control the commonwealth devote all their energies to increasing their private fortunes. Among such a people gravity is not a characteristic peculiar to certain men, but becomes a national trait.

We are told of small democracies in antiquity whose citizens gathered in public places garlanded with roses and spent the best part of their time dancing or at the theater. I do not believe in the existence of such republics any more than in that of Plato, or if things really did happen there in the way described, these supposed democracies must surely have been composed of very different elements from ours, and indeed had nothing in common with the latter but the name.

But no one must suppose that, for all their labors, the inhabitants of democracies think themselves objects of pity; quite the contrary. No men are more attached to their own way of life, which would lose its savor if they were relieved from the anxieties which harass them. They love their cares more than aristocrats love their pleasures.

I am led to inquire why these same serious-minded democratic peoples sometimes act in such an ill-considered way.

The Americans, who almost always seem poised and cold, are nonetheless often carried away, far beyond the bounds of common sense, by some sudden passion or hasty opinion. They will in all seriousness do strangely absurd things.

One should not be surprised by this contrast.

There is one sort of ignorance which results from extreme publicity. Under despotisms men do not know how to act because they are told nothing; in democratic nations they often act at random because there has been an attempt to tell them everything. The former do not know; the latter forget. The main features of each picture become lost in a mass of detail.

One is astonished at the imprudent suggestions sometimes made by public men in free countries, especially democracies, without their being compromised, whereas under absolute monarchies a few casual remarks are enough to ruin a man's reputation forever, without hope of recovery.

What I have said before provides the explanation. When a man addresses a large crowd, many of his words are not heard, or if heard, are soon forgotten. But where the masses dwell in silent stagnation, the slightest whisper strikes the ear.

In democracies men never stay still; a thousand chance circumstances constantly make them move from place to place, and there is almost always something unforeseen, something, if one may put it so, provisional about their lives. Hence they are often bound to do things which they have not properly learned to do and to say things which they scarcely understand; they have to throw themselves into actual work unprepared by a long apprenticeship.

In aristocracies every man has but one sole aim which he constantly pursues; but man in democracies has a more complicated existence; it is the exception if one man's mind is not concerned with several aims at the same time, and these aims are often very diverse. Unable to be an expert in all, a man easily becomes satisfied with half-baked notions.

In a democracy, if necessity does not urge a man to action, longing will do so, for he sees that none of the good things all around him are completely beyond his reach. Therefore he does everything in a hurry, is always satisfied with a "more or less," and never stops for more than one moment to consider each thing he does.

His curiosity is both insatiable and satisfied cheaply, for he is more bent on knowing a lot quickly than on knowing anything well.

He hardly has the time, and he soon loses the taste, for going deeply into anything.

Hence democratic peoples are serious-minded because social and political circumstances constantly lead them to think about serious matters, and their actions are often ill-considered because they give but little time and attention to each matter.

Habitual inattention must be reckoned the great vice of the democratic spirit.

Chapter 16

WHY AMERICAN NATIONAL PRIDE HAS A MORE RESTLESS AND QUARRELSOME CHARACTER THAN THAT OF THE ENGLISH

ALL FREE PEOPLES ARE PROUD OF THEMSELVES, but national pride does not take the same form in each case. (See Appendix I, W.)

In their relations with strangers the Americans are impatient of the slightest criticism and insatiable for praise. They are pleased by the mildest praise but seldom quite satisfied even by the most fulsome eulogy. They are at you the whole time to make you praise them, and if you do not oblige, they sing their own praises. One might suppose that, doubting their own merits, they want an illustration thereof constantly before their eyes. Their vanity is not only greedy but also restless and jealous. It makes endless demands and gives nothing. It is both mendicant and querulous.

I tell an American that he lives in a beautiful country; he answers: "That is true. There is none like it in the world." I praise the freedom enjoyed by the inhabitants, and he answers: "Freedom is a precious gift, but very few peoples are worthy to enjoy it." I note the chastity of morals prevailing in the United States, and he replies: "I suppose that a stranger, struck by the immorality apparent in all other nations, must be astonished at this sight." Finally I leave him to his self-contemplation, but he returns to the charge and will not stop till he has made me repeat everything I have said. One cannot imagine a more obnoxious or boastful form of patriotism. Even admirers are bored.

The English are not like that. Your Englishman quietly enjoys the real or supposed advantages he sees in his country. If he concedes nothing to other nations, he demands nothing from them. He is not in the least disturbed by a foreigner's criticism, and hardly flattered by his praise. His attitude to the whole world is one of contemptuous and ignorant reserve. His pride needs no nourishment, living on itself.

That two peoples, sprung so recently from the same stock, should feel and talk in ways so diametrically opposite is in itself remarkable.

The great men in aristocratic countries have immense privileges which sustain their pride without reference to the lesser advantages which accrue to them. These privileges having come by inheritance, they think of them in some degree as parts of themselves, or at least as natural rights inherent in their person. They have therefore a quiet assurance in their superiority; they do not think of boasting about prerogatives which all can see and none question. There is nothing so astonishing therein as to need comment. They stand unmoved in solitary grandeur, knowing that the whole world sees them without their needing to show themselves and that no one will attempt to drive them from their position.

When an aristocracy conducts public business, national pride naturally takes this reserved, indifferent, and haughty form, and all other classes in the nation imitate it.

But when, on the contrary, there is little difference in social standing, the slightest advantage tells. When each sees a million others around him all with the same or similar claims to be proud of, pride becomes exacting and jealous; it gets attached to wretched trifles and doggedly defends them.

In democracies, with their constant ebb and flow of prosperity, men have almost always acquired the advantages they possess recently. For that reason they take infinite pleasure in vaunting them, to show others and to convince themselves that they do enjoy them; and, as at any moment these advantages may slip from them, they are in constant alarm and anxiety to show that they have them still. The inhabitants of democracies love their country after the same fashion as they love themselves, and what is habitual in their private vanity is carried over into national pride.

This restless and insatiable vanity of democracies is entirely due to equality and the precariousness of social standing; that is why members of the haughtiest nobility display exactly the same characteristics in those minor aspects of their existence in which there is some instability and an element of struggle.

An aristocratic class is always profoundly different from the other classes in a nation on account of the extent and permanence of its prerogatives, but it sometimes happens that its members are distinguished among themselves by little fugitive advantages which can be gained or lost any day.

Members of a powerful aristocracy, assembled in a capital or at a court, have been known virulently to contest those frivolous privileges which depend on the caprice of fashion or their master's will. They have then shown just the same puerile jealousy toward each

other as men do in democracies, and have shown the same eagerness
to grasp the slightest advantages disputed by their equals, and the
same need to vaunt before the world those which they enjoy.

If the idea of national pride ever entered into the heads of courtiers, I have no doubt their brand of pride would be just like that
of democratic peoples.

Chapter 17

HOW THE ASPECT OF SOCIETY IN
THE UNITED STATES IS AT ONCE
AGITATED AND MONOTONOUS

ONE MIGHT HAVE thought the aspect of the United States peculiarly
calculated to arouse and feed curiosity. Fortunes, ideas, and laws are
constantly changing. Immutable Nature herself seems on the move,
so greatly is she daily transformed by the works of man.

In the long run, however, the sight of this excited community becomes monotonous, and the spectator who has watched this pageant
for some time gets bored.

In aristocracies each man is pretty firmly fixed in his sphere, but
men are vastly dissimilar; their passions, ideas, habits, and tastes are
basically diverse. Nothing changes, but everything differs.

But in democracies, contrariwise, all men are alike and do roughly
the same things. They certainly are subject continually to great vicissitudes, but as the same successes and the same reverses are continually recurring, the name of the actors is all that changes, the play
being always the same. American society appears animated because
men and things are constantly changing; it is monotonous because
all these changes are alike.

Men living in democratic times have many passions, but most of
these culminate in love of wealth or derive from it. That is not because their souls are narrower but because money really is more important at such times.

When every citizen is independent of and indifferent to the rest,
the cooperation of each of them can only be obtained by paying for

it; this infinitely multiplies the purpose to which wealth may be applied and increases its value.

When the prestige attached to what is old has vanished, men are no longer distinguished, or hardly distinguished, by birth, standing, or profession; there is thus hardly anything left but money which makes very clear distinctions between men or can raise some of them above the common level. Distinction based on wealth is increased by the disappearance or diminution of all other distinctions.

In aristocratic nations money is the key to the satisfaction of but few of the vast array of possible desires; in democracies it is the key to them all.

So one usually finds that love of money is either the chief or a secondary motive at the bottom of everything the Americans do. This gives a family likeness to all their passions and soon makes them wearisome to contemplate.

The constant recurrence of the same passion is monotonous; so, too, are the details of the methods used to satisfy it.

In a peaceful and well-ordered democracy such as that of the United States, where neither war nor public employment nor political confiscations open the door to wealth, love of money chiefly turns men to industry. Now, though industry often brings in its train great disorders and great disasters, it cannot prosper without exceedingly regular habits and the performance of a long succession of small uniform motions. The more lively the passion, the more regular and uniform must these motions be. One may say that it is the very vehemence of their desires that makes the Americans so methodical. It agitates their minds but disciplines their lives.

What I say about the Americans applies to almost all men nowadays. Variety is disappearing from the human race; the same ways of behaving, thinking, and feeling are found in every corner of the world. This is not only because nations are more in touch with each other and able to copy each other more closely, but because the men of each country, more and more completely discarding the ideas and feelings peculiar to one caste, profession, or family, are all the same getting closer to what is essential in man, and that is everywhere the same. In that way they grow alike, even without imitating each other. One could compare them to travelers dispersed throughout a huge forest, all the tracks in which lead to the same point. If all at the same time notice where the central point is and direct their steps thither, they will unconsciously draw nearer together without either seeking, or seeing, or knowing each other, and in the end they will be surprised to find that they have all assembled at the same place. All those peoples who take not any particular man but man in himself as the object to study and imitate are tending in the end toward similar mores, like the travelers converging on the central point in the forest.

Chapter 18

CONCERNING HONOR[1] IN THE UNITED STATES AND DEMOCRATIC SOCIETIES

PUBLIC OPINION EMPLOYS two very different standards in judging the actions of men: in the one case it relies on simple notions of right and wrong, which are common to all the world; in the other it assesses them in accordance with some very exotic notions peculiar to one age and country. It often happens that the two standards differ; sometimes they conflict, but they never either completely coincide or completely oust each other.

Honor, in times of the zenith of its power, directs men's wills more than their beliefs, and even when its orders are obeyed without hesitation or complaint, they still feel, by some dim yet powerful instinct, that there exists some more general, ancient, and holy law which they sometimes disobey, though they still acknowledge it. There have been actions which were considered both honorable and dishonoring—a refusal to fight a duel, for example.

I think that such phenomena can be explained by reasons other than the caprice of particular individuals or nations, which has been the reason given hitherto.

There are some universal and permanent needs of mankind on which moral laws are based; if they are broken all men everywhere at all times have connected notions of guilt and shame with the

[1] The word "honor" is not always used in the same sense either in French.

a. The first sense is the esteem, glory, or reputation which a man enjoys among his fellows; it is in that sense that one is said *to win honor*.

b. Honor includes all those rules by which such esteem, glory, and consideration are obtained. Thus we say that a man *has always strictly conformed to the laws of honor* and that he has *forfeited his honor*.

In the present chapter "honor" always has the latter sense.

breach. *To do wrong* meant to disregard them, *to do right* to obey them.

Within the vast community of mankind, lesser associations have been formed and called nations; within the nations further sub-divisions have been called classes or castes.

Each of these associations forms, as it were, a particular species of the human race, and though they differ in no essential from the mass of men, they stand to some extent apart and have some needs peculiar to themselves. It is these special needs which, to some extent and in certain countries, modify the way of looking at human behavior and the value attributed thereto.

It is a permanent and universal interest of mankind that men should not kill each other; but the particular and momentary interest of a nation or class may in certain cases make homicide excusable or even honorable.

Honor is nothing but this particular rule, based on a particular state of society, by means of which a people distributes praise or blame.

Nothing is so unproductive for the human mind as an abstract idea. So I hasten to consider the facts. An example will make my meaning clear.

I will choose the most extraordinary type of honor which has ever been seen in the world and the one which we know best, aristocratic honor sprung up within a feudal society. What I have already said will help to explain this, and it in turn will throw light on what I have said.

There is no need here to inquire when and how medieval aristocracy came into being, why it was so profoundly separated from the rest of the nation, and what established and consolidated its power. I shall take it as an established fact and try to explain why it viewed most human actions in such a peculiar light.

The first thing that strikes me is that in the feudal world actions were by no means always praised or blamed with reference to their intrinsic value, but were sometimes appreciated exclusively with reference to the person who did them or suffered from them, which is repugnant to the universal conscience of mankind. Some actions could thus have no importance if done by a commoner but would dishonor a noble; others changed character if the person who suffered them belonged to the aristocracy or was outside its pale.

When these various notions first arose, the nobility formed a distinct body amid the people, which it dominated from the inaccessible heights in which it was entrenched. To maintain this peculiar position from which its power was derived, it required not only political privileges but also standards of right and wrong for its special use.

That some particular virtue or vice was proper to the nobility rather than to the commons, that a certain action was harmless when it affected only a villein, but punishable when it touched a noble—these were often arbitrary questions; but that honor or shame should attach to a man's actions according to his condition—that was the result of the very existence of an aristocratic ordering of society. The same phenomenon appears in fact in every country which has had an aristocracy. As long as there is any trace of it left, these peculiarities will remain: to debauch a Negro girl hardly injures an American's reputation; to marry her dishonors him.

In some cases feudal honor enjoined revenge and stigmatized forgiveness of insults; in others it imperiously commanded men to master their own passions and forget themselves. Humanity and gentleness were no part of its law, but it praised generosity; it set more store by liberality than benevolence; it allowed men to enrich themselves by gambling or by war, but not by work. It preferred great crimes to small earnings. Greed struck it as less revolting than avarice. It often sanctioned violence but invariably reprobated cunning and treachery as contemptible. These fantastic notions were not exclusively due to the caprice of those who invented them.

A class which has succeeded in placing itself above all others and makes constant efforts to maintain this dominant position must especially honor those virtues which have their share of magnificence and renown and which easily go with pride and love of power. Such men were not afraid to invert the natural order of conscience so as to give these virtues precedence over all others. One can understand how they even came to set some of the bolder and more brilliant vices above quiet and unpretending virtues. Their standing in society in some way forced them to do so.

The medieval nobility reckoned military valor as the greatest of all the virtues, and indeed let it take the place of many of them.

That again was a peculiar notion arising of necessity from a peculiar state of society.

The feudal aristocracy was born of war and for war; it won its power by force of arms and maintained it thereby. So nothing was more important to it than military courage. It was therefore natural to glorify courage above all other virtues. Every manifestation thereof, even at the expense of common sense and humanity, was therefore approved and often even ordained by the manners of the time. The fantastic notions of individuals could affect only the details of such a system.

That a man should regard a tap on the cheek as an unbearable insult and feel bound to kill the man who struck him thus in single combat is an arbitrary rule; but that a noble should not tranquilly suffer an insult, and was dishonored if he let himself be struck without fighting—that was a result of the basic principles and needs of a military aristocracy.

It is therefore to some extent true to say that the laws of honor were capricious, but such caprices were always confined within certain necessary limits. So far am I from regarding the peculiar rules which our ancestors called the law of honor as an arbitrary law that I would gladly undertake to explain even its oddest and most incoherent manifestations as the result of a few fixed and invariable requirements of feudal society.

If one follows the conception of feudal honor into the domain of politics, it is no more difficult to explain its course.

The social conditions and political institutions of the Middle Ages were such that the central power in the nation never governed the citizens directly. Indeed, the latter may almost be said to have been unaware of it; each man was conscious only of another man, whom he was bound to obey. Through that personage he was linked, without realizing it, to all the rest. In feudal societies, therefore, the whole of public order depended on a feeling of loyalty to the actual person of the lord. With that destroyed, anarchy ensued.

Hence every member of the aristocracy daily saw the value of fidelity to a political chief, for each of them was both lord and vassal and had to give orders as well as to obey.

To be loyal to your lord, to sacrifice yourself for him if necessary, to share his good or ill fortune, and to help him in all his undertakings, whatever they might be—such were the first injunctions of feudal honor as far as politics were concerned. Public opinion was extraordinarily strict in its condemnation of treason. A particularly infamous name was invented for it, calling it "felony."

On the other hand, in the Middle Ages one finds few traces of that passion which was the lifeblood of the nations of antiquity: I mean patriotism. But even the word "patriotism" is far from ancient in our language.[2]

Feudal institutions kept the fatherland out of sight and made love of it less necessary. They let the nation be forgotten in passionate feelings for one man. Hence it was never a strict law of feudal honor to be loyal to one's country.

That does not mean that our ancestors had no feeling for their

[2] Even the word *"patrie"* was not used by French writers until the sixteenth century.

country in their hearts, but it was only some sort of dim and feeble instinct, which has now become brighter and stronger as classes have been destroyed and power centralized.

This point is well illustrated by the contradictory judgments of European peoples on various events in their past according to the generation which forms the judgment. The chief stain on the honor of the constable of Bourbon, in the eyes of his contemporaries, was that he bore arms against his king; we now think him most dishonored because he fought against his country. We brand him as deeply as our ancestors did, but for different reasons.

I have taken feudal honor to illustrate my meaning because its characteristics are both more marked and best known to us; but I could have taken other examples and reached the same destination by a different road.

We know less about the Romans than about our own ancestors, yet we do know that they held certain peculiar notions about glory and disgrace which were not solely derived from general notions of right and wrong. Much of human behavior was seen in a different light, according to whether a citizen or a stranger was in question, a free man or a slave; some vices were glorified and some virtues raised above all the rest.

"Now, at that time," writes Plutarch in the life of Coriolanus, "courage was more honored and valued at Rome than any other virtue. And that is proved by the fact that it was called '*virtus*,' using a generic term for one particular quality. So much was this so that in Latin 'virtue' came to mean 'courage.'"[3] Who fails to recognize there the peculiar needs of that remarkable community shaped to conquer the world?

Analogous observations could be made about any nation, for as I have said above, every time men come together to form a particular society, a conception of honor is immediately established among them, that is to say, a collection of opinions peculiar to themselves about what should be praised or blamed. The special habits and interests of the community are always the source of these particular rules.

This to some extent applies to democratic societies as to others. We shall find this proved again with regard to the Americans.[4]

Among opinions current among Americans one still finds some scattered notions detached from the old European aristocratic con-

[3] [Cf. Plutarch's *Lives*, "Life of Coriolanus", Bohn's edition (London, 1880), Vol. I, pp. 35 ff.]

[4] In this context I am speaking of those Americans who live in the parts of the country where there is no slavery. It is they alone who provide a complete picture of a democratic society.

ception of honor, but they have no deep roots or strong influence. It is like a religion whose temples are allowed to remain but in which one no longer believes.

Amid these half-effaced notions of an exotic honor some new opinions have made their appearance, and these constitute what one might call the contemporary American conception of honor.

I have shown how the Americans are continually driven into trade and industry. The origin, social conditions, political institutions, and even the very land they live in irresistibly impel them in this direction. Hence they now form an almost exclusively industrial and trading community placed in the midst of a huge new country whose exploitation is their principal interest. That is the characteristic trait which now distinguishes the Americans most particularly from all other nations.

Therefore all those quiet virtues which tend to regularity in the body social and which favor trade are sure to be held in special honor by this people, and to neglect them will bring one into public contempt.

But all those turbulent virtues which sometimes bring glory but more often trouble to society will rank lower in the public opinion of this same people. One could disregard them without forfeiting the esteem of one's fellow citizens, and perhaps by acquiring them one might run a risk of losing it.

The Americans make an equally arbitrary classification of vices.

There are some inclinations that common sense and the universal conscience of mankind condemn and that fit in with the particular and momentary needs of the American community. These are but feebly blamed, sometimes even praised. I cite in particular the love of money, and the secondary propensities connected with it. To clear, cultivate, and transform the huge uninhabited continent which is their domain, the Americans need the everyday support of an energetic passion; that passion can only be the love of wealth. So no stigma attaches to love of money in America, and provided it does not exceed the bounds imposed by public order, it is held in honor. The American will describe as noble and estimable ambition that which our medieval ancestors would have called base cupidity. He would consider as blind and barbarous frenzy that ardor for conquest and warlike spirit which led the latter every day into new battles.

In the United States fortunes are easily lost and gained again. The country is limitless and full of inexhaustible resources. The people have all the needs and all the appetites of a growing creature who believes that, however hard he tries, he will always be surrounded by more good things than he can grasp. For a people so situated the danger is not the ruin of a few, which is soon made good, but apathy and sloth in the community at large. Boldness in industrial undertakings is the chief cause of their rapid progress, power, and greatness. To them industry appears as a vast lottery in which a few men daily lose but in which the state constantly profits. Such a people is bound to look with favor on boldness in industry and to honor it. But any bold undertaking risks the fortune of the man who embarks on it and of all those who trust him. The Americans, who have turned rash speculation into a sort of virtue, can in no case stigmatize those who are thus rash.

That is the reason for the altogether singular indulgence shown in the United States toward a trader who goes bankrupt. An accident like that leaves no stain on his honor. In this respect the Americans are different not only from the nations of Europe, but from all trading nations of our day; their position and needs are also unlike those of all the others.

All those vices which tend to impair the purity of morals and the stability of marriage are treated in America with a severity unknown in the rest of the world. At first sight this seems in strange contrast to their tolerance in other matters. One is surprised to find in one and the same nation a morality both so relaxed and so austere.

But the contrast is not so incoherent as it seems. American public opinion but gently curbs love of money, for that serves the industrial expansion and prosperity of the nation. But it is particularly hard on bad morals, which distract attention from the search for well-being and disturb that domestic harmony which is so essential to business success. Thus, to win the esteem of their fellows, Americans are bound to conform to regular habits. In that sense one can say that it is a point of honor to be chaste.

American and European medieval conceptions of honor agree on one point: both rank courage first of virtues and count it the greatest moral necessity for a man. But the two conceptions envisage courage in a different light.

In the United States martial valor is little esteemed; the type of courage best known and best appreciated is that which makes a man brave the fury of the ocean to reach port more quickly, and face without complaint the privations of life in the wilds and that solitude which is harder to bear than any privations, the courage which makes a man almost insensible to the loss of a fortune laboriously acquired and prompts him instantly to fresh exertions to gain another. It is chiefly courage of this sort which is needed to maintain the American community and make it prosper, and it is held by them in particular esteem and honor. To betray a lack of it brings certain shame.

One last trait will serve to make the idea underlying this chapter stand out clearly.

In a democratic society such as that of the United States, where fortunes are small and insecure, everybody works, and work opens all doors. That circumstance has made the point of honor do an about turn and set it facing against idleness.

In America I have sometimes met rich young men temperamentally opposed to any uncomfortable effort and yet forced to enter a profession. Their characters and their wealth would have allowed them to stay idle, but public opinion imperiously forbade that and had to be obeyed. But among European nations where an aristocracy is still struggling against the current that carries it away, I have often met men whose needs and inclinations constantly goaded them to action, who yet remained idle so as not to lose the esteem of their equals, and who found boredom and discomfort easier to face than work.

No one can fail to see that both these contradictory obligations are rules of conduct originating in notions of honor.

That which our ancestors called, par excellence, honor was really only one of its forms. They gave the name of a genus to what was in fact only a species. Honor plays a part in democratic ages as well as in those of aristocracy, but it is easy to show that it presents a different physiognomy in the matter.

Not only are its injunctions different, but as we shall shortly see, they are fewer, less precise, and more loosely obeyed.

There is always something much more peculiar about the position of a caste than about that of a nation. Nothing in this world is more exceptional than a little society, always composed of the same families, such for instance as the medieval aristocracy, whose aim was to concentrate and keep all education, wealth, and power exclusively in its own hereditary hands.

Now, the more exceptional the position of a society, the more numerous are its special needs; and its notions of honor, which correspond to those needs, are bound to multiply.

The prescriptions of honor will therefore always be less numerous among a people not divided into castes than among any other. If ever there come to be nations in which it is hard to discover a trace of class distinctions, honor will then be limited to a few precepts, and these precepts will draw continually closer to the moral laws accepted by humanity in general.

Hence prescriptions of honor will be less odd and fewer in a democracy than in an aristocratic nation.

They will also be less well defined, for that is a necessary consequence of what has just been said.

The characteristic traits of honor being fewer and less peculiar, they must often be difficult to discern.

There are other reasons as well.

In the aristocratic nations of the Middle Ages generation followed generation without change; each family was like a man who never died or changed; ideas altered hardly more than conditions.

Each man therefore always had the same objects in sight and saw them in the same light; little by little his eye took in even the smallest details, and in the long run his vision was bound to become clear and accurate. Thus, not only did the men of feudal times have very extraordinary opinions that for them constituted honor, but each of these conceptions took a definite and precise shape in their minds.

That could never happen in such a country as America, where all the citizens are on the move and where society, itself subject to continual modification, changes its opinions with changing needs. In such a country men have glimpses of the rules of honor, but they seldom have leisure to consider them with attention.

Even if society stood still, it would even then be difficult to hold the meaning attached to the word "honor" fixed.

In the Middle Ages, each class having its own conception of honor, no very considerable number of men were ever agreed at the same time about its meaning, and this made it possible for it to take very limited and precise forms; this was so all the more because those who used the word, having a perfectly identical and very exceptional position, were naturally disposed to come to an understanding about the prescriptions of a law made expressly for themselves alone.

Thus the code of honor came to be complete and detailed with every possibility foreseen and provided for in advance, and it gave a fixed and always palpable rule for human behavior. In a democratic nation such as the people of America, in which ranks are confused and the whole of society forms one single mass composed of elements which are all analogous though not precisely similar, it is impossible ever to agree beforehand exactly what is allowed or forbidden by honor.

There are indeed for such a people certain national needs which give rise to common opinions concerning honor, but such opinions never present themselves at the same time, in the same manner, and with equal intensity to the mind of every citizen; the law of honor exists, but it is often left without interpreters.

The confusion is even greater in a democratic country such as France, where the different classes which composed the old society have been brought together but have not yet mingled, where these classes are constantly introducing each other to various and sometimes conflicting notions of honor, and where every man at his own caprice gives up one part of the opinions accepted by his ancestors while retaining another. So that amid so many arbitrary views it is never possible to establish a common rule. In such circumstances it is almost impossible to say in advance what actions will be honored and what stigmatized. Such times are wretched, but they do not last long.

Honor among democratic nations, being less defined, is of necessity less powerful, for it is hard to apply an imperfectly understood law with certainty and firmness. Public opinion, which is the natural and supreme interpreter of the law of honor, not seeing clearly to which side to incline in the distribution of praise and blame, always hesitates in giving judgment. Sometimes public opinion is self-contradictory; often it remains undecided and lets things slide.

There are several other reasons for the comparative weakness of honor in democracies.

In aristocratic countries identical notions of honor are always accepted by a few only, and these few often form a limited circle and are always separated from the rest of their fellows. Hence honor is easily associated and confused in their minds with everything which renders them peculiar. They think of it as the chief characteristic of the face they present to the world; they feel all the eagerness of personal interest in applying its various rules, and if I may put it so, there is something passionate in their obedience to its dictates.

This truth stands out very clearly if one studies the old applications of customary law to the question of trial by combat. The nobles, one finds, were bound to use lance and sword in their quarrels, whereas villeins fought only with sticks, "inasmuch," the old law books add, "as villeins have no honor." That did not mean, as a contemporary reader might suppose, that such men were contemptible, but simply that their actions were not judged by the same rules as applied to those of the aristocracy.

At first sight it is most astonishing to find that just when honor is at the zenith of its power its rules are at their strangest; apparently the further they get from common sense, the better they are obeyed. From this some people have drawn the conclusion that honor was strong just because of this exaggeration.

Both facts do spring from the same source, but the one is not derived from the other.

Honor becomes fantastic insomuch as it supports the peculiar requirements of a very few people, and just because it stands for requirements of this sort, it is strong. Honor therefore is not strong because of being fantastic, but it is fantastic and strong for the same reason.

I add a further remark.

In aristocracies all ranks are different, but all are fixed. Each man, in his own sphere, holds a position he cannot quit and in which he is surrounded by others similarly held in the same situation. In such nations no one can either hope or fear that he will not be seen. No man's social standing is so low but that he has a stage of his own, and no man can, by his obscurity, avoid praise or blame.

In democracies, on the other hand, where all are jumbled together in the same constantly fluctuating crowd, there is nothing for public opinion to catch hold of; its subject matter is ever vanishing from sight and escaping. In such circumstances honor must always be less binding and less urgently pressing. For honor is only effective in full view of the public, differing in that from sheer virtue, which feeds upon itself, contented with its own witness.

The reader who has followed my argument so far will see that there is a close and necessary connection between what we call honor and inequality of conditions, a connection which, if I am not mistaken, has never been clearly pointed out before. I shall therefore make a last effort to throw light on the matter.

A nation stands apart from the rest of mankind; as well as the general wants common to all humanity, it has some particular interests and needs. Certain opinions peculiar to this community about what should be praised or blamed are immediately established, and these are what the citizens call honor.

A caste comes to be established within this same nation, and it in turn keeps itself apart from all the other classes and contracts particular needs, which again give rise to special opinions. Among this caste honor composed of a strange mixture of the peculiar notions of the nation and the even more peculiar notions of the caste will get as far removed as it is possible to imagine from the simple, general opinions of men. That is the extreme point of the argument, from which we must now return.

Ranks mix and privileges are abolished. The members of the nation becoming again similar and equal, their interests and needs become identical, and all the peculiar notions which each class styled honor begin successively to disappear. The particular needs of the nation itself become the only source of honor, and that honor stands for the peculiar individual character of that nation before the world.

If one can further suppose that all races should become mixed, and all the peoples of the world should reach a state in which they all had the same interests and needs, and there was no characteristic trait distinguishing one from another, the practice of attributing a conventional value to men's actions would then cease altogether. Everyone would see them in the same light. The general needs of humanity, revealed to each man by his conscience, would form the common standard. Then one would see nothing in the world but simple, general notions of good and bad, to which nature and necessity would attach conceptions of praise and blame.

Thus, to conclude, compressing my essential thought into a single sentence, it is the dissimilarities and inequalities among men which give rise to the notion of honor; as such differences become less, it grows feeble; and when they disappear, it will vanish too.

Chapter 19

WHY THERE ARE SO MANY MEN OF AMBITION IN THE UNITED STATES BUT SO FEW LOFTY AMBITIONS

THE FIRST THING that strikes one in the United States is the innumerable crowd of those striving to escape from their original social condition; and the second is the rarity, in a land where all are actively ambitious, of any lofty ambition. Every American is eaten up with longing to rise, but hardly any of them seem to entertain very great hopes or to aim very high. All are constantly bent on gaining property, reputation, and power, but few conceive such things on a grand scale. That, at first sight, is surprising, since there is no obvious impediment in the mores or laws of America to put a limit to ambition or to prevent its taking wing in every direction.

Equality of conditions hardly seems a sufficient explanation of this strange state of affairs. For when this same equality was first established in France, it gave birth at once to almost unlimited ambitions.

Nevertheless, I think that we may find the chief reason for this in the social conditions and democratic manners of the Americans.

Every revolution increases men's ambition, and that is particularly true of a revolution which overthrows an aristocracy.

When the barriers that formerly kept the multitude from fame and power are suddenly thrown down, there is an impetuous universal movement toward those long-envied heights of power which can at last be enjoyed. In this first triumphant exaltation nothing seems impossible to anybody. Not only is there no limit to desires, but the power to satisfy them also seems almost unlimited. Amid this general and sudden change of customs and of laws, when all men and all rules share one vast confusion, when citizens rise and fall at such an unthought-of rate, and when power passes so quickly from hand to hand, no one need despair of snatching it in his turn.

It is also important to remember that those who destroy an aristocracy once lived under its laws; they have seen its splendors and have unconsciously imbibed the feelings and ideas which it conceived. At the moment, therefore, of the dissolution of an aristocracy, its spirit still hovers over the masses, and its instincts are preserved long after it has been conquered.

Thus ambitions are on the grand scale while the democratic revolution lasts; that will no longer be true some considerable time after it has finished.

Men do not in one day forget the memory of extraordinary events which they have witnessed; and the passions roused by revolution by no means vanish at its close. A sense of instability is perpetuated amid order. The hope of easy success lives on after the strange turns of fortune which gave it birth. Longings on a vast scale remain, though the means to satisfy them become daily less. The taste for huge fortunes persists, though such fortunes in fact become rare, and on all sides there are those who eat out their hearts in secret, consumed by inordinate and frustrated ambition.

But little by little the last traces of the battle are wiped out and the relics of aristocracy finally vanish. The great events which accompanied its fall are forgotten. Peace follows war, and order again prevails in a new world. Longings once more become proportionate to the available means. Wants, ideas, and feelings again learn their limits. Men find their level, and democratic society is finally firmly established.

When we come to take stock of a democratic people which has reached this enduring and normal state, it appears very different from the scene we have been contemplating. And we easily come to the conclusion that although high ambitions swell while conditions are in process of equalization, that characteristic is lost when equality is a fact.

When great fortunes have been divided up and education has spread, no one is absolutely deprived of either education or property. When both the privileges and the disqualifications of class have been abolished and men have shattered the bonds which once held them immobile, the idea of progress comes naturally into each man's mind; the desire to rise swells in every heart at once, and all men want to quit their former social position. Ambition becomes a universal feeling.

But equality, though it gives every citizen some resources, prevents any from enjoying resources of great extent, and for this reason desires must of necessity be confined within fairly narrow limits. Hence in domocracies ambition is both eager and constant, but in general it does not look very high. For the most part life is spent in eagerly coveting small prizes within reach.

It is not so much the small scale of their wealth as the constant and strenuous efforts requisite to increase it which chiefly diverts men in democracies from high ambitions. They strain their faculties to the utmost to achieve paltry results, and this quickly and inevitably limits their range of vision and circumscribes their powers. They could well be much poorer and yet be more magnanimous.

The few opulent citizens of a democracy constitute no exception to this rule. A man who raises himself gradually to wealth and power contracts in the course of this patient ascent habits of prudence and restraint which he cannot afterward shake off. A mind cannot be gradually enlarged, like a house.

Much the same applies to the sons of such a man. They may, it is true, have been born into a high position, but their parents were humble. They have grown up among feelings and ideas from which it is difficult later to escape. One may suppose that they inherit their father's instincts together with his property.

On the other hand, one may find some poor offshoot of a powerful aristocracy whose ambition is vast, for the opinions traditional to his race and the whole spirit of his caste for some time yet buoy him up above his actual fortune.

Another impediment making it far from easy for men of democratic ages to launch on great ambitions is the length of time that must elapse before they are in a position to undertake any such matter. "It is a great advantage," says Pascal, "to be a man of quality, for it brings one man forward at eighteen or twenty, whereas another must wait till he is fifty, which is a clear gain of thirty years."[1] Ambitious men in democracies generally have to do without those thirty years. Equality, while it allows any man to reach any height, prevents his doing so fast.

In a democratic society, as elsewhere, there are only a few great fortunes to be made. As the careers leading thereto are open without discrimination to every citizen, each man's progress is bound to be slow. When all candidates seem more or less alike and it is difficult to make any choice between them without violating the principle of equality which is the supreme law of democratic societies, the first idea which comes to mind is to make them all go forward at the same rate and submit to the same tests.

Therefore, as men become more alike and the principle of equality has quietly penetrated deep into the institutions and manners of the country, the rules of advancement become more inflexible and advancement itself slower. It becomes ever more difficult to reach a position of some importance quickly.

From hatred of privilege and embarrassment in choosing, all men, whatever their capacities, are finally forced through the same sieve, and all without discrimination are made to pass a host of petty preliminary tests, wasting their youth and suffocating their imagination. So they come to despair of ever fully enjoying the good things proffered, and when at last they reach a position in which they could do something out of the ordinary, the taste for it has left them.

In China, where equality has for a very long time been carried to great lengths, no man graduates from one public office to another without passing an examination. He has to face this test at every stage of his career, and the idea is now so deeply rooted in the manners of the people that I remember reading a Chinese novel in which the hero, after many ups and downs, succeeds at last in touching his mistress' heart by passing an examination well. Lofty ambition can hardly breathe in such an atmosphere.

What has been said about politics applies to everything else. Equality produces the same results everywhere. Even where no law regulates and holds back advancement, competition has this effect.

Hence great and rapid promotion is rare in a well-established democracy. Such events are exceptions to the general rule. Their very singularity makes men forget how seldom they occur.

The inhabitants of democracies do in the end get a glimpse of all these truths. They do at length appreciate that while the law opens an unlimited field before them, and while all can make some easy progress there, no one can flatter himself that his advance is swift. They see a multitude of little intermediate obstacles, all of which

[1] [Cf. Pascal, *Pensées*, edited by Brunschvicg, Fragment 322.]

have to be negotiated slowly, between them and the great object of their ultimate desires. The very anticipation of this prospect tires ambition and discourages it. They therefore discard such distant and doubtful hopes, preferring to seek delights less lofty but easier to reach. No law limits their horizon, but they do so for themselves.

I have said that high ambitions were rarer in democratic ages than under aristocracies. I must add that when, despite all natural obstacles, they do appear, they wear another face.

Under aristocracies the career open to ambition is often wide, but it does have fixed limits. In democratic countries its field of action is usually very narrow, but once those narrow bounds are passed, there is nothing left to stop it. As men are weak, isolated, and changeable, and as precedents have little force and laws do not last long, resistance to innovation is half-hearted, and the fabric of society never stands up quite straight or firm. As a result, when ambitious men have once seized power, they think they can dare to do anything. When power slips from their grasp, their thoughts at once turn to overturning the state in order to get it again.

This gives a violent and revolutionary character to great political ambitions, a thing which is seldom seen, to the same extent, in aristocratic societies.

A multitude of petty, very reasonable desires from which occasionally a few higher and ill-controlled ambitions will break out—such is the usual state of affairs in democratic nations. In them one hardly ever finds ambition which is proportionate, moderate, and yet vast.

I have shown elsewhere by what secret means equality makes the passion for physical pleasures and an exclusive interest in immediate delights predominate in the human heart. These instincts of different origin mingle with ambition, and it takes its color from them.

I think that ambitious men in democracies are less concerned than those in any other lands for the interests and judgment of posterity. The actual moment completely occupies and absorbs them. They carry through great undertakings quickly in preference to erecting long-lasting monuments. They are much more in love with success than with glory. What they especially ask from men is obedience. What they most desire is power. Their manners almost always lag behind the rise in their social position. As a result, very vulgar tastes often go with their enjoyment of extraordinary prosperity, and it would seem that their only object in rising to supreme power was to gratify trivial and coarse appetites more easily.

I think that nowadays it is necessary to purge ambition, to control it and keep it in proportion, but that it would be very dangerous if we tried to starve it or confine it beyond reason. The task should be to put, in advance, limits beyond which it would not be allowed to break. But we should be very careful not to hamper its free energy within the permitted limits.

I confess that I believe democratic society to have much less to fear from boldness than from paltriness of aim. What frightens me most is the danger that, amid all the constant trivial preoccupations of private life, ambition may lose both its force and its greatness, that human passions may grow gentler and at the same time baser, with the result that the progress of the body social may become daily quieter and less aspiring.

I therefore think that the leaders of the new societies would do wrong if they tried to send the citizens to sleep in a state of happiness too uniform and peaceful, but that they should sometimes give them difficult and dangerous problems to face, to rouse ambition and give it a field of action.

Moralists are constantly complaining that the pet vice of our age is pride.

There is a sense in which that is true; everyone thinks himself better than his neighbor and dislikes obeying a superior. But there is another sense in which it is very far from the truth, for the same man who is unable to put up with either subordination or equality has nonetheless so poor an opinion of himself that he thinks he is born for nothing but the enjoyment of vulgar pleasures. Of his own free will he limits himself to paltry desires and dares not face any lofty enterprise; indeed, he can scarcely imagine such a possibility.

Thus, far from thinking that we should council humility to our contemporaries, I wish men would try to give them a higher idea of themselves and of humanity; humility is far from healthy for them; what they most lack, in my view, is pride. I would gladly surrender several of our petty virtues for that one vice.

Chapter 20

CONCERNING PLACE-HUNTING IN SOME DEMOCRATIC COUNTRIES

IN THE UNITED STATES, when a citizen has some education and some resources he tries to enrich himself either by trade and industry or by buying a field covered in forest and turning into a pioneer. All he asks from the state is not to get in his way while he is working and to see that he can enjoy the fruit of his labor.

But in most of the countries of Europe, as soon as a man begins to feel his strength and extend his ambitions, the first idea that occurs to him is to get an official appointment. These different results, springing from the same cause, deserve a moment's attention.

When official appointments are few, ill-paid, and insecure, while at the same time industry offers numerous lucrative careers, all those in whom equality is daily breeding new and impatient desires naturally turn their attention to industry, not to administrative work.

But if, while ranks are moving toward equality, men's education is inadequate or their minds timid, or if trade and industry are hampered in their progress, so that they offer only a slow, hard road to fortune, the citizens, giving up hope of improving their lot by their own efforts, rush to the head of state and ask for his help. To increase their comfort at the expense of the public treasury strikes them as being, if not the only way, at least the easiest and most expeditious by which to escape from a condition which they no longer find satisfactory. The place-hunting attracts more recruits than any other trade.

Things are bound to be like that, especially in the great centralized monarchies, where there is an immense number of paid appointments and where the position of officials is fairly secure. In such circumstances no one need give up hope of obtaining an appointment and enjoying it in peace as if it were an inheritance.

There is no need for me to say that this universal and uncontrolled desire for official appointments is a great social evil, that it undermines every citizen's sense of independence and spreads a venal and servile temper throughout the nation, that it stifles manly virtues; nor need I note that such a trade only leads to unproductive activity and unsettles the country without adding to its resources. All that is obvious.

But I do want to point out that a government favoring this tendency risks its own peace and puts its very existence in great danger.

I know that in a time such as ours, when the love and respect which formerly waited on authority and power are gradually declining, it may seem necessary to governments to bind each man to them more closely by ties of interest, and they even think it convenient to make use of their passions in order to keep men orderly and silent, but such a method cannot work for long, and what may appear for a certain time to be a source of strength must in the long run prove a great cause of trouble and weakness.

In democratic countries, as in all others, there must be some limit to the number of public appointments; but among such peoples the number of men of ambition is not limited, but rather constantly increases, with gradual but irresistible progress, as equality becomes greater; the only check is the number of the population.

So, then, if administration is the only road open to ambition, the government in the end necessarily faces a permanent opposition, for it is bound to try and satisfy, with limited means, demands which multiply without limit. One must clearly understand that of all the peoples in the world, a nation of place-hunters is the hardest to restrain and direct. However hard its leaders try, it can never be satisfied, and there is always a danger that it will eventually overthrow the constitution and give new shape to the state simply for the purpose of cleaning out the present officeholders.

Those sovereigns of our day who try to concentrate on themselves alone all the new desires created by equality and to satisfy them will in the end, if I am not mistaken, regret that they ever embarked on such an undertaking. One day they will discover that they have put their own power in hazard by making it so necessary and that it would have been both safer and more honest to have taught their subjects the art of looking after themselves.

Chapter 21

WHY GREAT REVOLUTIONS
WILL BECOME RARE

WHEN A PEOPLE HAS LIVED for centuries under a system of castes and classes, it can only reach a democratic state of society through a long series of more or less painful transformations. These must involve violent efforts and many vicissitudes, in the course of which property, opinions, and power are all subject to swift changes.

Even when this great revolution has come to an end, the revolutionary habits created thereby and by the profound disturbances thereon ensuing will long endure.

As all this takes place just at the time when social conditions are being leveled, the conclusion has been drawn that there must be a hidden connection and secret link between equality itself and revolutions, so that neither can occur without the other.

On this point reason and experience seem agreed.

Among a people where ranks are more or less equal, there is no apparent connection between men to hold them firmly in place. None of them have any permanent right or power to give commands, and none is bound by his social condition to obey. Each man, having some education and some resources, can choose his own road and go along separately from all the rest.

The same causes which make the citizens independent of each other daily prompt new and restless longings and constantly goad them on.

It therefore seems natural to suppose that in a democratic society ideas, things, and men must eternally be changing shape and position and that ages of democracy must be times of swift and constant transformation.

But is this in fact so? Does equality of social conditions habitually and permanently drive men toward revolutions? Does it contain some disturbing principle which prevents society from settling down and inclines the citizens constantly to change their laws, principles, and mores? I do not think so. The subject is important, and I ask the reader to follow my argument closely.

Almost every revolution which has changed the shape of nations has been made to consolidate or destroy inequality. Disregarding the secondary causes which have had some effect on the great convulsions in the world, you will almost always find that equality was at the heart of the matter. Either the poor were bent on snatching the property of the rich, or the rich were trying to hold the poor down. So, then, if you could establish a state of society in which each man had something to keep and little to snatch, you would have done much for the peace of the world.

I realize that among a great people there will always be some very poor and some very rich citizens. But the poor, instead of forming the vast majority of the population as is always the case in aristocratic societies, are but few, and the law has not drawn them together by the link of an irremediable and hereditary state of wretchedness.

The rich, on their side, are scattered and powerless. They have no conspicuous privileges, and even their wealth, being no longer incorporated and bound up with the soil, is impalpable and, as it were, invisible. As there is no longer a race of poor men, so there is not a race of rich men; the rich daily rise out of the crowd and constantly return thither. Hence they do not form a distinct class, easily identified and plundered; moreover, there are a thousand hidden threads connecting them with the mass of citizens, so that the people would hardly know how to attack them without harming itself. In democratic societies between these two extremes there is an innumerable crowd who are much alike, who, though not exactly rich nor yet quite poor, have enough property to want order and not enough to excite envy.

Such men are the natural enemies of violent commotion; their immobility keeps all above and below them quiet, and assures the stability of the body social.

I am not suggesting that they are themselves satisfied with their actual position or that they would feel any natural abhorrence toward a revolution if they could share the plunder without suffering the calamities; on the contrary, their eagerness to get rich is unparalleled, but their trouble is to know whom to despoil. The same social condition which prompts their longings restrains them within necessary limits. It gives men both greater freedom to change and less interest in doing so.

Not only do men in democracies feel no natural inclination for revolutions, but they are afraid of them.

Any revolution is more or less a threat to property. Most inhabitants of a democracy have property. And not only have they got property, but they live in the conditions in which men attach most value to property.

If one studies each class of which society is composed closely, it is easy to see that passions due to ownership are keenest among the middle classes.

The poor often do not trouble much about their possessions, for their suffering from what they lack is much greater than their enjoyment of what they have. The rich have many other passions to gratify besides those connected with wealth, and moreover, the long and troublesome management of a great fortune sometimes makes them in the end insensible to its charms.

But men whose comfortable existence is equally far from wealth and poverty set immense value on their possessions. As they are still very close to poverty, they see its privations in detail and are afraid of them; nothing but a scanty fortune, the cynosure of all their hopes and fears, keeps them therefrom. The constant care which it occasions daily attaches them to their property; their continual exertions to increase it make it even more precious to them. The idea of giving up the smallest part of it is insufferable to them, and the thought of losing it completely strikes them as the worst of all evils. Now, it is just the number of the eager and restless small property-owners which equality of conditions constantly increases.

Hence the majority of citizens in a democracy do not see clearly what they could gain by a revolution, but they constantly see a thousand ways in which they could lose by one.

I have shown elsewhere in this work how equality naturally leads men to go in for industry and trade and that it tends to increase and distribute real property. I pointed out that it inspires every man with a constant and eager desire to increase his well-being. Nothing is more opposed to revolutionary passions than all this.

The final result of a revolution might serve the interests of industry and trade, but its first effect will almost always be the ruin of industrialists and traders, because it must always immediately change general habits of consumption and temporarily upset the balance between supply and demand.

Moreover, I know nothing more opposed to revolutionary morality than the moral standards of traders. Trade is the natural enemy of all violent passions. Trade loves moderation, delights in compromise, and is most careful to avoid anger. It is patient, supple, and insinuating, only resorting to extreme measures in cases of absolute necessity. Trade makes men independent of one another and gives them a high idea of their personal importance; it leads them to want to manage their own affairs and teaches them how to succeed therein. Hence it makes them inclined to liberty but disinclined to revolution.

In a revolution the owners of personal property have more to fear than all others, for their property is often both easy to seize and capable of disappearing completely at any moment. Owners of land have less to fear on this score, for although they may lose the income from it, they can hope at least to keep the land itself through the greatest vicissitudes. For this reason one finds that the latter are much less frightened of revolutionary movements than the former.

Therefore the more widely personal property is distributed and increased and the greater the number of those enjoying it, the less is a nation inclined to revolution.

Moreover, whatever a man's calling and whatever type of property he owns, one characteristic is common to all.

No one is fully satisfied with his present fortune, and all are constantly trying a thousand various ways to improve it. Consider any individual at any period of his life, and you will always find him preoccupied with fresh plans to increase his comfort. Do not talk to him about the interests and rights of the human race; that little private business of his for the moment absorbs all his thoughts, and he hopes that public disturbances can be put off to some other time.

This not only prevents them from causing revolutions, but also deters them from wanting them. Violent political passions have little hold on men whose whole thoughts are bent on the pursuit of well-being. Their excitement about small matters makes them calm about great ones.

It is true that from time to time in democratic societies aspiring and ambitious citizens do arise who are not content to follow the beaten track. Such men love revolutions and hail their approach. But they have great difficulty in bringing them about unless extraordinary events play into their hands.

No man can struggle with advantage against the spirit of his age and country, and however powerful a man may be, it is hard for him to make his contemporaries share feelings and ideas which run counter to the general run of their hopes and desires. It is therefore a mistake to suppose that once equality has become something long-established and undisputed, molding manners to its taste, men will easily allow themselves to be thrown into danger by some rash leader or bold innovator.

I am not suggesting that they resist him openly by means of well-thought-out-schemes, or indeed by means of any considered determination to resist. They show no energy in fighting him and sometimes even applaud him, but they do not follow him. Secretly their apathy is opposed to his fire, their conservative interests to his revolutionary instincts, their homely tastes to his adventurous passion, their common sense to his flighty genius, their prose to his poetry. With immense effort he rouses them for a moment, but they soon slip from him and fall back, as it were, by their own weight. He exhausts himself trying to animate this indifferent and preoccupied crowd and finds at last that he is reduced to impotence, not because he is conquered but because he is alone.

I am not making out that the inhabitants of democracies are by nature stationary; on the contrary, I think that such a society is always on the move and that none of its members knows what rest is; but I think that all bestir themselves within certain limits which they hardly ever pass. Daily they change, alter, and renew things of secondary importance, but they are very careful not to touch fundamentals. They love change, but they are afraid of revolutions.

Although the Americans are constantly modifying or repealing some of their laws, they are far from showing any revolutionary passions. One can easily see, by the promptness with which they stop and calm themselves just when public agitation begins to be threatening and when passions seem most excited, that they fear a revolution as the greatest of evils and that each of them is inwardly resolved to make great sacrifices to avoid one. In no other country in the world is the love of property keener or more alert than in the United States, and nowhere else does the majority display less inclination toward doctrines which in any way threaten the way property is owned.

I have often noted that theories which are basically revolutionary in that they cannot be put into practice without a complete, in some cases a sudden, change in property rights and personal status are infinitely less in favor in the United States than in the great monarchies of Europe. Though some individuals profess them, the mass of the people reject them with instinctive horror.

I have no hesitation in saying that most of the maxims which are generally called democratic in France would be outlawed by the American democracy. That is easily understood. In America there exist democratic ideas and passions; in Europe we still have revolutionary ones.

If there ever are great revolutions there, they will be caused by the presence of the blacks upon American soil. That is to say, it will not be the equality of social conditions but rather their inequality which may give rise thereto.

When social conditions are equal, every man tends to live apart, centered in himself and forgetful of the public. Should democratic legislators not seek to correct this fatal tendency, or actually favor it, thinking that it diverts the citizens' attention from political passions and avoids revolutions, it might happen in the end that they may bring about that very evil which they seek to avoid and that the moment may come when the unruly passions of certain men, aided by the foolish selfishness and pusillanimity of the greater number, will in the end subject the fabric of society to strange vicissitudes.

In democratic societies it is only small minorities who desire revolutions, but the minorities may bring them about.

I am far from asserting that democratic nations are safe from revolutions; I only say that the social state of those nations does not lead toward revolution, but rather wards it off. Democratic nations, left to themselves, are slow to embark on great adventures; they are only dragged into revolutions in spite of themselves; they may sometimes suffer from them, but they never make them. I would add that once they have gained education and experience, they will not allow them to occur.

I am well aware that, in this context, public institutions may have great influence; they can favor or restrain the instincts bred by the social state. I must therefore again make it perfectly clear that a nation is not safe from revolution simply because social conditions are equal there. But I do think that, whatever institutions such a people may have, great revolutions will be infinitely less violent and rarer than is generally supposed. I can easily, though vaguely, foresee a political condition, combined with equality, which might create a society more stationary than any we have ever known in our Western world.

What I have been saying about facts applies, in part, to ideas.

Two things in America are astonishing: the changeableness of most human behavior and the strange stability of certain principles. Men are constantly on the move, but the spirit of humanity seems almost unmoved.

Once an opinion has spread on American soil and taken root there, it would seem that no power on earth can eradicate it. In the United States general doctrines concerning religion, philosophy, morality, and even politics do not vary at all, or at least are only modified by the slow and often unconscious working of some hidden process. Even the very crudest prejudices take an unconscionable time to efface, in spite of all the froth and stir of men and things.

One hears people say that it is inherent in the habits and nature of democracies to change feelings and thoughts at every moment. That may have been true of such small democratic nations as those of antiquity, where everyone could assemble in the marketplace, and when there, be carried away by an orator's eloquence. But I have never seen anything like that happening in the great democracy on the other side of our ocean. What struck me most in the United States was the difficulty experienced in getting an idea, once conceived, out of the head of the majority and stopping their following the man of their choice. Neither writings nor speeches can have much success in that; only experience can do it, and that too must sometimes be repeated.

That is surprising at first sight, but closer examination gives the explanation.

I do not think it as easy as is generally supposed to eradicate the prejudices of a democratic people, to change its beliefs, to substitute new religious, philosophical, political, and moral principles for those which have once become established, in a word, to bring about great or frequent mental revolutions. Not that there the human mind is lazy; it is constantly active, but it is more concerned with infinite variations in the consequences to be derived from known principles and in finding new consequences rather than in seeking new principles. It turns around spryly on itself but has no straightforward impulse to rapid progress; slight, continual, hasty movements gradually extend its orbit, but it never changes position all at once.

Men with equal rights, education, and wealth, that is to say, men who are in just the same condition, must have very similar needs, habits, and tastes. As they see things in the same light, their minds naturally incline to similar ideas, and though any one of them could part company with the rest and work out his own beliefs, in the end they all concur, unconsciously and unintentionally, in a certain number of common opinions.

The more closely I consider the effects of equality upon the mind, the more I am convinced that the intellectual anarchy which we see around us is not, as some suppose, the natural state for democracies. I think we should rather consider it as an accidental characteristic peculiar to their youth, and something that only happens during that transitional period when men have broken the ancient links which held them together, but are still immensely different in origin, education, and manners. In such circumstances, having preserved very various ideas, instincts, and tastes, nothing any longer prevents them from airing them. Men's main opinions become alike as the conditions of their lives become alike. That seems to be the general and permanent fact; the rest is fortuitous and ephemeral.

It must, I think, be rare in a democracy for a man suddenly to conceive a system of ideas far different from those accepted by his contemporaries; and I suppose that, even should such an innovator arise, he would have great difficulty in making himself heard to begin with, and even more in convincing people.

When conditions are almost equal, one man is not easily to be persuaded by another. When all men see each other at close quarters, have together learned the same things and led the same life, there is no natural inclination for them to accept one of their number as a guide and follow him blindly; one hardly ever takes on trust the opinion of an equal of like standing with oneself.

It is not simply that in democracies confidence in the superior knowledge of certain individuals has been weakened. As I have pointed out before, the general idea that any man whosoever can attain an intellectual superiority beyond the reach of the rest is soon cast in doubt.

As men grow more like each other, a dogma concerning intellectual equality gradually creeps into their beliefs, and it becomes harder for any innovator whosoever to gain and maintain great influence over the mind of a nation. In such societies sudden intellectual revolutions must therefore be rare. For, taking a general view of world history, one finds that it is less the force of an argument than the authority of a name which has brought about great and rapid changes in accepted ideas.

It is also important to realize that since there is no link binding the inhabitants of democracies to each other, each man has to be convinced separately, whereas in aristocracies it is enough to influence the views of certain individuals, and the rest will follow. If Luther had lived in an age of equality and there had been no great territorial magnates and princes to listen to him, perhaps he would have found it harder to change the face of Europe.

Not that the inhabitants of democracies are naturally strongly convinced of the certainty of their beliefs; they often feel doubts which, in their view, no one can resolve. It sometimes happens in such times that a change of intellectual position is desired, but without the strong pressure of any directing force, nothing more than oscillation to and fro, without any progress, occurs.[1]

Even when one has won the confidence of a democratic nation, it is a hard matter to attract its attention. It is very difficult to make the inhabitants of democracies listen when one is not talking about themselves. They do not hear what is said to them because they are always very preoccupied with what they are doing.

Indeed, there are few men of leisure in democracies. Life passes in movement and noise, and men are so busy acting that they have little time to think. I want especially to stress that they are not only busy, but passionately interested in their business. They are always in action, and each action absorbs all their faculties. The fire they put into their work prevents their being fired by ideas.

I think it is an arduous undertaking to excite the enthusiasm of a democratic nation for any theory which does not have a visible, direct, and immediate bearing on the occupations of their daily lives. Such a people does not easily give up its ancient beliefs. For it is enthusiasm which makes men's minds leap off the beaten track and brings about great intellectual, as well as political, revolutions.

[1] Trying to discover the state of society most favorable to great intellectual revolutions, I think it must lie somewhere between complete equality for every citizen and the absolute separation of classes.

Under a caste system generation follows generation without a change in man's position; while some have nothing more to desire, the rest have nothing better to hope. The imagination slumbers in the stillness of this universal silence, and the mere idea of movement does not come into men's minds.

When classes have been abolished and conditions have become almost equal, men are constantly on the move, but each individual is isolated, on his own, and weak. For all the vast difference between these two states, they are alike in one respect, namely, that great intellectual revolutions become rare.

But between these two extremes in a nation's history there is an intermediate stage, a glorious yet troubled time in which conditions are not sufficiently fixed for the mind to sleep and in which there is enough inequality for men to exercise great power over the minds of others, so that a few can modify the beliefs of all. That is the time when great reformers arise and new ideas change the face of the world.

Hence democratic nations have neither leisure nor taste to think out new opinions. Even when they are doubtful about accepted ideas they still stick to them because it would take too much time to examine and change them. They hold to them not because they are certain but because they are accepted.

There are also other, and even stronger, reasons which prevent any great change in the doctrines of a democratic people coming about easily. I have already indicated them at the beginning of this book.

Whereas, in such a nation, the influence of individuals is weak and almost nonexistent, the power of the mass over each individual mind is very great. I have given the reasons elsewhere. What I want to stress now is that it would be a mistake to suppose that this depends on nothing but the form of government and that the majority would lose its intellectual sway with its political power.

In aristocracies men often have something of greatness and strength which is all their own. When they find themselves at variance with most of their fellows, they retreat into themselves and there find support and consolation. But in democracies it is not like that. There public favor seems as necessary as the air they breathe, and to be out of harmony with the mass is, if one may put it so, no life at all. The mass has no need of laws to bend those who do not agree to its will. Its disapproval is enough. The sense of their isolation and impotence at once overwhelms them and drives them to despair.

Whenever conditions are equal, public opinion brings immense weight to bear on every individual. It surrounds, directs, and oppresses him. The basic constitution of society has more to do with this than any political laws. The more alike men are, the weaker each feels in the face of all. Finding nothing that raises him above their level and distinguishes him, he loses his self-confidence when he comes into collision with them. Not only does he mistrust his own strength, but even comes to doubt his own judgment, and he is brought very near to recognizing that he must be wrong when the majority hold the opposite view. There is no need for the majority to compel him; it convinces him.

Therefore, however powers within a democracy are organized and weighted, it will always be very difficult for a man to believe what the mass rejects and to profess what it condemns.

This circumstance is wonderfully favorable to the stability of beliefs.

When an opinion has taken root in a democracy and established itself in the minds of the majority, it afterward persists by itself, needing no effort to maintain it since no one attacks it. Those who at first rejected it as false come in the end to adopt it as accepted, and even those who still at the bottom of their hearts oppose it keep their views to themselves, taking great care to avoid a dangerous and futile contest.

It is true that when a democratic majority does change its mind, a sudden, arbitrary, and strange intellectual revolution may ensue. But yet that majority's opinion has great difficulty in changing, and it is almost as difficult to be sure that it has changed.

Sometimes, though no change may be visible from outside, it does happen that time, circumstances, and the lonely workings of each man's thought do, little by little, in the end shake or destroy some belief. It has not been openly attacked. No meetings have been held to fight against it. But one by one its supporters quietly drop it, so that finally these small continual defections leave it with but a few upholders.

In such conditions it still prevails.

As its opponents still hold their peace or only stealthily exchange their thoughts, they are themselves long unsure that a great revolution has taken place, and when in doubt, they take no action. They watch and keep quiet. The majority no longer believes, but it looks as if it did believe, and this empty ghost of public opinion is enough to chill the innovators and make them maintain their silent respect.

We live in a time that has witnessed the swiftest changes in men's minds. But yet perhaps some of the main opinions of mankind may be soon more stable than ever before in the centuries of our history. Such a time has not yet come, but it may be at hand.

The more closely I examine the needs and instincts natural to democracies, the more am I convinced that if ever equality is established generally and permanently in the world, great intellectual and political revolutions will become much more difficult and much rarer than is generally supposed.

Because the inhabitants of democracies always seem excited, uncertain, hurried, and ready to change both their minds and their situation, it has been supposed that they want immediately to abolish their laws, adopt new beliefs, and conform to new manners. It has not been noted that while equality leads men to make changes it also prompts them to have interests which require stability for their satisfaction; it both drives them on and holds them back; it goads them on and keeps their feet on the ground; it kindles their desires and limits their powers.

That is something which one does not see at first sight. The passions that keep the inhabitants of democracies separated from each other are obvious enough, but the hidden force which holds them back and holds them together is not obvious at a glance.

Can I safely say this amid the surrounding ruins? What I most fear for succeeding generations is not revolutions.

If the citizens continue to shut themselves up more and more narrowly in the little circle of petty domestic interests and keep themselves constantly busy therein, there is a danger that they may in the end become practically out of reach of those great and powerful public emotions which do indeed perturb peoples but which also make them grow and refresh them. Seeing property change hands so quickly, and love of property become so anxious and eager, I cannot help fearing that men may reach a point where they look on every new theory as a danger, every innovation as a toilsome trouble, every social advance as a first step toward revolution, and that they may absolutely refuse to move at all for fear of being carried off their feet. The prospect really does frighten me that they may finally become so engrossed in a cowardly love of immediate pleasures that their interest in their own future and in that of their descendants may vanish, and that they will prefer tamely to follow the course of their destiny rather than make a sudden energetic effort necessary to set things right.

People suppose that the new societies are going to change shape daily, but my fear is that they will end up by being too unalterably fixed with the same institutions, prejudices, and mores, so that mankind will stop progressing and will dig itself in. I fear that the mind may keep folding itself up in a narrower compass forever without producing new ideas, that men will wear themselves out in trivial, lonely, futile activity, and that for all its constant agitation humanity will make no advance.

Chapter 22

WHY DEMOCRATIC PEOPLES NATURALLY WANT PEACE BUT DEMOCRATIC ARMIES WAR

THE SAME INTERESTS, the same fears, the same passions that deter democratic peoples from revolutions also alienate them from war. The military and revolutionary spirit grows feeble at the same time, and for the same reasons.

The ever-increasing number of men of property devoted to peace, the growth of personal property which war so rapidly devours, mildness of mores, gentleness of heart, that inclination to pity which equality inspires, that cold and calculating spirit which leaves little room for sensitivity to the poetic and violent emotions of wartime— all these causes act together to damp down warlike fervor.

I think one can accept it as a general and constant rule that among civilized nations warlike passions become rarer and less active as social conditions get nearer to equality.

Yet war is a hazard to which all nations are subject, democracies as well as the rest. No matter how greatly such nations may be devoted to peace, they must be ready to defend themselves if attacked, or in other words, they must have an army.

Fortune, which has showered so many peculiar favors on the inhabitants of the United States, has placed them in the midst of a wilderness where one can almost say that they have no neighbors. For them a few thousand soldiers are enough, but that is something peculiar to America, not to democracy.

Equality of conditions and the mores and institutions deriving therefrom do not rescue a democracy from the necessity of keeping up an army, and their armies always exercise a powerful influence over their fate. It is therefore peculiarly important to discover what are the natural instincts of those who compose these armies.

In aristocracies, especially where birth alone decides rank, there is the same inequality in the army as elsewhere in the nation; officers are nobles, soldiers serfs; the one is necessarily called on to command and the other to obey. In aristocratic armies, therefore, the soldier's ambition has very narrow limits.

That of the officers is also far from unlimited.

An aristocratic body not only is part of a hierarchy but also contains a hierarchy within itself. The people who compose it are ranked one above the other in a certain manner which does not alter at all. One is naturally called by birth to command a regiment, another a company. Once they have reached these ultimate goals of their hopes, they come to a halt of their own accord and feel themselves satisfied with their lot.

There is besides in aristocracies another strong reason why officers are not overanxious for promotion.

In aristocracies an officer, apart from his rank in the army, anyhow occupies a high position in society. He almost always regards his military rank as something secondary to his social position; a nobleman who joins the army as a career is less influenced by ambition than by a sense of the duties imposed by his birth. He goes into the army to find honorable employment for the leisure years of his youth and to have creditable stories of his soldiering life to recount later to his family and friends; it is not his principal aim to acquire property, reputation, or power, for he enjoys those advantages on his own account without any need to leave home.

In democratic armies all the soldiers may become officers, and that fact makes desire for promotion general and opens almost infinite doors to military ambition.

The officer, for his part, sees nothing that naturally and automatically stops him at one rank rather than another, and each promotion has immense importance in his eyes, because his standing in society almost always depends on his rank in the army.

In democracies it often happens that an officer has nothing but his pay and no claim to distinction but his military honors. Every new appointment, therefore, renews his fortune, and he is in some sense a new man. Something which was only a secondary consideration in aristocratic armies has become the chief thing, the only thing, and the essence of existence.

Under the old French monarchy officers were always addressed by their titles of nobility. Nowadays they are only given their military rank; this slight change in forms of speech is enough to show that a great revolution has taken place in the constitution both of society and of the army.

Desire for promotion is almost universal in democratic armies; it is eager, tenacious, and continual. All other desires serve to feed it, and it is only quenched with life itself. It is therefore easy to see that promotion in times of peace must be slower in democratic armies than in any other armies in the world. As the number of commissions is naturally limited, while the number of competitors is almost innumerable, and they are all subject to the unbending rule of equality, no one can make rapid progress, and many can make no progress at all. Thus the desire for promotion is greater and the opportunities for it are fewer than elsewhere.

Therefore all the ambitious minds in a democratic army ardently long for war, because war makes vacancies available and at last allows violations of the rule of seniority, which is the one privilege natural to a democracy.

We thus arrive at the strange conclusion that of all armies those which long for war most ardently are the democratic ones, but that of all peoples those most deeply attached to peace are the democratic nations. And the most extraordinary thing about the whole matter is that it is equality which is responsible for both these contradictory results.

All the citizens, being equal, constantly conceive the wish and discover the possibility of changing their condition and increasing their well-being; that inclines them to love peace, which favors industry and gives every man a chance to bring his little undertakings quietly to a conclusion. On the other hand, the same equality makes military honors seem more valuable to those who follow the career of arms, and by making these honors within the reach of all, causes soldiers to dream of battlefields. In both cases the restlessness of spirit is the same, and in both cases the taste for enjoyment is equally insatiable and ambition in both cases equally great. Only the means of gratifying it are different.

These contrary inclinations of nation and army cause great hazards to democratic societies.

When a nation loses its military spirit, the career of arms immediately ceases to be respected and military men drop down to the lowest rank among public officials. They are neither greatly esteemed nor well understood; therefore exactly the opposite happens to what occurs in aristocratic ages. It is not the leading citizens, but the least important who go into the army. A man only develops military ambitions when all other doors are closed. That forms a vicious circle, from which it is hard to escape. The elite of the nation avoid a military career because it is not held in honor, and it is not held in honor because the elite of the nation do not take it up.

There is therefore no reason for surprise if democratic armies are found to be restless, prone to complaint, and ill-satisfied with their lot, although their physical condition is generally much better and discipline less strict than in all other armies. The soldier feels that he is in a position of inferiority and his wounded pride gives him a taste for war which will make him needed, or a taste for revolutions, in the course of which he hopes to win by force of arms the political influence and personal consideration which have not come his way.

The composition of democratic armies makes this last danger much to be feared.

In democratic societies almost every man has some property to preserve, but democratic armies are usually led by men of the people, most of whom have little to lose in civil broils. The mass of the nation is naturally much more frightened of revolution than is the case in times of aristocracy, but the leaders of the army are much less so.

Moreover, as I have said before, because in democracies the richest, best-educated, and ablest citizens hardly ever adopt a military career, the army finally becomes a little nation apart, with a lower standard of intelligence and rougher habits than the nation at large.

But this little uncivilized nation holds the weapons and it alone knows how to use them.

The danger from the turbulent and warlike spirit of the army is actually increased in democracies by the pacific temper of the citizens. There is nothing more dangerous than an army amid an unwarlike nation. The citizens' excessive love of quiet puts the constitution every day at the mercy of the soldiers.

One can therefore make this generalization, that although their interests and inclinations naturally incline democracies to peace, their armies exercise a constant pull toward war and revolution.

Military revolutions, which are hardly ever a serious threat in aristocracies, are always to be feared in democracies. They should be reckoned among the most threatening of the perils which face their future existence. Statesmen must never relax their efforts to find a remedy for this evil.

When a nation sees that its internal peace is disturbed by the restless ambition of the army, the first thought which occurs is to provide a goal for this troublesome ambition by going to war.

I do not wish to speak ill of war; war almost always widens a nation's mental horizons and raises its heart. In some cases it may be the only factor which can prevent the exaggerated growth of certain inclinations naturally produced by equality and be the antidote needed for certain inveterate diseases to which democratic societies are liable.

War has great advantages, but we must not flatter ourselves that it can lessen the danger I have just pointed out. It only puts the danger off, to come back in more terrible form when war is over. For armies are much more impatient of peace when once they have tasted war. War could only be a remedy for a people always athirst for glory.

I foresee that all the great wartime leaders who may arise in the major democratic nations will find it easier to conquer with the aid of their armies than to make their armies live at peace after conquest. There are two things that will always be very difficult for a democratic nation: to start a war and to end it.

Again, if war has some peculiar advantages for democratic nations, it also entails certain dangers for them which aristocracies have no equal cause to dread. I will quote two examples only.

Although war satisfies the army, it annoys and often drives to desperation that countless crowd of citizens whose petty passions daily require peace for their satisfaction. There is therefore some danger that it may cause, in another form, the very disturbance which it should prevent.

Any long war always entails great hazards to liberty in a democracy.

Not that one need apprehend that after every victory the conquering generals will seize sovereign power by force after the manner of Sulla and Caesar. The danger is of another kind. War does not always give democratic societies over to military government, but it must invariably and immeasurably increase the powers of civil government; it must almost automatically concentrate the direction of all men and the control of all things in the hands of the government. If that does not lead to despotism by sudden violence, it leads men gently in that direction by their habits.

All those who seek to destroy the freedom of the democratic nations must know that war is the surest and shortest means to accomplish this. That is the very first axiom of their science.

One obvious remedy when the ambition of officers and soldiers becomes threatening is, by enlarging the army, to increase the number of commissions available. This affords temporary relief but makes the danger all the greater in the future.

To increase the army may produce a lasting effect in an aristocratic society, since military ambition is there limited to one class of men, and there is an automatic limit for the ambition of each, so that it is possible to satisfy almost all those stirred by ambition.

But nothing is gained in a democracy by increasing the army, because the number of men of ambition increases in exact proportion with the growth of the army itself. Those whose claims have been satisfied by the creation of new commissions are instantly succeeded by a fresh multitude who cannot be so satisfied, and even the first lot soon start complaining again. For the same restless spirit which prevails in the civil life of a democracy is seen in the army too; what men want is not a certain rank, but constant promotion. Their longings are not spectacular, but they constantly recur. Thus a democratic nation, by augmenting its army, allays the ambition of the military but for a moment; it soon revives in more formidable shape, since the number of those who feel it is increased.

For my part, I think that a restless, turbulent spirit is an evil inherent in the very constitution of democratic armies, and beyond hope of cure. The legislators in democracies must not flatter themselves that they will be able to find any way of organizing the army which will by itself calm and restrain military men. They would wear themselves out in frustrated efforts without attaining their end.

It is in the nation, not in the army itself, that one must look for the remedy for the army's vices.

Democratic peoples are naturally afraid of disturbances and despotism. All that is needed is to turn these instincts into considered, intelligent, and stable tastes. When once the citizens have learned to make peaceful and productive use of freedom and have felt its benefits, when they have conceived a manly love of order and have freely submitted to discipline, these same men, if they follow the profession of arms, will bring into it, unconsciously and almost in spite of themselves, these same habits and mores. The general spirit of the nation, penetrating the spirit peculiar to the army, tempers the opinions and desires engendered by military life, or by the all-powerful influence of public opinion, actually represses them. Once you have educated, orderly, upstanding, and free citizens, you will have disciplined and obedient soldiers.

Therefore any law which in repressing this turbulent spirit of the army should tend to diminish the spirit of freedom in the nation and to cloud conceptions of law and rights would defeat its object. It would do much more to increase than to impede the dangers of military tyranny.

After all, whatever one does, a large army in a democracy will always be a serious danger, and the best way to lesson this danger will be to reduce the army. But that is not a remedy which every nation can apply.

Chapter 23

WHICH IS THE MOST WARLIKE AND REVOLUTIONARY CLASS IN DEMOCRATIC ARMIES

IT IS OF THE ESSENCE of a democratic army to be very numerous compared to the population providing its manpower; I will give the reasons for that later.

But men living in times of democracy seldom choose a soldier's life.

Democratic peoples are therefore soon led to give up voluntary recruitment and fall back on conscription. The nature of their way of life forces them to do this, and it is safe to predict that that is what they will all do.

Military service being compulsory, the burden is spread equally and without discrimination among all the citizens. That too is a necessary result of their way of life and thought. A democratic government can do pretty well what it likes, provided that its orders apply to all and at the same moment; it is the inequality of a burden, not its weight, which usually provokes resistance.

Now, as every citizen is subject to military service, it is obvious that each of them can only remain a few years with the colors.

It is therefore in the nature of things that the soldier should do no more than pass through the army, whereas in most aristocratic nations the military profession is one which the soldier adopts or has imposed on him for the whole of his life.

This has important consequences. Some of the soldiers in a democratic army come to like a military life, but most of them, called to the colors against their will, are always ready to return home, not feeling seriously committed to a soldier's life, and only hoping to get out of it. Such men nether contract the needs nor ever more than half share the passions which that mode of life engenders. They perform their duty as soldiers, but their minds are still on the interests and hopes which filled them in civilian life. They are therefore not colored by the military spirit but rather carry their civilian frame of mind with them into the army and never lose it. In democracies it is the private soldiers who remain most like civilians; it is on them that national habits have the firmest hold and public opinion the strongest influence. It is especially through the soldiers that one may well hope to inspire a democratic army with the same love of liberty and respect for law as has been infused into the nation itself. The opposite is true of aristocratic nations, where soldiers eventually cease to have anything in common with their fellow citizens and come to live as strangers among them, indeed often as enemies.

In aristocratic armies it is the officers who have kept close ties with civilian society and never give up their desire sooner or later to take their place in it again. In democratic armies that is true of the soldier, and the reasons therefor are just the same.

On the other hand, it often happens in these same democratic armies that the officers contract tastes and desires entirely different from those of the rest of the nation. That is understandable.

In democracies the man who becomes an officer breaks all the ties attaching him to civilian life. He has left that life forever and has no interest in joining it again. His true fatherland is the army, since he has no importance apart from the rank he holds. He therefore follows the fortunes of the army, rising or falling with it, and that is where all his hopes are centered. An officer, having very different needs from those of the country, may perhaps eagerly desire war or work for a revolution at the very moment when the nation most longs for stability and peace.

There are, however, factors which modify his restless, warlike spirit. Though in democracies ambition is universal and perpetual, we have seen that it is seldom on the grand scale. A man sprung from the secondary classes of the nation who has worked his way up through the ranks to become an officer has already made an immense advance. He has won a footing in a sphere superior to his former standing in civilian society, and he has acquired rights which most democratic nations always consider inalienable.[1] He is willing to pause after that great effort and think about enjoying his achievement. Fear of risking what he has won tempers his heart's eagerness to acquire more. Having broken through the first and greatest obstacle to his promotion, he is resigned with less impatience to the slowness of further progress. This blunting of ambition goes a stage further when he reaches higher ranks and thereby has more to lose. If I am not mistaken, the least warlike and least revolutionary part of a democratic army will always be its leaders.

What I have just said about officers and soldiers does not apply at all to the numerous class which in all armies comes between these two, that of noncommissioned officers.

NCO's as a class have never before this century made any mark in history, but I think that now they are called on to play a part.

Like the officer, the NCO feels that he has broken all ties with civilian life; he too has made the army his career, and perhaps more than the officer, centers all his hopes on it. But unlike the officer, he has not reached a high or firm stage in his promotion, a stage at which he could halt and breathe more freely while awaiting further promotion.

By the very nature of his functions, which cannot change, the NCO is condemned to live an obscure, narrow, uncomfortable, and precarious existence. He still sees only the dangers of military life. He knows nothing but the privations and obedience, which are harder than dangers to bear. He suffers the more from his present discomforts because he knows that the constitution of society and of the army give him a chance to escape from them. He in fact can, from one day to another, become an officer. Then he will give the orders and have distinctions, independence, rights, and pleasures. But he is never sure of attaining this deeply coveted object of his hopes until he actually has it. There is nothing irrevocable about his rank; the whole time, he is completely subject to the arbitrary decisions of his commanding officers, for that is an imperious necessity

---

[1] The officer's position is in fact much more secure in democracies than elsewhere. The less importance an officer has on his own account, the more value he attaches to his army rank and the more does the legislature think it just and necessary to make his enjoyment thereof secure.

of discipline. Some slight fault or some caprice could make him in a moment lose the fruit of several years of laborious effort. So until he has reached the coveted rank, he has done nothing. It is only at that stage that he really seems to start his career. A man so constantly goaded by youth, want, passions, the spirit of the time, hopes, and fears cannot fail to kindle a desperate ambition.

Hence the NCO wants war; he always wants it and at any cost. If he cannot have war, he wants revolutions, which suspend the authority of rules and give him a hope, in the confusion of political passions, to chase his officer out and take his place. It is not impossible that he might bring about a revolution, for their common origin and habits give him great influence over the soldiers, though his passions and hopes are very different from theirs.

It would be a mistake to suppose that the differing dispositions of officers, NCO's, and men are peculiar to one age or country. They always occur at all times among all democratic nations.

In every democratic army it will always be the NCO who is least representative of the pacific and orderly spirit of the country, and the private who best represents it. The private will carry the strength or weakness of national mores with him into military life; he will provide a faithful reflection of the nation. If the nation is ignorant and weak, he will let himself be drawn by his leaders into disturbances, either unconsciously or even against his will. If the nation is educated and energetic, this fact will keep him within the bounds of discipline.

Chapter 24

WHAT MAKES DEMOCRATIC ARMIES WEAKER THAN OTHERS AT THE BEGINNING OF A CAMPAIGN BUT MORE FORMIDABLE IN PROLONGED WARFARE

ANY ARMY STARTING ON A CAMPAIGN after a long peace is in danger of defeat; any army that has long been fighting has good chances of victory; that truth applies particularly to democratic armies.

In aristocracies the military profession, being a privileged career, is respected even in times of peace. Highly educated and ambitious men of parts take to it; the army is in all respects on a level with the nation, and sometimes even above it.

But we have seen how in democracies the elite of the nation are gradually drawn away from the military profession to seek other paths to reputation, power, and above all, wealth. After a long peace—and in times of democracy the intervals of peace are long— the army is always inferior to the nation. War catches it in this condition, and until war has brought about a change, there is danger for the country and for the army too.

I have pointed out how in democratic armies in time of peace seniority is the supreme and rigid law of promotion. This is a consequence, as I have noted before, not only of the constitution of such armies but of the constitution of the nation itself, and it will always occur.

Moreover, as among such people the officer is of no account in the country apart from his army rank and derives all the distinction and comfort he enjoys therefrom, he does not retire and is not superannuated from the army until near the end of his life.

For these two reasons, when a democratic people does at last take up arms after a long peace, all the leaders of the army are found to be old men. I am not speaking only of the generals, but also of the subordinate officers, most of whom have stood still or only advanced step by step. If one takes a look at a democratic army after a long peace, one is surprised to find that all the soldiers are almost children and all the leaders in their declining years, so that the former lack experience and the latter energy. This is one great cause of defeat, for the first condition of successful leadership in war is youth; I would not have dared to say that if the greatest captain of modern times had not made the observation.

These two causes do not act in the same manner upon aristocratic armies; because in them men are promoted by right of birth much more than by right of seniority, there are in all ranks a certain number of young men who bring the early vigor of body and mind to the conduct of war.

Moreover, as those who seek military honors in an aristocracy enjoy an assured position in civilian society, it seldom happens that they stay in the army until old age overtakes them. Having devoted the most vigorous years of youth to the career of arms, they retire of their own accord and spend the remainder of their maturer years at home.

A long peace not only fills democratic armies with elderly officers but also gives all the officers habits of body and mind unfitting them for actual war. The man who has long lived in the quiet, unexacting atmosphere of democratic society is at first ill-inclined to adapt himself to the rough work and stern duties imposed by war, and if he has not absolutely lost his taste for arms, at least he has formed habits of life which prevent him from being victorious.

In aristocracies the softness of civilian life has less influence on military mores because in those nations it is the aristocracy who lead the army. Now, an aristocracy, however deeply plunged in luxurious pleasures, has always many other passions besides that for well-being and will readily sacrifice momentary well-being to better satisfy its other passions. (See Appendix I, X.)

I have pointed out the extreme slowness of promotion in democratic armies in times of peace. At first the officers are impatient of this state of affairs; they grow agitated, restless, and despairing; but in the long run most of them become resigned to this. Those of most ambition and resources leave the army; the others, finally adapting their tastes and desires to their humdrum lot, come in the end to look on a military career from a civilian point of view. What they value most is the comfort and security that goes with it. They base their vision of the future on the assurance of a small competence, and they ask no more than to be allowed to enjoy it in peace. So not only does a long peace fill democratic armies with aging officers, but it often gives even those who are still in the vigor of their years the instincts of old men.

I have also pointed out how in democracies in times of peace an army career is held in little honor and attracts few recruits.

Such public disapproval is a heavy discouragement to the army and weighs down the spirits of the troops; when war breaks out at last, they cannot immediately regain their spring and vigor.

The morale of aristocratic armies is not weakened by any such tendency. The officers never fall in their own esteem or in that of their equals, since, apart from their importance in the army, they have a high standing on their own account.

But even if the influence of peace were felt by both types of army in the same way, the results nonetheless will be different. When the officers of an aristocratic army have lost their warlike spirit and the desire for promotion in the army, they still have a certain respect for the honor of their order and an ingrained habit of being the first and setting an example. But when the officers of a democratic army have no taste for war or military ambition, nothing is left.

I therefore think that a democratic people undertaking a war after a long peace runs more risk of defeat than any other nation. But it ought not to let itself be easily discouraged by reverses, for its army's prospects of success increase as the war lasts longer.

When a war has at length by its long continuance roused the whole community from their peacetime occupations and brought all their petty undertakings to ruin, it will happen that those very passions which once made them value peace so highly become directed into war. War, having destroyed every industry, in the end becomes itself the one great industry, and every eager and ambitious desire sprung from equality is focused on it. For that reason those same democratic nations which are so hard to drag onto the battlefield sometimes perform prodigious feats once one has succeeded in putting arms in their hands.

As the war more and more focuses the attention of all on the army, and great reputations and huge fortunes are seen to be made quickly, the elite of the nation takes to a military career. Every naturally enterprising, proud, and bellicose man, not only in the aristocracy but in the whole nation, is drawn in this direction.

As the number of competitors for military honors is immense and war roughly forces each man to find his proper level, great generals always emerge in the end. A long war has the same effect on a democratic army as a revolution has on the people themselves. It breaks down rules and makes outstanding men come forward. Officers whose minds and bodies have grown old in peacetime are eliminated, retire, or die. In their place a multitude of young men, already toughened by war, press forward with ambitious hopes aflame. They want promotion at any price, and continual promotion. They are followed by others with the same passions and desires, and then by more still after these, the size of the army itself being the only limit. Equality allows every man to be ambitious, and death provides chances for every ambition. Death constantly thins the ranks, creating vacancies, closing and opening careers of arms.

Moreover, there is a hidden connection which war uncovers between the military and democratic mores.

The men of democracies are by nature passionately eager to acquire quickly what they covet and to enjoy it on easy terms. They for the most part love hazards and fear death much less than difficulty. It is in that spirit that they conduct their trade and industry, and this spirit carried with them onto the battlefield induces them willingly to risk their lives to secure in a moment the rewards of victory. No kind of greatness is more pleasing to the imagination of a democratic people than military greatness which is brilliant and sudden, won without hard work, by risking nothing but one's life.

Thus, while their interests and tastes divert the citizens of a democracy from war, their habits and their spirit fit them for success in it. They easily turn into good soldiers when once they have been torn from their business and their pleasures.

If peace is peculiarly hurtful to democratic armies, war secures advantages for them which no other armies ever possess; and these advantages, which attract little notice at first, cannot fail in the end to give them the victory.

An aristocratic people which, fighting against a democracy, does not succeed in bringing it to ruin in the first campaigns always runs a great risk of being defeated by it.

Chapter 25

OF DISCIPLINE IN DEMOCRATIC ARMIES

IT IS A VERY COMMON opinion, especially in aristocratic countries, that the great social equality prevailing in democracies makes the private soldier independent of the officer and thus destroys the bond of discipline.

That is a mistake. There are in fact two sorts of discipline, which should not be confused.

When the officer is a noble and the soldier a serf, the one rich and the other poor, the one educated and strong, the other ignorant and weak, in such a case it is easy to establish a bond of strict obedience between the two. The soldier has been broken in to military discipline, so to say, before he enters the army, or rather military discipline is only a more perfect form of social servitude. So in aristocratic armies the private soon comes to be insensible to everything except the orders of his leaders. He acts without thought, triumphs without excitement, and is killed without complaint. In such a condition, he is no more a man, but he is a very formidable animal trained for war.

Democratic peoples must despair of ever obtaining from their soldiers this blind, detailed, resigned, and equable obedience which aristocracies can impose without trouble. The state of society in no way prepares men for this, and there is a danger that they will lose their natural advantages by trying artificially to acquire this one. In democracies military discipline ought not to try to cancel out the spontaneous exercise of the faculties; it should aspire only to direct them; and the obedience thus trained will be less precise but more impetuous and intelligent. It should be rooted in the will of the man who obeys; it relies not only on instinct, but on reason too, and consequently will often spontaneously grow stricter as danger makes this necessary. The discipline of an aristocratic army is apt to relax in wartime, for it is based on habit, and war upsets habits. But in a democratic army discipline is strengthened in face of the enemy, for each soldier sees very clearly that to conquer he must be silent and obey.

Those nations that have achieved most in war have never known any other discipline than that of which I speak. In antiquity only free men and citizens were accepted for the army, and they differed but little from one another and were accustomed to treat each other as equals. In that sense the armies of antiquity can be called democratic, even when they sprang from an aristocratic society. As a result, in those armies a sort of fraternal familiarity prevailed between officers and men. To read Plutarch's lives of great commanders convinces one of that. The soldiers are constantly talking, and talking very freely, to their generals, while the latter gladly listen to what they say and answer it. Their words and their example led the army much more than any constraint or punishment. They were as much companions as leaders to their men.

I do not know if the Greeks and Romans ever brought the small details of military discipline to such perfection as the Russians have done, but that did not prevent Alexander from conquering Asia, and the Romans the world.

Chapter 26

SOME CONSIDERATIONS CONCERNING WAR IN DEMOCRATIC SOCIETIES

WHEN THE PRINCIPLE of equality spreads, as in Europe now, not only within one nation, but at the same time among several neighboring peoples, the inhabitants of these various countries, despite different languages, customs, and laws, always resemble each other in an equal fear of war and love of peace.[1] In vain do ambitious or angry princes arm for war; in spite of themselves they are calmed down by some sort of general apathy and goodwill which makes the sword fall from their hands. Wars become rarer.

As the spread of equality, taking place in several countries at once, simultaneously draws the inhabitants into trade and industry, not only do their tastes come to be alike, but their interests become so mixed and entangled that no nation can inflict on others ills which will not fall back on its own head. So that in the end all come to think of war as a calamity almost as severe for the conqueror as for the conquered.

Therefore, on the one hand it is difficult in democratic ages to draw nations into hostilities, but on the other, it is almost impossible for two of them to make war in isolation. The interests of all are so much entwined, their opinions and their needs so similar, that no one of them can stay quiet when the rest are in agitation. So wars become rarer, but when they do come about, they spread over a vaster field.

Neighboring democratic peoples do not only become alike, as I have just said, in certain respects, but in the end come to be alike in almost all matters.[2]

[1] I need hardly observe that the dread of war displayed by the nations of Europe is not due solely to the progress of equality among them. Apart from this permanent cause, there are several other chance ones which have great importance. I would mention above all the extreme lassitude supervening after the wars of the Revolution and the Empire.

[2] This is so not only because these nations have the same social condition but also because this same social condition by its nature leads men to imitate one another and identify themselves with one another.

When citizens are divided into castes and classes, not only do they differ from one another, but they have neither taste nor wish to be alike. Each, on the contrary, tries more and more to preserve intact his own peculiar opinions and habits and to remain himself. The spirit of individuality is very much alive.

When a people has a democratic state of society, that is to say, when there are no longer any castes or classes in the community and all its members are nearly equal in education and in property, the mental tide flows the other way. Men are alike, and what is more, it pains them in some way if they are not alike. Far from wishing to preserve their own distinguishing singularities, they only want to lose them so as to identify themselves with the general mass of the people, which is the sole representative, in their eyes, of right and of might. The spirit of individuality is nearly obliterated.

In aristocratic ages even those who are naturally alike strive to create imaginary differences between them; in democratic ages even those who are not alike are bent on becoming so and copy each other, so strongly is the

Now, this similarity between nations has important consequences when war is concerned.

When I inquire why the Swiss Confederation in the fifteenth century made the greatest and most powerful nations of Europe tremble, whereas at the present day the power of that country is in exact relation to its population, I find that the Swiss have become like all the inhabitants of surrounding countries, and those surrounding them like the Swiss. Therefore numerical strength now forms the only difference between them, and victory must go to the greater battalions. Thus one of the consequences of the democratic revolution taking place in Europe is to make force of numbers prevail on every battlefield and to constrain all small nations to incorporate themselves with the great ones, or at least to follow the political lead of the latter.

As numbers are the determining factor in victory, each people must strive by all means in its power to bring the greatest possible number of men on the battlefield.

When it was possible to enlist a type of soldier superior to all the rest, as were the Swiss infantry or the French cavalry in the sixteenth century, no need was felt to raise very large armies. But that is no longer the case now that all soldiers are as good as one another.

The same cause which begets this new need also supplies the means of satisfying it, for as I have already said, when men are all alike, they are all weak. The supreme power of the state is naturally much stronger in democracies than anywhere else. These nations both want to recruit the whole male population into the army and have the power to do so. The result is that in ages of equality armies seem to increase in size in proportion as the military spirit declines.

In the same ages, too, the manner of carrying on war is likewise altered by the same causes.

Machiavelli observes in *The Prince:* "It is much more difficult to subdue a people who have a prince and his barons to lead them, than a nation led by a prince with slaves."[3] To avoid

---

mind of every man always carried away by the general impulse of mankind.

Something of the same kind may be observed between nations; two nations having the same aristocratic social condition may remain thoroughly distinct and very different because the spirit of aristocracy favors strong individual characteristics. But if two neighboring nations have the same democratic social condition, they cannot fail at once to adopt similar opinions and manners, for the spirit of democracy tends to assimilate people.

[3] [This seems to be more a paraphrase of Machiavelli's meaning than a quotation. Cf. Machiavelli, *The Prince,* Everyman's edition, p. 78.]

offense, let us say "public officials" instead of "slaves" and this important truth applies very well to the matter in question.

It is very difficult for an aristocratic people to either conquer its neighbors or be conquered by them. It cannot conquer them because it can never assemble all its forces and hold them together for a long time; it cannot be conquered because the enemy everywhere finds small pockets of resistance which hold him up. One can compare war in an aristocratic country to war in the mountains. The defeated can always find new positions in which to rally and hold firm.

Exactly the opposite happens among democratic nations.

They easily bring the whole force at their disposal onto the battle-field, and if the nation is rich and numerous, it is soon victorious. But once you have defeated it and penetrated into its territory, it has few resources left, and once you get possession of the capital, the nation is lost. This can very well be explained; each citizen being individually very isolated and weak, none of them can either defend himself or offer a rallying point to others. Nothing is strong in a democracy except the state; once the military power of the state has been shattered by the destruction of the army and the civil government paralyzed by the capture of the capital, what is left is a mere disorderly and powerless multitude, unable to resist the organized power which assailed it; I realize that one can make the danger less by creating local liberties and, consequently, provincial powers, but that will always be an insufficient remedy.

In that case, not only will the population be unable to continue the war, but, I fear, they will not even want to try.

According to the law of nations adopted by civilized countries, the object of war is not to seize the property of private individuals but simply to get possession of political power. Private property is only occasionally destroyed for the purpose of attaining the latter object.

When an aristocratic nation is invaded after the defeat of its army, the nobles, although they are also the rich, prefer to go on defending themselves individually rather than submit, for if the conqueror remains master of the land, he will take away their political power, which they prize even more highly than their property; they therefore prefer to fight than be conquered, for that is the greatest of ills for them, and they easily carry the people with them, since the people have contracted a long habit of following and obeying them and, moreover, have practically nothing to lose in the war.

But where equality of conditions prevails in a nation, each citizen has but a small share of political power, and often none at all; on the other hand, all are independent and have property to lose;

as a result, they are much less afraid of conquest and much more afraid of war than the inhabitants of an aristocratic land. It will always be very difficult to make a democratic people decide to take up arms when hostilities have reached its own territory. That is why it is so necessary to provide such a people with the rights and the political spirit which will endow each citizen with some of those interests which influence the behavior of nobles in aristocratic lands.

The princes and other leaders of democracies should remember that it is only passion for freedom, habitually enjoyed, which can do more than hold its own against a habitual absorption in well-being. I can imagine nothing better prepared, in case of defeat, for conquest than a democratic people without free institutions. In the old days one took the field with few troops; one fought small engagements and conducted long sieges. Now one fights great battles, and as soon as it is possible to march straight ahead, makes for the capital to end the war with a single blow.

Napoleon is said to have discovered this new system, but it did not depend on one man, whoever he might be, to find that out. The way in which Napoleon carried on war was put into his head by the state of society in his time, and his system succeeded because it was wonderfully suited to the conditions of the day and because he was the first to put it in practice. Napoleon is the first man to march at the head of an army from capital to capital, but the road was opened for him by the ruin of feudal society. One may well think that had that extraordinary man lived three hundred years earlier he would not have reaped such a harvest from his system, or rather that he would have applied another method.

I shall add only a few words about civil wars for fear of exhausting the reader's patience.

Most of what I have said about foreign wars applies with even greater force to civil wars. The inhabitants of democracies do not naturally have any military spirit; they sometimes develop it when they have been dragged onto the battlefield; but to rise spontaneously in a body and voluntarily expose themselves to the miseries of war, especially civil war, is not a course of action inhabitants of democracies are likely to follow. Only the most adventurous of their citizens would be prepared to run such risks. The bulk of the population would stay quiet.

Even supposing the population were inclined to act, it would not be easy to do so. For there are no men of old and well-established influence whom they would be willing to obey, no acknowledged leaders to rally the discontented, control, and guide them. Nor are there any subordinate political powers below the central government which could supply effective support for resistance against the government.

In democratic countries the moral power of the majority is immense, and the material force of which it disposes is out of proportion to any which it would at first be possible to unite against it. Therefore the party which sits in the place of the majority, speaks in its name, and uses its power can easily triumph in no time over any individual resistance. It does not even leave it time to be born, but nips it in the bud.

Those who in such countries seek to effect a revolution by force of arms have no other recourse but suddenly to seize the whole machinery of government as it stands, and that can better be done by *coup d'état* than by a war, for as soon as there is a regular war, the party representing the state is almost always sure to win.

The only case in which a civil war could take place is if the army were divided, one part raising the standard of revolt and the other remaining loyal. An army constitutes a small society, very closely knit together and with great vitality, which is able to supply its own wants for a certain time. The war might be bloody, but it would not be long. For either the rebellious army would bring the government over to its side by a simple demonstration of its power or by its first victory, and then the war would be over; or else a struggle would take place, and that portion of the army which was not supported by the organized powers of the state would soon either disperse of its own accord or be destroyed.

One can therefore accept the general proposition that in ages of equality civil wars will become much rarer and shorter.[4]

---

[4] I must make it clear that I am here referring to *unitary* democratic nations and not to confederate democratic nations. In confederations the predominant power always resides, in spite of all political fictions, in the state governments, and not in the federal government. So civil wars are really foreign wars in disguise.

PART IV

On the Influence of Democratic Ideas

and Feelings on Political Society

I COULD NOT PROPERLY FULFILL the purpose of this book if, having pointed out the ideas and feelings prompted by equality, I did not in conclusion indicate the influence which these ideas and these feelings may exercise upon the government of human societies.

For this purpose it will often be necessary to go back over old ground. But I trust that the reader will not refuse to follow me when familiar paths may lead to some new truth.

Chapter 1

EQUALITY NATURALLY GIVES MEN THE TASTE FOR FREE INSTITUTIONS

EQUALITY, WHICH makes men independent of one another, naturally gives them the habit and taste to follow nobody's will but their own in their private affairs. This complete independence, which they constantly enjoy among their equals in the affairs of private life, makes them suspicious of all authority and soon suggests the notion and the love of political liberty. Men living at such times have a natural bias toward free institutions. Choose any man among them by chance and try and find out, if possible, his basic instincts, and you are sure to find that of all types of government, the one that enters his head first and which he most values is that whose leader he has chosen and whose actions he controls.

This love of independence is the first and most striking feature of the political effects of equality, and the one which frightens timid spirits most. Nor can it be said that they are completely wrong in this, for anarchy does have a more terrible aspect in democratic countries than elsewhere. As the citizens have no direct influence on one another, as soon as the central power that holds them in place begins to falter, it would seem that disorder must reach a climax and that, each citizen drawing separately aside, the fabric of society must fall into dust.

Nevertheless, I am convinced that anarchy is not the greatest of the ills to be feared in democratic times, but the least.

Two tendencies in fact result from equality; the one first leads men directly to independence and could suddenly push them right over into anarchy; the other, by a more roundabout and secret but also more certain road, leads them to servitude.

Nations easily see the former tendency and resist it. But they let themselves be carried along by the latter without seeing it. So it is most important to point it out.

For my part, far from blaming equality for the intractability it inspires, I am chiefly disposed to praise it just for that. I admire the way it insinuates deep into the heart and mind of every man some vague notion and some instinctive inclination toward political freedom, thereby preparing the antidote for the ill which it has produced. That is why I cling to it.

Chapter 2

WHY THE IDEAS OF DEMOCRATIC PEOPLES ABOUT GOVERNMENT NATURALLY FAVOR THE CONCENTRATION OF POLITICAL POWER

THE IDEA OF SECONDARY powers, between the sovereign and his subjects, was natural to the imagination of aristocratic peoples, because such powers were proper to individuals or families distinguished by birth, education, and riches, who seemed destined to command. Opposite reasons naturally banish such an idea from the minds of men in ages of equality; it can then only be introduced artificially and retained with difficulty; but the idea of a single central power directing all citizens slips naturally into their consciousness without their, so to say, giving the matter a thought.

Moreover, in politics, as in philosophy and religion, democratic peoples give a ready welcome to simple general ideas. They are put off by complicated systems and like to picture a great nation in which every citizen resembles one set type and is controlled by one single power.

Next after the idea of a single central power, that of uniform legislation equally spontaneously takes its place in the thought of men in times of equality. As each sees himself little different from his neighbors, he cannot understand why a rule applicable to one man should not be applied to all the rest. The slightest privileges are therefore repugnant to his reason. The faintest differences in the political institutions of a single people give him pain, and legislative uniformity strikes him as the first condition of good government.

But this notion of a uniform rule imposed equally on all members of the body social seems to have been strange to men's thoughts in ages of aristocracy. Either it did not enter their heads or else they rejected it.

In both cases these opposite mental attitudes in the end turn into instincts and habits so blind and invincible that, with few exceptions, they still control men's behavior. For all the variety of life in the Middle Ages, some people did live under precisely similar conditions; but that did not prevent the legislators from giving each of them different rights and duties. In contrast to which, nowadays governments wear themselves out imposing uniform customs and laws on populations with nothing yet in common.

As conditions become more equal among people, individuals seem of less and society of greater importance; or rather, every citizen, having grown like the rest, is lost in the crowd, and nothing stands out conspicuously but the great and imposing image of the people itself.

This naturally gives men in times of democracy a very high opinion of the prerogatives of society and a very humble one of the rights of the individual. They will easily admit that the interest of the former is everything and that of the latter nothing. They also freely agree that the power which represents society has much more education and wisdom than any of the men composing it and that it is its duty, as well as its right, to take each citizen by the hand and guide him.

If we look closely at our contemporaries and trace the very roots of their political opinions, we shall find some of the ideas that I have just pointed out, and perhaps we shall be surprised to see so much agreement between people who are so often at war.

The Americans believe that in each state supreme power should emanate directly from the people, but once this power has been constituted, they can hardly conceive any limits to it. They freely recognize that it has the right to do everything.

As for particular privileges granted to towns, families, or individuals, they have forgotten the possibility of such things. It has never come into their heads that one cannot apply the same law uniformly to all the parts of one state and all the men living in it.

The same views are spreading more and more in Europe. They even insinuate themselves among those nations that most vehemently reject the dogma of the sovereignty of the people. Such nations disagree with the Americans about the origins of power but see power in the same light. In all of them the idea of intermediate powers is obscured and obliterated. The idea of rights inherent in certain individuals is rapidly disappearing from men's minds; the idea of the omnipotence and sole authority of society at large is coming to fill its place. These ideas take root and spread as conditions become more equal and men more alike; equality brings them to birth, and they in turn hasten the progress of equality.

In France, where the revolution of which I speak has gone further than in any other European country, these opinions have got complete hold of the public mind. If we listen attentively to the voice of the various parties in France, we find that there is not one which does not adopt them. Most of them think that the government is behaving badly, but they all think that the government ought constantly to act and interfere in everything. Even those who attack each other most vehemently are nevertheless agreed on that. The unity, ubiquity, and omnipotence of the social power and the uniformity of its rules constitute the most striking feature of all the political systems invented in our day. They recur even in the most fantastic utopias. The human mind still pursues them in its dreams.

If such ideas arise spontaneously in the minds of private individuals, they strike the imagination of princes even more forcibly.

While the ancient fabric of European society is changing and dissolving, sovereigns acquire new conceptions about the scope of their action and duties. For the first time they learn that the central power which they represent can and should administer directly according to a uniform plan all affairs and all men. This opinion, which I am sure no king in Europe before our time ever thought of, has now sunk deeply into the minds of princes and stands firm amid the agitation of more unsettled thoughts.

Our contemporaries therefore are much less divided than is commonly supposed. They do argue constantly about who should have sovereign power, but they readily agree about the duties and rights of that power. They all think of the government as a sole, simple, providential, and creative force.

All secondary ideas about politics are unsettled, but that remains fixed, inalterable, and self-consistent. Publicists and statesmen adopt it; the crowd greedily snatches it up; both governed and governors agree to pursue it with equal eagerness; it was the first to come; it seems innate.

It is not due to any vagary of the human mind, but is a natural condition of the actual state of mankind. (See Appendix I, Y.)

Chapter 3

HOW BOTH THE FEELINGS AND THE THOUGHTS OF DEMOCRATIC NATIONS ARE IN ACCORD IN CONCENTRATING POLITICAL POWER

WHILE IN TIMES OF EQUALITY men readily conceive the idea of a strong central power, there is no doubt that both their habits and their feelings predispose them to accept and help it forward. I can very briefly make the point clear, as most of the reasons for it have been given already.

The inhabitants of democracies, having neither superiors or inferiors nor habitual and necessary partners, readily fall back upon themselves and think of themselves in isolation. I went into that matter at length when discussing individualism.

It is therefore always an effort for such men to tear themselves away from their private affairs and pay attention to those of the community; the natural inclination is to leave the only visible and permanent representative of collective interests, that is to say, the state, to look after them.

Not only are they by nature lacking in any taste for public business, but they also often lack the time for it. In times of democracy private life is so active and agitated, so full of desires and labor, that each individual has scarcely any leisure or energy left for political life.

I am certainly not the one to say that such inclinations are invincible, for my chief aim in writing this book is to combat them. I am only asserting that in our time a secret force constantly fosters them in the human heart, and if they are simply left unchecked, they will fill it all.

I have also had occasion to show how the increasing love of well-being and the shifting character of property make democratic peoples afraid of material disturbances. Love of public peace is often the only political passion which they retain, and it alone becomes more active and powerful as all the others fade and die. This naturally disposes the citizens constantly to give the central government new powers, or to let it take them, for it alone seems both anxious and able to defend them from anarchy by defending itself.

Since in times of equality no man is obliged to put his powers at the disposal of another, and no one has any claim of right to substantial support from his fellow man, each is both independent and weak. These two conditions, which must be neither seen quite separately nor confused, give the citizen of a democracy extremely contradictory instincts. He is full of confidence and pride in his independence among his equals, but from time to time his weakness makes him feel the need for some outside help which he cannot expect from any of his fellows, for they are both impotent and cold. In this extremity he naturally turns his eyes toward that huge entity which alone stands out above the universal level of abasement. His needs, and even more his longings, continually put him in mind of that entity, and he ends by regarding it as the sole and necessary support of his individual weakness.[1]

All that helps one to understand a frequent phenomenon in democracies, that men who are restive under any superior patiently submit to a master, proving themselves both proud and servile.

Men's hatred of privilege increases as privileges become rarer and less important, the flame of democratic passion apparently blazing the brighter the less fuel there is to feed it. I have already given the

---

[1] In democratic societies the central power alone has both some stability and some capacity to see its undertakings through. All the citizenry is ever moving and changing around. Now, it is in the nature of every government to wish continually to increase its sphere of action. Moreover, it is almost bound ultimately to succeed in this, for it acts with fixed purpose and determination on men whose position, ideas, and desires change every day.

Often the citizens, without intending to, play into its hands.

Democratic ages are times of experiment, innovation, and adventure. There are always a lot of men engaged in some difficult or new undertaking which they pursue apart, unencumbered by assistants. Such men will freely admit the general principle that the power of the state should not interfere in private affairs, but as an exception, each one of them wants the state to help in the special matter with which he is preoccupied, and he wants to lead the government on to take action in his domain, though he would like to restrict it in every other direction.

As a multitude of people, all at the same moment, take this particular view about a great variety of different purposes, the sphere of the central government insensibly spreads in every direction, although every individual wants to restrict it. In this way the simple fact of its continuing existence increases the attributes of power of a democratic government. Time works on its side, and every accident is to its profit; the passions of individuals, in spite of themselves, promote it; and one can say that the older a democratic society, the more centralized will its government be.

reason for this phenomenon. When conditions are unequal, no inequality, however great, offends the eye. But amid general uniformity, the slightest dissimilarity seems shocking, and the completer the uniformity, the more unbearable it seems. It is therefore natural that love of equality should grow constantly with equality itself; everything done to satisfy it makes it grow.

This ever-fiercer fire of endless hatred felt by democracies against the slightest privileges singularly favors the gradual concentration of all political rights in those hands which alone represent the state. The sovereign, being of necessity and incontestably above all the citizens, does not excite their envy, and each thinks that he is depriving his equals of all those prerogatives which he concedes to the state.

In democratic ages a man is extremely reluctant to obey his neighbor who is his equal; he refuses to recognize that the latter knows more than he; he mistrusts his fairness and regards his power with jealousy; he fears and despises him; he likes to make him feel the whole time their common dependence on the same master.

Every central power which follows its natural instincts loves equality and favors it. For equality singularly facilitates, extends, and secures its influence.

One can also assert that every central government worships uniformity; uniformity saves it the trouble of inquiring into infinite details, which would be necessary if the rules were made to suit men instead of subjecting all men indiscriminately to the same rule. Hence the government loves what the citizens love, and it naturally hates what they hate. This community of feeling which in democracies continually unites each individual and the sovereign in common thought establishes a secret and permanent bond of sympathy between them. The government's faults are forgiven for the sake of its tastes; only with reluctance is public confidence withdrawn, whatever its excesses or mistakes, and it is restored at the first call. Democratic peoples often hate those in whose hands the central power is vested, but they always love that power itself.

Thus two different paths have led me to the same conclusion. I have pointed out how equality prompts men to think of one sole uniform and strong government. I have just shown how equality gives them the taste for it; it must therefore be toward governments of this kind that nations nowadays are tending. Their natural bent of mind and heart leads them in this direction, and provided only that they do not hold themselves in check, that is where they are bound to arrive.

I think that in the dawning centuries of democracy individual independence and local liberties will always be the products of art. Centralized government will be the natural thing. (See Appendix I, Z.)

Chapter 4

CONCERNING CERTAIN PECULIAR AND ACCIDENTAL CAUSES WHICH EITHER LEAD A DEMOCRATIC PEOPLE TO COMPLETE THE CENTRALIZATION OF GOVERNMENT OR DIVERT THEM FROM IT

ALTHOUGH ALL DEMOCRATIC peoples are instinctively drawn toward centralization of power, this attraction is uneven. It depends on particular circumstances which may promote or restrain the natural effects of the state of society. There are many such circumstances, and I shall mention only a few.

Among people who have long lived in freedom before they have becomes equal, the instincts engendered by freedom to some extent combat the inclinations prompted by equality, and though in that case the central power does increase its prerogatives, private persons never entirely lose their independence.

But when equality starts developing among a people who have never known or long forgotten what freedom is, as one sees it happen on the Continent of Europe; as the former habits of a nation are suddenly combined, by some sort of natural attraction, with the new habits and principles engendered by the state of society, all powers seem spontaneously to rush to the center. They accumulate there at an astonishing rate and the state reaches the extreme limits of its power all at once, while private persons allow themselves to sink in one moment down to the lowest degree of weakness.

The English who emigrated three centuries ago to found a democratic society in the wilds of the New World were already accustomed in their motherland to take part in public affairs; they knew trial by jury; they had liberty of speech and freedom of the press, personal freedom, and the conception of rights and the practice of asserting them. They carried these free institutions and virile mores with them to America, and these characteristics sustained them against the encroachments of the state.

Thus, in America it is freedom that is old, and equality is comparatively new. The opposite obtains in Europe, where equality introduced by the absolute power of the kings and under their eyes had already penetrated into the habits of the people long before the idea of liberty had entered their thoughts.

I have said that among democratic nations the only form of government which comes naturally to mind is a sole and central power and that they are not familiar with the notion of intermediate powers. This applies particularly to those democratic nations which have seen the principle of equality triumph with the help of a violent revolution. The classes that managed local affairs were suddenly swept away in that storm, and as the confused mass which remains has as yet neither the organization nor the habits which would allow it to take the administration of these affairs in hand, the state alone seems capable of taking upon itself all the details of government. Centralization becomes a fact, and in a sense, a necessity.

One must not praise or blame Napoleon for concentrating almost all administrative powers in his own hands, for with the nobility and the upper ranks of the middle classes abruptly brushed aside, these powers fell automatically into his hands; it would have been almost as difficult for him to reject as to assume them. No such necessity has ever faced the Americans, for never having had a revolution and being from the beginning accustomed to govern themselves, they never had to call upon the state to act temporarily as guardian.

Hence centralization does not spread in a democracy simply in step with the progress toward equality, but also depends on the way in which that equality was established.

At the beginning of a great democratic revolution, when war between the various classes is just starting, the people make efforts to centralize public administration in the hands of the government so as to snatch control of local affairs from the aristocracy. But toward the end of such a revolution it is generally the defeated aristocracy which tries to put the control of everything into the hands of the state, dreading the petty tyranny of the common people who have become its equal and often its master.

So it is not always the same class of citizens that is eager to increase the prerogatives of power. But while a democratic revolution is in progress there is always a class in the nation, powerful through its numbers or its wealth, which is led by special and particular in·

terests to centralize administration, notwithstanding that hatred of being ruled by one's neighbor which is a general and permanent sentiment in democracies. It is worth noting that at the present moment it is the lower classes in England who are trying as hard as they can to destroy local independence and to shift administration from the circumference to the center, whereas the upper classes do their best to keep it where it was before. I predict that one day we shall see the roles reversed.

These observations suffice to explain why the social power is always stronger and individuals weaker in a democracy which has reached equality after a long and painful social struggle than in one where the citizens have been equal from the beginning. The American example completely proves that.

No privilege has ever kept the inhabitants of the United States apart. They have never known the mutual relationship between master and servant, and as they neither fear nor hate each other, they have never felt the need to call in the state to manage the details of their affairs. The American destiny is unusual; they have taken from the English aristocracy the idea of individual rights and a taste for local freedom, and they have been able to keep both these things because they have had no aristocracy to fight.

At all times education helps men to defend their independence, but this is especially so in ages of democracy. When all men are alike, it is easy to establish a single, all-powerful government; mere instinct will do that. But a great deal of intelligence, knowledge, and skill are required in these circumstances to organize and maintain secondary powers and to create, among independent but individually weak citizens, free associations which can resist tyranny without destroying public order.

In democracies ignorance as much as equality will increase the concentration of power and the subjection of the individual.

It is true that in unenlightened centuries governments often lack the knowledge necessary to make their despotism complete, just as the citizens, for the same reason, cannot shake it off. But the effect is not the same on both sides.

However rude a democratic people may be, the central power that rules them is never without some enlightenment, for it easily attracts to itself any skill to be found in the country and can if necessary call in assistance from outside. So if a nation is both democratic and ignorant, there is bound soon to be a huge difference between the intellectual capacity of the government and that of each of the governed. The government can easily get all power into its hands.

The administrative power of the state constantly increases, because it alone is capable of administration.

Things never go as far as that in an aristocratic nation, however unenlightened it may be, for what education there is, is equally divided between the ruler and the leading citizens.

The pasha who now rules Egypt found the inhabitants both extremely ignorant and very nearly equal, and he borrowed the knowledge and skills of Europe with which to govern them. The personal attainments of the ruler, helped by the ignorance and democratic weakness of his subjects, have made it easy to achieve the highest degree of centralization, and the pasha has made the country his factory and the people his workmen.

I think that extreme centralization of political power ultimately enervates society and thus, in the end, weakens the government too. But I do not deny that with the power of society thus centralized, great undertakings can be carried through at a given time and for a specific purpose. That is especially true of war, in which success depends much more on the capacity to bring all one's power to bear quickly at a given point than on the actual extent of one's resources. Hence it is chiefly in time of war that people wish, and often need, to increase the prerogatives of the central government. All men of military genius are fond of centralization, which increases their strength; and all men of centralizing genius are fond of war, which forces nations to put all power in the hands of the state. For this reason the democratic tendency constantly to multiply the prerogatives of the state and diminish those of individuals takes effect more quickly and continuously in democracies exposed by their position to great and frequent wars than in any others.

I have pointed out how fear of disorder and love of well-being unconsciously lead democracies to increase the functions of the central government, the only power which they think strong, intelligent, and stable enough to protect them from anarchy. So it is hardly necessary to add that all particular circumstances which tend to bring trouble and danger to the stability of a democratic society increase this widespread and powerful instinct and induce private persons to sacrifice more and more of their rights for the sake of tranquillity.

At no time, therefore, is a people more disposed to increase the functions of the central power than when it has emerged from a long and bloody revolution, which, having snatched their property from the former owners, has trod down all beliefs and filled the nation with fierce hatreds, conflicting interests, and contending factions. The taste for public tranquillity then becomes a blind passion, and the citizens are liable to conceive a most inordinate devotion to order.

I have dealt so far with several accidents which all help in the centralization of power, but I have left the chief one to the last.

The most important of all the accidental causes which, in a democracy, can bring control of all business into the ruler's hands is that ruler's own origin and inclinations.

Men who live in times of equality naturally love the central power and willingly extend its prerogatives. But if it happens that this power faithfully represents their interests and is an exact mirror of their instincts, there is hardly any limit to the confidence they will repose in it, for they feel that everything they give it is given to themselves.

Kings who are still in some way attached to an ancient aristocratic order will always draw administrative power to the center less easily and rapidly than new princes brought to power by their own exertions, whose birth, prejudices, instincts, and habits seem to bind them indissolubly to the cause of equality. I am certainly not saying that princes of aristocratic origin, living in times of democracy, do not try to centralize power. I think they are as diligently bent thereon as all the others. For them that is the advantage of equality; but their opportunities are less great, for the citizens, instead of naturally coming to anticipate their wishes, are often reluctant to fall in with them. In democratic societies centralization will always be greater the less aristocratic the ruler is; that is the rule.

When an ancient race of kings rules an aristocracy, the natural prejudices of the sovereign are in perfect accord with the natural prejudices of the nobles, and the vices inherent in aristocratic societies have free rein, with no corrective. The opposite is the case when the scion of a feudal stock is placed at the head of a democratic people. Education, habits, and memory constantly incline the prince to feelings whose origin derives from conditions of inequality. But the social condition of the people leads them as constantly toward mores engendered by equality. It thus often happens that the citizens try to restrain the central power not so much because it is tyrannical as because it is aristocratic; and they stoutly maintain their independence not only because they want to remain free but especially because they are determined to remain equal.

A revolution which overthrows an ancient royal family to put new men at the head of a democratic people may temporarily weaken the central power. But however anarchic it may at first appear, one can safely predict that the final and necessary result will be to extend and secure the prerogatives of that central power.

The chief and, in a sense, the only condition necessary in order to succeed in centralizing the supreme power in a democratic society is to love equality or to make believe that you do so. Thus the art of despotism, once so complicated, has been simplified; one may almost say that it has been reduced to a single principle.

Chapter 5

HOW THE SOVEREIGN POWER IS INCREASING AMONG THE EUROPEAN NATIONS OF OUR TIME, ALTHOUGH THE SOVEREIGNS ARE LESS STABLE

REFLECTING ON WHAT has already been said, one is both startled and alarmed to see how everything in Europe seems to tend toward the indefinite extension of the prerogatives of the central power and to make the status of the individual weaker, more subordinate, and more precarious.

The democratic nations of Europe share all the general and permanent tendencies which are leading the Americans toward the centralization of power, and they are also influenced by a great many secondary and accidental causes which do not apply in America. Each step they take toward equality seems to bring them nearer to despotism.

We need only to look at our surroundings and at ourselves to be convinced of this.

In the centuries of aristocracy before our time, the rulers of Europe had been deprived of or had voluntarily given up many of the rights inherent in their power. Less than a hundred years ago in most of the nations of Europe there were private persons or almost independent bodies who administered justice, raised and maintained soldiers, levied taxes, and often even made or interpreted the law. The state has everywhere reclaimed for itself alone these natural attributes of sovereign power. In all matters of government the state allows no intermediary between itself and the citizens, but directs them itself in matters of general concern. Far from criticizing this concentration of power, I simply point it out.

In Europe at that same time there were many secondary powers representing local interests and administering local affairs. Most of these local authorities have already vanished, and the rest are tending quickly to disappear or to fall into a state of complete subordination. From one end of Europe to the other seignorial privileges, the liberties of cities, and the powers of provincial governments have been or soon will be destroyed.

For half a century Europe has been shaken by many revolutions and counterrevolutions which have led it in opposite directions. But in one respect all these movements are alike: they have all undermined or abolished secondary powers. Some local privileges which the French did not abolish in the lands they conquered have perished at the hands of the rulers who defeated the French. Those princes rejected every innovation introduced by the revolution, except centralization; that was the one thing they were prepared to accept from it.

The point I want to make is that all these various rights which have been successively wrested in our time from classes, corporations, and individuals have not been used to create new secondary powers on a more democratic basis, but have invariably been concentrated in the hands of the government. Everywhere it is the state itself which increasingly takes control of the humblest citizen and directs his behavior even in trivial matters.[1]

In Europe in the old days almost all charitable establishments were managed by individuals or corporations. They are now all more or less under government control, and in several countries are administered by the government. The state almost exclusively undertakes to supply bread to the hungry, assistance and shelter to the sick, work to the idle, and to act as the sole reliever of all kinds of misery.

In most countries now education as well as charity has become

[1] There are a thousand indications of this gradual weakening of the status of the individual in face of society. I will choose an example from the law concerning wills.

In aristocracies it is usual to profess profound respect for a man's final testament. In the ancient nations of Europe this feeling sometimes even verged on superstition. The power of society, so far from interfering with a dying man's caprice, backed his slightest wish with all its strength and gave it permanent validity.

When all the living are weak, a dead man's will is less respected. A very narrow sphere is defined for its operation, and if it goes beyond that, the law annuls or modifies it. In the Middle Ages there was practically no limit to the power of testamentary disposition. In France now one cannot distribute one's property among one's children without the state's intervening. Having taken charge of the whole of his life, it even claims to control his final act.

a national concern. The state receives, and often takes, the child from its mother's arms to hand it over to its functionaries; it takes the responsibility for forming the feelings and shaping the ideas of each generation. Uniformity prevails in schoolwork as in everything else; diversity, as well as freedom, is daily vanishing.

It is also safe to say that now in almost all Christian nations, Catholic as well as Protestant, religion is in danger of falling under government control. It is not that the rulers are overzealous to fix dogma themselves, but they are getting more and more of a hold over the wills of those who do interpret it. They take their property from the clergy and give them salaries. They divert the priests' influence and use it purely for their own purposes. They make priests their ministers and often their servants, and with their help they reach right down into the depths of each man's soul.[2]

But that is still only one side of the picture.

The sovereign's power having spread, as we have seen, over the entire sphere of previously existing authorities, is not satisfied with that, but goes on to extend in every direction over the domain heretofore reserved for personal independence. A multitude of actions which formerly were entirely free from the control of society are now subject thereto, and this is constantly increasing.

The social power in aristocracies was usually limited to directing and supervising the citizens in all matters immediately and patently connected with the national interest. In all other respects they were freely left to choose for themselves. Among such peoples the government would often seem to forget that there comes a point where the mistakes or misfortunes of individuals compromise the general welfare, and that to prevent the ruin of a private person must sometimes be a matter of public importance.

The democratic nations of our time incline to the opposite extreme.

It is clear that most of our princes are not content simply to govern the nation as a whole. They seem to hold themselves responsible for the behavior and fate of their subjects as individuals, and have undertaken to guide and instruct each of them in all they do, and will, if necessary, make them happy against their will.

Private people also tend increasingly to see the power of society

[2] As the functions of the central government are multiplied, the number of officials serving it increases in proportion. They form a state within each state, and since they share the stability of the government, increasingly take the place of the aristocracy.

Almost everywhere in Europe rulers keep control in two ways: fear of their officials makes some of the citizens follow them, while the rest do likewise in hope of becoming officials.

in the same light. They turn to it for help whenever they are in need, and always look on it as teacher and guide.

I assert that there is no country in Europe in which public administration has not become not only more centralized but also more inquisitive and minute. Everywhere it meddles more than of old in private affairs. It controls in its own fashion more actions and more of their details, and ever increasingly takes its place beside and above the individual, helping, advising, and constraining him.

Formerly a sovereign lived on the income from his lands or the proceeds of taxes. But it is different now that his needs have grown with his power. In circumstances in which formerly a prince would have imposed a new tax, he now has recourse to a loan. So little by little the state comes to owe money to most of the men of wealth and thus centralizes the bulk of capital in its hands.

Another method draws the smallest capital into its keeping.

As men intermingle and conditions become more equal, the resources, education, and desires of the poor increase. The poor man gets the idea that he can improve his lot and tries to do so by saving. So daily savings create an infinite number of small capital accumulations, the slow fruit of patient labor. These savings are always increasing, but the greater part thereof would remain unproductive if it were still scattered. This has led to the creation of a philanthropic institution which will, if I am not mistaken, soon become one of the most important political institutions. Charitable men thought of the idea of collecting the poor man's savings and turning them to profitable use. In some countries these benevolent associations have remained entirely separate from the state, but in nearly all they are patently tending to identify themselves with the government, and in some cases the government has even taken their place and taken upon itself the enormous task of centralizing in one place and putting out at interest, on its own responsibility, daily savings of many million workers.

Thus the state draws to itself the wealth of the rich by loans and controls the poor man's mite through the savings banks. The wealth of the country is perpetually circulating around the government and falling into its hands. This wealth accumulates all the faster as equality increases, for in a democracy only the state inspires confidence in private persons, for it alone seems to them to have some force and permanence.[3]

---

[3] The taste for well-being is always increasing, and the government gets more and more complete control of the sources of that well-being.

Thus men are following two different roads to servitude. The taste for

Thus the sovereign does not limit himself to controlling the public treasure; he establishes a position for himself in private money matters too: he is the leader and often the master of every citizen, and in addition to this, becomes his steward and banker.

The central power not only fills the whole sphere of former authorities, extends, and goes beyond it, but also acts with greater speed, power, and independence than it had ever done.

All European governments have in our time introduced immense improvements in the science of administration. They both do more and do each thing more systematically, quickly, and cheaply. It would seem that all the initiative taken away from private people is constantly going to enrich that of the government. European princes daily bring their agents under ever stricter control and invent new ways of keeping a closer hold on them and supervising them more easily. They are not satisfied just to have agents to conduct all business, but try to control the conduct of their agents in all matters. As a result, public administration not only depends on one sole power but also is more and more controlled from one spot and concentrated in ever fewer hands. The government centralizes its activity at the same time that it increases its prerogatives; hence a twofold growth of power.

Two points stand out when one studies the former status of the judiciary in most European nations: the independence of its power and the extent of its functions.

Not only did the courts of justice decide almost all disputes between private persons, but in many cases also acted as arbitrators between the individual and the state.

I do not intend here to refer to the political and administrative functions which the courts in some countries usurped, but to the judicial functions proper to them everywhere. In all the countries of Europe there were, and still are, many private rights, mostly connected with the general right to property, which have been placed under the judge's protection and which the state could not violate without his permission.

It is this semipolitical power which chiefly distinguishes European law courts from all others. For all peoples have had judges, but they have not all given their judges the same privileges.

If we now come to look at what is happening among the democratic nations of Europe which are called free, as well as among the others, we find everywhere, by the side of the old courts, others

---

well-being diverts them from taking part in the government, and that love of well-being puts them in ever closer dependence on governments.

have been created which are more dependent and whose particular purpose is to exercise an exceptional jurisdiction over legal disputes arising between the public administration and the citizen. The old judiciary retains its independence, but its jurisdiction is restricted, and it tends increasingly to become no more than an arbitrator between private interests.

Both the number and the functions of such tribunals are constantly growing. Thus the government is daily more able to escape the obligation to have its will and its rights sanctioned by another power. Unable to do without judges, it likes at least to choose the judges itself and always to keep them under its hand; that is to say, it puts an appearance of justice, rather than justice itself, between the government and the private person.

Thus the state is by no means satisfied by attracting all business to itself, but is more and more successful in deciding everything by itself, without control and without appeal.[4]

In the modern nations of Europe there is one great cause, apart from those already indicated, which constantly aids the growth of government activity and extends its prerogatives, and it is one which has not attracted sufficient attention. I refer to the development of industry, which is favored by the progress of equality.

Industry generally brings together a multitude of men in the same place and creates new and complex relations among them. These men are exposed to sudden great alternations of plenty and want, which threaten public peace. Work of this sort may endanger the health, even the life, of those who make money out of it or who are employed therein. Therefore the industrial classes, more than other classes, need rules, supervision, and restraint, and it naturally follows that the functions of government multiply as they multiply.

That is a truth of general application, but there are some points which apply particularly to European nations.

In centuries before we were born, the aristocracy owned the land and was in a position to defend it. Therefore landed property was fenced in with guarantees, and landowners enjoyed great independence. From that laws and customs resulted which have survived the breakup of estates and the ruin of the nobility. In our day landowners and farmers are still better able than other citizens to escape the control of social power.

[4] In France there is a strange sophistry about this. When a lawsuit starts between the administration and a private person, it is not to be tried before an ordinary judge, in order, so they say, not to mix the administrative and judicial powers. As if this were not mixing the two powers, and mixing them in the most dangerous and tyrannical fashion, when the government has the right both to judge and to administer.

In those same aristocratic centuries in which all our history is rooted, personal property was of little importance, and its owners were despised and weak. Industrialists were a class apart in an aristocratic world. Disposing of no assured patronage, there was no one to protect them, and they were often unable to protect themselves.

Hence there arose a habit of considering industrial property as something of a peculiar nature, not entitled to the same respect and not deserving the same guarantees as property in general. And industrialists were regarded as a small, exceptional class in the body social, whose independence was of little importance and who could conveniently be sacrificed to the princes' passion for regimentation. If one studies medieval codes, it is amazing to find how, at a time of individual independence, the kings were constantly making rules for manufactures, even down to the most trivial details. In that matter centralization was as active and minute as it can ever be.

A great revolution has taken place in the world since that time. Industrial wealth, then no more than a seed, has spread till it covers Europe. The industrial class has grown and drawn strength from the ruin of all other classes. It has grown in numbers, importance, and wealth and is constantly growing. Almost all those not belonging to these classes are connected therewith in some respect at least. From being a class exceptional in society, there is a danger that it will become the chief and, one might almost say, the only one. Nevertheless, the notions and political habits which it engendered long ago have remained. These notions and these habits have not changed, partly because they are old and partly because they are in perfect harmony with the new ideas and prevailing habits of men today.

Consequently industrial wealth does not extend its rights in proportion to its importance. The manufacturing classes do not become less dependent as they become more numerous. On the contrary, it would seem that they bring despotism along with them and that it naturally extends in proportion to their growth.[5]

[5] I will quote some facts to support this thesis. Mines are the natural source of industrial wealth. As industry has developed in Europe, and as the output of the mines has become a matter of more general interest, while their successful exploitation has become harder, owing to the division of property resulting from equality, most governments have claimed a right of property in the subsoil and the right to supervise the workings. That has never been envisaged for any other type of property.

The mines, which were private property, subject to the same obligations, and enjoying the same security as other landed property, have thus been incorporated in the public sector. It is the state which exploits them or

In proportion as a nation becomes more industralized, it feels a greater need for roads, canals, ports, and other semipublic works which aid the growth of wealth. The more democratic the nation is, the harder it is for private people to undertake such works and the easier it is for the state to do so. I say confidently that there is a clear tendency for all governments now to undertake such matters on their sole responsibility. By such means they daily hold the populations under them in ever-greater dependence.

On the other hand, as the power of the state grows and its needs increase, the state itself consumes an ever-greater proportion of the industrial output, which is generally manufactured in its own arsenals and factories. Thus in every kingdom the government becomes the leading industrialist. It draws into its service and retains therein a vast number of engineers, architects, technicians, and craftsmen.

Not only is the government the leading industrialist, but it tends also to become the chief, or rather the master, of all the others.

The citizens, having become weaker as they grow more equal, can do nothing in industry without forming associations. But naturally public authority wants to put such associations under its control.

One must realize that these kinds of collective bodies known as associations are stronger and more redoubtable than any private person could be and that they have less responsibility than the latter for their acts. It therefore seems reasonable to grant each of them less independence from the power of society than would be proper in the case of an individual.

Rulers are all the more inclined to behave in this way, as it suits their natural taste. Among democratic peoples it is only through association that the citizens can raise any resistance to the central power. The latter therefore always looks with disfavor on associations that are not under its thumb. It is also very important to notice that in these very peoples the citizens often have secret feelings of fear and jealousy toward just these associations of which they

---

grants the right to do so. The owners have become tenants, deriving their rights from the state, and the state also almost everywhere retains powers of control. It lays down rules, enforces the adoption of particular methods, subjects them to continual supervision, and those who are refractory are dispossessed by an administrative tribunal. In that case the government hands over their rights to others. In that way the government not only owns the mines, but keeps control of those who work them.

Moreover, as industry develops, old mines are more actively exploited, and new mines are opened. The mining population expands and grows. Governments daily extend their sway beneath our feet and populate this domain with their servants.

stand in such great need, and this prevents them from defending them. The power of self-defense and the permanence of these little private societies amid the general weakness and instability are cause of astonishment and disquiet, and the free use which each association makes of its natural powers is almost regarded as a dangerous privilege.

Moreover, all the associations that spring up now are new corporate bodies whose rights have not been sanctioned by time; they come into the world just when the notion of private rights is weak and the social power knows no limits. It is not therefore surprising that they lose their freedom at birth.

In all European nations some associations cannot be formed until the state has examined their statutes and authorized their existence. In several countries efforts are made to extend this rule to all associations. One can easily see whither success in that would lead.

If once the sovereign had the general right to lay down certain conditions for associations of every sort, he would not be slow to claim the right to supervise and control them, so that they should not contravene the regulations laid down for them. In that way the state, having made all those who want to form associations depend on it, would do the same to those who have formed them, that is to say, almost every man alive in our day.

Governments thus appropriate to themselves and put to their own use the greater part of the new force which industry has created in the world of our time. Industry leads us along, and they lead industry.

I attach so much importance to all that I have just been saying that I am worried at the thought that, in trying to make myself clear, I may have done the opposite.

If, then, the reader thinks that the examples I have selected are inadequate or ill-chosen, or if he thinks that I have sometimes exaggerated the progress of the social power or that I have also excessively underestimated the sphere in which individual independence still operates, I beg him to put this book down for a moment and take a look for himself at the facts I have been trying to point out. Let him look attentively at what is daily happening among us and in other lands. Let him ask his neighbors, and finally look at himself. Unless I am much mistaken, he will reach, unguided and by other roads, the conclusion to which I have pointed.

He will see that in the last half century centralization has increased everywhere in a thousand different ways. Wars, revolutions, and conquests have aided its advance; all men have labored to increase it. In this same period, while men have succeeded one another at a tremendous rate at the head of affairs and while their ideas, interests, and passions have shown infinite variety, yet all have desired centralization in one way or another. The instinct for centralization has proved the one permanent feature amid the unusual mutability of their lives and their thoughts.

Then, if the reader, having investigated these details of human affairs, turns to look at the whole picture as one vast whole, he will be astonished.

On the one hand, the most stable dynasties have been shaken or overthrown. On every side peoples have violently shaken free from the restraint of their laws. They have abolished or limited the authority of their masters and princes. All nations, even those not in open revolution, are at least restless and disturbed, and all share the same spirit of revolt. And yet, at this time of anarchy and among these same unruly peoples, the social power is constantly increasing its prerogatives; it is becoming more centralized, more enterprising, more absolute, and more widespread. The citizens are perpetually falling under the control of the public administration. They are led insensibly, and perhaps against their will, daily to give up fresh portions of their individual independence to the government, and those same men who from time to time have upset a throne and trampled kings beneath their feet bend without resistance to the slightest wishes of some clerk.

So now two contrary revolutions seem to be taking place. One is continually weakening supreme power and the other constantly strengthening it. At no other time in our history has it appeared both so feeble and so strong.

But if one looks carefully at the state of the world, it appears that these two revolutions are intimately connected one with the other; they start from the same origin, and though they run a different course, they both finally lead men to the same goal.

I venture once more to repeat what I have already said or implied in several places in this book. One must be careful not to confuse the fact of equality with the revolution which succeeds in introducing it into the state of society and into the laws. In that lies the reason for almost all the phenomena which cause our surprise.

All the old political powers in Europe, the greatest as well as the least, have been founded in ages of aristocracy, and they represented and were more or less willing to defend the principle of inequality and privilege. To make the new wants and interests prompted by growing equality preponderant in the government, it was therefore necessary to overthrow or coerce the established powers. This led men to make revolutions and inspired in many of them that savage taste for lawlessness and independence which all revolutions, whatever their object, engender.

I do not think there is a single country in Europe where the progress of equality has not been preceded or followed by some violent changes in the status of property and of persons, and almost all these changes have been accompanied by much anarchy and license, because they have been brought about by the least self-controlled part of the nation in opposition to its most orderly members.

The two contrary tendencies I have mentioned result from this. In the heat of the democratic revolution, men busy destroying the old aristocratic powers which opposed it displayed a strong spirit of independence. But as the triumph of equality became more complete, they gradually gave way to the instincts natural to that condition, strengthening and centralizing the power of society. They had sought to be free in order to make themselves equal. But in proportion as equality was established by the era of freedom, freedom itself was thereby rendered more difficult to attain.

Sometimes these two conditions have occurred together. Our fathers demonstrated how a nation can organize a vast internal tyranny at the very moment when they were escaping from the authority of the nobility and flouting the power of every king, thus teaching the world both how to win freedom and how to lose it.

Nowadays men see that the ancient powers are crumbling on every side. They see what was once respected losing its influence, and all former barriers falling. This troubles the judgment even of the wisest. They can see nothing but the vast revolution taking place before their eyes, and they think that mankind will forever fall into a state of anarchy. Could they see the final result of this revolution, perhaps they would have other fears.

For my part, I own that I have no confidence in the spirit of liberty which seems to animate my contemporaries. I see plainly enough that the nations of this age are turbulent, but it is not clear to me that they are freedom-loving. And I fear that at the end of all these agitations which rock thrones, sovereigns may be more powerful than ever before.

Chapter 6

WHAT SORT OF DESPOTISM
DEMOCRATIC NATIONS HAVE TO FEAR

I NOTICED DURING MY STAY in the United States that a democratic
state of society similar to that found there could lay itself peculiarly
open to the establishment of a despotism. And on my return to
Europe I saw how far most of our princes had made use of the
ideas, feelings, and needs engendered by such a state of society to
enlarge the sphere of their power.

I was thus led to think that the nations of Christendom might
perhaps in the end fall victims to the same sort of oppression as
formerly lay heavy on several of the peoples of antiquity.

More detailed study of the subject and the new ideas which came
into my mind during five years of meditation have not lessened
my fears but have changed their object.

In past ages there had never been a sovereign so absolute and so
powerful that he could by himself alone, without the aid of secondary
powers, undertake to administer every part of a great empire. No
one had ever tried to subject all his people indiscriminately to the
details of a uniform code, nor personally to prompt and lead every
single one of his subjects. It had never occurred to the mind of
man to embark on such an undertaking, and had it done so, inadequate education, imperfect administrative machinery, and above
all the natural obstacles raised by unequal conditions would soon
have put a stop to so grandiose a design.

When the power of the Roman emperors was at its height, the
different peoples of the empire still preserved very various customs
and mores. Although they obeyed the same monarch, most provinces
had a separate administration. There were powerful and active
municipalities in profusion, and though the whole government of
the empire was concentrated in the hands of the emperor alone
and he could, if necessary, decide everything, yet the details of social
life and personal everyday existence normally escaped his control.

It is true that the emperors had immense and unchecked power,
so that they could use the whole might of the empire to indulge

any strange caprice. They often abused this power to deprive a man arbitrarily of life or property. The burden of their tyranny fell most heavily on some, but it never spread over a great number. It had a few main targets and left the rest alone. It was violent, but its extent was limited.

But if a despotism should be established among the democratic nations of our day, it would probably have a different character. It would be more widespread and milder; it would degrade men rather than torment them.

Doubtless, in such an age of education and equality as our own, rulers could more easily bring all public powers into their own hands alone, and they could impinge deeper and more habitually into the sphere of private interests than was ever possible in antiquity. But that same equality which makes despotism easy tempers it. We have seen how, as men become more alike and more nearly equal, public mores becomes more humane and gentle. When there is no citizen with great power or wealth, tyranny in some degree lacks both target and stage. When all fortunes are middling, passions are naturally restrained, imagination limited, and pleasures simple. Such universal moderation tempers the sovereign's own spirit and keeps within certain limits the disorderly urges of desire.

Apart from these reasons, based on the nature of the state of society itself, I could adduce many others which would take me outside the range of my subject, but I prefer to remain within these self-imposed limits.

Democratic governments might become violent and cruel at times of great excitement and danger, but such crises will be rare and brief.

Taking into consideration the trivial nature of men's passions now, the softness of their mores, the extent of their education, the purity of their religion, their steady habits of patient work, and the restraint which they all show in the indulgence of both their vices and their virtues, I do not expect their leaders to be tyrants, but rather schoolmasters. (See Appendix I, AA.)

Thus I think that the type of oppression which threatens democracies is different from anything there has ever been in the world before. Our contemporaries will find no prototype of it in their memories. I have myself vainly searched for a word which will exactly express the whole of the conception I have formed. Such old words as "despotism" and "tyranny" do not fit. The thing is new, and as I cannot find a word for it, I must try to define it.

I am trying to imagine under what novel features despotism may appear in the world. In the first place, I see an innumerable multitude of men, alike and equal, constantly circling around in pursuit of the petty and banal pleasures with which they glut their souls. Each one of them, withdrawn into himself, is almost unaware of the fate of the rest. Mankind, for him, consists in his children and his personal friends. As for the rest of his fellow citizens, they are near enough, but he does not notice them. He touches them but feels nothing. He exists in and for himself, and though he still may have a family, one can at least say that he has not got a fatherland.

Over this kind of men stands an immense, protective power which is alone responsible for securing their enjoyment and watching over their fate. That power is absolute, thoughtful of detail, orderly, provident, and gentle. It would resemble parental authority if, father-like, it tried to prepare its charges for a man's life, but on the contrary, it only tries to keep them in perpetual childhood. It likes to see the citizens enjoy themselves, provided that they think of nothing but enjoyment. It gladly works for their happiness but wants to be sole agent and judge of it. It provides for their security, foresees and supplies their necessities, facilitates their pleasures, manages their principal concerns, directs their industry, makes rules for their testaments, and divides their inheritances. Why should it not entirely relieve them from the trouble of thinking and all the cares of living?

Thus it daily makes the exercise of free choice less useful and rarer, restricts the activity of free will within a narrower compass, and little by little robs each citizen of the proper use of his own faculties. Equality has prepared men for all this, predisposing them to endure it and often even regard it as beneficial.

Having thus taken each citizen in turn in its powerful grasp and shaped him to its will, government then extends its embrace to include the whole of society. It covers the whole of social life with a network of petty, complicated rules that are both minute and uniform, through which even men of the greatest originality and the most vigorous temperament cannot force their heads above the crowd. It does not break men's will, but softens, bends, and guides it; it seldom enjoins, but often inhibits, action; it does not destroy anything, but prevents much being born; it is not at all tyrannical, but it hinders, restrains, enervates, stifles, and stultifies so much that in the end each nation is no more than a flock of timid and hardworking animals with the government as its shepherd.

I have always thought that this brand of orderly, gentle, peaceful slavery which I have just described could be combined, more easily than is generally supposed, with some of the external forms of freedom, and that there is a possibility of its getting itself established even under the shadow of the sovereignty of the people.

Our contemporaries are ever a prey to two conflicting passions: they feel the need of guidance, and they long to stay free. Unable to wipe out these two contradictory instincts, they try to satisfy them both together. Their imagination conceives a government which is unitary, protective, and all-powerful, but elected by the people. Centralization is combined with the sovereignty of the people. That gives them a chance to relax. They console themselves for being under schoolmasters by thinking that they have chosen them themselves. Each individual lets them put the collar on, for he sees that it is not a person, or a class of persons, but society itself which holds the end of the chain.

Under this system the citizens quit their state of dependence just long enough to choose their masters and then fall back into it.

A great many people nowadays very easily fall in with this brand of compromise between administrative despotism and the sovereignty of the people. They think they have done enough to guarantee personal freedom when it is to the government of the state that they have handed it over. That is not good enough for me. I am much less interested in the question who my master is than in the fact of obedience.

Nevertheless, I freely admit that such a constitution strikes me as infinitely preferable to one which, having brought all powers together, should then hand them over to one irresponsible man or body of men. Of all the forms that democratic despotism might take, that assuredly would be the worst.

When the sovereign is elected, or when he is closely supervised by a legislature which is in very truth elected and free, he may go to greater lengths in oppressing the individual citizen, but such oppression is always less degrading. For each man can still think, though he is obstructed and reduced to powerlessness, that his obedience is only to himself and that it is to one of his desires that he is sacrificing all the others.

I also appreciate that, when the sovereign represents the nation and is dependent on it, the powers and rights taken from each citizen are not used only for the benefit of the head of state, but for the state itself, and that private persons derive some advantage from the independence which they have handed over to the public.

To create a national representation of the people in a very centralized country does, therefore, diminish the extreme evils which centralization can produce but does not entirely abolish them.

I see clearly that by this means room is left for individual inter-vention in the most important affairs, but there is still no place for it in small or private matters. It is too often forgotten that it is especially dangerous to turn men into slaves where details only are concerned. For my part, I should be inclined to think that liberty is less necessary in great matters than in tiny ones if I imagined that one could ever be safe in the enjoyment of one sort of freedom without the other.

Subjection in petty affairs, is manifest daily and touches all citi-zens indiscriminately. It never drives men to despair, but continually thwarts them and leads them to give up using their free will. It slowly stifles their spirits and enervates their souls, whereas obedience demanded only occasionally in matters of great moment brings servitude into play only from time to time, and its weight falls only on certain people. It does little good to summon those very citizens who have been made so dependent on the central power to choose the representatives of that power from time to time. However im-portant, this brief and occasional exercise of free will will not prevent them from gradually losing the faculty of thinking, feeling, and acting for themselves, so that they will slowly fall below the level of humanity.

I must add that they will soon become incapable of using the one great privilege left to them. Those democratic peoples which have introduced freedom into the sphere of politics, while allowing despotism to grow in the administrative sphere, have been led into the strangest paradoxes. For the conduct of small affairs, where plain common sense is enough, they hold that the citizens are not up to the job. But they give these citizens immense prerogatives where the government of the whole state is concerned. They are turned alternatively into the playthings of the sovereign and into his masters, being either greater than kings or less than men. When they have tried all the different systems of election without finding one to suit them, they look surprised and go on seeking for another, as if the ills they see did not belong much more to the constitution of the country itself than to that of the electoral body.

It really is difficult to imagine how people who have entirely given up managing their own affairs could make a wise choice of those who are to do that for them. One should never expect a liberal, energetic, and wise government to originate in the votes of a people of servants.

A constitution republican in its head and ultramonarchial in all its other parts has always struck me as an ephemeral monstrosity.

The vices of those who govern and the weakness of the governed will soon bring it to ruin. Then the people, tired of its representatives and of itself, will either create freer institutions or soon fall back at the feet of a single master. (See Appendix I, BB.)

Chapter 7

CONTINUATION OF THE PRECEDING CHAPTERS

I BELIEVE THAT IT IS EASIER to establish an absolute and despotic government among a people whose social conditions are equal than among any other. I also believe that such a government once established in such a people would not only oppress men but would, in the end, strip each man there of several of the chief attributes of humanity.

I therefore think that despotism is particularly to be feared in ages of democracy.

I think that at all times I should have loved freedom, but in the times in which we live, I am disposed to worship it.

On the other hand, I am convinced that in the age now opening before us those who try to base authority on privilege and aristocracy will fail. All those who try to concentrate and maintain authority in the hands of one class only will fail. There is now no ruler so skillful and so strong that he can establish a despotism by restoring permanent distinctions between his subjects. Nor is there any legislator, however wise or powerful, who could maintain free institutions without making equality his first principle and watchword. Therefore all those who now wish to establish or secure the independence and dignity of their fellow men must show themselves friends of equality; and the only worthy means of appearing such is to be so; upon this depends the success of their holy enterprise.

There is therefore no question of reconstructing an aristocratic society, but the need is to make freedom spring from that democratic society in which God has placed us.

These two basic truths appear to me simple, clear, and fertile.

They naturally lead one to consider how a free government can be established among a people with equality of conditions.

The very constitution and needs of democratic nations make it inevitable that their sovereign power should be more uniform, centralized, extensive, and efficient than those of any other people. In the nature of things society there is more active and stronger, and the individual more subordinate and weaker: society does more and the individual less. That is inevitable.

One cannot therefore ever expect that in democracies the sphere of individual independence will ever be as wide as in aristocracies. But that is not something we should wish for, since in aristocracies society is often sacrificed to the individual and the prosperity of the greater number to the greatness of a few.

It is both necessary and desirable that the central power of a democratic people should be both active and strong. One does not want to make it weak or casual, but only to prevent it from abusing its agility and force.

What most helped to secure the independence of private people in ages of aristocracy was that the ruler did not attempt to govern or administer the citizens by himself. He was bound to leave part of this task to the members of the aristocracy. In this way the social power was always divided and never fell with all its weight from one source on one man.

Not only did the ruler not do everything by himself, but most of the officials who acted for him derived their power from the fact of their birth, and not from him, and so were not constantly under his thumb. He could not at any moment appoint or dismiss them capriciously or force them all uniformly to comply with his slightest wishes. That was some guarantee for the independence of private persons.

I well understand that one cannot now employ that method, but I do see some democratic procedures to replace it.

Instead of entrusting all the administrative powers taken away from corporations and from the nobility to the government alone, some of them could be handed over to secondary bodies temporarily composed of private citizens. In that way the freedom of individuals would be safer without their equality being less.

The Americans, who attach less importance to words than we do, have retained the word "county" to describe their largest administrative districts, but they have partly replaced functions of the county by those of the provincial assembly.

I freely agree that in such a time of equality as ours it would be unfair and unreasonable to institute hereditary officials, but there is no reason why one should not to some extent substitute elected officials for them. Election is a democratic expedient which secures the independence of officials in face of the central government even more effectively than it was secured by hereditary rank among aristocratic peoples.

Aristocratic countries abound in rich and influential persons who can look after themselves and cannot be easily or secretly downtrodden. Their existence instills general habits of moderation and restraint in those in power.

I am well aware that democratic countries do not naturally include persons of that sort, but something of like sort can be artificially created.

I am firmly convinced that one cannot found an aristocracy anew in this world, but I think that associations of plain citizens can compose very rich, influential, and powerful bodies, in other words, aristocratic bodies.

By this means many of the greatest political advantages of an aristocracy could be obtained without its injustices and dangers. An association, be it political, industrial, commercial, or even literary or scientific, is an educated and powerful body of citizens which cannot be twisted to any man's will or quietly trodden down, and by defending its private interests against the encroachments of power, it saves the common liberties.

In aristocratic ages each man is always bound by close ties to many of his fellow citizens, so that he cannot be attacked without the others coming to his help. In times of equality each man is naturally isolated. He can call on no hereditary friends for help nor any class whose sympathy for him is assured. He can easily be set upon alone and trodden underfoot. Nowadays an oppressed citizen has only one means of defense: he can appeal to the nation as a whole, and if it is deaf, to humanity at large. The press provides his only means of doing this. For this reason freedom of the press is infinitely more precious in a democracy than in any other nation. It alone cures most of the ills which equality may engender. Equality isolates and weakens men, but the press puts each man in reach of a very powerful weapon which can be used even by the weakest and most isolated of men. Equality deprives each individual of the help of his neighbors, but the press enables him to call to his aid all his fellow citizens and all mankind. Printing has hastened the progress of equality, but is also one of its best correctives.

I think that men living under aristocracies could, if need be, dispense with the freedom of the press. But the inhabitants of democracies could not do so. I should put no trust in great political assemblies, parliamentary prerogatives, or the proclamation of the sovereignty of the people to secure personal independence.

All those things can, to some extent, be reconciled with personal servitude. But such servitude cannot be complete if the press is free. The press is, par excellence, the democratic weapon of freedom.

Something analogous may be said of judicial power.

It is of the essence of judicial power to be concerned with private interests and gladly to pay attention to trivial subjects submitted to its consideration. Another essential element in judicial power is never to volunteer its assistance to the oppressed, but always to be at the disposal of the humblest when they solicit it. However weak a man may be, he can always compel a judge to listen to his complaint and give him an answer. That is inherent in the very nature of judicial power.

Such a power is therefore peculiarly adapted to the needs of freedom at a time when the ruler's eye and hand are constantly interfering in the tiniest details of human actions and when private people are too weak to defend themselves and too isolated to count on the help of their fellows. The power of the courts has been at all times the securest guarantee which can be provided for individual independence, but this is particularly true in ages of democracy. Private rights and interests are, then, always in danger unless the power of the courts grows and extends commensurately with the increase of equality of conditions.

Equality prompts men to indulge propensities very dangerous to freedom, and the legislator should always keep his eye on them. I shall only call attention to the most important of them.

Men living in democratic centuries do not readily understand the importance of formalities and have an instinctive contempt for them. I have explained the reasons for this elsewhere. Formalities arouse their disdain and often their hatred. As they usually aspire to none but facile and immediate pleasures, they rush straight at the object of any of their desires, and the slightest delay exasperates them. This temperament, which they carry with them into political life, makes them impatient of the formalities which daily hold up or prevent one or another of their designs.

But it is just this inconvenience, of which democracies complain, which makes formalities so useful to freedom. For their chief merit is to serve as a barrier between the strong and the weak, the government and the governed, and to hold back the one while the other has time to take his bearings. Formalities become more important in proportion as the sovereign is more active and powerful and private individuals become more indolent and feeble. Thus democracies by their nature need formalities more than other peoples, and by nature have less respect for them. This deserves most serious attention.

Nothing is more deplorable than the arrogant disdain of most of our contemporaries for questions of form, for the smallest of such questions have now taken on an importance they never had before. Many of the greatest interests of mankind depend upon them.

I think that although the statesmen of aristocratic ages might sometimes safely scorn formalities and often rise above them, those who are now leading the peoples ought to treat the slightest formality with respect, and only neglect it in case of imperious necessity. In aristocracies formalities were treated with superstitious reverence; our worship of them should be enlightened and well considered.

Another instinct which is very natural for democracies, and very dangerous, is a tendency to despise individual rights and take little account of them.

Generally men become attached to a right or feel respect for it because of either its importance or the long period over which it has been in force. Such individual rights as are found in democracies are usually unimportant or of very recent date and impermanent. As a result, they are often given up without trouble and almost always violated without remorse.

Moreover, it happens, at the same time and among the same peoples that have conceived a natural scorn for individual rights, that the rights of society are naturally extended and consolidated. This means that men become less attached to private rights just at the moment when it is most necessary to maintain and defend the few that still exist.

It is therefore especially necessary in our own democratic age for the true friends of liberty and of human dignity to be on the alert to prevent the social power from lightly sacrificing the private rights of some individuals while carrying through its general designs. At such a time no citizen is so insignificant that he can be trodden down without very dangerous results, and no private rights are of such little importance that they can safely be left subject to arbitrary decisions. There is a simple reason for this: when the private right of an individual is violated at a time when mankind is deeply convinced of the importance and sanctity of such rights, the injury is confined to the person whose right has been infringed. But to infringe such a right now deeply corrupts the mores of the nation and puts the whole of society in danger, because the very idea of this kind of right tends constantly among us to be impaired and lost.

There are some habits, some ideas, and some vices which are peculiar to a state of revolution and which any prolonged revolution cannot fail to engender and spread, whatever may be in other respects its character, object, and field of action.

When in a brief space of time any nation has repeatedly changed its leaders, opinions, and laws, the men of that nation will in the end acquire a taste for change and grow accustomed to see all changes quickly brought about by the use of force. Then they will naturally conceive a scorn for those formalities of whose impotence they have been daily witnesses, and they will be impatient to tolerate the sway of rules which they have so often seen infringed.

As ordinary ideas of equity and morality are no longer enough to explain and justify all the innovations daily introduced by revolution, men fall back on the principle of social utility, political necessity is turned into a dogma, and men lose all scruples about freely sacrificing particular interests and trampling private rights beneath their feet in order more quickly to attain the public aim envisaged.

Such habits and ideas, which I call revolutionary since all revolutions give rise to them, are seen as much in aristocracies as among democratic peoples. But in the former case they are often less powerful and always less permanent, because there they come up against habits, ideas, faults, and eccentricities which are opposed to them. They therefore vanish of their own accord when the revolution is at an end and the nation recovers its former political ways. However, that is not always the case in democratic countries, for in them there is always a danger that revolutionary instincts will mellow and assume more regular shape without entirely disappearing, but will gradually be transformed into mores of government and administrative habits.

Hence, I know of no country in which revolutions are more dangerous than in a democracy, because apart from the accidental and ephemeral ills which they are ever bound to entail, there is always a danger of their becoming permanent, and one may almost say, eternal.

I think that resistance is sometimes justified and that rebellion can be legitimate. I cannot therefore lay it down as an absolute rule that men living in times of democracy should never make a revolution. But I think that they, more than others, have reason to hesitate before they embark on such an enterprise and that it is far better to put up with many inconveniences in their present state than to turn to so dangerous a remedy.

I shall conclude with one general idea which comprises not only all the particular ideas with which this chapter treats but also most of those which this book is intended to expound.

In the ages of aristocracy which came before our time, there were very powerful individuals and a very feeble social authority. Even the bare outline of society was dim and constantly confounded with all the various powers ruling the citizens. It was right for the men of those times to devote their principal efforts to enlarging and strengthening the social power and to increasing its prerogatives and making them secure. It was also right for them to restrict private freedom within the narrowest bounds and to subordinate particular interests to the general good.

Other dangers and other needs face the men of our own day.

In most modern nations the sovereign, whatever its origin or constitution or name, has become very nearly all-powerful, and private persons are more and more falling down to the lowest stage of weakness and dependence.

Everything was different in the old societies. There unity and uniformity were nowhere to be found. In our day everything threatens to become so much alike that the particular features of each individual may soon be entirely lost in the common physiognomy. Our fathers were always prone to make improper use of the idea that private rights should be respected, and we are by nature inclined to exaggerate the opposite view, that the interest of the individual should always give way to the interest of the many.

The political world changes, and we must now seek new remedies for new ills.

We should lay down extensive but clear and fixed limits to the field of social power. Private people should be given certain rights and the undisputed enjoyment of such rights. The individual should be allowed to keep the little freedom, strength, and originality left to him. His position in face of society should be raised and supported. Such, I think, should be the chief aim of any legislator in the age opening before us.

It would seem that sovereigns now only seek to do great things with men. I wish that they would try a little more to make men great, that they should attach less importance to the work and more to the workman, that they should constantly remember that a nation cannot long remain great if each man is individually weak, and that no one has yet devised a form of society or a political combination which can make a people energetic when it is composed of citizens who are flabby and feeble.

Two contrary ideas are current among us, both equally fatal.

There is one lot of people who can see nothing in equality but the anarchical tendencies which it engenders. They are frightened of their own free will; they are afraid of themselves.

Others, who are fewer but more perceptive, take a different view. Beside the track which starts from equality and leads to anarchy, they have in the end discovered another road, which seems to lead inevitably to servitude. They shape their souls beforehand to suit this necessary servitude, and despairing of remaining free, from the bottom of their hearts they already worship the master who is bound soon to appear.

The former surrender liberty because they think it dangerous and the latter because they think it impossible.

If I shared this latter belief, I never should have written the book which you have just read, but would have contented myself with mourning in secret over the fate of my fellows.

I have sought to expose the perils with which equality threatens human freedom because I firmly believe that those dangers are both the most formidable and the least foreseen of those which the future has in store. But I do not think that they are insurmountable.

The men living in the democratic centuries into which we are entering have a natural taste for freedom. By nature they are impatient in putting up with any regulation. They get tired of the duration even of the state they have chosen. They love power but are inclined to scorn and hate those who wield it, and they easily escape its grasp by reason of their very insignificance and changeableness.

These instincts will always recur because they result from the state of society, which will not change. For a long time they will prevent the establishment of any despotism, and they will furnish fresh weapons for each new generation wanting to struggle for human liberty.

Let us, then, look forward to the future with that salutary fear which makes men keep watch and ward for freedom, and not with that flabby, idle terror which makes men's hearts sink and enervates them.

Chapter 8

GENERAL SURVEY OF THE SUBJECT

BEFORE I FINALLY BRING TO AN END the subject I have discussed, I should have liked to take one last look at all the various features of the new world and to form some considered view of the general influence which equality is likely to have over the fate of mankind. But the difficulty of such an undertaking holds me back. Faced by so vast a subject, I feel my vision hazy and my judgment hesitant.

This new society which I have tried to portray and would like to evaluate has only just begun to come into being. Time has not yet shaped its definite form. The great revolution which brought it about is still continuing, and of all that is taking place in our day, it is almost impossible to judge what will vanish with the revolution itself and what will survive thereafter.

The world which is arising is still half buried in the ruins of the world falling into decay, and in the vast confusion of all human affairs at present, no one can know which of the old institutions and former mores will continue to hold up their heads and which will in the end go under.

Although the revolution that is taking place in the social condition, laws, ideas, and feelings of men is still far from coming to an end, yet its results are already incomparably greater than anything which has taken place in the world before. Working back through the centuries to the remotest antiquity, I see nothing at all similar to what is taking place before our eyes. The past throws no light on the future, and the spirit of man walks through the night.

Nevertheless, in this vast prospect, both so novel and so confused, I can make out some salient features which I will point out.

I find that good things and evil in the world are fairly evenly distributed. Great wealth tends to disappear and the number of small fortunes to increase; desires and pleasures are multiplied, but extraordinary prosperity and irremediable penury are alike unknown. Everyone feels some ambition, but few have ambitions on a vast scale. Each individual is isolated and weak, but society is active, provident, and strong; private persons achieve insignificant things, but the state immense ones.

There is little energy of soul, but mores are gentle and laws humane. Though heroic devotion and any other very exalted, brilliant, and pure virtues may be rare, habits are orderly, violence rare, and cruelty almost unknown. Men tend to live longer, and their property is more secure. Life is not very glamorous, but extremely comfortable and peaceful. There is seldom great refinement or gross vulgarity in men's pleasures, little polish in their manners but little brutality in their tastes. One hardly ever finds men of great learning or whole communities steeped in ignorance. Genius becomes rarer but education more common. The spirit of man is advanced by the tiny efforts of all combined, and not by the powerful impulse given by the few. In the works of man there is less perfection but greater abundance. All the ties of race, class, and country are relaxed. The great bond of humanity is drawn tighter.

Seeking for the most general and striking of all these various characteristics, I notice that what has been said about personal fortunes applies to other things in a thousand different ways. Almost all extremes are softened and blunted. Almost all salient characteristics are obliterated to make room for something average, less high and less low, less brilliant and less dim, than what the world had before.

When I survey this countless multitude of beings, shaped in each other's likeness, among whom nothing stands out or falls unduly low, the sight of such universal uniformity saddens and chills me, and I am tempted to regret that state of society which has ceased to be.

When the world was full of men of great importance and extreme insignificance, very wealthy and very poor, very learned and very ignorant, I turned my attention from the latter to concentrate on the pleasure of contemplating the former. But I see that this pleasure arose from my weakness. It is because I am unable to see at once all that is around me that I am allowed thus to select and separate the objects of my choice from among so many others which it pleases me to contemplate. It is not so with the Almighty and Eternal Being, whose gaze of necessity includes the whole of created things and who surveys distinctly and simultaneously all mankind and each single man.

It is natural to suppose that not the particular prosperity of the few, but the greater well-being of all, is most pleasing in the sight of the Creator and Preserver of men. What seems to me decay is thus in His eyes progress; what pains me is acceptable to Him. Equality may be less elevated, but it is more just, and in its justice lies its greatness and beauty.

I therefore do all I can to enter into understanding of this divine view of the world and strive from thence to consider and judge the affairs of men.

No man on earth can affirm, absolutely and generally, that the new state of societies is better than the old, but it is already easy to see that it is different.

Some vices and some virtues were so inherent in the constitutions of aristocratic nations and are so contrary to the genius of modern peoples that they can never be introduced therein. There are some good inclinations and some bad instincts which were foreign to the former but are natural to the latter. Some ideas spontaneously strike the imagination of the one but are repugnant to the other. They are like two distinct kinds of humanity, each of which has its peculiar advantages and disadvantages, its good points and its bad.

One must therefore be very careful not to judge the nascent societies on the basis of ideas derived from those which no longer exist. To do so would be unfair, for these societies are so immensely different that direct comparison is impossible.

It would be just as unreasonable to expect from men nowadays the particular virtues which depended on the social condition of their ancestors, since that state of society has collapsed, bringing down in the confusion of its ruin all that it had of good and bad.

But these matters are still badly understood in our day.

I find that many of my contemporaries want to make a selection from the institutions, opinions, and ideas which sprang from the aristocratic constitution of the old society. They gladly abandon some of them, but would like to keep others and carry them along with them into the new world.

I think that such men are consuming their time and trouble in a sincere but sterile labor.

The task is no longer to preserve the particular advantages which inequality of conditions had procured for men, but to secure those new benefits which equality may supply. We should not strive to be like our fathers but should try to attain that form of greatness and of happiness which is proper to ourselves.

For myself, looking back now from the extreme end of my task and seeing at a distance, but collected together, all the various things which had attracted my close attention upon my way, I am full of fears and of hopes. I see great dangers which may be warded off and mighty evils which may be avoided or kept in check; and I am ever increasingly confirmed in my belief that for democratic nations to be virtuous and prosperous, it is enough if they will to be so.

I am aware that many of my contemporaries think that nations on earth are never their own masters and that they are bound to obey some insuperable and unthinking power, the product of pre-existing facts, of race, or soil, or climate.

These are false and cowardly doctrines which can only produce feeble men and pusillanimous nations. Providence did not make mankind entirely free or completely enslaved. Providence has, in truth, drawn a predestined circle around each man beyond which he cannot pass; but within those vast limits man is strong and free, and so are peoples.

The nations of our day cannot prevent conditions of equality from spreading in their midst. But it depends upon themselves whether equality is to lead to servitude or freedom, knowledge or barbarism, prosperity or wretchedness.

APPENDICES

Appendix I

TOCQUEVILLE'S NOTES TO VOLUME ONE

A, p. 25

SEE the two journeys undertaken by Major Long at the expense of Congress for all the countries of the West where Europeans have not yet penetrated.

In particular, Mr. Long says, speaking of the great American wilderness, that one should draw a line roughly paralled to the twentieth degree of longitude (meridian of Washington, corresponding approximately to the ninety-ninth degree of the meridian of Paris), starting from the Red River and ending with the river Platte. From this imaginary line to the Rocky Mountains, which border the Mississippi valley on the west, extend immense plains, generally covered with sand, that cannot be cultivated, or strewn with granitic rocks. They have no water in summer. There are only large herds of buffalo and wild horses to be found there. There are also some hordes of Indians, but in small numbers.

Major Long heard it said that in going above the river Platte in the same direction, to the left there would always be the same desert; but he was not able to verify himself the accuracy of this report. (*Long's Expedition*, Vol. II, p. 361.) [Cf. *Account of an Expedition from Pittsburgh to the Rocky Mountains* . . . under the Command of Major Stephen Long, compiled by E. James, 2 vols., Philadelphia, 1823.]

However much confidence one may put in Major Long's narrative, one must remember that he did no more than cross the country of which he speaks, without making any great zigzags to either side of the line he followed.

B, p. 26

In its tropical regions South America produces an incredible profusion of those climbing plants known under the generic name of liana. There are forty different sorts in the Antilles alone.

One of the most graceful of these creepers is the granadilla. This pretty plant, says Descourtilz in his description of the vegetation of the Antilles, uses its tendrils to cling to trees, thus forming waving arcades and colonnades that are rich and elegant with their purple and blue flowers, which exhale an enchanting scent. (Vol. I, p. 265.) [J. T. Descourtilz, *Flore Pittoresque et Médicale des Antilles* . . . 2nd ed., Paris, 1833, 3 vols.]

The large-podded acacia is a very thick liana which grows quickly, and running from tree to tree, sometimes covers more than half a league. (Vol. III, p. 277.)

C, p. 28

Concerning the Languages of America

The languages spoken by the Indians of America, from the North Pole to Cape Horn, are all said to be formed on the same model and subject to the same grammatical rules, and this makes it highly probable that all the Indian nations spring from one stock.

Every tribe on the American continent speaks a different dialect, but using the word strictly, there are very few languages, which is further evidence tending to show that the nations of the New World have no very ancient origin.

Finally, the American languages are extremely regular; it is therefore probable that the peoples using them have not yet experienced great revolutions and have not mingled, willingly or otherwise, with foreign nations, for it is usually the combination of several languages into one that produces grammatical irregularities.

It is only recently that the languages of America, particularly of North America, have attracted the serious attention of philologists. So it was an unexpected discovery to find that the idiom of this barbarous people was the product of a very complicated system of ideas and of very expert combinations. It was noticed that these languages were very rich and that their formation showed very sensitive attention to euphony.

The grammatical system of these American languages is different from all others in several respects, of which this the most important.

Several peoples of Europe, the Germans among others, have the faculty of combining various expressions at will, thereby creating words of complicated meaning. The Indians have extended this faculty in an astonishing way, bringing a very large number of ideas to bear on a single point. An example quoted by Mr. Duponceau in the *Transactions of the American Philosophical Society* will make the point clear.

When a Delaware woman is playing with a cat or a puppy, she is sometimes heard to pronounce the word *kuligatschis*. This word is composed as follows: *K* is the sign of the second person, meaning *thou* or *thy; uli,* pronounced *ouli,* is part of the word *wulit,* which means *handsome* or *pretty; gat* is part of the word *wichgat,* meaning *paw;* finally, *schis,* pronounced *chise,* is a diminutive termination implying smallness. So with a single word the Indian woman said: *Thy pretty little paw.*

Here is another example of the felicity with which the American savages put their words together.

In Delaware a young man is called *pilape*. This word is formed from *pilsit,* chaste, innocent, and *lenape,* man: that is to say, man in his purity and innocence.

This faculty for combining words is used with astonishing effect in the formation of verbs. The most complicated action is often expressed by a single verb; almost all the nuances of an idea act upon the verb and modify it.

Anyone wishing to study the details of this subject, on which I can only very superficially touch here, should read:

1. Mr. Duponceau's correspondence with the Rev. Mr. Heckewelder concerning the Indian languages. This correspondence is found in the first volume of the *Transactions of the American Philosophical Society,* published in Philadelphia in 1819 by Abraham Small, pp. 356–464.

2. The grammar of the Delaware, or Lenape, language, by Geiberger, with a preface by Mr. Duponceau. Both are to be found in Volume III of the same collection. [Actually "Geiberger" is David Zeisberger. He translated the Bible into the Delaware language in 1821 and published a Delaware Indian and English spelling book in Philadelphia in 1806, with notes by Duponceau. Cf. *Transactions of the American Philosophical Society,* Vol. I, Philadelphia, 1819, pp. 392 ff.]

3. A very good summary of these works at the end of Volume VI of the *American Encyclopaedia.* [The work appears to be the *American Encyclopedie* . . . New York, John Low, 1805–1810, 8 vols. We have not been able to locate the work.]

D, p. 29

Charlevoix [*Histoire et Description générale de la Nouvelle France avec le Journal historique d'un voyage fait par ordre du Roi dans l'Amérique septentrionale,* six vols., Paris, 1744], Vol. I, p. 235, gives an account of the first war, in 1610, between the French of Canada and the Iroquois. The latter, though armed with bows and arrows, put up a desperate resistance against the French and their allies. Charlevoix, though he is not a gifted descriptive writer, in this passage does bring out very well the contrast between the mores of the Europeans and of the savages, and the different ways in which the two races conceived honor.

"The French," he says, "seized some beaver skins which they found covering the Iroquois lying on the battlefield. Their allies, the Hurons, were scandalized at seeing this. For their part, the latter began to perform their usual cruelties on their prisoners and devoured one of those who had been killed, which horrified the French. And so," Charlevoix adds, "these barbarians gloried in a disinterestedness which they were surprised not to find in our nation, and did not understand that it was much less evil to plunder the dead than to devour their flesh like wild beasts."

Elsewhere (Vol. I, p. 230 [f.]) Charlevoix describes the first torture witnessed by Champlain and the return of the Hurons to their village.

"After they had gone eight leagues," he says, "our allies halted, and taking one of their captives, reproached him for all the cruelties he had perpetrated on the warriors of their nation who had fallen into his hands, and declared that he must expect to be treated in the same way, adding that if he was brave he would sing an accompaniment. He at once began to sing his war song, and all the songs he knew, but in a very sad tone, according to Champlain, who had not yet had time to appreciate that there is something lugubrious in all the music of the savages. His punishment, accompanied by all the horrors of which we shall speak later, shocked the French, who in vain did all they could to put a stop to it [. . .]. The next night, as one of the Hurons had dreamt that they were pursued, the retreat turned into a veritable flight, and the savages would not halt again anywhere until they were out of danger [. . .].

"As soon as they saw their village's huts, they cut long poles and fixed the scalps they had shared as booty to them, carrying them in triumph. At sight of this the women came running up, jumped into the water, and swam to the canoes; they then took the bleeding scalps from their husbands' hands and hung them around their necks.

"The warriors offered one of these horrible trophies to Champlain and also gave him some bows and arrows, the only spoils that they had wished to take from the Iroquois, asking him to show them to the king of France [. . .]."

Champlain lived alone for a whole winter with these barbarians without a moment's risk to his person or to his property.

E, p. 43

Although the strict puritanism that presided at the birth of the English colonies in America is already much relaxed, one does still find extraordinary traces of it in habits and in laws.

In 1792, that very year in which the antichristian French republic began its ephemeral existence, the Massachusetts legislature promulgated the following law to enforce Sunday observance. I quote the preamble and the main clauses of it, which are well worth the reader's closest attention.

"Whereas the observation of Sunday is in the public interest; inasmuch as it produces a useful suspension in labor, leads men to reflect upon the duties of life and the errors to which humanity is subject, permits the private and public worship of God the Creator and Ruler of the Universe, and dedication to the acts of charity which are the ornament and comfort of Christian societies;

"Whereas irreligious or light-minded persons, forgetting the duties which Sunday imposes and the advantages society derives from it, profane its sanctity by following their own pleasures or labors; inasmuch as this manner of acting is contrary to their own interests as Christians; that furthermore it is of such a nature as to upset those who do not follow their example, and bring a real prejudice to the whole society by introducing there the taste for dissipation and dissolute habits;

"The Senate and the House of Representatives ordain that:

"1. No one will be permitted on Sunday to keep open his shop or work-shop. No one on that day will occupy himself with any work or business whatsoever, attend any concert, dance, or entertainment, or indulge in any form of hunting, sport, or game, under penalty of fine. The fine will be not less than ten shillings and will not exceed twenty shillings for each infraction.

"2. No traveler, conductor, or driver, except in case of necessity, will travel on Sunday, under penalty of the same fine.

"3. Tavern keepers, retailers, innkeepers, will prevent any resident of their township from coming to their establishment on Sunday to spend time there for pleasure or business. In case of infraction, the innkeeper and his guest will pay the fine. Furthermore, the innkeeper can lose his license.

"4. Anyone who, being in good health and without sufficient reason, fails for three months to attend public worship, will be condemned to a fine of ten shillings.

"5. Anyone who, within a church, behaves improperly will pay a fine of from five to forty shillings.

"6. The tithingmen of the townships[1] are responsible for the execution of the present law. They have the right to visit all rooms of hotels or public places on Sunday. The innkeeper who refuses them entrance to his establishment will be condemned to a fine of forty shillings for this act alone.

"The tithingmen will stop travelers and inquire the reason why they are obliged to travel on Sunday. Whoever refuses to answer will be condemned to a fine which can be five pounds sterling.

"If the reason given by the traveler does not appear sufficient to the tithingman, he will prosecute the said traveler before the justice of the peace of the district." (Law of March 8, 1792, *General Laws of Massachusetts*, Vol. I, p. 410.) [Tocqueville condensed the legal text; cf. *op. cit.*, p. 407 ff.]

On March 11, 1797, a new law increased the rate of the fines, half of which was to go to the offender's prosecutor. (Same collection, Vol. I, p. 525.)

On February 16, 1816, a new law confirmed these same measures. (Same collection, Vol. II, p. 405.)

There are similar clauses in the laws of the state of New York, revised in 1827 and 1828. (See *Revised Statutes*, Part I, chapter XX, p. 675.) It is forbidden therein to hunt, fish, gamble, or frequent places where drink is sold on Sunday. No one may travel except in case of necessity.

This is not the only trace left in the laws by the spirit of religion and the austere mores of the first immigrants.

In Vol. I, p. 662, of the *Revised Statutes of the State of New York* there is the following clause:

"Whosoever wins or loses the sum of twenty-five dollars within the space of twenty-four hours by gambling or betting shall be guilty of a misdemeanor,

---

[1] These are annually elected officers whose duties resemble those of both the *garde champêtre* and the *officier de police judiciaire* in France.

and on proof of the fact will be condemned to a fine equal to at least five times the value of the sum lost or won; the said fine shall be handed over to the overseer of the poor for that township.

"Whoever loses twenty-five dollars or more can bring an action to recover it. If he fails to do so, the overseer of the poor can bring an action against the winner and make him pay the sum won, and threefold as much again, for the benefit of the poor." [Tocqueville summarizes the text of §§ 13, 14, 15, Article Third: cf. *Betting and Gaming,* Revised Statutes of the State of New York, Albany, 1829, Vol. I, pp. 662 f.]

The laws just quoted are recent ones, but who would be able to understand them without going right back to the origin of the colonies? I do not doubt that nowadays the penal part of that legislation is very seldom applied; laws remain rigid when mores have already bent with changing times. Nevertheless, Sunday observance in America is even now one of the things that strike a stranger most.

In one great American city in particular the whole movement of social life is suspended from Saturday evening on. If you go through the streets at the hour when you would expect grown-up people to be going to their businesses, and young ones to their pleasures, you will find yourself in profound solitude. It is not just that no one seems to be working; they do not even seem alive. One can hear no sound of folk at work or at play, and not even that confused noise which constantly rises from any great city. Chains are stretched around the churches, and the half-closed shutters reluctantly allow a ray of light to penetrate the citizens' houses. You may at long intervals just see some isolated man gliding noiselessly through the thoroughfares or along the empty city streets.

At daybreak the next day you will hear again the rumble of carriages, the strokes of hammers, and the shouts of men; the city is waking up; a restless crowd hurries to office or to factory; everything around you is stirring, agitated, and jostling. Feverish activity has succeeded after a sort of lethargic torpor; one might suppose that each man had but one day's chance of winning wealth and of enjoying it.

F, p. 47

There is no need to explain that this chapter does not pretend to give a history of America. My sole aim has been to enable the reader to appreciate the influence of the opinions and mores of the first immigrants on the destinies of the various colonies and the Union as a whole. So I have had to limit myself to some fragmentary quotations.

I do not know whether I am wrong, but I think that if one followed up the path I have here indicated, one could describe the infancy of the American republics in a way that would interest the general public and would certainly provide statesmen with material for reflection. As I cannot myself undertake this task, I should at least like to make it easier for others. So I think I should here give a short bibliography and abbreviated analysis of the works I consider most valuable to consult.

Of the documents of a general nature which one could profitably consult, I should place first a work entitled *Historical Collections, Consisting of State Papers and Other Authentic Documents, Intended as Materials for an History of the United States of America,* by Ebenezer Hazard.

The first volume of this compilation, printed in Philadelphia in 1792, contains the exact text of all the charters granted by the English Crown to the immigrants and all the principal acts of the colonial governments during the first period of their existence. Among other things, one finds a great number of authentic documents concerning the affairs of New England and Virginia during this period.

The second volume is almost entirely devoted to the acts of the Confederation of 1643. This was a federal pact between the colonies of New England, with the object of resisting the Indians, and was the first occasion on which the Anglo-Americans attempted a union. There were several other confederations of the same nature too, ending in that of 1776, which led to the independence of the colonies.

There is a copy of this work in the Bibliothèque royale.

Each colony also has historical records, some of which are very precious. I shall deal with Virginia first, which was the state to be populated earliest.

The first of all the historians of Virginia is its founder, Captain John Smith. Captain Smith has left us a quarto volume entitled *General History of Virginia, New England, and the Summer Isles, by Captain John Smith, Sometime Governor in Those Countries and Admiral of New England,* printed in London in 1627. (There is a copy of this book in the Bibliothèque royale.) Smith's work includes very remarkable maps and engravings, dating from the time it was printed. The historical narrative goes from the year 1584 down to 1626. Smith's work deserves its high reputation. The author is one of the most famous of adventurers, coming at the end of an age which saw so many of them; the book breathes that ardor for discovery and that spirit of enterprise characteristic of the men of that day; in it one finds an eye for business combined with chivalrous mores, both set to serve the acquisition of wealth.

But the most remarkable feature of Captain Smith was that he added to the virtues of his contemporaries qualities foreign to the greater part of them; his style is simple and clear, all his accounts have the stamp of truth, and his descriptions are not at all ornate.

This author throws precious light on the state of the Indians at the time of the discovery of North America. [There is also a copy at the British Museum.]

The second historian worth consulting is Beverley. His work, in duodecimo, was translated into French and printed in Amsterdam in 1707. The author begins his account in the year 1585 and finishes it in 1700. The first part of his book contains historical documents properly so called relating to the infancy of the colony. The second includes a remarkable description of the state of the Indians at that distant period. The third part gives very clear impressions of the mores, social condition, laws, and political habits of the Virginians of the author's day.

Beverley was of Virginian origin, and so he starts by begging his readers not to scan his work with too strictly critical eyes, for having been born in the Indies, he does not aspire to purity of language. Despite this colonial modesty, the author shows throughout his book his impatience in tolerating the supremacy of the motherland. There are many traces in his work of the spirit of civil liberty then animating the English colonies in America. One also finds signs of the divisions which so long subsisted among them and which delayed the day of independence. Beverley detests his Catholic neighbors in Maryland even more than the English government. His style is simple; his accounts are often full of interest and inspire confidence. The Bibliothèque royale has a copy of the French translation. [The British Museum possesses a copy with Robert Beverley's autograph subscribed to the dedication: *The History and Present State of Virginia,* London, 1705; French edition: *Histoire de la Virginie,* par un Auteur natif et habitant du Païs, Amsterdam, 1707.]

One book worth consulting I found in America, but have not been able to discover a copy in France; its title is *History of Virginia,* by William Stith. [*The History of the First Discovery and Settlement of Virginia Being an Essay Towards a General History of This Colony,* Williamsburg, 1747.] There are interesting details in this book, but it struck me as long and diffuse.

The oldest and best account of the history of the Carolinas is a little quarto volume entitled *The History of Carolina,* by John Lawson, printed in London in 1714. [*The History of Carolina,* by John Lawson, Surveyor-General of North Carolina, London, 1714.]

Lawson's book begins with a voyage of discovery in western Carolina. The account is in the form of a diary; the author's narrative is confused, and his observations are very superficial; but it does include a rather striking description of the ravages caused by smallpox and brandy among the savages at that time, and a remarkable picture of the corruption of mores prevailing among them, which the presence of the Europeans increased.

The second part of Lawson's book is concerned with the physical state of Carolina and advertising its produce.

In the third part the author gives an interesting description of the mores, usages, and government of the Indians at that time.

There is a good deal of sense and originality in that part of his book.

Lawson's history ends with the charter granted to Carolina in the time of Charles II.

The general tone of the book is light, often licentious, and it forms a complete contrast to the profoundly serious works published in New England at the same time.

Lawson's history is an extremely rare book in America and cannot be acquired in Europe. But there is a copy in the Bibliothèque royale.

I will pass from the extreme south of the United States to the extreme north. The country in between was not peopled until later.

I must first call attention to a very interesting collection entitled *Collection of the Massachusetts Historical Society,* first printed in Boston in 1792 and reprinted in 1806. There is no copy in the Bibliothèque royale, nor, I think, in any other library.

This collection, which is being continued, includes a great many very valuable documents concerning the history of the various states of New England. It includes unpublished letters and authentic records buried in provincial archives. The whole of Gookin's work about the Indians has been included. [Cf. *Collections of the Massachusetts Historical Society for the Year 1792,* Vol. I, Boston, 1792. See *Historical Collections of the Indians in New England,* by Daniel Gookin, pp. 140 ff.]

In the chapter to which this note refers, I have made several references to Nathaniel Morton's *New England's Memorial.* I have said enough to show that it deserves the attention of anybody who wants to understand the history of New England. It is an octavo volume, printed in Boston in 1826. There is no copy in the Bibliothèque royale.

The Rev. Cotton Mather's *Magnalia Christi Americana, or the Ecclesiastical History of New England, 1620–1698,* two octavo volumes, reprinted in Hartford in 1820, is the most highly reputed and the most important work concerning the history of New England. I do not think there is a copy in the Bibliothèque royale.

The author divided his work into seven books.

The first gives an account of everything that prepared for and led up to the foundation of New England.

The second gives the lives of the first governors and the principal magistrates who administered the country.

The third is devoted to the lives and labors of the ministers of the Gospel who guided men's souls during the same period.

In the fourth the author describes the foundation and growth of the University of Cambridge (Massachusetts).

In the fifth he describes the principles and the organization of the Church of New England.

The sixth is devoted to an account of certain events which, in Mather's view, proved the beneficent action of Providence on behalf of the inhabitants of New England.

Finally, in the seventh the author tells us of the heresies and troubles to which the Church of New England was exposed.

Cotton Mather was an Evangelical minister who was born in Boston and spent his life there.

All the ardor and all the religious passions which led to the founding of New England animate and enliven his narrative. There are many traces of bad taste in his way of writing, but he holds one's attention because he is full of an enthusiasm which in the end communicates itself to the reader. He is often intolerant, and still more often credulous, but one never feels that he is anxious to deceive; there are even some beautiful passages in his work and some true and profound thoughts, such as the following:

"Before the arrival of the Puritans," he says (Vol. I, chapter IV, p. 61[f.]), "there were more than a few attempts of the *English,* to people and improve the parts of *New-England,* which were to the northward of *New-Plymouth;* but the designs of those attempts being aimed no higher than the advancement of some *worldly interests,* a constant series of disasters has confounded them, until there was a plantation erected upon the nobler designs of *Christianity;* and that plantation, though it has had more adversaries than perhaps any one upon earth; yet, *having obtained help from God, it continues to this day."*

For all his austerity, Mather's descriptions are sometimes gentle and tender; speaking of an English lady who was led by religious ardor to go to America with her husband, and who soon succumbed to the fatigues and afflictions of exile, he adds: "As for her virtuous husband, Isaac Johnson, he tried to live without her, liked it not, and died." (Vol. I, p. 71.)

Mather's book is wonderfully successful in conveying a sense of the time and country he seeks to describe.

Wishing to explain the motives which led the Puritans to seek a refuge across the seas, he says:

"Briefly, the God of Heaven served as it were, a *summons* upon the *spirits* of his people in the English nation; stirring up the spirits of thousands which never saw the *faces* of each other, with a most unanimous inclination to leave all the pleasant accommodations of their native country, and go over a terrible *ocean,* into a more terrible *desart,* for the *pure enjoyment of all his ordinances.* It is now reasonable that before we pass any further, the *reasons* for this undertaking should be more exactly made known unto *posterity,* especially unto the *posterity* of those that were the *undertakers,* lest they come at length to forget and neglect *the true interest* of New-England. Wherefore I shall now transcribe some of *them* from a manuscript, wherein they were then tendered unto consideration.

"*'First,* it will be a service unto the Church of great consequence, to carry the *Gospel* into *those* parts of the world, and raise a *bulwark* against the kingdom of *antichrist,* which the *Jesuites* labour to rear up in *all* parts of the world.

"*'Secondly,* All other Churches of *Europe* have been brought under *desolations;* and it may be feared that the like judgments are coming upon *us;* and who knows but God hath provided this place to be a *refuge* for many, whom he means to save out of the *General Destruction.*

"*'Thirdly,* The land grows weary of her *inhabitants,* insomuch that *man,* which is the most precious of all creatures, is here more vile and base than the earth he treads upon: *children, neighbours* and *friends,* especially the *poor,* are counted the greatest *burdens,* which if things were right would be the chiefest earthly *blessings.*

"*'Fourthly,* We are grown to that intemperance in all *excess of riot,* as no mean estate almost will suffice a man to keep sail with his *equals,* and he that fails in it, must live in scorn and contempt: hence it comes to pass, that all *arts* and *trades* are carried in that deceitful manner, and unrighteous course, as it is almost impossible for a good upright man to maintain his constant charge, and live comfortably in them.

"'Fifthly, The *schools* of learning and religion are so corrupted, as (besides the unsupportable charge of education) most children, even the best, wittiest, and of the fairest hopes, are perverted, corrupted, and utterly overthrown, by the multitude of evil examples and licentious behaviours in these *seminaries*.

"'Sixthly, The *whole earth* is the *Lord's garden,* and he hath given it to the sons of *Adam,* to be tilled and improved by them: why then should we stand starving here for places of habitation, and in the mean time suffer whole countries, as profitable for the use of man, to lye waste without any improvement?

"'Seventhly, What can be a better or nobler work, and more worthy of a *christian,* than to erect and support a *reformed particular Church* in its infancy, and unite our forces with such a company of faithful people, as by a timely assistance may grow stronger and prosper; but for want of it, may be put to great hazards, if not be wholly ruined.

"'Eighthly, If any such as are known to be godly, and live in wealth and prosperity here, shall forsake all this to join with this *reformed church,* and with it run the hazard of an hard and mean condition, it will be an example of great use, both for the removing of *scandal,* and to give more *life* unto the *faith* of God's people in their prayers for the plantation, and also to encourage others to join the more willingly in it.' " [Cf. *Magnalia Christi Americana,* by Cotton Mather, London, 1702, p. 17 f.]

Further on, when he is expounding the principles of the Church of New England concerning moral questions, he inveighs violently against the habit of drinking toasts at table, which he calls a pagan and abominable habit.

With equal severity he proscribes all the ornaments that women put in their hair, and pitilessly condemns the fashion which, he says, they are adopting of uncovering the neck and arms.

Elsewhere in the book he tells us several cases of witchcraft which alarmed New England. Clearly the visible action of the devil in the affairs of this world seems to him an incontestable and proved truth.

The spirit of civil liberty and political independence characteristic of his contemporaries is to the fore in many places in the book. Their principles in matters of government are evident at every stage. Thus, for instance, one finds the inhabitants of Massachusetts in the year 1630, ten years after the foundations of Plymouth, devoting four hundred pounds sterling for the establishment of the University of Cambridge.

Passing from works concerned with the general history of New England to those relating to the various states there, the first to mention are the two octavo volumes of *The History of the Colony of Massachusetts* [Bay], by Hutchinson, *Lieutenant Governor of the Massachusetts Province.* [We have checked Tocqueville's references against its first edition, Boston, 1764.] There is a copy of this work, the second edition, printed in London in 1765, in the Bibliothèque royale.

Hutchinson's *History,* several times quoted in the chapter to which this note refers, begins with the year 1628 and finishes in 1750. A sense of truth-fulness prevails throughout the book; the style is simple and unaffected. The history is very detailed.

For Connecticut the best book to consult is Benjamin Trumbull's _A Complete History of Connecticut, Civil and Ecclesiastical, 1630–1764,_ in two octavo volumes, printed in New Haven in 1818. I do not think Trumbull's book is to be found in the Bibliothèque royale.

This history gives a clear and cool-headed account of all events occurring in Connecticut within the period stated. The author has gone to the best sources, and his accounts have the stamp of truth. All that he says about the earliest times in Connecticut is extremely remarkable. See especially what he says about the Constitution of 1639, Vol. I, chapter VI, p. 100[f.]; and also _The Penal Laws of Connecticut,_ Vol. I, chapter VII, p. 123.

Jeremy Belknap's _History of New Hampshire_ has a deservedly high reputation; it is in two octavo volumes, printed in Boston in 1792. See especially chapter III of the first volume. The author there gives extremely valuable details concerning the political and religious principles of the Puritans, the reasons for their emigration, and their laws. It includes this remarkable extract from a sermon delivered in 1663: "It concerneth New-England always to remember, that they are originally a plantation religious, not a plantation of trade. The profession of the purity of doctrine, worship, and discipline is written upon her forehead. Let merchants and such as are increasing cent per cent remember this, that worldly gain was not the end and design of the people of New England, but religion. And if any man among us make religion as twelve and the world as thirteen, such an one hath not the spirit of a true New-Englandman." [We quote from the 1784 Philadelphia edition in 2 vols.; Jeremy Belknap, _The History of New-Hampshire,_ Vol. I, p. 59.] The reader will find more general ideas and more strength of thought in Belknap than in any other American historian so far.

I do not know if this book can be found in the Bibliothèque royale.

New York and Pennsylvania are outstanding among the central states which have been in existence for some time and which deserve our attention. William Smith's _History of New York,_ printed in London in 1757, is the best history we have of that state. There is a French translation printed, also in London, in 1767 in a one-volume duodecimo edition. Smith furnishes useful details concerning the wars of the French and English in America. Of all American historians he is the most informative about the famous Iroquois confederation. [Cf. William Smith, _The History of the Province of New York from the First Discovery to the Year 1732,_ London, 1757; French translation, London, 1767.]

As for Pennsylvania, I cannot do better than refer to _The History of Pennsylvania, from the Original Institution and Settlement of That Province, Under the First Proprietor and Governor, William Penn, in 1681, Till After the Year 1742,_ by Robert Proud, in two octavo volumes, printed in Philadelphia in 1797.

This book particularly deserves the readers attention; it contains a large number of very remarkable documents concerning Penn, the doctrine of the Quakers, and the character, mores, and usages of the earliest inhabitants of Pennsylvania. As far as I know, there is not a copy in the Bibliothèque royale.

There is no need for me to add that the works of Penn himself and those of Franklin are among the most important books concerning Pennsylvania, for they are known to many readers.

I consulted most of the books here mentioned during my stay in America. The Bibliothèque royale kindly lent some of them to me. Others were lent to me by Mr. Warden, former consul general of the United States in Paris, himself the author of an excellent book about America. I do not want to finish this note without expressing my gratitude to Mr. Warden. [Cf. our note p. 18.]

G, p. 54

In Jefferson's *Autobiography* we read as follows:

"In the earlier times of the colony, when lands were to be obtained for little or nothing, some provident individuals procured large grants, and desirous of founding great families for themselves, settled them or their descendants in fee tail. The transmission of this property from generation to generation, in the same name, raised up a distinct set of families, who, being privileged by law in the perpetuation of their wealth, were thus formed into a Patrician order, distinguished by the splendor and luxury of their establishments. From this order, too, the king habitually selected his councillors of state."[1]

In the United States the principal provisions of the English law of inheritance have been universally rejected.

Mr. Kent states that the first rule which the Americans follow in questions of inheritance is this: "When a man dies intestate, his property passes to his heirs in direct line; if he has only one heir or heiress, he or she alone receives the entire succession. If there are several heirs of the same degree, they share the succession equally among themselves, with no distinction of sex." [Tocqueville summarizes here Kent's text. Cf. *Commentaries*, 1840 ed., p. 374.]

This rule was first prescribed in the state of New York by a statute of February 23, 1786 (see *Revised Statutes,* Vol. III, Appendix, p. 48); it has since been adopted in the revised statues of the same state. It is now in force throughout the whole of the United States, with the single exception of the state of Vermont, where the male heir takes a double share. (Kent's *Commentaries,* Vol. IV, p. 375.)

In Volume IV, pp. 1–22, of the same work, Mr. Kent recounts the history of American legislation concerning entails. The conclusion is that before the American Revolution the English laws of entail were the common rule in the colonies. Estates' entail was abolished in Virginia in 1776 (the motion for abolition was moved by Jefferson; see Jefferson's *Autobiography*) and in the

[1] [Cf. *The Writings of Thomas Jefferson* (Washington, 1853), Vol. I, p. 36.]

state of New York in 1786. North Carolina, Kentucky, Tennessee, Georgia, and Missouri abolished it subsequently. Entails were never the practice in Vermont, Indiana, Illinois, South Carolina, and Louisiana. The states that have felt they should preserve the English law of entail have modified it in a way that takes away its main aristocratic characteristics. "Our general principles of government," says Mr. Kent, "tend to favor free circulation of property."

A Frenchman who studies the American law of inheritance is particularly struck to find that our laws on the same subject are infinitely more democratic even than theirs.

American law divides a father's property equally, but only in the case where his will is not known: For each man in the state of New York, says the law (*Revised Statutes,* Vol. III, Appendix, p. 51 [Albany, 1829]), "shall have full and free liberty, power and authority to give, dispose, will or devise to any person or persons" (except bodies, politic and corporate "by his last will and testament . . .").

French law makes equal or nearly equal shares the rule for the testator.

Most of the American republics still allow entails and limit themselves to restricting their effects.

French law does not permit entails in any case.

If the social state of the Americans is even more democratic than ours, our laws are even more democratic than theirs. This is more easily explained than one might have thought: in France democracy is still busy demolishing; in America it reigns in tranquillity over the ruins.

H, p. 60

Summary of Electoral Qualifications in the United States.

All the states grant the enjoyment of electoral rights at the age of twenty-one. In all states it is necessary to have resided for a certain time in the district in which one votes. The time varies between three months and two years.

Property qualification: to be a voter in the state of Massachusetts you need an income of three pounds sterling or a capital of sixty.

In Rhode Island you must have landed property worth one hundred and thirty-three dollars.

In Connecticut property with a revenue of seventeen dollars. One year of militia service also gives electoral rights.

In New Jersey electors must have a fortune of fifty pounds sterling.

In South Carolina and Maryland electors must have fifty acres of land.

In Tennessee any property at all is enough.

In the states of Mississippi, Ohio, Georgia, Virginia, Pennsylvania, Delaware, and New York, if you pay any taxes you can vote. In most of those states militia service counts the same as paying taxes.

In Maine and New Hampshire it is enough not to be on the list of paupers.

Finally, in the states of Missouri, Alabama, Illinois, Louisiana, Indiana,

Kentucky, and Vermont there is no qualification based on the elector's property.

Only North Carolina, I think, imposes different qualifications for electors to the Senate from those to electors to the House of Representatives. The former must have fifty acres of land. But to elect representatives, it is enough to pay taxes.

I, p. 95

The United States has protective tariffs. The small number of customs officials and the extent of the coast make smuggling easy. However, there is much less smuggling than elsewhere, because everyone strives to suppress it.

As there is no precautionary organization in the United States, there are more fires than in Europe, but generally they are put out more speedily, because the neighbors never fail to come quickly to the danger spot.

K, p. 97

It is not right to say that centralization sprang from the French Revolution; the Revolution perfected it but did not create it. The taste for centralization and the mania for regulations date back in France to the time when lawyers came into the government; that takes us back to the time of Philip the Fair. Both these things have grown continually since then. This is what M. de Malesherbes, speaking in the name of the *Cour des Aides,* said to King Louis XVI in 1775:[1] ". . . Each body and each community of citizens retained the right to administer its own affairs, a right which we do not assert to be part of the primitive constitution of the kingdom, for it dates back further: it is a right of nature and of reason. Nevertheless, it has been taken away from your subjects, sire, and we are not afraid to say that in this respect the administration has fallen into childish excesses.

"Ever since powerful ministers have made it a political principle not to allow a national assembly to be convoked, precedent has followed precedent until it has come about that the deliberations of villagers may be declared null, if they have not been authorized by the Intendant. As a result, if that community has to make some expenditure, it has to get the approval of the Intendant's subdeputy, and consequently follow the plan he adopts, employ the workmen he favors, and pay them as he indicates; if the community has to face a lawsuit, that too must be authorized by the Intendant. The case has to be pleaded before that preliminary tribunal before it can be brought to court. And if the Intendant disagrees with the inhabitants, or if their adversary has some influence in his office, the community is deprived of the chance to defend its rights. Such, sire, are the means by which men have striven to stifle all municipal spirit in France and to extinguish, if possible,

[1] See *Mémoires pour servir a l'histoire du droit public de la France en matière d'impôts,* p. 654, printed in Brussels in 1779.

even the citizens' feelings; the whole nation has, so to say, been declared incompetent and provided with guardians."

What more could one say today, when the French Revolution has made its so-called *conquests* in the matter of centralization?

In 1789 Jefferson wrote from Paris to one of his friends: "Never was there a country where the practice of governing too much had taken root and done more mischief. . . ." (Letters to Madison, August 28, 1789.) [Cf. *The Papers of Thomas Jefferson*, ed. J. P. Boyd, Vol. 15, p. 364, Princeton, 1958.]

The truth is that in France for several centuries the central power has always done all it could to extend administrative centralization; nothing but the limits of its strength have checked this.

The central power which sprang from the French Revolution went further than its predecessors in this respect because it was stronger and knew more than any of them: Louis XIV subjected the details of municipal existence to the good pleasure of an Intendant, Napoleon to that of a minister. It is always the same principle, carried more or less far.

L, p. 101

This immutability of the French Constitution is a necessary consequence of our laws.

To speak first of the most important of all laws, that which regulates succession to the throne, what could be more immutable in principle than a political order based on the natural order of succession from father to son? In 1814 Louis XVIII had this right of political succession in perpetuity recognized in favor of his family; those who directed the results of the Revolution of 1830 followed his example; they simply established the same law of perpetual succession in favor of another family; in this they imitated Chancellor Maupeou, who in establishing the new parliament on the ruins of the old was careful to declare in the same ordinance that the new magistrates would be irremovable, as their predecessors had been.

No more than those in 1814 do the laws of 1830 indicate any method of changing the Constitution. So it is clear that ordinary means of legislation are not enough for that.

From what does the king derive his powers? From the Constitution. And the peers? From the Constitution. The deputies? From the Constitution. How, then, could king, peers, and deputies combine to change something in a law which is the sole source of their right to rule? They are nothing outside the Constitution, so on what ground could they stand in order to change the Constitution? There are just two alternatives: either their efforts are impotent against a charter which continues to be valid in spite of them, in which case they can continue to rule in its name; or they may succeed in changing the character, in which case the law from which their existence derives is gone, and they are nothing. By destroying the charter they have destroyed themselves.

This is even more apparent in the laws of 1830 than in those of 1814. In 1814 the royal power was, in a sense, placed outside and above the Constitution; but in those of 1830 it is on its own admission created by it, and is nothing without it.

Consequently one part of our Constitution is immutable, because it is tied to the destiny of one family; and the Constitution as a whole is equally immutable, because one can see no legal means of changing it.

None of this applies to England. England having no written constitution, who is to say that the constitution has been changed?

M, p. 101

The most highly reputed writers on the English constitution vie with one another to establish this omnipotence of Parliament.

Delolme says, Chapter X, p. 77: "It is a fundamental principle with the English lawyers that Parliament can do everything *except* making a woman a man, or a man a woman."[1]

Blackstone explains the matter even more categorically, if not more energetically, than Delolme; this is how he puts it:

"The power and jurisdiction of Parliament, says Sir Edward Coke (4 Inst., 36), is so transcendent and absolute, that it cannot be confined, either for causes or persons, within any bounds. And of this high court, he adds, it may be truly said, *'si antiquitatem spectes, est vetustissima; si dignitatem, est honoratissima; si jurisdictionem, est capacissima.'* It hath sovereign and uncontrollable authority in the making, confirming, enlarging, restraining, abrogating, repealing, reviving and expounding of laws concerning matters of all possible denominations, ecclesiastical or temporal, civil, military, maritime, or criminal: this being the place where that absolute despotic power, which must in all governments reside somewhere, is intrusted by the constitution of these kingdoms. All mischiefs and grievances, operations and remedies, that transcend the ordinary course of the laws, are within the reach of this extraordinary tribunal. It can regulate or new-model the succession to the Crown; as was done in the reign of Henry VIII and William III. It can alter the established religion of the land; as was done in a variety of instances in the reigns of King Henry VIII and his three children. It can *change and create afresh even the constitution of the kingdom* [the italics are Tocqueville's] and of parliaments themselves; as was done by the act of union, and the several statutes for triennial and septennial elections. It can, in short, do everything that is not naturally impossible; and therefore some have not scrupled to call its power, by a finger rather too bold, the omnipotence of Parliament.[2]

[1] [Cf. John Louis De Lolme, *The Constitution of England*, ed. by W. H. Hughes (London, 1834), p. 117. Tocqueville quotes this sentence in English.]

[2] [Cf. Blackstone, *Commentaries* (London, 1809), Vol. I, p. 160.]

N, p. 111

There is no matter in which all American constitutions are more in harmony than that of political jurisdictions.

All the constitutions deal with this matter and give the House of Representatives the exclusive right of bringing accusations, except for the Constitution of North Carolina, which gives the same right to grand juries (Article 23).

Almost all the constitutions give the Senate, or the assembly that takes its place, the exclusive right of pronouncing judgment.

The only penalties which political tribunals can pronounce are deprivation of public office and prohibition from public office in future. The Constitution of Virginia alone allows penalties of all sorts to be pronounced.

The crimes that can give rise to a political judgment are: in the Federal Constitution (Article I, section 3), in that of Indiana (Article 3, section 23 and 24) [Constitution of 1816], of New York (Article 5) [Constitution of 1812], of Delaware (Article 5): high treason, corruption, and other great crimes or offenses.

In the Constitution of Massachusetts (Chapter I, section 2), of North Carolina (Article 23) [Constitution of 1776], and of Virginia (p. 252) [?]: bad conduct and bad administration.

In the Constitution of New Hampshire (p. 105) [?]: corruption, malpractice, and bad administration. [Article 38.]

In Vermont (Chapter II, Article 54): bad administration.

In South Carolina (Article 5) [Constitution of 1790], Kentucky (Article 5), Tennessee (Article 4) [Constitution of 1796], Ohio (Article I, sections 23 and 24), Louisiana (Article 5), Mississippi (Article 5) [Constitution of 1817], Alabama (Article 6), Pennsylvania (Article 4) [Cf. Constitution of 1790]: offenses committed in office.

In the states of Illinois, Georgia, Maine, and Connecticut no crime is specified.

O, p. 170

It is true that the powers of Europe could wage great wars at sea against the Union, but it is always easier and less dangerous to face a naval war than a land one. A war at sea demands only one type of effort. A trading people ready to give its government the necessary money is always sure to have fleets. Now, it is very much easier to hide from nations' sacrifices of money than sacrifices of lives and personal endeavors. Besides, defeats at sea seldom bring the existence or independence of the nation suffering them into danger.

As for land wars, it is clear that the nations of Europe cannot wage any that would be dangerous to the American Union.

It is very difficult to transport and supply more than twenty-five thousand soldiers in America; that would represent a nation of about two million men. The greatest European nation fighting in this way against the Union would therefore be in the same situation as a nation of two million inhabitants waging war against one of twelve million. Besides this, the Americans have all their resources at hand, whereas the Europeans would be fifteen hundred leagues from theirs, and also the immensity of the territory of the United States in itself presents an insurmountable obstacle to conquest.

P, p. 186

It was in April, 1704, that the first American newspaper appeared. It was published in Boston. (See *Collection of the Historical Society of Massachusetts*, Vol. VI, p. 66.) [Cf. *Narrative of Newspapers, Collection of the Historical Society of Massachusetts*, Vol. VI, Boston, 1800, p. 64 ff.]

It would be a mistake to suppose that the periodical press has always been entirely free in America; there have been several attempts at establishing forms of anticipatory censorship and bail.

This is what appears in the legislative documents of Massachusetts under the date of January 14, 1722.

The committee appointed by the General Assembly (the legislative body of the province) to examine the affair of the newspaper called *The New England Courant* "thinks that the tendency of the said journal is to turn religion to derision and to bring scorn upon it; that the sacred writers are there treated in a profane and irreverent manner; that the conduct of the ministers of the Gospel is interpreted with malice; that his Majesty's government is insulted; and that the peace and order of his province are troubled by the said journal; in consequence, the committee proposes that James Franklin, the printer and editor, should be forbidden from printing or publishing in the future either the said journal or any other writing before he has submitted them to the secretary of the province. The justices of the peace of the county of Suffolk shall be responsible for obtaining bail from Mr. Franklin, to answer for his good behavior during the coming year."

The committee's proposal was accepted and became law, but its effect was nil. The newspaper escaped the prohibition by putting the name of *Benjamin* Franklin instead of *James* Franklin at the bottom of its columns, and public opinion found the expedient fair.

Q, p. 273

To be an elector in the counties (those representing landed property) before the Reform Bill passed in 1832, it was necessary to have a freehold or leasehold for life bringing in forty shillings net income. This law was made under Henry VI, about 1450. It has been calculated that forty shillings at the time of Henry VI might be taken as equivalent in value to thirty pounds sterling nowadays. However, this basis adopted in the fifteenth century was allowed to continue right down to 1832, which shows how far the English constitution became democratic with time, even while apparently immobile. (See Delolme; also see Blackstone, Book I, chap. 4.)

English jurors are chosen by the sheriff of the county (Delolme, Vol. I, chap. 13). [Cf. *op. cit.,* p. 748.] The sheriff is generally a man of considerable importance in the county; he has both judicial and administrative functions; he represents the king and is appointed annually by him (Blackstone, Book I, chap. 9). His position places him above suspicion of corruption by the litigants; moreover, if his impartiality is put in doubt, one can challenge the jury appointed by him as a whole, and then another officer is made responsible for choosing new jurors. (See Blackstone, Book III, chap. 23.)

To have the right to be a juror, one must have landed property worth at least ten shillings' income (Blackstone, Book III, chap. 23). It will be noticed that this condition was imposed in the reign of William and Mary, that is to say, about 1700, a time when money was infinitely more valuable than it is now. One sees that the English founded their jury system not on capacity but on landed property, as is the case with all their other political institutions.

Tenants were finally admitted to the jury, but their tenancies had to be very long and bring in an income of twenty shillings net, independent of the rent. (Blackstone, *idem.*)

R, p. 273

The federal Constitution introduced the jury into the tribunals of the Union in the same way as the states had introduced it into their own courts; moreover, the Union did not establish rules of its own for the choice of jurors. The federal courts draw upon the ordinary list of jurors that each state has prepared for its own use. Consequently it is the laws of the states that must be examined to discover the theory of the composition of the jury in America. (See Story's *Commentaries on the Constitution,* Book III, chap. 38, pp. 654–659, and Sergeant's *Constitutional Law,* p. 165. See also the federal laws of 1789, 1800, and 1802 on this matter.)

In order to understand the principles of the Americans concerning the composition of the jury properly, I have studied the laws of states widely separate from one another. Here are the general ideas resulting from this study.

In America all citizens who are electors have the right to be jurors. However, the great state of New York has established a slight difference between the two capacities, but it is in the opposite direction from our laws; that is to say, there are fewer jurors than electors in the state of New York. In general, one may say that in the United States the right of forming part of a jury, like the right of electing deputies, extends to everybody, but the exercise of this right is not indiscriminately entrusted to all.

Every year a body of municipal or district magistrates, called *selectmen* in New England, *supervisors* in the state of New York, *trustees* in Ohio, and *sheriffs of the parish* in Louisiana, choose for each district a certain number of citizens who have the right to be jurors and in whom they assume the existence of the capacity to be jurors. These magistrates, being themselves elected, arouse no distrust; their powers are very extensive and very arbitrary, like those of republican magistrates in general, and they often use them, it is said, especially in New England, to eliminate unworthy or incapable jurors.

The names of the jurors thus chosen are transmitted to the county court, and the jury for each case is drawn at random from this complete list.

Furthermore, the Americans have sought by all possible means to make jury service accessible to the people and to make it as little burdensome as possible. The jurors being very numerous, each citizen's turn to serve hardly comes more than once in three years. The sessions are held at the main town in each county, the county corresponding roughly to our *arrondissement*. Thus the tribunal comes near to the jury, instead of the jury having to go to it, as in France; finally, the jurors are indemnified, either by the state or by the parties. In general they receive a dollar a day, apart from traveling expenses. In America jury service is still regarded as a burden, but it is a burden easy to bear and submitted to without difficulty.

See Brevard's *Digest of the Public Statute Law of South Carolina,* Vol. II, p. 338; Vol. I, pp. 454 and 456; Vol. II, p. 218. [Exact title: *An Alphabetical Digest of The Public Statute Law of South Carolina,* by Joseph Brevard, 5 vols., Charleston, 1814.]

See *The General Laws of Massachusetts, Revised and Published by Authority of the Legislature,* Vol. II, pp. 331 and 187.

See *The Revised Statutes of the State of New York,* Vol. II; [Albany, 1829], pp. 720, 411, 717 and 643.

See *The Statute Laws of the State of Tennessee,* Vol. I [Knoxville, Tenn., 1831], p. 209.

See *Acts of the State of Ohio,* pp. 95 and 210.

See *Digeste général des actes de la législature de la Louisiane,* Vol. II, p. 55. [*A General Digest of the Acts of the Legislature of Louisiana,* 2 vols., New Orleans, 1828. Actually, the reference should read: Vol. II, pp. 239 ff.]

S, p. 275

When one examines the constitution of the civil jury in England closely, one readily discovers that the jurors never escape control by the judge.

It is true that the jury's verdict, in civil as in criminal cases, generally comprises, in one simple pronouncement, both fact and law. Example: a house is claimed by Peter, who says he has bought it; that is a question of fact. His adversary claims that the vendor had no right to sell; that is a question of law. The jury limits itself to saying that Peter should be put in possession of the house; it thus decides both fact and law. In introducing the jury into civil cases, the English have not kept to their view concerning the infallibility of jurors that applies in criminal cases when the verdict is favorable.

If the judge thinks that the verdict has made a wrong application of the law, he can refuse to accept it and send the jurors back to reconsider it.

If the judge lets the verdict pass without comment, the case is still not entirely closed; there are several ways open to appeal against the decision. The main one consists in asking the court to annul the verdict and summon a fresh jury. It is true to say that such a demand is rarely granted, and never more than twice; nevertheless, I have personally seen this happen. (See Blackstone, Book III, chap. XXIV; Book III, chap. XXV.)

TOCQUEVILLE'S NOTES TO VOLUME TWO[1]

T, p. 553

There are, however, some aristocracies which are eager in the pursuit of trade and successfully work in industry. The history of the world gives many striking examples of that. But in general one must say that aristocracy is not at all favorable to the progress of industry and trade. Aristocracies of wealth are the only exception to this rule.

In them there are hardly any desires that do not require money for their satisfaction. Love of wealth becomes, if one may put it so, the high road of human passions. All others end in it or cross it.

A taste for money and a thirst for consideration and power then become confused to such an extent in the same minds that it is hard to see whether men are avaricious from ambition or ambitious from avarice. That is what happens in England, where men want to get rich to win honors, and where honors are desired as a manifestation of wealth. The mind is then assailed from every direction and carried off toward trade and industry, which are the shortest roads to opulence.

This, however, strikes me as an exceptional and transitory circumstance. When wealth has become the only indication of aristocracy, it is very difficult for the rich to keep power for themselves alone and to exclude all the rest.

An aristocracy of birth and a pure democracy are the two extremes of the social and political state of nations. Aristocracy of wealth comes in between. It is like aristocracy of birth in conferring great privileges on a small number of citizens; it is like democracy in that these privileges can be acquired by all in turn. It frequently forms a natural transition between these two forms of society, and one cannot say whether it brings the reign of aristocratic institutions to an end or whether it is already ushering in the new era of democracy.

[1] [Whereas Tocqueville indicated his notes appended to Volume One (1835 edition) by alphabetical order, he adopted a different system for Volume Two (1840 edition): here the appended notes refer to pages. For the reader's convenience, we have used a unified system, that is to say, alphabetical references.]

U, p. 594

I find the following passage in my travel diary,[1] and it will serve to show what trials are faced by those American women who follow their husbands into the wilds. The description has nothing but its complete accuracy to recommend it.

". . . From time to time we came to new clearings. As all these settlements are exactly like one another, I will describe the place at which we stopped tonight. It will provide a picture of all the others.

"The bells which the pioneer is careful to hang round his beasts' necks, so as to find them again in the forest, warned us from afar that we were getting near a clearing. Soon we heard the sound of an ax cutting down the forest trees. The closer we got, the more signs of destruction indicated the presence of civilized man. Our path was covered with severed branches; and tree trunks, scorched by fire or cut about by an ax, stood in our way. We went on farther and came to a part of the wood where all the trees seemed to have been suddenly struck dead. In full summer their withered branches seemed the image of winter. Looking at them close up, we saw that a deep circle had been cut through the bark, which by preventing the circulation of the sap had soon killed the trees. We were informed that this is commonly the first thing a pioneer does. As he cannot, in the first year, cut down all the trees that adorn his new property, he sows corn under their branches, and by striking them to death, prevents them from shading his crop. Beyond this field, itself an unfinished sketch, or first step toward civilization in the wilds, we suddenly saw the owner's cabin. It is generally placed in the middle of some land more carefully cultivated than the rest, but where man is yet sustaining an unequal fight against the forest. There the trees have been cut, but not grubbed up, and their trunks still cover and block the land they used to shade. Around these dry stumps wheat and oak seedlings and plants and weeds of all kinds are scattered pell-mell and grow together on rough and still half-wild ground. It is in the midst of this vigorous and variegated growth of vegetation that the planter's dwelling, or as it is called in this country, his log house, stands. Just like the field around it, this rustic dwelling shows every sign of recent and hasty work. It is seldom more than thirty feet long and fifteen high; the walls as well as the roof are fashioned from rough tree trunks, between which moss and earth have been rammed to keep out the cold and rain from the inside of the house.

"As the night was coming on, we decided to go and ask the owner of the log house to put us up.

"At the sound of our steps the children playing among the scattered branches got up and ran to the house, as if frightened at the sight of a man, while two large, half-wild dogs, with ears prickled up and outstretched muzzles, came growling out of the hut to cover the retreat of their young masters.

[1] [This travel diary has now been published. Cf. Tocqueville, *Journey to America*, ed. by J. P. Mayer, Yale paperback series, New Haven, 1962.]

Then the pioneer himself appeared at the door of his dwelling; he looked at us with a rapid, inquisitive glance, made a sign to the dogs to go indoors, and set them the example himself, without showing that our arrival aroused either his curiosity or apprehension.

"We went into the log house; the inside was quite unlike that of the cottages of European peasants; there was more that was superfluous and fewer necessities; a single window with a muslin curtain; on the hearth of beaten earth a great fire which illuminated the whole interior; above the hearth a good rifle, a deerskin, and plumes of eagles' feathers; to the right of the chimney a map of the United States, raised and fluttering in the draft from the crannies in the wall; near it, on a shelf formed from a roughly hewn plank, a few books; a Bible, the first six cantos of Milton, and two plays of Shakespeare; there were trunks instead of cupboards along the wall; in the center of the room, a rough table with legs of green wood with the bark still on them, looking as if they grew out of the ground on which they stood; on the table was a teapot of English china, some silver spoons, a few cracked teacups, and newspapers.

"The master of this dwelling had the angular features and lank limbs characteristic of the inhabitants of New England. He was clearly not born in the solitude in which we found him. His physical constitution by itself showed that his earlier years were spent in a society that used its brains and that he belonged to that restless, calculating, and adventurous race of men who do with the utmost coolness things which can only be accounted for by the ardor of passion, and who endure for a time the life of a savage in order to conquer and civilize the backwoods.

"When the pioneer saw that we were crossing his threshold, he came to meet us and shake hands, as is their custom; but his face was quite unmoved. He opened the conversation by asking us what was going on in the world, and when his curiosity was satisfied, he held his peace, as if he was tired of the importunities and noise of the world. When we questioned him in our turn, he gave us all the information we asked and then turned, with no eagerness, but methodically, to see to our requirements. Why was it that, while he was thus kindly bent on aiding us, in spite of ourselves we felt our sense of gratitude frozen? It was because he himself, in showing his hospitality, seemed to be submitting to a tiresome necessity of his lot and saw in it a duty imposed by his position, and not a pleasure.

"A woman was sitting on the other side of the hearth, rocking a small child on her knees. She nodded to us without disturbing herself. Like the pioneer, this woman was in the prime of life; her appearance seemed superior to her condition, and her apparel even betrayed a lingering taste for dress; but her delicate limbs were wasted, her features worn, and her eyes gentle and serious; her whole physiognomy bore marks of religious resignation, a deep peace free from passions, and some sort of natural, quiet determination which would face all the ills of life without fear and without defiance.

"Her children cluster around her, full of health, high spirits, and energy; they are true children of the wilds; their mother looks at them from time to time with mingled melancholy and joy; seeing their strength and her weariness, one might think that the life she has given them exhausted her own, and yet she does not regret what they have cost her.

"The dwelling in which these immigrants live had no internal division and no loft; its single room shelters the whole family in the evening. It is a little world of its own, an ark of civilization lost in a sea of leaves. A hundred paces away the everlasting forest spreads its shade, and solitude begins again."

V, p. 595

It is not equality of conditions that makes men immoral and irreligious. But when men are immoral, irreligious, and also equal, the effects thereof are more easily manifest, for men have little influence on one another's behavior, and there is no class which can take over the duty of keeping society in order. Equality never creates moral profligacy, but it sometimes allows it to appear.

W, p. 612

Disregarding those who do not think at all and those who dare not say what they think, one still finds that the vast majority of Americans seem satisfied with the political institutions controlling their lives, and in fact, I think they are satisfied. I look on this state of public opinion as an indication, but not a proof, of the absolute excellence of American laws. National pride, legislation which satisfies certain ruling passions, chance circumstances, unnoticed vices, and above all, the interests of the majority, which shut its opponents' mouths, may over a long period delude a whole people as well as an individual.

Consider England in the eighteenth century. No nation has ever been freer with the incense; no people has ever been so perfectly pleased with itself; everything then was right in its constitution, and everything, even down to the most manifest defects, was above reproach. Nowadays a great number of Englishmen seem to have nothing else to do but point out a thousand defects in this constitution. Were the English of the last century or those of today right?

The same thing happened in France. It is certain that under Louis XIV the great mass of the nation were passionate supporters of the form of government then ruling their society. Those who imagine that the character of Frenchmen at that time was degraded are greatly mistaken. In some respects there may have been servitude in France then, but the spirit of the nation was certainly not servile. With a genuine enthusiasm, the writers of that age exalted the power of the king above all other authority, and even the humblest peasant in his hovel was proud of the glory of his ruler and would gladly die crying, "Long live the king." Such ways now excite our loathing. Who was right, the Frenchmen of the age of Louis XIV or their descendants of today?

Our judgment, then, of the laws of a people must not be based exclusively upon their attitude to them, for that is something which changes from century to century, but upon some higher principles and more general experience.

A people's love of its laws proves but one thing, that one should not be in haste to change them.

X, p. 656

In the chapter to which this note refers I have indicated one danger; I will now point to another, more rare indeed, but more formidable, if it should ever raise its head.

If the love of physical pleasures and the taste for well-being which are naturally prompted by equality should get such a hold on the spirit of a democratic people that they should come to absorb it altogether, national mores would become so antipathetic to the military spirit that even the army, in spite of the professional interest leading soldiers to desire war, would come to love peace. Living in such a soft society, soldiers would come to think that slow but convenient and effortless promotion in peacetime was better than a more rapid rise in rank paid for by all the toils and privations of the battlefield. In such a mood, the army would take up arms without eagerness and use them without energy. It would be more a question of allowing themselves to be led to face the enemy than of marching of their own will.

One should not suppose that such a pacific disposition in the army would remove the danger of revolution, for revolutions, especially military ones, which generally take place very quickly, often entail great dangers, but not protracted toil. They gratify ambition more cheaply than does war; only life is risked, and that is something to which the people of democracies attach less importance than to their comforts.

Nothing is more dangerous to the freedom and tranquillity of a people than an army afraid of war, for, no longer looking to the battlefield for its hopes of greatness and power, it must seek them elsewhere. It might therefore come about that the men forming a democratic army could lose a citizen's interests without acquiring the virtues of a soldier, and that an army, no longer warlike, might yet be turbulent.

I must repeat here something that I have said before. The remedy against such dangers does not lie in the army, but in the country. A democratic people which has kept its manly mores will always find courageous soldiers when it needs them.

Y, p. 670

Men think that the greatness of the idea of unity lies in means. God sees it in the end. It is for that reason that the idea of greatness leads to a thousand mean actions. To force all men to march in step toward the same goal—that is a human idea. To encourage endless variety of actions but to bring them about so that in a thousand different ways all tend toward the fulfillment of one great design—that is a God-given idea.

The human idea of unity is almost always sterile, but that of God is immensely fruitful. Men think they prove their greatness by simplifying the means. God's object is simple but His means infinitely various.

Z, p. 674

Not only is a democratic people led by its own tastes to centralize government, but the passions of all its rulers constantly urge it in the same direction.

It may easily be foreseen that almost all the able and ambitious men in a democratic country will labor constantly to increase the scope of social power, for they all hope sooner or later to control it themselves. It is a waste of time to demonstrate to such men that extreme centralization may be harmful to the state, for they are centralizing for their own interests.

The only public men in democracies who favor decentralization are, almost invariably, either very disinterested or extremely mediocre; the former are scarce and the latter powerless.

AA, p. 691

I have often wondered what would happen if, as a result of the laxity of democratic mores combined with the restless spirit of the army, a military government were ever to be established in any of the nations of our day.

I think that that government would not differ much from the sketch drawn in the chapter to which this note refers and that it would display the fierce characteristics of a military oligarchy.

I am convinced that in such a case there would be a sort of fusion between the ways of clerks and soldiers. The administration would adopt something of the spirit of an army, and the army would take over some of the ways of civil administration. The resulting government would be methodical, well defined, precise, and absolute; the people would become a reflection of the army, and societies would be regimented like barracks.

BB, p. 695

One cannot state in any absolute or general way whether the greatest danger at the present time is license or tyranny, anarchy or despotism. Both are equally to be feared, and both could spring from one and the same cause, that is, the *general apathy*, the fruit of individualism. It is because of this apathy that any day the executive power, having mustered a few troops, can commit acts of oppression, and the next day any party that can summon thirty men to the fray can also commit acts of oppression. Neither the one nor the other can establish anything that will last, those same causes which make success easy making its duration impossible. They rise because nothing resists them and they fall because nothing supports them.

We should therefore direct our efforts, not against anarchy or despotism, but against the apathy which could engender one or the other almost indifferently.

Appendix II

REPORT GIVEN BEFORE
THE ACADEMY OF MORAL AND POLITICAL SCIENCES
ON JANUARY 15, 1848,
ON THE SUBJECT OF M. CHERBULIEZ' BOOK ENTITLED
ON DEMOCRACY IN SWITZERLAND[1]

Gentlemen,

M. Cherbuliez, professor of public law at the Academy of Geneva, has published a book about the institutions and political mores of his country, entitled *On Democracy in Switzerland,* and he has presented a copy of this book to the Academy of Moral Sciences.

I feel, gentlemen, that the importance of the subject dealt with by the author makes a detailed examination of his work worthwhile. So, thinking that such an examination might prove of some use, I have undertaken it.

I mean completely to disregard the preoccupations of the moment, as is appropriate in this place, and to pass over in silence the events taking place, which do not concern us. I do not want to study the behavior of political society in Switzerland, but rather to study that society itself, the laws which shape it, and their origin, tendencies, and character. I hope that within these set limits my sketch will have some interest. What is happening in Switzerland is no isolated event, but a particular instance of a general movement which is driving to destruction all the ancient structure of European institutions. The stage may be small, but there is greatness in the play, and it has, moreover, some peculiarly original features. Nowhere else has the democratic revolution which is shaking the world taken place in such strange and complicated circumstances. We have one people, composed of several races, speaking several languages, with several religious beliefs, various dissident sects, two churches both equally established and privileged, all political

[1] [The French title of the work on which Tocqueville reports is: *De La Démocratie en Suisse,* 2 vols., Paris, 1843.]

questions quickly turning into religious ones, and all religious questions ending up as political ones, and finally two societies, one very old and the other very young, joined in marriage in spite of the difference of age. That is a fair sketch of Switzerland. To paint it properly the author should, in my view, have chosen a higher vantage point. In his preface M. Cherbuliez says, and I believe him to be sincere in this, that he has tried to be impartial. He is even afraid that the completely impartial quality of his work may make it a little dull. That fear is certainly unjustified. The author does indeed want to be impartial, but he does not succeed in that. In his book there is knowledge, perspicacity, real talent, and a manifest good faith which breaks through even where he feels most passionately. But impartiality is just what is lacking. The author is very intelligent but not broadminded.

To what forms of political society does the author incline? At first that seems hard to say. Although he to some extent approves the conduct of the most zealous Catholics, he is so decidedly opposed to Catholicism that he almost favors legislative impediments to prevent the spread of Catholicism to places where it is not predominant. On the other hand, he is very much against the dissident Protestant sects. He is opposed to both government by the people and government by the nobility. In religion, a Protestant church controlled by the state; in politics, a state ruled by a bourgeois aristocracy—that would seem to be the author's ideal. It is Geneva before the latest revolution.

But though it is not always easy to see what he likes, it is clear what he detests. What he detests is democracy. The democratic revolution which he describes was a blow to his opinions, to his friendships, perhaps to his interests, and he always speaks of it with hostility. He does not only attack democracy because of one or another of its results, but for its basic principles; he does not see its good qualities, and tracks down its defects. Of the ills that may result therefrom, he does not distinguish between what is fundamental and permanent and what is accidental and passing, what parts thereof must be tolerated as inevitable and what one should seek to remedy. But perhaps it is impossible for such a man as M. Cherbuliez, who has been so much involved in the disturbances of his country, to envisage the subject in such a way. Nevertheless, one regrets that. As we continue this analysis it will become clear that Swiss democracy badly needs someone to point out the imperfections of its laws. But to do that effectively, the first requirement was not to hate it.

M. Cherbuliez has called his book *On Democracy in Switzerland,* which might give the impression that the author thinks Switzerland can provide the basis for a book treating of the theory of democracy and that that country offers an opportunity to judge democratic institutions in themselves. That is the origin, in my view, of almost all the mistakes in the book. The title should have been *On the Democratic Revolution in Switzerland.* Switzerland has in fact for fifteen years been a country in a state of revolution. Democracy there is less a regular form of government than a weapon habitually used to destroy, and sometimes to defend, the old society. One can well study there the particular phenomena which go with a state of revolution, but one cannot take it as the basis for a description of democracy in its permanent and peaceful established state. Anyone who does not keep this point of departure constantly in mind will hardly understand the kaleidoscope of Swiss institutions. For my part, I should find it impossibly difficult to explain what now exists without saying how I understand what went before.

One has generally a false impression of the state of Switzerland at the time when the French Revolution broke out. As the Swiss had long been living in a republic, one is easily led to imagine that they came much closer than the other European peoples to the institutions which embody and the spirit which animates modern freedom. But the opposite is the truth.

Although Swiss independence was born amid a rebellion against the aristocracy, most of the governments then founded soon borrowed from the aristocracy most of their habits and laws, and even their opinions and inclinations. They never conceived of liberty as anything but a privilege, and the idea of a general pre-existent right of all men to be free was something as foreign to their understanding as it can ever have been to the princes of the house of Austria, whom they had vanquished. Hence all powers were soon brought into and kept in the hands of small aristocracies, which were either closed or self-recruiting. In the north these aristocracies took on an industrial character, and in the south they had a military constitution. But in both cases they were equally restricted and exclusive. In most of the cantons three quarters of the population were excluded from any participation, whether direct or even indirect, in the administration of the country. Moreover, each canton had subject populations.

These little societies, which had been established in the midst of such great upheavals, soon became so stable that no further movement was felt within them. The aristocracy, neither pressed by the people nor guided by a king, kept the social body immobile and dressed in the old garments of the Middle Ages.

The passage of time had long since allowed the new spirit to penetrate even the most monarchical societies of Europe, while Switzerland still remained closed to it.

The principle of the division of powers was approved by all writers, but in Switzerland it did not apply. Freedom of the press, which, in fact at least, existed in several absolute monarchies on the Continent, existed neither in fact nor in law in Switzerland; the right of political association was neither exercised nor recognized; freedom of speech was restricted within very narrow limits. Equal taxation, to which all enlightened governments were tending, was there as unknown as equality before the law. Industry there was hampered in a thousand ways, and there was no legal guarantee of individual liberty. Freedom of religion, which was beginning to penetrate even the most orthodox states, had still made no appearance in Switzerland. Dissident sects were entirely prohibited in several cantons, and discouraged in all. Differences in belief there almost everywhere resulted in political disabilities.

Switzerland was still in this condition in 1798, when the French Revolution broke into its territory by force of arms. For the moment it overthrew the

ancient institutions, but it put nothing solid or stable in their place. Napoleon, who some years later saved Switzerland from anarchy by the Act of
Mediation, granted equality but not liberty, the political laws that he imposed were so framed that political life was paralyzed. Power exercised in
the name of the people, but put well out of its reach, was all placed in
the hands of the executive authorities.

When, a few years afterward, the Act of Mediation shared its author's
fall, the Swiss did not gain liberty by this change, but only lost equality.
On all sides the old aristocracies again took up the reins of government
and again put into operation the exclusive and outdated principles that had
prevailed before the revolution. Matters then returned, as M. Cherbuliez
correctly states, to the condition they were in before 1798. The allied kings
are wrongly accused of having imposed the restoration by force on Switzerland. It was done in agreement with them, but not by them. The truth is
that the Swiss, in common with other peoples on the Continent, were
carried away by that passing but universal reaction which suddenly revived
the old society throughout Europe. Since, in their case, the restoration was
not brought about by the princes whose interests after all are different from
those of the former privileged classes, but by that class itself, it was more
complete, blind, and obstinate than in the rest of Europe. It did not prove
itself tyrannical, but very exclusive. Legislative power was entirely subordinated to the executive, and the latter was exclusively in the hands of
the aristocracy of birth; the middle class was excluded from the administration; the whole of the people were deprived of political life; such was the
state of almost every part of Switzerland down to 1830.

It was then that the age of democracy opened for her!

The object of this short exposition is to make two things clear:

First: that Switzerland is one of the countries of Europe in which the
revolution went least deep, and the following restoration was most complete.
So that, since institutions foreign or hostile to the new spirit had there
preserved or regained much of their sway, the impulse toward revolution
was bound to be more powerful there.

Second: that in the greater part of Switzerland up to our day the people
had never taken the smallest part in the government, so that judicial provisions guaranteeing civil liberty, freedom of association, freedom of speech,
freedom of the press, and religious liberty had always been as much, I
might almost say more, unknown to the great majority of the citizens of
these republics than they can ever have been, at the same time, to the subjects
of most of the monarchies.

That is something of which M. Cherbuliez often loses sight, but which we
should always bear in mind in the careful examination which we are going
to make of the institutions with which Switzerland has provided herself.

Everyone knows that in Switzerland sovereignty is divided into two parts;
there is the federal power on one side and the power of the cantonal
governments on the other.

M. Cherbuliez begins by speaking of what takes place in the cantons, and he is right to do so, for in them the real government of society resides. I will follow his example and discuss the constitutions of the cantons.

All the constitutions of the cantons are now democratic, but democracy does not show the same aspect in all.

In most of the cantons the people have handed over the exercise of their powers to assemblies which represent them, but in a few they kept it for themselves. The people come together as a body and govern. M. Cherbuliez calls the former *representative democracies* and the latter *pure democracies*.

I will ask the academy's permission not to follow him in his very interesting examination of the pure democracies. I have several reasons for that. Although the cantons living under a pure democracy played a great role in history and may still have a considerable part to play in politics, to study them satisfies a taste for oddity rather than any useful end.

Pure democracy is something almost unique in the modern world, and even in Switzerland very exceptional, for only one thirteenth part of the population is governed in that way. It is, moreover, a passing phase. It is not sufficiently realized that, even in those Swiss cantons where the people have most preserved the exercise of their power, there does exist a representative body entrusted with some of the cares of government. Now, it is easy to see, when studying recent Swiss history, that gradually those matters with which the people concern themselves are becoming fewer, whereas those with which their representatives deal are daily becoming both more numerous and more various. Thus the principle of pure democracy is losing ground gained by the opposing principle. The former is insensibly becoming the exception and the latter the rule.

Moreover, the pure democracies of Switzerland belong to another age; they can teach us nothing useful for the present or the future. Although we are obliged to use, in describing them, a name devised by modern learning, they live only in the past. Each century has its dominating spirit which nothing can resist. If any principles foreign or contrary to it are introduced within its domain, it is not slow to penetrate into them, and when it cannot abolish them, it adapts or assimilates them. In the end the Middle Ages came to give an aristocratic shape even to democratic freedom. In the midst of the most republican laws, side by side even with universal suffrage, the Middle Ages introduced religious beliefs, opinions, feelings, habits, associations, and families who, removed from the people, retained the real power. One can only regard the little governments of the Swiss cantons as the last venerable ruins of a vanished world.

But the representative democracies of Switzerland are the offspring of the modern spirit. They are founded on the ruins of a former aristocratic society; all are based on the sole principle of the sovereignty of the people; all have applied this principle in almost the same way in their laws.

As we shall see, these laws are very imperfect, and they would by themselves serve to show, without the testimony of history, that in Switzerland democracy and even liberty are new forces lacking in experience.

We must first note that, even in the representative democracies of Switzerland, the people have retained in their own hands the direct exercise of part of their power. In some cantons, when the chief laws have been approved by the legislature, they must still be submitted to the veto of the people. So that, as far as those particular cases are concerned, representative democracy has been turned back into pure democracy.

In almost all, the people must be consulted, usually at frequent intervals, as to whether they want to modify or to maintain the Constitution. That, at intervals, undermines all the laws at once.

All the legislative powers which the people have not retained in their own hands have been confided to a single assembly, which conducts its business in their sight and in their name. In no canton is the legislature divided into two branches, but is everywhere composed of one body; not only are its impulses not delayed by the need to come to an understanding with another assembly, but its desires do not even have to face the obstacle of prolonged deliberation. The discussion of general laws is subject to certain delaying formalities, but the most important resolutions can be proposed, discussed, and approved in a minute under the name of decrees. These decrees turn secondary laws into something as unforeseen, hasty, and irresistible as the passions of a crowd.

Outside the legislature there is nothing able to resist. The separation, and above all the relative independence, of the legislative, administrative, and judicial powers does not, in fact, exist.

In no canton are the holders of executive power directly elected by the people; it is the legislature which chooses them. Hence the executive power is endowed with no power properly its own. It is only the creation of another power, whose servile agent it is bound to be. That is one cause of weakness, but there are several others. Nowhere is executive power entrusted to a single man. It is confided to a small assembly, where responsibility is divided and action debilitated. Moreover, several rights essential to executive power are refused to it. It has either no veto or only an ineffectual one over the laws. It is deprived of any prerogative of mercy; it neither appoints nor dismisses its agents. One might even say that it has no agents, for it is usually obliged to make use of the municipal magistrates only.

But the chief defect in the laws of Swiss democracy lies in the bad Constitution and bad composition of the judicial power. M. Cherbuliez notices it but does not, in my view, stress it enough. He does not seem throughly to understand that in democracies it is above all the judicial power which must be both the protector from, and the protector of, the people.

The idea of judicial independence is a modern one. The Middle Ages missed conceiving it, or at least conceived it in only a very muddled way. One may say that in all European nations executive and judicial powers were intermingled in the beginning. Even in France, where by exceptional good fortune the judiciary developed a very vigorous individual existence, one can yet say that the division between the two powers remained far from complete. It is true that it was not the administration which kept justice in its hands, but the judiciary which took control of part of the administration. In Switzerland, on the other hand, perhaps more than in any other European country, justice was most completely confounded with political power and became most completely one of its attributes. One can say that our idea of justice as an impartial and free power which interposes between all interests and all other powers to call them all back to respect for the law is an idea which in the past has never entered the heads of the Swiss and which even today is very incompletely understood there.

The new constitutions have certainly given the tribunals more of a separate position than that which they had among the former powers, but it is not a more independent position. The inferior tribunals are elected by the people and subject to re-election; the supreme tribunal of each canton is chosen, not by the executive power, but by the legislature, and its members have no guarantee against the daily caprices of the majority.

Not only do the people, or the assembly which represents them, choose the judges, but they impose no restraints on their choice. In general, no professional qualifications are demanded. Moreover, the judge, whose duty is simply to enforce the law, has not the right to question whether the law conforms to the Constitution. In very truth it is the majority itself which judges, using the magistrates as its agents.

Besides this, even if the law had given the judiciary in Switzerland the independence and rights which are necessary for it, the judges would have found it difficult to play their part, for the power of justice is based on tradition and opinion, which need the support of judicial conceptions and mores.

It would be easy to stress the defects of the institutions I have just been describing and to show that they tend to make the people's government irregular in its action, hasty in its decisions, and tyrannical in its acts. But that would be too much of a digression. I will limit myself to comparing these laws to those of a more ancient, tranquil, and prosperous democratic society. M. Cherbuliez thinks that the imperfect institutions of the Swiss cantons are the only ones which democracy can prompt or even tolerate. My comparison will prove the contrary and show how, starting from the principle of the sovereignty of the people, elsewhere, with more experience, skill, and wisdom, it has been possible to derive different results. I take as example the state of New York, which contains as many inhabitants as the whole of Switzerland.

In the state of New York, as in the Swiss cantons, sovereignty of the people is the accepted principle of government, and it is universal suffrage which sets it in motion. But the people exercise their rights of sovereignty for one day only, when they choose their representatives. In general, in no case do the people retain in their own hands any part of the legislative, executive, or judicial power. They choose those who are to govern in their name, and until the next election, they abdicate.

Although the laws are changeable, their foundation is stable. The Swiss system, by which the Constitution is known to be subject to successive periodic revisions, so that each revision, or the mere anticipation thereof, keeps the organization of society in suspense, is a system which has never come into a New Yorker's head. In New York when some new need is felt, the legislature decides that a modification of the constitution has become necessary, and the ensuing legislature puts it into operation.

No more than in Switzerland can the legislature escape the pressure of public opinion, but it is organized in a way to resist its caprices. No proposal can become law until it has been considered by two assemblies. These two branches of the legislature are elected in the same way and composed of the same elements, so both originate in the people, but they do not represent it in exactly the same way: the function of the one is especially to reflect the impressions of the moment, whereas the other is concerned with habitual instincts and permanent inclinations.

In New York the division of powers exists not only in appearance, but in fact.

Executive power is exercised not by a body but by one man with full responsibility, who uses all his rights and prerogatives firmly and decisively. He is elected by the people but is not, as in Switzerland, the creature or agent of the legislature; he acts as its equal, being, like the legislature, the representative of the sovereign people, but in a different sphere. Both derive their power from the same source. He is not in name only the executive power, but actually exercises the natural and legitimate power thereof. He commands the armed forces and appoints their chief officers; he selects several of the most important officials in the state; he can grant pardons; his veto over the wishes of the legislature, though not absolute, is nonetheless effective. The governor of the state of New York is doubtless much less powerful than a European constitutional king, but he is certainly much stronger than a little Swiss council.

But the most striking difference is in the organization of judicial power.

The judge, though he emanates from the people and depends thereon, is a power to which the people themselves submit. This exceptional status of judicial power derives from its origin, permanence, professional competence, and above all, public opinion and mores.

The judges of the higher courts are not chosen, as in Switzerland, by the legislature, which is a collective power, often subject to passions, sometimes blind, and always irresponsible, but by the governor of the state. Once appointed, a judge is regarded as irremovable. No suit falls outside his jurisdiction, and no punishment can be imposed by anyone else. He not only interprets the law, but may be said to judge it; when the legislature, with its hasty moves of political parties, transgresses the spirit or letter of the Constitution, the courts bring it back to legality by refusing to enforce its decisions; in this way, though the judges cannot oblige the people to maintain the Constitution, they can at least make them respect it in its existing form. The judges do not direct the people, but do restrain and keep them within limits. The power of the judges, which hardly exists in Switzerland, is the real moderator of American democracy.

Nowadays, when one comes to examine that Constitution in its smallest details, one finds no trace of aristocracy. There is nothing which resembles a class, no privileges, the same rights everywhere, all powers deriving from the people and returning thereto, the same spirit animating all institutions, with no contradictory tendencies; the principle of democracy has penetrated everywhere and dominates everything. And yet these governments, so completely democratic, have a far greater stability, a much more peaceable aspect, and much more regular ways of conducting business than the democratic governments of Switzerland. One can safely say that this is partly due to different laws.

The laws of New York State, which I have just described, are framed in a way to combat the natural defects of democracy. But the Swiss institutions, which I have depicted, would seem to have been devised to make them worse. In New York they hold the people back, but in Switzerland they urge them on. The Americans fear that the people's power may turn into tyranny, but in Switzerland the only thought would seem to be how to make it irresistible.

I do not exaggerate the influence of legal mechanisms on the fate of peoples. I know that the great events in this world are chiefly due to deeper and more general causes. But one must appreciate that institutions have a certain virtue of their own and that they do contribute to the prosperity or wretchedness of societies.

If, instead of absolutely dismissing almost all his country's laws, M. Cherbuliez had pointed out their weak points and shown how they could be improved in detail without alteration of principle, he would have written a book of more lasting value and one more useful to his contemporaries.

Having shown how democracy works in the cantons, the author traces its influence over the Confederation as a whole.

Before following M. Cherbuliez in this, we must do something which he has neglected, that is to say, make it quite clear what the federal government is, how it is organized in theory and in practice, and how it works.

It is reasonable first to ask whether the lawgivers of the Swiss Confederation wished to establish a federal constitution or merely a league, in other words, whether they intended to sacrifice part of the sovereignty of the cantons in order to place it elsewhere or whether they did not mean to take any of it away. Considering that the cantons renounced several rights inherent in sovereignty and handed them over in permanent fashion to the federal government, and considering that, in questions entrusted to the federal government, the majority was to make the law, one cannot doubt but that the lawgivers of the Swiss Confederation intended to establish a true federal constitution and not simply a league. But one must admit that they set about this task very clumsily.

The Swiss federal Constitution strikes me as the most imperfect of all the constitutions of this kind yet seen in the world. Reading it, one might suppose oneself back in the Middle Ages, and it seems almost incredible that such a confused and incomplete work is the product of the learning and experience of our own century.[2]

---

[2] One must not forget that all this was written in 1847, that is to say, before the after-effects of the Revolution of 1848 had led to the reform of the former federal pact.

It is often and rightly said that the pact limited the powers of the Confederation unreasonably and that it left outside the sphere of the government representing it some essentially national questions which should, in the nature of things, have come within the competence of the Diet, such, for example, as the postal service, control of weights and measures, and coinage. . . . And the weakness of the federal power is thought to be due to the few matters entrusted to it.

It is perfectly true that the pact withheld from the government of the Confederation several rights which are naturally, even necessarily, its province. But that is not the true cause of its weakness, for the powers that it was given by the pact would have been enough if it could have used them to enable it soon to gain all those it lacked.

The Diet can raise troops, impose taxes, make war and conclude peace, negotiate commercial treaties, and appoint ambassadors. The constitutions of the cantons and the basic principles of equality before the law were placed under its protection, and that would, at need, have justified interference in all local affairs. Tolls and rights over the roads, etc., are controlled by the Diet, which gives it authority to direct and manage great public works. Finally, the Diet, according to Article IV of the pact, "takes all measures necessary for the internal and external security of Switzerland," and that gives it license to do everything.

The strongest federal governments have not had greater prerogatives, and far from thinking that the competence of the central power in Switzerland is too limited, I am led to feel that its limits have not been sufficiently carefully defined.

Whence, then, comes it about that the government of the federation, having such fine privileges, has in general so little power? The reason is simple: it has not been given the means of doing those things which it is allowed to desire. Never has a government been better kept in apathy and condemned to impotence by the imperfection of its organs.

It is of the essence of federal governments to act, not in the name of the people, but in that of the states composing the Confederation. Were things otherwise, the Constitution would no longer be a federal one.

Among other necessary and inevitable consequences of this, it results that federal governments are usually less bold in their decisions and slower in their movements than others.

Most of the legislators of confederations have striven, by means of more or less ingenious devices, which I need not go into here, partly to correct this natural defect of the federal system. But the Swiss have made this defect much more noticeable than it is elsewhere, owing to the particular forms which they have adopted. In their case, not only do members of the Diet act only in the names of the various cantons which they represent, but they generally cannot take any decision which has not been previously considered and approved by them. Hardly anything is left to their free initiative; each one of them thinks that he is subject to a binding mandate, imposed beforehand. As a result, the Diet is no more than a deliberating assembly where, to tell the truth, there is nothing to deliberate about and where one speaks not before those who must make the decision but before those who only have the right to carry it out. The Diet is a government which counts for nothing on its own but which is limited to giving effect to what has been decided by twenty-two other governments separately, a government which, whatever may be happening, can decide nothing and exercise no foresight or provision. One could not imagine any arrangement better suited to increase the natural inertia of the federal government and to turn this weakness into a sort of senile debility.

There are also many other reasons which, apart from the vices inherent in all federal constitutions, explain the habitual impotence of the government of the Swiss Confederation.

Not only has the Confederation got a weak government, but one might say that it has no government of its very own. Its Constitution in this respect is unique in the world. The Confederation puts at its head leaders who do not represent it. The directorate which forms the executive power in Switzerland is chosen not by the Diet, and still less by the people of Switzerland; it is a chance government which the Confederation borrows every two years from Berne, Zurich, or Lucerne. This authority, elected by the inhabitants of a canton to manage a canton's affairs, thus incidentally becomes the head and arm of the whole country. That may certainly count as one of the great political curiosities in the record of human laws. The effects of such a state of things are always deplorable and often very odd. Nothing could be more ridiculous than that which happened, for instance, in 1839. In that year the Diet was held at Zurich, and the Confederation had the directorate of the state of Zurich as its government. A popular insurrection overthrew the established authorities. The Diet immediately found that it had no president, and the life of the federation remained in suspense until the canton was ready to make itself new laws and appoint new leaders. The people of Zurich, by changing their local administration, had unintentionally decapitated Switzerland.

Even if the Confederation had an executive power of its own, the government would still be unable to make itself obeyed if it could not act directly and immediately on the citizens. That in itself is a greater cause of weakness than all the others put together; but to make that properly understood, one must do more than just mention it.

A federal government may have a pretty limited field of action and yet be strong if in its narrow sphere it can act without intermediary, as ordinary governments do in the unlimited scope of their activities; if it has officials who are in direct contact with each citizen, and tribunals which force each citizen to obey its laws, it can easily exact obedience, because it has nothing but individual resistance to face, and all obstacles put in its way can be dealt with by process of law.

On the other hand, a federal government may have a vast sphere of activity and yet have very weak and precarious authority if, instead of direct contact with the individual citizen, it has to turn to the governments of the cantons, for if the latter resist, the federal government at once finds itself faced not with a subject but with a rival who cannot be brought to reason except by war.

The power, therefore, of a federal government depends much less on the extent of the rights conferred on it than on the greater or lesser opportunity it is given to exercise them itself; it is always strong when it can give the citizens orders; it is always weak when it is reduced to giving its orders to the local governments.

The history of confederations gives examples of these two systems. But I know of no confederation in which the central government is as completely deprived of all action on the citizens as is that of Switzerland. There is, one may say, no single right of the federal government which it is able to exercise on its own account. There are no officials dependent on it alone and no law courts which represent its sovereignty exclusively. It would seem to be a being to whom life has been given but who has been deprived of all the organs of life.

Such is the federal Constitution as established by the pact. Now let us briefly follow the author of this book in seeing what influence democracy has on it.

One cannot deny that the democratic revolutions which have changed almost all the constitutions of the cantons in turn during the last fifteen years have had a great influence on the federal government; but this influence has been exercised in two very contrary ways. It is very necessary to take both sides of this phenomenon into account.

The democratic revolutions in the cantons have resulted in greater local activity with more power. The new governments created by the revolutions, relying on the people and urged on by them, have felt themselves both actually stronger and with a higher idea of their power than the governments which they supplanted. Since no similar renewal took place at the same time in the federal government, the natural, and in fact the actual, result was that the latter became weaker in comparison with the former than had previously been the case. Cantonal pride, the instinct of local independence, impatience of all control in the internal affairs of each canton, and jealousy of any supreme central authority—all these are feelings which have increased with the coming of democracy; from that point of view one can say that it has weakened the already feeble government of the Confederation and made the daily performance of its habitual work harder and more difficult.

But in other respects it has given it an energy, one might almost say an existence, which it never had before.

The establishment of democratic institutions in Switzerland has introduced two entirely new things.

Up to now each canton had its separate interests and separate spirit. The coming of democracy has divided all the Swiss, to whatever cantons they belong, into two parties, the one supporting democratic principles and the other opposed to them. It has created common interests and common passions which cannot be satisfied without some general common power operating at the same time continuously over the whole country. Thus for the first time the federal government has come to have a powerful force, something which it had always lacked before; it has been able to rely on the support of a party; that is a dangerous force, but one indispensable in free countries where the government can hardly do anything without it.

At the same time that democracy divided Switzerland into two parties, it made Switzerland join one of the two parties that are dividing the world between them; it has brought the need for a foreign policy; it has provided both natural friends and inevitable hostility; to cultivate and keep her friends and to watch and guard against her enemies, Switzerland has felt an irresistible need for a government. Local patriotism has been replaced by national.

Those are the direct ways in which democracy has fortified the federal government. The indirect influence which it exercises, and more especially, which it will exercise in the long run, is equally important.

The more different the population is in institutions, feelings, customs, and ideas, the greater will be the resistance to a federal government and the more numerous and harder to solve will be its difficulties. Similar interests play less part in making the United States so easily governed than do the perfect similarity of laws, opinions, and social conditions. By the same token, one can say that the strange weakness of the former Swiss federal government was chiefly due to the immense difference and strange contradiction between the spirit, outlook, and laws of the various populations over which it had to rule. It was a very laborious task to keep men so naturally dissimilar and remote from one another under a uniform control and within the same political system. A much better-constituted government, and one with a wiser organization, would not have succeeded in this. The democratic revolution now taking place in Switzerland has the effect in each canton in turn of establishing the sway of certain institutions, maxims of government, and ideas of similar tendency; while the democratic revolution strengthens the spirit of independence in the cantons in face of the central government, on the other hand it makes it easier for that government to act; to a great extent it abolishes the causes of resistance, and without making the cantonal governments more anxious to obey that of the federation, it makes obedience to its wishes infinitely easier for them.

To understand the present and foresee the future of the country, it is necessary to study very carefully the two contrary effects which I have described.

If one pays attention to only one of these tendencies, one is led to believe that the coming of democracy in the cantonal governments will lead immediately and easily to legislation extending the sphere of the federal government and the concentration in its hands of the normal direction of local affairs; in a word, to modify the whole organization of the pact in the direction of centralization. I am convinced, for my part, that such a revolutionary change would still for a long time encounter much greater resistance than is generally supposed. The cantonal governments of today show no greater taste than their predecessors for such a revolutionary change, and will do all they can to avoid it.

But I nevertheless think that in the end the federal government is destined to increase its power. Circumstances will help this on more than laws. Maybe it will not in any very manifest way increase its prerogatives, but it will use them differently and more often. It will in fact grow in strength, even if in law it remains the same; it will develop more by interpreting the pact than by changing it; and it will dominate Switzerland before it is in a position to govern her.

One can also foresee that those very people who, till now, are most opposed to the methodical extension of its power will not be slow to wish for it, either to escape from the intermittent pressure of such an ill-constituted power or to seek protection from the nearer and heavier tyranny of the local governments.

The one certain fact is that henceforth, whatever may be the modifications to the letter of the pact, the Swiss federal Constitution has been profoundly and irrevocably altered. The Confederation has changed its nature. It has become something new in Europe; a policy of action has succeeded there to a policy of inertia and neutrality; whereas only the life of the municipalities used to count, it now has a national existence—an existence which is more laborious, more troubled, and more precarious, but also more dignified.

Appendix III

SPEECH PRONOUNCED IN THE CHAMBER OF DEPUTIES ON JANUARY 27, 1848, DURING THE DISCUSSION OF THE PROPOSED ANSWER TO THE SPEECH FROM THE THRONE

Gentlemen,

It is not my intention to continue the particular discussion which has been started. I think it could be taken up again more profitably when we come to discuss the law about prisons. My object in rising to speak now is a more general one.

Paragraph 4, which is being discussed today, naturally leads this house to consider the general state of internal politics, and in particular that aspect to which attention has been drawn by my honorable friend M. Billault's amendment referring thereto.

It is to that part of the discussion on the address that I wish to call the attention of the house.

Gentlemen, I may be mistaken, but it seems to me that the present state of things, the state of opinion and of men's minds in France, gives cause for alarm and sorrow. For my part, I tell the house candidly that, for the first time for fifteen years, I feel a certain fear for the future; and the knowledge that this impression is shared goes to show that I am right; I think I can ask all my hearers, and they will answer that such an impression exists in the constituencies they represent; a certain malaise, a certain fear, possesses men's minds; for the first time in, perhaps, sixteen years, there is a feeling, a consciousness, of instability, and that is a feeling which goes before revolutions, often announcing them and sometimes bringing them about, and that feeling is there to a very serious extent in the land.

If I rightly understood the concluding remarks a few days ago of the Minister of Finance, the cabinet itself admits the reality of the feeling of which I speak; but it attributes it to certain particular causes, to certain recent accidental happenings in the political world, to meetings which have disturbed men's minds and words which have aroused their passions.

Gentlemen, I think that to attribute the admitted evil to such causes is to mistake the symptoms for the disease. For my part, I am convinced that the disease does not lie there; it is more general and deeper. It is a disease which must be cured at all cost if it is not, believe me, to sweep us all away. All of us, I repeat, if we do not take care, for such is the state of public opinion and of public mores. Now, in what does the disease lie? That is the point to which I wish to call your attention. I think that public mores and public spirit are in a dangerous state; moreover, I believe that the government has contributed, and is contributing, in the most serious way to the growth of the danger. That is what makes me rise to speak.

When, gentlemen, I look carefully at the class which governs, at the class which has political rights, and then at the governed, what is happening both in the one and in the other disturbs and frightens me.

To speak first of what I have called the class which governs (note that I use the words in their most general sense; I am not speaking of the middle class only, but of all those citizens, in whatsoever situation, who possess and make use of political rights); I say, then, what is happening in the class which governs disturbs and frightens me. What I see, gentlemen, can be put in a word: public mores are changing and have already profoundly changed; the change grows greater from day to day; common opinions, feelings, and ideas are more and more being replaced by particular interests, particular aims, and points of view carried over from private life and private interests.

I do not wish to force the house to dwell more heavily than is necessary on these sorry details; I will be content to address my adversaries themselves, and my colleagues in the government majority. I ask them, for their own information, to make a sort of statistical review of the electoral colleges which have sent them to this house; let them make a first list of those who vote for them, not on account of any political opinion, but from motives of private friendship or good neighborliness. Then, let them make a second list of those who vote for them, not with any public or general interest in mind, but for reasons of purely local interest. Let them add to this a third list of those who vote for them from motives of purely private interest, and I would ask them whether there are many voters still left over. I ask them whether those who vote from a disinterested feeling of public spirit, on account of political opinions and passions of a public nature, form the majority of the electors who have conferred on them the mandate of deputies. I am sure they will easily discover that it is just the opposite. I would also ask them to allow me to inquire whether, to their knowledge, in the last five years, ten years, fifteen years, the number of those who vote from reasons of personal and private interest has not been increasing continually, whereas the number of those who vote from political opinion has not been decreasing continually. Finally, I would ask them to tell me whether or not, among those around them and under their eyes, some strange sort of tolerance of the facts of which I speak has little by little established itself in public opinion, whether little by little a sort of base and vulgar moral concept has been formed, according to which a man with political rights owes it to himself, to his children, wife, and relations to make a personal use of those rights in their interest; whether this is not gradually being elevated into a sort of duty for the father of a family. Whether this new morality, unknown in the great ages of our history and unknown at the beginning of our Revolution, is not spreading more and more and daily invading men's minds. That is my question.

But what is all that, if not a deep and continuing degradation, a more and more complete corruption of public mores?

And if, turning from public to private life, I consider what is happening there and pay attention to all the things you have witnessed in the last year, particularly all those blatant scandals, all those crimes, all those shortcomings, all those offenses, all those extraordinary vices which it would seem that every circumstance brought to light on all sides, and which have been re-vealed by every matter brought into court; if I pay attention to all that, have I not reason to be frightened? Am I not right to say that it is not only our public mores which are changing, but that our private mores are becoming corrupt? (Cries of dissent in the center.)

Note that I do not say this as a moralist, but as a politician; do you know what is the general, effective, deep cause which makes private mores turn corrupt? It is the change in public mores. It is because morality does not prevail in the main acts of life, that it does not find its way down into the least important ones. Because interest has replaced disinterested feelings in public life, interest sets the tone in private life.

It has been said that there are two moralities, political morality and morality in private life. Most certainly, if what happens among us is as I see it, the falsity of such a maxim has never been proved more strikingly or with more unhappy effect than here and now. Yes, I do believe that something is happening to our private mores of a nature to cause disquiet and alarm to good citizens, and I believe that what is happening in the case of our private mores is in great part due to the state of public mores. (Cries of dissent in the center.)

Well, gentlemen, if you do not believe me about this, at least believe the impression created in Europe. I think I am as familiar as anyone in this house with what is printed and said about us in Europe.

Well, then, in all sincerity, from the bottom of my heart, I am more than made sad, I am heartbroken at the things I daily read and hear; I am heartbroken when I see the use made against us of the things of which I speak, the exaggerated deductions drawn therefrom about the whole nation, and the whole national character; I am heartbroken to see how the power of France has slowly been brought lower and lower in the world; I am heartbroken when I see that it is not only the moral power of France which has grown feeble . . .

M. Janvier: I ask leave to speak. (Stir.)

M. de Tocqueville: . . . but the power of her principles, her ideas, and her feelings.

It was France who first threw into the world, amid the thunders of her first revolution, principles which since then have become principles of regeneration in all modern societies. That was once her glory and the most precious part of herself. But now, gentlemen, it is just those principles which are enfeebled today by our example. The way in which we ourselves seem to apply them makes the world lose faith in them. Europe, with its eyes on us, begins to wonder whether we were right or wrong; Europe wonders whether in fact, as we have so often claimed, we are leading human societies toward a happier and more prosperous future or whether we are dragging them in our train down into moral squalor and ruin. That, gentlemen, is what chiefly pains me in the picture we present to the world. It harms not ourselves only, but our principles and our cause; it harms that fatherland of the mind, which I, for my part, as a Frenchman, value more than the physical and material fatherland which we see before our eyes. (General commotion.)

Gentlemen, if this spectacle makes such an effect when seen from afar, from the distant boundaries of Europe, what must be its results in France even on those classes who have no rights and who, in the leisure of the political inactivity to which our laws have condemned them, see us alone act on the great stage on which we are placed? What do you suppose they think of such a spectacle?

For my part, I am afraid. Some say there is no danger because there is no uprising, that because there is no manifest disorder on the surface of society revolutions are far from us.

Gentlemen, allow me to say that I think you are mistaken. Undoubtedly there is no physical disorder, but disorder has entered deeply into men's minds. Look at what is happening among the working classes, who are, I agree, at the moment tranquil. It is true that they are not troubled by political passions, in the narrow sense of the word, in the way they once were. But can you not see that their passionate feelings, once concerned with politics, now turn to social questions? Can you not see that little by little there are spreading among them opinions and ideas which are not concerned just with overthrowing this or that law, this or that administration, even this or that government, but society itself, shaking the very foundations on which it now rests? Do you not hear what is being said every day among them? Do you not understand that they are constantly repeating that all who are placed in authority over them are incapable and unworthy to rule them? That the present distribution of property in the world is unjust? That property rests on foundations that are not those of equity? Do you not believe that when such opinions take root, when they spread almost universally, when they go right down deep into the masses, they must sooner or later, I do not say when, I do not say how, but they must sooner or later lead to the most dreadful revolutions?

Such, gentlemen, is my profound conviction. I think that we are slumbering now on a volcano. (Protests.) I am profoundly convinced of that. (Various reactions.)

Now let me explain, in few words but with complete candor and sincerity, who are the real authors, the chief authors, of the ills I have described.

I know very well that evils such as those of which I speak do not all derive, perhaps do not even chiefly derive, from the actions of governments. I know very well that the prolonged revolutions which have so often disturbed and shaken the basis of this land must have left behind an unusual instability in the minds of men. I know very well that one can find some secondary but important causes which help to explain the deplorable phenomenon, now under examination, in the passions and the agitations of parties. But I have too high an idea of the part which power plays in the world not to be convinced that when there is some great ill in society, some great political ill, some great moral ill, power has much to do with the matter.

What, then, has power done to produce the ill described? What has power done to introduce this deep perturbation in public morality first and then in private mores? How did it contribute to this result?

I think, gentlemen, that one may say, without hurting anybody's feelings, that the government has recaptured, in the last few years especially, greater rights, greater influence, more considerable and more numerous prerogatives than it had ever possessed at any other epoch. Its power is much greater than could have been imagined by anybody, not only among those who granted the powers but also among those who received them, in 1830. On the other hand, one can assert that the principle of liberty has expanded less than anyone then would have expected. I pass no judgment on events, but seek the result thereof. If such a peculiar and unexpected consequence, such a strange twist in human affairs, has unleashed some ill passions and some guilty hopes, do you not think that the sight thereof has stifled many noble feelings and disinterested passions? That as a result many honest souls have felt a sort of disillusionment with politics and a real depression of spirit?

But it is especially the way in which this result was attained, a roundabout and to some extent surreptitious way, which has dealt a fatal blow to public morality. It was by recapturing some ancient powers that men had thought abolished in July, by reviving former rights which seemed to have been annulled, by again putting in force ancient laws which were thought to have been repealed, and by applying new laws in a sense different from that intended in making them—it was by all these roundabout means applied with skillful and patient industry that the government in the end regained wider scope for its activity and influence than had perhaps ever been enjoyed at any time in France.

That, gentlemen, is what the government has done and what, in particular, the present ministry has done. And do you think, gentlemen, that this method which I have just called roundabout and surreptitious, by which power has gradually been regained, capturing it in some sense by surprise, using other means than those supplied by the Constitution; do you think that this strange exhibition of juggling and manipulation, publicly given during several years and in a vast theater to all the watching nation, do you think that such an exhibition was designed to improve public mores?

For my part, I am profoundly convinced of the opposite; I do not wish to attribute to my adversaries dishonest motives which they did not have; I will admit, if you like, that in using means which I reprobate they believed they were acquiescing in a necessary evil and that the greatness of their aim obscured from them the danger and immorality of the means. I should like to believe that; but were the means therefore any less dangerous? They believe that the revolution which has taken place in the rights of power during the last fifteen years was necessary; let that be so; and they did not act from motives of private interest; I like to believe it; but it is nonetheless true that they worked by means which public morality discountenances; it is nonetheless true that they worked by approaching men on their evil, not their honest, side, appealing to their passions, weakness, interest, and often to their vices. (Stir.) Thus, though their aim may perhaps have been honest, they did things which were not so. And to do these things, they had called to their aid, and honored with their favor, and introduced into their daily company men who had no desire for an honest aim, nor for honest means, but only wanted the vulgar satisfaction of their private interests by the help of the power entrusted to them; in this way they offered a sort of prize for immorality and vice.

I will only cite one example to demonstrate what I mean. It is the case of that minister, whose name I will not mention, who was asked to become a member of the cabinet, although the whole of France, and his colleagues too, knew that he was unworthy to be seated there, who left the cabinet because this unworthiness became too notorious, and who was then placed—where? On the highest judge's bench, from whence he soon had to come down to sit in the dock.

For my part, gentlemen, I do not regard that as an isolated fact. I consider it the symptom of a general ill and the most salient feature of a whole policy. If you walk in the ways you have chosen, you have need of such men.

But it is especially through what the Minister of Foreign Affairs has called the abuse of influence that the moral ill of which I have been speaking has spread and become general and penetrated throughout the land. It is in that way that you have acted directly, and without intermediary, on public morality, no longer by example only, but by acts. In that respect too I do not want to make out that the position of the members of the government is worse than I really see it to be; I know well that they have been exposed to an immense temptation; I well know that at no time and in no country has a government had to face anything similar, that nowhere has power had in its hands such means of corruption, nor had to face a political class so restricted or exposed to such wants, so that there had never been such a good chance of working on it by means of corruption, nor had the desire so to work on it seemed so irresistible. I admit therefore that it was not a premeditated wish only to play on the chord of private self-interest in men that made ministers commit so great an offense: I well know that they were carried along down a steep slope where it was very difficult to stop; I know that; so the only thing for which I blame them is that they put themselves in such a position and acquiesced in a point of view which made it necessary, in order to rule at all, not to appeal to opinions, feelings, and general ideas, but to private interests. Once they had started down that road, I hold it certain that however much they may have wished and longed to turn back, a fatal power pushed them, and was bound to drive them, continually forward, everywhere where in fact they have since been. Only one thing was needed for that result: to live. From the moment when they put themselves in the position I have just described, they only had to go on existing for eight years in order to do everything which we have seen them do, not only using all the ill means of government of which I have just been speaking, but exhausting them.

It was that fatality which first made them increase the number of places beyond measure; which then, when they came to run short, led them to divide them up and break them, if one may put it so, into fractions, so as to have in their gift, if not more places, at least more salaries, as was done in all the offices concerned with finance. It was that same necessity which, when, in spite of all their hard work, places again began to run short, led them, as we saw the other day in the Petit affair, artificially to create vacancies by roundabout means in places which had already been filled.

The Minister of Foreign Affairs has often told us that the opposition was unjust in its attacks and made violent, ill-founded, and false accusations. But I would ask him to his face, has the opposition ever in its most vicious moments made accusations such as are now proved true? (Stir.) The opposition has certainly made grave charges against the Minister of Foreign Affairs, charges which may, for all I know, be exaggerated; but it had never accused him of doing that which he has recently confessed himself to have done.

For my part, I declare that not only did I never accuse the Minister of Foreign Affairs of such things, but I never even suspected him of them. Never, never would I have believed, when I heard the Minister of Foreign Affairs on this tribune explaining in wonderfully well-chosen words the claims of morality in politics, and in spite of my opposition to him felt proud of my country to hear such language, certainly I should never have believed that what has happened could happen. I should have felt that I was not only doing something wrong to him, but also something wrong to myself as well if I had even imagined that which was nevertheless the truth. Should I believe, as someone recently said, that when the Minister of Foreign Affairs used this fine and noble language, he was not saying what he thought? For myself, I would not go as far as that; I think that the minister's instinct and taste was to do other than what he did. But he was urged on, carried away in spite of himself, uprooted, if one may put it so, out of his own will by that kind of political and governmental fatality which he had imposed on himself and which I have just depicted.

Recently he asked in what this action, which he called a small matter, was so serious. What was so serious was that it was imputed to you, that it was you, you of all men in this house, who by your language had given the least reason to suspect that you had done acts of this sort, that it was you who were convicted thereof.

And if such an act, such a sight, is bound to make a deep, painful, and deplorable impression on morality in general, what must be its effect in particular on the agents of government? There is a comparison which seemed to me peculiarly striking when I came to know the facts.

Three years ago an official in the Ministry of Foreign Affairs, a high official, differed from the minister on some point of political opinion. He did not express his disagreement in any ostensible way but voted silently.

The Minister of Foreign Affairs declared that he could not live in the official company of a man who did not think entirely as he did; he dismissed him, or rather, to put it plainly, he chased him out. (Stir.)

And now here is another official, not placed so high in the hierarchy, but closer to the minister personally, who does the things you know of. (Hear! Hear!)

At first the Minister of Foreign Affairs did not deny that he knew about them; he did deny it afterward; for the moment I will grant that he did not know . . .

On the left: No! No!

M. de Tocqueville: But if he denies that he knew these facts, he at least cannot deny that they are such and that he knows them now; they are established. Now, it is here not a case of some political disagreement between you and an official, but of a moral disagreement about something close to the heart and conscience of man. In this case it is not only the minister who is compromised, it is, note well, the man too.

Well, then. You could not tolerate a more or less serious political disagreement with an honorable man who had done no more than vote against you. But instead of blaming, you actually reward an official who, if he did not act in accordance with your wishes, has unworthily compromised you and put you in the most painful and serious position in which you have ever been certainly since you entered political life. You retain that official; even more, you reward and honor him.

What do you expect to be thought? How do you expect us not to think one of two things: either that you have a strange partiality for disagreements of this sort or that you are no longer free to punish them? (Sensation.)

I defy you, in spite of all your immense talents, to escape from that circle. If, in fact, the man of whom I speak has acted against your will, why do you keep him near your person? If you keep him near you and reward him, if you refuse to blame him even in the slightest way, one must necessarily come to that conclusion to which I have just come.

On the left: Very good! Very good!

M. Odilon Barrot: That is conclusive.

M. de Tocqueville: But, gentlemen, even granted that I am mistaken about the great ill of which I have just spoken, and granted that the government in general and the cabinet in particular has no share therein— even granting that for the sake of argument, is the ill, gentlemen, therefore any less immense? Do we not owe it to our country, to ourselves, to make the most energetic and sustained efforts to overcome it?

I told you just now that this ill will sooner or later—I do not know how or whence it will come, but sooner or later it will bring about most serious revolutions in this country; make no mistake about that.

When I come to inquire at different times and periods, and among different peoples, into what has been the effective cause which has brought the class which governed to ruin, I certainly notice this or that event, this or that man, and this or that accidental and superficial cause; but, believe me, the real cause, the effective cause, which makes men lose power is that they have become unworthy to wield it. (Renewed sensation.)

Gentlemen, consider the ancient monarchy; it was stronger than you, stronger because of its origin; it had better support than you in ancient usages, old customs, and ancient beliefs; it was stronger than you, and yet it fell into dust. And why did it fall? Do you think it was due to some particular accident? Do you think it was caused by some particular man, by the financial deficit, or by the Tennis Court Oath? By Lafayette or by Mirabeau? No, gentlemen; there is a deeper and truer cause, and that cause is that the class which governed then had become by its indifference, egoism, and vices incapable and unworthy to rule. (Very good! Very good!)

That is the true cause.

Now, gentlemen, if at all times it is right to be thus concerned for the honor of our country, is not this more right at the present hour? Does not some instinctive intuition, which cannot be analyzed but is certain, tell you that the ground in Europe is again trembling? (Stir.) Do you not feel—how shall I say?—a wind of revolution in the air? One does not know whence this wind comes nor whither it goes, nor, believe me, whom it will sweep away. And it is at such a time that you remain unmoved in face of corruption in public mores, for the word "corruption" is not too strong.

I speak here without bitterness; I think I even speak without party spirit; I attack men against whom I feel no anger; but it is my duty to tell my country what is my profound and considered conviction. Well, my profound and considered conviction is that public morality is being corrupted and that this corruption will lead you in a short time, immediately perhaps, to new revolutions. Is the life of kings supported by stronger ties and ones harder to break than the lives of other men? Have you, in this moment of time, any certainty of the morrow? Do you know what may happen in France in a year from now, in a month, in a day perhaps? You do not know; but you do know that there is a storm on the horizon and that it is coming in your direction; will you let it take you by surprise? (Interruption in the center.)

Gentlemen, I implore you not to do that; I do not ask, I implore. I would gladly fall on my knees before you, so real and serious do I think the danger, so convinced am I that to point it out is no vain rhetorical flourish. Yes, the danger is great; take steps to deal with it while there is time; cure the ill by effective means, by attacking not the symptoms but its essence.

There has been talk of changes in legislation. I am much inclined to think that these changes are not only useful but necessary; I believe that electoral reform is useful and parliamentary reform urgent; but I am not so mad, gentlemen, as not to know that it is not only mere laws that decide the destiny of peoples; no, it is not the mechanism of the laws that causes the great events of this world; what does decide events, gentlemen, is the essential spirit of the government. Keep your laws, if you like, though I think you would make a great mistake in keeping them; even keep the same men if you want to, and I will put no obstacle in your way; but, for God's sake, change the spirit of the government, for that spirit, I repeat, is leading you to the abyss. (Loud applause on the left.)

(Quoted from the "Moniteur" of January 28, 1848.)

INDEX

Abolition of slavery, dangers of, 354, 357; effect of, on Negroes, 349–52; effect of, on whites, 351–52; effects of, on race prejudice, 342–43; hindrances to, in South, 352–55; motive for, 343–44; in North, 343–44; probable consequences of, in South, 357–59, 360–63

Abstract expressions, use of, in democracies, 481

Adams, John, 134

Administration of government, centralized, 262–76; in counties, 74–75; court of sessions, 76–78, 81; decentralization of, 86–98; effect on, of power of majority, 248–50; in England, 88; in Europe, 682–84; in France, 88, 92, 97; instability of, 207–8; justices of peace, 75–76; in New England, 71–80; in townships, 73–74; in U.S., 61–98; uniformity of, how attained, 74

Administrative despotism, in democracies, 690–95

Agriculture, 580–82; in France, 583–84; progress of, in democracies, 551–52; in U.S., 554

Alabama, state of, 320; Indian policy of, 335n.; protest of, against tariff, 390

Alexander the Great, 659

Allegheny Mountains, 24, 25, 372, 379

Ambassadors, 143

Ambition, of Americans, 627; in aristocracies, 629, 631; of citizens of democracies, 628–30; effect of revolution on, 628

Americans, absence of revolutionary passion among, 639; ambition of, 627; devotion of, to individual welfare and freedom, 540–41; free social intercourse of, 566–67; humanitarianism of, 571–72; individualism

of, 430; manners of, 605–8, 609–11; philosophical method of, characteristics of, 429; religious practices of, 542; restlessness of, 535–38; and Russians, 412; sensitiveness of, in Europe, 569; vanity of, 612–13

American society of 1650, compared with European society, 45–46

Amphictyonic League, 156n.

Amusements, lack of, in U.S., compared with aristocratic countries, 609–11

Anabaptists, discrimination against, 42n.

Anglo-Americans, business habits of, 285; destiny of, in New World, 409–12; enterprise of, 403–4; laws and customs of, reasons for some peculiarities in, 48–49; maritime genius of, 400–3; origin of, 31–49; point of departure of, 32–49; political consequences of the social state of 56–57; political education of, 69–70; pride of, 373–75; restlessness of, 284–86; social state of, 50–57; superiority of, in navigation, reasons for, 401–4; unity of, 372–73

Archives, lack of, 200

Aristocracies, ambition in, 629–31; amusements of, 609; armies of, 646–47, 652, 655, 658, 662; attitude of, toward labor for profit, 550; belief and, 435; caste in, effect of, on sympathies, 561–65; comfort in, 530–32; domestic service in, 572–76, 579; drama in, 499–500; family in, 586–89; fine arts in, 467–68; historians in, 493–96; honor in, ideas of, 617–20, 622–26; human perfectibility and, idea of, 452–54; ideas and, general, 438; individualism in, 506–8, 696; language in, state of, 477–79, 480–81; limits to

Colonization of New World, 32ff.

Color prejudice, *see* Race prejudice

Combinations, manufacturing, *see* Companies

Comfort, *see* Well-being

Commerce, American, causes of prosperity of, 400–7; commercial genius of Anglo-Americans, 400–3; future development of, probable, 403–7; imports and exports, 400–2; relation of, to South America, 405–6; *see also* Trade

Committal, 48

Commune, 63, 68

Companies, manufacturing, effect of, on power of state, 685–86

Confederation, Articles of, 112–14; weakness of, 113

Congress, U.S., 499; *see also* House of Representatives; Senate

Connecticut, colony of, code of laws of (1650), 40–43; founding of, 40

Connecticut, state of, 35n.; attitude of, toward federal government during War of 1812, 169; cession of western lands, 388n.; congressional representatives born in, 282; electoral body in, 43; historical work concerning, discussion of, 720; privileges and obligations of citizens of, 41–44; westward movement from, 281

Conscription, 651–52, 661; unlikelihood of adoption of, 22–23

Constantinople, fall of, effect on western European languages, 478

Constituent Assembly, French, 441

Constitution, English, 725; French, 724

Constitution, federal, 112–70; adoption of, 114; amendment of, 101–2; Art. II, Sec. 2 subsection 2, *quoted,* 226n.; compared with French and English constitutions, 101, 102, 104; federal constitutions compared, other, 155–58; framers of, character of, 152; framing of, 114; history of, 112–14; impeachment of public officials, 109; judicial decisions founded on, 100 ff.; provision of, for divided sovereignty, 363 ff.; provisions concerning foreign affairs,

226; state constitutions and, compared, 151–55; strengthened by interpretation, 385–87; summary of, 114–15; weakened by interpretation, 386–87; *see also* Federal courts; Federal government; Federal system; President, U.S.

Constitutional principles, modern, in New England colonial law, 43–44

Constitutions, state, American, 726; frequent amendment of, 249

Convention, French, 441

Corruption in U.S., 233; France and England, compared, 220–21

Cortes, Hernando, 470

Cotton culture, 554

Council of State, French, 105

Counties, administration of, outside of New England, 81; administration of government, 73 f.; compared with townships, 70; court of justice, 70; New England, compared with French *arrondissements,* 70; officers of, 69, 70–71

County assemblies in U.S., 81, 696

Cour de cassation, 141n.

Court of sessions, administrative and judicial functions of, 76–77, 81

Courts of justice, as instruments for control of democracy, 269; political influence of, 99 ff.; power of, to declare laws unconstitutional, 269; *see also* Federal courts

Creeks, 329n., 333, 335n., 336n.; expulsion of, from tribal homes, 335; letter of Andrew Jackson to, *quoted,* 337n.; petition of, to Congress, 334–35; treatment of, by Southern states, 334–35; treaty of 1790 with, *quoted,* 336n.

Crime, punishment of, 95–96; in Southwest, 225

Criminals, reform of, 249–50

Crusades, 11

Dartmouth College case, 146n.

David, Jacques Louis, Raphael compared with, 468

Debating clubs, 243

Debts, national, in Europe, growth of, 682

Decentralization of administration, 87–98